WORDSWORTH CLASSICS
OF WORLD LITERATURE

General Editor: To...

THE VOYAG...
THE *DISCOV...*

CAPTAIN ROBERT F. SCOTT

The Voyage of
the *Discovery*

❖

*with an introduction
by Beau Riffenburgh*

WORDSWORTH CLASSICS
OF WORLD LITERATURE

In loving memory of
MICHAEL TRAYLER
the founder of Wordsworth Editions

1

Customers interested in other titles from
Wordsworth Editions are invited to visit our
website at www.wordsworth-editions.com

For our latest list and a full mail order service contact
Bibliophile Books, Unit 5 Datapoint,
South Crescent, London E16 4TL
Tel: +44 0207 515 9222
Fax: +44 0207 538 4115
e-mail: orders@bibliophilebooks.com

This edition published 2009 by Wordsworth Editions Limited
8B East Street, Ware, Hertfordshire SG12 9HJ

ISBN 978 1 84022 177 0

This edition © Wordsworth Editions Limited 2009
Introduction © Beau Riffenburgh 2009

Wordsworth® is a registered trademark of
Wordsworth Editions Limited

Typeset in Great Britain by Roperford Editorial
Printed and bound by Clays Ltd, St Ives plc

CONTENTS

ILLUSTRATIONS

DIAGRAMS

INTRODUCTION

Robert Falcon Scott is remembered as one of the greatest heroes of Antarctic exploration. For generations, children in homes and schools throughout Britain have been told the story of his 'race' against Roald Amundsen to be the first to the South Pole. It remains one of the most memorable tales in the history of exploration: how, with his support groups having turned back, Scott and four colleagues continued on, man-hauling all the way to the Pole, only to find the Norwegian flag flying over a tent that Amundsen had used to mark the southernmost place on Earth. On the return journey of some 800 miles, devastated emotionally and struggling against both inadequate supplies of food and fuel and worsening weather conditions, the members of Scott's party slowly wore out.

First, Petty Officer Edgar Evans died after he broke down near the base of the Beardmore Glacier. Then, having sledged most of the way across the Great Ice Barrier, Captain L. E. G. Oates, whose feet were so badly damaged by frostbite and gangrene that he felt he could not travel at the rate necessary to safely reach the next depot, walked out of the tent to his death so that he would not hinder his companions' progress. Nevertheless, only days later, Scott and his last two companions – Edward Wilson and Henry Bowers – were halted by a terrible storm, and the three eventually weakened and then died in their tent, only 11 miles short of a depot holding large quantities of the food and fuel that would have saved them.

Scott's diaries and final letters – found the next spring by a search party – were edited and published posthumously as *Scott's Last Expedition*, and his eloquent prose made the work a classic of exploration literature, one that immediately was translated into several different languages. More significant to the majority of Scott's countrymen, however, was that in a time when increasing

German and American economic, technological, and military success – combined with the decline of British production, military might, and political influence throughout Europe – had made Britons anxious that their age of greatness had passed, Scott's tale proved to a doubting public that Britons could show as much strength, courage, stamina, and fortitude as ever. The valiant struggle of the polar party, and their deaths marked by supreme self-sacrifice, dignity, and perceived Christian values, served as an inspiration of the highest order to the British public and propelled Scott to the same pantheon of heroes as earlier martyrs of the British Empire such as General Henry Havelock, Dr David Livingstone, and General Charles Gordon.

But although the tragic events of Scott's second expedition – in conjunction with his literary masterpiece that so touched the British soul – immortalised him, they did not provide his first encounter with fame. That had come in the previous decade, when Scott had led one of the initial efforts to penetrate into the mysteries of the Antarctic continent, the British National Antarctic Expedition (BNAE). Despite Scott being the leader of the BNAE, however, the concept of the enterprise far predated his involvement. In fact, the expedition was the culmination of the dream and goal of one man and one man only: Sir Clements Markham.

Born in 1830 in Stillingfleet in Yorkshire, the second son of a local vicar, Markham first became fascinated by polar exploration in his early school years, when he read an account of William Edward Parry's Arctic voyages in the first decades of the nineteenth century. At the age of 13, Markham entered the Royal Navy as a cadet, and two years later he was advanced to the rank of midshipman. Although he was not enamoured of the harsher aspects of naval discipline, he remained in the Senior Service long enough to be appointed to HMS *Assistance*, which, under Captain Erasmus Ommanney, was part of a fleet of four ships commanded by Captain Horatio Austin sent to search for the missing men and ships of the Northwest Passage expedition under Sir John Franklin.

Austin's expedition sailed in May 1850 and wintered in the waterways of the Canadian archipelago. The next spring, man-hauling sledge parties were sent out looking for traces of the

Franklin expedition. Although they were unsuccessful, they did discover and chart several hundred miles of new coastline. But for Markham there was much more than just the excitement of discovery. He was completely taken with the camaraderie of the officers, with the team effort and spirit of the sledging parties, and with the elaborate winter routine, which, following the practices of Parry decades before, included school lessons, lectures, producing a newspaper, and staging theatricals. All of this determined just how Markham thought polar exploration should be conducted, and thus later shaped the organisation of the BNAE.

Markham's return to regular service brought home his dissatisfaction with the Royal Navy, and he resigned within months of the search expedition's homecoming. He eventually drifted into a position at the India Office in London, and around the same time was elected a Fellow of the Royal Geographical Society (RGS). While at the India Office, he conceived a plan to liberate Britain from its dependence on several South American countries for its supply of quinine, which was required to fight malaria throughout the tropical regions. Quinine came from the cinchona tree, which was found in the Andes. Markham suggested ignoring local opposition and laws, and smuggling cinchona seeds and saplings out of Peru, Ecuador, and Bolivia, thence taking them to India, where they could be cultivated to provide Britain's own supply. The eventual success of this project, of which Markham was one of the active participants, led to his promotion at the India Office and to his rise to prominence at the RGS, where in 1863 he was made Honorary Secretary.

In 1867–68, Markham served as the geographer for the British punitive expedition against Emperor Theodore of Abyssinia. But his attention increasingly was given to the polar regions, and particularly to a plan to revive British exploration there, which had lapsed since the ending of the Franklin searches in 1859. In 1865, Markham's old shipmate Sherard Osborne read a paper at the RGS, advocating an attempt on the North Pole via Smith Sound, between Greenland and Ellesmere Island. With the backing of the RGS and eventually the Royal Society, Markham and Osborne spent years pushing for this Arctic re-involvement, until the government finally agreed to send out a naval expedition financed by the Treasury.

In 1875, under the command of Sir George Strong Nares, the British Arctic Expedition went north with great hopes. However, in retrospect, it had little chance of extensive success because the Arctic veterans who made up the organising committee, Markham among them, were so firmly entrenched in the past that the expedition was little more than a carbon copy of those of the 1840s and 1850s on which they had served. This meant there was little advance in either equipment or technique, and using the decades-old methods eliminated any real chance of reaching the North Pole. Despite Markham's cousin, Albert Hastings Markham, leading a sledging party that reached the farthest north that any men had ever been – 83° 20' 26"N – the expedition returned south a year early, to a great extent due to widespread scurvy. In all, the expedition was considered a serious disappointment to the government and the Admiralty, and yet little was learned from its failures, particularly by Markham.

In the 1880s, Markham launched another campaign: for the renewal of British Antarctic exploration. It followed the same, exceptionally slow progress of the previous one, although his position as an advocate for it was strengthened significantly when, in November 1893, he was elected President of the R.G.S. Markham now began pushing his cause much more actively, and his case benefited enormously from the Sixth International Geographical Congress being held in London in 1895. With Markham in the president's chair, and strongly supported by the powerful German meteorologist and geophysicist Georg von Neumayer, the conference passed a resolution stating that the exploration of the unknown Antarctic was the greatest piece of geographical exploration remaining and that it should be explored before the turn of the century.

In April 1897, Markham gained the full support of the Council of the RGS to support such an expedition, and within a year the Royal Society joined the effort. But raising funds was no easy thing, and it was not until March 1899 that Markham's efforts turned the corner. That month, Llewellyn Longstaff, a Fellow of the RGS, donated £25,000 to launch the project. That inspired more individuals to make contributions, and the societies began to develop plans for a purpose-built ship. Then the Prince of Wales agreed to become patron of the venture. That in turn led to Arthur

Balfour, the First Lord of the Treasury, adding his support, which resulted three weeks later in the government extending a grant of £45,000. The BNAE had become a reality.

That did not end the problems, however, as it was not long before the RGS and the Royal Society were confronted with the fact that the organisations' goals and plans for the expedition were decidedly different. At the heart of the disagreements was a fundamental difference of opinion about the objectives of the expedition and, based on those, the relative roles of the naval and civilian staff. Markham and the RGS believed that geographical discovery was the primary purpose of the expedition, whereas the representatives of the Royal Society supported scientific research as its basic aim.

This difference became a serious issue in 1900, not long after the expedition ship *Discovery* was launched. The distinguished geologist John W. Gregory – who also had extensive exploring and polar experience – had been named scientific director, and to the Royal Society this meant that he would have absolute responsibility for operations on land. To Markham, the Royal Society's notion would reduce the naval staff to little more than boat handlers, and this was totally contrary to how he envisioned the expedition, which was as a Royal Navy enterprise with a small scientific party under the direct command of the ship's captain.

Markham's choice for that captain – and therefore the leader of the expedition – was the 32-year-old torpedo lieutenant of HMS *Majestic*, Robert Falcon Scott. Scott had initially come to Markham's attention in 1887, when, as a midshipman, he had won a sailing race that Markham had been watching. Markham now fully supported him for the position, and, despite objections from the Royal Society, engaged in a series of behind-the-scenes man-oeuvres that saw Scott and Lieutenant Charles Royds released from naval duties to become expedition commander and executive officer, respectively. Shortly thereafter, Scott was promoted from lieutenant to commander.

In December 1900, when Gregory returned to England from Australia, where he had been appointed professor of geology at the University of Melbourne, he expressed serious reservations about Markham's draft instructions for the expedition, which placed him and his scientific staff under the command of Scott. As a justification of the Royal Society's position, Edward Poulton, the professor of zoology at Oxford, pointed out that Scott 'has had no experience in either Arctic or Antarctic seas . . . has not as yet the slightest reputation as a naturalist, a geologist, or an investigator of glacial problems . . . and is without experience in the branches of science.'[1]

But Markham would not budge, and, with the help of the manipulative Sir George Goldie, the power behind the Royal Niger Company and a member of both societies, he led an offensive that resulted in Gregory's resignation. And with that, according to the famed Antarctic expert Hugh Robert Mill, the emphasis of the expedition shifted from serious scientific research to adventure.

The great venture began on 31 July 1901, when *Discovery*, the first British vessel designed specifically for scientific research, sailed from the East India Dock. After a long voyage to, and respite in, New Zealand, the expedition headed south toward the Ross Sea, and on 9 January 1902, the men landed at Cape Adare at the northern tip of Victoria Land. It was the first time any of them had set foot on Antarctica other than Louis Bernacchi, the expedition physicist, who had been a member of Carsten Borchgrevink's expedition when it had made the first wintering on the continent in 1899.

Discovery then proceeded deeper into Antarctic waters, tracing the western margins of the Ross Sea and following the edge of the Great Ice Barrier (now known as the Ross Ice Shelf). This Wonder of the World is the result of numerous East Antarctic outlet glaciers and West Antarctic ice streams merging, along with snow that accumulates on the surface, to form a vast, roughly triangular sheet of floating ice that averages some 1200 feet thick. It is hundreds of miles long on its seaward face and covers 209,000 square miles, an area larger than Spain.

Near the eastern edge of the Barrier, Scott turned back west due to the threat of being caught between the Barrier and the numerous large, floating icebergs that had calved off it. On 3 February, a landing was made at a natural quay on the Barrier, which sloped down to the water's edge. While a party under the expedition's second-in-command, Albert Armitage, made an initial ski and sledge jaunt to the south, Scott had a balloon inflated and became the first man to make an ascent over Antarctica. His altitude was soon surpassed by the expedition's third lieutenant, Ernest Shackleton, one of a few British merchant mariners who had joined what was a primarily Royal Navy expedition.

Scott now sailed into McMurdo Sound between Ross Island and the mountains of Victoria Land. At its southern end, Ross Island terminated in a long cape near where the island abutted the Barrier. Just north of the tip of what they named Cape Armitage was a protected embayment, where *Discovery* was intentionally frozen in for the winter. They named the adjacent strip of land land Hut Point, and on it they erected a good-sized hut, which was used for work, while the men lived aboard the ship.

There was much for this group of novices to learn. In early March, two sledging parties, led by Royds and Reginald Skelton, the chief engineer, left for Cape Crozier on the eastern corner of Ross Island. Several days later, bad weather forced a party of men to be sent back under the command of the second lieutenant, Michael Barne. But as they neared Hut Point, a blizzard blew in, and they unwisely decided to continue on. Suddenly three of the men – including Barne – disappeared in the swirling snow, and, leaderless, the others continued in the dangerous conditions. While making a descent, one of the seamen, George Vince, was unable to stop on a slick surface and shot over the edge of a cliff into the sea, never to be found. The other men managed to reach base – as did Barne and the men with him – but the dangers of their situation had been brought home clearly.

The winter was spent in the region of Hut Point, with a strict social separation between officers and crew. Although the scientific programme was conducted with regular observations and measurements, and there was a great deal of preparation for the coming sledging season, the period was also marked by some of those things so dear to Markham: lectures, theatricals, and the production of *South Polar Times*, a monthly journal edited by Shackleton and illustrated primarily by Edward Wilson, the junior surgeon.

After much preparation and several spring reconnaissance journeys, at the beginning of November 1902 the expedition's most important sledging effort began. Scott, Shackleton, and Wilson, along with a team of dogs, headed south onto the Great Ice Barrier in an attempt to reach the South Pole. Unfortunately, none of them knew how to drive the dogs effectively, and before long the animals were hardly pulling and the men had little idea of how to improve their performance. The three were forced to go into harness themselves and begin man-hauling, a terrible task once described as the hardest work ever done by free men. For more than a month they relayed, dragging part of the load forward and then returning for the rest, thus making only one mile south for every three travelled. Nevertheless, they still managed to sledge deep onto the Great Ice Barrier, only to find that rather than the flat, smooth surface for which they had hoped, it was home to huge crevasses, steep ridges, and heavy snow that made pulling the sledges far harder than had been expected.

On 9 December, a dog died, an unfortunate portent of things to come. The next week, the men cached some of their supplies, which allowed them to advance without relaying. But they still suffered painfully from overwork, lack of food, and snowblindness. By 20 December, five of the 19 dogs had died, and in the following days Wilson detected the first symptoms of scurvy in Shackleton. But still they carried on, until, on 30 December, they halted at 82° 17 ' S, a record for the farthest south ever reached by man.

With supplies dwindling, they turned for home. The journey was a misery, as they had to man-haul the entire way. The remaining dogs could only follow behind the sledges, and, as they died one by one, they were fed to the others. Even though the men's rations increased when they reached their cache, they were now all showing symptoms of scurvy. Shackleton particularly suffered from it; he also was short of breath and spat blood in coughing fits. For a while he was given the only remaining pair of skis, and Scott and Wilson pulled the sledge. Then Wilson's eyesight began to fail, and the weather, which had been glorious on the way out, turned ugly. But still they struggled on. One night, as a blizzard roared and Shackleton lay gasping for breath in the tent, he heard Wilson tell Scott that he did not expect him to last through the night. That made him determined, Shackleton later said, to survive, and somehow, by the morning, he was ready. But all three men were 'nearly done', and it was something of a miracle that on 3 February 1903 they were able to arrive back safely at Hut Point.

The southern party was not the only one to have faced adventure and adversity. At the end of November 1902, Armitage – who had the most polar experience of any expedition member, having spent several years exploring Franz Josef Land in the high Russian Arctic – led a party across McMurdo Sound. Their goal was to find a route through or over the mountains of Victoria Land into the unknown interior and, if possible, carry on to the South Magnetic Pole.

The party spent days breaking a trail up through the mountains, before coming to a high plateau from which they could see sprawled below them the Ferrar Glacier, named for the expedition geologist. Armitage had rejected using the glacier as a highway at an earlier stage due to it being riddled with crevasses, and to that danger now was added that there seemed to be no safe way to descend to it. He therefore decided to continue on the mountain route, but within several days found high, rocky, impassable ridges ahead. The only way forward was to retreat to where they could attempt to reach the Ferrar Glacier. Ultimately, this meant a trip down Descent Glacier, an effort that proved the most dangerous challenge of the journey. For two days and a distance of three miles, the men had to lower the unwieldy sledges hand–over–hand, down gradients of up to 40 per cent. But they finally reached the Ferrar Glacier and were able to follow it cautiously to the west.

By 1 January 1903, Armitage's team had reached an altitude of about 7500 feet. But then one of the men, William Macfarlane, collapsed. Some of the others were in little better condition, so Armitage left a number behind, with Petty Officer David Allan in charge. He then pushed on, and on 4 January, at an elevation of about 9000 feet, the remainder of his party reached the top of the glacier and the start of the Polar Plateau, thereby becoming the first men ever to stand on the world's largest icecap. Concerned about Macfarlane and the others, Armitage decided to turn back rather than investigate further. The retreat followed the route taken, including ascending the nearly impossible Descent Glacier, an effort that almost proved too much for Macfarlane. The final descent to the coast down the Blue Glacier was not without problems either, as at one time Chief Engineer Skelton, Petty Officer Evans, and Royal Marine Gilbert Scott were simultaneously hanging in three separate crevasses by their traces that connected them to their sledges. Eventually all three were pulled out, and the party managed to reach Hut Point after 52 days in the field.

Four days after Armitage's return, smoke in the distance heralded the approach in McMurdo Sound of a relief ship, *Morning*, sent out after another frantic round of fund-raising by Markham. However, more than eight miles of ice separated *Discovery* from open water, meaning that, unless the weather soon broke up the ice, she and most of Scott's party would be forced to winter again.

The situation had not changed much when Scott returned on 3 February, and he quickly agreed with William Colbeck, master of *Morning*, that the relief expedition should sail north in a month lest *Morning* herself be trapped. In the interim, Scott decided to reduce the land party from 45 to 37 men, ridding it of 'one or two undesirables' and those individuals who did not wish to stay a second year. Thus, on 2 March, when *Morning* sailed north, she took several men who did not want to remain – and one who did. Despite Shackleton's objections, Scott 'invalided' home the junior officer on medical grounds, claiming he had not recovered his health after the southern journey. He was replaced as the third lieutenant by an officer from *Morning*, George Mulock.

As the long polar night again began to fall, *Discovery*'s company settled into the same winter routine as before. During that period, several spring journeys were planned, with the intention of all participants returning by mid-December, so that the entire man-power of the expedition could be turned to trying to free the ship from the ice. On one of the spring treks, Royds, Wilson, and four others travelled to the far side of Ross Island to Cape Crozier in order to collect emperor penguin eggs. However, they arrived too late and found many adults and chicks but no eggs still being incubated. This surprising development would lead Wilson and two companions to return to the site in the midst of winter on Scott's next expedition, a terrible experience made famous as 'the worst journey in the world'.

Meanwhile, Scott's major focus was extending the limits of Armitage's discoveries, and proceeding well onto the Polar Plateau. Guided by Skelton, and with four other men, he pushed up the Ferrar Glacier and onto the barren, featureless plain. But after nine terrible days on the Plateau, with ferociously icy winds blowing constantly into their faces, two of the men were exhausted, so Scott sent them back with Skelton, while proceeding onwards with Evans and Leading Stoker Bill Lashly. On 30 November, Scott ordered an about-face, and, with failing food and fuel, the three raced against time to reach their depot. At one stage, Scott and Evans both went down a crevasse, and only Lashly's quick thinking and remarkable strength prevented the sledge from following them. He then protected the sledge while simultaneously holding the ropes of both of his companions until they were able slowly to struggle out.

When Scott, Evans, and Lashly returned to Hut Point on Christmas Eve, they found that about 20 miles of ice still remained between *Discovery* and the open sea, and that Armitage was overseeing relatively ineffective efforts to saw through it. Then, in early January, *Morning* returned, accompanied by another relief ship, *Terra Nova*. Scott was given the unwelcome news that unless the expedition ship could be freed in six weeks, she would have to be abandoned. Fortunately, in the following weeks most of the ice broke up, and, on 16 February, explosives were used to free *Discovery* from the last remnants of it. Scott and his party headed north, with his eventual return to England promising both a promotion to captain and a hero's welcome.

As tough as the man-hauling on the sledging journeys had been for most of the men, Scott – physically powerful, driven, and seemingly tireless – had absolutely revelled in both the challenge and the process. But like many explorers, he found the greatest difficulties to come not in the field, but after he arrived home, for nothing was more tedious for him than joining the lecture circuit, nor required more effort or was harder than the process of writing his expedition account.

Soon after his return, Scott was granted six months' leave at half pay by the Admiralty in which to lecture and write. Initially, he crisscrossed the country to fulfil what seemed a never-ending demand for speeches, lectures, and other appearances. Even during these, he tried to produce the initial stages of his expedition account, struggling to put words together in hotel rooms or train carriages. 'Of all things I dread having to write a narrative,' he confessed to Hugh Robert Mill, 'and am wholly doubtful of my capacity.'[2]

When finally he tried to settle into the work, he used a room first at Markham's home in Ecclestone Square and then at a house he took with his mother in Chelsea. But he found it hard to be productive at either place: 'I can't tell why I find it impossible to work in London but so it is, my ideas refuse to flow and I get a cramped inexpansive feeling which hinders me badly.'[3] The result was that in April 1905 he retreated to The Burlington, a large but quiet establishment by the sea in Sheringham, Norfolk. And there he was able to grind out the rest of the book, sending each chapter to his publisher – Reginald Smith of Smith, Elder – as it was completed, along with a series of nervous letters about the quality of his efforts and the difficulty of his task: 'this is weary work, a treadmill business.'[4]

Smith, however, did not concur, but rather found the writing delightful, a remarkable combination of descriptive prose, lyrical impressions, and careful and disciplined observation. Even more impressed was Leonard Huxley, a reader and editor for Smith, Elder, who would later edit and arrange *Scott's Last Expedition*. 'When I received the script of *The Voyage of the 'Discovery'* I was amazed,' he later told one of Scott's biographers. 'I had only to read a few pages to realise that it was literature, unique of its kind . . . Scott's mind was like wax to receive an impression and like marble to retain it.'[5]

Huxley was not the only one with such an opinion. When the two-volume work appeared on 12 October 1905, the reviewers recognised it as a masterpiece and extolled it accordingly. 'The narrative of Capt. Scott easily takes rank among the foremost books of travel and discovery which a half-century has brought out,' stated a critic in *The Nation*.[6] And *The Spectator* called it 'the ablest and most interesting record of travel to which the present century has yet given birth.'[7] Even Scott's old rival Professor Gregory gave it fulsome praise in a review in *Nature*.

The book was equally successful in the shops: the public responded resoundingly, with the first printing of 3000 copies selling out virtually immediately and being quickly followed by a second print run of 1500 more. By the end of the year, Scott had received royalties of more than £1500, almost four times his current salary.

The reasons for such a response are obvious when one opens *The Voyage of the 'Discovery'*. Compared to many traditional, rather lifeless expedition accounts of the polar regions, this work was bursting with a rare combination of minute and fascinating detail and lucid, even exquisite description. Scott did not just record events and mention places as if they were spots on a map, but made the reader feel as if he, too, could experience the brilliance of the aurora in the long winter night; the slow build-up of ice on one's beard brought about by breath; the frostbite, snowblindness, and hunger of sledging trips; and the strange combination of isolation and ecstasy at being the first ever to see previously unknown locations. 'I had no idea you had been through such trials,' wrote Admiral Sir Lewis Bayly. 'I held my breath as you shot down the ice following your two companions. I trembled when you were down the crevasse.'[8]

The reader also learned a multitude of facts that allowed one to feel an intimacy with the expedition that was not usually a part of earlier accounts. What food and equipment were selected? What was the difference in life aboard ship at sea and when frozen in the ice? What questions and problems arose during the expedition, and how were they resolved? All of these and many more details set the book on a far-different plain than its predecessors.

Scott also instilled the book with one other unusual aspect: not just the character of the place, but of himself. Perhaps never before had an author of such an account given so freely of 'his deep if not brooding sense of responsibility, his loyalty to tradition, his sense of justness, and his commitment to science and discovery'.[9] For Edwardian readers, such insights of a now-famous man were true revelations. Surprisingly, these character insights did not extend to most of his fellow participants on the expedition. Perhaps the closest Scott came to this was with the two bluejackets with whom he finished his final sledging trip, Evans and Lashly. Yet by comparison, his two companions on the farthest south – Shackleton and Wilson, his closest friend – received little character development.

Intriguingly, in addition to their roles in the farthest south, Wilson and Shackleton each made more direct contributions to *The Voyage of the 'Discovery'*. It was lavishly illustrated, both with watercolours by Wilson and photographs, most of which were taken by either Skelton or Shackleton. Altogether, there were no fewer than 13 full-colour Wilson watercolours, 33 other illustrations by Wilson, five double-page sets of panoramas, 225 photographs, and five maps. As with the writing, these images set the book apart from most of its contemporary accounts.

Perhaps because of the initial excellent sales and the effusive praise for Scott's book, Smith, Elder did not follow the common practice of the time of abridging the two-volume, first edition into a one-volume 'Popular' or 'Cheap' edition within a short period. Instead, Smith, Elder published a smaller format two-volume edition in 1907 and 1912, the latter because 'the reissue of this book in a handy and compact form at a much cheaper rate should give it a new lease of life'.[10] Little did anyone in Britain know that the very month that reprint was published, Scott, Wilson, Bowers, and Oates would all die on the Barrier. In the following few years, with the interest in the BNAE increased due to the events of Scott's last expedition, John Murray, Scribner's Sons, and Thomas Nelson & Sons each brought out new two-volume editions.

Thus, it was not until 1929 that John Murray first published a one-volume abridgement of *The Voyage of the 'Discovery'* – which is the one that is reproduced here. As were its predecessors, that edition was very well received, at least in part because Scott's basic story was left untouched. Rather than condensing or tightening his account, the book was reduced in length primarily by eliminating most of the illustrations. In addition, three elements that had been at the end of the second volume were removed: a general survey of observations, an appendix on geological observations by Ferrar, and an appendix on the wildlife of the region by Wilson. Concurrently, an introduction was added by the famed Norwegian explorer Fridtjof Nansen.

It has now been many years since any one-volume edition of *The Voyage of the 'Discovery'* has been published, and, as with the original two-volume work, copies of the first 'Popular' edition can now demand a high price. When combined with the fact that most of the attention paid to Scott in recent decades has focused on his last expedition, the difficulty of finding copies of his first expedition account means that the story of the BNAE is not nearly so well-known as it could or should be. This is a highly unfortunate loss, as the expedition was, in a sense, the effort that truly began the opening up of the Antarctic continent and that established much of the groundwork for what became known as the 'Heroic Age' of Antarctic exploration. Therefore, it is to be much appreciated that this current volume allows the reader to become familiar not only with what was a hugely significant expedition, but with a classic account by a man who was not simply a remarkable explorer but one of the most talented, commanding, and articulate writers in the field of polar exploration.

BEAU RIFFENBURGH
Scott Polar Research Institute, Cambridge

References

1. 'The National Antarctic Expedition'. *Nature* 64 (1651), page 103.

2. R. F. Scott, letter to H. R. Mill; quoted in E. Huxley, *Scott of the Antarctic*, page 177.

3. R. F. Scott, letter to H. Scott, 24 April 1905; SPRI MS 1542/8/13.

4. R. F. Scott, letter to R. Smith; quoted in G. Seaver, *Scott of the Antarctic*, page 19.

5. G. Seaver, *Scott of the Antarctic*, page 35.

6. *The Nation* 82 (2114), pages 13–14.

7. 'Farthest South'. *The Spectator* 14 October 1905, pages 566–567.

8. Quoted in R. Pound, *Scott of the Antarctic*, page 122.

9. M. Rosove, *Antarctica 1772–1922: Freestanding Publications Through 1999*, page 342.

10. 'New Books'. *Scottish Geographical Magazine* 28 (1912), page 444.

THE VOYAGE OF
THE *DISCOVERY*

TO

SIR CLEMENTS MARKHAM, K.C.B., F.R.S.

THE FATHER OF THE EXPEDITION
AND ITS MOST CONSTANT FRIEND

PREFACE TO NEW EDITION

By his whole career, his achievements, his wonderfully heroic end, Robert Falcon Scott differs from all other travellers, and has got a position of his own in the history of Polar exploration. The message of his death in the great silence of the South made a deep impression in the whole civilised world, and we felt most keenly the loss it was to humanity and to exploration. Since then the Great War has passed, and the world has been much altered. Does Scott look different after this deluge of events? To the writer it seems that his important achievements, the great results of his journeys, the deep, noble qualities that distinguished him, the beauty of his character, will be even more highly appreciated today than they could be at that time.

It is strange to note that this man, who has made such a mark in Polar history and has inaugurated a new era in Antarctic exploration, had been led into this work quite accidentally. As he tells himself, he had no predilection for Polar exploration; he had not, like what we hear about so many other Polar travellers, taken any keen interest in Arctic adventures ever since his boyhood. It was by mere chance that he happened one day in June 1899 to walk down the Buckingham Palace Road in London and meet Sir Clements Markham, who unbeknownst to Scott had had his eye on him ever since seeing him at work as a *mere lad*.

Scott learned then 'for the first time that there was such a thing as a prospective Antarctic expedition'. He had just served as first lieutenant of the *Majestic*, then flagship to the Channel Squadron; he was an unusually able, accomplished, and very promising young officer, who had obviously a great future before him in the Navy. Nevertheless, two days later, encouraged by Sir Clements, he 'wrote applying to command the expedition and a year after that he was officially appointed'.

His education hitherto had not prepared him specially for what was going to be his life's great work, and he had had no training which made him specially fit for the task. He had not been a sportsman of the kind one may expect as the future Polar traveller; he had had no experience in snow and ice, in cold and snowstorms, had never tried skiing or sledge-travelling or living in the snow. He was not a literary man who had studied the history of Arctic or Antarctic travelling and exploration. He was not a man of science who had studied the Polar problems.

He was, however, what was of more worth than all these things together, an excellent specimen of the human race, both physically and mentally, and he was a born leader of men.

When he was appointed leader of the coming expedition, in June 1900, there was only a year left till the expedition was expected to start. He had had nothing to do with the preparations of it before that time, and very little had been done, except that the building of the ship had begun in March 1900. Considering that he now had to study from the beginning the history of Polar exploration, the technique of Polar travelling, all the different problems before him, both practical and scientific, one is filled with amazement and with great admiration for the man who in that short time mastered all difficulties as he did and managed to fit out the expedition and to start only a year after he had taken over the command.

I have a vivid recollection of our first meeting when he came to my home in Norway with my friend Sir Clements Markham. I still can see him, a very attractive young naval officer who made an unusually good impression, and at once inspired confidence. We discussed the problems of the Antarctic and all details of sledge-travelling, as well as Polar and oceanographic research, etc. Although most of these subjects were more or less new to him, he at once grasped the points and the various details with his clear and well-balanced intelligence; one easily understood that it would not take him long to acquire the necessary knowledge.

If one wishes to form a just opinion of the value of Scott's great achievements on his first expedition as compared with those of later explorers, one has to consider how very little any of us knew at that time about the conditions in the Antarctic regions, how uncertain everything was, and how much harder it was to prepare an Antarctic expedition when so little was known about the possible difficulties, than it has been in later years, when after Scott's discoveries we knew so much better what might be expected, and the explorers could profit by the experiences made during the first journeys.

Before the voyage of the *Discovery* our knowledge of the outer parts as well as the interior of the Antarctic was very scanty indeed, and the views of the Polar authorities differed widely. The prevailing idea was perhaps that the South Polar region was covered by an extensive Antarctic Continent, and according to the discoveries made during my own crossing of the Greenland Inland ice, it was expected that this continent was covered by a similar ice-cap, whose surface would rise slowly inland from the outer continental coasts. Assuming that the Antarctic Continent had a very great width one of my apprehensions was, that the surface of this ice-cap might rise to very considerable altitudes in the interior which might make travelling difficult. On the other hand, it was to be expected that this glacial surface would be very even and convenient for sledge-travelling. Other authorities held, however, that the Antarctic was probably not covered by one extensive continent, but that there were several different lands and groups of islands. These lands were probably covered by great ice-caps, which might possibly extend more or less continuously across the intervening sea, from one and to another. Very little was also known about the ice conditions of the sea in the different seasons of the year, along the Antarctic coasts and along the Great Ice Barrier, and what the possibilities of navigation might be in those waters.

Scott had to work out his plan and to make his careful equipment with all possibilities in view, and had to be prepared for every eventuality. He did it in a masterly way, and his discoveries during this first expedition, completed by those of his last great journey, have thrown an entirely new light upon the Antarctic problems. His discovery of the Victoria mountain range extending inland with the low almost horizontal glacial surface at its foot, and the extensive ice-cap covering the land behind the mountains and extending towards the Pole, his examination of the ice surface and determination of its altitudes, his discovery of King Edward Land, etc. etc., have entirely changed our views and have formed the foundation for a new understanding of the Antarctic problems.

It is remarkable how Scott, who was not a man of science by his education, had a perfect understanding of the importance of all kinds of scientific research in Polar exploration; and how the value of an expedition may be said to be proportional to its scientific results. This view grew so strong with him that, when he prepared his last expedition, his ambition was that it should be as completely equipped for scientific work, both as regards men and material, as was in any way possible, and he had on board a fuller complement of scientists of different kinds and surveyors than ever before composed the staff of a Polar expedition.

The scientific researches and results of that expedition are accordingly of the very greatest value in different branches of science. Scott was unable to complete the scientific work projected, and direct the presentment of it; a great loss was thus inflicted on Science; but, nevertheless, the work which was accomplished and the rich material of scientific observations collected during the series of years and with the many important results obtained give this great expedition a unique importance, and will more and more prove fundamental for our knowledge of the Antarctic and its conditions.

It is also striking how Scott, who, as was mentioned before, had not the advantage of being educated from his boyhood to skiing and a life in the snow, nevertheless learned to master the technicalities of sledge-travelling so perfectly that his last journey to the South Pole and back is really a unique feat in the history of travelling. It is strange that with our common friend Sir Clements Markham he seemed to be opposed to the use of dogs for the more strenuous sledge-travelling. Had he used more dogs and less man haulage, he might have made an easy and brilliant journey to the Pole and back again. As it is, we are filled with admiration for the wonderful exploit accomplished, most of the enormous distance being covered on foot by him and his comrades without the help of any beasts of draught; and had it not been for the breakdown of some of his comrades, whom Scott could never think of leaving behind, he could easily have pulled through.

But Robert Scott was much more than a very prominent traveller and discoverer: he was a great man with a noble and generous character. No-one can read this book about his first expedition and still less his diary written on his last journey without being thrilled with admiration for this unusual man and his fine qualities. Always and on every occasion we are struck by the startling selflessness of the man. His thoughts are for his country, his comrades, his navy, and for science, never for himself – a selflessness that does not fail even in the hardest moments.

When my memory goes back to the days when we met, I see him before me, his tight, wiry figure, his intelligent, handsome face, that earnest, fixed look, and those expressive lips so seriously determined, and yet ready to smile – the features of a kindly generous character, with a fine admixture of earnestness and humour. He was keen and intense in what he was doing, but always ready to enjoy a joke, or to lighten a strenuous moment with his whimsical humour. It is characteristic of him that his nearest never saw him lose his temper. One understands how on his last death march he has been able to cheer up his comrades almost to the last moment. The history of Polar exploration has got many a leaf that bears evidence of the noblest qualities of man in his struggle for unselfish goals, in his sacrifices for what he considers to be the aim of his life. But one of the most beautiful leaves is, in its tragic greatness, the one which tells about the last journey of Scott and his comrades. We find nowhere a finer revelation of the superiority of the spirit and will of man in his stubborn fight against the forces of Nature. Can one read anything more thrilling than Scott's simple narrative of the homeward journey after they had reached the Pole; how they, with one comrade already broken down and dying, with the difficulties piling up ahead of them, nevertheless carry out their scientific work, stop to examine the rocks, to collect samples and important fossils throwing light on the origin and history of the great mountain range which he had discovered. And then, further on, on their last terrible death march, in the cold and blizzard and snowdrift, they carry with them their journals and notes of observations, their instruments, and their valuable samples of rocks and fossils, they save them for humanity, while they themselves must perish, instead of throwing everything away and only thinking of saving their lives: it is as if death had no power.

For all future generations he has set an inspiring example of how a man takes struggle and suffering for a cause he has chosen as his. From the leaves of his diary, written under the impression of the moment, from day to day, rises the picture of a great man, a great leader, a character of the finest and noblest that ever lived, and who never failed, even under the heaviest test, ever the same unbribable spirit, with thoughts for the others and none for himself, just to the end – upright, and indomitable on the threshold to the long journey into the eternal stillness. A *man* he was – a *man* wholly and fully – a *man* till the last.

FRIDTJOF NANSEN

PREFACE

Strange as it may seem, the greater part of this story had been enacted before I realised that it would devolve on me to narrate it in book form.

When first I saw vaguely this unwelcome task before me there was fresh in my mind not only the benefit which we had derived from studying the records of former Polar voyages, but the disappointment which we had sometimes suffered from the insufficient detail which they provided. It appeared to me in consequence that the first object in writing an account of a Polar voyage was the guidance of future voyages; the first duty of the writer was to his successors.

I have done my best to keep this object in view, and I give this explanation because I am conscious that it has led me into descriptive detail which will probably be tiresome to the ordinary reader. As, however, such matter is more or less massed into certain portions of the book, I take comfort from reflecting that the interested reader will have no difficulty in avoiding such parts as he may consider tedious.

I have endeavoured to avoid the use of technicalities, but in all cases this has not been possible, as the English language is poor in words descriptive of conditions of ice and snow. I take the opportunity, therefore, of defining some technical words that I have used freely.

Névé – the packed snow of a snowfield, an accumulation of minute ice crystals. This word is, of course, well known to mountaineers.

Nunatak – an island of bare land in a snowfield. Where an ice-sheet overlies the land, the summits of hills thrust through the sheet present this appearance.

Sastruga [plural *Sastrugi*] – an irregularity formed by the wind on a snow-plain. 'Snow-wave' is not completely descriptive, as the sastruga has often a fantastic shape unlike the ordinary conception of a wave.

Ice-foot – properly applied to the low fringe of ice formed about Polar lands by the sea-spray. I have used the term much more widely, and perhaps improperly, in referring to the banks of ice of varying height which skirt many parts of the Antarctic shores, and which have no connection with sea-spray.

Beyond explaining these few words I make no apology for the style or absence of style of this book; I have tried to tell my tale as simply as possible, and I launch it with the confidence that my readers will be sufficiently indulgent to its faults in remembering the literary inexperience of its writer.

For me the compilation of these pages has been so weighty a matter that I must always feel the keenest gratitude to those who assisted me in the task. I cannot think that the manuscript would ever have been completed but for the advice and encouragement I received from its publisher, Mr Reginald Smith, nor can I forget to thank Sir Clements Markham and other friends for hints and criticisms by which I profited, and Mr Leonard Huxley for his judicious provision of the 'hooks and eyes' to many a random sentence. How much I owe to those of my comrades who are responsible for the originals of the illustrations, will be evident.

R. F. S.
August 28, 1905

THE SHIP'S COMPANY

Officers

ALBERT B. ARMITAGE, Lieutenant R.N.R.
CHARLES W. R. ROYDS, Lieutenant R.N.
MICHAEL BARNE, Lieutenant R.N.
ERNEST H. SHACKLETON, S. Lieutenant R.N.R.
GEORGE F. A. MULOCK, S. Lieutenant R.N.
REGINALD W. SKELTON, Lieutenant (E.) R.N.
REGINALD KOETTLITZ, surgeon and botanist
EDWARD A. WILSON, surgeon, artist, vertebrate zoologist
THOMAS V. HODGSON, biologist
HARTLEY T. FERRAR, geologist
LOUIS C. BERNACCHI, physicist

Warrant Officers (all R.N.)
Thomas A. Feather, boatswain
James H. Dellbridge, 2nd engineer
Fred. E. Dailey, carpenter
Charles R. Ford, ship's steward

Petty Officers
Jacob Cross, P.O. 1, R.N.
Edgar Evans, P.O. 2, R.N.
William Smythe, P.O. 1, R.N.
David Allan, P.O. 1, R.N.
Thomas Kennar, P.O. 2, R.N.

Marines
Gilbert Scott, Private R.M.L.I.
A. H. Blissett, Private R.M.L.I.

Civilian
Chas. Clarke, ship's cook

Seamen
Arthur Pilbeam, L.S. R.N.
William L. Heald, A.B. R.N.
James Dell, A.B. R.N.
Frank Wild, A.B. R.N.
Thomas S. Williamson, A.B. R.N.
George B. Croucher, A.B. R.N.
Ernest E. Joyce, A.B. R.N.
Thomas Crean, A.B. R.N.
Jesse Handsley, A.B. R.N.
William J. Weller, A.B.

Stokers
William Lashly, lg. stoker R.N.
Arthur L. Quartley, lg. stoker R.N.
Thomas Whitfield, lg. stoker R.N.
Frank Plumley, stoker R.N.

R. F. SCOTT, *Captain*

Historical

> Till then they had deemed that the Austral earth
> With a long unbroken shore
> Ran on to the Pole Antarctic,
> For such was the old sea lore. – RENNELL RODD

A bibliography of the Arctic Regions would occupy a large volume; that of the Antarctic Regions compiled by Dr H. R. Mill in 1901 contained 878 references, and included all books, pamphlets, and maps even remotely touching the subject that had been published in any country. This great difference in the published matter relating to the two ends of our globe justly represented the relative knowledge concerning them in 1901, to whatever extent the disproportion has been modified since that year.

The history of the Arctic Regions stretches back for many centuries, to the adventurous voyage of Oht-here, the friend of King Alfred, and to the exploits of the Norsemen in Greenland; the history of the Antarctic Regions commences at a much later period, and attention was drawn to them, not so much by the voyages of discoverers as by the persistent delineations of a great Southern continent by the map makers. The idea of this conjectural continent probably arose at a very early date, and when there was much excuse for such a view; but it was retained with extraordinary pertinacity throughout several centuries, being held long after the voyages of many navigators had disproved the existence of parts and thrown strong doubt on the accuracy of the whole conception.

Ortelius, in his *Typus orbis terrarum*, published in 1570, boldly draws the coast of '*Terra australis nondum cognita*' round the world and well to the north, even crossing the Tropic of Capricorn in two places. The editions of Mercator follow this delineation pretty exactly down to the one published by Hondius in Amsterdam in 1623, and although the famous map of the world prepared for Hakluyt in 1599 has the merit of omitting the Southern continent as unauthenticated, the fictitious coastline continued to appear in later maps and naturally attracted the attention of enterprising navigators.

There are three legends on the Southern continent of Ortelius's map: one is to the effect that it is named by some the Magellanic Region; the second tells us that the Portuguese called the part south of the Cape '*Psittacorum regio*' (region of parrots), because of the incredible number of these birds; and the third, opposite to Java, refers to Marco Polo and Varthema for statements of very extensive land to the south. At this time a fanciful idea prevailed among cartographers that there must be a great mass of land to the south to balance the known land to the north.

The earliest references to the climatic conditions of the Antarctic Regions are perhaps to be found in the statement of Amerigo Vespucci; this famous person acted as pilot of a Portuguese expedition which, after surveying the coast of Brazil in 1501, is supposed to have sailed to the south and to have sighted the land of South Georgia, of which Vespucci remarks: 'A rocky coast without any port or inhabitants. I believe this was because the cold was so great that no-one in the fleet could endure it.' Another curious indication of the same nature is to be found in the conversation which the Italian traveller Ludovico di Varthema, referred to by Ortelius, had with the Malay captain who took him to Java in 1506. The skipper knew how to steer by the compass and by a certain star of the Southern hemisphere as well as by the pole-star. He told Varthema of a region far beyond Java where the day only lasted for four hours, and said that it was colder than any other part of the world. Varthema concludes his account of the conversation by saying, 'We were pleased and satisfied'!

The manner in which the veil of mystery was first lifted from the Southern hemisphere was naturally enough by the extension of exploration along the coastlines of the Northern land masses, but it was long before the facts thus ascertained ceased to be distorted by cartographers. The circumnavigation of the Cape by Vasco da Gama in 1497 did not extend sufficiently far south to upset calculations greatly, but when in 1520 Magellan discovered the strait which bears his name, Tierra del Fuego, to the south, was at once seized upon as an evident part of the *Terra australis*, and its coasts were unhesitatingly joined to the main outline of that continent. And when Sir Francis Drake in 1577 'came finally to the uttermost part of the land towards the South Pole; the extreme cape or cliff lying nearly under 56° S., beyond which neither continent nor island was to be seen; indeed the Atlantic and the Pacific Oceans here unite in the free and unconfined open,' his discovery seems to have been completely misrepresented, and his accounts were garbled in such a manner as to have taken centuries to unravel.

How complete was the ignorance of Southern conditions at the commencement of the seventeenth century can be gathered from the voyage of Quiros. Pedro Fernandez de Quiros was a Portuguese pilot in the Spanish service; favoured by the Pope Clement VIII, he obtained an order from the King of Spain, Philip III, to prosecute a voyage to annex the South Polar continent and to convert its inhabitants to the true faith. He sailed from Callao in 1605 and steered to the W.S.W., but after proceeding a month on this course his heart failed him, and in latitude 26 S. he turned to the W.N.W. On this track he discovered the largest of the New Hebrides group, named it '*Australia del Espiritu Santo*', and, firmly believing it to be part of the Southern continent, solemnly annexed it, with the South Pole itself, to the crown of Spain!

Of the early voyages of the seventeenth century, that of the Dutchmen Schouten and Le Maire in 1616 went to establish Drake's discovery of the meeting of Atlantic and Pacific Oceans south of Cape Horn, and to curtail the extent of the Southern continent in this direction; but more important was the voyage of Tasman, who actually set forth in search of the continent, and in 1642, after crossing the Indian Ocean between the latitudes of 45 and 49 S., discovered Tasmania and the northern island of New Zealand. This was a heavy blow to the theory of a great Southern continent, because it was in this region that its most northerly extension had been suggested by the early cartographers, and

Tasman showed that it could not lie much beyond the 50th parallel either in the Indian Ocean or to the south of Australia, then known as New Holland. How slowly even important information of this sort must have travelled in those days is shown by the fact that in 1660, when Wells published his 'new set of maps', he says: 'New Holland is esteemed to be part of the Southern unknown continent.'

The result of these voyages was to give a great impetus to others; especially it encouraged ships to venture to make the passage about Cape Horn, and this in turn led to a considerable increase of knowledge in this region. Voluntarily or involuntarily ships attained a comparatively high latitude reaching the 62nd or 63rd parallel, and, for the first time encountering the great Southern icebergs, obtained some idea of the severity of the Southern Regions.

But the idea of a great and populous Southern continent, though weakened, was by no means dissipated, and the eighteenth century saw several expeditions despatched in search of it. Of these, some of the most important were the French ventures under Bouvet, Marion du Frezne, and De Kerguelen-Tremarec, which led to the discovery of Bouvet Island, the Crozets, and Kerguelen, and collected much further evidence to show the great extent of the Southern Seas.

During the latter half of the eighteenth century there came a marked change in the objects which were set before the Southern voyagers. Hitherto men seemed to have thought of little but the aggrandisement of themselves or their State by the discovery of some new America; but now for the first time we find an eagerness in exploration for its own sake. Science had made rapid strides, and it was felt that its ends should be furthered by a completer know-ledge of the distribution of land and water on our globe, and by an investigation of natural phenomena in its less-known regions. This new view of exploration was held most strongly in France and England, and both Marion and Kerguelen in their voyages in 1771–2 were accompanied by a staff of learned men whose sole object was to add to the scientific knowledge of the regions visited. Curiously enough, the last of these voyagers, starting as he did under these more favourable conditions for exploration, succeeded in retarding rather than in advancing the cause of geography, for he interpreted the island which bears his name as part of a larger land mass, and boldly concluded that the great Southern continent had at last been found.

But this error, with many another, was soon to be rectified, and the whole mythical conception of the Southern continent to be swept away once and for all, when the great English navigator James Cook made known the results of his famous voyages. To give even a summary of the far-reaching effects of these wonderful voyages is beyond the scope of this chapter, but it may be briefly noted how each bore on the Antarctic problem that is before us.

In his first voyage in 1768, Cook circumnavigated New Zealand and laid down the eastern coast of New Holland, thus definitely cutting off these lands from any connection with the Southern Regions; this alone cleared up great misconceptions, but speculative geography continued to suggest that there was a continent further to the south, and finally Cook undertook to set the matter definitely at rest by a second voyage. This voyage is the most important incident in the history of Antarctic research, and may therefore be given in outline.

Cook sailed from Deptford in 1772 with two ships, the *Resolution*, 462 tons, and the *Adventure*, 336 tons. From the Cape he steered due south, and in spite of icebergs, fogs, and stormy weather, boldly pushed on to the 58th parallel, where he turned to the S.E. On January 17, 1773, he succeeded in crossing the Antarctic Circle for the first time, in longitude 38 E. Finding his progress blocked by ice, he turned again to the N.E., but not without giving us the impression that he must have been the first to see that icy barrier which appears to fringe the greater part of the Antarctic lands.

Passing to the south of Kerguelen, he showed the very limited dimensions of that island, and reached the 62nd parallel in longitude 95 E. Thence he continued more or less in the same high latitude to the 148th meridian, where he turned towards New Zealand. In November of the same year he again steered to the south, and reached the 60th parallel in 174 W.; constantly repulsed by the ice, he fought his way on east and south; in longitude 142 W. he crossed the Antarctic Circle a second time, but so arduous had been the labour of working the ship continuously among the ice that he was obliged to retreat to the north to give his crew some rest. It was not for long, however, for towards the end of January he was again on the Antarctic Circle in longitude 109 W. This time he was able to push on still further to the south, and it was not until he had reached latitude 71.10 S. in longitude 107 W. that he was forced to turn. What Cook actually saw in this advanced position is a matter of great interest; he describes a belt of pack with an unbroken sheet of ice beyond, which appeared to him to rise in level and in which he counted ninety-seven ice-hills. He does not definitely state that he saw ice-covered land, but many authorities have believed that his description could mean nothing else; with some experience of the deceptive appearances of ice masses, however, I am inclined to think that the evidences are by no means sufficient to support this view.

After turning, Cook retreated to the north, and spent the winter amongst the Pacific Islands; in November he once more turned south and made his way towards Cape Horn between the parallels of 50 and 60 S., and thus for the first time traversed the Pacific in a high southern latitude. After doing much valuable surveying work in the region of Cape Horn and South Georgia, he again steered to the east, and now crossing the Atlantic in a high latitude, between 58 and 60 S., he finally returned to the Cape.

The importance of this voyage can scarcely be exaggerated; once and for all the idea of a populous fertile Southern continent was proved to be a myth, and it was clearly shown that whatever land might exist to the south it must be a region of desolation hidden beneath a mantle of ice and snow. The vast extent of the tempestuous Southern Seas was revealed, and the limits of the habitable globe were made known. Incidentally it may be remarked that Cook was the first to describe the peculiarities of the Antarctic icebergs and floe-ice.

One might pause here to consider the extent of human knowledge as regards the Antarctic Regions at the end of the eighteenth century after Cook's voyages, because it can be stated with brevity. The ocean was known to encircle the world completely about the 60th parallel; beyond this lay a region of icebergs and intense cold; attempts to penetrate this inhospitable region had seemed to show that in many places ships might force their way to the Antarctic Circle, but at about this latitude they were stopped by impenetrable obstacles; if land lay beyond this, it was, in Cook's words, as 'countries condemned to everlasting rigidity by nature, never to yield to the warmth of the sun, for whose wild and desolate aspect I find no words'. Generally speaking, therefore, people had come to the conclusion that if land existed beyond the 60th parallel, it was not of much account.

After the return of Cook no important expedition was sent to the Southern Seas until 1819, when Bellingshausen sailed from Kronstadt with two well-equipped vessels. The object of this voyage was to emulate the achievement of Cook in circumnavigating the globe in a high southern latitude, and well was this mission fulfilled. With wonderful pertinacity the intrepid Bellingshausen again and again steered his ships to the south, and he succeeded no fewer than six times in crossing the Antarctic Circle. Although he did not reach such a high latitude as his predecessor, on the whole his course lay to the southward, and he still further narrowed the limits of the southern land which had been so greatly reduced by Cook. Further, Bellingshausen was the first definitely to discover land within the Antarctic Circle. In the longitude of 90 W. he saw a small island which he named Peter I Island, whilst farther to the eastward he sighted in the distance a more extensive coast which he called Alexander I Land. Unfortunately, little is known of Bellingshausen's voyage, as the narrative was never translated into English from the original Russian.

As regards the Southern Seas the early years of the nineteenth century were memorable for the development of the great whaling and sealing industries which flourished for half a century, and passed away only with the practical extermination of the animals on which they depended. It is strange to think that regions which before Cook's famous voyage were utterly unknown to man should have so speedily become the scenes of great activity, but no sooner was the existence of whales and seals in the Southern Seas reported than hundreds of English and American adventurers crowded in pursuit of them, and as late as 1840 it was reported that there were no fewer than 400 vessels occupied in this manner.

Amongst the owners of these vessels were men of broad public spirit, and the captains who commanded them included not a few of larger intelligence or more liberal education, who were keenly interested in the prosecution of geographical discovery. Conspicuous amongst the former were the famous firm of Enderby, who instructed the commanders of their ships never to neglect an opportunity for discovery and exploration, and who more than once sent forth an expedition largely for that purpose; whilst amongst the more enterprising commanders may be named Weddell, Biscoe, and Balleny. The result of this enlightenment was to add considerably to our knowledge of the Southern Regions.

The most important voyage made in these circumstances was that of James Weddell. After doing some excellent surveying work among the Southern islands in 1823, Weddell, in his small brig the *Jane*, and accompanied by the cutter *Beaufoy*, crossed the Antarctic Circle in longitude 32 W., and, passing innumerable bergs, found himself in an open sea, through which he sailed, and eventually reached a latitude of 74.15 S., more than three degrees to the south of Cook's farthest point. In this position, and when he could see nothing to the south but the clear sea horizon, he was forced to turn on account of the state of his crew and his provisions. For nearly twenty years this remained the most southerly point reached, and the extraordinarily open condition of the sea as reported by Weddell has rendered the region to this day one of the most fascinating to which prospective explorers can turn their thoughts.

Biscoe was one of Enderby's officers, and had been a mate in the Royal Navy. Like Weddell's, his voyage was made in a small brig, the *Tula*, accompanied by a tiny cutter, the *Lively*. He crossed the Antarctic Circle in longitude 2 E., and succeeded in running to the eastward on an exceedingly high latitude. On February 25, 1831, he discovered an ice-barrier which he likened in height and appearance to the North Foreland. He added: 'It then ran away to the southward with a gradual ascent, with a perfectly smooth surface, and I could trace it in extent to at least 30 or 40 miles from the foretop with a good telescope.' His ship at this time was in latitude 66.2 S., longitude 43 W., but apparently he again saw this icy barrier farther to the eastward and observed several indications which denoted the proximity of land. It was this coast to which he gave the name of Enderby Land. Biscoe wintered in New Zealand, and in the following season he sailed to the south again, and continuing his circumnavigation of the earth in a high latitude, discovered Graham Land, which, although connected with lands already known to the sealing community, gave a considerable extension to them.

Another voyage of great importance was made by John Balleny, also under the auspices of the enterprising firm of Enderby. Balleny started his voyage of discovery from New Zealand, in 1839, sailing in a schooner, the *Eliza Scott*, in company with the cutter *Sabrina*. He crossed the Antarctic Circle in longitude 177 E., but, unlike former voyagers, directed his course to the west instead of the east. On February 9 he discovered the group of islands which bear his name, and which I shall describe more fully in the course of my narrative. From this region Balleny was obliged to steer to the N.W., but later he was able to turn to the south again, and on March 2, when in latitude 64.58 S., longitude 121 E., he made the following laconic entry in his log: 'Saw land to the southward, the vessel surrounded by drift-ice.' On the following day he noted 'every appearance of land', and other entries tell of the large number of birds seen. On such slender evidence rests Sabrina Land, and yet after personally demonstrating the accuracy of Balleny's observations with reference to his islands, I should be sorry to undertake to sail over the spot where he 'saw land to the southward'. Balleny was evidently a man of few words, but of his ability as a navigator there can be no doubt.

This ends a brief retrospect of the discoveries made in connection with the whaling and sealing industries of the south, and shows that it is entirely honourable to the commercial enterprise of our country; for to the disinterested exertions of Mr Charles Enderby and to the zeal of his officers was due the discovery of Graham Land, Enderby Land, Sabrina Land, Kemp Land, and the Balleny Islands, whilst with an English sealer, Weddell, rested the honour of having achieved the highest southern latitude.

The necessarily bald outline of fact which it is alone possible to give in these pages can convey no idea of the extraordinary hardships and difficulties successfully overcome by these men. In the smallest and craziest ships they plunged boldly into stormy ice-strewn seas; again and again they narrowly missed disaster; their vessels were wracked and strained and leaked badly, their crews were worn out with unceasing toil and decimated by scurvy. Yet in spite of inconceivable discomforts they struggled on, and it does not appear that any one of them ever turned his course until he was driven to do so by hard necessity. One cannot read the simple, unaffected narratives of these voyages without being assured of their veracity, and without being struck with the wonderful pertinacity and courage which they display.

In the light of subsequent events, it is convenient to pause again at the close of Balleny's voyage to consider the further extent of Antarctic discovery. It must now have appeared to men that, after all, the South Polar area was occupied by land, and that the coast of this land clung very persistently to the Antarctic Circle. South of the Pacific, Cook and Bellingshausen had shown a dip towards the Pole, and south of the Atlantic Weddell had indicated another deep bay; but south of the Indian Ocean and of Australia it must have seemed highly probable that the coastline followed the Circle with little divergence. It can well be imagined, therefore, that explorers who were about to sail to the south in this direction must have been strongly disposed to expect land in that latitude.

At about this time there sprang up a new motive to encourage polar exploration, in the shape of terrestrial magnetism. The development of this science had gradually converted it into a subject of great interest, its practical importance in connection with the navigation of ships was now fully realised, and it was known that no complete study could be made of its phenomena without extensive observations in the polar regions. Amongst the scientific men who devoted their energies to achieve a more general recognition of these facts were Humboldt and Sir Edward Sabine, and as a result of their labours in 1838 the British Association petitioned the Government to send a scientific expedition to the Antarctic regions. The Government responded nobly to this petition, and organised an undertaking which was destined to achieve the most brilliant results, and to open up the Antarctic Regions in a manner which must have been wholly unexpected by its promoters.

But whilst Captain James Ross, the commander of this expedition, was diligently and carefully preparing and equipping his ships for this great venture, two other expeditions of importance had been despatched by other countries. One of these had left the shores of France in 1837. It consisted of two ships, *L'Astrolabe* and *La Zélée*, under the command of Dumont D'Urville, an experienced navigator. D'Urville first descended on the Antarctic area in the region of Graham Land, with the intent to follow Weddell's course and reach a higher latitude; but in this he was frustrated by the pack-ice, and after making some minor discoveries in the neighbourhood of Louis-Philippe Land and Joinville Island he returned to pursue his investigations in milder climates. In the end of 1839 D'Urville was at Hobart Town, Tasmania, where for the moment we will leave him and follow the fortunes of the other and more imposing expedition, consisting of five vessels, which left Chesapeake Bay in 1837 under the command of Commodore Wilkes.

In relating the history of the voyages of Wilkes and D'Urville I touch only on those parts which have a relation to the Antarctic Regions, though it must be understood that both these expeditions pursued scientific investigations in other parts of the world.

On reaching the Southern waters Wilkes divided his forces, and whilst he turned his attention to minuter surveying work, he sent the *Peacock* and *Flying Fish* south-west towards Graham Land and Alexander Land. These vessels, after much struggling with the ice, reached the vicinity of Peter I Island, but failed to attain a higher latitude than Bellingshausen or Cook had previously done in this region. The close of the season obliged them to retreat and rejoin the squadron without the achievement of any important result.

Towards the close of 1839 Wilkes, like D'Urville, had found shelter in Australian waters. By this time news of the prospective British expedition had been spread abroad, and it was known that, fully equipped for magnetic work, it proposed to sail directly for the position assigned to the magnetic pole by the calculations of the great German magnetician Gauss; this position was approximately in latitude 76 S., longitude 146 E. It was known also that Ross could not be in a position to attempt to reach it until the following year. How far Wilkes and D'Urville were guided by this information in their future actions it is impossible to say; that they must have received it is certain, and, considering that neither expedition was completely equipped for magnetic work, the fact that both immediately set sail in the direction of the magnetic pole must be regarded at least as showing questionable taste on the part of the commanders.

D'Urville left Tasmania early in January 1840, and, after a comparatively easy passage, on January 19, when in latitude 66 S., longitude 140 E., sighted land to the south. At first he seems to have seen nothing but the long ice-barrier so typical of Antarctic coasts, but later he found beneath the icy wall eight or ten small islets on which his people were able to land and to collect specimens of rock. He named this coast Adélie Land, and, continuing his explorations to the west, again sighted the ice-barrier somewhat more to the north, and named it Côte Clarie. Satisfied with the result of his voyage, D'Urville then turned to the north. Although it is to be deplored that he did not take full advantage of the season to continue his explorations, the discovery of Adélie Land was an extremely important matter, and possesses a definition which is sadly lacking in other reports.

Wilkes with his five ships sailed from Sydney at the end of December 1839. His ships took various tracks, but he himself in the *Vincennes* reached latitude 66 S., longitude 158 E., on January 16, and at this point he claimed to have first seen land to the south. Hence he cruised to the westward, approximately on the latitude of the Antarctic Circle, with a comparatively open sea to the north and masses of pack-ice to the south; and beyond the latter he again and again claimed the discovery of high mountainous land. He passed close to Adélie Land and Côte Clarie only a few days after their first discovery by D'Urville, and, continuing his course, alleged the discovery of further extensive lands to the westward.

On his return to civilisation Wilkes claimed a vast discovery. The courses of his ships had practically traversed an arc of the Antarctic Circle of no less than 70°, and, although he did not assert that he had seen land continuously south of this arc, he reported its existence at such frequent intervals as to leave little doubt that it was continuous.

At a later date a great controversy arose as to the accuracy of Wilkes's observations, and resulted in much discredit being thrown on work which in many respects was important. Whilst there can be no possible object in attempting to revive such a controversy, it is evident that the true geographical conditions should be known, and therefore I make bold to give my opinion of the matter. In the course of this narrative I shall show that the mountainous lands reported by Wilkes to the eastward of Adélie Land do not exist, and it must be recognised that those to the west may be equally unsubstantial, but it is not clear that Wilkes wilfully perverted the truth; only those who have been to these regions can realise how constantly a false appearance of land is produced, and no position could be more favourable to such an illusion than that in which this expedition was placed when it skirted the edge of a thick pack containing innumerable icebergs. It must be supposed also, for reasons which I have given, that Wilkes, in common with other explorers, expected to find land about the Antarctic Circle, and when after his return he learned of D'Urville's discoveries, the position of Adélie Land would naturally have tended to dispel any doubt which he may have had as to what he or his people had seen.

Wilkes's ships were ill adapted for battling with the ice, and, apart from their discoveries, the fact that they continued so long in high latitudes reflects great credit on their navigation. Had he been more circumspect in his reports of land, all would have agreed that his voyage was a fine performance.

Whilst Wilkes and D'Urville were pursuing their explorations, Ross had sailed from England. James Ross had taken part in the Northern voyages of Parry and of his uncle John Ross; in the course of these he had spent no fewer than eight winters in the Arctic Regions, and he therefore brought an unrivalled experience to the task of fitting out his Southern command.

For the purposes of the expedition, two old bomb vessels were chosen, the *Erebus*, 370 tons, and the *Terror*, 340 tons; though slow sailers, these vessels had the advantage of great structural strength, and when Ross had further fortified their bows he possessed two ships capable of navigating amongst the pack-ice, the first of such that had ever sailed for the Southern Regions. Towards the end of the year 1840, Ross arrived in Tasmania to learn that others had already explored the route which he proposed to take. Whatever his feelings may have been at the time, the incident proved exceedingly fortunate, for it was this alone which decided him to proceed south on a more easterly meridian, it being 'inconsistent with the traditions of British exploration to follow in the footsteps of other nations'.

Sailing from Hobart in November, Ross reached the Antarctic Circle on New Year's Day in longitude 171 E., and at the same time found himself opposed by heavy masses of pack-ice. Here was the critical point at which the course taken by the expedition differed from that of its predecessors. Up to this time such an obstacle would have been deemed insuperable, and the older navigators would have sailed their light ships along its edge; Ross, with his heavy ships, plunged directly into it and continued to buffet his way to the south. Making all allowance for the fortified condition of the ships, it was a bold stroke, and it met with the most ample reward. After pushing onward for five days through the closely packed floes, the vessels burst forth to the south into an open sea. Remembering the main object of his journey, Ross steered to the west towards the magnetic pole, and on January 8, 1841, discovered the glorious mountainous country of Victoria Land.

Ross's discoveries are so closely connected with my narrative, that it is unnecessary to refer to them in detail here. Twice he visited this great open sea, and the results of these extraordinarily interesting voyages may be summed up as follows: The high mountain ranges and the coastline of Victoria Land were laid down with comparative accuracy from Cape North in latitude 71 to Wood Bay in latitude 74, and their extension was indicated less definitely to McMurdo Bay in latitude 77½. In the same latitude, but slightly to the eastward, the lofty volcanoes of Erebus and Terror were discovered, and the former was found to be active. Stretching away to the eastward for 400 miles beyond these, Ross observed that great wall of ice which he named the Great Barrier. At the eastern end of this wall he achieved his highest latitude, 78.11 S., an advance of nearly four degrees on his predecessor Weddell. Ross was not able to disembark on this great mass of land which he had discovered, but managed to reach the shore of some off-lying islands which he named the Possession Islands.

There are many reasons why Ross's wonderful voyage should not have attracted the wide popular interest which it deserved, but when the extent of our knowledge before and after it is considered, all must concede that it deserves to rank among the most brilliant and famous that have been made. After all the experiences and adventures in the Southern Seas which I have briefly described, few things could have looked more hopeless than an attack upon that great ice-bound region which lay within the Antarctic Circle; yet out of this desolate prospect Ross wrested an open sea, a vast mountain region, a smoking volcano, and a hundred problems of great interest to the geographer; in this unique region he carried out scientific research in every possible department, and by unremitted labour succeeded in collecting material which until quite lately has constituted almost the exclusive source of our knowledge of magnetic conditions in the higher southern latitudes. It might be said that it was James Cook who defined the Antarctic Region, and James Ross who discovered it.

This great expedition is brought curiously close to our own time when it is remembered that of those who took part in it there is yet one survivor. The young assistant surgeon of the *Erebus* has become the renowned botanist and traveller Sir Joseph Hooker, and has lived not only to take a share in sending forth a second expedition to the same region, but to welcome it back to our shores nearly sixty years after his own return from the Far South.

The *Erebus* and *Terror* reached the shores of England in September 1843, and for fifty years the map of the Antarctic remained practically unaltered, though during this period some important light was shed on the general conditions of the region, and the advance of science caused a gradual awakening of interest in it. The results of the few voyages to the Antarctic area during this long period, or indeed down to the close of the nineteenth century, may be summed up in a very few words.

Tempted by Sir James Ross's report of the large number of whales seen during his voyage, in 1892 a number of Scotch whalers set sail for the south, and touching the Antarctic lands in the neighbourhood of Joinville Island, threw some further light on that region; but as they found no sign of the whales which they sought, the voyage was commercially a failure, and the vessels soon turned to the north again. In the following year, however, Captain Larsen, of the whaler *Jason*, bent on much the same errand, managed to sail down the east coast of Graham Land, and to reach a latitude of 68.10 S. in longitude 60 W. This voyage has been very little noticed, though from a geographical point of view it is of great importance, as with Biscoe's discovery to the west, it showed the attenuated form which Graham Land possesses, at any rate until it is well south of the Antarctic Circle. Looking over the whole Antarctic area, I can scarcely see a place where geographical discovery is more urgently needed than in the extension of this bold effort of Larsen's.

Whilst Larsen pursued his investigations on the east coast of Graham Land, his compatriot Evenson, in the *Hertha*, descended on the west side, and reached the high latitude of 69.10 S. in longitude 76 W. He sighted Alexander Land, but unfortunately does not appear to have extended its coasts, though there can be little doubt that it is connected with Graham Land.

A similar object, the hope of discovering a whale fishery, induced the veteran shipowner Svend Foyn, of Tonsberg, to send one of his ships, the *Antarctic*, to the Ross Sea area. This resulted in the first landing on Victoria Land, which was made by her captain, Christiansen, at Cape Adare in 1894. Three years later Sir George Newnes sent an expedition to this spot, under Mr Borchgrevink; the party landed safely, and spent a winter in a hut which will be introduced to the reader in the course of my narrative. Unfortunately this party did not travel far from its base, and so was unable to throw any light on the geographical conditions of the interior; but its scientific observations were of importance, and its geological collection especially interesting. Before leaving the south Mr Borchgrevink landed from his vessel, the *Southern Cross*, towards the eastern end of Ross's Great Ice Barrier, and thus reached a higher latitude, by a few miles, than that achieved by the great explorer.

Whilst Sir George Newnes's expedition was wintering at Cape Adare, another band of explorers was living beyond the Antarctic Circle in a widely different region. The energies of M. de Gerlache had succeeded in equipping a small vessel, the *Belgica*, for a polar voyage, and this ship, passing down the west coast of Graham Land through an unexplored channel, had become beset in the ice to the south-west of Alexander Land. Here, the first vessel to spend a winter beyond the Antarctic Circle, she drifted to and fro throughout a long imprisonment. Reaching at one time a latitude of 71.30, she was gradually carried to the westward, and at length freed near the farthest point reached by Cook in 1773. Equipped with modern apparatus and ideas, this expedition, if it did not add greatly to geographical knowledge, contributed much by its investigations in other scientific departments to the general cause of Antarctic discovery.

But by far the most important event in the history of Antarctic research, after the great voyage of Ross and before the close of the nineteenth century, remains yet to be described. This was the crossing of the Antarctic Circle by the famous *Challenger* Expedition in 1874.

The *Challenger*, under Sir George Nares, stood to the south on the meridian of 80 E., and after crossing the Circle turned to the north-east, and later to the east, remaining altogether some three weeks in the region of icebergs. During this time she pursued her customary employment of sounding and dredging in the depths of the ocean, and here, as elsewhere, this resulted in a rich harvest of fresh information. Amongst the specimens thus secured were numerous rocks of continental origin; there could be no doubt that these had been borne by ice from some Southern land, and therefore they showed that continental land must exist within the Antarctic Circle almost as conclusively as if the land itself had been seen.

But the importance of the *Challenger* expedition as regards the Antarctic Regions lay not so much in the discoveries made as in the fact that they drew the attention of scientific men to the interest of the problems which yet remained to be solved in that area. From the return of this famous expedition and the publication of its results dates that revival of interest in the Far South which, fostered by a few eminent men, continued to spread and culminated in the despatch of the various expeditions which co-operated with the *Discovery*.

This desire for further Antarctic research arose principally in Germany and England, but in both countries it was equally slow in arriving at a practical result. In Germany the repeated and energetic representations of the great magnetician Georg Neumayer gradually bore fruit, and resulted eventually in the despatch of our German colleagues under Professor von Drygalski in his good ship the *Gauss*.

In England, whilst there were many Arctic explorers and others who were keenly interested in the subject, it was the written appeals of Sir John Murray that first secured for it a wider appreciation. Soon after the completion of his labours on that monumental work the *Challenger* publication, Sir John Murray exerted his great abilities to stimulate a fresh interest in the Southern Regions; in 1886 he published an important treatise in the *Scottish Geographical Journal*, which led to the despatch of the Dundee whalers to which I have alluded; this in turn tended to direct further attention to Southern exploration, and in 1893 Sir John read a second paper to the London Geographical Society which still more clearly and ably advocated the cause.

Meanwhile other events had occurred which, although unproductive, were significant of the tendency of public thought. In 1885 an Antarctic Committee was appointed by the British Association, which two years later made a strong report in favour of further exploration. In 1887 the Victorian Government, through its agent Sir Graham Barry, offered to join the Home Government in sending out an expedition, but this scheme likewise fell through.

The actual birth of the *Discovery* Expedition may be dated from July 1893, when Sir Clements Markham resolved that an expedition should be sent. The extraordinary strength and pertinacity of Sir Clements' character were already well known to his intimates, and they at least must have known that this resolve was momentous and signified that by hook or by crook an expedition would go. In virtue of his position as President of one of the greatest and richest societies in the world, Sir Clements was favourably placed for carrying out his determination, but few could deny that in the years of struggle and difficulty which followed, however ably and generously he was supported by his colleagues and others, it was mainly through his own unique, unconquerable personality that the expedition became a living fact.

As a result of the discussion on Sir John Murray's paper in November 1893, it was suggested that the Government should be approached with a view to sending out an expedition consisting of two ships. This proposal was supported by many eminent men of science, including the late Duke of Argyll, Sir Joseph Hooker, and the late Sir William Flower, and by such naval officers as Admirals McClintock, Vesey Hamilton, Hoskins, Colomb, Markham, and Lord Charles Beresford. It was on this occasion that the Duke of Argyll remarked on the incongruity of the fact that we knew more about the planet Mars than about a large area of our own globe.

The Council of the Royal Geographical Society therefore appointed a special Antarctic Committee. In a lengthy report the Committee enumerated the objects to be gained by such an expedition, and concluded with the following words: 'Apart from the valuable scientific results of an Antarctic expedition, great importance must be attached to the excellent effect that all such undertakings, in which our country has been prominent, have invariably had on the Navy by maintaining the spirit of enterprise.'

To the appeal which followed this report in 1896 the Government opposed the existing state of public affairs, which made it inconvenient for the Navy to undertake such a task as was proposed; but in a later letter the Lords Commissioners of the

Admiralty expressed their sympathy with the objects desired, and signified their willingness to assist any expedition that might be despatched.

Failing Government assistance, in May 1897 it was resolved by the Council of the Geographical Society that every effort should be made to start an expedition on a proper scale under its own auspices, but it was soon seen that this was a task of such magnitude that the assistance of all who were interested in the scheme would be required.

During the early months of 1898 the Royal Society was invited and agreed to co-operate; henceforth the undertaking was to be considered as under the auspices of two great Societies instead of one, and was demonstrably supported by the whole scientific opinion of the country. An important report by a sub-committee of the Royal Society clearly detailed the scientific objects which were to be sought, and laid particular stress on the extreme value of the magnetic work. Meanwhile Sir Clements Markham commenced and continued his indefatigable efforts to raise the necessary funds; the Geographical Society headed the subscription list with 5,000l., and circulars were issued to the public.

In March 1899 this appeal met with a noble response, when Mr Llewellyn Longstaff came forward with a munificent donation of 25,000l. When the *Discovery* eventually sailed it was to act on a concerted plan between expeditions of various nationalities; it is quite certain that Britain would not have been represented in this exploring effort had it not been for Mr Longstaff's public-spirited and patriotic gift. But whilst our countrymen complacently reflect that the British tradition for exploration has been maintained, they appear entirely to have forgotten the man who made it possible.

The position of the promoters of the enterprise was now greatly strengthened, and was made yet stronger when His Majesty the King, then Prince of Wales, graciously consented to become its patron, and the Duke of York vice-patron. Later in the year it was decided to make a further appeal to the Government; a deputation consisting of some of the most eminent men in both Societies waited on Mr Balfour and re-stated the objects of the enterprise. Mr Balfour expressed strong sympathy with the objects and a lively interest in the undertaking, and it was entirely owing to his generous attitude that the Government eventually yielded and agreed to contribute 45,000*l*., provided an equal sum could be raised by private subscriptions.

Again Sir Clements Markham issued appeals for money, and gradually the private fund crept up. After Mr Longstaff, amongst the largest and most generous contributors were Sir Alfred Harmsworth with 5,000*l*., the Misses Dawson Lambton with 1,500*l*., the Royal Society with 1,000*l*., and the Government of Queensland, Australia, with 1,000*l*.; many others were equally generous in accordance with their means, and with a further sum of 3,000*l*. from the Geographical Society the private subscriptions were raised to 47,000*l*., the Government grant was secured, and the whole available fund was carried to the adequate total of 92,000*l*. Financially all was now comparatively plain sailing.

As soon as Mr Longstaff's gift had placed the expedition within the bounds of practical politics, the question of the vessel in which its members were to sail came under consideration, and the appointment of a special Ship Committee, consisting of several distinguished Admirals and Arctic explorers, was followed by the decision to build a new ship for the purpose.

Mr W. E. Smith, C.B., Chief Naval Constructor, was invited and consented to prepare the plans and supervise the construction of this new vessel, and the Committee, in consultation with Mr Smith, accepted the tender of the Dundee Shipbuilding Company to build her. In March 1900 the keel was laid in the Company's yard.

In the summer of this year the position of the National Antarctic Expedition, as it was now called, was briefly as follows. The money had been subscribed for the venture, the control of which was vested in the hands of a body named the Joint Committee, containing sixteen members appointed by each of the two Societies. The names which figured on the list of this Committee were those of gentlemen eminent in many branches of science, and of distinguished Admirals and explorers – in fact, of all those who were best able to give advice concerning the multifarious details of a scientific exploring expedition. As, however, this body, as a whole, was obviously too large to deal with matters of detail, it had appointed nine sub-committees; these were for the purpose of considering the various branches of science which were to be investigated, to supervise the construction of the ship, &c.;

whilst one, the Executive Committee, was to act for and report to the larger body.

Such was the position of affairs when I received my appointment to command the expedition on June 10, 1900, and therefore, in making my bow to the public, I will digress slightly to show how this had come about. I may as well confess at once that I had no predilection for polar exploration, and that my story is exceedingly tame, but such as it is it shows how curiously the course of one's life may be turned. I suppose the tale really starts in 1887, when Sir Clements Markham, then the guest of his cousin, the Commodore of the Training Squadron, made himself the personal friend of every midshipman in the four ships which comprised it, and when I became one of those midshipmen and first made his acquaintance. But there is a long interregnum – until 1899, in fact; in that year I was serving as first lieutenant of the *Majestic*, then flagship to the Channel Squadron. Early in June I was spending my short leave in London, and chancing one day to walk down the Buckingham Palace Road, I espied Sir Clements on the opposite pavement, and naturally crossed, and as naturally turned and accompanied him to his house. That afternoon I learned for the first time that there was such a thing as a prospective Antarctic expedition; two days later I wrote applying to command it, and a year after that I was officially appointed. On June 30, 1900, I was promoted to the rank of commander, and a month later my duties in the *Majestic* lapsed, and I was free to undertake the work of the expedition. The year which followed was in many respects the busiest I have ever spent, and in view of the novelty and importance of the work this cannot be considered surprising; but, great as my difficulties were, I have to acknowledge that they would have been much greater had it not been for the numerous acts of kindness and the invariable courtesy which I received from the many persons who were directly or indirectly connected with the expedition.

The first month after my release from the Navy I spent in endeavouring to collect the threads of what was going forward, and in gaining some further instruction in magnetism, which was to form so important a part of our undertaking; but early in October I met Sir Clements Markham in Norway, and gathered a great many practical suggestions from Dr Nansen, to which I shall refer later; from Norway I went to Berlin to meet the leader of the

German expedition, Professor von Drygalski, and here, again, I met with the greatest kindness and consideration. The German expedition was to sail from Europe at the same time as our own, but its preparations were far more advanced. In Berlin I found the work of equipment in full swing; provisions and stores had already been ordered, clothing had been tried, special instruments were being prepared, the staff of the expedition had been appointed and was already at work, and the *Gauss* was well on towards completion. I was forced to realise that this was all in marked contrast with the state of things in England, and I hastened home in considerable alarm.

I found, as I had expected, that all the arrangements which were being so busily pushed forward in Germany were practically at a standstill in England; many of them, in fact, had not yet been considered. The construction of the ship was the only task which showed steady progress, and here there were many interruptions from the want of someone who could give immediate decisions on points of detail. It was clear that no time must be wasted if the lost ground was to be regained.

I have already outlined the machinery by which the expedition was now being guided. In spite of its individual efficiency it was necessarily ponderous: the members of the various committees and sub-committees were busy men; each was deeply engaged in his own work; many lived out of London, and all found it impossible to meet frequently and consistently. It was evident that the prompt and vigorous action which was necessary could not be expected from such bodies, and that in some manner I must obtain the power to act on their behalf. But here arose a considerable difficulty: out of the thirty-two members who constituted the Joint Committee I was personally known to only four or five; the responsibility vested in them was a large one, and it was not to be supposed that they would immediately place it in my hands without the showing of a strong case and reasonable guarantees. In this dilemma I have to acknowledge most gratefully the advice and assistance of Sir Arthur Rücker, then Secretary of the Royal Society, who, seeing my case, clearly pointed out the difficulties and offered to support me, provided I could produce a reasonable scheme by which they could be overcome.

On November 4 the Joint Committee met to consider such a scheme, and after some discussion passed it.

This resolution was of great importance; it left me practically with a free hand to push on the work in every department under a given estimate of expenditure in each, whilst to safeguard the interests of the Societies it provided that this expenditure should be supervised by a Finance Committee, which should control the business arrangements and sign the necessary cheques.

This plan has worked successfully down to the present time; that it has done so is mainly due to the generous manner in which the members of the Finance Committee have given their services to the business of the expedition, and to the complete accord with which they have worked together. It would be impossible to exaggerate the importance of the vast amount of business transacted by this Committee, and certainly no history of our expedition would be complete without a due acknowledgment of the individual and collective services of its members.

It was originally arranged that it should consist of the Presidents and Treasurers of the two Societies, but the President of the Royal Society desired that his place should be taken by an official from the Treasury, and the constitution eventually became: Sir Clements Markham (Chairman); Mr A. B. Kempe, K.C., Treasurer of the Royal Society; Mr Chalmers, C.B., of the Treasury; and Mr E. L. Somers Cocks, Treasurer of the Geographical Society; whilst Mr Cyril Longhurst, the indefatigable Secretary of the Expedition, became also the Secretary of this Committee.

The Joint Committee, after arranging for this new order of things, proceeded to consider the instructions which were to guide the movements of the expedition, and as there were many scientific interests to be served there was naturally considerable divergence of opinion on points of detail, and it was many months before these were finally decided.

In the meantime my first task was to collect, as far as possible, the various members of the expedition. It was evident that there was far more work than I could hope to do single-handed, and the best assistance I could have would be from those who were to take part in the voyage. I shall give some account of the individual officers and men in a future chapter, confining myself here to the part they played in the work of preparation.

From a very early date I had set my mind on obtaining a naval crew. I felt sure that their sense of discipline would be an immense acquisition, and I had grave doubts as to my own ability to deal with any other class of men. Mr Goschen had originally limited the Admiralty assistance in this respect to two officers, myself and Mr Royds, who was already at work in our service. At a later date, however, the Admiralty extended this limit to include Mr Skelton, our engineer, a carpenter, and a boatswain, and this gave us at any rate a small naval nucleus. But beyond this for a long time the Admiralty hesitated to assist us, and before the tide turned I was almost reduced to despair of a concession which I thought so necessary.

In this matter and in many others I can never forget the assistance which was given me by the late Sir Anthony Hoskins. Sir Anthony loved to do his good deeds silently, and it was not until long after that I learnt how frequently he had lent a helping hand to the expedition. But any hesitation the Admiralty may have had in granting naval seamen did not spring from coldness towards the enterprise. The Sea Lords were at this time Lord Walter Kerr, Sir Archibald Douglas, and Admiral Durnford, and both individually and collectively they never failed to evince an interest in it, so that at length the active assistance of Sir Archibald Douglas overcame objections of principle, and the men were granted.

But this concession, perhaps the most important which the expedition received, did not come until the spring of 1901; and as, after this, steps had to be taken to select the most fitting volunteers, the chosen men did not join until very shortly before the sailing of the expedition.

Many of the officers, however, came on the scene much earlier, and whilst our new vessel was yet a skeleton the first lieutenant, the chief engineer, and the carpenter were standing by her, and were able to look into the numerous small difficulties that arose, and to inform me of them during my flying visits to Dundee. My own headquarters I was obliged to make in London, and I fixed them in the University buildings of Burlington House, where rooms were kindly placed at my disposal by Lord Esher, then Secretary to His Majesty's Office of Works.

It would not be possible for me to describe half the work that went on in this office; suffice it to say that it kept me extremely busy for six days in the week. My room soon became a veritable museum of curiosities: sledges, ski, fur clothing and boots were crowded into the corners, whilst tables and shelves were littered with correspondence and innumerable samples of tinned foods. In the midst of this confusion I worked steadily on with all the ups and downs that such occasions will bring, sometimes in high hope that all was going well, and sometimes with the dreary feeling that by no possibility could we be ready to start at the required date.

Luckily, throughout this busy, trying time I had much assistance. Our indefatigable Secretary, Mr Longhurst, was always willing to take fresh troubles on his already overburdened shoulders, and devoted his whole energies to the work. Of Mr Armitage's help in matters of equipment I shall speak later on. At about this time also Mr George Murray, F.R.S., received his appointment as temporary director of the scientific staff, and many of the details of the scientific equipment passed into his hands, where I soon became conscious they rested with safety. Mr Murray also undertook to edit that very important publication the *Antarctic Manual*, which provided us with a great deal of scientific and historical instruction concerning the regions we were about to visit.

But it was not all plain sailing with those who were gathered around me at this important time; not all were such staunch supporters as those I have mentioned. Amongst my most careful selections had been the person who was to hold the responsible position of ship's steward. At this time a good ship's steward would have been invaluable, but my choice proved unfortunate, and first and last caused us a great deal of trouble, although I am glad to say we were rid of him before the expedition sailed.

In this manner and with varying fortune the work of equipment proceeded. First a lengthy provision list was drawn up, the amounts being calculated for a three-years' absence; tinned meats, vegetables, flour, biscuit, butter, sugar, and every other necessary article were ordered in due proportion, and even such minor requirements as dubbin and plate-powder were not forgotten. After this came a consideration of the clothing, and with what an assortment of this we were provided will be gathered from the pages of this narrative; for it will be seen that we had need to be prepared for every variety of climate, from the sultry heat of the tropics, through the storms of the Southern Seas, to the intense cold of the Far South. Next came the provision of the travelling equipment – sledges, tents, furs, &c., had to be thought of and selected with a care which I shall explain in a future chapter.

But the above by no means exhausts the list of subjects for which arrangements had to be made in that small office in Burlington House. Few people can realise what an extraordinary variety of articles is required on such an expedition as ours, where a ship and its crew are to be banished from all sources of supply for a lengthened period. For, besides the provision of food and clothing and such things as were obviously necessary, it is possible to enumerate a host of articles which, whilst we were equally forced to procure them, will probably not have occurred to the ordinary reader.

For instance, there were boatswain's stores, with rope, canvas, and everything necessary for the refitting of the top-hamper of the ship; carpenter's stores, with all requisites for work in that department; engineer's stores, including a vast variety of articles; ice implements of various kinds, explosives for destroying the ice, guns and ammunition, and fireworks for signalling. There were tobacco, soap, glass, crockery, furniture, mattresses, and all such requisites for personal comfort; oil-lamps and candles for lighting, and stoves for heating; medicines and medical comforts; a photographic outfit; a library of many hundreds of volumes; also a balloon equipment; canvas boats of various kinds, huts for our shore station, instruments of many descriptions; and so on almost ad infinitum.

It may be imagined that, large as this list of requirements was, with the sum of 92,000*l.* there should have been no financial difficulty, nor, indeed, was there; but it has to be remembered that of this large sum 51,000*l.* went to the complete cost of building the new vessel, and it was necessary to reserve more than 25,000*l.* for the wages and the contingent expenses of the voyage.

The sum which remained was sufficient to equip the expedition in the most thorough manner, but it had to be administered with economy; and though I am now conscious of many mistakes which were made from lack of experience, I think little money was wasted.

On the whole the firms with which we dealt treated us with great liberality, and supplied us with excellent goods. Many took an especial interest in the expedition, and made a very considerable reduction in the prices of the articles they supplied. Whilst it is impossible to quote all the instances of this nature, I take the opportunity of most gratefully acknowledging three* cases in which goods were supplied as an absolutely free gift, and in which the donors took exceptional care that the packing should be in exact accordance with our requirements. These firms were Messrs. Colman, Limited, who supplied us with nine tons of flour and a quantity of mustard; Messrs. Cadbury, who gave 3,500 lbs. of excellent cocoa and chocolate – all that we required of these articles, in fact; Messrs. Bird & Sons, who presented us with eight hundredweight of baking and custard powders; and Messrs. Evans, Lescher & Webb, to whom we were indebted for all our lime-juice.

During these busy months of preparation which I have briefly described, the various important posts in the expedition had been gradually filled up, and now expeditionary work was being carried on in many places. Some officers were in Dundee, superintending the building of our good ship; others were working on their especial subjects at the British Museum; others were preparing themselves at the Physical Laboratory at Kew; and others, again, were travelling in various directions, both at home and abroad. Of all these movements and doings the central office was obliged to have cognisance, and therefore, as can be imagined, there were not many idle moments for its occupants.

Long ago it had been decided that the *Discovery* should be loaded with her valuable freight in London, and on June 3 she was brought round from Dundee and berthed in the East India Docks. The courtesy of the London Docks Company had placed at our disposal a large shed near this berth and soon after the centre of interest was transferred to this spot.

Here, therefore, during the two following months, busiest of all, were gathered all those stores which were to minister to our comfort and aid our work throughout our long voyage; and here also we loaded the staunch vessel which, with her solid wooden walls, was to form our home for more than three years.

* Though he goes on to acknowledge four.

CHAPTER 2

Preparation

> Ere long we will launch
> A vessel as goodly, strong, and staunch
> As ever weathered a wintry sea. – LONGFELLOW

In deciding to build a vessel for the purposes of the expedition the Ship Committee made a new departure, for the *Discovery* was the first vessel ever built in England for scientific exploration.

Few details in the great voyages of the early adventurers are more interesting to a sailor than those concerning the ships in which such voyages were accomplished. If one is inclined to wonder at the deeds of those mariners, wonderment must be greatly increased on realising the extraordinary vessels in which they were performed. Space does not permit me to touch on such a subject, but it may be interesting to note some of the vessels which have been used since the commencement of the era of scientific exploration to which I referred in the last chapter.

All four ships, the *Endeavour*, *Resolution*, *Adventure*, and *Discovery*, which took part in Cook's famous voyages, had been built and used for the coal trade; they ranged from 300 to 462 tons, and Cook expressed himself very well satisfied with them, deeming them well suited for his purpose.

The *Erebus* and *Terror*, as I have noted before, had been bomb vessels. They had been built in the old French war, and were designed to carry mortars which discharged shells at an angle of 45°. It was these same vessels which, after they had returned from their famous Southern voyage, were lost with the ill-fated

Franklin Expedition in 1845. The *Hecla* and *Fury*, which took part in Parry's famous voyages to the Arctic Regions, were also bomb vessels of the same class, but many of the early Arctic ventures were provided with old whalers: it soon came to be recognised what a useful type of vessel this was for ice-work.

The majority of ships employed in the Franklin Search Expedition were ordinary merchant vessels purchased into the navy and strengthened at considerable expense. Some of these which did good service, such as the *Enterprise* and *Investigator*, were over 530 tons. Most of these early vessels were sailing ships; the first steamers used were the *Pioneer* and *Intrepid*; they were about 430 tons burden, and both had been traders under different names.

In the latest Government Arctic Expedition of 1875 the two vessels employed were, as is well known, the *Alert* and the *Discovery*. The *Alert* was an old 17-gun sloop especially strengthened for the service, but the *Discovery*, though also strengthened at Portsmouth, had been the whaler *Bloodhound*, built at Dundee for the Greenland whale trade. The contrast between these two ships for ice-work was remarkable. The *Alert* had a bluff straight bow, whilst the *Discovery* had the more recently designed overhanging stem, and as a result the *Discovery* had often to be sent ahead to force a passage in order that the *Alert* might follow.

The lines of the *Discovery* represented the experience gained in the whaling trade; this industry, which had flourished for so many years, and which at one time had employed more than a hundred vessels sailing out of Hull, Peterhead, and Dundee, was slowly dwindling, but then, and even much later, fresh ships were launched from time to time to compete in it. The whale, however, was growing timid, and had to be sought in new waters; the difficulties with the pack-ice were ever increasing, and success lay more and more with those ships which were capable of forcing their way through it.

As a natural result of these conditions, a class of vessels was evolved which, whilst capable of taking the same hard knocks as the older ships, had a greatly increased power for making progress through the pack-ice, and to this class belonged the old *Discovery*. As regards lines, she probably reached the best form for such a vessel; for although others have been launched since, they have achieved greater efficiency mainly by increased engine-power. It was generally admitted by those who witnessed her performances in 1875 that the old *Discovery* was the best ship that had ever been employed on Arctic service.

The Ship Committee which was appointed to consider the design of the new vessel for the Antarctic Expedition had all these facts vividly before it, since some of its members had occupied the most important positions in the expedition of 1875. Without giving the names of all the members, as the Committee was a large one, I may mention that amongst the most active were Sir Leopold McClintock, Sir George Nares, Sir Vesey Hamilton, Sir Albert Markham, Sir Anthony Hoskins, and Captain E. W. Creak.

This Committee, therefore, after due deliberation, decided that the new vessel should be built more or less on the lines of the old *Discovery*; and here it is necessary to explain more exactly why this decision was made, as it wholly rejected another and newer type of Arctic vessel suggested by the *Fram*.

I have so often been asked whether the *Discovery* was like the *Fram*, and if not, why not, that I wish to make this point clear. The *Fram* was built for a specific object, which was to remain in safety in the North Polar pack in spite of the terrible pressures which were to be expected in such a great extent of ice.

This object was achieved in the simplest manner by inclining the sides of the vessel until her shape was something like that of a saucer, and lateral pressure merely tended to raise her above the surface. Simple as this design was, it fulfilled so well the requirements of the situation that its conception was certainly a stroke of genius. But what is generally overlooked is that this quality was only got by the sacrifice of others, which, though they might not be needed on that expedition, might be very much required on future ones. In short, the safety of the *Fram* was achieved at the expense of her sea-worthiness and powers of ice-penetration.

Hence it will be seen that since the advent of the *Fram* there are two distinct types of polar vessels, the one founded essentially on the idea of passive security in the ice, the other the old English whaler type, designed to sail the high seas and push forcefully through the looser ice-packs.

A very brief consideration of Southern conditions will show which of these two types is better suited for Antarctic exploration, for it is obvious that the exploring ship must be prepared to navigate the most tempestuous seas in the world and then to force her way through the ice-floes to the mysteries beyond. As yet the Southern Regions have shown no uses for the type which achieves safety at the expense of progress. It will be seen, therefore, that the Committee had a clear issue in deciding to adopt good and well-tried English lines for its vessel, and certainly in the excellent qualities which the *Discovery* showed, the decision was justified.

It is fair to add, however, that whilst this view commended itself so clearly to the English Committee, it was not adopted in Germany. Speaking at the Geographical Congress at Berlin in 1899, Nansen strongly recommended for South Polar work a vessel of the *Fram* type with fuller lines; this was, in fact, an attempt to produce all qualities by a compromise, and those responsible for the construction of the *Gauss* adopted the idea. I am not in possession of any detailed information concerning the perform-ance of the *Gauss* as a sea-boat or in pushing through the ice; but with a knowledge of her lines and her small engine-power, and my experience in the Southern Regions, I cannot believe she was so efficient an exploring vessel as the *Discovery*.

The art of building wooden ships is now almost lost to the United Kingdom; probably in twenty or thirty years' time a new *Discovery* will give more trouble and cost more money than a moderate-sized warship. This is natural enough: it is the day of steel, of the puncher and the riveter; the adze and the wood-plane are passing away. It must become increasingly difficult to find the contractors who will undertake to build a wooden ship, or the seasoned wood and the skilled workmen necessary for its construction.

The technicalities of the business may still remain in the memories of the older constructors, but have grown vague from disuse, and very few persons have cause to refresh their memories. And so it is all passing away; even the quaint old Scotch foreman, John Smith, who played so important a part in the building of the *Discovery*, has finished his work and vanished from the scene. It is a strange ending to an industry which a century ago produced those stout wooden walls that were the main defence of the kingdom.

In October 1899, when tenders for the new ship were invited, there were few replies, and only one from a firm which had recent experience of such a task. This was the Dundee Shipbuilding Company, the owners of a small yard on the Tay, which had been better known in the flourishing days of the whale trade as Stevens's Yard. Stevens had been a very well-known character in Dundee, the builder and owner of many a fine whaling ship.

Arrangements were therefore entered into with this Company to build the new vessel, and in the meanwhile the Committee's architect, Mr W. E. Smith, had thoroughly overhauled the plans of the old *Discovery* and drawn up a masterly specification for the new one. In March 1900 the keel of the new vessel was laid, and in a few months the massive oak frames had been raised and the busy scene of construction was in full swing.

I have spoken of this new ship as the *Discovery*, but it was not until June that her name was selected. Many names came up for discussion, and not a few of these had already done service in the older English expeditions. It was generally considered that the most appropriate plan was to revive some old time-honoured title, and as it was seen that few names carried a greater record than *Discovery*, that name was chosen. It is perhaps interesting, therefore, to give some idea of its history. There have now been six *Discovery*s. The first made no fewer than six Arctic voyages from 1602 to 1616 to the regions of Hudson Bay and Baffin Bay, on one of which she was commanded by the famous navigator William Baffin. The second also voyaged to Hudson Bay in 1719. *Discovery* No. 3 took part in Cook's third voyage in 1776. *Discovery* No. 4 was Vancouver's ship when he discovered the insularity of the land which is named after him. *Discovery* No. 5 took part in the 1875 expedition to the Arctic; she was commanded by the present Sir Henry F. Stevenson, and I have already shown her fitness for the work. Our own *Discovery* was therefore the sixth of that name and the heir to a long record of honourable service, and, what was equally important, of fortun- ate service, as the name *Discovery* seems never to have been associated with shipwreck or disaster.

And here I should like to introduce the reader to this good ship which was to carry us and our fortunes through many adventures. I can do so without going into technical details, as, thanks to the interest which Mr W. E. Smith took in his handiwork and the enterprise of the Institution of Naval Architects, a permanent record of the vessel has been established. The *Discovery*, alas! has passed away from the paths of exploration, but the future architect of such a ship will find all the information he needs concerning her in the *Proceedings* of the Institution I have named (April 1905).

The displacement of the *Discovery* was 1,620 tons, but her registered tonnage, by which her size can be compared with other ships I have mentioned, was 485. Her length between perpendiculars was 172 feet, and her breadth 34 feet.

By consulting the profile drawing of the ship, the reader will get some idea of the internal arrangements, but he will scarcely realise the extraordinary solidity of the structure. Most people who have voyaged in modern ships know that between them and the sea there has only interposed a steel plate the fraction of an inch in thickness; they may, therefore, be interested to know what the side of the *Discovery* was like. The frames, which were placed very close together, were eleven inches thick and of solid English oak; inside the frames came the inner lining, a solid planking four inches thick; whilst the outside was covered with two layers of planking, respectively six and five inches thick, so that, in most places, to bore a hole in the side one would have had to get through twenty-six inches of solid wood.

It will give some idea of the complexity of the construction of such a ship to name the various woods that were employed in the side, for in each place the most suitable was chosen. The inner lining was of Riga fir, the frames of English oak, the inner skin, according to its position, of pitch pine, Honduras mahogany, or oak, whilst the outer skin in the same way was of English elm or greenheart. The massive side structure was stiffened and strengthened by three tiers of beams running from side to side, and at intervals with stout transverse wooden bulkheads; the beams in the lower tiers were especially solid, being eleven inches by eleven inches in section, and they were placed at intervals of something less than three feet.

All this went to give the ship a frame capable of resisting immense side strains, but, strong as she was in this respect, the rigid stiffness of the sides was as nothing to that of the bows. Some idea of the fortification of this part can be gathered from the drawing, which shows the numerous and closely placed girders and struts that went to support the forefoot. Such a network of solid oak stiffeners gave to this portion of the vessel a strength which almost amounted to solidity. It will be seen, too, how the keel at the fore-end of the ship gradually grew thicker till it rose in the enormous mass of solid wood which constituted the stem. No single tree could provide the wood for such a stem, but the several that were employed were cunningly scarfed to provide the equivalent of a solid block; and, in addition to the strong fastenings which held piece to piece, long strengthening bolts were used which ran fore and aft and securely held all together. Some of these bolts, running entirely through wood, were as much as 8½ feet in length.

The bow of the *Discovery* was, therefore, a part which ran little risk of damage, and a knowledge of its strength was a pleasing possession when we came to ramming the ice-floes. In further preparation for such service the stem itself and the bow for three or four feet on either side were protected with numerous steel plates, so that when we got back to civilisation not a scratch remained to show the many hard knocks which the bow had received.

The shape of the stem was a very important consideration. It will be seen how largely it overhangs, and this was carried to a greater extent than in any former polar ship. The object with which this was fitted was often very prettily fulfilled during our voyage. Many a time on charging a large ice-floe the stem of the ship glided upwards until the bows were raised two or three feet, then the weight of the ship acting downwards would crack the floe beneath, the bow would drop, and the ship would gradually forge ahead to meet the next obstruction. This is the principle on which the ice is broken by all modern ice-breakers; and here, perhaps, I may be allowed to interpolate a remark. I have often been asked why the now well-known ice-breakers are not employed for such expeditions as ours. It is because the ice-breaker is built of steel, and, except when breaking very thin ice, is in constant need of repair; nothing but a wooden structure has the elasticity and strength to grapple with thick polar ice without injury.

The *Discovery*'s greatest strength lay in her bows, as I have just shown; next to this, and as far aft as the mainmast, the structure, supported by numerous beams and bulkheads, still remained very strong; but further aft there was a distinct weakening, for although the sides remained equally thick, the position of the engines and boilers necessitated the omission of many of the crossbeams.

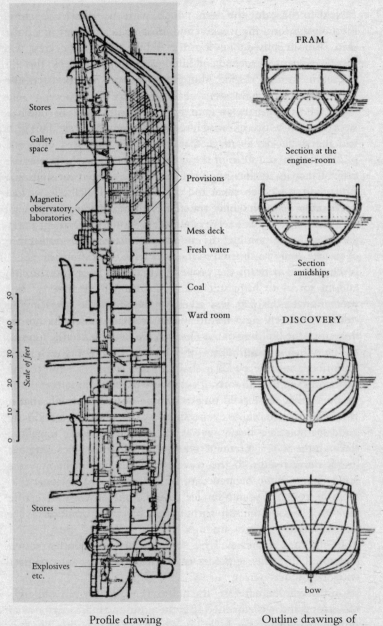

FRAM

Section at the
engine-room

Section
amidships

DISCOVERY

bow

Stores

Galley
space

Provisions

Magnetic
observatory,
laboratories

Mess deck

Fresh water

Coal

Ward room

Scale of feet

50 40 30 20 10 0

Stores

Explosives
etc.

Profile drawing
of *Discovery*

Outline drawings of
Discovery and *Fram*

Next to this came the stern, which, with the rudder and screw, must always form the weakest and most vulnerable part of a polar ship. Nansen aptly defines it as the Achilles' heel. Our screw was capable of being detached and lifted up through the deck; this is a common enough device, though, as I shall remark later, the manner in which it was done in the *Discovery* was new.

But Mr Smith made an entirely new departure in providing us with a rudder which likewise lifted up through the deck. This plan had the single disadvantage that the rudder possessed only one pintle and brace instead of the several that are customary; on the other hand, its advantages in the facilities it offered for shifting a damaged rudder were great and easily seen. As I shall tell, we had occasion to be exceedingly grateful for these advantages.

Protection for our keel was afforded, firstly, by making every part as strong as possible; the rudder-post was an enormous piece of timber, and was secured to the keel with extra strengthening – pieces placed beneath the propeller; it would have taken tremendous forces to have strained or distorted these fixtures. But protection to this part was given yet more by the overhanging stern, an entirely new feature in this class of vessel. As can be imagined, the building of the *Discovery* excited the keenest interest in the whaling community of Dundee. Few novelties passed unnoticed, and the peculiar shape of our stern gave rise to the strongest criticism; all sorts of evils were predicted, the commonest being that we should one day come down so heavily that it would be broken off! As events showed, this stern was a distinctly good feature: in a heavy seaway, as long as we were travelling through the water, it tended to keep the ship drier by causing her to lift more readily to the waves; to a certain extent it was a disadvantage if we happened to be becalmed and stationary, as then the rounded under-surface would come down with terrific violence, shaking the ship throughout; but these occasions were rare, and when we got amongst the ice we reaped great benefit from it, for then, as will be seen, it formed a buffer which prevented the heavier pieces of ice from coming into contact with the rudder.

On the whole, therefore, the hull of the *Discovery* was a splendidly strong and well-fortified structure, and the machinery was in all respects equal to the hull. The ship had two cylindrical boilers arranged to work at a pressure of 150 lbs. per square inch, and a set of triple expansion engines. The latter were designed to give 450 indicated horse power, but actually on trial gave over 500. Whilst there was nothing particularly novel in these engines and boilers, many details in connection with them had to be considered with especial care in view of the service for which they were required; more particularly was this the case with regard to the leads of steam pipes and the position of sea inlets.

In the shape of auxiliary machinery, besides that in connection with the main engines, the *Discovery* possessed a small condenser for making fresh water, a small dynamo for supplying electric light, a strong deck winch amidships, and a very powerful capstan engine under the forecastle. In connection with the last-named, and placed close to it, there was also a small auxiliary boiler which on one occasion at least did yeoman service. All these various machines were supplied by different firms, but our excellent set of main engines and boilers were built and placed by Messrs. Gourlay Brothers, of Dundee, and to the energetic manager of this firm, Mr Lyon, we owe the really novel feature which was embodied in our arrangement for lifting the screw.

For the benefit of those who are interested in engineering details I may briefly explain this device, as it is certainly worthy of record. As I have said, a lifting screw is a common fitting, but it has always had one disadvantage in the fact that the joint between the shaft and the screw has tended to get loose, and this has caused a very uncomfortable jarring when the engines have been revolving. The fittings in the *Discovery* entirely avoided this in the following manner: The tail end of the shaft was made hollow, and inside it was placed an inner shaft; the outer shaft fitted into the boss of the screw on a taper; inside the boss beyond this taper was a large nut in which the inner shaft could engage; the outer shaft and the screw were kept in close connection by the inner shaft and nut, and therefore there was no loose connection to jar. To disconnect the screw, a small section of the main shaft, in front of the tail shaft, could be lifted bodily, the inner tail shaft could then be turned and freed from the nut, when both inner and outer shafts could be withdrawn together, and the screw was free for lifting. This fitting was naturally expensive, but it is certainly the most efficient that has been devised for a lifting propeller.

In the profile drawing which is reproduced, on the middle of the upper deck will be seen a deck-house marked 'Magnetic Observatory'; this was an important place, both in the building and in the subsequent work of the *Discovery*. I have already given reason to show why the greatest stress was laid on the accuracy of our magnetic observations, and it will be clear that accurate magnetic observations cannot be taken in a place closely surrounded with iron. The enthusiasm of the magnetic experts on the Ship Committee had at first led them to request that there should be no iron or steel at all in the *Discovery*, and when it was pointed out that this could scarcely be, they demanded the exclusion of the metals from the vicinity of the magnetic observatory. At last a compromise was arrived at, which stipulated that no magnetic materials should be employed within thirty feet of the observatory. It is difficult to realise what immense trouble and expense this decision involved. This thirty-foot circle swept round, down by the foremast, under the bottom of the ship, and up in front of the mainmast; everything within this radius had to be made of brass or some other non-magnetic material, and when all the fastenings of the hull and all the fittings and furniture of the ship are considered, some idea may be gathered of the difficulty; even much of the rigging, which would ordinarily have been of wire, had to be made of hemp, of a size which is rarely, if ever, used in these days. And yet when all these elaborate precautions had been taken we could not banish magnetic objects from the sacred ring, for as a critic might well have pointed out in the first place, the provision-rooms within it could not possibly have their contents preserved in brass.

Nevertheless, this care in building was by no means lost. The magnetic observations taken on board throughout the voyage required astonishingly little correction, and though the condition of perfection looked for was not achieved, it was certainly more nearly approached than it would have been in an ordinary wooden steamship.

There were several curious results of this magnetic ordinance. I might mention, for instance, that the officers outside the circle slept on modern spring mattresses, whilst those within had to content themselves with wooden battens. There was quite a small stir, too, when the buttons of some cushions were found to be made of iron, and these were immediately ripped off and replaced by leaden ones. Of course, also, the magnetic regulations caused some amusement: at one time those who lived within the circle were threatened with the necessity of shaving with brass razors. The careful rounds made by the navigator before he commenced his observations were another subject of jest: knives and all sorts of instruments had to be summarily confiscated and placed beyond the pale, much to the annoyance of their owners; and on our way home from New Zealand I remember one awful case where it was discovered that throughout a whole set of observations a parrot had been hanging on the mess-deck. It was not the inoffensive bird that was objected to, but the iron wires of its cage.

The general distribution of ourselves and our stores inside the *Discovery* can be seen in the plan. The wardroom was a good-sized apartment, about thirty feet long and nearly twenty feet across; on each side were comparatively roomy cabins for the officers, whilst at the after-end, between it and the engine-room, lay my own cabin and that of the navigating officer. This position was by no means a catch, for in the tropics when steam was up it had the doubtful benefit of the heat given off by the boilers, whereas in the polar winter, when we had no steam, the engine-room naturally became the coldest place in the ship, and the after-cabin suffered accordingly. The crew-space was a little shorter than the ward-room, but as it extended the full breadth of the ship it was larger; compared with other vessels it gave ample room for its occupants. The galley-space was narrowed by having compartments cut off on each side; however, it was quite big enough for our require-ments. Between the fore-end of the galley-space and the after-end of my cabin were comprised the living-spaces, and the ship was designed so that this part might be kept especially warm in a polar climate. Concerning our advantages and difficulties in this respect I shall speak more fully in the course of my story, but whilst the plan of the ship is under discussion, it may be as well to point out how we were situated. Naturally, if one wants to keep warm one must exclude the cold on every side. During our polar winters, owing to the insulation of the upper deck, and to the fact that we piled snow on top of it, we had nothing to fear from that direction. As regards the sides, we had small difficulties which I shall men-tion, but the fact that cold might creep up from beneath was overlooked in providing for the comfort of our living-spaces.

It will be seen that beneath the men's quarters were the provision-rooms and holds; these, owing to the temperature of the sea outside and the space above, never fell much below freezing point, and so the men suffered little discomfort from below, but the coal-space or bunker under the wardroom was a different matter. This was only shut off from the engine-room by a steel bulkhead, and consequently it became extremely cold and communicated its temperature to the wardroom. This difficulty would not have arisen had the decks of the living-spaces been thoroughly well insulated.

Daylight was admitted to the living-spaces through central sky-lights and small round decklights. There were no portholes or sidelights in the *Discovery*.

Reference to the drawing will show the reader that the space devoted to our provisions and stores was divided into many compartments. It was very much smaller than the drawing might lead one to suppose, as a great deal of the room was taken up by the beams and girders provided for the strengthening of the ship. I do not know the exact weight of provisions and stores we carried when fully loaded, but I believe it to have been about 150 tons. And here I may add that the manner in which provisions and other stores are packed is of great importance in such an expedition as ours. The tinning of foods has advanced greatly of late years, but it is still necessary to exercise great care in selecting tins; the shape, the thickness, the care of manufacture, and the paint or lacquer employed, are all points to be observed, and as a general rule they give a good indication of the quality of the food within. Damp and rust are enemies which can be resisted successfully only by a well-made tin. The same care is necessary in selecting the cases in which these tins are stowed. For the *Discovery*, we had them made to reduce bulk as much as possible, while for convenience of hand-ling we limited the weight of each case to 50 or 60 lbs.

The position of our fresh-water tanks will be seen on the drawing; the full stowage of these tanks was 25 tons. As they lay within the magic circle they also had to be subservient to the magnetic rule, and were made of zinc. The zinc was too thin, and the arrangement was not satisfactory; however, as the tanks were not used during the winter we did not suffer much inconvenience.

Our coal supply was amongst our most precious possessions, and I shall show how things went for us in this respect. The outline of

the problem can be gathered from the following figures. The main
bunker held 240 tons; to this two small pocket bunkers added 53
tons, and the deck cargo we took south was 42 tons. For our
Southern campaign we had therefore 335 tons in all. At sea,
steaming economically, we used between 5 and 6 tons a day, or
with one boiler only, about 4 tons; on the occasions when we had
to lie with banked fires the consumption was about 1½ ton. It will
be seen, therefore, that each day made a marked difference in our
stock of coal when fires were alight in the main boilers. But of
course throughout our long imprisonment in the ice these fires
were not lighted, and then our consumption was only such as was
necessary for cooking and for warming the ship, and during our
second winter we reduced this to the very moderate figure of 15
cwt. per week.

A description of the *Discovery* would scarcely be complete
without a word or two about the spread of canvas which assisted
our voyage so greatly. The ship was under-masted: the mainmast
from truck to keelson was only 112 feet, and this is extremely
short for such a vessel, while comparatively speaking for this
height of mast the yards were square (i.e. long), the mainyard
being 60 feet in length.

The *Discovery* was extraordinarily stiff, and could have carried a
much larger sail area with advantage. As it was, the mainsail and jib
were the only sails we took off for a gale, and I think rarely, if ever,
have top-gallant sails been carried through such weather as ours.
For the non-nautical reader I may explain that in a gale there
comes a time when certain sails cannot be furled: to relieve the
ship they must be either cut or blown away. That we allowed our
top-gallant sails to remain spread in such weather shows our
confidence in the *Discovery*'s stability as well as in our canvas and
our boatswain.

But the comparatively small spread of sail was a great drawback
in light winds, and the ship was an extremely sluggish sailer.
Matters were rendered much worse also by the masts being placed
in the wrong position. They should have been put much nearer
the bows. When sailing 'on a wind' in the *Discovery* we had to trim
our sails so that everything forward was clean full while the sails on
the mainmast were almost shivering. These details are somewhat
technical, I fear, but it is very necessary that they should be noted

for the guidance of future explorers. Masts, yards, and sails are rapidly passing away from the seas, but where the saving of coal is of such prime importance, as in the case of the polar exploring ship, they must long remain a useful auxiliary. Although the *Discovery* was very slow under sail alone, unless running before a strong breeze, there were many occasions when the sails proved an immense assistance to the engines.

In the foregoing pages I have endeavoured to give some description of the ship which was built at Dundee, 1900–1, and which on March 21 of the latter year was launched and named the *Discovery* by Lady Markham. When, after gliding smoothly into the waters of the Tay, she was brought back to the dock side, it was to be invaded by a small army of workmen, to receive her engines and boilers, to undergo her successful trials, and generally to be prepared for that voyage to the Thames in June which I have already mentioned.

From the brief manner in which I have dealt with the *Discovery* it will be seen that the initial labours of the Ship Committee and the high intelligence of Mr W. E. Smith had provided us with the finest vessel which was ever built for exploring purposes. If I had little cause to complain concerning the instrument thus put into my hands, I had equally little concerning the officers and men who were to assist me in using it. The manner in which they did their work and the loyalty with which they supported me will appear in these pages; but here I would wish to introduce the reader individually to that roll whose members faced hardships and difficulties with invariable cheerfulness and elected to remain at their posts whatever might betide.

Ten officers besides myself messed together in the small wardroom of the *Discovery*. The senior of these was Lieutenant Albert B. Armitage, R.N.R. Armitage had spent a great number of years at sea, joining the training ship *Worcester* in 1878. He had passed through that ship with credit, and after an excellent practical seamanship training in sailing ships, had been appointed to a position in the P. and O. Company's service. In this service he had remained nominally ever since, but in 1894 he had been granted leave of absence to join the Jackson-Harmsworth Expedition to Franz-Josef Land. The expedition was absent for four years, and on its return Armitage's services were not only gratefully recognised by his employer, but were acknowledged by the Royal Geographical Society, which presented him with its Murchison Award. After this he had returned to his ordinary duties as first mate on one of the P. and O. Company's ships until January 1901, when his services were again lent for polar work, and he joined our expedition as navigator and second in command. Armitage was an excellent practical navigator, and of the value of his polar experience I shall speak later on. He was thirty-seven when he joined us.

Another member of our community who had seen Arctic service was our senior doctor, Reginald Koettlitz. Koettlitz was English in all but name, as his father, a minister of the Reformed Lutheran Church, had married an English lady and settled at Dover in the 'sixties. He had been educated at Dover College, and thence passed to Guy's Hospital. After qualifying he had settled down in the quietest of country practices, where he remained for nearly eight years, and might have remained to the present time but for a sudden impulse to volunteer his services as doctor to the Jackson-Harmsworth Expedition. This act had made him a wanderer, for after four years in the Arctic he accompanied expeditions to Abyssinia, Somaliland, and Brazil; and finally, with experiences gathered in many parts of the globe, he applied for and received his appointment as medical officer to the Antarctic Expedition. As his medical duties were expected to be light, he also acted as botanist to the expedition. As far as the land flora was concerned, this post was something of a sinecure, as the Antarctic lands produce only some poor forms of mosses and lichens, but Koettlitz had also to study and collect the various marine forms of plant life which are known to science under the name of phyto-plankton.

Our biologist, Thomas V. Hodgson, was a native of Birmingham. With a strong desire to qualify in medicine and natural science, he had been obliged to spend many years in business. His career shows well the pertinacity which we all came to recognise in his character, for during the years when he had been tied to a business which he disliked, he had devoted his spare hours with ceaseless diligence to scientific study. At last his chance had come, and he had been appointed to a small post in the Plymouth Biological Laboratory. From this time until he joined the expedition in August 1900 his life had been identified with Plymouth, at first in work connected with the laboratory and with a science lectureship, and later as curator of the Plymouth Museum, of which, in one sense, he may be said to have been the creator, as he guided its first tottering footsteps. Hodgson's task was to collect by hook or by crook all the strange beasts that inhabit our polar seas, and of the manner in which he went about it these pages will tell.

Koettlitz was forty years of age when he joined the expedition, and Hodgson thirty-seven. The average age of the remaining members of our wardroom mess was little over twenty-four years, so that it may be said they had most of their lives before them, and after my experience of their services I have little doubt as to the value of youth for Polar work.

Charles W. R. Royds was our first lieutenant, and had all to do with the work of the men and the internal econo ny of the ship in the way that is customary with the first lieutenant ∈f a man-of-war. He had passed into the *Britannia* from the *Conway* in 1890, and so joining the Naval Service had reached the rank of lieutenant in 1898. He joined us from H.M.S. *Crescent*, then serving as flagship on the North America station, and came with an excellent record of service for so young an officer. Throughout our voyage he acted as our meteorologist, and secured the most valuable records in this important branch of science in face of difficulties which this narrative will present.

Our second naval lieutenant was Michael Barne, who had only recently been promoted to that rank. He had been educated at Stubbington School in preparation for the Navy, and had joined the *Britannia* in 1891. Later he had served with me in the *Majestic*, and I had thought him, as he proved to be, especially fitted for a voyage where there were elements of danger and difficulty.

The original idea in appointing two doctors to the *Discovery* was that one should be available for a detached landing party; but, although this idea was practically abandoned, there were few things for which we had greater cause to be thankful than that it had originally existed, for the second doctor appointed to the expedition was Edward A. Wilson. Wilson was a native of Cheltenham, and had been educated at the college of that name and at Caius College, Cambridge; after taking his degree he had qualified in medicine at St George's Hospital, London, but on leaving the hospital ill-health had obliged him to spend some years abroad. His health was not wholly re-established when he joined the *Discovery*, but he was evidently on the mend, and his fitness for the post in other respects was obvious. In addition to his medical duties he was appointed vertebrate zoologist and artist; in the first capacity he dealt scientifically with the whales, birds and seals; in the second he was perhaps still more active, and it would take long even to number all the pictures and sketches he has produced of the wild scenes amongst which we lived.

I was still serving in the *Majestic* when I received my appointment to the expedition, and it was at that time I realised that among my messmates was just the man for the post of chief engineer of the *Discovery*. This was Reginald W. Skelton. He was a Norfolk man, and had joined the Navy as an engineer-student in 1887; subsequently he had served in various ships on various stations until at last he had been appointed as senior engineer of the *Majestic*, where I first got to know him well. One of my earliest acts on behalf of the expedition was to apply for his services, and it was certainly a very fortunate one: from first to last of our voyage we never had serious difficulty with our machinery or with anything concerning it. But Skelton's utility extended far beyond his primary duties. I shall have reason to tell of the many ways in which he assisted the scientific work of the expedition, whilst, thanks to his ability with the camera, in the course of his work as photographer-in-chief he produced the most excellent pictures that have ever been obtained by a polar expedition.

Our geologist, Hartley T. Ferrar, joined us only shortly before the *Discovery* sailed. Though born in Ireland he had spent the early years of his life in South Africa, but he had returned home to be educated at Oundle School and at Sidney Sussex College, Cambridge. Events went very rapidly for Ferrar at the end of his university career; in June 1901 he took honours in the Natural Science Tripos, in July he was appointed to the Antarctic Expedition, and in August he sailed for the Far South. He had very little time, therefore, to prepare himself for his important work, but he did his best to make up this deficiency by a steady application to his books and an increased activity when he arrived at the scene of his work. As will be seen later, the result of Ferrar's work was to throw considerable light on the structure of a vast land mass, no inconsiderable portion of the surface of the earth; it was a result, therefore, that cannot but be highly important to geological science, and it was achieved by physical labour which might not have been within the powers of a more experienced geologist.

Owing to the medical rejection of a former candidate for the post our physicist, Louis Bernacchi, did not join us until we reached New Zealand. Bernacchi had been born and educated in Tasmania; in 1895 he had joined the Melbourne Observatory as a student, and had there gained his knowledge of the special physical work which he has since steadily pursued. In July 1898 he had joined Sir George Newnes's Expedition to Cape Adare, and the valuable magnetic observations which he then made showed that he was capable of undertaking the more extensive programme connected with this science proposed for our shore station. The delicate instruments which he manipulated, and the difficulties he had with them, will be described in due course.

In the roll of the *Discovery* I have inscribed the names of two officers who did not serve throughout the whole term of the voyage; my reason will, I think, be clear.

One of these, Ernest H. Shackleton, was forced to leave us by ill health in 1903, when he was relieved by the other, George F. A. Mulock, who remained with us until the end of the voyage. Shackleton was born in Ireland and educated at Dulwich College; but at an early age he had taken to the sea, and as a merchant-service officer had drifted about to various parts of the world. From casual and irregular voyages he had passed to the more settled employment of the Union-Castle Line, and had already begun to make steady progress in that service when he was appointed to the *Discovery*. His experience was useful to us in many ways, and as he was always brimful of enthusiasm and good fellowship, it was to the regret of all that he left us in 1903.

His successor, Mulock, was a sub-lieutenant in the Navy when he joined us; he was then only twenty-one years of age, but having received some excellent instruction as a surveyor in H.M.S. *Triton*, and having a natural bent for this work, his services proved invaluable. Of this, however, I shall speak at a later date.

From what I have said of the individuals of our wardroom mess, the reader will see that, taking them as a whole, there were two rather noticeable features. The first was youth, concerning the advantages of which for a polar expedition I could write many pages; the second was diversity of experience: no two of us were likely to look at a matter from precisely the same standpoint. This, I think, was also an advantage: it gave us larger interests, and generally encouraged that attitude which is so necessary to the members of a small community – the determination to live and let live.

Be this as it may, we certainly had reason to congratulate ourselves on the selection of our officers, for of this there could be no clearer proof than the fact that we lived together in complete harmony for three years.

It has been said in the Navy of that useful class of individuals the warrant officers that they form the backbone of a ship's company, and certainly on board the *Discovery* the warrant officers played a highly important part. They lived in a small berth occupying one corner of the mess-deck, and comprised the boatswain, carpenter, second engineer, and ship's steward. With one exception I had known nothing personally of these men before they joined the expedition, but I had fully realised the importance of their duties and had taken great pains to select them from amongst other men who were recommended to me by my friends. In no case could I have made a happier choice; it would be impossible to exaggerate the admirable manner in which they all did their duties throughout the voyage.

Our boatswain, Thomas Feather, was a thorough seaman, and took that intense pride in his charge which was so well known in the old sailing days. A sailor will understand well the merits of a boatswain who can make the proud boast that the *Discovery* circumnavigated the world without losing a rope or a sail. Our boatswain, like the rest of us, under new conditions had to turn his talents into fresh channels; in the Far South all that pertained to our sledge equipment was placed in his charge, and with him rested the responsibility that everything was in readiness when we started out on our sledge journeys. And here, as before, he proved his excellence, for I do not remember a single complaint or breakdown that could have been obviated by more careful preparation.

In his own department our carpenter, F. E. Dailey, worked with the same zealous care as the boatswain. He possessed the same 'eye' for defects and the same determination that his charge should be beyond reproach.

I speak feelingly in these matters; anyone who has been captain of a ship will know the countless things that continually get out of order, and he will know, on the one hand, how annoying it is to have constantly to call attention to them, and, on the other, how pleasant it is to feel that close supervision is not necessary. I speak feelingly, therefore, because I was saved all these minor worries. I knew that whatever was 'adrift' with the rigging, the hull, or the machinery of the *Discovery*, it would be put right in the shortest possible space of time by the warrant officer in whose department it lay.

J. H. Dellbridge was our chief engineer's right-hand man. As the responsibilities of the carpenter and boatswain lay with the hull and rigging, so his lay in the engine-room; his duties implied that the engines must never be found wanting, and in what manner they were carried out this narrative will show.

A ship's steward is a specially important individual in an exploring vessel; he has to keep the most exact account of the stores that are expended, and of those that remain; he has to see that provisions are properly examined and properly served out, and that everything is stowed below in such a manner that it is forthcoming when required. I had difficulty in filling this post, to which I have referred, but eventually I decided to give it to C. R. Ford, who, although a very young man without experience, showed himself to be well fitted for it in other respects. He soon mastered every detail of our stores, and kept his books with such accuracy that I could rely implicitly on his statements. This also was no small relief where it was impossible to hold a survey of the stores which remained on board.

And now I pass on to that long list of petty officers and men which completes the roll of honour of the *Discovery*. I would that space permitted me to give to each that notice which his services deserved. There is not one name on the list that does not recall to me a pleasant memory or does not add to the splendid record of loyalty and devotion with which I was served. But gladly as I would stay my pen to discuss individual merits, I have to remember that to tell of the things we did and the things we saw are the main objects of this book, and reluctantly I leave the personalities of my sailor friends to emerge in a more casual manner from its pages.

Yet I cannot pass on without some acknowledgment of their collective efficiency and some explanation of the manner in which such a fine body of men was brought together. It will be remembered that I was serving in the Channel Squadron before joining the expedition; consequently, when the Admiralty gave permission for naval men to serve in the *Discovery*, I had friends in each ship of this fleet to whom I could write asking them to select one or two men from those who volunteered for the service. It was a simple plan, and relieved me of the difficulty of picking out names from the very long list which would have resulted had volunteers been generally called for. I knew well that amongst British blue-jackets there would be no lack of good men to volunteer for a voyage that promised to be so adventurous. Our men, therefore, came to us singly or by twos and threes from various ships; Evans, Allan, and Quartley came from my old ship the *Majestic*, Cross and Heald from the *Jupiter*, Smythe from the *St Vincent*, and so on.

All brought with them that sense of naval discipline which they displayed so noticeably throughout the voyage. It must be understood that the *Discovery*, not being in Government employment, had no more stringent regulations to enforce discipline than those which are contained in the Merchant Shipping Act, and however adequate these may be for commercial purposes, they fail to provide that guarantee for strict obedience and good behaviour which I believe to be a necessity for such exceptional conditions as exist in polar service. Throughout our three years' voyage in the *Discovery* the routine of work, the relations between officers and men, and the general ordering of matters were, as far as circumstances would permit, precisely such as are customary in His Majesty's ships. We lived exactly as though the ship and all on board had been under the Naval Discipline Act; and as everyone must have been aware that this pleasing state of affairs was a fiction, the men deserve as much credit as the officers, if not more, for the fact that it continued to be observed.

Since the return of our expedition it has been acknowledged that our labours met with a large measure of success, and it has been recognised that each officer in his particular department has added something to the advancement of scientific knowledge; and they, as well as I, will be the last to forget how much they owed to the rank and file. For my part I can but say that success in such an expedition as ours is not due to a single individual, or to a few individuals, but to the loyal co-operation of all its members, and therefore I must ever hold in grateful memory that small company of petty officers and men who worked so cheerfully and loyally for the general good.

I have now endeavoured to give the reader some idea of the good ship *Discovery*, and of the gallant crew which manned her; it remains to give a clearer account of the mission on which she was despatched.

It was Sir Clements Markham who first suggested that for convenience of reference the Antarctic area should be divided into four quadrants, to be named respectively the Victoria, the Ross, the Weddell, and the Enderby. Having given a brief outline of the history of Antarctic research, I will pause here for a moment to point out the prospects which each of these quadrants offered for exploration.

The Victoria quadrant included that region which had been investigated by Wilkes and D'Urville. Whilst it offered an interesting problem in the discovery of the true extension of Adélie Land, the prospect of getting to a high latitude in it did not seem hopeful.

Very little was known of the Enderby quadrant, but much attention had been called to it by the scientific voyage of the *Challenger*, and this, with certain evidences connected with drifting ice, had caused some people to believe that a high latitude might be reached in this region. This opinion was especially held in Germany, and it was therefore in this direction that the *Gauss* was steered.

The Weddell quadrant I have already noticed as a region of exceptional interest. More than once ships had attempted to penetrate to the open sea reported by Weddell, but they had invariably found it impossible to do so. But these vessels had not possessed the power of steam; with a steamer there seemed little doubt that Weddell's farthest point could be reached, and an explorer might determine what lay in the clear sea which had been seen beyond.

In spite of the undoubted fascination of this region, however, it appeared to the promoters of our enterprise that in the Ross quadrant lay even a fairer prospect of important results. Though this was the region of which most was known, the discoveries of Ross, like those of all great explorers, had given rise to a host of fresh problems. Here it was certain that a high latitude could be reached, and that the work of the expedition could be conducted in the heart of the Antarctic area. Geography saw in this region a prospect of the reproduction of those sledging journeys which had done so much to complete the mapping of the Far North; meteorology grasped at a high latitude for the fixed observation of climatic conditions; magnetism found in the Ross Sea that area which most nearly approached the magnetic pole; geology was attracted by the unknown mountainous country which fringed its shores. There was no branch of science, in fact, that did not see in the Ross quadrant a more hopeful chance of success than was promised by any other region. When, therefore, Sir Clements Markham proposed that this direction should be taken by the expedition, the proposition met with complete and unanimous assent from all who were interested in the venture, and long before the *Discovery* was built her prospective course had been finally decided.

It might be thought that with an exploring expedition such as ours, little more was necessary than to indicate the direction in which it should go, and to leave the uncertain future in the hands of those who conducted it. There is much in this view, and there is no doubt as to the wisdom of leaving to the commander of an expedition the greatest possible freedom of action, so that at no time may his decision be restricted by orders which could not have been conceived with a full knowledge of the conditions.

But instructions for the conduct of an expedition may serve a most useful purpose, both for the authorities who issue them and the commander who receives them, if, without hampering conditions, they contain a clear statement of the relative importance of the various objects for which the expedition is undertaken.

I need not recall the several branches of science which it was proposed that our expedition should investigate, but I may point out that there were bound to be innumerable instances in which their interests clashed. The best-conducted expedition cannot serve two masters, and in pursuance of one object is often obliged to neglect others. Although circumstances will generally determine the object which can be pursued most profitably at the moment, where what may be described as so many vested scientific interests are concerned, it is obviously of advantage to the commander that he should know in what light these interests are regarded by those responsible for the expedition.

The value of instructions, then, is to place before the leader a general review of the situation, a statement of the order in which the objects of the expedition are held, and as much information as can be given without prejudice as to the wishes of his chiefs. Of such a nature were the instructions I received before sailing for the South. The original draft had been prepared by Sir Clements Markham at a very early date, and, as I have already mentioned, it came subsequently under the consideration of the Joint Committee of thirty-two members.

The draft contained many clauses relating to matters of opinion, and it was not to be expected that so large a Committee, containing representatives of so many interests, should at once agree as to their relative importance or as to the manner in which the expedition should be conducted.

In consequence of this there was much discussion, with delay that threatened to impede the progress of the expedition; but at this point the Societies wisely decided to submit the whole question to a body of smaller dimensions, and a Committee of four was appointed to decide the matter finally.

The four members of this Committee were Lord Lindley, Sir George Goldie, Sir Leopold McClintock, and Mr A. B. Kempe. Thanks to the practical manner in which it dealt with the question, and perhaps especially to the great administrative experiences of Sir George Goldie, all difficulties were speedily solved, and the instructions were finally drafted.

There can be no doubt that the expedition, as well as the Societies, owes much to this Committee, which, after piloting a difficult question through rough waters, furnished instructions of such a nature as I have previously indicated. In quoting these instructions I confine myself to such parts as relate to the conduct of the expedition, disregarding, for obvious reasons, those which have reference to the conditions of our service. I also omit several paragraphs which, owing to a subsequent alteration in the organisation of our officers, became non-effective.

Extracts from the Instructions under which we Sailed

... The objects of the expedition are (a) to determine, as far as possible, the nature, condition, and extent of that portion of the South Polar lands which is included in the scope of your expedition; and (b) to make a magnetic survey in the southern regions to the south of the 40th parallel, and to carry on meteorological, oceanographic, geological, biological, and physical investigations and researches. Neither of these objects is to be sacrificed to the other.

... We, therefore, impress upon you that the greatest importance is attached to the series of magnetic observations to be taken under your superintendence, and we desire that you will spare no pains to ensure their accuracy and continuity. The base station for your magnetic work will be at Melbourne or at Christchurch, New Zealand. A secondary base station is to be established by you, if possible, in Victoria Land. You should endeavour to carry the magnetic survey from the Cape to your primary base station south of the 40th parallel, and from the same station across the Pacific to the meridian of Greenwich. It is also desired that you should observe along the tracks of Ross, in order to ascertain the magnetic changes that have taken place in the interval between the two voyages.

... It is desired that the extent of land should be ascertained by following the coastlines; that the depth and nature of the ice-cap should be investigated, as well as the nature of the volcanic region, of the mountain ranges, and especially of any fossili-ferous rocks.

... You will see that the meteorological observations are regularly taken every two hours ... It is very desirable that there should, if possible, be a series of meteorological observations to the south of the 74th parallel.

As regards magnetic work and meteorological observations generally, you will follow the programme arranged between the German and British Committees, with the terms of which you are acquainted.

Whenever it is possible, while at sea, deep-sea soundings should be taken with serial temperatures, and samples of sea-water at various depths are to be obtained for physical and chemical analysis. Dredging operations are to be carried on as frequently as possible, and all opportunities are to be taken for making biological and geological collections.

. . . The chief points of geographical interest are as follows: to explore the ice-barrier of Sir James Ross to its eastern extremity; to discover the land which was believed by Ross to flank the barrier to the eastward, or to ascertain that it does not exist, and generally to endeavour to solve the very important physical and geographical questions connected with this remarkable ice-formation.

Owing to our very imperfect knowledge of the conditions which prevail in the Antarctic seas, we cannot pronounce definitely whether it will be necessary for the ship to make her way out of the ice before the winter sets in, or whether she should winter in the Antarctic Regions. It is for you to decide on this important question after a careful examination of the local conditions.

If you should decide to winter in the ice . . . your efforts as regards geographical exploration should be directed to three objects, namely – an advance into the western mountains, an advance to the south, and an exploration of the volcanic region.

. . . In an enterprise of this nature much must be left to the discretion and judgment of the commanding officer, and we fully confide in your combined energy and prudence for the successful issue of a voyage which will command the attention of all persons interested in navigation and science throughout the civilised world. At the same time we desire you constantly to bear in mind our anxiety for the health, comfort, and safety of all entrusted to your care.

Such were the principal paragraphs of the instructions which were signed by the Presidents of the Royal and Royal Geographical Societies and delivered into my hands, and when my tale is told I think it will be acknowledged that they were closely observed.

That part of my story which concerns the preparation of our venture is almost accomplished, and the reader will now understand how and why in July 1901 the *Discovery* lay in the East India Dock equipped for her long voyage.

Of the difficulties which threatened to avert this happy accomplishment, space has only permitted me to give the briefest outline. Dr Nansen has observed that the hardest work of a polar voyage comes in its preparation, and my remembrance of the years 1900–1 fully corroborates this dictum; but even the troubles and trials of this anxious time had their bright side, and it is only with pleasure that I can look back on the kindly assistance which was freely given to the expedition, and to one who like myself was treading unaccustomed paths to further its ends.

Briefly and inadequately I have already mentioned the services of many eminent men who bore a share in our enterprise, but such references have by no means included all to whom our gratitude is due. It is not generally understood that in undertaking the management of our expedition the two great Societies concerned assumed an unprecedented responsibility. A great Government department like the Admiralty would have had little difficulty in preparing a dozen such ventures, because it has all the machinery necessary for dealing with these matters; but a learned Society possesses no such facilities, because as a rule it has no need of them. Neither the Royal nor the Royal Geographical Society was organised for the equipment of expeditions, and consequently for them such a task was beset with difficulties. That all obstacles were successfully overcome is to the lasting credit of these bodies, but especially is it to the honour of those who bore the chief responsibility as officers of the Societies. I think there is little doubt that these gentlemen would acknowledge that during the troublous youth of the Antarctic Expedition they were more worried over its details than by all the other business of the Societies which they guided.

Of those who were thus forced to give much attention to the affairs of the expedition, and who did so for its benefit, were the successive Presidents of the Royal Society, Lord Lister and Sir William Huggins; the Honorary Secretaries, Sir Arthur Rücker and Sir Michael Foster; and the Permanent Secretary, Mr Harrison. In speaking of my own experiences, I have ever to remember the courteous and kindly treatment I received from these gentlemen. There were many reasons why my lot was still more closely cast with the Geographical Society at this time, and here, also, I can speak in the warmest manner of the treatment I received. Its Secretary, Dr Scott Keltie, has always taken the keenest interest in the expedition, and the services he has rendered to it and to me might alone occupy a chapter of this book. To the Honorary Secretaries of this Society also, Major L. Darwin and Mr J. F. Hughes, my thanks are due for their continual efforts to make my path smooth; and of the important services of Dr H. R. Mill, who was at this time Librarian of the Society, I shall speak at a later date.

Though on the officers of the Societies fell the greatest share of the difficulties which beset the expedition, there were several other gentlemen who in the midst of busy lives spared many an hour for its service.

As Hydrographer of the Navy, Sir William Wharton undertook the supply of the greater part of the instruments which we carried, and in this, as in many other ways, he showed his deep sympathy with the objects of the expedition.

On Captain E. W. Creak, at that time Director of Compasses at the Admiralty, fell all the difficulties of arranging our long and complicated magnetic programme, and of drawing up such instructions concerning it as were necessary for our guidance.

Amongst those who gave their services freely on various committees, in arranging the details of departmental work, and in adding to the interest of that excellent publication the *Antarctic Manual*, may be mentioned Mr R. H. Scott, Mr Howard Saunders, Mr J. Y. Buchanan, Dr W. T. Blanford, Mr P. L. Sclater, Captain T. H. Tizard, Sir Archibald Geikie, Mr J. Teall, Professor E. B. Poulton, Sir John Evans, and Dr A. Buchan. Not less valuable to me, starting as I did with no experience of polar work, was the kindly advice and assistance I received from those officers who had taken part in Arctic Expeditions; and for my guidance in numerous respects I have to thank many a conversation with such eminent travellers as Sir Vesey Hamilton, Sir George Nares, Sir Albert Markham, Sir Leopold McClintock, Admiral Aldrich, Admiral Chase Parr, and perhaps most of all with my old Captain, now Admiral G. Le C. Egerton.

As will be seen, there were many who had a share in the building of our Antarctic Expedition; but even with all this kindly assistance it is doubtful whether it would ever have started had it not been that amongst the many who gave to it some hours from their busy lives was one who, from the first, had given his whole and undivided attention.

After all is said and done, it was Sir Clements Markham who conceived the idea of an Antarctic Expedition; it was his masterful personality which forced it onward through all obstruction; and to him, therefore, is mainly due the credit that at the end of July 1901 we were prepared to set out on our long voyage and eager to obey the behest:

> Do ye, by star-eyed Science led, explore
> Each lonely ocean, each untrodden shore.

CHAPTER 3

Voyage to New Zealand

Arrival at Cowes – Visit of the King – Sailing from Cowes – Madeira – Crossing the Line – South Trinidad – Arrival at the Cape – Simon's Bay – At Sea in the Westerlies – Alarm of Fire – First Encounter with the Ice – Southern Birds – Macquarie Island – Lyttelton, New Zealand – Preparations for Final Departure – Departure from Lyttelton – Fatal Accident – Final Departure from Civilisation.

> They saw the cables loosened, they saw the gangways cleared,
> They heard the women weeping, they heard the men who cheered.
> Far off – far off the tumult faded and died away,
> And all alone the sea wind came singing up the Bay. – NEWBOLT

In spite of difficulties and delays in the delivery of the ship and in stocking her with the complicated equipment which had been provided, the *Discovery* left the London Docks on the last day of July 1901, and slowly wended her way down the Thames.

Late on August 1 we arrived at Spithead, here to carry out that most important matter of swinging the ship. It may not be generally known that all ships, before proceeding on a voyage, are 'swung' – that is, are turned slowly round, whilst the errors of their compasses on each point are eliminated by the application of correcting magnets. Although the great care taken in building the *Discovery* to keep all iron away from the neighbourhood of the compass rendered the use of correcting magnets unnecessary, yet it had been impossible to banish the disturbing causes wholly, and it was most necessary to find out exactly what influence they had, not only on the compass, but on the position in which it was proposed to work the rarer magnetic instruments – that is to say, in the small central magnetic deck-house. This work was completed during the week, and on Monday morning, August 5, we made fast to a buoy in Cowes Harbour, at this time crowded with yachts assembled for the famous 'Cowes week'. In the midst of vessels displaying such delicate beauty of outline, the *Discovery*, with her black, solid, sombre hull, her short masts, square spars, and heavy rigging, formed a striking antithesis, a fit example to point the contrast of 'work' and 'play'. Shortly before noon we were honoured by a visit from their Majesties the King and Queen. The visit was quite informal, but must be ever memorable from the kindly, gracious interest shown in the minutest details of our equipment, and the frank expression of good wishes for our plans and welfare.

In those days we thought much of the grim possibilities of our voyage. There was ever present before us the unpleasant reflection that we might start off with a flourish of trumpets and return with failure. But although we longed to get away from our country as quietly as possible, we could not but feel gratified that His Majesty should have shown such personal sympathy with our enterprise, and it was a deep satisfaction to know that our efforts would be followed with interest by the highest in the land, as well as by others of our countrymen more particularly occupied with the problems before us.

On the afternoon of the 5th the ship was crowded with visitors, whilst we did our best to make the final preparations for sea. At noon on the 6th we slipped from our buoy and, after receiving a visit from the First Lord of the Admiralty, steered to the west; a few of our immediate relatives who had remained on board hastened to say their last farewells, and, descending into their boats off the little town of Yarmouth, waved their adieux as the *Discovery* steamed towards the Needles Channel.

How willingly would one dispense with these farewells, and how truly one feels that the greater burden of sadness is on those who are left behind! Before us lay new scenes, new interests, expanding horizons; but who at such times must not think sorely of the wives and mothers condemned to think of the past, and hope in silent patience for the future, through years of suspense and anxiety?

Early on the 7th the Start was still in sight, but gradually it shaded from green to blue, till towards noon it vanished in the distance, and with it our last view of the Old Country.

At this time we had much to learn about the *Discovery*. Great as may be the advantage of having a new ship, it can be readily understood that there are also serious drawbacks. In addition to our want of familiarity with the details of such a vessel, her construction, her engines, and so forth, we were ignorant of her capacity of performance under steam or sail, and we could not predict with any degree of certainty the length of time which would be necessary for our long voyage to New Zealand.

As we steered our course across the Bay of Biscay with varying baffling winds, it soon became evident that the *Discovery* did not possess a turn of speed under any conditions; that with favourable winds we could hope for little more than seven or eight knots, whereas a very moderate head-wind might reduce her to a fraction of this speed.

Under these conditions our voyage to New Zealand promised to occupy a very long time, and it became obvious that we could not stop by the way longer than was absolutely necessary, since delay in the date of our arrival was limited by the desire to take full advantage of the Southern summer of 1901–2 for our first exploration in the ice.

This proved a most serious drawback, as I had confidently looked for ample opportunities to make trial of our various devices for sounding and dredging in the deep sea whilst we remained in temperate climates. Some of these devices were new, and with all we were unfamiliar; and the fact that we were unable to practise with them during our outward voyage was severely felt when they came to be used afterwards in the Antarctic Regions.

On August 14 we sighted the island of Madeira, and late that night anchored off Funchal. The directors of the Union-Castle Line had generously placed a small quantity of coal at our disposal at this port, and we hoped to take it in and to complete some small repairs on the following day; but, as luck would have it, this proved a 'Fiesta' (feast day), and we were unable to get to sea until the afternoon of the 16th, though our courteous agents, Messrs. Blandy, did their best to hasten the work. On sailing from Madeira we reluctantly bade farewell to Dr H. R. Mill, who, as an expert in oceanography and meteorology, had accompanied us on the first stage of our journey to assist us in arranging the various branches of work in these departments.

By this time, however, the routine of our scientific observations had taken form, and departments had been allotted to various officers who continued to be responsible for them throughout the voyage; and now was commenced that steady, patient record of observation on which so much of the success of an expedition must depend.

The analysis of the records of many thousands of ocean voyages in all parts of the world has resulted in the issue of sailing directions which give the best advice as to the course to be taken by various classes of vessels. As a rule full-powered steamers alone can proceed directly from port to port; small-powered steamers and, still more, sailing ships are obliged to shape a devious course in order to take advantage of favourable winds and currents. The progress of the *Discovery* was so wholly dependent on wind and weather that in making ocean passages she was obliged to be considered in this respect as a sailing ship, and to make long detours which involved the traversing of many hundreds of miles more than would be required on the direct track.

With the help of the N.E. trade wind we made steady progress to the south during the third week in August, but losing the trade in 17 N. lat., our daily run was so reduced by baffling winds that we did not cross the line till August 31.

The traditional customs of this event were fully observed. Father Neptune and his Tritons held their court on a platform immediately above a large canvas bath, and the numerous members of our company who had not yet been introduced to His Majesty succeeded one another in this rather trying ordeal. The victim was blindfolded, and seated on the bare edge of a plank over the bath; in front of him stood the barber, with a huge jagged pantomime razor, and the barber's assistant, with a whitewash brush and a bucket of soft soap; the unfortunate tyro was then asked questions, and the barber's assistant showed his deftness with the lather when he opened his mouth to reply; after a good deal of such rude horseplay, usually prolonged in proportion to the victim's reluctance as shown by his struggles to escape, a last push sent him floundering into the bath below.

Immediately on crossing the line we fell in with the S.E. trade wind, and stopped our engines to give them a much-needed refit. Remaining under sail during the ensuing nine days, we had some opportunity of gauging the sailing qualities of the ship, and found to our chagrin that they were exceedingly poor. Although we made some progress through the water, the course laid and the leeway made carried us far to the westward, and comparatively close to the South American coast. On September 9 we raised steam and shaped our course for South Trinidad Island. Since our departure from Madeira we had suffered some trouble from the leaking of the *Discovery*. Much of it sprang from the hopeful prediction of the builders that there would be no leak, and in consequence of this no flooring had been placed in the holds to lift the provisions above any water which might collect, and the provision cases had been packed close down to the keel. When the water began to enter, therefore, there was no well in which it could lie, and it rose amongst the cases, causing a good deal of damage. In the old days it had always been expected that a wooden ship would leak, and the more pleasing hope with regard to the *Discovery* was based on the fact that she possessed two layers of planking on the outside of her frames and one on the inside. In this respect, however, the fact proved rather a disadvantage than otherwise, as it made it most difficult to localise the spot at which the water was entering, and there was every chance that it passed through the inner skin at quite a different place from that at which it had penetrated the outer. As soon as we were assured of calm seas the holds were unstowed and a flooring built, but this was not effected before we had suffered considerable damage to our provisions, which we were afterwards put to some expense in replacing.

Later on we had the annoyance of seeing the report of our leak exaggerated and represented as a danger to the ship. This it never was, but of course the water that entered had to be pumped out; and if the whole voyage is considered, the sum total of hours spent in pumping out the *Discovery* is a large one.

The island of South Trinidad is an isolated mass of volcanic rock lying some 500 miles to the east of the continent of South America. It has been frequently visited, thought not regularly, and a fascinating description is given of it in *The Cruise of the 'Falcon'* (E. F. Knight). Few naturalists have landed on it, and as it lay on our route I thought our time would not be wasted in giving our officers an opportunity of a run ashore. We sighted it on the morning of the 13th, and, approaching the western side, manned our boats and pulled for the shore. The ocean swell was breaking heavily along the whole coast, and the prospect of landing looked doubtful, but at length we found a small natural pier which seemed to afford some shelter from the heavy rollers; even here, however, our small boats were at one moment lifted high above the rocks, and at the next had dropped many feet below them. The attempt to land seemed hazardous, and on inquiring if all on board could swim, I found that one at least could not; but the shore looked too enticing to our sea-accustomed eyes to be abandoned without an effort, and, handling the boats with care, we eventually succeeded in taking advantage of the lift of each wave to leap one by one on to the rocks, and at length all except the boat-keepers were safely landed.

On the rocky shore we scattered in various directions, some of us climbing to a line of tree-ferns 1,200 feet above the sea; and the day passed pleasantly as we rambled about in search of specimens of life peculiar to the island. Little of novelty could be expected from a stay of six hours, but we had the satisfaction of finding a few species new to science, of which perhaps the most important was a new petrel, afterwards named *Aestrelata Wilsoni* after our zoologist, Dr Wilson. We left South Trinidad the same night and steered to the south to get into the region of westerly winds. On the 18th our coal supply was getting so short that I decided to proceed under sail and husband what remained of our limited stock. The wind proved very fitful, but by keeping well to the south we received it from the westward, and made slow but sure progress towards our destination.

On October 2 we arrived within 150 miles of the Cape, and, getting up steam, rounded Green Point and entered Table Bay at four o'clock on the 3rd. On the 4th we refilled our bunkers with coal, and that night put to sea once more, to take up our quarters off the naval station at Simon's Bay. It was during this short passage that we first appreciated the *Discovery*'s ability to roll: on meeting a heavy swell off the Cape Peninsula during the night, our small ship, without any sail to steady her, was swung from side to side through an angle of 90°, and as some of our furniture was not well secured, chaos reigned below and discomfort everywhere.

The main object of our stay at the Cape was to obtain comparisons with our magnetic instruments. The instruments which are used in a ship for taking observations of the various magnetic elements are unfortunately subject to change, and consequently the observations at sea are of little value unless such changes are known. Whenever it is possible, therefore, the sea instruments are compared with absolute values on land, and by this means the sea observations are corrected. The observations to be taken on our voyage to New Zealand were an important part of our magnetic survey, and it was highly desirable that the errors of the instruments to be used should be obtained before and after the voyage – that is, at the Cape and in New Zealand.

To compare all our instruments with suitable care was a long and tedious operation. There being no fixed magnetic observatory at the Cape, the work was done in tents, kindly lent by the Admiral and pitched on a plateau beyond the hills immediately surrounding the port. It was carried out by Lieutenants Armitage and Barne, with the kind assistance of Professors Beatty and Morrison, of the Cape University; and as it could only be continued during the daylight hours, ten days passed before all the observations were completed. On board the ship every advantage was taken of this spell to refit. The rigging was set up afresh, the deck and top sides of the ship were re-caulked, the engines were overhauled, and the weed was removed from the bottom by the divers of the fleet.

At this time the war was proceeding, and things were in an unsatisfactory state; guerilla bands had penetrated so far into the Colony that martial law had been proclaimed at Capetown; the termination of hostilities seemed very remote; officials and residents took a gloomy view of the outlook. Under these circumstances it is additionally pleasing to record the great kindness which we received at all hands, the ready assistance which was offered us, both in our scientific work and in the more practical requirements of the ship, and the kindly hospitality which made our visit so pleasant. Our peaceful mission was regarded with sympathy and interest by all, and we remember with gratitude the entertainment provided for us by His Excellency the Governor, Sir Walter Hely-Hutchinson, by Sir David Gill and the members of the Philosophical Society, and by Mr Andrews, of the Union-Castle Line. But above all we owed thanks to the Naval Commander-in-Chief, Sir Arthur Moore, who placed at our disposal the resources of the naval dockyard for our repairs, and most generously extended to our officers the hospitality of Admiralty House. It is difficult to express how much we owed to these attentions, which smoothed our difficulties and obviated all chance of unnecessary delay.

By October 14 our refitting and the magnetic observations had been completed, and all preparations had been made for sea. In the morning Mr George Murray bade us farewell, much to our regret; he had originally been appointed to accompany the ship to Melbourne, but owing to the unexpected delays of our voyage, I had perforce decided to go direct to New Zealand without calling at that port. The additional length of the voyage, and the delay already experienced, would have prolonged his absence from his regular work at the British Museum to such an extent that Mr Murray thought it best to return direct from the Cape. After a last farewell to all our naval friends, at noon we slowly steamed out of the harbour, accompanied by the cheers of the warships, and proud of this last tribute of their generous sympathy.

For nearly a week after our departure from the Cape we had light westerly winds – an unusual experience, especially as we were now well in that belt known to sailors as the 'Roaring Forties'; but after the first week we had little to complain of on the score of wind, and our daily run became a much more satisfactory thing to contemplate. Towards the end of the month we had a succession of heavy following gales, and although we had put out our fires and were dependent on sail power alone, we frequently exceeded 200 miles in the day, an exceedingly good run for a ship of the *Discovery*'s type.

As time went on we became more and more satisfied with the seaworthy qualities of our small ship; she proved wonderfully stiff, and as her sail area was small, it was rarely, if ever, necessary to shorten sail even in the most violent gales; she rose like a cork to the mountainous seas that now followed in her wake, and, considering her size, was wonderfully free of water on the upper deck.

With a heavy following sea, however, she was, owing to her buoyancy, extremely lively, and we frequently recorded rolls of more than 40°. The peculiar rounded shape of the stern, to which I have referred, and which had given rise to so much criticism, was now well tested. It gave additional buoyancy to the after-end, causing the ship to rise more quickly to the seas, but the same lifting effect was also directed to throwing the ship off her course, and consequently she was more difficult to steer. Our helmsmen gradually became more expert, but at first when some mountainous wave caught us up, we narrowly escaped broaching-to, and on one occasion we actually did so. I happened to be on the bridge at the time, with some other officers, as our small vessel swerved round and was immediately swept by a monstrous sea, which made a clean breach over her; we clutched instinctively at the bridge rails, and for several moments were completely submerged, whilst the spray dashed as high as our upper topsails. A great deal of water found its way below, flooding the ward-room and many of the cabins, from the decks of which people were soon busily picking up books and garments in a more or less sodden condition. Needless to say, we did our best to avoid 'broaching-to' again.

On October 31 we accomplished our record run under sail alone, driving before a very heavy gale. This amounted to 223 miles in the twenty-four hours. We were now gradually increasing our latitude, until on November 12 we were in lat. 51 S., long. 131 E., when we arrived in an extremely interesting magnetic area, and I decided to steer to the south to explore it more effectively.

The exact reason for this decision is somewhat technical, but I may briefly recall that amongst the elements that came within the purview of our magnetic survey was that of magnetic force or the actual pull exercised by the earth at various places. The only data previously available seemed to show a curious inconsistency in the distribution of this force to the northward of the Magnetic Pole, where we had now arrived, and consequently it was desirable to make our survey in this region as extensive as possible. This new course took us well to the south, far out of the track of ships and towards the regions of ice.

It was almost on arrival in these lonely waters that I was awakened one night by a loud knocking and a voice shouting, 'Ship's afire, sir.' I sprang up full of 'Where?' 'When?' and 'How?' only to find that my informant had fled. As may be imagined, I was not long in getting on the deck, which was very dark and obstructed by numerous other half-clad people, who knew no more than I. Making my way forward I at length found, amidst streams of water and a slight smell of burning, the officer of the watch, who explained that the fire had been under the forecastle, but had been easily extinguished when the hose had been brought to bear on it. It eventually transpired that the rolling of the ship had brought some oilskins dangerously close to a police light, and that this had not been discovered until the woodwork round about was blazing merrily. In these days, steel ships and electric lights tend to lessen the fear of fire, but in a wooden vessel the possible consequences are too serious not to make the danger a very real one, nor to allow such a report as was made to me to be received without alarm. The risk of fire was one which was very constantly in my thoughts; it must always loom large in a wooden ship, and I am not at all sure that it is much lessened in a polar climate, whereas in polar regions the consequences may be vastly increased. It can be imagined that after such an experience as this, I was not less likely to realise the peril, but as events turned out, I am happy to say, this was the first and last occasion on which an alarm of fire was raised: we were never again scared with such a report.

On November 15 we crossed the 60th parallel, and on the following morning much excitement was caused by our first sight of the sea-ice. At first we saw only small pieces, worn into fantastic shape by the action of the waves, but as the afternoon advanced signs of a heavier pack appeared ahead, and soon the loose floes were all about us, and the *Discovery* was pushing her way amongst them, receiving her baptism of ice.

As night closed down on us we became closely surrounded by the pack, which consisted of comparatively small pieces of ice from two to three feet in thickness and much worn at their edges by the constant movement of the swell. The novelty of our surroundings impressed us greatly. The wind had died away; what light remained was reflected in a ghostly glimmer from the white surface of the pack; now and again a white snow petrel flitted through the gloom, the grinding of the floes against the ship's side was mingled with the more subdued hush of their rise and fall on the long swell, and for the first time we felt something of the solemnity of these great Southern solitudes.

We had now reached lat. 62.50 S., long. 139 E., and were within 200 miles of Adélie Land, discovered by Dumont D'Urville. With steam we should have had small difficulty in pushing on towards the land; but already our delays had been excessive, and we knew that we could not add to them if we were to reach New Zealand betimes. Reluctantly the ship's head was once more turned towards the north and we passed again into looser ice. On the following day we passed a small iceberg, the only one seen in this region. Two soundings taken about this time gave depths of 2,500 and 2,300 fathoms respectively, showing that the ocean depths must extend moderately close to Adélie Land; but a third taken at our more southerly position gave 1,750 fathoms, rather indicating that the shoaling of the greater depths was commencing.

The tempestuous seas of the Southern oceans have one great feature, lacking in other oceans, in the quantity and variety of their bird life. The fact supplies an interest to the voyager which can scarcely be appreciated by those who have not experienced it, for not only are these roaming, tireless birds seen in the distance, but in the majority of cases they are attracted by a ship and gather close about her for hours, and even days. The greater number are of the petrel tribe, and vary in size from the greater albatrosses, with their huge spread of wing and unwavering flight, to the small Wilson stormy petrel, which flits under the foaming crests of the waves. For centuries these birds have been the friends of sailors, who designated them by more or less familiar names, some of which have been preserved, whilst others have been dropped for more definite titles. In the older accounts of voyages it is often difficult to recognise the birds referred to; for instance, the term 'Eglet' seems to have been applied to various species. But the 'Wanderer', 'Sooty', 'Cape Hen', 'Cape Pigeon', 'Giant Petrel', and many others are survivals which the ordinary man still prefers to employ in preference to the scientific designation. It was the shooting of a 'Sooty' albatross by one Simon Hartley in Shelvocke's voyage that supplied the theme immortalised in the *Ancient Mariner*.

Our zoologist Dr Wilson was possessed of the necessary knowledge to distinguish and name our various visitors, and with his assistance most of us soon became familiar with even the rarer species. This not only added greatly to the interest of the voyage, but enabled us in turn to assist in keeping the record of such visits.

Various devices were resorted to in our endeavours to capture birds for our collection, and sooner or later examples of most of the species were brought on board. The larger albatrosses were caught by towing a small metal triangle, well baited; when a bird settled, the line would be slacked, and as it pecked at the bait a jerk of the line would sometimes catch its beak in the sharp angle of the triangle, when by keeping a steady strain on the line the bird could be landed. The smaller birds were usually caught by becoming entangled in long streamers of strong thread which were allowed to float away in the wind. A lead weight on the end of a string was also a means of capturing such birds as flew close to the ship.

The weight would be thrown over the bird so that, in falling, the string would descend across the wings. All such devices required much patience and deftness to be effective, and our most successful bird catchers, the chief engineer, Mr Skelton, and the second engineer, Mr Dellbridge, spent many a patient hour before they were rewarded with a capture.

The larger albatrosses rarely go as far south as the ice, but the smaller species of white albatrosses, as well as the dusky, sinister-looking 'Sooty', accompanied us as far as the edge of the pack. But the birds which live in the regions of ice are rarely met with in the more northerly seas, though a few are widely distributed. It may be taken for granted that all the birds inhabiting the icy seas are now known; sooner or later during our voyage we saw all, but we were not often in circumstances to make such a good bag as during our short visit to the ice in November. It was then that for the first time we saw and captured the southern fulmar, a beautiful bluish-grey petrel; the Antarctic petrel, a white bird with brown barred wings and head; the snow petrel, with its pure white plumage; and two species of the small blue prion or whale-bird.

On November 22 we sighted Macquarie Island, which lies about 600 miles S.W. of New Zealand, and as we came abreast of it early in the afternoon I thought we might devote the few hours of daylight which remained to an excursion on shore. We accordingly anchored in Fisherman's Cove, a poorly-sheltered spot to the eastward of the island, and after pushing through thick kelp we succeeded in landing on a sheltered beach, and our naturalists were soon busily at work making collections. The western slopes of the island are bare, but on the eastern side a coarse tussock grass grows thickly and makes walking rather difficult. Our attention was principally devoted to the penguin rookeries on the beach, of which there were two inhabited by different species of birds, the larger and more numerous kind being the richly coloured King penguin, and the other a small crested penguin (*Schlegeli*).

It was the first time that any of us had seen a penguin rookery, and every detail of their strange habits proved absorbingly inter-esting; we were lucky enough to have arrived during the nesting season, and were able to collect specimens of eggs and of the young in various stages of development. Perhaps the most excited member of our party was my small Aberdeen terrier 'Scamp', who was highly delighted with his run on shore, until he came to the penguins, when he was most obviously and comically divided between a desire to run away and a feeling that he ought to appear bold in such strange company. The result was a series of short rushes, made with suppressed growls and every hair bristling, but ending at a very safe distance. I may add that 'Scamp' found a comfortable home in New Zealand; it was felt that an Antarctic climate would prove too much for him; and in becoming the idol of a household he quickly forgot his former acquaintances.

As night fell we weighed our anchor and proceeded to the north, sighting the Auckland Islands on the 25th, and rather foolishly shaping our course to pass to windward of them. As we came abreast of the land the wind became very fresh, and with a strong set to leeward we were for some time anxious about our prospect of weathering it. Eventually, however, we were lucky enough to clear the rocks at the northern end just before the wind increased to a full gale, which, with a heavy sea, caused us to lurch on one occasion to an angle of 55°, and kept us in considerable discomfort below. Late on the 29th we arrived off Lyttelton Heads, and on the following day were berthed alongside a jetty in the harbour.

It is most difficult to speak in fitting terms of the kindness shown to us in New Zealand, both at this time and on our return from the Antarctic Regions. The general kindness and hospitality of New Zealanders are well known to every stranger who has visited the country, but in our case there was added a keen and intelligent interest in all that concerned the expedition, and a wholehearted desire to further its aims. Officers and men were received with open arms and quickly made friends – friends who hastened to assure them that although already separated by many thousands of miles from their native land, here in this new land they would find a second home, and those who would equally think of them in their absence and welcome them on their return.

But it is not only for private but for public kindness and sympathy that we have to thank the people of New Zealand: on all sides we received the most generous treatment. All charges for harbour dues, docking, wharfage, &c., were remitted to us by the Lyttelton Harbour Board, and the sum thus saved to the expedition throughout the voyage was very large. The railway authorities gave us many facilities for the transport of our stores, and issued free tickets to officers and men for passage over their lines. On every side we were accorded the most generous terms by the firms or individuals with whom we had to deal in business matters. By the Christchurch Magnetic Observatory and by the Christchurch Museum we were offered numerous facilities in carrying on our scientific work. Later on, to add to this noble record of sympathetic help, the Government of New Zealand subscribed 1,000*l*. towards the expenses of the relief ship.

In considering such general kindness it is almost invidious to mention particular names, but the following gentlemen are amongst those who must be especially remembered by us for the manner in which they were ever ready to assist us: His Excellency the Governor, Lord Ranfurly; the Premier, Mr Seddon; the Hon. C. C. Bowen; Captain Hutton, of the Christchurch Museum; Mr Kinsey, Mr Waymouth, Mr A. Rhodes, Mr Coleridge Farr, of the Christchurch Observatory, and Mr H. J. Miller, of Lyttelton.

A great deal of work lay before us at Lyttelton. The rigging had to be thoroughly overhauled and refitted; this was taken in hand at once, and the work was much expedited by assistance given by working parties sent by H.M.S. *Ringarooma*. The *Ringarooma* had been directed to lend us all possible aid by the Admiral, Sir Lewis Beaumont, who, as an old Arctic traveller, took an especial interest in our mission, and the Admiral's wishes were most thoroughly carried out by Captain Rich, of that vessel. Meanwhile our magneticians were forced to undertake again the comparison of their delicate instruments, and as this was the last occasion on which it could be done, special care and attention were necessary; but now, instead of camping in tents on a heathery hill plateau as they had done at the Cape, they were able to carry on their work in an observatory equipped with every modern convenience, and directed by an official who was not only eager to render them every assistance, but was preparing himself to take an important part in the international programme of observations which were to be taken in connection with our magnetic work in the Far South. Even with such facilities a long and troublesome task lay before our observers, but luckily their complement was now complete, for we found the last of our officers, Mr Bernacchi, awaiting us on our arrival; so pushed had we been with many of our arrangements in England that this officer had been obliged to remain behind and to spend the weeks which could be saved by a rapid steamer voyage in getting together and studying the delicate recording instruments which were needed for our Southern station. And so, for the time being, the members of our small community were scattered once more, and whilst each was working at his special task in more than one place there was bustle and hurry to be prepared for the date of our final sailing.

At Lyttelton we found awaiting us large quantities of stores ready to be shipped for our long voyage, and since, as I have already mentioned, some of the stores in the *Discovery* had been damaged by the leaky state of the ship, it was necessary to replace these by purchases in New Zealand. It was when I appreciated the excellence of the goods obtained in this manner I regretted that we had not relied on New Zealand for the greater part of our provisions. Were I to go again on such an expedition, I should certainly do this. Tinned meat, flour, cheese, and, in fact, every necessary for a voyage, can be obtained at moderate prices and of most excellent quality; and the fact that in such an expedition as ours these provisions would not have had to come through the tropics, is, I think, of very great importance.

The case of butter may be especially mentioned. The tinned Danish butter which we had brought from Europe was as satisfactory as tinned butter could be, but in New Zealand we were able to purchase fresh butter which is largely exported in cases of white pine, and we found that it was quite possible to keep these cases sound through the short voyage to the Antarctic Circle, after which they could be relied on to keep for any length of time.

Owing to the damage done to our provisions, and wishing, moreover, to know exactly where everything was stowed, we thought it advisable to re-stow our holds at Lyttelton, a task which meant a good deal of labour, but ensured our being able to take advantage of every corner of the hold-space. As soon as it could conveniently be done, the *Discovery* was docked and every effort was made to stop the leak. This, as I have pointed out, was a difficult matter owing to the several layers of planking. A thorough examination of the ship's bottom revealed not a few defects which should have been remedied before the ship was launched, but though these defects were made good and the bottom was thoroughly caulked, we found, when the ship was again afloat, that the leak was not stopped. The chagrin of our excellent contractor, Mr H. J. Miller, was as deep as our own, and for his own satisfaction he begged that the ship might be docked again at his expense: this time he removed all the heavy steel plates that protected the bow of the ship, hoping that the fault might be found beneath them; but though more defects were made good and every inch of the bottom was examined, we had the intense annoyance of seeing the water again entering when the ship was once more afloat. Every effort had been made, we could do no more; and the result served to show the extreme difficulty of localising such a fault in a ship of this kind. Amongst the many skilled workmen whose united labour had produced the solid structure of the *Discovery*'s hull, had been one who had scamped his task, no doubt knowing full well that he was free from all chance of detection, and for this we were condemned to suffer throughout our voyage. The leak never grew serious, and when we were in the ice it was very much reduced; but, as I have said, first and last we spent on the pumps many a weary hour that could ill be spared with so much other work to be done.

As the month of December advanced the *Discovery* became a very busy scene; parties of men were employed in stowing every hole and corner of the available storage-space, the upper deck was littered with packing cases of all sorts, whilst many truck-loads of stores still stood waiting on the wharf. As usual in such cases, the prospect of getting everything stowed seemed hopeless. Meanwhile, whenever permitted, flocks of curious visitors added to the confusion but as many of these had come from a long distance, it was impossible not to accede to their almost pathetic requests to be allowed to see the ship.

At last came the day for sailing from Lyttelton, but not for our final departure from civilisation, for we yet proposed to make a short visit to Port Chalmers in the south to complete our stock of coal. On Saturday, December 21, the *Discovery* lay alongside the wharf ready for sea and very deeply laden. Below, every hold and stowage-space was packed to the brim – even the cabins were invaded with odd cases for which no corner could be found. But the scene on deck was still more extraordinary. Here, again, were numerous packing-cases for which no more convenient resting-place could be found; the afterpart of the deck was occupied by a terrified flock of forty-five sheep, a last and most welcome present from the farmers of New Zealand. Amidst this constantly stampeding body stood the helmsman at the wheel; further forward were sacks of food, and what space remained was occupied by our twenty-three howling dogs in a wild state of excitement. Above the deck, the skid-beams, fitted for the carriage of our boats, were in addition piled high with the woodwork of our huts, adding, as we estimated, a weight of some thirty tons, and therefore requiring to be secured with many lashings and much care. Here and there stood little groups of our friends waiting for the last handshake and to wish us Godspeed, and incidentally doing their best to separate the combatants in a dog-fight.

As may be imagined, the ship was not in a condition in which one could look forward with pleasure to crossing the stormiest ocean in the world. One could reflect that it would have been impossible to have got more into her, and that all we had got seemed necessary for the voyage; for the rest we could only trust that Providence would vouchsafe to us fine weather and an easy passage to the south.

Before noon our small company was collected on the mess-deck and a short service of farewell was held by the Bishop of Christchurch – a simple, touching ceremony gratifying to all. At 2 p.m. we cast off our warps and steamed slowly out of the harbour, but New Zealand was determined we should know how thoroughly it was interested in our venture and how heartily it wished us success. Special trains from Christchurch had borne thousands to the port to bid us farewell. Wharves and quays were packed with enthusiastic figures. It was indeed a great 'send-off'; two men-of-war – the *Ringarooma* and *Lizard* – steamed out slowly ahead of us, whilst no fewer than five gaily dressed steamers, crowded with passengers, and with bands playing and whistles hooting, thronged about us. Cheer followed cheer as we steamed out towards the 'Heads'; assembled in the rigging, on mast or spar, our small party of adventurers did their best to respond to this kindly expression of good feeling, until, as we entered the open sea, with a last burst of cheering and a final flutter of handkerchiefs, our kind friends turned away, and slowly we steamed out between the warships that seemed to stand as sentinels to the bay.

And now, whilst our hearts were full of this leave-taking, whilst with our glasses we could still discern the forms of our friends in the receding vessels, there happened one of those tragedies that awake one to the grim realities of life. Amongst our enthusiastic ship's company who had crowded into the rigging to wave their farewells, was one young seaman, named Charles Bonner, who, more venturesome than the rest, had climbed above the crow's-nest to the top of the mainmast. There, seated on the truck, he had remained cheering with the rest, until in a moment of madness he raised himself into a standing position, supported only by the slender wind vane which capped the mast. Precisely what happened can never be known; possibly the first of the sea swell caused him to lose his balance; we below only know that, arrested by a wild cry, we turned to see a figure hurtling through the air, still grasping the wind vane from the masthead. He fell head foremost on the corner of an iron deckhouse, and death was instantaneous. The body was borne through the confused obstructions on the deck to the stern gratings, and covered reverently with the Union Jack, whilst sadness and gloom descended on the ship and damped for the time all thought of our future in the South. Though this was on Saturday, it was not until Monday that we arrived at Port Chalmers, owing to delay from a strong head wind. Captain Rich, of the *Ringarooma*, had kindly promised to make arrangements for the funeral of our poor shipmate, and though we only arrived at 4 p.m., an inquest was immediately held, and the body buried with naval honours at 6 p.m. Bonner was a smart young seaman, already popular on board, and his untimely death was much felt; but in the busy life we were now leading there was little time for sad thought, and the gloom of this unfortunate accident was rapidly dispelled in the activities of the voyage.

Of all the stores we carried, coal was perhaps the most important, and I had determined to wedge in every ton we could carry, more especially as, through the generosity of Mr John Mill, of Port Chalmers, such coal as we received there was a free gift.

Early on the morning of the 24th we managed to increase our already crowded deck cargo by the addition of 45 tons of coal, which with 285 tons already in the bunkers, brought our total up to 330 tons, a quantity which, although it may not sound great to those who know the consumption of modern steamers, sufficed for all our needs for more than two years.

At 9.30 a.m. we left the wharf after saying farewell to the few friends who had gathered in the port even at this early hour. The *Ringarooma*, to whose officers and men we were so deeply indebted for assistance in the past, 'manned ship' and cheered us yet once again, and soon, in company with a tug, we were wending our way down the long, tortuous channel which leads to the sea.

By noon we were clear of the harbour bar, with a good offing, and with a fresh breeze from the N.E., we loosed our sails, and were soon briskly bowling along towards the south under steam and sail. A hoarse shout and a hoarser whistling from our friendly tug, a final wave from the signal station on the cliff, and we were away. The last view of civilisation, the last sight of fields, and trees, and flowers, had come and gone on Christmas Eve, 1901, and as the night fell, the blue outline of friendly New Zealand was lost to us in the northern twilight.

CHAPTER 4

Southward ho!

Steering to the South – Fog – Icebergs – Entering Pack-ice – Life in the Pack –
Nature of Pack – Slow Progress – 'Watering Ship' – Southern Edge of Pack –
The Ross Sea – First Sight of Victoria Land – Cape Adare – Danger in the
Pack – Coulman Island – Heavy Gale – Landing in Lady Newnes Bay – Killing
Seals – Wood Bay – Cape Washington – Coasting South – Landing in Granite
Harbour – A Well-sheltered Spot – McMurdo Sound – Stopped by the Pack –
Turning to the East.

> In fog and heavy weather,
> Through wildering sleet and snow,
> We fought the ice together,
> On a track where no ships go. – ANON.

Christmas Day, 1901, found us on the open expanse of the
Southern Ocean, but after such a recent parting from our friends
we had none of us much heart for the festivities of the season, and
the day passed quietly.

The wind held fair for our voyage, at first from the N.E., but
gradually shifting round to the west. At noon on the 26th we
were able to stop engines, and our heavily laden ship plunged
on towards the south under all the canvas that could be spread.

Although as a rule there are fewer gales to the south of New
Zealand at this time of the year than at any other, it is not at
all possible to rely on fine weather, and in the fact that we
escaped a 'blow' whilst traversing these stormy seas we had to
congratulate ourselves on exceedingly good fortune. The *Discovery* had little to fear from the worst gales when in good sea
trim, but at this time had we encountered a heavy sea the
consequences would have been exceedingly unpleasant. We must
inevitably have lost much of our large deck cargo: the masses of
wood on the superstructure would have been in great danger,
whilst all our sheep and possibly many of the dogs would have
been drowned.

As the days went by and we approached the Antarctic Circle, we felt how exceptionally fortunate we were in the continuance of fine weather. Although on the 28th the wind failed us and we were obliged to raise steam, on the 29th we were again favoured by a fresh breeze, and fell back once more on our policy of using the sails and saving the coal.

On the 31st we were in lat. 61 S., the temperature of both sea and air had fallen to 39°, and we had daylight throughout the twenty-four hours; but we now fell in with one of the commonest evils in these latitudes, a thick fog, and as we did not know how soon we might come upon icebergs, a very sharp 'lookout' was necessary.

The fog remained with us until the afternoon of January 2, occasionally lifting for a few hours, but again descending like a thick pall, and giving us at least one reason for being resigned to our very limited speed of five knots. A fact that adds to the depressing effect of a fog is that one's friendly companions the sea birds disappear, and one realises a curious sense of desertion as one peers into the unbroken grey, wondering when some monster iceberg will loom up, and prepared for instant action to avoid collision with it.

On the afternoon of the 2nd the weather cleared, and shortly after we sighted our first iceberg in lat. 65½ S. Other bergs soon rose above our horizon, and in the evening we counted seventeen about us, none more than four or five hundred yards in length, and although generally of a tabular shape, they were not more than 90 or 100 feet in height.

The nature and origin of the southern iceberg have always been a subject of some mystery. In the Northern Hemisphere, where glaciers push down into the sea, fragments, often of considerable size, become detached and are carried by currents to decay in milder climates.

Early Southern voyagers had doubtless a knowledge of these northern bergs, but in the southern oceans they met with masses of ice incomparably larger than anything known in the North, and to these they gave the name of Ice Islands, or often enough went yet farther and named them as new lands. Even Cook preserves the name of Ice Island in describing the long tabular berg so typical of the Southern Regions.

Except in cases where they have suffered denudation or have lost their stability and capsized, the shape of Antarctic icebergs is uniform: they have all a flat top and wall sides, and appear to have broken quietly away from some huge sheet of ice of which they formed a part. In 1854 an iceberg of this description was reported as fifty miles in length and 150 feet in height. Several accounts give thirty or forty miles as the length, and the height has been even stated to be as much as 400 feet. The longest berg reported by Ross was four miles long and 150 feet in height, but he gives a greater height for many others. The *Challenger* saw bergs of at least four miles in length and 200 feet in height. The largest berg we saw was aground off King Edward's Land, and we estimated it as about seven miles long and 200 feet high. Doubtless some of the larger dimensions here given are exaggerated, but in view of the fact that, as I hope to show, icebergs can be detached from a fixed but floating mass of ice, I see no reason why their length should be limited.

The whole subject of Antarctic icebergs is of more than purely polar or scientific interest, since they drift into more northerly latitudes, and become a formidable danger in the navigation of the Southern Seas. In the southern trade routes, voyages would be shortened greatly by taking a high latitude, but the danger of encountering these huge masses of ice has recommended a longer but safer route, and of late, I understand, the steamships of the New Zealand Company have been accustomed to take a yet more northerly course for this reason.

The bergs we now saw were comparatively small, and our course did not take us close to any, but even at a distance it was possible to realise the unpleasant shock that would be experienced by suddenly encountering them on a dark night, or in such a fog as that from which we had just emerged. Before our voyage ended we had ample opportunity of appreciating what unpleasant neighbours they may prove under such conditions.

On January 3 we had left our first group of bergs behind us; early in the morning we crossed the Antarctic Circle, little thinking how long a time would elapse before we recrossed it. We had at length entered the Antarctic Regions; before us lay the scene of our work; the struggles and trials of preparation and the anxiety of delays were over, and the haste of our long voyage was forgotten in the fact that we had reached the field of our labours in time to take advantage of the best part of the short open season in these ice-bound regions. During the night we had encountered the first of the scattered fragments of sea-ice which form the outriders of the pack, and soon we were passing through loose streams of ice, feeling again the slight shocks as our iron-clad prow forced a way through the honeycombed floes.

Having raised steam in one boiler, at 2.30 we stopped and took a sounding, finding bottom at 2,040 fathoms. The pack was now on all sides of us, but so loose that there were many large pools of open water, in one of which we stopped for our sounding and to put over our dredge. It is almost impossible to sound or dredge in thick pack-ice, owing to the danger of entanglement of the lines, and this was to us a very great drawback, because in pursuing our general explorations it was constantly necessary to enter the pack, and consequently the opportunities for carrying out such interesting operations as sounding and dredging were largely reduced.

The belt of pack-ice into which we had now entered was that which was traversed for the first time by Sir James Ross in 1840. We had therefore fully expected to meet it more or less in the latitude in which we actually did so. In general terms it is the ice which freezes over the Ross Sea in the winter, and which is broken up by the spring gales and drifts to the north, forming a band across the sea on this meridian. Later in the year, still drifting northward, it becomes scattered, leaving for a brief season an open sea route to the south.

During our long stay in our winter quarters we were able to observe to some extent the breaking-up and clearing of the Ross Sea, which goes to form this line of pack, and I shall refer to it in due course. In our passage through it we had usually an overcast sky; this affords the best condition for that noticeable phenomenon the 'ice-blink', the name given to the white reflection thrown on the clouds by the snowy surface of the pack. The polar voyager, when cruising in an open sea, soon becomes familiar with the patchy white sky which indicates the presence of ice long before it is visible from the deck; and in like manner when forcing his way through the pack he looks eagerly for the dark sky shadows which surmount the pools of open water, by entering which he may hope to find his progress made easier.

And now for several days we were destined to force our way through grinding floes, making for the open pools, and taking advantage of every favourable lead when the ice loosened. The pack is far from being a desert; life abounds in many forms. As we receded from the open sea the albatrosses and various oceanic petrels silently vanished, but their place was taken by other and equally interesting birds; around us flew the blue-grey southern fulmar and the Antarctic petrel, with brown barred wings and head, and a white breast; now and again a giant petrel would come lumbering by, an unwholesome scavenger, ready to gorge himself to repletion on such carrion as might catch his vulture eye. These birds are met with far and wide; they vary much in colour from black to the lighter shades of brown, whilst there are a very large proportion of pure albinos. Occasionally a pugnacious skua gull would flap past, pausing to make some less formidable bird disgorge his hard-earned dinner. But the pleasantest and most constant of our winged visitors was the small snow petrel, with its dainty snow-white plumage, relieved only by black beak and feet and black, beady eye. These charming little birds are everywhere in the pack-ice, capturing for their food the small crustaceans which the sea washes over the surface and into the caves of the worn floes.

The squawk of the penguin was constantly heard, at first afar and often long before the birds were seen; curiosity drew them to the ship, and suddenly their small figures appeared on a floe at some distance, only to skurry across and leap into the water on the near side, when with what seemed extraordinary rapidity they bobbed up again, shooting out on to the surface of some floe quite close to the ship. Here they paused and gazed at us with open-eyed astonishment, occasionally uttering a prolonged call, apparently to attract any of their fellows that might be in the neighbourhood. As the ship forced her way onward, these merry little companions would again and again leap into the water, journeying from floe to floe in their effort to find out what it all meant. Some of the sailors grew very expert in imitating their call, and could not only attract them from a long distance, but would visibly add to their astonishment when they approached.

In all parts of the pack seals are plentiful and spend long hours asleep stretched out on the floes. The commonest kind is the crab-eater or white seal, but the shorter species, the Ross seal, is not infrequently met with; whilst here and there is found the sea leopard, ranging wide and preying on the penguins, or even on the young of its less formidable brethren. It is curious to observe that both seals and penguins regard themselves as safe when they are out of the water. In the sea they gain their livelihood as best they can with the chance of being snapped up by each other or by the voracious killer whale, and in that element Nature has made them swift and alert to prey or to avoid being preyed on. But once on the ice or on land they have known no enemy, and can therefore conceive none. The seal raises his head only on your near approach, and then with but little alarm, whereas it is often difficult to drive the penguin into the water; even when chased it will still avoid the water under the impression that the sea is really the sole source of danger.

To add to our collection, whenever seals were seen ahead, the ship's course was altered towards them, and when sufficiently close a bullet gave the quietus to our intended specimen; the best shots were requisitioned for this purpose in order that the skin and skull should be damaged as little as possible, and to avoid unnecessary pain. Once or twice the animals thus killed had to be secured with a boat, but generally it was possible to carry a rope over the floe and take a hitch round the body, when willing hands would soon hoist it over the side.

We had not proceeded far into the pack when our upper deck became a busy but gory scene, for in one part men were skinning our prizes in the shape of seals and penguins, whilst elsewhere it was thought advisable to turn our sheep into mutton, and soon we had an array of carcases which made an excellent show, but which, alas! did not represent a great supply when the number of mouths on board was reckoned. However, we determined to consider this mutton a luxury to be kept for the winter, and to be eked out with the greatest care. Fresh meat will generally keep for a long time when hung in the rigging of a ship at sea, but here we had the advantage of temperature, and our carcases soon became to all intents and purposes frozen mutton.

The preservation of seal skins is not a light task: the skin is taken off with the thick layer of coarse fat or blubber which surrounds the body, and has then to be flensed or freed from this blubber, when it is placed in a cask with brine.

Sunday, January 5, we determined to keep as a somewhat belated Christmas day, and after the morning service and a special dinner, we tied the ship up to the largest piece of floe-ice we could find, and although this only measured 100 yards across, it proved sufficient for our purpose, which was to make our first attempt to use the Norwegian snow shoes or ski. With very few exceptions we had none of us used ski before, and consequently our first trial caused vast amusement; but even in such a short time it was possible to see signs of improvement, and before the afternoon ended races were organised and figures were darting about in all directions, with constant collisions and falls and much laughter. In the evening we pushed on once more, and whilst the ice crashed against our bows and came grinding along the side, a singsong was held below with choruses that went far to drown the outer tumult.

The position of officer of the watch in the pack was no sinecure: he had to be constantly on the alert to avoid contact with the heavier floes and to pick out the easiest path for the ship. When the pack was open his best position was in the 'crow's-nest', where he could first see the open patches of water and the heavier streams of ice, but in thicker pack he could often handle the ship better by 'conning' from the bridge, and at such times he had to be constantly giving fresh directions for the movement of the helm. Progress through the pack depended very largely on the care with which the ship was handled; often, after forging slowly ahead for some time, an incautious movement of the helm would bring us in collision with some heavy piece of ice, and the ship would be brought to a dead stop; sometimes by pushing on, the obstruction would be slowly forced aside, but oftener it was necessary to reverse the engines and seek a new direction.

The floes of this pack-ice through which we were now passing varied very greatly in character. Generally speaking, they increased in area as we advanced to the south, and this might well be expected, as we did not lose the ocean swell until we were 100 miles south of the northern edge. There were very few signs of pressure; only here and there a more ancient floe could be seen with ridged hummocks evidently produced far from its present position, but everything seemed to give the impression that the ice had been constantly opening out and allowing fresh ice to form in the channels thus left free. This would produce sheets of ice of varying ages, and when the sheets broke into pack, rupture would naturally take place along the joints and would produce in close association floes of varied thickness and character. The nature of sea-ice depends largely on the temperature at which it is produced, and, in turn, when the ice arrives in warmer water the process of decay seems to depend on its nature. All the ice we met with in the pack was undergoing decay, but whilst the older snow-covered floes were more or less completely honeycombed, the younger ice seemed to have become merely very sodden and brittle. Progress was not rapid in the pack; on January 6 our latitude was 68.20 S., in long. 175 E., and we had only made thirty-five miles in the last twenty-four hours. The ice was now so close that we could make no headway with the power of the single boiler, and we were obliged to light up both.

Whilst waiting for our second boiler to be prepared, we took the opportunity of replenishing our stock of water. Although fitted with condensers, to have produced water for the engines and general ship purposes with them would have necessitated a large expenditure of coal. By far the most economical plan was to obtain water by melting ice, and for this purpose we had immediately inside the engine-room, two long tanks fitted with steam coils, in which blocks of ice or snow could very speedily be converted into water and supplied to the engines, or wherever else it might be required. Our fresh-water tanks had a considerable capacity, but every now and again we were forced to stop and refill them, and after selecting the most promising floe the ship would be secured to it, and all hands set to work to dig out and pass on board the blocks of snow.

'Watering ship' was always a very busy scene, and since the hours spent at it were so much loss to our exploring season, it soon became the custom for the officers as well as the men to share in the work. As the pack-ice is frozen sea-water, it may be a surprise to many that fresh water can be obtained from it, and it should be explained that for making the fresh water one does not take the ice itself but the snow which has fallen on its surface; in many cases this is only a thin layer, so that it is always advisable to secure a floe which has been hummocked, as about the pressure ridges the snow will lie deeper than in other parts. At first we were rather inclined to scorn floes that were not very irregular in surface, but we soon found that what meant a great deal of snow to us made a very small hole in their burden, and that we could easily satisfy our requirements from comparatively insignificant ice-floes. After the first few occasions, therefore, as soon as we had decided on 'watering ship', it took us very little time to select our floe and to run the ship alongside it, when ready men would leap out with the ice-anchors, and after planting them securely would attach our ropes; directly the ship was secured the digging party would swarm over the side with picks and shovels and boxes, a few would dig away with the picks whilst others bore the filled boxes or large blocks across the floe, and others again stood ready to transport these over the side and on to the deck; the heap that was thus made was reduced as fast as the tanks could be fed, but generally the work was so vigorously carried on that the supply exceeded the immediate demand and a large deck-heap had to be gauged to determine the moment at which it would be wise to say, 'Hold, enough!' These words spoken, all would troop on board, the ice-anchors would be uprooted, the engines revolved, and we would push on through the pack once more; in this systematic manner we could provide ourselves with many tons of water with a halt of one or two hours.

We made better progress again with both boilers, and as we ground through and overturned broken fragments, it was astonishing to see the extent to which the under-ice was honeycombed. Many of the overturned blocks showed under-strata of a reddish yellow colour due to the presence of diatoms; it was surprising to find that these microscopic plants could be caught in the freezing water in such vast quantities, although our surface tow-nets at this time were producing large hauls.

Tow-netting had been a very great source of interest to many of us throughout our voyage from England; our original tow-nets were designed for use only when the ship was drifting; constructed of very fine meshed silk, they were intended to capture the microscopic plants which inhabit the surface waters of the sea. By increasing the length of the net and largely reducing its aperture, we found that we could use it whilst the *Discovery* was travelling through the water at her ordinary speed, and thus daily explore this most interesting form of life. Although Dr Koettlitz performed all the serious work in this department, many of us, in a more amateurish fashion, were interested in examining the strangely beautiful forms revealed by the microscope in these catches. It was strange to have sailed the sea for many years in entire ignorance that such things were. Our attempts to manufacture a speed-net to capture the small crustaceans and other surface beasts were not so successful. Mr Hodgson, our biologist, in whose department these were, reported that the delicate organisms were hopelessly destroyed, and came up 'all heads and tails'. The phyto-plankton, or plant life of the surface-waters, changed greatly on our advance to the south, and many beautiful forms of the tropic and sub-tropic seas gave place to vast quantities of diatoms. Since this life possesses no power of locomotion, under certain conditions it must form a guide to the surface currents of the ocean, and when further exploration has been made, as startling facts will be obtained from such data in the South as have already been established in the North.

On January 6 the swell ceased and floes increased to four or five acres in extent, and late at night they were almost a mile in length, but very rotten; a touch from our iron prow caused long cracks to fly out in all directions, into one of which the ship would glide and gradually gather way for the next obstruction. By the 7th we were in lat. 68.32 S., having only made thirty-two miles in the past twenty-four hours, but in the evening a considerable amount of 'open-water sky' appeared ahead, and soon after the ice slackened greatly, and we passed through a number of large water-holes. A fine following breeze in the evening enabled us to shut off steam in all but the thickest places.

Since our capture of seals we had been regularly feeding on seal-meat, and on the whole, even at this time, we found it palatable: there are naturally prejudices to be overcome in taking to a new meat, and the seal being a very full-blooded animal, his flesh does not look pleasing before it is cooked, and afterwards it has a very dark mahogany colour, which is not attractive. It is almost imposs-ible to describe the taste of a seal; it has a distinctive flavour in a similar degree to beef and mutton, but it cannot be called 'fishy', or like anything else that is generally known. It is a very strong meat, and in food value quite equal to the best beef. But the great drawback to the seal is that there is no fat other than blubber, and blubber has a very strong rancid taste and a most penetrating smell.

At this time blubber was to us an abomination both in taste and smell, and the smallest scrap that had inadvertently been cooked with the meat was sufficient to put us off our dinner. Later on we grew indifferent to this smell, and to some extent to the taste, but except under the stress of great hunger we have no record of blubber being enjoyed. Later on, moreover, we came thoroughly to enjoy our seal steaks and to revel in the thought of seal liver or kidneys; whereas I find my diary records very doubtful expressions of pleasure with regard to all these things at this time.

Early on the morning of the 8th, behind the ice-blink to the south, could be seen a strong water sky, and soon the officer of the watch hailed from aloft the glad tidings of an open sea to the south, the ice-floes became smaller, and we soon entered a belt where the ice lay in comparatively small pieces, closely packed and grinding together on the slight southerly swell. This extended for about 1½ mile, and pushing through it with steam and sail, we at length reached the hard line where the ice abruptly ended, and from whence to the south could be seen nothing but a clear sea.

Such a well-defined limit to the pack clearly indicates the prevalence of southerly winds at this season; it is obvious that the wind will get better hold on the floes in loose streams of ice than on those in the main pack, and hurry them along until they join the slower-moving main body.

Our pleasure in once more reaching open water may be imagined. During the past four days we had made little more than 200 miles, expending the precious coal which would have taken us three times that distance in an open sea. Although we could congratulate ourselves on getting through, it was evident that we had encountered a heavier obstruction than had Sir James Ross in first entering this sea in 1840, when, even in his slow sailing ships, he had been able to penetrate this pack in four days.

As we entered the open sea the thick pall of leaden clouds, which had remained persistently over us in the pack, rolled away, and the sun shone forth in a clear sky. Furling our sails, we obtained in lat. 70.3 a sounding of 1,480 fathoms, indicating that we were on the verge of the Antarctic land plateau. We celebrated our successful penetration of the pack by splicing the mainbrace, and at our modest dinner in the wardroom we drank to the future in champagne, so that the shout of 'Land in sight' at 10.30 p.m.

only added to an already joyful frame of mind. All who were not on deck quickly gathered there, to take their first look at the Antarctic Continent; the sun, now near the southern horizon, still shone in a cloudless sky, giving us full daylight. Far away to the south-west could be seen the blue outline of the high mountain peaks of Victoria Land, and we were astonished to find that even at this great distance of more than 100 geographical miles we could clearly distinguish the peaks of the Admiralty Range.

The course was directed for Robertson Bay, but when within forty or fifty miles we again fell in with loose streams of pack-ice, and once more repaired to the crow's nest to 'con' the ship through. At 4 p.m. on the 9th, after much turning and twisting to avoid the heaviest masses of ice, we arrived off the entrance of Robertson Bay, and forcing our way through a heavy band of pack-ice at the entrance, eventually reached the open water within the bay. Robertson Bay is formed by the long peninsula of Cape Adare, within which, standing but slightly above the level of the sea, is a curious triangular spit, probably the morainic remains of the vaster ice conditions of former ages.

It was on this spit that the expedition sent forth by Sir George Newnes, and commanded by Mr Borchgrevink, spent their winter in 1896, the first party to winter on the shores of the Antarctic Continent. We came to anchor under its shelter in 15½ fathoms, and soon had our boats ready to carry us to the shore.

We landed as best we could over the grounded floe-ice which fringed the shore, and beyond which lay the level plateau or beach of pebbled basalt, extending for about three-quarters of a mile to the foot of the cliffs, which rose abruptly with dark frowning aspect to a height of over 1,000 feet; a few ponds of melted snow occupied the slight depressions in the plateau, which elsewhere formed the nesting-place of countless thousands of Adélie penguins, and these small creatures were not content with the beach, but had formed their nests on the steep hillsides, even to a height of 1,000 feet.

Members of the extended colonies were constantly moving up and down on the regular beaten tracks, which lead from the sea to their elevated nests; they walked erect, and evidently found it a most difficult and laborious task to climb the steeper places. There can be little doubt that the occupants of the highest nests must take considerably over an hour to make this journey, and when it is considered that this is all waste time out of their day's fishing, it is difficult to understand why they should choose these very elevated positions. But we found later on that there were far more of these penguin rookeries than we supposed, and a little thought showed that a rookery has certain requirements that are not often found in the Antarctic Regions. It must have comparatively easy access to the sea at a spot where the fast ice breaks early in the season, and where the floating ice is not likely to pack. As long stretches of the coastline are fringed by an ice-cliff, such places are not too frequently met with, and I am inclined to think that in most cases, if not in all, they are tenanted by colonies of this pushing, energetic little penguin; and it may be, therefore, that it is want of room alone that causes them to nest in such apparently inconvenient places.

In every respect these small birds afford a fund of interest. Their winter is spent in the pack-ice to the north, but with regular migratory habits they suddenly appear at their rookeries in September or October, and crowding in every available spot, they scrape a few pebbles together into the rudest form of nest and lay their eggs. In due course the little brown-coated chicks are hatched out and begin and continue their life in an almost ceaseless clamour for food, which the parent birds provide with indefatigable patience and zeal. Things continue thus until the chicks have grown to full stature and have shed their brown coats of down for their maturer white-breasted plumage, when they are led to the water by the older birds, and, in spite of much protest, rudely pushed in. Henceforth, it is to be supposed, they must fend for themselves, and the rookery once more becomes a desert.

On our arrival at Cape Adare the young birds were already well grown, and despite the very pungent and decided odour of penguin which assailed our nostrils, we continued to watch the antics of these queer inhabitants with absorbing interest.

Round and about the clusters of penguins, with their busy comings and goings and their ceaseless chatter, were gathered a number of the light-brown skua gulls. One could have imagined them to be dwelling on the greatest terms of friendship with the penguins until one saw some unfortunate penguin chick wander from its immediate company, when with a swift swoop a watchful skua would descend on it and in an instant its life was ended, and its yet quivering little form was being torn by its rapacious enemy, whose own nest and chicks might lie but a few yards away.

In the centre of the Cape Adare beach still stands the hut used by the members of the Southern Cross Expedition, and scattered about it we found a considerable quantity of provisions. The hut is in very good condition, and in such a climate might well remain so for many years to come. Should some future explorers traverse this region, it is well to know that here they possess a retreat in case of emergency, as, although they may not find all the provisions in good condition, a fair proportion is likely to be found so, and at this spot there would always be abundance of food in the shape of seals or penguins.

There is always something sad in contemplating the deserted dwellings of mankind, under whatever conditions the inhabitants may have left. We could only wander about and imagine the daily life of the party until our physicist, Mr Bernacchi, joined us. This officer had been one of this small party of eight souls, and here on this spot he recalled the past and told us of the unhappy death of one of his comrades, the naturalist Hanson, now lying buried on the hilltop 1,000 feet above our heads. The dying man had requested that he should rest there, and slowly and laboriously his body was borne up the steep hillside to the chosen spot. So there rest the remains of the only human being who has found burial on this great southern continent, and above his body still stands, in touching memorial, a plain wooden cross.

Our energetic magnetic observers, Armitage, Bernacchi, and Barne, were soon at work with their instruments amongst the penguins, whilst the naturalists wandered farther afield in search of specimens. The search was not without result, as, besides specimens of moss and rock, several species of birds were collected. Amongst the high rocks the small Wilson petrel was found nesting, and two eggs were obtained. On the beach were collected some white giant petrels as well as the commoner brown ones. On entering the bay we had disturbed one of these greedy birds taking a siesta on a floe, and so gorged with food that it could barely fly.

The scene in the bay after we had returned for our late evening meal was very beautiful; the surface was calm and placid, beyond it the sunlight fell on the bold peaks and splendid glaciers of the

Admiralty Range, the sharp summits of Mount Minto and Adam were well defined against a clear sky, whilst the lofty peak of Sabine was lost in a mystery of fleecy cloud. The placid, deep-shadowed sea was dotted with streams of brilliantly white pack-ice, whilst here and there a table-topped iceberg showed the sharpest contrast of light and shadow as the sun fell on its smooth, steep sides. The tide was making out of the bay with considerable strength, and now and again it bore past us a floe alive with busy, chattering penguins.

Somewhat later Bernacchi and some others landed again to visit once more the grave of poor Hanson, and to see that all was well with it. They took with them a tin cylinder containing the latest information with regard to our voyage, with directions to place it in some conspicuous part of the hut. The following year this cylinder was found by the *Morning*, and gave the first information that the *Discovery* had succeeded in reaching these southern regions.

At 3 a.m. on January 10, when it was still gloriously calm and bright, we weighed our anchor and again stood out to sea, steering close around the high land of Cape Adare in hopes of finding a clear channel close to the land. At first it appeared as though we should do so, but soon the tidal stream began to make from the south, and the whole aspect of the streams of heavy pack-ice rapidly changed; before we could decide to turn, the pack was all about us, and we were being rapidly borne along with it. Across the entrance to the bay there was a chain of grounded icebergs, and it was towards these that we were now being carried; we could see and almost hear the heavy floes grinding and overriding one another against these barriers: For the first time we faced the dangers of the pack, and became aware of its mighty powers. For we could do little or nothing, the floes around us were heavier than anything we had yet met; twist and turn as we would, we could make no appreciable advance, and in front of one monster floe we were brought to a standstill for nearly half an hour. Still we battled on; Armitage remained aloft working the ship with admirable patience, the engine-room, as usual, responded nobly to the call for more steam, and soon the *Discovery* was exerting all her powers in the fray, but the progress was still so slow that it looked almost inevitable that we should be carried down amongst the bergs. It was one of those hours which impress themselves for ever on the memory. Above us the sun shone in a cloudless sky, its rays were reflected from a myriad points of the glistening pack; behind us lay the lofty snow-clad mountains, the brown sun-kissed cliffs of the cape and the placid glassy waters of the bay; the air about us was almost breathlessly still; crisp, clear and sun-lit, it seemed an atmosphere in which all Nature should rejoice; the silence was broken only by the deep panting of our engines and the slow, measured hush of the grinding floes; yet, beneath all ran this mighty, relentless tide, bearing us on to possible destruction. It seemed desperately unreal that danger could exist in the midst of so fair a scene, and as one paced to and fro on the few feet of throbbing plank that constituted our bridge, it was difficult to persuade oneself that we were so completely impotent. It is curious here to note that, except myself, only those who were actually on watch were on deck. The hour was early, and the majority were resting after their labours of the previous night, and so, asleep in their bunks below, they were happily unconscious of the uncomfortable possibilities before them; and that they were not told bears testimony to the fact that a fuss was rarely made in the *Discovery* unless there was some good reason. Our release from this danger was so gradual that it would have been difficult to say when it happened; perhaps on these occasions one is always a little slow to realise that things are getting better. It came from the gradual weakening of the tide, and most unexpectedly, because we had not looked for change in this for some hours to come. But gradually the tidal stream slackened, the close-locked floes fell slightly apart, and under her full head of steam the *Discovery* began to forge ahead towards the open sea and safety. By 8.20 we had won through, and could breathe a sigh of relief. For me the lesson had been a sharp and, I have no doubt, a salutary one; we were here to fight the elements with their icy weapons, and once and for all this taught me not to undervalue the enemy.

During the forenoon we were able to stand within seven or eight miles of the high bold coastline to the south of Cape Adare, but later we were obliged to turn outwards to avoid the heavy streams of pack-ice drifting along the land, and this took us well outside the group of rocky islets on which Ross landed, and which he named the Possession Islands. Our navigator took advantage of fine weather to swing the ship; this means that the ship was gradually turned round, and as her head pointed in certain directions, observations of the sun were taken from which the error of the compass could be computed. I have already explained how highly important the finding of the compass errors at various places was, but it should be added that since the error in any spot might differ according to the direction of the ship's head, it was also necessary that an allowance should be made for the particular direction of the ship's head when an observation was made. It was to obtain this allowance that the *Discovery* was swung, and therein we held an immense advantage over Sir James Ross, who had been unable to manœuvre his sailing-ships in this manner; but although we realised the advantage of swinging, it involved not a few trials and tribulations: sometimes when we had stopped for this work, clouds would come flying across the face of the sun, and we had to wait patiently until they had passed; at others, the wind would spring up and make the ship so difficult to handle that it was some time before we could get her steadied on the various courses; and as these delays tended to fritter away the valuable hours of our open season, it can be imagined that we did not regard them with complacency.

Owing to our being continually forced to edge out to seaward to avoid streams of pack, by the morning of the 11th we were well clear of the land, which, however, could be very distinctly seen in the distance, and gave us much to think and talk about as we recognised the various peaks and headlands which Sir James Ross had named.

We still stood to the south, but our progress was slow owing to a brisk S.E. wind, and to the fact that we were only using one boiler. As I have pointed out, of all economies practised on board, the most important was that of coal, and every device by which a saving could be effected in this respect was worthy of consideration. It is still doubtful, however, whether my decision to use one boiler commonly, instead of two, really effected the saving I intended. At this time the *Discovery*, with both boilers alight, would burn from five to six tons of coal a day, and for this she could maintain a speed of six or seven knots in calm water; with one boiler, she would burn from three and a half to four tons, productive of a speed of four to five knots in calm water. So far the problem, though not very exact, is capable of solution; but the trouble is that a calm sea is a rarity, and the *Discovery* was so dependent on wind and sea that when these conditions were included, the question was complicated out of all recognition. The problem as to whether the ground could more economically be got over with one boiler or two was therefore one that could only be decided by experience. At this time we had no experience to guide us; for good or ill I decided on using the single boiler, and with rare exceptions this became our custom throughout the summer cruise.

On such occasions as the present, however, it meant that our progress against an adverse wind was exceedingly slow. On the 11th we only made fifty-five miles, and on the 12th only thirty-two miles, on our southerly course. The wind gradually increased, and the weather became very unsettled. On the afternoon of the 11th we had a succession of snowstorms, and the land was blotted out in thick haze. During the misty evening we were surrounded by large flocks of Antarctic petrel, which stayed with us for a time, and vanished as suddenly as they had come. Almost immediately after we were surrounded with flocks of snow petrel, quaint little ghostly forms flitting about in the mist, and dropping now and again to the edge of a floe to capture the small *Euphausia* on which they feed.

During the 12th we scarcely made any headway at all. The wind increased from the S.W., and occasionally bore down on us in heavy snow squalls. The low black rock and bold capes of the coastline stood out distinctly; but heavy, ominous clouds obscured the mountains. We could now distinguish Coulman Island on our bow, and by the morning we had brought it almost abeam; but by this time the weather bore a still more threatening aspect. A heavy swell came up from the south and the glass was falling. There could be little doubt that a gale was brewing, and in order that it should not carry us far to the north I thought it wise to try to seek shelter under Coulman Island. We turned in and were soon amongst the loose pack-ice and in smoother water, but the wind was momentarily increasing, and we were obliged to light up our second boiler in order to gain the open-water shelter which we could now see under the high cliffs of the island.

Coulman Island, like all the coastal land, is a mass of volcanic rock, rising about 2,000 feet above the sea. It is comparatively flat on the top, which is covered with an ice-cap of considerable thickness, and it is surrounded by steep and in some places almost vertical cliffs. Beneath the heaviest falls of névé from the ice-cap, and clinging to the steep cliffs, are fan-shaped masses of ice with vertical faces, rising as much as 100 feet above the sea. These have all the appearance of glacier tongues, though they can scarcely be called by that name, and they form an intermittent ice-foot fringing the coast. The land as we approached it looked illusively near; the sky was overcast, and the higher land was hidden in cloud, but beneath this sheet of grey the black rocks stood out with such distinctness that one was wholly deceived as to their distance. So strong was this deception that the engines were eased when we were nearly two miles from the cliffs, under the impression that they were only a few hundred yards away; we only discovered our mistake when we saw a colony of penguins, and found that even with glasses it was impossible to distinguish the individuals. I find also I noted in my diary that there was on our right 'a curious indentation like the crater of a volcano', and this was really the strait between the island and the mainland, some ten miles across.

Afterwards in our winter quarters, and during our sledge journeys, we got to know very well how easily one could be deluded in respect to distance, and what extraordinarily false appearances distant objects would assume. The matter is of more than passing interest, because it shows that one must be exceedingly cautious in believing even what appears to be the evidence of one's own eyes, and it largely helps to explain some errors which we found had been made by former explorers, and which we knew must have been made in all good faith.

During the night of the 13th we lay under the shelter of the high cliffs on the N.E. side of Coulman Island, over which had now gathered a heavy storm cloud; the wind had risen to a full gale at sea, but only reached us in occasional squalls which swept down from the high cliffs. To occupy our time, a trawl-net was put over in about 100 fathoms of water, and great was the delight of Mr Hodgson when it was found to be well filled with specimens. At such times our biologist was in his element; on one side of him would be arrayed a number of glass jars, before him would lie in one mass the mud, stones, and animals which the net had produced. And thus, surrounded by a circle of eager, curious faces he would work with fingers and forceps, sorting fish, sponges, crustaceans, and polyzoa into their proper receptacles. It was as much as anyone's life was worth to approach without invitation, but questions were allowed and would be answered, generally with a string of lengthy scientific terms which left the questioner about where he was before.

By the morning of the 14th the wind had increased to a furious gale, and the squalls now swept down over the cliffs with such terrific violence that we were forced to exert all our one-boiler power to keep the ship in her station, and even thus we began to lose ground. The ship would not face the wind directly, and we were obliged to carry it on the bow with the yards braced sharp up; in this position she would gradually edge away sideways until it became necessary to bring the wind on the other bow and edge back again. We had so little control over her that we could not alter our course by 'tacking', but were obliged to set a head sail and so 'wear' round with our stern to the wind. In the afternoon the wind force, as measured by the Robertson anemometer, was ninety miles an hour, and as we continued to lose ground we got into a more choppy sea, which sent the spray over us in showers to freeze as it fell. As evening approached we drove down on a line of pack and amongst several small bergs, raising clouds of spray in the driving gale. Our situation was not pleasant; to avoid one berg we were forced to go about, and in doing so we ran foul of another. As we came down on it our bowsprit just swept clear of its pinnacled sides, and we took the shock broad on our bows; it sent us reeling round, but luckily on the right tack to avoid further complications, and we rebounded clear of our dangerous neighbour. The night which followed was dismal enough; again and again small bergs appeared through the blinding spray and drift, and it was only with great difficulty that our unmanageable ship could be brought to clear them. Meanwhile, in spite of our continuous steaming we were being driven farther and farther to leeward. But even gales must have an end, and towards morning there was a visible moderation in the wind, when we were able to creep up towards the island once more. In the afternoon an arch of clear sky appeared in the south and the wind fell rapidly. We were able to steam up close to the island once more; and there, between two high tongues of ice off Cape Wadworth, we landed on the steep rocks and erected a staff bearing a tin cylinder with a further record of our voyage.

By the time this was accomplished the wind had fallen completely, and the sun shone forth with great brilliancy. We entered the strait between the island and the mainland and found it to be considerably narrower than was expected, so that we soon approached the high land of Cape Jones on the other side. At this time, although there was a quantity of pack in the southern limits of the strait, from our crow's-nest it looked as if it would not be difficult to find clear leads to the open sea beyond, and thus to pass completely through the strait, but when we attempted this some hours later we found the pack closely locked in the entrance.

To the southward of Cape Jones the land recedes abruptly and sweeps round, forming a long bay, behind which we now saw rising in a clear sky the magnificent sharp peaks of Mounts Monteagle and Herschel, and the high snow-covered ranges between. From the summits many vast glaciers sweep down with majestic curves to the sea, and on these we looked with a keen eye, calculating the chances of reaching the interior over surfaces which looked so smooth at this distance. But the most remarkable physical feature of this neighbourhood is the fact that the whole of this bay, called by Mr Borchgrevink 'Lady Newnes Bay', is filled with a vast mass of what we subsequently came to call 'barrier' ice, a sheet of such thickness that its towering ice-cliffs stand in many places 150 feet above the water. On the origin and nature of these extraordinary ice-formations I shall have more to say in a future chapter. At this time, although few of us had much knowledge of ice conditions in other parts of the world, we felt that we were gazing on a phenomenon unlike anything reported elsewhere.

On our passage across the strait we had a very remarkable instance of the influence of volcanic rock on the compass. Two successive bearings taken of a distant cape showed us that the card had swung 8°. At this time we were more than a mile from the cliffs of the island, and on sounding found forty fathoms of water beneath us. The directive force of the compass was of course extremely small, but such a large deflection is astonishing.

In the evening we entered a long inlet between Cape Jones and the barrier-ice, and later turned out of this into a smaller inlet in the barrier-ice itself. After pushing through heavy detached floes we secured to some sea-ice which, although cracked in all directions, had not yet broken away. We were now in a remarkably well-sheltered spot; on each side we had high ice-cliffs, whilst across the mouth of the inlet lay the high land of Cape Jones. On the sea-ice of the inlet, which ran for some distance ahead of the ship, more than a hundred seals lay basking in the sun, and elsewhere a small colony of Emperor penguins in process of moulting exhibited the most dishevelled appearance, and evidently hated to be seen with their usually smooth glossy plumage in such an untidy state.

As so often in the Antarctic Regions, we resolved to turn night into day, and, although it was 10 p.m., to start about our work at once. Our work was not a pleasant task, but one we regarded as very necessary – namely, that of adding to our larder sundry joints of seal. We felt fairly confident of finding a wintering spot before the season closed, but we had no guarantee that we should find seals in its vicinity, and it seemed the wisest plan to get them whilst we could.

The seal possesses the most astonishing vitality, and though nothing can be easier than to catch and wound these poor creatures, it is difficult to kill them outright, and until our men had had practice and knew exactly where to strike, many a futile knife-thrust was given.

It seemed a terrible desecration to come to this quiet spot only to murder its innocent inhabitants and stain the white snow with blood; but necessities are often hideous, and man must live. Some of us were glad enough to get away on our ski and to climb the steep snow slopes at the end of our creek. We found that the surface of this 'barrier' mass undulated in long waves, some of which we crossed; but knowing we had no prospect of reaching the land, we soon turned and employed ourselves in sliding down the steep slopes of the inlet on our ski, an amusement which cost us many falls.

Leaving the men to get in the seal carcases and some ice for our boilers, I turned in at two to get a few hours' rest before we again put to sea. On returning to the deck at 7.30 I was told that all work was completed, but that some five hours before a party consisting of Dr Wilson, Mr Ferrar, Cross and Weller had got adrift on a floe, and that no-one had thought of picking them up. Although the sun had been shining brightly all night, the temperature had been down to 18°, and afar off I could see four disconsolate figures tramping about to keep themselves warm on a detached floe not more than fifteen yards across. When at length our wanderers scrambled over the side, it was very evident they had a big grievance, and it was only after some hot cocoa that they could talk of their experiences with ease. They had been obliged to keep constantly on the move, and when they thought of smoking to relieve the monotony of the situation, the smokers found they had pipes and tobacco, but no match. It was whilst they were dismally discussing this fact that Dr Wilson, a non-smoker, came nobly to the rescue and succeeded in producing fire with a small pocket magnifying glass – a fact which shows not only the resource of the officer, but the power of the midnight sun in these latitudes.

As we turned the corner of the barrier-ice cliff I saw to my disgust that the channels of open water which I had observed to the south on the previous evening had now closed up, and only thick pack lay in that direction. There was nothing for it but to pass again round the north side of Coulman Island, which, owing to many buffetings with loose pack, it took us the whole day to circumnavigate.

On the 17th we had to stand out farther and farther from the land to clear the pack; on our return voyage we also found much pack in this vicinity, and it is evident that Coulman Island forms a sort of cul-de-sac, delaying the ice as it passes up the coast.

It was not easy under our varying conditions to arrive at the currents along this coast. We found that there was evidently a tidal stream setting alternately north and south. Whilst we were delayed under Coulman Island we had been influenced by this fact, and had on occasions seen small bergs travelling against the wind; a change of direction in the stream had appeared to us to occur only once in twelve hours, and this was supported by subsequent tidal observations.

It is probable that the north-running stream is stronger than the south, as undoubtedly the bergs as well as the pack-ice move gradually to the north. The pack-ice is of course mostly influenced by the wind, which at this season of the year appears to blow pretty constantly from a southerly direction.

At 2.30 a.m. on the 18th we arrived in the entrance to Wood Bay, only to find it heavily packed. I had hoped to be able to land here and leave a record, but to have attempted to force through this heavy ice would have involved an unjustifiable expenditure of coal. The ice we faced was evidently that which had been formed in the bay; it was from six to seven feet thick, and far more solid than anything we had yet encountered. Very little snow had fallen on the surface of the floes, and except where some volcanic sand and rubble had been carried on to them by the wind, there was no sign of decay. To run into floes of this description was a very different matter to charging the comparatively rotten ice which we had met in the pack.

Away to the N. and N.W. of us we could now see the sharp peaks of Monteagle and Murchison, amongst bewildering clusters of lesser summits; across the bay rose the magnificent bare cliff of Cape Sibbald, rising 2,000 feet above the sea; to the west one could trace the breaks in hill-outline suggestive of the windings of the arms of the bay and the glacier valleys beyond, but the eye lingered most pleasantly on the uniform outline of Mount Melbourne to the S.W. This fine mountain rears an almost perfect volcanic cone to a height of 9,000 feet, and, standing alone with no competing height to take from its grandeur, it constitutes the most magnificent landmark on the coast. Cape Washington, a bold, sharp headland, projects from the foot of the mountain on its eastern side, and finding such heavy pack in Wood Bay, we now turned to the south to pass around this cape.

From this point our voyage promised to be increasingly interesting, since the coast to the south of Cape Washington was practically unknown. Ross seems to have satisfied himself that there was a continuance of land to Mount Erebus, but he saw it only at a very great distance – a fact which is attested by the absence of names from individual mountains and capes. He probably did not see more than the dim outline of hills far beyond his horizon, and the only particular name he supplies – that of Cape Gauss – was probably given to some darker patch of bare mountain-side, as at this spot there is no such conspicuous cape as he imagined. I have already pointed out how easily one may be deceived in such a matter, and it can be imagined that we looked forward eagerly to exploring this unknown land.

As we passed within half a mile of the sheer headland of Washington we were surprised to get shallow soundings. Our lead gave us eighteen fathoms, then fifteen, then eight, and in this shallow water our compass was again largely disturbed.

It should be understood that we were now south of the magnetic pole, and as the south-seeking end of the compass needle continued to point towards that spot, our ship's head, although directed to the true south, appeared by the compass to be travelling in a northerly direction. To find out the actual amount of this error in different places was, of course, one of our most important missions, but throughout our voyages in these seas, where the error was so great and so constantly changing, the compass proved a most confusing instrument, and in thick weather much calculation was necessary to determine the true direction in which any new course would take one.

On rounding Cape Washington we were delighted to find that the coast was comparatively free of pack. We could now see that the western slopes of Melbourne merged into a range of comparatively low hills, which continued to the south till they rose to the steep sides of a long, high table mountain beyond which a snow-covered ridge carried the outline to farther mountains of a less perfect but distinctly tabular form. We were destined to find this tabular form of mountain to be a feature of Victoria Land for many hundreds of miles to the south, and largely a key to the geological formation of the whole country; but at this time the majority of us failed to appreciate the importance of this new development, though we were aware of the novelty of outline.

The coastline from Cape Washington sweeps back in a deep bay, and then runs directly to the south, in places fringed by a steep ice-foot, while in others bare, rocky slopes descend to the water's edge. Curiously enough, there was but little snow on the higher mountains, but the foothills in front were almost covered with a thick glacial crust.

As we got to the southward of our table mountain we could see that the high snow ridge beyond it represented an immense overflow of the ice-mass of the interior. Some vast store of ice beyond seemed to take advantage of the break in the mountain chain, and to pour down in one great river of ice to the sea.

The glistening white surface of this great overflow, fully fifteen miles across, rose gradually to a height of some 4,000 feet at the crest of the ridge, and no doubt continued to rise to greater height beyond. It was broken only in the centre, where a huge beehive-shaped nunatak thrust its head through the mass and left deep furrows in its snowy surface. The rich brown of the bare basaltic rock of this nunatak is conspicuously contrasted with the vast surface of white snow about it, and therefore constitutes one of the most striking landmarks on the coast, a most remarkable and distinctive feature.

And now as we skirted the ice-foot on our right we found ourselves suddenly brought up in a curious inlet, with ice-walls on every side, and were obliged to turn and retrace our steps for some way, when, still keeping the ice-wall on our right, we found ourselves going due east directly away from the land. For many hours we steamed along this ice-cliff, which varied in height from 70 to 100 feet, until, after travelling more than twenty miles, we came where the cliff rose to 150 feet in height and turned abruptly to the south, and after a mile or more again abruptly to the west. We now perceived that we had encountered another example of the barrier-ice which we had seen in Lady Newnes Bay, but this time the ice ran out in a long snout to seaward, and we could fit no theory to the fact that the extremity of the snout was higher than many parts behind it. Off the end of the snout we obtained 368 fathoms of water – another rather puzzling circumstance, when the flotation of ice was considered.

On turning the corner to the south we were again brought in full view of our ancient enemy the pack-ice. Here, as further north, it is evidently detained in its passage along the coast. The extent of the pack carried us some way to the south before we could find a 'lead' towards the land. It was a gloriously bright Sunday morning – so clear that at midday we sighted Mount Erebus at a distance of 120 miles, and in the afternoon could even see the vapour rising from the summit of that lofty volcano. The day was so perfectly clear that at one time we could see Melbourne, Monteagle, and even Coulman Island to the north, and Erebus to the south; that is an included range of vision of 240 geographical miles.

It is here that I find a note in my diary to the effect that the ice-cap of the interior appeared to rise beyond the coastal mountains, and that patches of rock could be seen farther inland, but that it was impossible, owing to the mirage, to define the height or distance of such patches. This note is of great importance in connection with our subsequent exploration of the interior ice. At 6 p.m. we were able to turn towards the land, and later in the night made out a very conspicuous bluff cliff in marked contrast to the white snow slopes behind.

We were now in a latitude where it was most desirable that we should make a diligent search for safe winter quarters for the ship. Wood Bay had been thought by many in England to be the most southerly spot in which we were likely to find security, but we had seen enough of the coastline to the south of that place to realise the impossibility of travelling along it in sledges, and to assure us that if we wished to make any advance to the south we must find a harbour in some higher latitude. The sight of this bluff cliff seemed to give promise of finding an inlet in its neighbourhood, and I decided to make an effort to explore the coast. But to approach the land was not such easy work, as we had constantly to force our way through streams of pack-ice, and the floes were more solid than any we had yet met. If one charged them with any speed the shock of meeting was tremendous; the ship would stop dead with masts and yards quivering, anyone below might have imagined an earthquake, and to be in the swaying, trembling crow's-nest on such an occasion was anything but a pleasant sensation. The only comfortable way was to push quietly through, and so it was not until 4 p.m. on the 20th that we could convince ourselves that we had been right in expecting an inlet behind the conspicuous mass of rock for which we had been steering. An hour later, as we entered it, we met ice which had evidently been formed inside and but recently broken up. It was perfectly smooth, showing absolutely no sign of pressure, and therefore indicating what a secure wintering harbour the inlet would make. But what struck us as most curious was that every floe was a rectangle and looked as though it had been purposely shaped with accuracy and precision; it is difficult to comprehend how an irregular ice-sheet can be broken naturally in this manner; the swell which breaks it must be extremely regular, and the ice-sheet must be astonishingly uniform. One must infer also that very placid conditions exist in this well-sheltered inlet both in winter and spring.

As we gradually worked our way into the inlet we could see on our right a few small crevassed glaciers between high cliffs showing faulted rock strata, of which our geologist at this time could make little. On the left and nearer shore the steep slopes were formed of broken angular boulders, with here and there the native rock peeping through. Two or three miles ahead the inlet took a sharp turn to the left. As no boat could be used in such an ice-strewn bay, we were forced to reach the shore by other means, and a large party was soon bounding from floe to floe, now and then encountering a breach too wide to be leaped and having to raft themselves across.

On shore we found that the boulders which had looked so dingy from the ship were mostly composed of granite, and a little chipping provided us with such a variety of this beautiful crystalline rock that we afterwards named the inlet Granite Harbour. Ice scratchings were visible on a few of the boulders, but much weathering had taken place.

Enclosed by so much bare rock capable of absorbing the sun's rays, and well protected from the wind, this inlet is probably the most sheltered spot in many a league of coastline, and in this calm, bright weather we thoroughly enjoyed our run on shore, and, except for the ice in the bay, could have imagined ourselves in a far milder climate. We found small streams of water meandering over the stones, and it was pleasant to hear their music and to drink the pure snow water, and still pleasanter to find in their sheltered courses small banks of moss of almost luxuriant growth. We headed up the bay to see where the inlet ended after its sharp turn, and disturbed several skuas guarding their fluffy slate-coloured chicks. They showed their annoyance by wheeling round and swooping down straight at us, only turning their course at the very last moment, so that one was sometimes brushed by their wings as they swept past with wild cries. The skua is a heavy bird with a very formidable bill, and such attacks appear alarming, as doubtless they are intended to do; but though we often saw them under similar conditions, I do not think anyone was ever actually struck.

After scrambling over rocks for some time, we reached the corner from which we could see the extremity of the inlet, where the snout of a glacier of no great size dipped into the sea. We saw at once that the inner recesses of this inlet would have afforded us excellent shelter for the winter. In a week or two the ice would have pushed out to sea, leaving a free surface on the placid waters of the bay. Around the second corner the sea swell had fallen to a small rhythmic movement which could have caused little inconvenience. The steep shores around were skirted everywhere with a low strip of fast ice on which it would have been easy for us to land, and across which we could have carried the heavy materials for constructing our huts. Here and there on this ice-foot lay a somnolent seal, giving assurance of winter food; and although the waters of the inlet were doubtless very deep, as they are in most fiords, it is probable that in the vicinity of the glacier we should have found some bank of morainic material on which we could have cast our anchors; in fact, altogether there was a promise of snugness and security about this spot which we met nowhere else.

It is only on looking back on our experiences that I can see how much we should have missed had we succumbed to the allurements of this tempting spot. Surrounded as we should have been by steep and lofty hills, we could have obtained only the most local records of climatic conditions, and our meteorological observations would have been comparatively valueless; but the greatest drawback would have been that we should be completely cut off from travelling over the sea-ice beyond the mouth of our harbour. There can be no doubt that the sea-ice was constantly broken up along this coast in the winter of 1902, and an attempt to travel to the south along the coast without the assistance of the sea-ice would have been beset with such innumerable dangers and difficulties that it is possible we should never have reached even as far south as the spot at which we eventually wintered. It is when one remembers how naturally a decision to return to this place might have been made that one sees how easily the results of the expedition might have been missed.

When, after a stiff climb, we again came abreast of the ship, we found the swell had increased, and it was only with some difficulty that we regained the ship over the swaying floes. Shortly after midnight we pushed out to sea, satisfied that we had discovered a place which would serve us for wintering in default of a better.

Turning again to the south, we found an open sea, and crossed the 77th parallel; but early on the 21st the inevitable pack appeared ahead, and we were forced away from the coast in trying to pick

the easiest channels. The ice we met with at first was not formidable, but in the afternoon we entered a pack of the hard solid ice
which we were now getting to know so well and to associate with
the inlets on the coast. The moment of entering this pack could
be detected exactly from the astonishing increase in the shocks
sustained by the ship.

At this time I still cherished a hope of being able to find more
southerly winter quarters than Granite Harbour, and, searching
the coastline with powerful glasses, thought I could detect the
promise of such on our starboard bow, and so spent some hours in
trying to push through the heavy obstruction that now met us. By
4 p.m., however, as we had progressed only a few hundred yards,
we edged away to the eastward, where things appeared more
promising; here we got into ice which looked much heavier, as it
was thickly covered with snow, whereas the ice which we had
been attacking was practically bare and blue. The line of demarc-
ation was well defined, and the difference in the nature of the ice
was felt the moment we crossed it – the heavy shocks ceased and
the ship was able to make gradual though slow progress.

I have dwelt somewhat fully on the nature of the pack-ice
through which we passed at various times, because the differences
are so great, and because the subject is not only of great interest but
of vast importance to the navigator in these seas. It was always a
fascinating study to observe the pack-ice, to infer the various
conditions under which the ice had been produced, and to note
the extraordinary differences of form that frozen sea-water can
assume.

The night of the 21st was gloriously fine. By 8 a.m. we were in
the middle of McMurdo Sound, creeping slowly, very slowly,
through the pack-ice, which appeared from the crow's-nest to
extend indefinitely ahead. But a few miles separated us from the
spot where we were ultimately to take up our winter quarters,
and as we got to know this scene so well it is interesting to recall
some extracts from what I wrote when first we gazed on it: 'To
the right is a lofty range of mountains with one very high peak far
inland, and to the south a peculiar conical mountain, seemingly
ending the coastline in this direction; on the left is Mount Erebus,
its foothills, and a glimpse of Mount Terror. The Parry Mountains cannot be seen ahead of us. In the far distance there is a small

patch like a distant island. Ross could not have seen these patches, and a remnant of hope remains that we are heading for a strait, and not a bay.'

This was written shortly after four, and at eight I added: ' . . . as we drove slowly southward the apparent islands ahead broadened out, and there was no longer a doubt as to their being connected to form the end of the bay. But it is highly satisfactory to note that there are no mountains in the background, and that so far as the eye can see there must be a plain stretching directly south. . . . We now see that if fortune allows us to winter in either of the two harbours we have found, we shall have good prospect of getting to the south. . . . In this manner the coastline to the south for nearly 40° of arc is suggested by five dark rock patches and their connecting snow slopes, this space being flanked on the right by the conical hill and on the left by a spur of Erebus, which appears to form a sharp headland.' It was easy afterwards to recognise each point here noticed when, actually situated at the 'spur of Erebus', we named the conical mountain after our ship, and the high western mountains in honour of the Royal Society; but it is curious to think that at this time I should have been prepared to affirm that continuous land ran from Erebus to the mainland.

So at 8 p.m. on the 21st we thought we knew as much of this region as our heavy expenditure of coal in the pack-ice would justify us in finding out, and as before us lay the great unsolved problem of the barrier and of what lay beyond it, we turned our course with the cry of Eastward ho!

Along the Great Barrier

> She skirts the icy margin of the main,
> And where unchanging from the first of time
> Snows swell on snows amazing to the sky,
> And icy mountains high on mountains pil'd
> Seem to the shivering sailor from afar
> Shapeless and white, an atmosphere of cloud. – THOMSON

In our journey from Cape Washington to the south we had already done something to justify the despatch of the expedition.

A coastline which had hitherto been seen only at a great distance, and reported so indefinitely as to leave doubts in many minds with regard to its continuity, had been resolved into a concrete chain of mountains; the positions and forms of individual heights, with the curious ice formations and the general line of the coast, had been observed. The lofty peaks of Northern Victoria Land had been seen to be succeeded by a comparatively low mountainous country of peculiarly suggestive topographical outline, behind which a vast interior ice-cap appeared to rise to greater heights. Towards the 78th parallel the flanking ranges of the continent again rose to great altitudes, and yet farther south we could see no tendency in them to turn towards the east as had been supposed.

In all this we had been aided by the most astonishingly fine weather; instead of the gales, thick weather, and snowstorms which we had expected, since the heavy weather off Coulman Island, we had daily enjoyed bright sunshine, cloudless skies, and calm seas. We could but hope such good fortune would continue on our journey to the eastward.

As we turned on the night of the 21st to push our way to the open sea once more, we had a rather curious and exciting adventure. Owing to some inexplicable wounds found on the bodies of seals, it had been suggested that a land mammal might exist in these regions, though hitherto unseen by man. Most of us were incredulous of this theory, but on that night we suddenly came on a floe covered with soft snow which bore the impress of footprints wide apart and bearing every appearance of having been made by a large land animal. The excitement was great, and observers with cameras were soon over the side and breathlessly examining this strange spoor; but, alas! it was soon detected that the impress was that of a webbed foot, and gradually we came to the conclusion that the footprints were those of a large giant petrel, and that their distance apart was due to the fact that they had been made when the bird, half-flying and half-walking, had been lazily rising on the wing. Even the most imaginative had to concede that we had not increased the prospect of finding a polar bear or any kindred animal in these inhospitable regions. Shortly after midnight we reached the open water and shaped our course to pass between Beaufort Island and the long snow capes of Erebus.

In the morning we stopped to sound and dredge in this channel; we found a depth of 470 fathoms, but the fouling of our trawl rendered our catch of sea beasts somewhat disappointing.

The volcanoes of Erebus and Terror lie west and east, united by a high humped ridge; to the N.W. of Erebus extends the long and lofty Cape Bird, whilst to the N.E. of Terror, the slopes, blistered with innumerable volcanic cones, descend to the splendid basaltic cliffs of Cape Crozier.

The northern face of this land is heavily glaciated, masses of crevassed névé descending to the sea, with a precipitous ice-foot, except on the northern and N.E. slopes of Terror, where the snow only occupies the deeper valleys, and where there are such extensive areas of bare land that it looks quite possible to ascend Mount Terror without encountering snow slopes. In this region the land has therefore a very dark appearance from the water's edge to the summit of Terror.

It was this northerly view of Erebus and Terror that Ross saw in his early voyages, and it is interesting to note that the sketches made at that time show no extent of bare land; moreover, Sir

Joseph Hooker, the great survivor of that expedition, has told me he is almost certain that the slopes of Terror were covered with snow when he saw them. Can it be possible that the sheet of ice which exists elsewhere can have disappeared from this region within the comparatively short space of sixty years?

At 8 p.m. we arrived off the bare land to the westward of Cape Crozier, where the dark volcanic hillside reached the sea in gentle slopes; thousands of small Adélie penguins were passing to and fro on the shelving beach, hurrying up steep winding paths to their nests, or springing into the curling breakers to seek their food.

We thought at first it might prove impossible to land, owing to the northerly swell which broke high on the rocky promontories, but immediately off the beach of the rookery lay a number of grounded bergs which promised to form some protection from the waves. One of our staunch whaleboats was soon lowered into the water, and, somewhat crowded with sixteen persons and a number of magnetic instruments, we pulled for the land. On nearing the shore we found that in spite of the icebergs the surf was considerable, and as we did not at all wish to be upset into this icy sea, we approached the beach with great caution. With our bows pointing to the shore we waited for a heavy wave, when a sharp order was followed by a strain on the oars, and we were carried to the beach on its crest; regardless of wet feet, all hands had then to leap out, and heaving lustily on the painter and thwarts we soon had the boat high and dry.

We proposed at this place to complete our chain of records, and had brought with us a post, a tin cylinder containing an account of our doings, and the necessary implements for erecting them. A spot was chosen in the centre of the penguin rookery on a small cliff overlooking the sea, and here our post was set up and firmly anchored with numerous boulders. In spite of all our efforts to mark the place at a few hundred yards it was almost impossible to distinguish it, and one could not help thinking that, should disaster come to the expedition, what a poor reed was this on which alone we could trust to afford our friends a clue to our whereabouts. Yet it was this small post on the side of a vast mountain, in the midst of the most extensive penguin rookery we had seen, that eventually brought the *Morning* to our side.

Whilst Bernacchi and Barne set up their magnetic instruments and started on their chilly task of taking observations we others set off in twos and threes to climb the hillside in various directions; it was long before we could get clear of the innumerable penguin colonies and the all-pervading odour which they emit; and as they occupy every inch of available land we found ourselves clambering up steep screes of loose stones, and climbing still steeper friable rock faces, getting what hold we could on the deeply weathered surface. With Royds and Wilson I at length reached the summit of the highest of the adjacent volcanic cones, for which our aneroids gave a height of 1,350 feet; there we were rewarded by a first view of the Great Ice Barrier. Perhaps of all the problems which lay before us in the south we were most keenly interested in solving the mysteries of this great ice-mass. Sixty years before Ross's triumphant voyage to the south had been abruptly terminated by a frowning cliff of ice, which he traced nearly 400 miles to the east; such a phenomenon was unique,and for sixty years it had been discussed and rediscussed, and many a theory had been built on the slender foundation of fact which alone the meagre information concerning it could afford. Now for the first time this extraordinary ice-formation was seen from above. The sea to the north lay clear and blue, save where it was dotted by snowy-white bergs; the barrier edge, in shadow, looked like a long narrowing black ribbon as it ran with slight windings to the eastern horizon. South of this line, to the S.E. of our position, a vast plain extended indefinitely, whilst faint shadows on its blue-grey surface seemed to indicate some slight inequality in level; further yet to the south the sun faced us, and the plain was lost in the glitter of its reflection. It was an impressive sight, and the very vastness of what lay at our feet seemed to add to our sense of its mystery.

But there was now 16° of frost, the chill air soon counteracted the warmth generated by our climb, and we were glad to be again on the move. As we stumbled down the steep inclines of the penguin rookery the astonished chicks ran helter-skelter in all directions; following blindly the direction in which their beaks were pointing they frequently collided with each other and ran full tilt into our legs. It was often difficult to avoid treading on them; but as the chicks scattered, the old birds raised their ruffs in anger, and, quite devoid of fear, rushed at us with hoarse cries of rage. After beating wildly at our shins with their beaks and flippers they would fall back growling and cursing in the most abominable manner. Shortly after we regained the beach our magnetic observers completed their task, and when they had taken a short run to rouse up their chilled circulation we all assembled to launch the boat.

This did not prove by any means an easy matter. Awaiting our opportunity, we rushed her down on a receding wave, and up to our knees in water we endeavoured to launch her clear of the surf and at the same time to spring on board; but the next wave caught our stern, and in a moment we were broadside on and in imminent risk of being swamped. It was an occasion which called for instant action, and when it was good to have a boat manned by sailors. At the critical moment Mr Barne leapt over the side and seized the stern of the boat, and his example was instantly followed by two or three of the sailors; and though the next curling wave swept over these devoted people, the boat luckily met it stern on and was poled out to sea as it receded. It was not a time when one would willingly take a bath, and our wet companions were glad to seize the oars and pull as hard as they could towards the ship; but by this time Mr Armitage, in swinging the ship, had been carried some way to the west, so that when we got on board, teeth were chattering and hot cocoa or grog was felt to be very desirable.

From Cape Crozier the land turns sharply to the south in a magnificent black volcanic cliff in parts 700 or 800 feet sheer above the sea. The barrier edge extends at right angles from the southern end of the cliff, and at first has a very rugged appearance where the ice-mass presses past the land, but within a few miles it settles down into its uniform wall-like aspect.

Early on the 23rd we started to steam along this long ice-face, hoping that fortune would favour us in discovering more facts concerning it, and especially in finding out what lay at its eastern extremity. In order that nothing important should be missed, it was arranged that the ship should continue to skirt close to the ice-cliff; that the officers of the watch should repeatedly observe and record its height, and that thrice in the twenty-four hours the ship should be stopped and a sounding taken. In this manner, during the following days, we were able to make a comparatively accurate survey of this northern limit of the barrier, and the result is indicated on the chart.*

On the morning of the 23rd we found that the barrier edge did not exceed sixty or seventy feet in height, and though the weather was slightly overcast we could see for a long distance over the ice to the S.W. from our crow's-nest. It was on looking in this direction, but from a greater distance, that Ross thought he distinctly saw a high range of mountains running to the south from Mount Terror. He described them as 'probably higher than anything we have yet seen', and named them the Parry Mountains. It will be remembered that when in McMurdo Sound I had some doubt as to these mountains, and it is therefore of interest to note the entry made in my diary on this occasion.

'Over the barrier and to the S.W. could be seen some small or apparently small hills, showing bare rock patches, but nothing could be seen of the Parry Mountains, and judging by our position two days ago we seem to have been viewing the hills which form or are close to the limits of McMurdo Bay.

'... The southern slope of Erebus can be distinctly seen.... There seems every probability of getting over this slope on to the ice-plain if we winter west.'

Already there was a strong case against the Parry Mountains, and later we knew with absolute certainty that they did not exist; it is difficult to understand what can have led such a cautious and trustworthy observer as Ross to make such an error. I am inclined to think that in exaggerating the height of the barrier in this region, he was led to suppose that anything seen over it at a distance must necessarily be of very great altitude; but, whatever the cause, the fact shows again how deceptive appearances may be and how easily errors may arise. In fact, as I have said before, one cannot always afford to trust the evidence of one's own eyes.

On steaming along the barrier, we soon found that Ross had exaggerated not only its height, but its uniformity. This was perhaps natural, as in a sailing ship he dared not approach too closely, and often had to estimate the height when at a great distance; and the want of uniformity can only be determined by close measurement. It can be readily imagined that even if the height changes from 70 to 240 feet in ten miles, the change is so gradual that it cannot be

* Not reproduced in this edition.

detected by the eye at a distance, as the higher part will only appear to be closer. The only way in which the inequality can be detected is to follow the wall closely, when the change of height must be obvious. Ross had to judge his barrier from the very few places in which he was able to approach it closely.

Though we started with a long stretch of barrier not more than 70 feet high, by the evening of the 23rd it had risen to 240 feet. During the night the wind came off the barrier, and the temperature fell to 10°; shortly after, it again came from the sea, and the temperature rose to 25°. Later, this change of temperature with a shift of wind became still more marked, and already we began to wonder what that great snow plain would be like in winter if it produced this great fall in the warmer summer air. Up to this time our clothing had been little out of the ordinary, but we now found that standing about on the bridge or sitting in the crow's-nest was chilly work, and warmer garments were dug out of our various drawers and lockers.

Though we were several days steaming along this ice-wall, the passage was by no means monotonous. Every few hours some new variation showed itself: now a sharp inlet or other irregularity of outline, now a more than ordinary alteration in height, now a change in appearance showing a difference in the length of time that the ice-face had been exposed; and throughout we could watch the gradual shoaling or deepening of the sea-floor as shown by the sounding machine. My diary is principally devoted to figures giving the definite data concerning these matters; but a few more general extracts may serve to give an idea of our progress along the ice-wall from day to day.

'January 24. – Barrier fell from 240 feet to 80, and later to 50, but gradually rose again in the evening to 90. Soundings both over and under 400 fathoms. Barrier sometimes very broken and rugged in outline. Passed some bergs and sharp inlets. Noon, long. 176.45 E., progress 86½ miles. In evening weather became overcast with snow.'

'January 25. – Barrier fell in night to 30, gradually rose to 80 feet, when there was a sudden dip for 200 yards to 15 feet. In afternoon irregular rise to 100 feet at midnight. Put sail on the ship in morning watch, but, wind hauling ahead, obliged to clew up. Passed over fifty icebergs in course of the day, the first

we have seen since leaving Cape Crozier. They were mostly
irregular in shape, but two, close to the barrier, had evidently
recently calved off that mass; the line of separation was very
regular and even, and the bergs floated in precisely the same
manner as they had when they formed part of the ice-sheet.
Noon, long. 184 E., progress 91 miles. Evening, appear to be
passing inside a very large berg detached from the barrier. Sounding 350 to 300 fathoms.'

'January 26. – The iceberg on the port bow turned out to be
attached to the barrier; we appeared to be steaming through a long
channel until 5 a.m., when we found ourselves at the head of an
inlet. The ice on our right-hand side gradually sloped down from
120 feet to 20 feet at the extremity of the inlet; here it suddenly
dropped to 8 feet, and on our left very gradually rose again to
90 feet. Our sounding here was 315 fathoms, and our lat. 78.36 S.,
the highest we have reached. The weather was very misty and
overcast, and we could not see the ending of our channel until we
were close on it. There was nothing to be done but to turn round
and come out again, and on reaching the end of the ice-cliff, now
on our right, we found a stiff E.N.E. breeze blowing, with a short
sea causing the ship to pitch heavily. The temperature had risen to
31°. As we could not hope to make headway against this wind, we
made plain sail on clearing the inlet, and allowing our steam to
drop, we stood to sea close-hauled on the starboard tack. Later, the
wind, which never blew above force 7, backed to the S.E., and not
wishing to run too far from the barrier, we put about at 8 p.m. The
glass, which has been low, is again rising.'

'January 27. – During the night the glass rose and the wind fell,
and as we approached the barrier we put over our "Agassiz" trawl;
the contents were not plentiful, but, I understand, contain several
new species. In the afternoon we furled sails and steamed towards
the barrier. When we started to steam along it, we were evidently
making little or no headway against a westerly set of at least three
knots. Our very slow progress hitherto has been to a great extent
due to an adverse current, which is much stronger at some times
than at others: it is not improbable that there is a tidal effect which
alternately accelerates and retards the current, but the net result is a
strong set to the west. The present excessive force of the stream is
probably due to the recent wind. We shall have to light up our

second boiler. Along the barrier there is a heavy vapour rising from the water, and the water temperature has risen half a degree.

'Noon, long. 174.22 W.; negative progress for the day, and only a very few miles to the eastward of our position on the 25th. . . . Two whole days practically wasted; one requires a great deal of patience for this sort of work. Tried a new sounding tube, made with the object of getting mud from below the surface; the tube brought up a column of mud 18 inches in length, but there appeared to be no difference in consistency between the upper and lower layers.'

'January 28. – Passed abeam of the ice peninsula inside which we steamed on the night of the 25th. It rose from 90 to 150 feet, and soundings off its edge were all about 300 fathoms. About noon a lot of loose ice appeared ahead. It was found to consist of very low bergs and pieces of bergs, apparently broken from the barrier where it is quite low, and probably some way to the east, as the westerly drift is strong. We were obliged to stand some way off the barrier to avoid this ice, and at 4 p.m. a thick fog came down on us. In the evening the weather cleared, and we stood in towards the barrier again, passing a prominent ice peninsula with a cliff 200 feet in height. The barrier was again very irregular, and detached bergs could be seen in the various indents. Noon, long. 167.44 W. Progress, 80 miles. We are passing on slowly but surely to Ross's most easterly position.'

'January 29. – The barrier became very rugged and broken during the night, and soon after twelve it dropped to a few feet. We were running close to it in a fairly thick fog, but the speed was not great, and with a sharp lookout, the ice could be seen in good time. At 2.30 we ran into a small creek, only noticing our position by finding ice on both sides; that on the right was barely three or four feet above the water, sloping gradually up to 30 to 40 feet; that on the left was from 30 to 40 feet and sheer. The inlet was most irregular in shape, as, indeed, was the ice surface.

'This morning the low edge continued for several hours, and during the day we passed along a very smooth, straight cliff of uniform height, and again to our annoyance, found the current making to the west so strong that our progress was practically stopped until we could raise more steam. Soundings for day all about 360 fathoms. Noon, long. 162.6 W.; lat. 78.18 S. Passed a curious subsidence in the uniform ice-wall, where for some 300 yards there was a depression filled with hummocky ice.'

We had succeeded thus far in making a fairly complete investigation of the northern face of the barrier in spite of not a little thick and unpleasant weather, and, as will be gathered, we had found not only that it differed considerably from the rather uniform ice-wall which Ross had led us to expect, but that there were many puzzling features which seemed to increase rather than diminish as we approached its eastern extremity. It was not until later, when our positions were plotted, that we fully realised the significance of the fact that our course throughout had been to the southward of Ross's barrier, and that we had sailed continuously over ground which in his day had been covered with a solid ice-sheet.

What we thought of it all I do not propose to set down at present, but I hope that, having added other facts which we were able to glean concerning it, I shall be able to throw some light at least on this very extraordinary ice formation.

By noon on this day, January 29, we had arrived at a particularly interesting place, as we were to the southward and eastward of the extreme position reached by Sir James Ross in 1842. From that extreme position he reported a strong appearance of land to the south-east, and in most minds there rested the conviction that land had actually been seen at that time. It was therefore with great curiosity that all eyes were directed over the icy cliffs to the south-east. The afternoon was bright and clear, and if Ross had seen land it must evidently be well within our view.

But alike from below and from aloft we could see nothing, and were obliged to conclude that the report was based on one of those strange optical illusions which are so common in this region, and against which, now more than ever, we were determined to guard ourselves.

In spite of our disappointment at being unable to report that Ross's 'appearance of land' rested on a solid foundation, as we steamed along this high ice-wall on the afternoon of the 29th we had an indescribable sense of impending change. The constant differences which we had observed in the barrier outline during the past twenty-four hours seemed to us to indicate strongly the proximity of land, though probably none of us could have produced a very tangible argument to support this view. We all felt that the plot was thickening, and we could not fail to be inspirited by the facts that we had not so far encountered the heavy pack-ice which Ross reported in this region, and that consequently we were now sailing in an open sea into an unknown world.

Many an eager face peered over the side; now and then a more imaginative individual would find some grand discovery in the cloud-forms that fringed the horizon, but even as he reported it in excited tones his image would fade and he would be forced to sink again into crestfallen silence.

Meanwhile we were making comparatively rapid progress along the uniform high wall on our right. Perhaps the engines, as well as those in charge of them, were eager to find out what lay beyond. Our course lay well to the northward of east, and the change came at 8 p.m., when suddenly the ice-cliff turned to the east, and, becoming more and more irregular, continued in that direction for about five miles, when it again turned sharply to the north.

Into the deep bay thus formed we ran, and as we approached the ice which lay ahead and to the eastward of us we saw that it differed in character from anything we had yet seen. The ice-foot descended to varying heights of ten or twenty feet above the water, and behind it the snow surface rose in long undulating slopes to rounded ridges whose height we could only estimate. If any doubt remained in our minds that this was snow-covered land, a sounding of 100 fathoms quickly dispelled it. But what a land! On the swelling mounds of snow above us there was not one break, not a feature to give definition to the hazy outline. Instinctively one felt that such a scene as this was most perfectly devised to produce optical illusions in the explorer, and to cause those errors into which we had found even experienced persons to be led. What could be the height of that misty summit? And what the distance of that shadowy undulation? Instruments provided no answer – we could but guess; and although guesses gave an average height of 800 or 900 feet to the visible horizon, one would have been little surprised to learn that the reality was half or double that amount.

Around us were several icebergs grounded in the shallow sea; some lay on their sides, and in these for the first time we saw discoloured layers caused by embedded sand and dirt. Our geologist departed in a boat to inspect these bands, whilst we lowered a small net and delighted the biologist's heart with a good haul from the sea floor.

It was late at night before all was ready for proceeding, and by this time the eastern sky was banking up, and later the air was thick with falling snow. A sounding at 2 a.m. gave us the bottom at 265 fathoms, and at six the snow ceased and we could see a 200-foot ice-wall again with slopes estimated to rise to 500 feet behind. But an hour or more later, when all were once more astir for the day's work, a thick fog descended on us, blotting out for the time all hope of seeing what lay beyond the ice-foot.

Throughout the morning and afternoon of the 30th we continued to grope our way along, endeavouring to keep close to the ice masses on our right, whilst avoiding the deeper bays. Now and then the foggy curtain lifted slightly and revealed what lay within a mile or two of us, but beyond that all was tantalisingly obscure. Soundings were taken frequently, and, varying from 90 to 100 fathoms, showed that we were again in comparatively shallow water.

During the night the trend of the ice-foot had carried us due north, but in the morning we turned sharply to the east, and throughout the day seemed to be passing from cape to cape of a very indented coastline. When the fog allowed us to see them more clearly, we found that these capes were detached masses of ice of curious shape. Varying from a half to a mile or more across, and surrounded by a steep but low ice-cliff, they rose on all sides to a rounded ridge 200 or 300 feet in height. Soundings taken close to these curious ice-masses showed them to be aground, and we were much puzzled to account for them, as, although they were irregular in outline and differed in detail, all had the same feature of gradually rising to a rounded central eminence. It was difficult to imagine that grounded icebergs could have assumed this shape, and almost as difficult to think that under each ice-cap lay some rocky islet. In our then bewildered frame of mind we called them ice islands, and it was not until we had a larger experience and could take a more general view of the glaciation of the whole region that we arrived at any plausible theory to account for their formation. In the fog we headed more than once to pass between and inside these ice islands, but always to run into a deep bay bounded by fast sea-ice, which formed a hummocky junction with the inner end of each island.

Early in the day we became aware that the pack-ice, which we had so long avoided, lay thick in our offing. Occasionally we had to push through narrow streams which opened out into broader masses on our left. It seemed as though we were threading a narrow channel left along the shore by the effect of the easterly wind on the moving ice.

At 4 p.m. (January 30) a more promising lift in the fog enabled us to gather information with regard to our surroundings. Beyond the extensive sheet of fast sea-ice which abutted on the ice islands, we could see the customary ice-cliff of varying height which marked the coastline, but behind this cliff there was now no doubt that the snow surface rose in altitude. The rise in places was gradual, much as we had seen it on the previous night, but in others the slope must have been much steeper, for here the ice-sheet was torn and distorted and descended in heavily crevassed falls. Even in the uncertain light the contrast of light and shadow made it evident that it rose to an altitude of many hundred feet, and consequently that land must lie beneath it; but, peer as we would into the misty distance, amongst the steep and rugged icy slopes, we could see no sign of bare land, without which our discovery must remain so barren to ourselves.

It was as the bell sounded for our evening meal, and all save the officer of the watch were preparing to descend, that over the summit of the ice island for which we were making, appeared two or three little black patches, which at first we took for detached cloud. We gazed idly enough at them till someone remarked that he did not believe they were clouds; then all glasses were levelled; assertions and contradictions were numerous, until the small black patches gradually assumed more and more definite shape, and all agreed that at last we were looking at real live rock, the actual substance of our newly discovered land.

Dinner had to wait until on rounding the ice islands we could approach these fascinating patches as near as the fast ice would allow; but this still separated us from them by a great distance, and in the misty, overcast weather we could add but little to our knowledge, as the following extracts from my diary will show.

' . . . At a height of about 2,000 feet several rock patches could be seen. The snow slope from which they emerged seemed to be otherwise gradual and unbroken. One could not say to what height it rose beyond, but the rock alone was sufficient to prove that the tall ice ridges which we saw yesterday and today cover solid land of considerable altitude. . . . These particular patches appeared in the centre of a long ridge, the outline of which it was very difficult to distinguish for want of adequate contrast. The wind has changed to the east, so that we may hope for clearer weather.'

It is curious to reflect now on the steps which led us to the discovery of King Edward's Land, and the chain of evidence which came to us before the actual land itself was seen: at first there had been the shallow soundings, and the sight of gently rising snow slopes, of which, in the nature of things, one is obliged to retain a doubt; then the steeper broken slopes of snow, giving a contrast to convey a surer evidence to the eye; and, finally, the indubitable land itself, but even then surrounded with such mystery as to leave us far from complete satisfaction with our discovery.

As we continued our course to the N.E. we held close along the fast ice which prevented us from approaching to the land. The weather was still dull and overcast, but we could see that the fast ice on our right was no longer plain sea-ice; at the edge it stood seven or eight feet above the water, and seemed to rise to fifteen feet or more on the slope of the cornice that overhung the edge, after which the surface ran back on the level for many miles. We could see hazily the extent of this plateau and the rocky exposure of the land which lay beyond. It is difficult to account for this ice-sheet; it was too thick to be considered sea-ice, and yet was far thinner than any land-ice or barrier formation that we saw elsewhere. Both before and after this we passed at sea very low tabular bergs, which must have come from such a sheet as this. Our soundings running along this edge gradually increased from 88 fathoms at 8 p.m. to 265 fathoms at midnight; but later we came to several more of the curious ice islands which I have described, and close to these we again got 100 fathoms. During the night some more patches of exposed rock had been sighted, but we seemed in the uncertain light to be increasing our distance from them.

On the morning of the 31st the weather outlook was as dismal as ever, and all outward and visible signs of the land had vanished;

we could only guess its proximity by the continuously shallow soundings as we circumnavigated the overhanging capes of occasional ice islands. As the fog lifted slightly in the forenoon we found ourselves surrounded by mighty masses of ice. On the right the ice islands showed more clearly, and on the left were numerous lofty bergs, some of very great extent; one, indeed, we estimated as at least six miles in one direction, and as probably more in another. But yet more unwelcome to our eyes than this formidable array of bergs was the vast amount of heavy pack-ice which lay scattered in all directions, and blocking the channels between the bergs. Though our hearts sank at the thought of so much obstruction, we could afford to admire such a majestic and impressive ice scene. Under a dark, threatening sky the pack-ice showed intensely white in an inky sea, whilst the towering walls of the icebergs frowned over us, shaded from the palest to the most intense blue.

Most of the icebergs seemed aground, and as their height often exceeded 200 feet and our soundings were comparatively shallow, I have little doubt that the majority were at least temporarily at anchor. For a few brief minutes we could see the distant outline of our snow-covered land as we threaded our way amongst these great ice-masses and through the shifting streams of pack which lay between them, then for the time all attention had to be devoted to navigation. As our water supply was getting short, early in the afternoon we were obliged to secure to a large floe in order to replenish it. We had little difficulty in finding a suitable one, as the pack-ice about us was heavier than anything we had yet seen. It is evident that in this region there is much pressure and a considerable snowfall, as the floes were very hummocky and their snow-covering thick; but the ice itself was by no means so hard as that which we had met near the coast of Victoria Land.

During the afternoon the weather cleared somewhat, and for the first time for many days the sun shone forth. There was little wind, and the low temperature was already forming young ice over the calmer patches of sea. After a few hours' delay we pushed on once more, and, passing through a very narrow channel between two bergs, reached a sheet of open water which appeared to stretch for a long distance to the north, but this was bounded on the right by a sheet of fast sea-ice, whose edge ran almost due north and threatened to carry us farther from the land which we had last seen trending in a north-easterly direction.

As we could not penetrate this sheet, there was no choice but to follow its edge, which we proceeded to do, hoping that it would eventually turn in a more promising direction.

During the last few days of fog and mist we had seen a few seals and a large number of penguins of both the species which inhabit these regions. The latter appeared to live on the most amicable terms, and it was a common sight to see a few alert, busy little Adélies preening themselves amidst a group of dignified, ponderous Emperors; both showed great curiosity as we passed, and leapt into the water in our wake with loud squawks. What great speed these birds must possess in the water is shown by the manner in which they shoot out of it and land erect on a floe two or three feet above the surface. Occasionally on an exceptionally high ice-edge they miss their aim and, dashing heavily against the ice, fall sprawling back into the sea with wild complaints; but this does not appear to disconcert them, for with wonderful pertinacity they will try again and again to reach their goal. As we advanced, the Emperors grew more numerous, until it was rare not to have two or three groups of a dozen or more birds in sight from the bridge.

In the comparatively clear weather which we enjoyed on the afternoon of the 31st we could get a good view over the immense sheet of sea-ice, which appeared to be gradually carrying us farther from the land. It was quite smooth and showed no sign of pressure, but here and there the ice was sunken and sodden, giving the appearance of large pools of water. At that time we could hazard no guess as to the cause of this decay, though doubtless it is the same effect as we afterwards witnessed in the ice-sheet about the *Discovery* in places where the current ran over a shallow bottom.

Far in on the ice-sheet we could see a few small bergs securely frozen in and drifted up with snow, and grouped about the base of one or two of these were many hundreds of Emperor penguins. The steady increase in the groups we had met with and their final discovery in such great numbers seemed to indicate that we had at length found their breeding-place, and as this had never yet been seen, our excellent zoologist was all eagerness to explore it; but in the circumstances I thought it hopeless to attempt to cross the treacherous, slushy sheet of ice which lay between, and reluctantly we were forced to steam past this interesting spot, hoping that we might have better fortune on our return journey. In the light of fuller information which we were able to obtain concerning these birds, it seems doubtful whether this really was their breeding-place, but at any rate it would have been interesting to know what they were doing in such numbers.

Our eager outlook for land beyond the great ice-sheet was only partly rewarded; far to the south-east we could see the faint undulating lines of the high snow slopes, but in the dim expanse of white no sign of exposed rock appeared, and even the outlines vanished as the sun travelled lower towards the south.

At midnight an appearance of land was reported in the E.N.E.; a bank of cloud hung low upon the horizon, and its fixed position and unchanging form seemed to indicate that land lay beneath it. Though glasses were constantly directed towards it, no more definite form was ever revealed, but it is curious to note that on the following day a similar cloudy indication was visible in this direction.

It was after midnight on the 31st that we got lost. Leaving the ship steaming along the edge of the fast ice in a northerly direction, as I have described, I went below to snatch a few hours of the sleep of which the late exciting times had robbed me, and have only a dim recollection of constant reports that the ship had to take a more westerly course owing to ice islands, bergs and pack, and in obedience to a general order to keep in the open water, westerly gradually became southerly, and so on until, as we were headed off again and again, the ship must have worked round a complete circle. She was well on towards a repetition of this manœuvre when I again reached the bridge, and nobody knew exactly where we were. It was evident that the stretch of open water which we had entered through a very narrow channel on the previous evening was surrounded by a chain of immense bergs, between which the channels were sometimes blocked by fast ice and sometimes by heavy pack, and the latter was constantly altering its position and streaming across the bay in the most confusing manner. The only way out of this cul-de-sac seemed to be to take the same narrow road by which we had entered, but where was it? Meanwhile the whole bay was covered with a rapidly thickening coating of tough young ice, through which it was by no means easy to force a passage, and it looked as though, had we stopped to consider matters, we should have had some difficulty in starting again. Our bewilderment was, if anything, increased by suddenly coming across the very floe from which we had watered on the previous afternoon. What was it doing here? It was certainly a long way from where we had seen it before. For more than an hour we splintered through the young ice in a very confused frame of mind, when the sharp eye of Mr Royds brought to our notice a conspicuous feature which we all recognised as belonging to one of the bergs between which we had entered, and soon we skirted round it and to our relief found the narrow passage still open.

The rapid formation of young ice at this season of the year was to some extent alarming. To be obliged to winter in these regions would have been a great calamity, since we could scarcely hope to have travelled far from our base. At a later date, when we knew more of the seasonal changes and appreciated how frequently young ice is formed and dissipated, even in the height of the Antarctic summer, we should not have regarded this phenomenon as serious, but at this time we had very little to go upon, and were exceedingly glad to get into a clearer sea once more.

At noon on February 1 we were five miles south of our position on the previous day, looking in all directions for some lead which would take us through the thick pack to the N.W. and again allow us to approach the coast at a farther point; but though we entered several promising channels, they speedily ended, where from the crow's-nest one could see nothing but one vast sea of ice.

It now became a question what to do. Should we remain here and wait for the pack to open? There was still a chance that we might be able to push farther to the eastward with patience. But then what of the coast of Victoria Land and what of our coal supply? With young ice forming so rapidly here, it well might be that in a fortnight the harbours to the west would be closed and we could ill afford the loss of coal that waiting here would entail.

I decided to return, but it is natural enough that sometimes vague regrets should arise that we did not attempt to push farther to the east. That we need not have feared the closing of the season is obvious, but that we should have been hard put to it for coal at a later date is equally certain. One can never do quite what one would wish in these matters. In the afternoon the wind came from the east and rapidly cleared the sky as we steered back on the course by which we had come, and, with wind and current fair, so rapidly cleared the ground that by night we were again abreast of the icy plateau beyond which we had first seen the exposed rock of King Edward's Land.

We could now see the coastline clearly for many miles. On the left was the low barrier formation of which I have already spoken, and which I now note as 'ten to twelve feet high and sloping up for a short distance, when it runs horizontally for ten or eleven miles to the base of a range of well-defined hills'. To the right and left of two groups of hills which lay opposite to us, a thin stratus cloud partially hid the outline of continuously high snow-covered ridges, and the same thin veil hung in the broad valley between the groups; but the sharp peaks of the groups were clearly outlined against the sky, and with a sextant and the distance given by four-point bearing, we were able to calculate the altitude as between 2,000 and 3,000 feet.

The outline suggested a volcanic country, but although many of the slopes were steep, the bare rock appeared only in a very few places; and where some lofty spur was flanked by a sheer precipice, the more gradual slopes at the base of the hills and the deep-cut valleys presented a uniform white surface, save where, here and there, it was broken by crevasses or ice cascades.

Behind the broader valley which separated the hill groups the outline of farther ranges was strongly indicated, and convinced us that the high land extended far back beyond the coastal hills, and that our new-found land was not a group of islets, but a country of considerable altitude and extent. But although we gazed for hours through our glasses and endeavoured to drink in every detail of this distant view, we could not but long to traverse the snowy plain and throw yet more light on our discovery. Had we then known our sledge equipment and dogs as we afterwards came to know them, had we been as prepared for such adventures as we afterwards were, I should certainly have made a dash towards the distant hills. As we were then situated, the plan, though it occurred to us, seemed to involve unjustifiable risk and delay. Such are the disadvantages of inexperience.

Tabular berg, 280 feet high

Throughout the night the bridge was well occupied until the low skimming sun, gradually facing us, obscured all detail in its glaring path, and the officer of the watch was left to face the chill morning hours alone. By the morning our course had turned again from west to south, and in bright weather we skirted a lofty ice-cliff which before we had only seen dimly through the fog. Throughout the day this ice-cliff rose and fell; when it was low, we could see high rising snow-slopes in the background, and whilst calculating that they rose to a height of 950 feet, had again to deplore the want of definition which rendered exact observations impossible.

Many grounded and tilted bergs lay in the offing, and here and there was one which, though detached from the cliff, had tilted and remained at anchor close to it. The conditions were quite different from those which obtained along the barrier edge, and we could not doubt that the ice which we saw was firmly planted on the ground and broke away as it became water-borne. In the afternoon for a brief space the ice-cliff rose to a height of 280 feet, and we passed close to this sheer wall of ice, the highest that we were ever fated to see in the Antarctic Regions; as we passed by this huge stationary object, we could see how strongly the current was making with us: it increased our speed by at least two knots. As night approached, the wind, which had been increasing throughout the day, descended on us with great violence from the high ice-cliffs, filled with whirling clouds of drifting snowdust swept from the plains beyond; the temperature fell to 5°, and soon the rigging was festooned with icicles and the decks covered with a thin layer of ice. The date corresponded with August 2 in England, and we wondered how flannel-clad holiday-makers would enjoy an Antarctic summer, and, as this sort of thing was the Antarctic summer, what the Antarctic winter would be like.

We steered away from the ice-wall and escaped from the clouds of drift, only to get into a sharp sea where the wind raised clouds of spray which froze solid as it fell.

Later in the night the wind fell to a flat calm, and before the temperature rose the whole sea was covered with pancake ice, but as the sun gained power the temperature crept up to 22°, and with a slight breeze the young ice quickly vanished. In reflecting on recent experiences, although at this time our ideas were not thoroughly sifted, I vaguely realised that indications pointed to the fact that the Great Barrier did not rest on land, and since the ice which we had seen to the east undoubtedly did, there must be some place where the conditions changed, some junction which we ought to explore. Somewhere abreast of us now should be one of those deeper indentations in the ice-mass, where we might reasonably suppose the change took place, and it occurred to me that we might glean further knowledge by re-examining this part. As we had been driven some way to the northward, it was several hours before we were sufficiently close to recognise the deep bight for which I had determined to make, and it was well on in the afternoon before we turned into it and had the ice on each side of us. We found that the inlet had several branches; selecting the most southerly, we turned sharply into it and entered a creek facing towards the east, inside which we were completely shut off from a view of the sea. The ice-wall which surrounded us rarely rose above twenty feet, and in places descended almost to the water level. Selecting a spot on a level with the ship's bulwarks, we placed the ship alongside it and secured her with our ice-anchors so closely that we were able to step from the rail on to the snow surface beyond. The valley of the inlet was continued between rising snow-slopes for several miles to the west, and in its hollow a continuous crack ran through ice standing only a few feet above the water level. Along this crack were numerous seal holes, and quite a hundred of these animals lay asleep on the snow within easy reach of them.

As it was now late, and the light was poor, and as we appeared to be in a secure position, it was decided that work should be deferred till the morrow, and the more energetic were soon mounted on ski and pursuing a very uncertain course over the rough snow. Armitage had asked permission to take a small sledge party in a southerly direction, and with Bernacchi and four men and a light sledge equipment he was soon marching up the valley; and later a black dot on the snow showed us that the party had turned to the south and were mounting the rise.

Skiing did not prove such good sport as was expected. The wind had raised quantities of irregular waves or sastrugi on the snow surface, and in the uncertain light these could not be seen until one actually tumbled over them, and as no-one progressed more than a few yards at a time without a fall, it was not long before all, except the sledge party, were on board once more, when we took a sounding, and found that there was a depth of 315 fathoms under the ship. On our arrival in the inlet not a fragment of loose ice could be seen, but as we were trying to take the temperature of the water at different depths we found our work much impeded by small ice-floes, which were being crowded into the inlet by a strong surface current that now ran towards and under the ice at the head of the inlet. Feeling in some security, I had looked forward to a quiet night, after many broken ones, but the sight of this ice was not reassuring, especially when amongst the floes there appeared two or three small icebergs. One of these bore down on the ship before we had sufficient steam to move her, and by the few on deck it was watched with very anxious eyes. As it approached we breathed a sigh of relief, imagining that it would just clear our side by a foot or two, but on coming abreast of us it slowly turned and a small projection on it caught and grazed our side. As far as the berg was concerned it was the merest glancing touch, but, wrenching a large piece out of the solid oak covering board, it gave the *Discovery* a squeeze which caused every beam and frame to groan, and brought all hands on deck with scared faces. This berg was not more than twenty yards across, and its top, which was irregular and pinnacled, was nowhere more than twenty feet in height, nor was it travelling with any great speed; yet the shock of a mere graze from it was great enough thoroughly to alarm every-one below, and there can be little doubt that had it met us fair and square the consequences might have been most serious. It is difficult to realise what an overwhelming force even a small berg may represent, until one remembers that it is, perhaps, barely one-sixth of its mass that is visible, and that there must be always thousands of tons submerged to support the hundreds which are seen.

Even with this knowledge, after beholding the stupendous masses of ice which are borne high on the great flat-topped bergs, we had been perhaps inclined to pay too little attention to the more insignificant-looking ones, but we learnt now that an iceberg of any dimensions is not to be trifled with, and it can be imagined that whilst we remained in the inlet we had steam at very short notice as well as a bright lookout. On the following morning our berg, as well as the pack-ice, took its way out to sea again, clearly showing that there is a regular tidal stream in this region; and as, in spite of this, we and the barrier-ice about us rose and fell together, there was no doubt that at least this part of the barrier was afloat.

At an early hour on this day, February 4, we commenced to make preparations for a balloon ascent to extend our knowledge of the surrounding region.

It was Sir Joseph Hooker who first suggested the carriage of a balloon for obtaining a view over the great southern ice-wall, and when, after much difficulty, the necessary funds for this equipment had been raised, we had decided that the best thing for our purpose was one of the small captive balloons used by the army for lifting a single observer.

Thanks to the sympathy of the War Office we had been enabled to purchase a complete equipment of this description, consisting of two balloons, which, when neatly folded, occupied very little space, and a quantity of hydrogen gas, carried in steel cylinders at high pressure, which occupied a great deal. Indeed, it had been a great problem where in our small ship to stow these cylinders, of which there were more than fifty, containing something over three fills for the balloon, and it was only by placing them on top of the deck-houses and by utilising every other spare space about the deck that we had managed to solve it.

And as it was of little use to carry such a costly oufit without a knowledge of how to employ it, before leaving England I had taken advantage of the kind suggestion of the chief of the ballooning department at Aldershot, Colonel Templer, R.E., and had sent two officers and three men to receive some instruction at his hands.

I now found that although officers and men had regarded their short course as a most excellent diversion, they had picked up most of the wrinkles and had learnt to proceed about their work in the most business-like manner.

First a large sail-cloth was spread on the snow, and a number of cylinders carried out and placed nearby. Then the balloon was taken out with tender care, laid on the sailcloth and connected to the cylinders with many small pipes. As the gas gradually inflated the empty case the sticky folds were carefully straightened out until the time came for the process of 'crowning' the balloon, when the gradually filling carcase was centralised and covered with its net, well weighted with sandbags.

The contents of cylinder after cylinder were added, until gradually our balloon became a thing of life swaying about in the gentle breeze; but the temperature was down to 16°, and owing to the contraction of the gas wrinkles were still visible on its surface after it had absorbed its correct allowance of sixteen cylinders containing 500 cubic feet apiece, and it was not until we had brought out and emptied three additional ones that its name *Eva* could be read on a smooth, unwrinkled surface.

The honour of being the first aeronaut to make an ascent in the Antarctic Regions, perhaps somewhat selfishly, I chose for myself, and I may further confess that in so doing I was contemplating the first ascent I had made in any region, and as I swayed about in what appeared a very inadequate basket and gazed down on the rapidly diminishing figures below I felt some doubt as to whether I had been wise in my choice.

Meanwhile the balloon continued to rise as the wire rope attached to it was eased, until at a height of about 500 feet it was brought to rest by the weight of the rope; I heard the word 'sand' borne up from below and remembered the bags at my feet; the correct way to obtain greater buoyancy would have been gradually to empty these over the side of the car, but with thoughtless inexperience I seized them wholesale and flung them out, with the result that the *Eva* shot up suddenly, and as the rope tightened commenced to oscillate in a manner that was not at all pleasing. Then, as the rope was slackened I again ascended, but, alas! only to be again checked by the weight of rope at something under 800 feet. Our wire rope was evidently too heavy to allow greater altitude, and the only lighter one we possessed seemed not quite within the bounds of safety should the wind increase.

But, as it was, my view was very extended, and probably afforded as much information as would have been obtained in a loftier position. The following I take from my diary.

'Here the nature of the barrier surface towards the south could be seen well. South of the rising slope ahead of the ship I had expected to see a continuous level plain, but to my surprise found that the plain continued in a series of long undulations running approximately east and west, or parallel to the barrier edge; the first two undulations could be distinctly seen, each wave occupying a space of two or three miles, but beyond that, the existence of further waves was only indicated by alternate light and shadow, growing fainter in the distance. In the far south a bank of cloud had all the appearance of high land, but such indications are now too well known not to be received with caution, and even as I looked through my glasses, faint changes in outline were perceptible. Far over the snow expanse a small black dot represented our sledge party; they must have been nearly eight miles away, and their visibility shows how easily a contrast can be seen on the monotonous grey of the snow.'

When I again descended to the plain, Shackleton took my place, armed with a camera. I had hoped that in the afternoon other officers and men would have been able to ascend, and especially our engineer, Mr Skelton, and those of his department who had so successfully inflated the balloon, but the wind was gradually increasing, and our captive began to sway about and tug so persistently at its moorings that it became necessary to deflate it.

The sight of so many seals on the previous evening had reminded us that our winter stock was to be thought of, and whilst ballooning operations were in progress, the majority of our people had been despatched once more on a murderous errand. The work of killing and skinning was now performed with greater dexterity, but the labour of transporting the carcases to the ship was found to be very great, and it was late in the day before it was accomplished and all hands tumbled aboard dead tired.

Meanwhile our sledge party had returned. Armitage reported that he had crossed two undulations before camping for the night, and in the morning had left his camp, and pushing ahead on ski had crossed two further ones. Their temperature during the night had fallen to 0°, whilst at the ship it was +4°; but as six people slept in a tent with bare accommodation for three, instead of suffering from the cold, one or two members had found the quarters so close that during the night they had extricated themselves from the general mass, preferring to spend the remaining hours in the open. It was noted for future guidance that these members reported most unfavourably on the snoring capabilities of the others.

Curiously enough this party was able to report that the undulations were not gradual as we had supposed on seeing them from the balloon, but that the crest of each wave was flattened into a long plateau from which the descent into the succeeding valley was comparatively sharp. Rather than crossing a series of undulations, the party had appeared to be travelling on a plain intersected by broad valleys, the general depth of which as measured by aneroid was 120 feet. The actual distances travelled were difficult to guess. At this time we were very prone to exaggerate our walks, and it was not until we came actually to measure them later on that we appreciated how slowly we travelled on snowy surfaces. One thing was certain, however; the waves were by no means regular in extent, nor the slopes regular in inclination. At 7.30 in the evening we cast off from the ice and put out to sea, having no desire to spend another night on the lookout for icebergs. During the night the wind carried a heavy drift off the barrier, and covered the rigging with a thick rime, giving the ship a very wintry appearance. We now shaped course directly for Victoria Land, having no longer an object in following the irregularities of the barrier. On the following day, February 5, the wind came fair, and we were able to make sail and so effect better progress.

On the 6th we sighted a large number of icebergs, and suddenly recognised one which had been seen and sketched on January 25 on our passage to the eastward. It was a curious, dilapidated berg, shaped somewhat like a ship, and had one tall column in the centre which one might liken to a dissipated funnel; we had consequently called it the 'Belleisle' berg, in recollection of the woebegone appearance of the ironclad of that name after she had served as target to a more modern battleship.

We were naturally eager to find out how far this berg had travelled in the interval, and were most surprised to learn that now after twelve days it had only drifted seventy miles to the westward, an average of six miles a day. As I have pointed out, the ship experienced a strong westerly set when cruising along the barrier, and there can be no doubt that the pack-ice and smaller bergs are carried along by this at a far greater speed than is represented by the above figures; one can only suppose that the current experienced was merely a surface current, and that the larger bergs are influenced by the deeper water which is not moving so rapidly. Possibly also the current in the surface waters, like those in McMurdo Sound, are seasonal and only follow a seasonal prevalence of easterly winds. At this time easterly winds were certainly prevalent, but there seems some reason to doubt whether they are so at all seasons.

On our return along the barrier we had experienced much lower temperatures than on the outward journey, and as this strongly suggested an early closing of the Victoria Land harbours we were anxious to delay our western journey as little as possible. In some alarm lest we were already over-late, we were anything but reassured when on the morning of the 7th the temperature fell to +2° and we were enveloped in a thick fog of ice-crystals. We could only console ourselves by reflecting that these exceptionally cold temperatures were produced by a wind from off the great snow-plains of the barrier, where probably at no time of the year were the temperatures other than severe.

Early on the 7th we caught glimpses of the land through the patchy fog, and now, being under sail alone, we were obliged to haul to the north to give it a wide berth. The icy fog had so stiffened the ropes and sails, and had made the decks so slippery, that it was only with difficulty we could brace round the yards, and the men, who had frequently to work with bare hands, suffered much from frozen fingers before we had settled down to the new course. The wind dropping later, we were obliged to get up steam, and soon after to furl sails, but by this time the fog had cleared, and we could see clearly the massive outlines of Terror and Erebus. In the evening we rounded Cape Bird, but in such repeated and heavy snowstorms that frequently we could not see the bowsprit from the bridge, and were forced to stop and wait for the clearer intervals. The temperature, however, had risen nearly 20° and the air felt mild and soft in comparison with that which we had lately experienced. By the morning of the 8th we were once more in McMurdo Sound; a south-easterly wind and a falling temperature were gradually clearing the skies and revealing the same magnificent scene of mountain and glacier on which we had so recently gazed.

The heavy pack which had obstructed us before seemed now to have vanished, and as we eagerly scanned the coast of the mainland our hopes rose high that we should find some sheltered nook in this far south region in which the *Discovery* might safely brave the rigours of the coming winter, and remain securely embedded whilst our sledge-parties, already beyond the limits of the known, strove to solve the mysteries of the vast new world which would then lie on every side.

CHAPTER 6

Finding winter quarters: a fatal accident

In McMurdo Sound – A Glacier Tongue – Landing South of Erebus – Selection of
Winter Quarters – Prospects – Difficulty in Maintaining our Station – Erection of
Huts – Amusements – A Trip to White Island – Sledge Party to the Cape Crozier
Record – Accident to Returning Sledge Party – Fatal Result to poor Vince – Results
of Search Parties – Frostbites – Wonderful Escape of Hare – Visit to Danger Slope

> Beholde I see the haven near at hand
> To which I mean my wearie course to bend;
> Vere the main sheet and bear up to the land
> The which afore is fairly to be ken'd.
>
> SPENSER: *The Faerie Queene*

In remembering the extraordinary distinctness with which we
had been able to see distant mountains in fine weather, owing
to the clearness of the atmosphere, the reader may have been led
to suppose that under these conditions the 'crow's-nest' of the
Discovery would have commanded a very extensive view of the sea
surface. This was by no means the case: unless indicated by an ice-
blink, the presence of pack could never be detected at more than
four or five miles even from that elevated position, and it was often
our lot to be steaming towards an apparently open sea, and in less
than an hour to find ourselves surrounded by ice-floes. Similarly, it
was not possible when steering through the pack to see the open-
water leads, or to extend the prospective track to a greater distance
than two or three miles.

It can therefore be understood that although on the morning of
February 8 we were steaming across McMurdo Sound in open
water, and could clearly see the high mountains on each side, we
could not see more than a very limited portion of the extensive
surface of the Sound, nor tell when we might again find ourselves
obstructed by masses of pack-ice.

On January 21 we had been foiled in an attempt to follow closely
the coast of Victoria Land to the south of Granite Harbour, and

especially we had been unable to examine a spot where the configuration of the rocky cliffs gave promise of a second and more southerly harbour for our wintering.

We now headed directly for this spot, and my diary records the proceedings of the day as follows.

' . . . On this occasion we got within eight miles before meeting with the same slabs of pack-ice which caused us so much trouble before. On closer approach, the deep valley between the bluff headlands turned out to be partially filled with an immense glacier, and at first sight it appeared as though very little shelter could be hoped for. Later, however, as we skirted the pack towards the south, we found that a long ice-tongue projected partly across the entrance, and undoubtedly good shelter could be found behind this. . . . But now, the ice being so free to the S.E., we pushed on in that direction, seizing the opportunity of examining the bay, and hoping to find quarters still further to the south. Gradually the sky cleared, and shortly after noon the sun shone forth and the clouds rolled away from the hills, leaving us in possession of a magnificent scene. To the left was Erebus puffing forth light clouds of vapour, and, slowly opening to the south of it, the clear outline of Terror. The slopes of Erebus ran gradually down into the bay, almost completely snow-covered, but here and there an ink-black rock jutted into the sea and gave definition to the hazy coastline. The very high mountain which had been so conspicuous behind our harbour now passed to the left of it, and extended itself into a range exhibiting three magnificent peaks. . . . Some thirty degrees from this our former cone mountain' (afterwards Mount Discovery) 'stood out, impressively isolated; many declared it to be also an active volcano. The western coastline, after leaving the ice-foot protecting our new harbour, runs back into a deep bay, the southern horn of which touches the slopes of the cone mountain; ranges of comparatively low foothills stand behind the inner part of the bay, and five or six islets in the bay form a strong contrast to the snow behind. Another low range of hills flanks the cone mountain on the left, and separated from these by a long and barely perceptible snow bank is yet another low range. This snow bank is due south, and over it in the dim distance the faint outline of very distant hills can be seen. But from the left extremity of the last range to the long cape which bounds the slopes of Erebus, nothing could be seen; so with renewed hope of finding a strait we skirted the pack in this direction.

'During the forenoon and afternoon we passed through extensive sheets of young ice two or three inches in thickness, and all day a school of grampus (*Orca gladiator*, killer whale) were playing about the ship, often coming within a few feet of the side and scattering the young ice as they rose to breathe. Early in the afternoon we came suddenly on a low foot of fast glacier ice, which appears to be the extremity of a long tongue running for many miles out of the bay to the right of the cone mountain. Its formation is most peculiar. The surface is covered with numerous spiky pinnacles and ridges many feet in height; I can think of no less fanciful resemblance than to compare them to tombstones in a cemetery.

'A boat was got out to examine it, and we found that the surface of the ice between the pinnacles was covered with a thick deposit of volcanic sand, amongst which were evidences of numerous water-courses now dried up; evidently the heat absorbed by the sand has melted these channels, leaving the pinnacles between. It was by no means easy to clamber over this confusion of ice and rubble, and it would be quite out of the question to drag a sledge through it; it is to be hoped, therefore, that we do not meet many such obstructions on our journeys. A few hundred yards from the edge, the winding of the water-channels had produced some very beautiful, as well as curious, effects. In places the rush of the stream had undercut the channel till the bank overhung its base by many feet, leaving a deep cave beneath, in which the intensest shades of blue could be observed, whilst from the overlapping edge hung a fringe of sparkling icicles; in others a platform of stones and rubble stood poised on a slender shaft of ice, high above the bed of the stream; here the water had run placidly over a smooth, polished ice-floor, and there its surface had been broken as it glided over a bank of rounded boulders. From the ship it had seemed that the disturbed ice would not rise more than breast-high as one stood amongst it, but as one descended into the courses of these streams the fantastically twisted pinnacles of ice rose high above one's head and completely shut out all view of the ship and the mountainous scene beyond.

'We found on the ice the skeleton of a fish eighteen inches in length, probably carried here by a seal; it is interesting to find that fishes of such size exist in these cold seas. Off the edge of the ice we got a sounding in ninety-five fathoms, and whilst the ship was being swung for her compasses, a small dredge produced a fairly rich haul of animals from the bottom. Our biologist, Hodgson, being on the sick list with a chill, we proceeded to make this catch with all possible secrecy, hoping to reward him with the result; but, unfortunately, the secret leaked out, and, zeal overcoming caution, our sick man was soon in the thick of it, with openly expressed scorn for our amateurish efforts; entreaties had to be extended to commands before, for his own sake, he could be driven back into the milder atmosphere below.

'Rounding this tongue of ice we found our further progress to the south barred by a sheet of fast sea-ice, and skirting along the edge of this, we now find ourselves steering almost due east, and heading towards the long ridge of small uncovered hills which extends from the southern slopes of Erebus, and ends in an abrupt and conspicuous cape which we hope will point us yet further south.'

It was 8 p.m. before we found that the ice edge which we had been skirting extended continuously to this cape, and hopes of an open strait vanished; but we continued our course until at ten we were close to the black, bare volcanic land of the cape. We made for a small rocky promontory without getting soundings with our hand lead, until our bows gently grounded on a bank within a few yards of the shore; backing off from this we found deep water alongside the ice-foot in the small bay on its northern side, and here we secured the ship with our ice-anchors. Later I write.

'We have now to consider the possibility of making this part of the bay our winter quarters. From the point of view of travelling, no part could be more seemingly excellent; to the S.S.E. as far as the eye can reach, all is smooth and even, and indeed everything points to a continuation of the Great Barrier in this direction. We should be within easy distance for exploration of the mainland, and apparently should have little difficulty in effecting a land communication with our post office at Cape Crozier. There are no signs of pressure in the ice; on the other hand, the shelter from wind is but meagre, and one can anticipate intense cold and howling gales. On the whole tonight I feel like staying where we are.'

Hut Point to Cape Armitage

It is interesting to recall our first impressions of a region which we were destined to know so well, and to observe that in a general sense these impressions were correct; in the south only the outlook seemed mysterious, and evidently we did not realise that the southern ranges of hills were detached islands surrounded by a practically level ice-sheet, but, misled by refraction, still imagined them to be connected by comparatively high snow-covered ridges.

On the 9th, the day following our arrival, we set out to explore our immediate surroundings; the ship, as I have mentioned, lay on the north side of a small promontory. Our first discovery was that there was an excellent little bay on the south side. The sea-ice had not yet broken away in this bay, but it was evident that it would only be a matter of a few days before it did so, as the ice was cracked in all directions. Here, then, was a promising spot in which to establish ourselves for the winter; my determination to remain in this region was much strengthened, and I wrote.

'The small bay completes the shelter from pressure in all directions from S.S.E. to W.N.W., and the remaining space faces the main coastline, from which pressure cannot be expected; the water is shallow enough to prevent danger from drifting icebergs; little difficulty will be found in securing the ship or in finding sheltered spots for the huts within easy reach of the ship. . . . This afternoon the ship broke away from her ice-anchors, leaving a number of officers and men on shore, but before we had drifted far, steam was raised and we secured to the sea-ice on the south side of the promontory. It seems very difficult to get a good grip with our ice-anchors, and we have now bedded them well, and have supplemented them with the small kedge buried in the snow; our position is not altogether satisfactory, as there is a slight swell and the ship bumps occasionally against the ice-foot. There is apparently only a small rise and fall of tide, I think not more than twelve or eighteen inches. After tea I went for a long walk with Skelton; we struck out over the sea-ice to round the cape, starting on ski, but quickly abandoning them as the snow was hard enough to walk on and too smooth for the ski to grip properly. We found a curious water-hole off the cape, surrounded for a long distance by thin ice which we only discovered when it began to bend ominously under us and we were obliged to separate very rapidly and retire in different directions.' This thin sheet and the open water in the midst of solid sea-ice puzzled us greatly, and it was not until the following year that we discovered that thick winter-ice is actually melted through in the summer where the current flows over a shallow bank. 'We quickly left this doubtful spot, and, skirting further round, headed for a strait which we can now see surrounds Erebus and Terror, placing them on an island. A clear, smooth snow plain can be seen to the further ridge of Terror, the ridge which lies close to Cape Crozier, where the barrier edge meets the land. The presence of an inky-water sky confirms the sea beyond. From the ridge to the right through 120° of arc naught can be seen but the plain level white surface of the Great Barrier. As we mounted a pass in the hills on our return to the ship, we could see these things still more distinctly.

'The ice south of the cape was evidently comparatively thin sea-ice, and we could rejoice in beholding thousands of seals scattered over the white surface – a promising sign that we shall have no lack of these animals in the coming winter. The ridge of hills under which we shelter is apparently a spur extending from the southern slopes of Erebus.

'Tonight there have been most excited arguments. Everybody seems to have been in a different direction, and either, as one would imagine, has seen quite a different scene, or else prefers to describe things in his own language. At any rate, all agree in the insularity of Erebus and the final decease of the Parry Mountains; for the rest, there is nothing that we shall not be able to investigate more definitely at a later date.'

As I have mentioned, in seeking our winter quarters on the coast of Victoria Land so early in February we had been firmly under the impression that the season was closing in, and that the harbours and inlets would shortly be frozen over. With no previous experience to guide us, our opinion could only be based on the very severe and unseasonable conditions which we had met with to the east. But now to our astonishment we could see no sign of a speedy freezing of the bay: the summer seemed to have taken a new lease, and for several weeks the fast sea-ice continued to break silently and to pass quietly away to the north in large floes.

Meanwhile our situation was surrounded with thorny difficulties. Although the ice broke farther afield, it refused to move out of the small bay on which we had set our eyes, and we were forced to cling to the outskirts of the bay with our ice-anchors, in depths that were too great to admit of the larger anchors being dropped to the bottom. The weather changed frequently and rapidly, and often after the ship had lain quietly for several hours a sudden squall or snowstorm would fling her back on her securing ropes, uprooting the ice-anchors and ultimately sending her adrift. Whilst such possibilities remained, in spite of the most earnest wish to save coal it was necessary to retain facilities for getting up steam at short notice, and the constant work of securing and re-securing the ship was a most harassing addition to the men's work.

At other times the tide and swell would carry the ship into awkward positions with regard to the ice-foot or the shallow bank which lay immediately off it. On February 10 I wrote: ' . . . Later, owing to current, the ship forged ahead and forced herself into the fast ice; this brought the bow into deeper water, but the stern swung into the ice-foot and bumped a good deal; in this position she has made a bed for herself, and we cannot haul her out.'

'February 11. – . . . The ship bumped heavily during the night and worked herself into a very uncomfortable position, her stern obliquely against the ice-foot, and her bow jammed into the thick fast ice. In the morning we made some attempt to haul her stern out, but only succeeded in carrying away a hawser. In the after-noon all hands were turned on to free her, a boiler was run down, balloon cylinders and other weights transported forward, and a party was set to free the ice at the fore-foot. The kedge anchor was buried fast in the floe, and a large hawser brought from it through the stern to the winch. At seven, when we could get a good strain on the hawser, the ship was gradually freed from her awkward position.'

By the 12th we had managed to get an anchor on the bottom, but the stern had been hauled in to assist the work on shore. 'This morning it blew fresh from the E.S.E. directly over the hills, and, with an off-setting tide and some swell, we began to drag our ice-anchors, the two kedges. For an hour in heavy snowdrift we were endeavouring to check the drag by backing the anchors, but to no avail; at last both dragged out, when there was only just sufficient time to get all hands on board before the ship drifted off.'

In spite of the difficulty of keeping the ship in position, how-ever, steady progress was made with the work on shore, which consisted mainly in erecting the various huts which we had brought with us in pieces. The main hut had been brought from Australia, and was, in fact, a fairly spacious bungalow of a design used by the outlying settlers in that country. The floor occupied a space of about thirty-six feet square, but the overhanging eaves of the pyramidal roof rested on supports some four feet beyond the sides, surrounding the hut with a covered verandah. The interior space was curtailed by the complete double lining, and numerous partitions were provided to suit the requirements of the occupants. But of these partitions only one was erected, to cut off a small portion of one side, and the larger part which remained formed a really spacious apartment.

It had been originally intended that the *Discovery* should not attempt to winter in the Antarctic, but should land a small party and turn northward before the season closed; the hut had been pro-vided for this party and carried south under the impression that circumstances might yet force the adoption of such a plan. Having discovered a spot in which we felt confident the *Discovery* could winter with safety, the living-hut was no longer of vital importance; but, even retaining the ship as a home, there were still many useful purposes to which a large hut might be adapted. It was obvious that some sort of shelter must be made on shore before exploring parties could be sent away with safety, as we felt that at any time a heavy gale might drive the ship off her station for several days, if not altogether. With the hut erected and provisioned, there need be no anxiety for a detached party in such circumstances. Later on, too, we hoped that the large room would come in useful as a workshop or as a playroom, or for any purpose which might tend to relieve the congestion of the ship.

We found, however, that its erection was no light task, as all the main and verandah supports were designed to be sunk three or four feet in the ground. We soon found a convenient site close to the ship on a small bare plateau of volcanic rubble, but an inch or two below the surface the soil was frozen hard, and many an hour was spent with pick, shovel, and crowbar before the solid supports were erected and our able carpenter could get to work on the frame.

In addition to the main hut, and of greater importance, were the two small huts which we had brought for our magnetic instruments. These consisted of a light skeleton framework of wood covered with sheets of asbestos. The numerous parts were of course numbered, and there would have been no great difficulty in putting them together had it not been that the wood was badly warped, so that none of the joints would fit without a great deal of persuasion from the carpenter. One of these huts was designed to hold instruments which should keep a continuous record of the change of the magnetic elements on a photographic drum, and it was highly desirable that the record should be commenced as soon as possible.

As may be imagined, with so much work going on on shore and the frequent necessity of looking after the ship, our time was well occupied. But life was not all work, and we found plenty of interest and amusement in our surroundings, as well as relaxation of a more usual character, as the following extracts from my diary will show.

'After working hours, all hands generally muster on the floe for football. There is plenty of room for a full-sized ground in the bay, and the snow is just hard enough to make a good surface.'

'February 13. – We hauled the stern into the ice-foot in the morning and carried on hut-building operations. It was calm and clear, and we made good progress. We tried a team of dogs to tow the light sledge up the hill with pieces of the small huts. Some pulled well, but others are evidently young and untrained; some were extremely timid and grovelled at the least attempt to drive them, others fought whenever and wherever they could. It was not rapid, but eventually all the pieces were got up the hill. . . . Repeated walks are taken to the hilltops in the immediate vicinity, and eyes are turned towards the south – the land of promise. Many are the arguments as to what lies in the misty distance, and as to what obstacles the spring journeys will bring to light. . . . The officers played the men at football tonight, and won by a goal, but the wind rather spoilt the fun. It is now blowing fresh from the usual E.S.E. direction. Two bergs were seen moving up the bay. This is interesting as showing that the bottom waters must be moving in.'

'February 14. – . . . We have landed all the dogs, and their kennels are ranged over the hillside below the huts. They complain bitterly, but they are a good riddance from the deck, which is again assuming some appearance of cleanliness. . . . It is surprising what a number of things have to be done, and what an unconscionable time it takes to do them. The hut-building is slow work, and much of our time has been taken in securing the ship; an annoyingly large number of hours have to be devoted to pumping her out; the pumps get frozen and have to be opened up and thawed out with a blow-lamp. Much work is before us when the huts are up: we must land a store of provisions and a boat for emergencies; then there are the instruments to be seen to, more seals to be killed for the winter, arrangements made for fresh-water ice, sledges and tents to be prepared, and a hundred-and-one details to be attended to.

'The sun is now very near dipping at midnight, and will soon give us an appreciable night. In the morning and evening it is therefore low, and gives the effect of sunset or sunrise for many hours together. The scene is wonderfully beautiful at such times; the most characteristic feature is a soft pink light, that tinges the snow-slopes and ice-foot and fades into the purple outline of the distant mountains. Here and there a high peak is radiantly gilded by a shaft of sunlight.

'Names have been given to the various landmarks in our vicin-ity. The end of our peninsula is to be called "Cape Armitage", after our excellent navigator. The sharp hill above it is to be "Observation Hill"; it is 750 feet high, and should make an excellent lookout station for observing the going and coming sledge-parties. Next comes the "Gap", through which we can cross the peninsula at a comparatively low level. North of the "Gap" are "Crater Heights", and the higher volcanic peak beyond is to be "Crater Hill"; it is 1,050 feet in height. Our protecting promontory is to be "Hut Point", with "Arrival Bay" on the north and "Winter Quarter Bay" on the south; above "Arrival Bay" are the "Arrival Heights", which continue with breaks for about three miles to a long snow-slope, beyond which rises the most conspicuous landmark on our peninsula, a high precipitous-sided rock with a flat top, which has been dubbed "Castle Rock"; it is 1,350 feet in height.

'In spite of the persistent wind, away up the bay it is possible to get some shelter, and here we take our ski exercise, and find it increases in interest as we make rapid strides towards maintaining our stability. Now that we are able to turn, we can start from several hundred feet up the hillside and come down on an incline for half a mile or more before we reach the sea-ice. It is most exhilarating exercise, and figure after figure can be seen flying down the hillside, all struggling hard to keep their balance, but generally failing at some critical turn, and coming an "awful purler" to the amusement of the others.'

On February 16 our football and general athletic ground broke away, leaving only a small corner of the bay filled with ice, and skiing became a still more popular amusement. Some days later I find: 'The party of officers who disport themselves on ski is getting more ambitious, and today we started from a much higher place. The course started with a quick slope of 120 feet in height, covered with soft snow, on which a tremendous pace was acquired; a sudden lessening in the inclination shot one out on rough hard snow, which not only had to be taken at the same pace, but involved a double turn to left and right, then a slightly milder slope slackened the pace to a sharp corner, where a turn of 120° had to be made before one plunged down the final slope to the sea-ice. One or two of us got down safely, but it was generally touch-and-go at the corners. Skelton is by far the best of the officers, though possibly some of the men run him close.

'February 17. – The forenoon was gloriously fine. In a dead calm the sun shone in a cloudless sky; the western mountains were very distinct, but the foreshore was raised and exaggerated by strong mirage. The work is now so far ahead on our huts that we can contemplate some sledge parties. Barne and Shackleton tossed a coin as to who should take the first, and the latter won. Wilson and Ferrar will accompany him. The ice has broken away so far round the corner that I have told them they must take a pram until they get beyond the sea-ice; it will be a heavy drag, but I don't expect they will have to drag it far. All three are very busy making preparations.

'All that remained of the sea-ice in our bay moved out very quietly this morning, nearly taking away Hodgson, who was fishing on the floe with a tow-net, quite unconscious of what was happening until he looked up and saw his retreat cut off. There was quite an excitement in rescuing him. The wind sprang up again suddenly in the afternoon; we seem fated not to be long without it. It came sweeping down the gullies in bitter gusts. I went up the hill for exercise, and was glad to turn back and sail home.

'Late this evening Walker suddenly appeared, reporting that Ford had met with an accident on the eastern slope of the Gap and needed assistance. It appeared that Ford, Buckridge, and Walker has been "running" the slope on ski in a rather bad light, and that Ford, whose sight is not good, had failed to see a steep drop from the ice-foot and had fallen over it, with the result that his leg had caught in the tide crack and was injured. A party were soon away with a sledge on which they brought back the invalid, the first to occupy our small sick berth. The doctors found that there was a simple fracture, which, though not a very serious matter, will rob us of our ship's steward for some weeks.' The fracture healed with remarkable rapidity, and in less than six weeks Ford was able to resume his duties.

'February 18. – It blew hard from the S.E this morning, but about eight the wind dropped, and during the rest of the working hours it was quite calm and we were able to push ahead with the huts.

'As the ice has broken away around the cape, the sledge party have had stiff work in dragging their sledge and pram over the "Gap"; they will start fair from that side tomorrow.

'There have been arguments lately as to the necessity of a whip in driving dogs, and today the two keenest controversialists,

Armitage and Bernacchi, who are respectively for and against coercive methods, had a competition. They selected their own teams, and, whether by accident or design, Armitage selected all the fighting element, whilst Bernacchi's team were mostly the younger and timider dogs. At first neither team could be got to start at all; there was a wild confusion of twisted traces and some exciting fights; but eventually, amidst the cheers of the onlookers, Bernacchi succeeded in coaxing his animals into a trot, from which they broke into a gallop, and, heading up the steep snow-slope, left the driver breathless behind. Whilst this was scarcely the exhibition of control that had been intended, the other team had refused to trot at all, and the honours of the day were of necessity given to the advocate of gentle persuasion.

'It is surprising how suddenly the wind rises and drops here. At 6.30 tonight it came on to blow from the north, and, without warning, in the space of a few minutes a strong breeze was blowing. The hawser securing our stern to the ice-foot parted, the ship swung off, and we were obliged to lower a boat in haste to pick up the men who had stayed to secure the half-built hut. By the time they were on board, it was blowing a gale; we had good shelter from Hut Point, but the swell got up very quickly, and there was soon a considerable commotion in our small bay. . . . At midnight the wind dropped as suddenly as it had risen, and we have now to be prepared for being carried against the ice-foot, which with this swell would probably mean some heavy bumps.' On the following day the wind came as suddenly from the south, and we bumped so heavily on the ice-foot that I thought it advisable to get up steam.

'Later the wind increased to force 8, and we had a scare with a mass of ice bearing straight into the bay. At the last moment it diverted its course and passed harmlessly round the point. . . .'

From such extracts as the above it will be seen that it is no easy matter to secure a peaceful anchorage on the Antarctic coastline.

'February 20. – We have had the first continuous bright windless day since we arrived. The glass was steady at 29.4, the sun shone brightly, and although the temperature did not rise above 18° it was pleasant to loll about in the sun during the dinner hour, when we smoked our pipes in great comfort, sitting on pieces of the hut which are not yet fixed. The dogs are now allowed to run loose, so many at a time; there is much less fighting than would be expected. They are losing their coats, I suppose at about the time they would shed them in the north in preparation for summer, but it seems an awkward lookout when they ought to be preparing for winter. We took advantage of the fine evening to re-secure the ship. I let go two anchors in the bay and middled, then veered both cables till we could just bring her stern up to the ice-foot for landing our gear. She ought to lie much more comfortably now.'

On the 21st our energetic first lieutenant, Royds, had a very narrow shave. Late at night, when everyone else was below, he jumped on to a grating which had been placed over the side and carelessly secured; the lashing slipped, and the next moment he was in the water with nothing to hold on by or to assist him in climbing out; with the water at 29° and the air at zero he realised that there was no time to be wasted if he was to reach the deck again safe and sound, and that the chance of his being heard was so small, he would only be wasting his breath by attempting to shout. In this serious position he luckily remembered that a rope ladder had been left over the stern, and husbanding his strength he swam for it. It could have been no light matter climbing that ladder under such freezing conditions, but fortunately he managed to do it, and to swing himself over the side. The first we knew of the accident was when he appeared in the wardroom with his clothes dripping and his teeth chattering.

On the 22nd our small reconnoitring sledge party returned. After leaving on the 19th they had made directly south towards the White Island, eventually reached it, and climbed one of the nearer volcanic peaks. They were so naturally bubbling over with their experiences that it was some time before we could get answers to our eager questions. From the summit of their peak, for which the aneroid gave a height of 2,700 feet, they had seen the great snow plain of the barrier still stretching without limit through east and south-east to south, and curling a long white arm around the island on which they stood. To the west the same level sea of snow seemed to run deep into the fretted coastline, and again they could see it beyond the high cape which limited our view from the ship. In the dim distance south of our lofty western ranges more high snow-covered peaks appeared. But of the roads it was more difficult to speak; they had crossed ridges and hummocks and crevasses, and had come to see that these things did not advertise themselves afar, but lay hidden in unexpected places under the deceptive smoothness of the plain. It looked as though the best road would lie to the east of the island and well clear of it, but our travellers shook their heads over the bright prospect of a smooth highway, in visions of which many had indulged up to this time.

Altogether we felt that our outlook on affairs was considerably enlarged by this small journey, and we stopped up late as we discussed its bearings and listened for the first time to the woes of the inexperienced sledger. Although the temperature had not been severe, our travellers had nearly got into serious trouble by continuing their march in a snowstorm. They found themselves so exhausted when they did stop to camp that they were repeatedly frostbitten. They could only get their tent up with great difficulty, and then followed all sorts of troubles with the novel cooking apparatus. It is strange now to look back on these first essays at sledging, and to see how terribly hampered we were by want of experience. Perhaps the most curious note I have of the report of these three is to the effect that in their opinion our pemmican wouldn't do at all. It was far too rich, they said, and when made into soup it was so greasy that none of them could touch it. Our pemmican contained 60 per cent. of lard, but after knowing how it tasted to a true sledging appetite and seeing the manner in which it was scraped out of the cooking pots in later times, it needs such a reminder as this to recall that it might not be always grateful to a more civilised taste.

This sledge party did something to dispel curious illusions which existed amongst us with regard to distances. On certain days every detail of our surroundings was so clear that it was impossible to persuade oneself that much on which we looked was in the far distance. Shortly after our arrival, for instance, two of our company had started off with the serious intention of taking an afternoon walk around this very 'White Island', and it was only after they had walked for some hours without noticing any appreciable change in the appearance of the island that they were convinced they had undertaken a task beyond their powers. On another occasion two officers discussed the advisability of making a day's excursion to the top of Mount Erebus and back.

When we had learnt to discount the deceptive appearance of nearness, many of us were inclined to go to the opposite extreme, and to imagine our distances much greater and our mountains much more exalted than they really were. One was led to this by an exaggerated conception of the distance one could walk in a given time. It was not until instruments and observations had shed the cold light of reason on our sledge marches that we came to know that two miles an hour is very good going on a soft snow surface.

Though our work was much impeded by the cutting winds, we continued to make progress as the month advanced; as yet, however, there were no signs of the sea freezing over, and the old sea-ice still continuing to break away, had left a large extent of open water to the southward and eastward of Cape Armitage. The seals had no longer a resting-place within two or three miles of the ship, and we had been forced to kill them at this distance in providing for our winter consumption. Not wishing to drag the carcases such a long distance until they were required, we had left them partly buried in snow, but on revisiting the spot somewhat later we found to our dismay that the skua gulls had been at our cache and had wrought great havoc. It was extraordinary to see the manner in which they had torn the frozen flesh from the bones with their powerful bills.

'February 26. – . . . The main hut is roofed and the windows placed; there is little more to be done outside, though the whole of the inner lining has to be put up. The first magnetic hut is almost finished; a good quantity of provisions and oil has been landed, with fifteen tons of coal. I feel we can now leave the ship without anxiety, and have been pushing forward our arrangements for the first trip, which I hope to lead myself. The object will be to endeavour to reach our record at Cape Crozier over the barrier, and to leave a fresh communication there with details of our winter quarters.

'The snow on the "ski" slopes has become very hard and rough, and we can no longer enjoy that exercise.'

'February 27. – I went out with Barne on ski, and was foolish enough to try to run the upper slope, which is now covered with hard sastrugi (wind waves). As I was coming down at a good pace, my right ski was turned by one of these, and in falling I brought a heavy strain on my right knee, and damaged the hamstring. I was forced to limp back and get it bandaged.' On the following day I found my leg much swollen, and could scarcely put foot to the ground, and to my great annoyance, as the days went on, the improvement was so slow that I had to abandon all idea of accompanying the sledge party to Cape Crozier, and to content myself with deputing the charge to Royds. I already foresaw how much there was to be learnt if we were to do good sledging work in the spring, and to miss such an opportunity of gaining experience was terribly trying; however, there was nothing to be done but to nurse my wounded limb and to determine that never again would I be so rash as to run hard snow-slopes on ski.

By March 4 the preparation of the sledge party was completed. The party consisted of four officers, Royds, Koettlitz, Skelton, and Barne, and eight men, and was divided into two teams, each pulling a single sledge and each assisted by four dogs. I am bound to confess that the sledges when packed presented an appearance of which we should afterwards have been wholly ashamed, and much the same might be said of the clothing worn by the sledgers. But at this time our ignorance was deplorable; we did not know how much or what proportions would be required as regards the food, how to use our cookers, how to put up our tents, or even how to put on our clothes. Not a single article of the outfit had been tested, and amid the general ignorance that prevailed the lack of system was painfully apparent in everything. Though each requirement might have been remembered, all were packed in a confused mass, and, to use a sailor's expression, 'everything was on top and nothing handy'.

Even at this time I was conscious how much there was to be learnt, and felt that we must buy our experience through many a discomfort; and on looking back I am only astonished that we bought that experience so cheaply, for clearly there were the elements of catastrophe as well as of discomfort in the disorganised condition in which our first sledge parties left the ship.

However, at the time few of those actively employed had time or inclination to consider their unfitness; all was bustle and hurry to depart, and at length the order to march was given and the party stepped out briskly for the steep snow-slopes. By this time the sea-ice had broken past the eastern slope of the 'Gap', the peninsula could be crossed only by climbing the higher passes, and the sledges had to be dragged to an altitude of nearly 800 feet before the level plain of the barrier could be reached. It was not until the following day, therefore, that the retreating figures of the party were lost to our watchers on the hilltops, and we settled down to wait for their return.

It was about this time that we first began to notice the strange relation between the direction of the wind and the temperatures we experienced in our small bay. 'With the wind from north or south, or anywhere to the westward of these points, the thermometer rises above 20° and the air is soft and mild. But should an easterly wind arise – and this is the most constant direction of our winds – the temperature falls to zero or below, and the air is rendered more biting by fine particles of snow blown from the hill surfaces. Last night light airs were succeeded by a squally southerly breeze; the thermometer showed a maximum of 25°; I noticed my bunk unusually warm, and in the morning found water on the upper deck. To the eastward is the barrier, and doubtless the cold weather is due to air carried from its extensive surface. . . . The northerly breeze coming from the sea would naturally be warmed, but it is difficult to account for the warmth of the southerly winds, unless it is an effect of descending currents from the higher levels. We should welcome both northerly and southerly breezes were it not that the first brings a swell and the last a continual prospect of being beset by drifting ice. Of the several evils, the least is undoubtedly the cold, and with a southerly wind especially one does not feel that our bay affords a good protection; luckily, so far, it has not lasted at any time for more than a few hours, nor has it blown with any great force. We have only experienced the lightest puffs of air from the west, in which direction our bay affords least protection.

'We have now got our windmill up, and it revolves merrily. The mill regulates itself to a certain extent by its large rudder, which causes it to face more obliquely to the wind as its force increases, but this is only partial regulation, and with changes in the wind there is considerable variation in the speed of the mill. The dynamo stands on deck beneath the mill, and has an ingenious contrivance with a sucking magnet to regulate the current output by altering the resistance in the field magnets. This does not work so well as one could wish, and though the cells are gradually charging I do not like the variations in the current which is effecting this. Dellbridge and I have been going into the matter, but I fear the sucking magnet will never be very satisfactory. Tonight we had electric light below for a few hours; it made our quarters look wonderfully bright and comfortable, and will be the greatest boon if we can only keep it going during the winter; but besides the dynamo, the cells will need a lot of attention; one or two are already showing signs of sulphating.

'The main hut is now finished and looks quite a palatial residence. The Eschenhagen magnetographs have been in full swing since the term day, March 1, thanks to Bernacchi's energy; there will be much difficulty, he thinks, in maintaining an equable temperature for these instruments. I hope it can be overcome to some extent by banking the hut with snow.'

'March 9. – The young ice forms quickly when it is calm, especially at night, but when the wind springs up it is soon driven out.

'I was able to get about sufficiently to go rounds and perform our short service. Without Royds and the harmonium the hymns were a difficulty, but we chose the simplest tunes. A calm but dull morning was succeeded by the most glorious afternoon. The sun was warm and bright, and it was pleasant to sit about in its rays. I was sorely tempted to try to walk abroad, but wisdom kept me chained on board. We have now been here a month and a day; it is odd to think that we expected to be frozen in on arrival, a miscalculation of a whole month; but what could one suppose from the evidence we then had before us? In addition to the records of former expeditions to these seas, I find that the *Belgica* ceased to move after March 4 when far to the north of us. The bay is full of young ice and the swell has almost gone; it appears as if our little corner was at last to be frozen in. Tonight the sun sinks behind our western range in a sky of rosy glory, and deep shadows fall across the frozen bay.'

'March 10. – . . . Again a fine bright day, though there was some wind in the night. My leg better, and was able to hobble to the shore station on a tour of inspection. Quite a number of small round sponges have been picked up on the hillsides; they must have been cast up on the ice-foot and there dried, until they became so light that the wind caught them up and whirled them to the rocky crannies above. The men go out very regularly for exercise; they have mostly given up their ski and have taken to tobogganing. Toboggans are made of a pair of ski and the end of a packing case. As many of the slopes are extremely steep, the pace is sometimes terrific, and the least unevenness of surface inevitably causes a capsize, when toboggan and man come whirling down in a cloud of snow, much to the delight of the onlookers.

'The sun circles so low now that the effects of sunset are visible for many hours, and the changes of light are very gradual and very beautiful. As I returned from my walk at six, the western sky bore a saffron tint, deepening to crimson where the dark blue mountains were clearly outlined against it; the fleecy clouds showed dark, with bright gilded edges where they stood against the sky, and whitish grey where they nestled in the distant valleys. And yet now, five hours later, though heavier cumulus clouds have spread overhead, the saffron tint can still be seen through breaks in the cloudy mantle, whilst the clear horizon has only turned to a richer crimson. The beauties of the sky are reflected in deeper tone on the patchy surface of the young ice, in which a few puffs of wind have traced ink-black leads of open water. But it is still sunset, as it was five hours ago.'

Tuesday, March 11, was to be one of our blackest days in the Antarctic, but we had little suspicion of this as the daylight hours passed quietly, and we remained snugly in our comfortable quarters on board the ship. Since the departure of our sledge party the weather had been exceptionally fine; but we awoke on the 11th to find the wind blowing from the east; in the afternoon it increased in strength, and the air was filled with thick driving snow. The main part of our outdoor work was accomplished, and as there was plenty to be done on board we did not attempt to face the inclement conditions outside, but sat down in comfort to our tasks with an occasional thought for our fellows who were less happily circumstanced. On the previous evening a report had been brought in from the hilltop that a spot had been seen in the distance, which was thought to be our sledge party returning. Though we considered it rather soon for them to appear, we did not imagine that anything could be wrong, and only lamented for their sakes that they should be obliged to support this weather in a tent rather than with our own comfortable surroundings. At the worst no-one suspected that they could be anything but weather-bound and uncomfortable. It was not until half-past eight, when it was quite dusk without, that our tranquillity was rudely shaken by a report that four men were walking towards the ship. The sense of trouble was immediate, and all hastened on deck; we could scarcely recognise the newcomers as they climbed over the side in the thick whirling drift, but the first disjointed sentences were enough to show that all was amiss, and we hurried them below. As they emerged from their thick coverings we recognised them as Wild, Weller, Heald, and Plumley, and it was evident that though thoroughly exhausted they were labouring under strong excitement. In such circumstances, and from so many mouths, it was almost impossible to get a connected tale, and it was not until I had selected Wild, as obviously the most cool and collected of the party, and had called him aside, that I was able to get an idea of what had happened; and even then I could only get a meagre outline such as follows.

They had been sent back, he said, a party of nine, in charge of Mr Barne, and early in the day had reached the crest of the hills somewhere by Castle Rock; besides the three with him now, there had been Mr Barne, Quartley, Evans, Hare, and Vince; they had thought they were quite close to the ship, and when the blizzard came on they had left their tents and walked towards her supposed position. They found themselves on a steep slope; couldn't see anything, but tried to keep close together; suddenly Hare had disappeared, and a few minutes afterwards Evans went. Mr Barne and Quartley had left them to try to find out what had become of Evans, and neither had come back, though they waited. Afterwards they had gone on, and then suddenly found themselves at the edge of a precipice with the sea below; Vince had shot past him over the edge. After much trouble they had climbed back, reached some rocks, and groped their way to the ship; he feared all the others must be lost; he was sure Vince had gone. Could he guide a search party to the scene of the accident? He thought he could – at any rate, he would like to try.

The information was little enough; at any rate, it was something on which to act, and the details could be filled in later. But meanwhile the practical common sense on board had outstripped orders, and already warmer clothing and wind coverings were being hurried on by all, and a sledge with a fur sleeping-bag and medical comforts had been equipped. But the ship could not be deserted even for such an errand as this, and when Mr Armitage had chosen four officers and ten men to accompany him, it was felt that numbers had already reached the limit of usefulness, and that others like myself must wait in dreary inaction whilst the few laboured. Though the first disastrous tidings had been brought to us at 8.30, it was still before nine when the relieving party tumbled over the side and vanished into the gloom.

It will be as well to relate now the actual story of the original sledge party, as we learnt it in after-times, and to trace the steps which had led to the accident.

The party, after crossing the hills on March 4 on their outward journey, had descended to the level ice and directed their course into the deep bay which lies on the eastern side of our peninsula and south of Erebus and Terror. After crossing some ice-ridges they found fairly easy travelling for ten miles or more, but then came to very soft snow, where at each footstep they sank to a depth of eighteen inches or two feet. The labour was excessive, and the dogs were of no assistance, but they struggled on in hopes of coming to better conditions. After three days Royds saw that it was useless to continue as they were going, and that the only chance of making progress was to use snow-shoes, but unfortunately there were only three pairs of ski with the party. He decided, therefore, to push on for his mission at Cape Crozier with two officers only, and to send the remainder back in charge of Barne. The separation took place on the 9th, and the returning party, finding a somewhat easier road, were able to retrace their steps at a more rapid pace. They came abreast of Castle Rock on the morning of the 11th; and, although this was not the way by which they had descended from the hills, Barne thought that the incline at this place looked more gradual and would prove an easier road to the summit than that by which they had come, and so decided to take it. In expectation of a stiff and slippery climb, he directed his men to put on the loose leather ski boots which they carried instead of the softer fur boots. The ski boots were frozen hard, and although most of the party got them on after much difficulty, Vince and Hare had to give up the attempt and were allowed to continue in their fur boots. Barne's report proceeds: 'Neither Primus lamp could be used on account of the prickers being broken. At 9.45, the weather being clear, we started, particular care having been taken to pack the sledges securely to prevent damage in case of capsize during the ascent. The hill can be easily ascended by taking a zigzag course, the surface of the snow being in broad natural steps. Finding, however, that we could haul the sledges straight up, I did so, making for Castle Rock. We stopped twice for rests, and reached the top of the ridge about half a mile south-west of Castle Rock at 1 p.m. We had scarcely gained the ridge when it began to blow from the south-east, and the air was filled with snow. I had just time to take a bearing of Crater Hill before it was obscured, and I intended to make for it along the ridge, but as several of the crew were getting frostbitten and the sledges were being blown over, I thought it best to camp, and made for the shelter of some rocks which I had seen before the wind sprang up. On finding them we got as much as possible under their lee and pitched our tents, getting the men in as quickly as possible.'

The tents being up, the party crept into them, already exhausted from their heavy pull up the long incline, and more or less frostbitten from their last efforts in the driving snow. At ordinary times hot tea or cocoa would have revived their spirits, but now neither cooking apparatus was in order, and they could not even melt the snow to drink with their icy cold lunch. We afterwards weathered many a gale in our staunch little tents, whilst their canvas sides flapped thunderously hour after hour, and we, ensconced in our sleeping-bags, passed our time, if not in comfort, at least without sense of danger. But to this party the experience was new; they expected each gust that swept down on them would bear the tents bodily away, and meanwhile the chill air crept through their leather boots and ill-considered clothing, and continually some frostbitten limb had to be nursed back to life. It was small wonder that the position seemed intolerable, that their thoughts turned to the comforts of the ship which they imagined to be within a mile or so of them; and after some discussion the fatal decision was made to abandon their sledges and attempt to reach her.

We knew well enough afterwards the rashness of attempting to move in an Antarctic snowstorm, but at this time it was impossible for us to have known fully the serious nature of such an act and the utter confusion which must ensue. It was an experience which had to be bought, and this party were destined to pay the price.

At this juncture Barne's report proceeds: ' . . . The tents were rolled up and secured, the dogs unharnessed, and we left the sledges. Before leaving I impressed on the men, as strongly as I could, the importance of keeping together, as it was impossible to distinguish any object at a greater distance than ten yards on account of the drifting snow. The two men wearing fur boots had a man on either side to prevent them from slipping. Our progress was very slow, as we were greatly delayed by the men in fur boots, who had difficulty in walking on the slippery, uneven surface. As we proceeded the surface inclined to our right front until it was evident we were crossing a steep slope on which it was more and more difficult to keep a foothold. . . . About ten minutes after we had left the sledges, Hare, who was at the rear of the party, was reported to be missing, and at this moment an unusually violent squall prevented us from seeing even one another. I immediately ordered a chain to be formed at right angles and extending across our track, each man keeping in touch with the next with the idea of intercepting Hare when he came on. We shouted and blew whistles, and whilst this was going on, Evans stepped back on to a patch of bare smooth ice, fell, and shot out of sight immediately.'

Thinking the slope to be one of the short ones so common in the folds of the hills, Barne cautioned his men to remain where they were; and sitting down, deliberately started to slide in Evans's track. In a moment or two the slope grew steeper, and soon he was going at a pace which left him with no power to control his movements; he whipped out his clasp knife and dug it into the ice, but the blade snapped off short and failed to check his wild career. In the mad rush he had time to realise the mistake that had been made and to wonder vaguely what would come next. In a flash, ice changed to snow, which grew softer until, in a smother of flying particles, his rapid flight was arrested, and he stood up to find Evans within a few feet of him. They had scarcely exchanged greetings when a third figure came hurtling down on them out of the gloom and was brought to rest at their feet. This was Quartley, who, growing impatient at Barne's absence, and of course ignorant of what lay below, had started to slide down on the same track, and had been swept down the descent in the same breathless manner. Realising the impossibility of ascending again by the way they had come, they started to descend, but within four paces of the place at which they had been brought to rest they found that the slope ended suddenly in a steep precipice beyond which they could see nothing but the clouds of whirling snow. Even as they recoiled from this new danger and dimly realised the merciful patch of soft snow which had saved them from it, a yelping dog flew past them, clawing madly at the icy slope, and disappeared for ever into the gloom beyond.

Movement of any sort seemed impossible in this whirling storm, and they sat for long huddled together, forlornly hoping for some respite from the blinding drift. At last, chilled to the bone, they felt that whatever happened they must be again on the move, and in a dazed fashion they gathered themselves together and slowly moved along the cliff to the right; they found that it gradually fell, and then suddenly they caught a glimpse of the sea at their feet, and for the first time realised that it was from this they had been saved by the patch of snow almost on the cornice of the cliff.

In a short break in the storm they now saw Castle Rock towering over their heads, and close ahead of them a rocky ridge which ran from its foot. Slowly and painfully they made their way up the stony incline until they stood beneath the high rock cliffs, and here again they crouched together, seeking what shelter they could behind a huge boulder, and thus they must have remained for some hours.

Meanwhile the party which had been left at the head of the slope, in obedience to orders, waited long for their absent leader, shouting again and again in the lulls of the whirling storm. At length they felt that something must be amiss, and that it was hopeless and dangerous to remain where they were. As usual on such occasions, the leading spirit came to the front, and the five who now remained submitted themselves to the guidance of Wild and followed him in single file as he again struck out for the direction in which they supposed the ship to lie. As they proceeded they found the slope growing steeper and the difficulty of foothold increased, especially for Vince, who was wearing fur boots, but they never doubted they would soon come to the bottom and find themselves in one of the valleys which would guide them to our winter quarters. In this manner they must have proceeded for about 500 yards, when their leader suddenly saw the precipice beneath his feet, and far below, through the wreathing snow, the sea. Another step would have taken him over the edge; he sprang back with a cry of warning, and those behind him, hearing it, dug their heels instinctively into the slippery surface, and with one exception all succeeded in stopping. What followed was over in an instant. Before his horror-stricken companions had time to think, poor Vince, unable to check himself with his soft fur boots, had shot from amongst them, flashed past the leader, and disappeared. It was difficult to discover from the men's account exactly what happened after this catastrophe. In some sort of hazy way they seem to have realised that they must make upwards and away from the danger, and they started to ascend the slope.

All spoke of that ascent with horror, and wondered how it was ever accomplished. They could only hold themselves by the soles of their boots, and to fall or even to slip to their knees meant inevitably to slide backwards towards the certain fate below. Literally their lives depended on each foothold, and they possessed no implement to make these more secure. Of the party, Wild alone had previously armed the soles of his boots with a few light nails; this gave him a great advantage, and, to his great credit, he used it to go from one to another of his companions with a helping hand. As they crept laboriously upwards, the slope became steeper and more icy, but now, here and there, they found a stone which had rolled from the heights above and become firmly frozen in the icy surface. These afforded some anchorage and rest to the weary climbers. The storm still whirled the snow about them with unabated fury, but they pushed upwards in its teeth from stone to stone, until to their joy the stones grew thicker, and close above them they saw the black outline of the rocky summit. A final scramble, and they were once more on safe ground, with the nightmare of the climb behind them.

But their troubles were far from over, as they were still ignorant of the position of the ship. Wild again took the lead: the sea behind them must be north of the ship, he argued, and therefore they must keep the wind on their left front, and if possible keep always to the rocks. It is difficult in such circumstances to gauge time, and none of the party knew how long they walked on in dogged silence before their eyes fell on a well-remembered landmark, and cautiously descending a steep rocky incline, they saw the ship looming through the grey whirl of snow; but between the breaking-up of their camp and the moment when they clambered over the side to make their report to me, six hours had elapsed. It is little wonder that after such an experience they should have been, as I have mentioned, both excited and tired.

The hours which followed the departure of Armitage and his search party on this fatal night were such as one could scarcely forget; exhausted as our returned wanderers were, we questioned them again and again to get greater light on the accident, but nothing could alter the fact that five of our small company were lost or wandering helplessly about in this dreadful storm. Hatefully conscious of my inability to help on account of my injured leg, my own mind seemed barren of all suggestion of further help which we might render; but, as was always my experience in the *Discovery*, my companions were never wanting in resource. Dell-bridge thought he could soon raise steam enough to blow the syren, and before long its shrill screams were echoing amongst the hills. Then, as we reconstructed the story of Vince's loss and pictured the cliff over which he had fallen, the bare possibility of some remaining fragment of sea-ice clinging below was suggested. Was it possible that we could reach it? The only possibility was by boat. Who would volunteer? Of course everyone. In ten minutes a whaler was swinging alongside and being rapidly loaded with provisions, cooking apparatus, and fur clothing; in ten more, with a picked crew of six men in charge of Shackleton, she disappeared around Hut Point.

Then we could do nothing but peer through the driving snow and wait. It was a trying time, and a full three hours elapsed before there was a hail from without, and through the drift appeared Ferrar leading three of the lost – Barne, Evans and Quartley. Ferrar's tale was soon told. He had accompanied Armitage's party, and, guided by Wild, they had made for Castle Rock and eventually found the abandoned sledges, and, at first, nothing near them but two dogs cosily coiled up beneath the snow; but later, as they circled round on their ropes, they had providentially come on the three with whom he had returned. Armitage had picked him to return because his geological work had given him an exceptional knowledge of the locality.

An hour later the main search party returned; they had done all that men could do in such weather. A completer search was impossible, but it had to be admitted that the chance of seeing Hare or Vince again was very small. Soon after our whaler reappeared with her crew thoroughly exhausted; they had pulled easily whilst under the shelter of the nearer hills, but as they proceeded to the north they had come under the influence of heavy squalls which had driven them away from the land. It was only with the most strenuous exertion, and after hours of arduous struggling, that inch by inch they had gradually been able to regain the shelter of Hut Point, and so reach the ship.

As we prepared to snatch some few hours of rest after the anxieties of the night, we had sadly to realise the calamity that had befallen us in what appeared to be the certain loss of two of our comrades; but as the details of the story were unfolded, we could well appreciate that we had been almost miraculously preserved from a far greater tragedy. It seemed almost wonderful that the whole party had not disappeared, to leave us only the terrible discovery of the abandoned sledges or perhaps a frozen silent figure in the snow. Even now we could not clearly understand how the officer of the party and his two companions had been rescued; all were too dazed to complete their story on this woeful night. Later we learnt that after hours of crouching beneath the boulder under Castle Rock, they had heard the faint shriek of the syren. It had revived their waning faculties, and they staggered once more to their feet to make towards the welcome sound, and thus it was that as they dragged themselves along they mercifully fell into the arms of our sledge party. All three were badly frostbitten, and on the following day their ears, cheeks, and noses were swollen to a prodigious size; but as this meant a return of circulation, there was nothing worse for them in this respect than a great deal of pain and discomfort. But one of Barne's hands was in a much more serious condition; the blood obstinately refused to return to the dead white fingers, and, whilst he swathed them in well-greased bandages, the doctor informed me that there was little hope of saving them. For many days the prospect of amputation seemed imminent, and it was not until a week after the accident that the blood began to extend slowly and painfully towards the tips of the fingers. Although the hand was left in a shockingly mangled and painful condition, the fingers were saved.

It may be of interest to those whose fortune has not taken them to the colder regions of the earth to say a word or two concerning frostbites.

Even in the coldest places it is necessary to keep one's face and sometimes one's fingers uncovered; consequently it is these parts of the body that are most likely to suffer, and in the Antarctic Regions we were all so frequently frostbitten in them that we learnt to regard such an evil as part of the ordinary course of events: and indeed there was very little to fear as long as the frostbite was noticed and the remedy taken in time. Under ordinary conditions one has a distinct sensation on being frostbitten; the blood seems to recede from the veins in the exposed part with a suddenness that almost conveys the sound of a 'click' and the feeling of a prick with a sharp instrument. At such times all that is necessary is to apply gentle warmth to the frostbitten member. For instance, if one's cheek or nose is gone, one simply covers it for a minute or two with the palm of one's hand. There is a fiction that the best remedy is to seize a handful of snow and rub the offending member, but as the snow in the polar regions has the consistency of sharp sand or emery powder, the application of such a remedy would speedily remove the skin, with anything but a pleasant result.

Frostbites such as I have described are merely superficial, and, as I have said, they were of such frequent occurrence that under ordinary conditions we learnt to regard them very little, and often, if one found it inconvenient to nurse one's own limb back to life, one called on the kindly offices of a neighbour.

But the frostbites that come when people are doing hard work are more serious, as the first prick may pass unnoticed and the superficial freezing continues to take deeper hold without any further sensation. Should the frostbitten person be exhausted, the evil may spread with alarming rapidity, and then, too, limbs which are well covered and protected may be attacked, and the seriousness of such a condition needs no comment. Hence in our subsequent hard sledging work, whilst we treated the superficial frostbite with scant respect, we learnt to be cautious to prevent the evil from becoming deep-seated. On long, tiring marches in a wind, frostbites were bound to come frequently, and in nine cases out of ten were unfelt, so that our custom at such times was to pause occasionally and peer into each other's faces in search of white patches. More important still, we learnt not to continue exhausting marches too long in heavy weather, but to reserve a margin of energy for the chill work of making the camp, during which any unduly tired person was bound to be in great danger of serious freezing.

A frostbite must be very superficial and very quickly dealt with not to leave an after-effect. This effect is a blister, more or less painful in proportion to the seriousness of the frostbite. To all intents and purposes the effect is precisely the same as that of a burn. In anything but a very superficial frostbite, moreover, the actual sensation of returning circulation is very distinctly painful.

Places which have been frostbitten become extraordinarily susceptible to a recurrence of the evil. In our second winter in the Antarctic there were few of us whose fingers had not 'gone' at one time or another, and consequently it was much rarer to see people working with bare hands than it was in the first winter, when many delighted to show their scorn of cold fingers. So for a long while after Barne had recovered the use of his hand he had to nurse it with far greater care than the uninjured one.

For the events which succeeded the distressing night of March 11 I draw on my diary.

'March 12. – Though the glass has risen continuously and uniformly, the wind has only grown steadier without diminishing, but there is very little of the driving snow which made last night so hideous. Another search party were out early under Wilson; they went well provided with ice-axes, rope, and crampons, and even thus had to use great care in venturing on the fatal slope where so much happened yesterday. They brought back the sledges and two more dogs, but could see no sign of the missing men. But indeed it would be beyond hope to find them alive after such a night; at least, we now know the worst. Some of the men are overwrought; twice today it has been reported that someone thought he saw a figure crawling down the hillside, and on one occasion the illusion was so strong that two or three ran to the other side of the bay, only to find a boulder over which the drift was sweeping in fantastic curls.'

'March 13. – It is still blowing, and the temperature is –6°; but the air is clear, and, the glass having reached a maximum, there are hopes of a change for the better. We are raising steam, as I want to view the scene of the accident from the sea, and to make certain as to Vince's fate at least.'

Later I write: 'A very extraordinary thing has happened. At 10 a.m. a figure was seen descending the hillside. At first we thought it must be someone who had been for an early walk; but it was very soon seen that the figure was walking weakly, and, immediately after, the men who were working in the hut were seen streaming out towards it. In a minute or two we recognised the figure as that of young Hare, and in less than five he was on board. He was taken into the magnetic house, as it was thought unwise to take him into the full warmth of the living-quarters at once. We soon discovered that, though exhausted, weak, and hungry, he was in full possession of his faculties and quite free from frostbites. He went placidly off to sleep whilst objecting to the inadequacy of a milk diet.

'It was much later that we learnt his story. It appears that he had left his companions intentionally, on finding that it was impossible to stand alone in his fur boots. He had shouted to the others that he meant to return to the sledges and change into leather boots, and he was under the impression that they had heard him and had quite understood the reason. He made the best of his way in the direction in which he supposed the sledges to be, but, as was natural, in the thick snowdrift he could see no sign of them. For long he wandered forward and backward, intent on his search; but gradually he got exhausted, and then he was conscious that his footsteps were aimless. The last thing he remembered was making towards a patch of rock, where he hoped to find some shelter from the raging wind. When he awoke this morning he found himself covered with snow, but, on raising himself on his elbow, he saw that he was on a slope under Castle Rock, and, glancing about him, recognised Crater Hill and other known eminences, and realised exactly where he was and the direction in which the ship lay. He started towards her, but found himself so stiff that for a long way he was obliged to crawl on hands and knees. But the stiffness wore off, and he was able to raise himself at length, and, with some rests, to reach the slope where we had first seen him.

'He must have lain under the snow for thirty-six hours, but it took a long time to persuade him of this; he found it hard to believe that this was the second day after the accident. I cannot but believe that his preservation is unique, and almost miraculous. The boy, who is only eighteen, has been forty hours without food, and sixty without warm food; he must possess great stamina to have come through without hurt. The incident is also a tribute to our clothing. He was luckily wearing a heavy woollen blouse and complete gaberdine wind-covering over his warm under-clothing. Unconsciously he withdrew his arms inside the blouse, and covered the opening in his thick helmet, and so saved his hands and face from freezing. The fur boots alone saved his feet from the same fate, and the snow, which rapidly covered him, must have done the rest. Tonight his temperature has gone up to 100°, but he is otherwise quite well.

'In the afternoon we weighed our anchors and steamed round to the scene of the accident, when every detail of what we now called "Danger Slope" could be clearly seen. It is very steep for about 400 or 500 yards, and ends in a sheer drop into the sea. Though partly covered with hard white snow, it has extensive patches of smooth bare ice; and, as the tracks of the various parties were worked out, it seemed more wonderful than ever that any should have escaped to tell the tale.

'Every incident could now be closely followed, and all shadow of doubt as to Vince's fate is gone. At least, we have the satisfaction of knowing that nothing could have been done either by his own party or by those on board to have averted it.'

We had now finally and sadly to resign ourselves to the loss of our shipmate, and the thought was grievous to all. From the moment when he joined us at the Cape of Good Hope, Vince had been popular with all; always obliging and always cheerful, I learnt that he had never shown these qualities more markedly than during the short sledge journey which brought him to his untimely end. His pleasant face and ready wit served to dispel the thought of hardship and difficulty to the end. Life was a bright thing to him, and it is something to think that death must have come quickly in the grip of that icy sea.

Preparing for winter

> Experience be a jewel that we have
> Purchased at an infinite rate. – SHAKESPEARE

Of late the temperature had crept steadily down and the young ice seemed more and more reluctant to yield to the blustering winds and quit the surface of the strait. Our short voyage to 'Danger Slope' was made through patches of sludgy, sodden ice which were even then increasing in thickness. As we dropped our anchors again in our small bay we felt that it was for the last time before the winter closed in on us, and that soon further movement would be impossible; indeed, the only wonder was that such conditions had not come long before. But now the wind alone kept the water open, and in the short intervals of calm the icy crust formed with great rapidity. I was anxious to be frozen in with our bow pointing out to sea, and with the ship at such a distance from the ice-foot that she should run no chance of being pressed against it; but as the wind always blew out of the bay, this was not easily accomplished, and we had to content ourselves with being ready to turn her at the critical moment. For this purpose anchors were bedded on the ice-foot, and wire hawsers attached to them ready to haul the stern round when the wind permitted it. In the meantime we could only get to the shore by means of boats, and when the wind grew very strong our communication was interrupted altogether, since under such circumstances we scarcely liked to send a boat away, for fear it should be carried out to sea by some more than usually fierce gust.

It was for this reason that we were impotent to prevent the murder of two of our dog-team, though we actually witnessed it, and bitterly regretted the incautious but kindly policy which had allowed these animals to run free, when they should have been chained up.

Here, again, we erred from want of experience. The dogs had been particularly quiet of late; each had his own kennel, and his own bountiful supply of food; they had been given plenty of exercise and were allowed to run about at their own sweet will; there seemed to be absolutely nothing that they could quarrel about, and for days they had lulled us into false security by appearing to be quite contented and to be living on the most amicable terms. But alas for dog morals! As we well understood when we knew them better, they were only biding their time. Some of their number had been away sledging; why should they have been chosen? What treats and petting had they been receiving from the hands of man that by right belonged to the whole community?

They were objects of suspicion. Nothing they could do was quite right; it was no use their wagging their tails and pretending to be friendly when they had played a lowdown game like that! it was all mere impertinent deception! One can only suppose that such thoughts pass through the doggish mind, because the result is always the same. Let a dog be unduly petted or receive more than his share of food, or be taken away sledging: he inevitably becomes an object of suspicion to the rest. The first growl, the first step beyond the rigid limits of propriety, and not one, but the whole pack are upon him, and even the thickest coat is a poor protection against those bloodthirsty fangs. Of course there are exceptions; here and there is a dog of such commanding temper or such truculent demeanour that he can afford to be treated differently from the rest; but even he seems to have to silence criticism by being more than usually aggressive, if he should have been absent for any length of time. Such a dog becomes the natural leader of the pack; he is unceasingly watchful; he never pauses to parley, but attacks at the first sign of insolence, for he knows well that the sharpest and quickest fang commands the situation.

These revelations of dog nature came to us gradually. It was on March 15, whilst we were cut off from the shore, and were casually watching the dogs as they idly trotted about on the snow, that we witnessed the first attack. There was a growl, a wild rush to a central spot, a heap of heaving, snarling forms, and the horrid deed was done, almost before we realised that the peace had been disturbed. We shouted and whistled, but might just as well have held our breath. The deed done, peace once more prevailed, and one would scarcely have imagined that anything had happened but for the stiff, lifeless form on the snow.

On the following day the wind still blew hard. We had determined, however, that we must risk the passage to get these bloodthirsty wretches chained up; but even whilst the boat was being manned the last night's tragedy was re-enacted, and another poor beast lay mangled on the ice-foot. As the boat's crew landed, the murderers welcomed them as though nothing out of the ordinary had happened, and with a few exceptions they were easily caught and chained up. Then, one by one, they were led out and severely chastised in front of their victims. The punishment helped to relieve our righteous indignation, but otherwise, I think, we might have spared our energy again, for the dogs evidently didn't know what it was all about. You cannot change dog nature.

Meanwhile, however, we had lost two good sledge dogs, which we could ill afford, and we decided that, however trying it might be to their feelings, the remaining animals must be kept on their chains. As we expected, the victims proved to be two harmless, quiet animals which had recently returned from sledging.

The fatal mishap which had attended the main portion of our first sledge party left us in some anxiety for the remaining members who were still absent. We knew them to be ill provided for very severe conditions, and saw already that sledging in the Antarctic was not a thing to be approached in a lighthearted, irresponsible spirit, but was one which called for great care, attention, and forethought. Our anxiety for the absentees was not lessened when we saw Skelton descending the hills alone on the 19th. However, when he was safely on board we learnt that he was only a forerunner, and that the others were close behind; and soon they appeared, and in turn were ferried off to the ship. There was much to be learnt on both sides: it was for us to tell the sad tale of the recent disaster, and for them to set forth the incidents and difficulties of their attempt to reach the Record cairn. Royds's report was so laconic that extracts from it may well convey an idea of the troubles which beset the inexperienced sledge-traveller.

'March 4. – . . . On the summit "Nigger" bit "Gus" so badly through the mouth that I had to send the latter back. . . . 6.0. Stopped for tea, erected two tents; Barne's ear frostbitten, several men had cramp in left leg, myself very bad. . . . On starting again Vince and I had frostbites under the nose. Dogs pulled well; some fights and a little trouble; "Boss" ran away. 8.15. Camped. Dogs wouldn't eat anything; one sledging lamp broken – a great nuisance, as now one lamp has to cook for six men. Cramp prevalent amongst all hands.'

'March 5. – Very heavy going. Quartley's foot giving much pain. Got up tent and had it examined. Not frostbitten, but intensely cold; made him wear fur boots. . . . Several dogs got bleeding feet; snow getting heavier; all hands perspiring very much, feet sinking 9 inches to 1 foot at every step. . . . 5.45. Men completely "cooked", dogs tired out; so camped.'

'March 6. – . . . Snow getting thicker and softer, and steered towards the land hoping for better conditions. . . . Barne's dogs lying down and refusing work. . . . Find it best for sledges to run on fresh snow, and not over footmarks. . . . 6.50. Forced to call a halt; men and dogs completely done. The dogs' feet give them a lot of trouble; they lick them hard at every halt. Several men have cramp; we feel back muscles and legs awfully. Weller was so done when we stopped that he flopped across the sledge and broke the sling thermometer. . . . Made good only four miles. . . .'

This, with more to the same effect, goes to show that the party were doing a great deal of hard work without much result. By steering towards the land they only got into softer and deeper snow, and therefore it was little to be wondered at that on the 8th Royds decided to divide the party and to attempt a further advance with Mr Skelton and Dr Koettlitz, who, besides himself, were alone provided with ski. By this time they were almost beneath the steep cliffs which fringe the southern snow-slopes of Mount Terror. The level plain had given place to long, steep undulations formed by the pressure of the land-ice, and the silence about them was repeatedly broken by the thunderous roar of an avalanche. On the 9th the three officers set out on their ski, and with only one light sledge behind them made much better progress until, getting

'Terror' party in deep snow

towards the eastern slopes of Terror, they again found themselves on a hard, windswept snow surface. They had still some miles to go before they came to the junction of the barrier edge with the land, and the calm weather which they had hitherto enjoyed now deserted them, making it most difficult in the drifting snow to see their exact whereabouts or the nature of the snow conditions about them. Skirting the slopes of the mountain, however, they pushed on until they were forced to rise on a snow incline which came abruptly to an end and was succeeded by long stretches of bare land over which it was impossible to take the sledge. Here they made their camp, and from it they could see the open Ross Sea and the confused hummocked ice of the barrier where it forces its way around the land. The penguin rookery in which our record had been placed was still some distance from them, as they knew, and they remembered that the north-eastern side of the mountain was so free from snow that there could be nothing now but bare land between them and it.

But this bare mountain-side was extensive, and covered so thickly with small volcanic craters that it was difficult to select the best path for their walk to the rookery, or, within limits, to estimate their distance from it. There was risk also, in a country where one landmark was so much like another, that on their return they might have great difficulty in finding their camp; and if the wind should rise during their absence this risk would be greatly increased, so that they ran the chance of being landed in a very sorry plight. In fact, at their first attempt on March 13, they had barely gone half a mile from the camp when a thick blizzard came on, and they only regained their tent by luckily falling across their ski, which had been planted at some distance from the camp as a possible guide.

On the following day, however, they again sallied out and succeeded in getting some miles towards their goal, if not actually above it, before the wind came on and, blotting out all features of the landscape with snowdrift, obliged them to turn back and seek shelter with all possible speed.

It was now evident that the Record post could be reached, but a fine day was essential, and here, as elsewhere, small matters of detail connected with the special circumstances must be attended to. One could not conveniently climb over sharp, jagged rocks in the foot-gear which was worn with comfort on the snow plains, as the bruised, sore feet of the party witnessed; another time it would be necessary to come properly prepared with some arrangement for protecting the sole of the foot.

The attempt to reach the Record was finally abandoned on the 15th; but not until it was evident that a better-equipped party with more favourable weather would have no difficulty in getting to it. It will be understood that it presented itself to me as a most important matter that this record should be reached, as here lay the only chance of communicating our position to any who should follow in our footsteps, but it was immaterial whether it was reached now or after the coming winter; the assurance that it could be reached was the comforting fact that this party discovered, and in any case a spring expedition would have been necessary to bring the news up to date.

No sooner had the party turned towards the ship than the wind fell, and with it the temperature. It was something to know that the wind which had swept past this corner throughout their stay was not perpetual, but the rapid fall of the thermometer found them ill prepared. It had not occurred to anyone that within such a short distance of the ship there might be any large difference of temperature, and as the summer was barely over, the officers had provided themselves with a light wolf-skin fur suit only, for night wear. They had found this clothing all too meagre when the thermometer stood at −10° or −15°, but on the night of the 16th sleep proved impossible, and for the first time they found themselves subjected to uncontrollable paroxysms of shivering. Huddle together as they might, they could get no warmth, and on creeping out to consult the thermometer they found it had fallen to −42°. They were luckily able to boil some cocoa, and thus to get some warmth into their chilled bodies, but as the long sleepless hours crept by they had ample opportunities of learning the value of adequate clothing, and the wisdom of being prepared for the unexpected rigours of a fickle climate.

With the morning the cold snap ended, and three days later they reached the ship without further adventure.

On comparing notes with this party we realised for the first time what a difference there might be in the weather conditions of places within easy reach of the ship. It was not only in the matter of temperatures, as I have already described, but also in the force and direction of the wind. On the 17th at the ship we had had a very strong blow from the south, at one time rising in force to a full gale, but the party only some twelve miles to the eastward had felt nothing of this; with them the day had been calm, though overcast. This difference of weather conditions could be observed throughout the journey; neither those on board nor those away could have told from their own meteorological conditions what the weather might be with the others, and this fact was again and again impressed on us throughout our stay in this region. Already we had learnt that the prevalent wind at our winter quarters blew from the S.E. through the 'Gap', and that this wind was usually local and frequently ceased within a mile or two of the ship. To this we could now add some further conclusions. It was evident that the eastern slopes of Terror were terribly windswept, and that there the prevalent direction was from the south, whilst the deep bay immediately to the eastward of our peninsula was a particularly windless area where the snow lay thick and soft, and was only occasionally stirred by whirling squalls.

Meanwhile the position of the ship towards the latter end of March was anything but satisfactory; that the temperature should have fallen to −40° to the eastward was a clear sign that the winter conditions were upon us, but although the ice forming about us sometimes reached a thickness of two or three inches the sheet never held for any length of time, but broke up rapidly when the wind grew strong. Under these conditions it became increasingly difficult to keep up communication with the shore; when it was not blowing a stiff gale our boats had to force their way through a tough elastic sheet of young ice which clung to the sides in the most exasperating fashion, and sometimes the short passage could only be made after much hauling on ropes and the systematic use of poles to break up and thrust aside the sheet. On one occasion our light skiff was brought to a stop half-way across in such a manner that the crew could neither advance nor retreat, and it was quite an hour before, by manning a heavier boat, we were able to break a way through and free her.

In this wholly unexpected state of affairs at such an advanced date there were many drawbacks. Until we were solidly frozen in, the security of our position must be doubtful; economy of coal had long ago necessitated the extinction of fires in the boilers, and should a heavy gale drive us from our shelter we could only have raised steam with difficulty and after the lapse of many hours. If driven off by such a gale, should we be able to get back? It seemed doubtful, and meanwhile it would certainly be unsafe to send a large party away from the ship, because with the ship adrift it was obvious that most of them would be needed. If, on the other hand, the fates were going to allow us to remain in this spot, there was much to be done in preparing for the winter; especially it was desirable that the engines should be taken to pieces and the steam joints be broken before the severer cold came upon us; but in our present position we dared not attempt such work. One of the most annoying circumstances was that until we had a solid sheet of ice about us we could not set up our meteorological screen, nor communicate regularly with the magnetic huts, nor, in fact, properly carry out any of the routine scientific work which was such an important object of the expedition.

Our proposed winter station was so far beyond that of any former expedition that, as I have already pointed out, we had nothing to guide us as to what the winter climate might be, and our astonishment at the prolonged open conditions left us almost in doubt as to whether the sea was ever going to freeze over satisfactorily. The breaking away of the old ice had ceased, and the open water was now at its maximum for the season; as will be seen from the chart,* it ran from the decayed glacier tongue, which we had visited on February 8, to the S.E., circling about Cape Armitage with a radius of four or five miles, and forming a deep bay to the eastward of the peninsula. The ice-edge which limited the open water could be seen very distinctly from the hills in the vicinity of the ship – a long, irregular ribbon of white, gradually circling round, the edge itself standing in some places two or three feet and in others ten or fifteen feet above the sea level, and showing that what remained was ice of a different character from that which had broken away, and constituted the limit of a more ancient ice-sheet.

At this time I was anxious to make one more sledging effort before the winter set in. The ostensible reason was to lay out a depot of provisions to the south in preparation for the following spring, but a more serious purpose was to give myself and others a practical insight into the difficulties of sledge-travelling. One saw already that a great deal of our sledging outfit was unsuitable and would have to be rearranged; one saw, too, that in the minor details of clothing and so forth there were points on which there was much difference of opinion, and with regard to which, therefore, it was desirable that every man should fend for himself, providing for things as best suited his own ideas; above all, it was evident that in a sledging campaign, as in any other, the best work would be done by the trained man. Before us lay the long winter with ample time to organise our parties and to make the most detailed preparations, but one could not hope to do this without a full knowledge of the conditions to be met and a ready and intelligent co-operation amongst all who were engaged in the work. My wish, therefore, was to make a final autumnal expedition which should include all those who had not been away already; but as this included the majority on board, we were forced to await the greater security of the ship, not only for reasons which I have already mentioned, but also because until the deep bay to the south became re-frozen we could only travel in that direction by the most circuitous and difficult route. When the ice became safe, the simplest way lay around the cape; failing this, we could manage without much difficulty to get through the 'Gap'; but if the sea-ice opposite that was unsound, we should have been

* Not reproduced in this edition.

forced to climb to a height of nearly 1,000 feet, and after descending on the other side to traverse a number of high, broken ridges.

The freezing-in of the *Discovery* was a very gradual process. The ship, secured by her stern hawsers, had held in place a small wedge of ice which had formed in the corner of the bay. On March 24 this small patch was strong enough to bear, and, whilst the bow of the ship was in open water, for the first time we were able to walk on shore from the stern; and this wedge of ice held, and gradually increased in thickness, in spite of the strong breezes of the week which followed.

For instance, on March 27 I write: 'Blowing with −10° temperature during forenoon, but quite fine in afternoon and evening. Our ice, having held during the late wind, may fairly be considered to have come to stay. At 4.30 a party of us went over the hill through the "Gap" to investigate the chance of getting sledges down by that route. We found the sea frozen over, and evidently, from the snowfall on it, the ice has been formed for several days. It looks firm and hard, but there is a drop of eleven feet from the ice-foot, which will be a difficulty for the sledges, but will save the necessity of going round by the seal crack. Nothing could exceed the beauty of the scene this afternoon; the snow was bathed in rosy light, gorgeous shafts of gold sprang up from the sun, and the sky was blood-red behind the hills in its wake. The moon was up, a vast yellow disc to the east. It will be a companion for at least the first part of our journey. Now and again, as we trod on the snow-covered slopes of the hillsides, the icy crust cracked with a sharp report like a pistol-shot. Evidently it is in high tension from the recent cold.'

'March 28 (Good Friday). − The day has been beautifully calm and bright, though the temperature has not risen above −4°. After service our people spent the day wandering over the hills; it was quite pleasant to see little parties dotted about here and there, with a dog or two for company. The sea is at last frozen over, and if this weather lasts the ice should become firm enough to withstand future gales. We have completed the packing of our sledges, though I cannot say I am pleased with their appearance; the packing is not neat enough, and we haven't yet got anything like a system. Tomorrow, if the weather holds, we take our sledges across to the other side, so as to make a fair start on Monday.'

'March 30 (Easter Sunday). – Like yesterday, a fine day, with a light northerly breeze. This is a season of flowers, and behold! they have sprung up about us as by magic: very beautiful ice-flowers, waxen white in the shadow, but radiant with prismatic colours where the sunrays light on their delicate petals. It was a phenomenon to be expected in the newly frozen sea, but it is curious that they should come to their greatest perfection on this particular day. The ice is about five inches thick and free from snow; consequently the ice-flowers stand up clear-cut and perfect in form. In some places they occur thickly, with broad, delicate, feathery leaves; in others the dark, clear ice surface is visible with only an occasional plant on it; in others, again, the plants assume a spiky appearance, being formed of innumerable small spicules. The more nearly one examines these beautiful formations, the more wonderful they appear, as it is only by close inspection that the mathematical precision of the delicate tracery can be observed. It is now established that on the freezing of salt water much of the brine is mechanically excluded. Sea-ice is much less salt than the sea itself, and what salt remains is supposed only to be entangled in the frozen water. The amount of salt excluded seems to depend on the rate at which the ice is formed, and whilst some is excluded below the ice-surface, some is also pushed out above, and it is this that forms the ice-flowers. The subject is very fascinating, and we have already started to measure the salinity of ice taken from different depths and formed under various conditions: the ice-flowers themselves do not seem to constitute a saturated solution of brine, and why they should differ in form in various places seems beyond explanation.

'Today we saw a group of penguins far over the ice, and after church Hodgson, Shackleton, and I walked out towards them. They turned out to be Emperors, and were all standing about very contentedly near a crack much too narrow to allow them to get through. It is difficult to see how these birds can now get north, and it looks as though they winter more or less in these regions, probably close to spots where the ice is certain to open from the effect of tide or wind. If so, this would throw a new and interesting light on their habits, and one can only hope that they will give us the pleasure of their company in our immediate vicinity.

'Tonight as I was walking back from the hills I was frostbitten in the lobe of the ear. I describe it because it was a typical example.

There was very little wind, and as I came down the slope I distinctly heard or felt a sort of snap in my ear, but, feeling nothing, I paid no heed until when I got on board I realised that I had no feeling in the ear. It very quickly thawed out – much too quickly, in fact; for now it is swelled up to a great size, and there will be no escaping the coming blister.'

· On the following day we made our start, a party of twelve, divided into two teams, each with a string of sledges and nine dogs. A strong south-easterly wind with snowdrift was pouring through the 'Gap', but a mile or two to the south we got clear of this and plodded on in comparative calm. Our loads were arranged theoretically, 200 lbs. to each man and 100 lbs. to each dog, and the first discovery we made was that the dogs entirely refused to work on our theory; the best of them only exerted a pull of about 50 lbs., and this with very dispirited and downcast mien; the rest hung disconsolately back on the traces and had to be half led, half dragged over the frozen surface. The whole thing was extremely troublesome, and, what with the heavy pulling and the constant necessity of clearing the traces, as may be imagined, our progress was extremely slow, and we heartily wished we had left the whole dog-team safely chained up. It was a curious reversal of our expectations. I don't know that we had any very good reason, but we had never thought but that our dogs, when they got the chance, would be found straining at their traces with heads and tails held high. To see them now with both ends at the maximum depression was a severe shock to our inexperience.

We learnt later on that it was a bad plan to combine dogs and men on a sledge; the dogs have a pace and a manner of pulling of their own, and neither of these is adapted to the unequal movement caused by the swing of marching men. Both men and dogs like a light load, but the former are much less easily dispirited by a heavy one.

But on this occasion there was a stronger reason for the inefficiency of the dogs. They were losing their coats; the thick fur was coming out in handfuls, and the young downy coat underneath formed a wretched protection against the bitterly cold winds that headed us. The habits of the animals were of course adapted to their northern home, where at this time the warm summer would be just commencing and where no doubt they would have been glad enough to be free of their thick winter garment; but that Nature should oblige them to discard it at the same season in this hemisphere was obviously ill-timed. As a matter of fact, our poor dogs suffered a great deal from their poorly clothed condition during the next week or two, and we could do little to help them; but Nature seemed to realise the mistake, and came quickly to the rescue: the new coats grew surprisingly fast, and before the winter had really settled down on us all the animals were again enveloped in their normally thick woolly covering. It may here be remarked that they moulted again in the spring; what would have happened in the following autumn cannot be said, for by that time, alas! all our team had ceased to be; but it seems as though they were already adapted to their new environment.

The fact that the dogs refused to do their share of the work on this trip meant of course that we had to do a good deal more than ours, and the resultant load per man was a great deal more than we ever afterwards sought to inflict on a party. We were practically doomed to failure, but each hour was an invaluable experience. On the first day we had already travelled some way over the new sea-ice when we realised that we must cross it before camping, as on it we could get no snow, either to fill our cookers or to secure our tents. This meant a long pull, and the night fell on us as we struggled with all the unaccustomed details of pitching camp. The thermometer fell to $-40°$ before we could climb into our ill-made fur clothing, and the hours which followed were comfortless enough to have discouraged the most ardent sledger. For two more days we pushed on in the same disorganised fashion, the men straining hard at a heart-breaking load, the dogs at each step flinching more determinedly from the cutting wind and the light pricking drift which it carried to the level of their noses; the thermometer never rose above $-30°$, and the third night it fell to $-47°$. The daylight hours were now very short, and all too many were wasted in the unavoidable delays of inexperienced camp work, and from the want of facility in the details of our arrangements. After three days' labour we were only nine miles from the ship, and it was quite evident that under present conditions we could not expect a better speed. On April 3 I decided to turn, and 'caching' our heavy loads we reached the ship that night, and could then fully realise what an extraordinarily sheltered position she occupied, for I find in my diary: 'The temperature on board has never fallen below −23°, so that it appears we can count on about 20° better in our snug winter quarters than occurs on the open barrier. But if one can get nearly −50° on the barrier before the sun has set, what is it going to be like in mid-winter? And what also in the early spring, when our sledging begins again?'

Our autumn sledging was at an end, and left me with much food for thought. In one way or another each journey had been a failure; we had little or nothing to show for our labours. The errors were patent; food, clothing, everything was wrong, the whole system was bad. It was clear that there would have to be a thorough reorganisation before the spring, and it was well to think that before us lay a long winter in which this might be effected.

I have described these early troubles in some detail, partly because they show how much we learnt by our failures and partly because it is necessary to realise that sledging is not such an easy matter as might be imagined.

That we were eventually able to make long and successful sledge journeys is no doubt due to the mistakes which we made and to the experience which we gained during the first barren attempts of this autumn, and yet more to the fact that we resolved to profit by them, and thoroughly took our lesson to heart. I do not mean to imply that our education was complete − as a matter of fact, we never ceased to learn new tips or to adopt new devices, and the general sledging work of the second summer was vastly superior to that of the first − but it was the crushing ineffectiveness of our early efforts which taught us the first great lesson.

The daylight hours were now getting rapidly shorter, and we knew that before the end of the month we should lose the sun. We were left with little time to complete all our outside arrangements, which had been necessarily delayed until the formation of the ice-sheet; although we felt anything but certain that the ice had come to stay, the losses which its break-up would entail must now be risked.

One of our first cares was to get up the meteorological screen; this erection, made under the superintendence of our meteorologist, Mr Royds, consisted of a framework supported by four stout poles; special louvred box-screens were placed high on this, and inside them were fitted the various thermometric and hygrometric instruments, whilst the corner poles were utilised for anemometers and wind vane. The whole of this somewhat elaborate erection was placed about 100 yards astern of the ship, and consequently in a direction which would be to windward of her with the prevalent south-easterly winds. At first the actual screens were some eight feet above the surface of the ice, but we soon found that our small bay was a focus for driving snow, and after each storm the surface was raised a foot or more and the comparative height of the screens proportionately reduced; once the whole structure had to be dug up and moved for this reason, but this could not be repeated often, and the net result was that the screens were reduced to an average height of five or six feet above the surface. We found it was quite time that these screens were placed, as we were getting very inaccurate temperature readings on board; for instance, I find a note of one comparison made about this time: 'The thermometer on the gunwale shows −20°, that in the screen on board 4° higher, and that in the screen on the ice some 5° or 6° lower.'

We possessed one recording anemometer of the 'Dyne' type. The instrument itself had to be placed in shelter, and we allotted one of our small deck-houses to it. The funnel vane was secured in the mizen cross-trees, some forty or fifty feet above the deck, and two small lead pipes connected it to the recording instrument. Finally, the barometer was placed in the magnetic deck-house and the barographs in suitable positions close by.

To obtain a complete record of meteorological observations was one of the most important scientific objects of the expedition, and it had been decided that the instruments should be read and recorded every two hours. And so in calm or storm, night and day, some member of our community had to be on the alert and every other hour to make the rounds of the various instruments. First the barometer would be visited, its reading and that of the attached thermometer registered; then at the screen the readings of the wet and dry bulb thermometers and of the minimum thermometer would be noted; then the anemometers and the wind direction had to be observed; then an estimate made of the force of the wind and notes added concerning the nature, amount, and direction of movement of the clouds; and, finally, the various recording instruments must be visited to see that they continued in good order. On a fine night this was no great hardship, but in stormy weather the task was not coveted by anyone. On such occasions it was necessary before going out to prepare oneself carefully to resist the wind and snowdrift, and the round itself was often attended with exasperating annoyances. During the winter it was always necessary to carry a lantern, but it is not easy to construct a lantern which will remain alight in all conditions of weather. At first we tried a small electric glow-lamp, but batteries and leads so easily got out of order that this was abandoned. Finally a candle lantern was evolved which was fairly satisfactory, but in the meanwhile many a time was the hapless observer forced to desist in the middle of his work to return and obtain a fresh light. The necessity of writing up the record sheet in the open was also trying in windy, cold weather; not only would one's fingers freeze very rapidly, but one's breath would form an icy film on the paper through which it was difficult to make the pencil-mark. The most annoying instrument with which we had to deal was called the Ashmann's aspirator; it consisted of a wet and dry bulb thermometer, but the air was circulated around the bulbs by a clockwork fan. At each observation it was necessary to wind up the clockwork, to wait for the fan to have full time for action, and then to read the result on two distressingly thin threads of mercury. As all these operations had to be done with bare fingers, a more angering cold-weather instrument can hardly be imagined.

The trials and tribulations of the meteorological observer were, in fact, numerous, and it was arranged that throughout the winter each officer should take it in turn to make the night observations from 10 p.m. to 6 a.m. Dr Wilson nobly offered to take the 8 a.m. observation regularly, but the lion's share of the work fell on the meteorologist himself, who, besides taking his share of the night work, throughout the first winter and a great part of the second, took all the observations between 10 a.m. and 10 p.m.

The most dreaded day for Mr Royds, however, was Monday, as on that day it became necessary to change the papers on the recording instruments. Anyone who is familiar with the ordinary barograph or thermograph can imagine that when the temperature was below $-20°$, with a brisk wind, this task could appear attractive to no-one.

I may remark generally that it is quite a mistake to suppose that one grows hardened or more callous to the cold, either in one's fingers or in any other part of the body; what does happen, however, is that one becomes more expert in keeping oneself warm. For instance, in handling cold metal one learns when to stop and to plunge one's fingers back into a warm mit, and how best to restore one's circulation; and so in the long run, when a cold job has to be done, it is done more expeditiously and with less suffering after experience has been gained.

Before quitting the subject of meteorology I may say that other observations were added as we gradually came to see our way more clearly and took our winter walks abroad. One had only to walk a few hundred yards from the ship to get sight of the smoking summit of Erebus, and we soon saw that the direction of move-ment of its vapour afforded us the most excellent indication of the upper air currents, and few days passed without some recorded observation of this fine beacon.

Later, too, our energetic walkers established subsidiary observ-atories where the temperatures could be taken and compared with those read near the ship. We were thus able to get interesting comparisons with observations taken on the top of the highest hill in our neighbourhood, 1,080 feet above us, and with a spot on the other side of Cape Armitage, and therefore more directly affected by the barrier conditions.

Another routine observation I was anxious to get into working order was that of the tide, and here we were faced with a good deal of difficulty in attempting to make a gauge which would work successfully through the ice. We had endeavoured to get some observations before the sea froze over, but the long pole which we placed against the ice-foot soon became so crusted with ice that the markings were obscured, and as it was impossible to clear this ice except from a boat, we were not able to get continuous readings. But later on we succeeded in getting a continuous record over a long period; and as the arrangement was only arrived at after some thought and numerous trials, the method is worth description for the benefit of future explorers who may be similarly situated.

Our first essay was to take a length of the single pianoforte sounding-wire, of which we carried a great quantity. One end of this was attached to a heavy weight resting on the bottom; the wire was then taken through a block held up by means of a tripod firmly planted on the ice, and to its other end was attached a second weight having about half the mass of the first. It is evident that with such an arrangement, as the tripod rose and fell with the tide, the upper weight would record its movement, always providing that the wire did not become too firmly gripped by the ice. As the wire was strong enough to admit of comparatively heavy weights, I had hopes that the pull would always be sufficient to overcome the friction of the ice, and for a long time this was so; but at length the ice became thick enough to hold the wire, and then of course the arrangement failed.

We had already improved on the tripod, by fixing up a second gauge working over the ship's side, with the second weight inside, when this difficulty arose. The problem now was, how to get the wire to work freely through the ice, and it was solved in a very simple manner. Someone – I think it was Wilson – conceived the brilliant idea of surrounding the wire with paraffin, which does not freeze, and our excellent engineers had soon turned out a small copper tube more than eight feet in length. The new tide-gauge was quickly completed; the wire was now brought up through a small wooden plug at the bottom of the tube, then through the tube and up over a freely working pulley which hung from the forecastle, through another pulley on the deck, and down to the inside weight, which hung opposite a well-marked scale. When the copper tube, filled with paraffin, was firmly frozen in the ice, we had the satisfaction of seeing the wire working through it practically without friction, and this it continued to do throughout the winter and spring. In searching for possible causes of error, we had, of course, to assure ourselves that the ship rose and fell regularly with the surface of the water, and to make allowance for any alteration in trim which might take place from time to time; but, with all its advantages and disadvantages, the arrangement must be considered about as satisfactory a one as could well be arrived at in the circumstances.

I have given some account of the erection of our magnetic huts. It would perhaps be as well to give here an idea of the purpose for which they were used. They and all that appertained to them were Mr Bernacchi's special business, and many times a day this officer could be seen journeying to and fro in attendance on his precious charge. Within the larger of the huts, mounted on a solidly bedded oak plank, could be seen three small instruments, set at different

Bernacchi at entrance to magnetic hut

angles, but each containing a delicately suspended magnetic needle to which was attached a tiny mirror; a shaded lamp and a roll of sensitised photographic paper were so arranged that the light reflected from each small mirror was thrown on to the roll, and the latter was slowly but continuously revolved by clockwork. The sensitised paper came off the roll in long strips, and after being developed exhibited fine wavy lines drawn by the points of light focussed from the mirrors. The three small instruments recorded respectively the declination, horizontal force, and vertical force, or the elements of the earth's magnetic pull from which its nature could be calculated at any moment.

The general reader may well wonder why so much trouble should be taken to ascertain small differences in the earth's magnetism, and he could scarcely be answered in a few words. Broadly speaking, the earth is a magnet, and its magnetism is constantly changing; but why it is a magnet, or why it changes, or indeed what magnetism may be, is unknown, and obviously the most hopeful road to the explanation of a phenomenon is to study it. For many reasons the phenomenon of magnetism could be recorded in few more useful places than our winter station in the Antarctic.

These record strips were a source of great interest to us all when Bernacchi showed them from time to time. They varied much in character; sometimes the lines would run with long gradual waves, at others they were distinctly jerky and unsettled, and occasionally, there were magnetic storms when they would fly off the paper altogether. There was a fourth line, which I have not yet mentioned; this was the line of temperature, and was necessary for the correction of the others. It was this that gave Bernacchi most of his trouble and drew to an alarming extent on our oil supply. The desire was to keep a constant temperature inside the hut, but with the frequent change outside this was most difficult to do, and although attempts were made to regulate the burning of a hanging lamp within, the variations were at first very great though they were lessened when we could get a sufficient supply of soft snow to bank the house up thoroughly outside.

Besides the magnetic variometers the larger hut contained another instrument of importance in the seismograph, which also kept a continuous record on a long roll of sensitised paper. I do not know that we had any good reason for so thinking, but, situated so close to an active volcano, we had expected this instrument to show much activity; contrary to our expectation, however, our region proved a particularly quiet one, and throughout our stay we were singularly free from earth tremors.

It should be understood that the magnetic instruments which I have briefly mentioned above were purely differential instruments. Whilst they would faithfully record the changes from hour to hour and day to day they were liable to small derangements which might prevent the comparison of one month with another. To obviate this difficulty, from time to time check observations were taken with absolute instruments, and for this purpose the second and smaller hut had been provided. In this small, dark cabin Bernacchi would occasionally be forced to shut himself, with only the magnetometer and the cold for company.

In addition to the establishment of the routine of regular scientific work, there was a great deal of work to be done for the comfort and well-being of the ship before the winter set in, and this, together with many unexpected tasks, kept all hands busy and amused. The incidents of this time are perhaps best given in extracts from my diary.

'April 5. – Some seals were observed close to the cape this afternoon; a killing party managed to get six. The skua gulls have gone, so that the carcases can now be left about with safety. Except for this reason, we rather miss the skuas; the absence of bird life adds to the deserted appearance of our outlook. There is still a slight swell, most noticeable at the crack beyond Hut Point; from the Point and from Cape Armitage there are numerous radial cracks, gradually widening and extending in length. Two "crab-eater" seals were found on the ice close to the ship tonight; we have very rarely seen these seals since our arrival in winter quarters; they seem to live mostly in the open sea. These animals must have come up through one of the holes, and then, possibly attracted by the ship, they appeared to have lost their bearings, as they crawled in any direction rather than towards an opening in the ice.

'We were still desirous of increasing our stock of seal-meat, but had we killed these animals at once we should have had great difficulty in skinning them in the dark, and by morning we knew the carcases would be hard frozen. In this dilemma orders were given to tie them up, and this resulted in quite an amusing scene. This species of seal is much more lithe and agile than the Weddell, and no sooner had a noose been cunningly drawn around the neck of one of these animals than he whipped round with such a ferocious snapping of the jaws that the holder of the rope incontinently fled; at length double nooses were drawn tight under the flippers of each animal, and with a precautionary extra rope around the tail we had them, as we thought, securely tied to the ship's chain cables; but ten minutes later we heard that both had freed themselves by slipping through their lashings. By this time everyone was turning in, but the matter was now growing into a serious reflection on our ability; that a party of sailors should confess themselves unable to tie any animal up securely was not to be thought of, so out we all sallied again. This time, after much struggling, each seal was lashed up like a hammock with frequent turns of rope round the body from the nose to the tail, and finally they were once more secured to the cable.' In spite of all our efforts, however, in the morning we found that one of these animals had slipped through everything and disappeared.

'April 7. – Today we found the sea open northward of a line from Hut Point, evidently the result of the late gale. The temperature today has risen to +10°, and, possibly in consequence, tonight furious squalls come from the E.S.E. towards the open water. I think our bay-ice is safe enough, but one can never tell. If it breaks now, we shall be in a very uncomfortable position, as both our boilers are run out and the engines are in pieces. A party with two large sledges and the dogs brought back eleven seals today, and will bring in some more tomorrow, so that we are now getting pretty secure for our winter stock.

'The work of getting comfortably settled is progressing. The winter awning is spread; it did not fit at all well, and we were obliged to make several alterations. It is made of a thick, rough, flaxen material, called, I think, "waggon cloth", which I was at great pains to get, on advice. I believe we should have done better to have had it made of ordinary stout canvas. The winter awning ends at the mainmast, but we propose to construct a further covered way aft to the engine-room with our summer awnings and odd pieces of canvas. There will probably be a good deal of work in the engine-room during the winter, and it is well to have complete shelter to and from it. With the awning spread over the living spaces, we are obliged to use artificial light all day; but we should get little enough natural light even if the awning were not there.

'The men are building a snow-bank for our gangway, and another at the ice-foot to make a road to the hut; but the difficulty at present is to get snow. None has fallen recently, and that on the land is hard and icy. As our awning would not spread well over the boats, we have got them out, and hauled them over towards the ice-foot. They are now ranged in a line close to it, and there, it is to be hoped, they will remain safely during the winter.'

This latter step with regard to the boats was a fatal error, and afterwards gave us a vast amount of labour and trouble. It was yet another case in which we had to buy our experience sadly. Our principal anxiety had been to find a place where they would not be exposed to the full force of the winter gales, and we never thought of the danger which actually overtook them. It was not until the middle of the winter that we realised that what had been the surface of the ice was, under the weight of newly fallen snow, gradually sinking below the water-level, carrying the boats with it;

and then, as it was impossible to commence rescuing operations till the daylight returned, we were forced helplessly to watch them getting into a worse and worse plight.

On the night of the 8th there was a great Emperor penguin hunt. 'It was blowing half a gale of wind, and the snow was driving rapidly past when someone espied a company of dignified "Emperors" advancing towards the ship. Our zoologist pointed out that here was the chance to complete our collection of skins, as the birds would now be in their finest plumage; and in spite of the weather a large party had soon surrounded the unfortunate birds. I was not present myself, but I hear there was much excitement. It is no easy matter to hold an Emperor; they are extraordinarly strong both in their legs and flippers, and are capable of moving even with a man on top of them. They could of course have been clubbed, but this would have damaged them as specimens. The proper method was to get hold of them firmly and give the *coup de grâce* in a scientific manner by inserting the blade of a penknife at the base of the skull. The confusion in the dark, when everyone was trying to capture a bird and these powerful creatures were dashing in every direction, can better be imagined than described. Report says that frequently one man was trying to capture another under the impression that he was a penguin, and more than one of the party seem to have been temporarily floored by the wild dashes of the intended victims. It was late at night before sufficient specimens had been slain, and then the party returned with a plentiful supply of frost-bites, of which they had been quite oblivious in the excitement of the chase.' The above scene may sound somewhat bloodthirsty, but it is just to remark that we never slew animals except for the practical object of obtaining food or specimens or both; and, indeed, the more we came to see the extraordinary, unsuspicious tameness of the animal life about us, the more compunction we were forced to feel at the necessity of killing at all. It was difficult to realise at first the full extent of this tameness – one is so little accustomed to total ignorance of man as an enemy – yet the attitude of both seals and penguins towards life is a very simple one. In the sea they prey and are preyed upon, and are adapted to such a condition; in that element they are swift, agile, and doubtless suspicious. But on the ice or on land they have never known an enemy – from all time it has been sanctuary, where they can mate, sleep, and rest without fear; and so the presence of an utterly unknown danger produces at first only consuming curiosity, and even when a vague feeling of alarm steals on their dull senses, they instinctively recoil from seeking safety in the sea, where alone safety is. It is interesting to think how different are the corresponding conditions in the far North, where for countless years the bear and the Esquimaux have ranged the floes, and the seal has become so timid that it is often difficult for the traveller to get within rifle-shot.

We found later on that the care which was taken on this night to shepherd the flock of penguins together before the victims were slain was quite unnecessary. So unsuspecting are these birds that they will stand stupidly by, without thought of flight, whilst individuals are cut out one by one from the group and killed. Even the last surviving member of such a group seems to remain unalarmed.

'April 9. – We found that the Emperor penguins killed last night are in splendid plumage. Many of them weighed over 80 lbs., and the largest turned the scale at 90 lbs. – quite a record weight. Rather a touching scene occurred when four or five stragglers from last night came boldly up to their dead companions, evidently at a loss to understand what it all meant.

'The sea is again open up to Hut Point, and possibly the inrush of cold air to the open water causes the extraordinary difference of weather conditions which exist in different localities within our view. Some of the hills are clear and bright with sunshine, whilst others are dark with hovering clouds; at certain places it is undoubtedly calm, but at others the drift snow can be seen rising in clouds and sweeping furiously along. Towards Cape Bird there are heavy, low cumulus clouds with black under-shadows; there must be a great deal of open water in this direction. The various sky effects are very beautiful.'

'April 13. – The ice has broken away enough to show open water around Hut Point ahead of the ship; it has been snowing all day, the snow falling in large, soft flakes, with a temperature of +17°. This afternoon we had several strong gusts from the south, and later the wind became more constant from the same direction and gradually increased to a full gale, when it shifted slowly to the S.E. with a rapidly falling temperature. Unfortunately, the windmill was left running after dinner, when it should have been feathered to the wind. The result is that some of the fans are badly twisted. I am rapidly losing faith in this unfortunate device, but I don't think that it had a fair chance today, and I shall suggest to the engine-room staff that it ought to be repaired if it is not too far gone.' For days after this the windmill was under repair, all the bent fans were taken down and carefully straightened below, but the task of replacing them was anything but pleasant, and hour after hour our excellent engine-room people spent aloft in the bitter wind, seated on cold metal, clinging to cold metal, and often obliged to handle their cold metal tools with bared fingers. Nothing would persuade them to give up, however, until the work was completed and the windmill once more revolving merrily.

'April 17. – All our former ski runs are now impossible; most of the snow-slopes are covered with hard high sastrugi raised by the late winds. Everywhere the snow is packed by the same cause, and the surface is so hard that it is impossible to climb the steeper inclines even in boots. Some of the men are out occasionally with a football, but the wind interferes sadly with all forms of sport, and in anything like calm weather most of us prefer to take walks to spy out the land. There are such a number of old volcanic craters close about us that it will be long before we become thoroughly acquainted with all the folds and valleys between, and for many a month yet we may hope to find new features in our neighbourhood and some fresh interest in our daily exercise.

'The sun does not now rise sufficiently high to shine on the ship, but about noon one can see it from the eminence of Hut Point. . . .'

'April 20. – A bright day with moderate northerly wind. The young ice just formed over the open strait crowded down on the old and rode over it in many places. The sun is very near its departure; today it appeared a highly refracted elliptical ball of red, giving little light and no appreciable heat. For a few minutes it bathed the top of Observation Hill in soft pink light, then vanished beneath a blood-red horizon.'

This was the last we saw of the sun till it returned to us more than four months later. Its actual date of disappearance was the 23rd, but after the 20th we had a return to what, at this time, appeared the normal weather conditions, and for the three following days my daily journal opens with the same remark: 'Wind still blowing hard with an overcast sky.' It was not a very enlivening prelude to the coming darkness, but it would have taken far more than this to depress us in our novel surroundings, and all felt the propriety of the celebrations on the night of the 23rd, when hilarity reigned supreme, and with a liberal allowance of extra grog we drank to a speedy passage of the long night.

The winter was now upon us. The ice about the ship had been firmly fixed for nearly a month, and there seemed little reason to suppose that the heaviest gale could move it before the following summer. For good or ill we were now a fixture, destined to spend our winter nearly 500 miles beyond the point at which any other human beings had wintered, and therefore about to face conditions at which we could only guess.

Before us lay a weary spell of darkness, but we came to it in full health and vigour, and all that skill could devise to provide for our comfort and lighten its monotony seemed within our grasp. Each day would bring us nearer to the longed-for spring, and to the day when, with high hopes, we should step forth on those new trails which met at our door and vanished in the unknown.

CHAPTER 8

The polar winter

Winter Routine – Obtaining Water – Meals and Meal-hours – Pastimes – Officers' Routine – Debates – Exercise – Work of the Officers – Weather Conditions – Heavy Blizzard and its Effects – Incidents of the Winter – Winter Clothing – Remarks on our Food – Sunday Routine – Discomforts of the Living-quarters from Ice – Heating and Ventilation – Mid-winter Day

> The cold ice slept below,
> Above the cold sky shone,
> And all around
> With a chilling sound
> From caves of ice and fields of snow
> The breath of night like death did flow
> Beneath the sinking moon. – SHELLEY

Long before the sun left us we had settled down into a regular routine of daily life, and although when it was above the horizon the hours of work were modified and generally increased, our meal-hours remained unaltered during the two years which saw us in the grip of the ice.

The following description of our daily life on board is contained in my diary of the early months of our first winter.

'The first task of the day is to fetch the ice for the daily consumption of water for cooking, drinking, and washing. In the latter respect we begin to realise that many circumstances are against habits of excessive cleanliness, but although we use water very sparingly, an astonishing amount of washing is done with it, and at present the fashion is for all to have a bath once a week. To fetch the ice in the morning a party of men are roused out somewhat earlier than their comrades, and dressing themselves according to the weather, they proceed to the ice-quarry with a heavy sledge specially fitted for the work. The harder and bluer the ice, the better it is adapted for melting and the less fuel is required to melt it; had we been obliged to use snow, either hard or soft, the daily task would have been much heavier; but by good fortune we have a very solid icy slope on the land not more than 200 yards from the ship, and here we have made our quarry.' For two years we dug in an area no greater than twenty yards across, and yet at the end of that time, when we must have removed many tons of ice, we scarcely seemed to have scratched the surface of the slope: such are the puny efforts of man!

'A quarter of an hour of hard delving with pick and shovel each morning is sufficient to supply our daily needs; the sledge, loaded with ice-blocks, is towed back to the ship, and the blocks are then carried on board and placed in a convenient storage close to the main hatchway. The pile thus made is kept well in advance of our needs in preparation for spells of bad weather when digging may be impossible. Long before the departure of the ice-diggers the cook's mate has been astir with the galley fire alight and the coppers and ice-melters filled so that by 8.30 the men's breakfast is prepared. By this time all hammocks except those of the night watchmen are lashed up and stowed away, and the linoleum-covered mess-deck has been washed and cleared up. Breakfast is a very simple meal, and consists always of a large bowl of porridge with bread and butter and marmalade or jam. For a long time a hash or stew was prepared, but as appetites fell off with our comparatively confined life this was rarely touched, and is now practically discontinued; on the two mornings of the week when seal's liver replaces the more ordinary meat, however, there is no such abstinence; everyone partakes of this excellent dish and wishes heartily that the seal was possessed of more than one liver.'

I may here mention that when we came to slaughter seals for our second winter there was a strong temptation to kill them for their livers only, and I think it is a creditable fact that we refrained from obtaining this luxury at a rate so expensive to life, but confined ourselves to the due proportions which fell to our share in treating the whole animal as food.

It is extraordinary how our liking for porridge grew upon us; we none of us cared much for it at first; naval sailors rarely do, and I believe it has lately been struck off the list of food supplied to the naval service; but with us the taste for this excellent food grew ever stronger both with officers and men, until we not only made our breakfast exclusively from it, but decided to include the more easily cooked variety in our sledge rations.

'After breakfast the mess-deck is again cleared up in preparation for prayers at 9.15, after which the men are assembled and told off for the work of the day, which is arranged as far as possible so that each man gets his fair share of the outside tasks.' I do not remember a time when there was not a great amount of work to be done. During the latter part of the first winter, and throughout the whole of the second a large party were constantly employed on our sledging outfit, making or repairing sleeping-bags, sledges, tents, cookers or other details of equipment. Out of doors there was generally some work in the digging line, either piling snow around the ship or the huts, or digging out various objects which had become buried, or making holes in the sea-ice for fish traps, or freeing the entrances and the paths to and from the huts, or many other lighter tasks. Then, again, the awning, the chimneys of the stove, and many outdoor instruments needed attention and repair, and few of our heavy winter gales passed without creating some havoc which had to be rectified.

'Dinner for the men is at one. This varies with the day, but consists always of soup, seal or tinned meat, and either a jam or a fruit tart. After dinner the rum is served out in accordance with naval custom. I am not at all sure the men would not be better without it, but perhaps some would feel aggrieved if it was stopped, and the small daily allowance can do little harm; of course it will be stopped when the sledging comes on. Smoking has been allowed on the mess-deck and at all times since we entered winter quarters; there are few non-smokers, and no-one who dislikes the smell of tobacco. After two in the afternoon the men return to work until five; up to the present there has been enough to keep them going, but if, as is probable, it falls off, I propose to leave their afternoon free; there is no object in making work. Supper is at five; a few with good appetites make up dishes out of what remains of the tinned meats or seal left over from dinner, but many confine themselves to bread and butter and tea, with perhaps some jam or cheese. Those men who have not been employed outside during the day take their exercise after supper; there is no constraint, but luckily the men are intelligent enough to appreciate the advantage of good health and the benefit of a daily walk. There

has been a difficulty in this respect with regard to the cooks and
stewards, whose duties lie naturally inside the ship; with a little
thought, however, we have been able to arrange a routine by
which each has some spare time daily to devote to a walk abroad.
In the evening all the men are free, and a glimpse at the mess-deck
at such a time leaves the impression that the greatest comfort and
contentment reigns throughout. Many have some special work in
hand, such as wood-carving, netting, mat-making, &c., which
serves to fill in the spare hours; others play games or read; whist,
draughts, and even chess are popular, and much time is beguiled
by a peculiar but simple game called "shove-ha'penny". This
pastime needs only a long board with numbers marked in squares
at one end and a halfpenny, which is placed on the edge at the
other; the coin is jerked along the smooth board towards the
numbers by striking the palm of the hand against the edge of the
board, and the player of course scores the number at which the
coin stops; whence this game came I know not, but I think it
must bear a strong resemblance to the older pastime called
"shovel-board". At any rate at present it affords much amusement
and produces shouts of laughter; tournaments are constantly held
in this, as well as in draughts and whist. At ten o'clock hammocks
are slung, and soon all are in bed and asleep; only one or two
sleep in the daytime, and perhaps in consequence all sleep well at
night. There is no doubt that hammocks are far preferable to the
bunks at one time suggested for the men; the large clear space
which is left when the hammocks are stowed for the day is alone
sufficient to prove this, but it is also certain that a hammock is
drier and more snug than a bunk would be under our present
conditions of life.'

Later in the year, on July 18, I note: 'During the darkest days,
when work was slack, nothing was done by the men after their
dinner, and I do not think anything is gained by making work;
now that preparation for sledging has commenced, however, there
is plenty to be done and perhaps it is better to have such employment. Entertainments have been few and far between, but have
counted for something, and Hodgson, Ferrar, and others have
given little scientific expositions on their special subjects which
have proved very popular. It was a very usual thing in the old
Northern expeditions to hold classes for school amongst the men,

but in those days many could not read or write; with these accomplishments men are able to amuse themselves, as we have proved, and the officers have had the more time for their own in consequence. I have endeavoured to suit everything to the requirement of the moment, and was prepared if monotony and dulness crept in to attempt to dispel them, but there has been no necessity; laughter and good cheer accompany warmth and comfort in the crew space as well as aft in the wardroom, and all in all a brighter or more contented company than ours it would be difficult to conceive.

'Reading on the mess-deck is of a very desultory character; Arctic books of travel are of course much sought after, simple and popular histories are frequently read; especially in request are such books as *Fights for the Flag*, *Deeds that Won the Empire*, and stories of the sea are much appreciated also. Novels are not very popular, though Dickens and Marryat find readers; old magazines seem to go the round many times and become much thumbed. Books of a quite different character from the above are often asked for, however; last week one man was deeply immersed in *The Origin of Species*, another is studying navigation, and not a few have the evident intention of improving themselves. There is a good deal of writing as well as reading on the mess-deck, and the excellent articles that have been contributed to the *South Polar Times*, show that much that is written would be well worth perusal. A goodly number of diaries are kept, some as personal records, but others for transmission home to the most-thought-of individual. It is difficult to say for certain, but as one looks on the cheerful, contented scene on the mess-deck at night, one rather gathers the impression that the regular organisation of lectures and entertainments would disturb rather than add to the comfort of the community. Perhaps, however, a second winter would necessitate more effort on the part of the officers to amuse the men; without doubt the novelty of the first season counts for much.'

The contentment of the men was no transient condition dependent on novelty such as at this time I surmised that it might be. We afterwards settled down to our second winter with even greater cheerfulness, and, far from finding such a life monotonous and dreary, the men with the officers adapted themselves with ease to its placid course.

'The officers' routine is somewhat different from that of the men. Breakfast aft starts at nine and is concluded at ten; few are exactly punctual, but all have finished by the latter hour. The breakfast meal itself is precisely the same as that served to the men, as are all our other meals. I made this rule at the start of the expedition, and it has been observed ever since and will be observed throughout; without subverting discipline, it silences complaint. Two or three months ago, for instance, one of the few troublesome men in the ship, a merchant seaman, asked to see me to complain of some cake. When I appeared on deck he held a slice of cake in his hand and plaintively informed me that it was not fit for human food. I immediately sent down for a slice from a cake in the wardroom which we had been eating with pleasure, and of course found that the slices were precisely similar. As a consequence I could express my opinion of the complaint and its maker with the utmost freedom, and proceeded to do so. That officers and men should mess apart, and that the officers should have the privacy of their cabins for their work, &c., is all very right and proper, and marks a distinction which is in the best interests of discipline; but in other respects it is an advantage on such an expedition as ours that all should share the same hardships, and, as far as possible, live the same lives. My rule does not of course apply to luxuries sent by officers' friends, to wines, or to a few delicate but indigestible trifles by which we increase the wardroom fare on the rare occasions when we have a special dinner; it is only a rule for ordinary circumstances, and one which will receive great extensions when we come to the hard sledging work that is before us, for then officers and men must live and work alike in every respect.

'From ten to two the officers have a good round interval for the routine work of the day; at two we have tea, the actual beverage being accompanied with jam, cakes, and toast. The latter is made at our own fire; the bread is cut off in huge chunks, and numerous patent toasting forks are brought into action. The toast made, it is spread thickly with butter until it is a sopping, dripping mass, suitable to nothing but a robust appetite; then the meal and the arguments begin, the latter being pursued to such lengths that the clock usually shows three before we break up. On the whole I think we all find this the most enjoyable meal of the day. In the afternoon those who have not been out already, start on their daily exercise; the rest melt away to their various tasks, self-imposed or otherwise, and it is not until 6 p.m. that we all meet again for dinner.

'This is the biggest and most formal meal of the day; each officer takes it in turn to be president for a week at a time, and during his term of office sits at the head of the table. Although we do not dress, we come as near to it as we can with a general tidy-up of costume; all are supposed to be seated before grace is said, and those who are not must duly apologise to the president for their absence.

'The dinner which follows is the same as that which is served to the men earlier in the day, though with us it is served in courses on a comparatively clean, if not a white, tablecloth. Few of us drink any alcohol, except possibly an occasional glass of wine after dinner, or a small bottle of beer on Sunday with our mutton. We have a supply of "sparklets" that make excellent ginger-beer or lemonade, and some cider, which is sometimes drunk; but the total consumption of alcoholic drink is ridiculously small, and that not from any rule of living or example, but simply because no-one seems to have any appetite for it. The consequence is we have a great deal of whisky and wine on board which will certainly never be touched.

'After dinner the table is cleared, grace said, the wine passed round, and the King's health formally drunk, when the functions of the president cease. Whilst the latter is in office the proprieties have to be observed on pain of a fine. No-one is allowed to contradict the president, no bets can be made, and no reference-books can be consulted; these limitations, with a few others which are more rarely transgressed, cause a good deal of amusement. Arguments are started on every imaginable subject under the sun, and the flattest contradictions are given and returned; as the president joins in the conversation, the chances are that in the heat of debate someone will directly traverse his statements or back his own opinion by saying, "I bet you so and so"; in either case his eager messmates call immediate attention to his breach of etiquette, and he is promptly fined "wine all round"; no appeal is possible, and complaint is met by an increase of the penalty. "Wine all round" doesn't mean much in our abstemious community, but sometimes even those who are practically teetotalers will relax to drink the health of a hardened offender. After "The King" has been drunk there is generally a rush for reference-books, and then a good deal of twisting of position to suit the reference. Our reference-books are fairly numerous, but (though we feel the lack of the *Encyclopædia Britannica*) the *Century Dictionary*, the Atlas, Haydn's *Dictionary of Dates*, *Whitaker's Almanack*, *Hazell's Annual*, the *Statesman's Year Book*, and some others, provide an ample field for supporting one's own opinion, refuting one's opponent, or at least for confusing the issue. I am not sure we get much "forrader" by our heated discussions, but it is a great deal better than being dull and silent; we have never yet sat through a meal without continual conversation, and I hope we never may.

'Dinner is followed by an hour or two of recreation, discussion, or work, a go-as-you-please arrangement; some finish off their daily work, some write, some read, and some play games. For some time now a game of "bridge" has been the evening amusement; five or six play, "cutting in" in the usual manner. No doubt the popularity of "bridge" will wane as has that of other games; chess was played for a long while, and will probably come to the front again. Most of us straggle off to bed between eleven and twelve, but some, myself amongst others, often stay up later. A few find that sleep does not come at all uniformly, but for my own part I sleep like a top.

'Every Tuesday after dinner we have a debate in the wardroom. I think Bernacchi first suggested this, and it was decided to have a technical subject one week and a lay one the next. The proceedings have always been very orderly, and throughout the winter nearly everyone has attended, though now their popularity is waning. On technical evenings we have discussed the barrier, the climatic conditions, the prospects of getting east and west, the seals, and the penguins, with results that have been both instructive and amusing. There is so much in these subjects that remains unexplained and mysterious that everyone must gain fresh ideas from their free discussion; of the barrier we still seem to know all too little, but that little is contrary to preconceived notions, and the ideas it suggests are confused enough to need sorting, if we are to continue our exploration systematically in the spring. In the climatic conditions we have yet to explain the astonishing differences of temperature in different localities and with different winds, and to discuss methods by which we can get some notion of the snowfall and evaporation in our region; while with regard to seals and penguins, we feel there is yet much to be learned as to their winter habits, their breeding, and their migrations. In fact, our discussions, whilst helping to elucidate minor points in the problems in debate, have served to set those problems more clearly before us, and to indicate the manner in which we may hope to arrive at their solution. People are so very genuinely interested in all this that I think the lapse of enthusiasm in the debates arises merely from the knowledge that we can only hope to throw more light on the subjects by further exploration and observation.

'The non-technical nights are of course devoted entirely to amusement, and the subjects selected accordingly are such as to encourage the most startling statements and lines of argument; thus we have had "The Trade of the Empire", "Conscription", &c., subjects on which, without knowing anything, everyone can talk. Needless to say, such debates generally end in more or less of an uproar.

'The day's routine for the officers gives four clear hours before tea and three after; during these hours all without exception are busily employed except for the hour or more devoted to exercise; the best time for this is now about noon, but during the very dark days the moon was a potent influence in fixing the time. In this, as in other matters, I have endeavoured to avoid all irksome rules and regulations. The officers are only too eager to go out for a breath of fresh air; the men have outside employment in fetching ice, tending their dogs, taking observations, &c., and in fine weather need no spur to be out and about with a football or on ski; the only class for which it has been necessary to make special arrangements are the cooks and domestics, whose duties are apt to tie them to the ship.

'My own time is taken up in organising the spring sledging, drafting instructions, calculating weights, searching up references, &c.; it would be difficult for an outsider to understand what a mass of detail this lands one in. I try also to keep touch with the work which is going on in the various departments, and am endeavouring to do some physical work in connection with the ice and snow which would otherwise be neglected; but such matters are attended with great difficulty to an untrained observer, and it is only when one comes to make the attempt that one finds that a simple experiment is almost an impossibility; every condition is complicated by outside variable causes.'

To give an instance of what was evidently meant by this paragraph I may mention that it was suggested in our *Antarctic Manual of Instructions* that a block of ice should be suspended in the sea and its rate of increase in winter and decrease in summer should be measured. Had we attempted to do this, probably we should have arrived at an utterly false conclusion, because in no two places would the result be the same; in one place, for example, the block would most certainly have disappeared early in the summer, whereas in another it would have been diminished by little throughout that season. This difference was dependent on the movement of the sea-water, but it shows the impossibility of carrying out experiments of this sort, however easily they may be conceived in the quiet of an English study.

'I find time also to read up Arctic literature, of which I am woefully ignorant; most unfortunately, our library is deficient in this respect, as owing to the hurry of our departure many important books were omitted. We have Greely, Payer, Nares, Markham, McClintock, McDougall, Scoresby, Nansen's *Greenland*, and a few others of less importance; but, sad to relate, Nordenskjold, Nansen (*Farthest North*), and Peary are absent, and two of these at least would have been amongst our most valuable books of reference. Yesterday I was pleasantly astonished to find that Wilson had some notes on Nansen's *Farthest North*, giving extracts of his sledge weights, &c., and these may be of great use in calculating our own weights.

'The work of the various officers is so distinct, and keeps them so busily employed, that we rarely meet except at meal hours and in the evenings. Armitage is reworking the observations for position taken during the summer cruise, and correcting his magnetic data. This is a very sedentary employment, but occasionally he is to be seen out on the floe with the large theodolite taking star observations for the rating of the chronometers – a very cold job, both for the observer and for the timekeeper, in which capacity I sometimes attend.

'It is satisfactory to find that all four chronometers are keeping a steady rate, notwithstanding that the temperature in the chronometer-box frequently falls below freezing-point. Every morning the clocks are set by the chronometer, so that our daily routine is timed to the minute.

'Luckily Koettlitz has not much to do in connection with his medical duties, as there is little sickness, but occasionally there are wounds and cuts to be dressed and small ailments to be doctored. In his daily walk he has undertaken the important duty of reading the thermometer off Cape Armitage. It is an instrument with a minimum indicator, and is attached to a post about 1½ mile from the ship. As I have before remarked, even at this very short distance the common difference of temperature between it and the ship's screen is from 10° to 15°. There are regular duties in the medical line which are of great importance, and which are shared by the two doctors. Every tin of food has to be examined by them after it is opened and before it is served out. This is no light task when hours are considered; for instance, Wilson has to be out early to examine the milk for the day. Another self-imposed duty of the doctors is to take weights and measurements and examine the blood of everyone, fore and aft, once during the month; all the information thus obtained is tabulated by Koettlitz, forming a very interesting record of the changes in different individuals living more or less under similar conditions.

'Soon after the first of each month in the evening we all gather in the wardroom clad in pyjamas, and are put through our paces as follows: Our weight is taken, and then the measurement of chest, filled and empty, waist, calf, forearm and upper arm; then, by means of a small spring instrument, our power of grip with right and left hand is recorded, and finally the capacity of our lungs is measured as we discharge one long breath into the spirometer.

'This performance is an entertainment in itself, and bets are freely offered and taken on the results, especially by those who fondly hope for a smaller waist or a stronger grip.

'Generally on the following night the same scene is enacted on the mess-deck, with the same display of chaff and good-humour. One has but to cast one's eye over the records that come from this quarter to realise what a splendid set of men we have from the point of view of physique. Some turn the scale at over 190 lbs., and several at over 180 lbs., without an ounce of superfluous fat; and though in some cases we can equal the blowing powers of these individuals, we cannot compete with their grips; in fact, a specially strong instrument is usually employed to prevent all chance of the ordinary one being wrecked.

'The further monthly examination of our physical condition consists in an examination of our blood. Our senior surgeon goes to each individual in turn with a special needle and a small test-tube; the former is plunged into the finger of the victim, and as the blood oozes out, it is drawn up and transferred to the test-tube. The first test is to dilute a given quantity with water and to compare the resultant colour with a standard; water is added until the colours are equalised in shade, and the richness of the blood is of course in proportion to the quantity of water added. The next test is carried out by putting a drop of blood on a graduated slide under the microscope and counting the numbers of red and white corpuscles which lie in one square millimetre. To obtain samples of blood from forty-five people and to examine them in this manner takes a considerable time, and Koettlitz is kept extremely busy for some days. So far we have always published the results of the examination as well as the weights and measurements, principally because they display no sign of any change in the general condition; there has been a falling-off in weight in a few cases, but others have put on more than the number of pounds lost; measurements and strength have shown merely slight fluctuations, but with few exceptions the blood has grown richer. I have no clear idea as to what the meaning of this may be, and I do not think that the doctor has either, but we are inclined to look upon it as a hopeful sign of our well-being.

'But to return to the manner in which our officers pass their days. It would be difficult to say who is the most diligent, but perhaps the palm would be given to Wilson, who is always at work; every rough sketch made since we started is reproduced in an enlarged and detailed form until we now possess a splendid pictorial representation of the whole coastline of Victoria Land. Wilson starts his day early by an examination of the breakfast food; his next business is to see to the ventilation of the living-spaces, which he does so thoroughly that when we come to breakfast there is no complaint about the freshness of the air, though occasionally people appear in fur mits as a mute protest against the temperature. He next takes the eight o'clock meteorological observations, and after the men are told off for the work of the day his business takes him to the superintendence of those who are detailed for bird-skinning and who carry on this work in the main hut. Under his direction a few of the men, and especially Cross, have become quite expert taxidermists, and the collection of prepared skins is gradually growing.

'The rest of his day is devoted to working up sketches and zoological notes, making those delightful drawings for the *South Polar Times*, without which that publication would lose its excellence, and performing a hundred and one kindly offices for all on board. He and Shackleton generally journey together to the top of Crater Hill, a height of 950 feet, each day, and return with a record of the temperature at our second outlying station. It is curious that although this temperature is generally lower than that in the ship's screen, it is rarely as low as that off Cape Armitage, and the fact almost seems to point to an inverted temperature gradient over the great ice-plain.

'The day starts early with Royds, our first lieutenant, also, for he must be up to see the men started at their various jobs. His special care is the meteorology, and the manner in which he sticks to what might well be considered a monotonous task is beyond praise. Rough or fine, every two hours from 10 a.m. to 8 p.m. he journeys forth on his round of observations. Regularly each morning the fair record books are produced on the wardroom table, and the rough observations of the previous day neatly entered in their columns. With the care of the ship's work, the maintenance of the various instruments in good working order, and many a stray task, it can be imagined that he has few idle hours. But one at least he finds – that immediately before dinner, when he goes to the piano and plays it, sometimes with and sometimes without the aid of the pianola; in either case we others in our various cabins have the pleasure of listening to excellent music and feel that the debt of gratitude we owe to our only musician is no light one. This hour of music has become an institution which none of us would willingly forego. I don't know what thoughts it brings to others, though I can readily guess; but of such things one does not care to write. I can well believe, however, that our music smooths over many a ruffle and brings us to dinner each night in that excellent humour, when all seem good-tempered, though "cleared for action" and ready for fresh argument.

'Shackleton is editor of our monthly journal, the *South Polar Times*; he is also printer, manager, typesetter, and office boy, and consequently a week before that publication appears he is kept pretty busy. At slacker seasons he conducts experiments to determine the salinity of the sea-ice and the sea-water about the ship, sees that the dogs are properly cared for, besides many other odd jobs, and at all seasons he is responsible for the serving-out of provisions and for the proper regulation of the cooking and general galley arrangements.

'Hodgson, our biologist, goes steadily on with his outdoor work, and I think this is the first instance of dredging being carried on throughout a polar winter. He is rather inclined to scorn assistance, and seems almost to prefer to do everything himself – the manual as well as the expert work connected with his task. Lately he has accepted the assistance of a single man, but it is currently reported that this individual is required to look on whilst Hodgson digs, and much digging and a great deal of preparation is necessary before the nets can be actually used, so that it is only occasionally that a frozen mass is borne into the wardroom, which, on being thawed out, discloses the queer creatures that crawl and swim on the floor of our polar sea. Hodgson tells me he had expected to be obliged to devote the winter to working out his summer catches, and that it was a pleasant surprise to find that he could continue his collecting work during the dark season. No doubt it is also an excellent thing for his health, and he certainly remains surprisingly fit.

'Bernacchi up to the present has found plenty of employment in the care of his magnetic instruments; in addition to taking and developing the records, he has spent much time in tending the heating lamps in the huts and in endeavouring to render them more efficient. By banking up the principal hut with snow he has been able to keep it at a more equable temperature, but he tells me that even yet it is by no means satisfactory, which I very much regret to hear, as we are making very great sacrifices of oil in order that his lamps should be kept going – sacrifices which would land us in an uncomfortable predicament were we obliged to remain a second winter. In Bernacchi's department are also included electrometer, auroral, seismic, and gravity observations; the which leave him no time for other physical work. As far as I can see at present, this is the point at which we are most lacking; with such curious formations of land and sea ice around us, we should possess a physicist and chemist who could devote his time principally to the many curious phenomena which they present.

'Of the lovers of fresh air, Barne is pre-eminent; it seems to bore him much to be cooped up on board; at any rate, in nearly all weathers he is out and about. He generally leaves the ship early in the day with his own special sledge, on which are mounted a sounding machine and a box containing reversible sea thermometers. With these he vanishes into the darkness and rarely reappears much before dinner. It is a curious sort of picnic life, and one which I imagine would be appreciated by very few. With a few sticks of chocolate in his pocket he journeys away to some distant crack or seal-hole, and there with the assistance of a flickering lantern he spends long hours, often in the intensest cold, letting down a string of thermometers, laboriously winding them to the surface, and recording the temperatures shown at the various depths. Could a more uninviting task be imagined? Indeed, it is doubtful if it even possesses the advantage of being useful. He sounds in depths of 200 to 400 fathoms, and rarely gets differences of much more than a tenth of a degree in the various layers, as naturally all the water in the strait is close on the freezing-point or something under 29° F. There will be interest, however, if we can continue the series when the summer approaches.

'Unlike the other officers, our geologist, Ferrar, inhabits a cabin at the fore-end of the ship, and there also is situated his small laboratory, the only one that is habitable under present conditions. Between meals Ferrar is rarely to be seen, for his tasks are numerous. Out on the hillsides and on the floes signs of him can be observed — here a line of sticks, and there a few stones so weirdly disposed that one might almost imagine they served some fetish or enchantment rather than the object of discovering the physical conditions of our surroundings. On board one may see a shaft of ice bending under a weight with a notice, "Do not touch. – H. T. Ferrar". Below one may find the officer himself, sorting a box of geological specimens or polishing a section on his lapidary's wheel, but always busy in some way or another. It is a curious fact that I rarely meet Ferrar in my walks and yet cannot speak of any feature of the numerous hill-slopes and valleys about our winter quarters without finding out that he knows it well.

'Skelton, our invaluable engineer, is also our photographer in chief, and has had a great deal of work in sorting and arranging the large numbers of photographs taken by various members of the expedition; the prints which he has already managed to get together are extraordinarily interesting, and if we can get good photographic results on our sledge journeys our collection should be quite unique. But photography is now the smallest part of Skelton's duties; every officer in every department has had need sooner or later to solicit his services. The amount of mechanical work that is needed to make good every defect in such an expedition as this is truly surprising, and the work varies from the roughest to the most delicate task; without mechanical skill we should have been hopelessly at sea, and it is not too much to say that the majority of our scientific observations would have been brought to a standstill. To give only a few instances of the jobs which have been done of late sufficiently illustrates this statement: a short while ago the clockwork of the Dyne's recording anemometer refused to act, and it was found that the hair-spring was rusted through; the only spare escapements were of a different pattern, but by drilling new holes one was eventually fitted to the instrument, which has been going continually since, though not of course at precisely the same speed as it maintained before.

'Last week, again, Hodgson found that his implements were unsuited to digging the slushy ice in his fishing holes. The only possible remedy was to forge new ones on a fresh design, and of course this was done. Quite lately our engineering skill has been called on for an extraordinarily delicate task connected with the cover of the gravity apparatus. This cover is placed over the pendulums, and its metal flange is supposed to rest so truly on the base that it forms an airtight joint when the space beneath the cover is exhausted; on trial of our instrument, however, it was found that the joint was not true, and there was considerable leakage. How the flange became strained is not known, but the delicacy of bringing it into perfect truth again can be easily imagined. Yet this has now been done, and the pendulums are being swung as they should be in a good vacuum, which would certainly not have been the case had we not possessed engineering skill competent to deal with the situation. These instances are only some of many; all day long repairs, great and small, pour in upon the engine-room department, and one cannot exaggerate the importance of possessing a staff which is capable of under-taking them.

'I have written much today concerning our daily life, but as I proceeded it occurred to me to think of the view which those at home would take of a party of their fellow men condemned to four months of darkness, and I have thought that they would probably imagine a life in which there was a maximum amount of sleep and little more activity than was necessary for the preparation and consumption of food. How far otherwise is the reality can be gathered herein, and to explain this must be my excuse for carrying description to such detail. Also, at home many no doubt will remember the horrible depression of spirit that has sometimes been pictured as a pendant to the long polar night. We cannot even claim to be martyrs in this respect: our life seems in every way normal; with plenty of work the days pass placidly and cheerfully.'

Life throughout our polar winters ran so smoothly that there was little to record from day to day but the changes of weather and those trifling adventures and incidents which loom so large at the moment, but diminish in importance as they recede into the past. My diary presents a running record of such circumstances and events, with here and there some lengthy digression explanatory of the general conditions under which we lived. It is difficult to extract from these memoirs in connected fashion, and at the same time to observe a chronological sequence of events, without falling to some extent under the influence of the diary form, but in adopting this form I shall suppress as far as possible the repetition of entries which might weary the reader.

It can be readily understood, however, that what is usually conceded to be an easily exhausted conversational topic, the weather, was to us at this time a matter of extraordinary importance. In this respect it has rarely, if ever, been the lot of a polar expedition to be so unfortunately circumstanced as we were, and consequently we had much that was novel in our situation, even when the experiences of former expeditions are considered. Almost without exception the North Polar winter has been recorded as a period of quiescence, when, although the thermometer has fallen to low limits, the atmosphere has remained comparatively undisturbed; but with us calm weather was the exception, and we eagerly looked to take full advantage of such breaks as occurred in the monotonous round of windy days.

'April 30. – . . . Wind still blowing from the old quarter, with temperature fallen to −27°.'

'May 2. – . . . A moderate breeze in the forenoon developed into a southerly gale during the afternoon, and in the evening it was blowing in furious squalls. Word was brought down that the windmill was straining badly, although it was feathered to the storm – a precaution which the engine-room staff have been careful to take in good time since the last breakdown; at about 8 p.m. it snapped off short, and now lies a wreck on the forecastle. So this is the last of our electric light, though for some time it has seemed hopeless to expect the system to work satisfactorily. It is some comfort to know that this last breakdown could not have been prevented; it reveals a radical weakness in the windmill itself, and entirely supports an opinion expressed to the expert who fitted it.

'Outside the snowdrift is so thick that one cannot see a yard in front of one's face; it is whirling and eddying about the ship in such a manner that were one to lose touch of a guide-rope he would be immediately lost. No-one has been outside for more than a few minutes, except the observers, and tonight even they are not going beyond the ship. Five minutes in the open is sufficient to powder one from head to foot, and though the temperature is comparatively high, the snow crystals lash so sharply in one's face that it is necessary to protect it with a mit, and even thus there is imminent danger of frostbites. The awning is swaying about in the most alarming manner – it seems a great question if it will last the night; the drift is almost as thick beneath it as outside. The tops of the chimney-funnels have come off and gone heaven knows where; the result is a down-draught in the chimneys which at first filled the living-spaces with choking smoke until the fires were put out and skylights and doors opened. The latter have now been closed again, and as we sit in rather chilly comfort below we can hear the wind howling through the rigging and the awning flapping noisily in its wild efforts to escape.

'Notwithstanding her icy surroundings one can actually feel the ship give to the more furious squalls, and the tide-gauge is moving up and down as much as five or six inches at irregular intervals; it looks as though the ice-crust of the strait is depressed as the heavier gusts sweep over it. In spite of the din without, the fireless condition within, and some anxiety as to what we shall find missing after the gale, we have had quite an interesting debate in the wardroom on "Women's Rights"; each man was allowed a period of twelve minutes in which to set forth his views, and managed to cram into it as much nonsense as he could think of in that space of time; even the married men felt that it was an occasion on which they could speak with the utmost freedom.'

The gale continued throughout the whole of the 3rd. In the short lulls we could see that the snow was drifting high about the ship; all our instruments had long been choked up; the temperature in the fireless living-spaces fell to 35°, outside the thermometer stood at −5°, but we had some comfort on seeing the gradual accumulation of snow weigh down the awning into a more secure position.

'May 4. − The wind has gone to the S.E., and though there is still some drift, we have been able to get out and observe the results of the gale. The first discovery was that the strait was clear of ice within 150 yards of the ship, and here, almost in the middle of winter, we find open water little more than a couple of ships' lengths ahead of us. Not only has all the ten-days-old ice gone, but a considerable portion of that which was formed five weeks ago has broken away. I once thought of the possibility of wintering in Arrival Bay; that place is now quite free of ice, and where we should now be had we adopted that plan is beyond the power of guessing. The snow lies in mountainous drifts around the ship; from a few hundred yards' distance she looks to be buried. On the starboard and lee side the drift slopes down from the gunwale itself, and on the port side it stands higher, but between it and the ship there is a deep trench almost free of snow; this is always the manner in which snow drifts about an object.

'The meteorological screen has drifted up to six feet, and some-where far beneath the present surface lies the snow-gauge − a fact that makes comment on the utility of that instrument unnecessary. The Dyne's anemometers have been drifted up since the earlier hours of the storm, and thus fail to record the wind at exactly the time when such a record would have been most valuable. On such occasions even the Robertson anemometer seems unreliable, as the caps get partially filled with the clinging snow-crystals. The awning is heavily weighted with snow and sadly torn: the boats' crutches and other projections have made clean breaches in it. The windmill lies an ugly wreck on the forecastle, and the shaft and standards which still remain up look particularly forlorn. We cannot yet get at the chimneys to repair them, and though the fires have been restarted we get a plentiful supply of smoke in our quarters.

'The dogs, or rather their kennels, were dug out this morning and found none the worse; we have lately brought them from the shore and disposed them near the bows of the ship, and luckily none were placed where the worst drifting took place. It is evident, however, that the dogs do not like the idea of being drifted up; very few had used their kennels during the storm, preferring to coil themselves down outside, where they could break out when the weight of snow got too great.'

'May 5. – We still have some wind from the eastward, but curiously the temperature has gone up to +5°, so that it is positively enjoyable to walk about outside. The storm has buried the ice in the bay by about three feet on an average, though the snow is very much deeper about the ship and close to the ice-foot. It is strange that we had little or no warning of this gale from the barometer, though the pressure fell during the blow. Bernacchi found exceptionally high electrometer readings as much as twelve hours before the wind came on; one wonders whether this instrument can be relied on to give warning of a blow – it would seem not altogether improbable. The dogs have now got over their recent unclothed state and have grown very thick, shaggy coats.'

Except when we said farewell to our winter quarters, I do not think we ever had quite so heavy or so prolonged a gale as that which has just been described. The wind swung round also in a manner which gave all the indication of a revolving storm whose centre had narrowly missed us, and the gale was followed by a result which we did not experience again, or at least only to a much smaller extent. The temperature remained extraordinarily high for several days after the storm; on one occasion it rose to +17°, and it was not until the 9th that it fell again below zero, and then it fell rapidly. On other occasions the temperature rose regularly with a southerly wind, but fell when the wind dropped or changed direction. The whole subject of this astonishing and inexplicable wave of warm air is so interesting that it is well to remember that the conditions under which it occurred were not always precisely the same. With the warm air on this occasion came a comparatively high degree of evaporation; the drifts about the ship diminished rapidly as the snow settled down and packed, and we could observe for the first time some of the extraordinary conditions under which packed snow-crystals adhere.

'The snow has drifted and hardened against the side of the magnetic hut, forming a coating from three inches thick at the bottom to about one and a half inch at the top. For some reason, possibly change of temperature, the inner surface has been severed from the side of the hut, and the sheet has gradually bent back until it described a complete semicircle. A similar sheet curled back from the ship's stern shows her name clearly impressed on its surface.'

Around the cape the gale had produced high under-cut snow-waves or sastrugi, whose thin overhanging edges would reverberate with a deep note when struck with a ski pole. Again from the summit of each perpendicular ice-face there were now single, double, and even triple cornices hanging in graceful festoons, actually formed by the adhesion of the whirling snow particles, but appearing to be formed by the overflow of the white sheet on the slopes above. This ever-changing condition of the snow was to many of us a fascinating study; it was not only that it lent to our walks a delightful variety, but we realised that it had a highly practical bearing on our sledge-travelling. From start to finish of our journeys we must haul our sledges over this fickle substance, and according as its surface was hard or soft, sticky or clean, waved or smooth, so must our progress be measured. Those who have only seen snow under the soft, flaky guise which it assumes in a temperate climate must find it difficult to appreciate its infinite variety and bewildering changes under more rigorous conditions, which even the sledge-traveller, whilst he is forced to appreciate, finds it impossible wholly to explain.

'May 12. – Fine, calm day; quite pleasant to be out in the morning. In the afternoon the temperature fell to −37°; as it fell the calm stillness on deck was interrupted by the continuous crackling of the contracting rigging, a succession of sharp, clear reports like muffled rifle-shots. In such calm weather, too, there are similar but intermittent reports at the tide-crack; as the water rises or falls with the tide the ice at the edge appears to hang for several minutes and then to break up or down suddenly, starting from one end of the bay and running quickly through to the other with the sound of a miniature cannonading. The western sky was very beautiful this afternoon when I went for my walk after tea; the hills in deep shadow were sharply outlined against a background of crimson, fading through saffron to pale green, which merged into the slaty blue of a greater altitude. As the light failed the stars shone forth wonderfully bright and clear. . . . '

'May 13. – For a wonder another fine day, temperature down to −43°, the lowest we have had in winter quarters. It is not the low temperatures that annoy, but the wind and foul weather, and we should suffer few inconveniences if we had not the latter to face so constantly. A party of four of us went round to Seal Bay to examine the ice-ridges, where the temperature was evidently much lower, though we had no thermometer. Beyond the necessity of occasionally warming our noses and cheeks, however, we were quite warm and comfortable. We passed a seal blow-hole at which the owner remained placidly breathing under a dome-shaped covering of snow, even when the dogs barked and scratched the snow down on his nose. There is not much light now, even at noon, and by two it is quite dark. Can one hope that the last few days of calmer weather are an earnest of better conditions to come?'

'May 16. – Wind blowing harder than yesterday – in fact, over forty miles an hour – with temperature down to −35°. There is happily no sign of the ice breaking up again, but this is scarcely in keeping with the more settled conditions hoped for. Nobody is very anxious to be out: the wind cuts like a knife at this temperature. Poor Bernacchi had a very bad night, as it was his term-day, and he had to make several visits to the hut, and got frostbitten in consequence.'

'May 17. – . . . Had an alarming evening. The wind having lulled this afternoon, the boatswain and second engineer started off at 2.30 for a walk round Castle Rock, without giving warning of their intention except by a few casual remarks dropped in their mess. Later it came on to blow hard with heavy drift, but I was not informed of the absence of the men till eight o'clock, some hours after their messmates had begun to grow anxious. We immediately organised two search parties, and having made elaborate plans and fully dressed ourselves to face the elements, we stepped forth – to meet the absentees returning over the gangway. It appears they had an idea that our peninsula was an island, and started to walk round it. Not finding the other end, they got farther from the ship than they had intended, and then the drift coming on, they had to feel their way along the land to get back, and so reached the ship in a very exhausted and frostbitten condition. There must be no more of this casual wandering about.'

'May 19. – Still the never-ceasing easterly wind; the barometer has risen very high, but, high or low, the wind persists, lulling and rising, and again lulling and rising, till one grows heartily sick of it.'

'May 21. – . . . Wind from the eastward, increasing during the day to a howling gale between five and nine. It is curious how clearly I can hear the wind in my bunk at night. Each gust is distinct as it shrieks through the rigging, and it is not inspiriting to lay awake and think to this weird and rather dismal accompaniment; one begins to wonder whether it ever will be calm again. On the other hand, as the sound is precisely that of a storm at sea, one cannot but take great comfort in reflecting how infinitely pleasanter it is to listen to it under such restful conditions rather than when tossed about on the mountainous seas of the Southern Oceans. Overhead today it is calm and bright, with peculiar luminous cirro-stratus cloud towards the south, but for some feet from the surface the air is thick with driving snow. How used we are getting to the sound of this driving snow! I seem to have heard the same as the dust was swept along a hard, sandy road; it is almost like the patter of hail; to all intents and purposes our snow is fine sand.'

'May 22. – A day of hard wind, ending in a beautifully fine calm moonlight night. We all went out in the evening, and in the clear silvery light were able to see about us for the first time for many days. The scene was perfect in the pale white light and silence. Later there was a curious effect of frozen fog; the nimbus cloud seemed to descend on the hills and roll over us, leaving the ship free, but though all around us was clear, there was a heavy deposit of ice-crystals on masts and ropes which shone and sparkled in the moonlight. Now the ship looks spectral in her white shimmering robe, the mist-clouds are rolling down the hillsides into the snow-covered hollows, and a strong wind can be heard high above us, though all below is calm. The whole scene is so weird that it gives one a positively eerie feeling.'

The foregoing extracts show how persistently the wind annoyed us about this time, and, indeed, so matters continued, with occasional calms, when we could enjoy our outdoor strolls, and occasional gales from the south, when, though the temperature rose comparatively high, it was unsafe to venture far from the ship.

'May 31. – Temperature abnormally high (+8°). Went well out over the ice to the westward, where the recent snowfall has improved the surface for ski; found three seals up on the ice, the first that have ventured up for a long time. In the cold weather they never seem to quit the water; evidently they know when the thermometer rises. It is now pretty dark, even at noon, and dismal enough when the fine snow is driving past and the sky overcast. Regret to say one of the dogs, "Paddy", was found dead this morning. A post-mortem revealed a deep wound in his side, and when "Nigger", acknowledged king of the pack, approached with the most innocent air and wagging tail, and it was found that he must have slipped his collar in the night, there was little difficulty in guessing the cause of the disaster and fixing the guilt. The curious thing is that "Paddy" appeared to be "Nigger's" sole and only friend; their kennels were adjacent, and as "Paddy" was always content to play second fiddle, there seemed no chance of a rupture. The deed must have been done in the silent hours of the night, and alas! we shall never know the cause. There is nothing to be done but to bore an extra hole in "Nigger's" collar. I trust we are not to lose more of our dog-team: this is the second loss since the winter set in, as poor "David" died last Sunday from causes unknown.

'I do not think it would be possible to take more care of the dogs than we do. Each dog has his own particular master among the men, and each master seems to take a particular delight in seeing that his animal is well cared for. The most thoughtful are constantly out building extra shelters, covering the kennels with sacking, and generally endeavouring to make their charges comfortable.'

'June 2. – . . . As far as winter conditions are concerned, our clothing arrangements are satisfactory, and although the outlay in this direction was heavy, the excellent quality of our garments fully justifies it. Practically men and officers are clothed alike, such minor differences as exist serving only as a useful distinction of costume on board the ship, and not signifying any difference in the quality or comfort of the garments worn by either.

'Everyone wears the thick warm woollen drawers and vests supplied by the expedition, and over these a flannel or woollen shirt and pilot-cloth trousers. On board the ship the outer upper garment of the men is a dark woollen jersey, but that of the officers a brown "cardigan" jacket. Some of the more chilly individuals put on an extra waistcoat, but few wear the thick jacket which is supplied with the pilot-cloth trousers, the jersey or cardigan giving excellent freedom to the limbs and movements. The men's jerseys come well up around the throat, and they need no additional neck protection; but the officers wear a variety of comforters or scarves, or sometimes a flannel collar. Dressing for dinner is a more or less punctilious performance, and generally means the donning of the Sunday cardigan and neck-scarf.

'For ship wear there are some warm, comfortable slippers provided for both officers and men, but many prefer to remain in their Russian felt boots. These were especially obtained from Russia at a very small cost, and are perhaps the most satisfactory footwear we possess for general purposes, now that we have modified them to suit our requirements. The modification consists in adding a sennet sole made from ordinary spun yarn and secured to canvas which is closely fitted and sewn to the boot; by this device the felt of the boot is protected from wear, and our people are able to do a great deal of work both inside and outside the ship in this comfortable foot-gear. The only drawback is that when it is snowing or drifting the fine powdery snow clings to the felt, and on being brought into the living-spaces melts and wets the boots. Even in fine weather this happens to the sole, and for the sake of the boot it is really wiser to change before going out of doors. For walking abroad or climbing over rocks these boots are not well adapted, though there are individuals who from perversity or laziness continue to wear them for the purpose; the majority, however, change their foot-gear when they leave the immediate neighbourhood of the ship.

'English leather boots were soon found to be far too chilling to wear on such excursions, though better adapted to climbing over the sharp, jagged rocks than anything we possess; but for a long time we clung to the Norwegian leather ski boot, which is a looser and easier fit, and therefore allows a much freer circulation in the foot; in fact, ski boots are still worn, and in some cases have been fitted with a stouter sole by the cobbling abilities of that excellent man-of-all-trades, Lashly. But most of us have by this time taken to wearing fur boots on our walks abroad, and now that we can always dry them on our return they are the most warm and comfortable foot-gear imaginable; the only trouble is that they wear out rapidly, especially on the sharp, stony, hillsides, and as we may need many pairs for our sledge journeys we cannot afford to be too lavish in serving them out during the winter.

'These fur boots are made of selected reindeer skin and sewn with gut; the sole is made from the covering of the forehead both on account of the thickness of the pelt in this part, and also to obtain the twist in the growth of the hair which gives the boot a better chance of gripping on a slippery surface; the upper part of the boot is made from neck-pieces and is soft and pliable. Already we see that our stock varies greatly in quality, and that for our sledge journeys we shall have to make a most careful selection; but by wearing them now we are gaining experience of what constitutes a good boot, which is not at all the sort of fact that can be discovered at the first glance. Some officers and men have already resoled their "finneskoes", as these fur boots are called, with sealskin, but it is doubtful if there is much wear in the latter, though it is thick and hard; however, it is interesting to try the purposes to which the natural productions of our desolate region can be put, and it is to be hoped that our sealskin will be available for something more useful than the leggings, tobacco pouches, and knife sheaths which have so far been made from it.'

I may add that we never found this sealskin of much use: it was far too weak and brittle. Though possibly we were not very expert in preparing it, it may be added that similar skins landed in Dundee some years ago were found to be practically valueless for the purposes for which the skin of the Northern hair-seal is employed. I do not know the reason for this fact, but it is evident that it should go far to ensure a peaceful existence to the Southern seal.

'Everyone is provided with a complete suit of wind covering for outdoor wear, and a second suit is held in readiness for sledging.

This is made of a thin waterproof gaberdine material supplied by Messrs. Burberry, and will doubtless be excellent for our sledging, but for constant winter wear it is not adequate, and already we have strong regrets that we do not also possess suits of a thicker, tougher material. A light canvas would be just the thing for this rough winter wear, though it might become too stiff and icy on a sledge journey. It would have been better also and cheaper had we brought the material only, instead of the made-up garments, for our wind clothing; both officers and men can ply a needle more or less handily, and although everyone conforms to the same general cut of trousers and blouse, each has his own ideas in matters of detail, concerning the collars and cuffs, &c. It is doubtful if the original making of garments would have taken much more time than the very numerous alterations that have been made to suit individual taste, and even if it had, there is now ample opportunity for such work.

'The necessity of continually facing a blighting wind is calling forth original genius and inventive talent in devising a headgear which shall protect one's necessarily exposed features. Our helmets are made of a thick fleecy material woven of camel's hair, which is satisfactory enough for winter wear, though many of us are not in favour of it for sledging. When buttoned across, this helmet comes low on the forehead and circles round over the chin and close under the mouth, leaving only the cheeks and nose exposed; but in a cold wind it takes all one's time to keep even these members from being frostbitten. At first talent was devoted to finding some practicable form of 'nose-nip', a semi-attached piece which can be disposed to cover the nose and cheeks in windy weather, but in spite of all efforts the same difficulty always arises: one's breath is caught as it ascends and freezes on it, gradually accumulating until one's face is covered with a mass of ice. The same drawback is found to occur to a greater degree with any form of face-mask. A new departure is now being developed by which a sort of blinker is placed on each side of the helmet, and each blinker is capable of being pushed forward according to the direction of the wind.'

The development of this new idea finally put us in possession of a device which proved really admirable, and which I can confidently recommend to expeditions that may be called on to face equally windy conditions. A light peak about two or two and a quarter inches deep, constructed of gaberdine stiffened with canvas, was carried across the forehead and down on each side of the face well below the chin, and attached to the edge of the helmet aperture; in its ordinary position, it lay flat back against the helmet, but either side could be thrust forward separately, or both together. The beauty of this device was that with the wind on either side one had but to push forward the guard on that side to obtain shelter, whereas if the wind was ahead one pushed forward both sides and, securing the lower edges together, obtained a funnel-shaped protection which held the air immediately in front of the face in comparative rest. With a very strong wind and a low temperature, no possible device can prevent frequent frostbites, but this one went a long way towards mitigating the evil, and it had also the advantage that by peering beneath the guard of a companion, one could readily tell if the frost had attacked him.

'We find not only that furs are unnecessary for winter wear, but cannot imagine that they would be otherwise than positively objectionable. It is reported that some of the old Arctic expeditions wore furs; the mess-deck under such conditions cannot have been very attractive. We wear furs only on our feet and hands, the latter are also protected by excellent woollen half-mits, which extend from the knuckles nearly to the elbow; armed with these and with one's fists thrust into a lined fur mit, one's hands may be comfortable in any weather. We have also excellent felt and woollen mits, which the men use for outdoor work. Should the wind get through these, the best plan is to wet them, as the ice forms the best possible protection.

'I regret to say that the clothing issue displays the fact that the sailors are extremely careless of their clothes; they seem to have an idea that there is an unlimited stock of socks, mits and such like, and have an obvious contempt for the "stitch in time". Of course there are the few careful ones by whom the others can be judged. More than once I have had to speak seriously about the wasteful use of food, clothes, and various articles of our equipment, but I am bound to confess that my words have not had any great result; in fact, even the cutting off of supplies does not seem to have any lasting effect. One may well wonder whether, in any circumstances, it would be possible to alter their happy-go-lucky-nature. On the other hand, such a nature has its obvious advantages. One knows with these men that their resource will always be equal to the occasion, and even if they run short of clothing, one has a feeling that they will manage somehow.'

'June 10. – . . . In considering the excellent manner in which we are getting through the long winter and the good health enjoyed by all, the share which our material comforts have had in the result must not be forgotten. We have fresh well-baked bread continuously, seal-meat three times a week, pies and other dishes of tinned meat three times, and fresh mutton once. To this is added a good supply of butter, milk, cheese, jam, and bottled fruits, whilst cakes are constantly made for all. There is, of course, a certain amount of sameness in the diet, and preserved foods are more likely to become wearisome than fresh, and of course, also, appetites are tending to grow fastidious from the inactive life; but, taking it all in all, the food is quite good enough to tempt us to eat a sufficiency, whilst, as may perhaps be equally fortunate, it is not so attractive as to leave us with any desire to take more than that sufficiency. The main point is that we all seem to thrive well on it. Perhaps the articles we miss most are fresh vegetables; tinned vegetables are always a poor substitute, and with the exception of the potatoes ours are unfit for food. Our preserved potatoes are as good as such things can be, but the best preserved potatoes are dull and uninteresting. The greatest drawback to the galley productions, however, is the cook. We shipped him at the last moment in New Zealand, when our trained cook became too big for his boots, and the exchange was greatly for the worse; I am afraid he is a thorough knave, but what is even worse, he is dirty – an unforgivable crime in a cook. I think if the men were free to deal with him it would be "something slow with boiling oil"; but, alas! one cannot be rid of the most undesirable in this far-off land: one is forced to make the best of a bad job. Luckily, he is a comparatively isolated blemish. Luckily, also, our cook's mate is a good man and an excellent baker; it is he who provides us with our good bread and toothsome cakes.'

'June 12. – . . . We keep a very regular weekly routine; each day has its special food and its special tasks, and as far as possible we stick to what the sailor calls "man-of-war fashion". The week's work ends on Friday; Saturday is devoted to "clean ship", and though we don't polish bright work, we do our share of scrubbing.

In the forenoon the living-spaces are thoroughly cleaned, lockers and other articles of furniture are moved, holes and corners are searched, and whilst the tub and scrubber hold sway, the deck becomes a "snipe marsh". At this time also the holds are cleared up, the bilges pumped out, the upper deck is "squared up", and a fresh layer of clean snow is sprinkled over that which has been soiled by the traffic of the week. On this follows a free afternoon for all hands, and after dinner in the wardroom the toast is the time-honoured one of "Sweethearts and Wives".

'On Sunday we don a different garment; it need not necessarily be a newer or cleaner one – the thing is for it to be different from that which has been worn during the week. By 9.30 the decks have been cleared up, the tables and shelves tidied, and the first lieutenant reports "All ready for rounds". Then follows a humble imitation of the usual man-of-war walk-round Sunday inspection, and in solemn procession we pass through the now empty mess-deck and on to the other inhabited parts of the ship. I am more than ever convinced that this routine is an excellent thing; not only has it the best effect on the general discipline and cleanliness of the ship, but it gives an opportunity of raising and discussing each new arrangement that is made for the better comfort of all on board.

'After the inspection of the ship comes that of the men, who are fallen in under the awning on deck. Though it is only possible to see them in the rays of the flickering lantern which the boatswain bears ahead of me, I see enough to assure me of the general good health and cheerfulness of the company. Then come the only military orders of the week. The first lieutenant says, "Front rank, one pace forward – march." We pass between the ranks, and the men are dismissed.

'After this the mess-deck is prepared for church; harmonium, reading-desk, and chairs are all placed according to routine, and the bell is tolled. The service is read by me, the lessons by Koettlitz, and Royds plays the harmonium. As he plays it extremely well, the responses are chanted and the three hymns are so heartily sung that I have no doubt they could be heard far over the floe. Service over, all stand off for the day, and look forward to the feast of "mutton", which is also limited to Sunday; by using it thus sparingly the handsome gift of the New Zealand farmers should last us till the early spring. But it is little use to think of the sad day when it will fail; for the present I must confess that we always take an extra walk to make quite sure of our appetites on Sunday.'

'June 15. – . . . It would be idle to say that we live in complete comfort below; perhaps it is as well that there should be difficulties to overcome. We have several weak places as regards damp and cold; the mess-deck is the best part of the ship; except for a little damp on the side there is not much to complain of; but the wardroom in general, and the after cabins in particular, are not so happily situated. We can now see that our insulation scheme is very imperfect. The upper deck is lined with asbestos, and is satisfactory; but the ship's side is not lined, and wherever the bolts come through the region inside is covered with a hard, spiky mass of ice. This ice accumulates in time, especially in the region of the bunks, and lately several people have had literally to chip out their mattresses, which were solidly frozen to the ship's side. At the after-end of my cabin there is an iron bulkhead; it is lined with asbestos, but I imagine the latter must have slipped down, as the whole bulkhead inside is a solid mass of ice. Another very stupid arrangement is the plan of the small cabin deck-lights; these are made in a single metal casting, with double glasses; of course the metal forms a free conductor between the outside and in, and the fitting is consequently a natural ice-trap.

'But the worst feature of the wardroom is the deck below it, which has no lining, and out of which the caulking has fallen into the bunker. Except for the linoleum on top there is little in this floor to protect us from the temperature of the bunker, and the latter, being in direct communication with the engine-room and thence with the open air, is always considerably below freezing-point. As a consequence of this we get very cold draughts in the wardroom, and a thermometer placed on the deck anywhere but near the stove falls to 32° or 34°. A week or two ago it was so bad that I was obliged to sit in my cabin with my feet in a box of hay, an efficient but inconvenient foot warmer.

'Before the gale in May, when we had no snow about us, the ship was getting very badly iced up inside, but after that gale we were able to improve matters, and now they are a good deal better. At the end of April the temperature in my cabin averaged about 40° during the daytime and 33° during the night, a condition under which one was not tempted to dawdle over the processes of dressing and undressing; now the temperature keeps up to nearly 50°, except near the floor, where it is much colder. The course of improvement was accompanied by much thawing, and for some time we had a general dripping, which was much worse than the ice and infinitely more ruinous to our effects, amongst which mildew is already making rapid strides. In this way, as in others, we have had to buy our experience, and since May we have been fighting the evil by banking up snow without and by nailing up quantities of felt within.

'The most difficult place to fight is the galley-space, because here it is impossible to avoid the volumes of steam given off by the cooking; directly this steam strikes against the cold sides of the compartment it condenses, and during cooking-hours this space is very much like a shower bath. We have improved matters a little by trying to guide the steam up through the skylight, but the place is still very bad.

'Our stoves have also been a source of trouble to us, and are likely to continue to be so. They are of the slow-combustion type, designed to burn anthracite coal, and though it was claimed that they would be equally efficient with our steaming-coal, we find that to burn it at all we must greatly increase the draught, and consequently we do not achieve the economy of fuel we expected. Under the impression that we should require them whilst magnetic observations were being taken on board, they were made of phosphor bronze (a non-magnetic material), and we now find that this metal burns so easily that one stove is already practically destroyed, and the other is in a bad way; luckily we have spare ones which are made of iron. But the worst trouble in this connection is perhaps not so much the fault of the stove itself as of the chimney; we find that with certain directions of wind it is impossible to avoid a down-draught, and directly the wind turns to this quarter we have to draw fires with all speed and remain fireless till the weather becomes more favourable.

'But the stove arrangement has its good points as well as its bad: it is satisfactory to find that we can do well with a single stove in each compartment instead of the two that were originally fitted, and the flat stove itself, with its broad grate and transparent talc windows not only forms a very cheerful object, but affords an

excellent toasting surface, and as we gather round it before our
cheerful midday tea we are not inclined to quarrel with its shape.

'It is laid down by Parry, I think, that no artificial ventilation is
necessary in a ship wintering in polar regions, as the difference in
temperature without and within is sufficient to cause a speedy
interchange of air through the cracks or on the opening of doors.
Such a dictum would hold at a time when it was exceedingly
difficult to make a ship tight, and no doubt it would hold also in
the present condition of the *Discovery*; but if our decks had been
thoroughly caulked some form of air inlet would have been
necessary, and an ideal living-space for polar regions should
certainly possess a ventilating system capable of regulation and an
entire freedom from casual draughts. An efficient ventilating
system, however, is a difficult thing to provide in a ship at the best
of times, and under polar conditions there are many circumstances which tend to increase the difficulty.'

As ventilation must always be a subject of serious consideration
to polar explorers, it may be of interest to describe the somewhat
ingenious system which was fitted in the *Discovery*, and to point
out in what respects it failed.

The idea was that fresh air entering should pass into a chamber
and there become warmed by a small stove before entering the
compartment; the vitiated air was to be drawn up through the
exhaust which surrounded the funnel of the ordinary heating
stove, the heat of the funnel being expected to cause an up-
draught. Of course, in addition to the air passing out at the exhaust
under this system, a large volume of air would have to enter to
supply the combustion of the stoves, but as long as there was an
up-draught through the exhaust the heated vitiated air in the
upper part of the compartment would be drawn off. When we
found that we obtained sufficient heat from the ordinary stove
alone, much of the theoretical benefit of this scheme vanished.
With changes of wind we had often to contend with practical
difficulties, and there were times when the system was the object
of universal contumely.

The question of fresh air and ventilation was one which afforded
us a constant field for argument, and even our medical officers
were divided in opinion, one making a bold stand for equable
warmth, whilst the other contended that at all costs the purity of

the air we breathed should be assured. In consequence of this, the community was divided into two camps, for and against the opening of the skylights; and as the members of each camp were desirous of arranging matters to suit themselves, the skylights were constantly flying up and down until a compromise was effected. It was decided that the skylight and the door of the companion should be opened every morning at 7.30, and not closed until the air in the compartment was thoroughly renewed, and that after that hour it should only be opened by general consent, and should the temperature rise above 60°.

'June 23. – We kept our mid-winter festival today, as yesterday was Sunday, and the ship has been *en fête*. The mess–deck was gaily decorated with designs in coloured papers and festooned with chains and ropes of the same material, the tables were loaded with plum puddings, mince pies, and cakes, mostly of home manufacture, but none the less "Christmasy" in appearance. It seems that there has been quite a rivalry amongst the messes with respect to their adornment, and the results which have been achieved with little more than brightly coloured papers, a pair of scissors, and a paste pot are really quite astonishing. On each table stands some grotesque figure or fanciful erection of ice, cunningly lighted up with candles from within and sending forth shafts of sparkling light.

'At 12.30, when all was ready, I went round in procession with the officers, exchanging greetings for the season and accumulating sweetmeats, cakes, and such dainties, offered by each mess as a tribute of good will, and incidentally an evidence that we possess no inconsiderable amount of confectionery talent. Next came the unpacking of a large box of presents provided by the kindly thought of Mrs Royds, the mother of our first lieutenant, and the distribution of these and other Christmas gifts sent by friends in the Old Country to gladden our winter season. Everyone was remembered, and with all in high spirits the distribution occupied the time with jest and laughter, until we left the men to enjoy their Christmas fare with an extra tot of grog.

'At six we had our dinner in the wardroom, with the table decorated and the display of all our plate. Starting with turtle soup, we passed on to a generous helping of mutton, and from that to plum pudding, mince pies, and jellies, all washed down with an excellent dry champagne. With a largely assorted dessert of crystal-lised fruits, almonds and raisins, nuts, &c., came the port and liqueurs, which brought us into good form for the enthusiastic speeches that followed. With such a dinner we agreed that life in the Antarctic Regions was worth living, and those who didn't make speeches felt that they must sing; and starting with "For he's a jolly good fellow", twice repeated, the evening continued with a regular "sing-song", when everyone, regardless of talent, had to contribute something for the common entertainment. One could not help wondering what would have been the feelings of those sympathetic friends who imagined the polar night to be filled with gruesome horror, had they been permitted a glimpse of this scene of revelry.

'In the early hours we went out to cool our heated brows. It was calm and clear, and the full moon, high in the heavens, flooded the snow with its white, pure light; overhead a myriad stars irradiated the heavens, whilst the pale shafts of the aurora australis grew and waned in the southern sky. It was sacrilege to disturb a scene of such placid beauty, but for man it was a night of frolic, and as the dogs quickly caught the infection, the silence was soon broken by a chorus of shouts and barking which was continued long after the bare ears and fingers should have warned their possessors that the temperature was nearly into the minus thirties. Eventually even exuberance of spirit was forced to give way to rapidly growing frostbites, and we retired within to contemplate, rather sadly, our extremities swelling as they thawed. Clearly under no conditions can one play tricks with our climate.

'We are half-way through our long winter. The sun is circling at its lowest; each day will bring it nearer our horizon. The night is at its blackest; each day will lengthen the pale noon twilight. Until now the black shadow has been descending on us; after this, day by day, it will rise until the great orb looms above our northern horizon to guide our footsteps over the great trackless wastes of snow. If the lighthearted scenes of today can end the first period of our captivity, what room for doubt is there that we shall triumph-antly weather the whole term with the same general happiness and contentment?'

CHAPTER 9

Winter passing away

> Here Winter holds his unrejoicing court,
> And through his airy hall, the loud misrule
> Of driving tempests is for ever heard. – THOMSON

>   Morn
> Dawns on this mournful scene, the sulphurous smoke
> Before the icy wind slow rolls away,
> And the bright beams of frosty morning dance
> Along the spangling snow. – SHELLEY

'July 18. – . . . The moon has greatly favoured us this winter by achieving its full dimensions during its monthly stay above our horizon; or, in other words, the full moon has approximated with its most southerly declination. The clear outline of the hills, the cold blue of the sky crowded with brilliant stars, and the luminous sparkle of the snow make our moonlit days more beautiful than can be easily imagined. I have just returned from a walk around the settlement, when the moon to the south was yellowed by the mysterious noon twilight and the northern sky was a flame of crimson. One dresses with care even on these calm days, knowing that the thermometer stands low and that there will be a keen bite in the lightest flickering puffs of air. Well protected, therefore, one closes the wardroom door on the bright yellow light and comfortable warmth within, and climbs the steep ladder to the entrance porch. These porches, with their double doors and insulated sides, are eminently satisfactory, and although they are thickly crusted with ice inside, and have occasionally to be chipped out, they save us from the keenest draughts and give space in which the snow of the outer world can be shaken off by those who enter. On arriving on deck one treads carefully over its soft snow covering, for here, beneath the winter awning, the gloom is deep, obstacles are numerous, and although fur boots may be an excellent protection against the cold, they are but a poor one against the sharp corner of a hatchway or the business end of a pick-axe; and indeed one is lucky if one reaches the flap-door of the awning without coming into violent collision with some obstacle, and feeling tempted to use equally violent language concerning the person or persons unknown who have unwittingly prepared the trap. From the ship's starboard or inshore side a gangway of stout poles and planks slopes to a snow platform, and is fitted with battens and guard rails, from the ends of which one guide rope supported on poles leads sharply to the right towards the meteorological screen, whilst the other shows the way to a cutting on the ice-foot, whence an easy path leads to the rocky patches on which stand our little group of huts. The main hut is of most imposing dimensions and would accommodate a very large party, but on account of its size and the necessity of economising coal it is very difficult to keep a working temperature inside; consequently it has not been available for some of the purposes for which we had hoped to use it. One of the most important of these was the drying of clothes; for a long time the interior was hung with undergarments which had been washed on board, but all these water-sodden articles became sheets of ice, which only dried as the ice slowly evaporated. When it was found that this process took a fortnight or three weeks the idea was abandoned, and the drying of clothes is now done in the living-spaces on board. A drying-room would be an excellent thing to have on a polar expedition, and had the space under our forecastle been properly insulated and fitted with a stove it might well have served the purpose. As it is, with the present system, the dampness of the living-spaces must be increased, though, curiously enough, we do not notice it. We have erected long clothes-lines on each side of the wardroom, which carry a full exposé of our clothing economy, but whatever is ludicrous in this Arcadian simplicity, whatever is incongruous with the more artistic background, we have long ceased to notice. We find that we can eat our dinner with the usual regard to the forms of social politeness even when seated beneath our socks and nether garments.

'But although the hut has not fulfilled expectation in this respect, it is in constant use for other purposes. After the sledging it came in handy for drying the furs, tents, &c.; then it was devoted to the skinning of birds for a month or more, a canvas screen being placed close around the stove, whereby a reasonable temperature was maintained in a small space; then various sailorising jobs, such as the refitting of the awnings and the making of sword matting, were carried on in it; and finally it has been used both for the rehearsal and performance of such entertainments as have served to lighten the monotony of our routine, and in this capacity, when fitted with a stage and decked with scenery, footlights, &c., it probably forms the most pretentious theatre that has ever been seen in polar regions. Of late a solid pedestal of firebricks has been built in the small compartment and on this Bernacchi will shortly be swinging his pendulums for gravity observations; while in the spring I hope that we may be able to use the larger compartment as a centre for collecting, weighing, and distributing the food and equipment of the various sledge parties.

'On the whole, therefore, our large hut has been and will be of use to us, but its uses are never likely to be of such importance as to render it indispensable, nor cause it to be said that circumstances have justified the outlay made on it or the expenditure of space and trouble in bringing it to its final home. It is here now, however, and here it will stand for many a long year with such supplies as will afford the necessaries of life to any less fortunate party who may follow in our footsteps and be forced to search for food and shelter.

'Beyond the large hut stand the smaller magnetic huts, and from the eminence on that point the little cluster of buildings looks quite imposing. In the midst of these vast ice-solitudes and under the frowning desolation of the hills, the ship, the huts, the busy figures passing to and fro, and the various other evidences of human activity are extraordinarily impressive. How strange it all seems! For countless ages the great sombre mountains about us have loomed through the gloomy polar night with never an eye to mark their grandeur, and for countless ages the windswept snow has drifted over these great deserts with never a footprint to break its white surface; for one brief moment the eternal solitude is broken by a hive of human insects; for one brief moment they settle, eat, sleep, trample, and gaze, then they must be gone, and all must be surrendered again to the desolation of the ages.'

'July 19..– ... One of the most important considerations for our comfort during the polar night is the manner of lighting the ship. The breakdown of the windmill was a blow, as a supply of electric light would have been the greatest boon; but, luckily, we never over-estimated the possibility of success in this respect, and the breakdown found us amply supplied with alternative means. From the first, paraffin suggested itself as the most suitable illuminant for our purpose, and from the first also it had been decided to use this oil as fuel during our sledge journeys. On the other hand, paraffin is not a desirable oil to carry in a ship in any quantity, and in our case it was rendered less desirable by the fact that we had to take it at a low flash-point in order that it might remain liquid at the lowest temperatures. The flash-point of our oil is 105°, it begins to turn milky when the thermometer falls below −40°, and we have not yet experienced a temperature in which it will not flow freely.

'We decided in London that the best position to carry the large quantity which we required was on the upper deck, and consequently we had a number of tanks of considerable capacity constructed to fit into odd spaces where they would be least likely to obstruct the working of the ship. In this manner we managed to find room for over 1,500 gallons, which is now served out under the care of the engine-room department.

'Our luckiest find was perhaps the right sort of lamp in which to burn this oil. Fortunately an old Arctic explorer, Captain Egerton, presented me with a patent lamp in which the draught is produced by a fan worked by clockwork mechanism, and no chimney is needed. One could imagine the great mortality there would be in chimneys if we were obliged to employ them, so that when, on trial, this lamp was found to give an excellent light, others of the same sort were purchased, and we now use them exclusively in all parts of the ship with extremely satisfactory results. We also have on board a goodly number of candles, which are served out as occasion requires; but over both oil and candles it is necessary to keep a very tight hold, as people are inclined to be extraordinarily wasteful.

'The necessity of heating the magnetic huts was not included in our estimate, and is therefore an unexpected drain on our resources; but apart from this our expenditure of both oil and candles is a great deal too large at present, and everyone has been warned that in case of a second winter the allowance will be largely curtailed. Although I realise that we are going too strong in this respect, I have not the heart to cut things down at present; the probability is we shall only do one winter; why not let it be as comfortable as possible? It is in the nature of a gamble, but if the worst comes to the worst, we can always fall back on blubber.'

It was perhaps a fortunate oversight that in the general comfort of our situation with regard to light we gave no thought to the adaptation of a still brighter illuminant which lay within our reach in the shape of acetylene. For when it became evident that we should have to spend a second winter in the same spot and there was no guarantee that this might not be prolonged to a third or even a fourth, the question of lighting the ship became a much more serious problem, and our thoughts flew at once to the calcium carbide which had been provided for the hut and which we had not previously thought of using. Once brought into working order, this illuminant proved to be the most delightful and the most easily worked that it would be possible to imagine. All that was necessary was to arrange a system of piping which led to the entrance porch; here the generator which regulated the mixture of the carbide with water, and so the production of gas, was placed, and here it continued to work in spite of the temperature, as the chemical action by which the gas was produced gave off sufficient heat to prevent the water from freezing on the coldest days. In this manner the darkness of our second winter was relieved by a light of such brilliancy that all could pursue their occupations by the single burner placed in each compartment. I lay great stress on this, because I am confident that this is in every way the best illuminant that can be taken for a polar winter, and no future expedition should fail to supply themselves with it. The single drawback is the danger of carrying the carbide on shipboard. It must of necessity be kept in a dry place, but the danger can be greatly diminished by careful packing, and there is no reason why the sealed tins containing it should not be stowed in boxes, which are likewise made watertight, and so assurance be made doubly sure.

I may mention that our stock of candles had also to be carefully considered in the second winter, and we thought it good policy to exaggerate our destitution to encourage greater care. As the result of a limited allowance it was possible to see widely different methods of consumption, and each person preserved with care a box in which he kept the grease which had guttered over from his own candles or from any others that he could lay his hands on. As soon as sufficient was collected he would set about casting fresh candles, and so eke out his own scanty supply; later it was found that by mixing this surplus grease with blubber still greater economy could be achieved, and in the end comparatively firm candles were made containing two parts of blubber to one of the original composition. Such are the teachings of adversity!

'The subjects of illumination and paraffin lead me naturally enough to consider the question of fire, which at first gave me some anxiety, and the adequacy of our pumps to meet this important contingency. During the summer cruise the ship continued to leak, the main hold slightly, the fore peak rapidly; this leakage continued for some time after we were frozen in, but gradually, as the ice thickened around the ship, it diminished until finally it practically ceased. But our experience with the pumps in relieving the leak was sufficient to show their defects. Whilst the temperature was high they acted well, but when it fell they froze solid immediately after use, and to be brought into action again they had to be opened up and thawed out with a blow-lamp, a task which occupied from twenty minutes to half-an-hour. Obviously it would be futile to rely on such pumps for coping with a fire during the winter, and I could see no possible object in keeping open a firehole in the ice on the vain supposition that we should then have water at our disposal. Consequently, I had to consider the possibility of fighting a fire without water. Some reflection showed me that with a few precautions the risk of fire would be reduced to a minimum, and that if in spite of these it should break out, the strong probability was that it would be discovered at once.

'In the living-spaces safety lies in the fact that they are always occupied; with the additional safeguard of a box of earth it may be granted that a fire could not make any headway in these parts. On the rare occasions when people work in the holds or other parts there is always a responsible officer in charge, as well as the most stringent regulations with regard to lights. In the engine-room it would be very difficult to start a fire, and an officer goes round after working-hours to see that all is in order. Should fire occur despite such precautions our best means of coping with it would be to stifle it with fur and woollen clothing, of which there is always an abundance to hand. On the whole, one feels that there is much less risk of fire whilst the ship is steady than when she is knocking about at sea, but the grave consequences keep one always alive to the risk.'

'July 20. – . . . A southerly gale blew all yesterday and through the night, bringing quantities of snow, as in May; the temperature rose as high as +12°, and all the out-stations show a corresponding increase. The fore-end of the awning was split, the boats entirely covered, and the drifts about the ship again raised to a height of ten or twelve feet. The fine snow penetrated everywhere; it raised our deck layer several inches under the awning, crowded in through a small ventilation hole in the magnetic observatory, completely covering the instruments, and snowed-up the kennels, the occupants of which have had to be temporarily housed on board. More than once our efforts to light the stove filled the wardroom with thick smoke, until we were glad to fly on deck for fresh air, and subsequently to go fireless. Luckily, the high temperature made this no great inconvenience. Today the wind has gone back to the eastward, from which direction it sweeps along the loose snow with a rapidly falling temperature and a most comfortless outlook.'

'July 21. – . . . It was my "night on" last night. As I have said, we take it in turn to make all the two-hourly observations from 10 p.m. to 6 a.m. Each of us has his own way of passing the long, silent hours. My own custom is to devote some of it to laundry-work, and I must confess I make a very poor fist of it. However, with a bath full of hot water I commence pretty regularly after the ten o'clock observation, and labour away until my back aches. There is little difficulty with the handkerchiefs, socks, and such-like articles, but when it comes to thick woollen vests and pyjamas, I feel ready to own my incapacity; one always seems to be soaping and rubbing at the same place, and one is forced to wonder at the area of stuff which it takes to cover a comparatively small body. My work is never finished by midnight, but I generally pretend that it is, and after taking the observations for that hour, return to wring everything out. I am astonished to find that even this is no light task: as one wrings out one end the water seems to fly to the other; then I hang some heavy garment on a hook and wring until I can wring no more; but even so, after it has been hung for a few minutes on the wardroom clothes-line, it will begin to drip merrily on the floor, and I have to tackle it afresh. I shall always have a high respect for laundry-work in future, but I do not think it can often have to cope with such thick garments as we wear.

'Washing over, one can devote oneself to pleasanter occupations. The night watchman is always allowed a box of sardines, which are scarce enough to be a great luxury, and is provided with tea or cocoa and a spirit-lamp. Everyone has his own ideas as to how sardines should be prepared, and of course puts tl em into practice when his turn of night duty comes, but the ma,ority like them cooked in some form, so that nearly every night the sizzling of the frying-pan can be heard in the early hours and the odour of cooking is wafted into the adjacent cabins. I scarcely like to record that there is a small company of gourmets who actually wake one another up in order that the night watchman may present his fellow epicures with a small finger of buttered toast on which are poised two sardines "done to a turn". The awakened sleeper devours the dainty morsel, grunts his satisfaction, and goes placidly off into dreamland again.

'I find that after my labours at the wash-tub and the pleasing supper that follows, I can safely stretch myself out in a chair without fear of being overcome by sleep, and so, with the ever-soothing pipe and one's latest demand on the library bookshelves, one settles down in great peace and contentment whilst keeping an eye on the flying hours, ready to sally forth into the outer darkness at the appointed time. The pleasure or pain of that periodic journey is of course entirely dependent on the weather. On a fine night it may be quite a pleasure, but when, as is more common, the wind is sweeping past the ship, the observer is often subjected to exasperating difficulties, and to conditions when his conscience must be at variance with his inclination. Sometimes the lantern will go out at the screen, and he is forced to return on board to light it; sometimes it will refuse to shine on the thin threads of mercury of the thermometer until it is obvious that his proximity has affected the reading, and he is forced to stand off until it has again fallen to the air temperature. He will climb to the indicator of the Robinson anemometer, and find it so difficult to see that the glass has frosted over before he has accomplished the reading, and he is obliged to scrape away the film of ice that covers it with his bare hand. Occasionally he has to cherish water with tender care against its freezing until he can re-wet the wet-bulb thermometer; and, again, he may have to remain stationary with upturned face for several minutes to determine the direction of motion of some elusive upper cloud. All these and many other difficulties in taking observations which may be in themselves valueless are met in the right spirit. I think we all appreciate that they are part of a greater whole whose value must stand or fall by attention to detail.'

'July 24. – . . . "Pipe, money, baccy, matches." I have forgotten the origin of this formula, but it is one which I have used for many years to remind myself of the indispensable contents of my pockets for a run on shore. I thought of it as I went out today, and, wondering what formula would replace it under present conditions, decided that there was none, as one has no requirement out of doors here but suitable apparel. Few, if any, smoke outside – in fact, it would be an impossible performance when the wind is blowing; and as for money, I look with mixed feelings at a sovereign which is gradually growing tarnished in the drawer of my desk; few coins have had such a restful time as this sovereign – and for the matter of that, few persons such a restful time as its owner – but I expect for neither of us will there be much repose when we get back to civilisation. Meanwhile it is rather fascinating to consider the moneyless condition in which we live. With absence of wealth, community of interest, and a free sharing of comforts and hardships, we must realise much that is socialistically ideal, yet in recognition of rank and supremacy of command the government must be considered an autocracy; and, indeed, just at present I can the more fully realise my position as autocrat when I see how eagerly everyone is awaiting the sledging programme which is to foreshadow their lives for the coming season.

'Although no-one smokes out of doors, many smoke within, and a few, amongst whom I must number myself, are inveterate victims of the habit. And yet, speaking generally, the consumption of tobacco is not so great as might be expected in the circumstances. Of eleven officers in the wardroom three are pretty constant smokers, four indulge moderately, and four are practically non-smokers. The first three may possibly consume about 1½ lb. each month, the moderate men may account for something over ½ lb. apiece, whilst the amount used by the remainder is practically negligible, so that the whole consumption for the eleven officers does not exceed 6 or 7 lbs. per month, at which rate our stock will last for many a year. On the mess-deck also there are a few who do not smoke at all, and many who are extremely moderate. The allowance is 1 lb. per month, and there has never been any request for an increase. No doubt the moderate smokers help those who are more addicted to the habit, but I should doubt whether any consume much more than their allowance, though from force of habit they prefer a very much stronger tobacco than that smoked aft, and in readiness for this preference we shipped a quantity of tobacco in the leaf which has proved very popular; the men like rolling it up for themselves in the good old naval fashion. There is now little or no restriction as to time or place of smoking, and apart from the sympathy that I should naturally have with freedom in this respect as a great smoker myself, I cannot see that anything would be gained by limiting the practice as long as there is no-one who is inconvenienced by it – and, luckily, we are in the happy position of possessing non-smokers who have not the least objection to sitting amongst many pipes.

'There is another habit indulged in by a few of the men which I thought had almost universally died out of fashion – namely, that of chewing. The objection to this, in my mind, is that it is carried on during the outdoor work, and it will, therefore, be a temptation for them to continue it during the sledging, and I feel sure that such a habit will detract from their marching powers. I have said nothing at present, but I propose that both smoking and chewing shall be forbidden on the march, and though a small allowance of tobacco will be permitted for smoking in camp, I hope to discourage chewing altogether.'

'July 25. – . . . The fourth number of our excellent monthly publication, the *South Polar Times*, has recently appeared, and maintains the same excellence as former issues. The scheme for this publication was discussed long before the sun left us, and by general consent Shackleton was appointed editor. It was decided that each number should contain, besides the editorial, a summary of the events and meteorological conditions of the past month, certain scientifically instructive articles dealing with our work and our surroundings, and certain others written in a lighter vein. As the scheme developed it was found that other features, such as full-page caricatures, acrostics, and puzzles, could be added; and now each month sees the production of a stout volume which is read with much interest and amusement by everyone. One of the pleasantest points with regard to it is that the men contribute as well as the officers; in fact, some of the best and quite the most amusing articles are written by the occupants of the mess-deck, of whom one or two show extraordinary ability with the pen. But beyond all else the journal owes its excellence to the principal artist, Wilson, who carries out the greater part of the illustration and produces drawings whose charm would be appreciated anywhere.

'Once or twice lately we have discussed the possibility of these volumes being interesting to a larger public, though there was no such idea in anyone's mind at the start. It is certain, however, that the journal is more ambitious in intention, and far more effective in its realisation, than any of its predecessors of the North Polar regions. On the one hand, we have some reading matter and many delightful sketches that would be appreciated by all; on the other, it has to be remembered that the humour and many of the references are local and would convey little or nothing to the uninformed reader, however much they may appeal to us "who are in the know". It is obvious that we cannot decide this matter for ourselves, but must take the opinion of outsiders more capable of judging.

'Before the appearance of the first number of the "S. P. T.", which came out with the departure of the sun, the editor had to face a rather delicate situation: it was announced that contributions need not be signed, but must be dropped into the editor's box by a certain date. When the date arrived it was found that the novelty of the venture had aroused such widespread interest that the box was crammed with manuscripts, and though there was not much difficulty in making a selection, there was some danger of wounding the feelings of those literary aspirants whose contributions were rejected. In this dilemma the editor decided to issue a supplementary journal, to be named the *Blizzard*, and one number

of this redoubtable publication was produced, but fell so lament-
ably short of the "S. P. T." that the contributors realised that their
mission in life did not lie in the paths of literary composition, and
thereafter the editor's box contained only what that astute individual required for the original periodical.

'The anonymity of articles could not long be observed in such a
small community, and after the appearance of the first numbers the
style of different individuals was more or less easily recognised; but
even the later numbers have contained some articles concerning
the authorship of which there has been much erratic guessing. In
mentioning the *Blizzard* I ought to remark that it has redeeming
features in some capital line caricatures and a distinctly humorous
frontispiece by Barne.'

'July 26. – . . . On the whole, the displays of the aurora australis
have been disappointing; we had expected them to be more
brilliant. When the sky is clear there is generally some auroral light,
but it is rarely vivid, and never bright enough to be photographed.
In hopes of obtaining the spectrum of this light, a rapid plate has
been exposed to it for hours, and even days together, but as yet
there has not been the least impression on it. In general the light is
so faint that stars of even a small magnitude can be seen distinctly
through it; but of late there has been an improvement, and the
contrast on the dark nights has given us a very beautiful, if not a very
brilliant, effect to the southward. Lately it has commenced about
three by a bright but low curtain to the E.N.E., where unfortunately the hills partly hide the view; but later it seems to spread up
and towards the south, so that usually in the evening there are shafts
and patches of light scattered about in full view of the ship with
sometimes a well-formed corona to the south.

'Often when the weather has been calm and clear I have been up
and over the hills in the afternoon to see the easterly display. There
is something very weird and awe-inspiring in a phenomenon so
fleeting, so intangible and so difficult to describe. The light grows
and wanes, but one cannot mark the moment of its coming or its
going. It distinctly moves, but one cannot say how; sometimes it
appears to roll forward or to the side, sometimes it seems to spread
itself as though anxious for greater space. For no two instants is it
the same, and yet the change is so subtle that one cannot grasp it
until some new development has robbed one of the picture.

'As I arrived on the hill summit today the sky was clear and dark, but as I walked forward a narrow arched band of light appeared across the east; it seemed to rise, to halt. Little fibrous shafts spread out above and below; a moment more, and the fibres became luminous cloud masses rolling towards the south; in the next they had ceased to move; the light was spreading and waning, was gone. Then shafts of light flashed up like mighty search-light beams cast to the zenith; but before I could well note them, they were bent in fantastic convolutions, some curling to spiral columns. In a few moments all this had come and gone, and the broad clean arch of a corona seemed to be rushing towards me from the south. As it rose, a second arch flashed up beneath; then, as though some giant hand had swept across the skies, the whole scene was changed, and only some vague luminous patches remained.

'It appears to me that the sharpest contrasts are formed by the vertical shafts, or at the lower edge of the arches where the light is brightest and is clearly outlined against the vaulted blue of the sky; elsewhere the light merges indefinitely into shade.

'Since the phenomenon of the aurora has been reproduced artificially, its study has advanced to a stage rather beyond the comprehension of the ordinary man, and after the countless observations which have been made in the North it does not seem likely that our observations or any observations of the actual phenomenon itself can add greatly to our knowledge; but considering that the luminosity of the aurora must be an electrical effect closely connected with the magnetism of the earth, it may be of some interest that in our observation it always appears to the south-east or away from the magnetic pole. The auroral light is usually a pure white, but we have observed it with a distinct green tinge, and on rare occasions with a reddish shade. Last night there were large patches of light in the zenith, and, what is also rare, several shafts in the west.'

'July 28. – . . . The latest southerly gale has awakened us to a most unpleasant fact, though at present it is impossible to gauge the exact extent of our difficulty. The question of the moment is, What has become of our boats? Early in the winter they were hoisted out to give more room for the awning, and were placed in a line about 100 yards from the ice-foot on the sea-ice. The earliest gale drifted them up nearly gunwale high, and thus for two months they remained in sight whilst we congratulated ourselves on their security. The last gale brought more snow, and, piling it in drifts at various places in the bay, chose to be specially generous with it in the neighbourhood of our boats, so that afterwards they were found to be buried three or four feet beneath the new surface. Although we had noted with interest the manner in which the extra weight of snow in other places was pressing down the surface of the original ice, and were even taking measurements of the effects thus produced, we remained fatuously blind to the risks our boats ran under such conditions. It was from no feeling of anxiety, but rather to provide occupation, that I directed that the snow on top of them should be removed, and it was not until we had dug down to the first boat that the true state of affairs dawned on us. She was found lying in a mass of slushy ice, with which also she was nearly filled. For the moment we had a wild hope that she could be pulled up, but by the time we could rig shears the air temperature had converted the slush into hardened ice, and she was found to be stuck fast. At present there is no hope of recovering any of the boats: as fast as one could dig out the sodden ice, more sea-water would flow in and freeze. The only hope is to prevent bad going to worse before the summer brings more hopeful conditions. The danger is that fresh gales bringing more snow will sink them so far beneath the surface that we shall be unable to recover them at all. Stuck solid in the floe they must go down with it, and every effort must be devoted to preventing the floe from sinking. At present all hands are removing the snow on top of the boats and for a distance of ten yards around, and are forming a snow-wall on the outskirts of this area. It is a long job, and will probably have to be repeated after every gale. Meanwhile our stupidity has landed us in a pretty bad hole, for we may have to leave this spot without a single boat in the ship.'

From this time we had a hard fight for our boats. Day after day parties were digging away at their snow covering, and in the course of months many tons must have been removed. After each gale our hearts sank, as to all appearance we were forced to begin all over again; but we knew that, although there was so little to show for our labours, our work must tell in the long run, and that in it lay the only hope of keeping the boats within our grasp until the climate should be more favourable. So, however deeply the snow fell after each new southerly blow, the work was renewed with vigour, and we bowed to the inevitable whilst we heartily cursed the folly which had landed us in such a predicament. It was not until December, five months later, that Mr Royds and our excellent boatswain were able to attack the question of release with any chance of success, and it was in this month that, after much sawing and blasting, the boats were finally liberated, though by no means without injury.

'August 1. – There can be few scenes more beautiful than that which is about us on a calm moonlight night. During the noon hours the silver rays are lost, and the moon itself is changed to a deep orange yellow in the diffused twilight cast by the gleaming crimson band to the north; but as the red glow slowly travels around and is lost behind the western hills, our white world is left alone with the moon and the stars. The cold, white light falls on the colder, whiter snow against which the dark rock and intricate outline of the ship stand out in blackest contrast. Each sharp peak and every object about us casts a deep shadow, and is clearly outlined against the sky, but beyond our immediate surroundings is fairyland. The eye travels on and on over the gleaming plain till it meets the misty white horizon, and above and beyond, the soft, silvery outlines of the mountains. Did one not know them of old, it would sometimes be difficult to think them real, so deep a spell of enchantment seems to rest on the scene. And indeed it is not a spell that rests on man alone, for it is on such nights that the dogs lift up their voices and join in a chant which disturbs the most restful sleepers.

'What lingering instinct of bygone ages can impel them to this extraordinary custom is beyond guessing; but on these calm, clear moonlit nights, when all are coiled down placidly sleeping, one will suddenly raise his head and from the depths of his throat send forth a prolonged, dismal wail, utterly unlike any sound he can produce on ordinary occasions. As the note dies away another animal takes it up, and then another and another, until the hills re-echo with the same unutterably dreary plaint. There is no undue haste and no snapping or snarling, which makes it very evident that this is a solemn function, some sacred rite which must be performed in these circumstances. If one is sentimentally inclined, as may be forgiven on such a night, this chorus almost seems to possess the woes of the ages; as an accompaniment to the vast desolation without, it touches the lowest depths of sadness.

'But if one is not sentimentally inclined, and rather bent on refreshing sleep, it possesses so little charm that one endeavours to correct matters by shouts and pieces of ice. As a rule the animals are so absorbed in their occupation and so lost to their surroundings that even these monitions have no power to disturb them, and one has at length to bribe them basely with a biscuit or a piece of seal-meat.

'Generally in calm, bright weather, the temperature is low, and tonight, when the thermometer stood below −40°, we observed a curious fact which I do not remember to have seen mentioned before. If one is standing still and bareheaded, and exhales a deep breath, one can actually hear one's breath freezing a moment or two after it has left the mouth. What one hears I do not precisely know, unless the actual formation of ice-crystals produces a sound, as appears to be the case. The sound itself is not easy to describe; it is rather like that produced by the movement of sand on a beach when a wave washes up. Koettlitz says it is like the minutest crepitations, and though few of us knew what the word meant till we consulted the dictionary, we have adopted his description.

'A curious effect of the cold snaps is a mist which arises off the land, very thin and very white, and in the silvery moonlight beautiful beyond description. It spreads like the finest gauze-web over the sharp outlines of the near hills; the white snow-slopes and dark shadows of the rocks are softened in its shimmering folds, and seem to rest on the lightest foundations of silvery cloud.'

'August 4. − . . . The driving snow has again enveloped everything. The boat clearance is covered. The only thing is to go on steadily digging away at it; but if the snowfall continues in the spring it will mean a lot of work. Still, by hook or by crook the boats must be kept above water. We now feel a great drawback in the scarcity of picks and shovels. It is wonderful what has been done already with the mere dozen which were supplied, considering that they have been in use every day and all day; but a good many are now hopelessly broken, and the remainder are not very efficient. We shall have to rely on the engine-room department once more, but although they can make shovels, I doubt if they will be able to cope with the picks for want of materials. The temperature since the gale has been extraordinarily high. Today it has been above zero, and light snow is falling. The daylight is coming on apace; at noon, when it is cloudless, the details of the land can be seen very clearly on all sides, and it is pleasant to be out when the snow is not driving.

'Bernacchi and Skelton are just completing a set of pendulum observations in the main hut, and last night when the gale was rising with blinding drift they had an adventure from which they were extremely lucky to escape unscathed. In the evening the hut was fully occupied, Bernacchi and Skelton being at work in the smaller compartment, whilst Royds was busily rehearsing his nigger minstrel troupe in the larger one; but shortly after the rehearsal began, either because it proved a somewhat disturbing element or because their work was finished, the two scientific workers left to return to the ship. It was fully an hour and a half after this that, the rehearsal being finished, Royds and his party, numbering more than a dozen, started back. They found that the gale had increased, and that in the whirling snow they could see nothing; but, being in such numbers, they were able to join hands and sweep along until they caught the guide rope leading to the gangway. As they travelled along it, they heard feeble shouts wafted on the storm, and again extending their line they swept on in a chain and suddenly fell on Bernacchi and Skelton, who, although they had left the hut an hour and a half before, had entirely lost their bearings and were reduced to shouting on the poor chance of being heard and rescued.

'Meanwhile on board the ship we had not the smallest suspicion that anything unusual had taken place, and remained in ignorance until the rescuers and the rescued burst in upon us; the latter were severely frostbitten about the face and also in the legs, as they had not been prepared for such a long stay in the open; and as they had not been provided with wind covering, their garments inside and out were thickly coated with ice and snow. As soon as we had revived them we learnt what little tale they had to tell.

'On leaving the hut they had started for the ship, steering through the blinding drift as best they could. After walking for some distance they came to the conclusion they must have missed her, and proceeded to grope their way back to the land. When they reached the tide crack they found some difficulty in deciding which way they should go, but finally they reached a spot which they recognised, and, calculating the position of the ship, they again made tracks for her, and again found that they had missed the mark. They then decided to try to search around in circles, and so the time passed whilst they wandered more or less aimlessly about until they became alarmed, and tried to attract attention by shouting. In the nick of time they were rescued within thirty yards of their goal, but without any knowledge of the fact.

'The hut is certainly not more than 200 yards from the ship, and the ship is not only a comparatively big object, but is surrounded by guide ropes and other objects which if encountered would have informed the wanderers of their position. These officers were neither of them likely to have lost their heads, and both might be trusted to take the most practical course in such a difficulty. In these circumstances the fact that they should have been lost for two hours would have been incredible had it not actually occurred. It is the most convincing lesson on the blinding, bewildering effect of a blizzard that we have had, and shows clearly what care will be necessary with our sledge parties if such weather continues in the spring. Throughout the greater part of the winter we have had a guide rope which continued as far as the hut, and had this been in order last night all trouble would have been avoided; but recently it has sagged between the poles and become buried beneath the snow, and it was not available, therefore, for parties leaving the hut.'

Throughout our stay in these regions I had constantly a lurking anxiety that disaster might attend the overbold habits of some of our officers in making long excursions from the ship, especially during the winter months. The trouble lay chiefly in the impossibility of predicting the weather conditions; the barometer told nothing, and such other signs of bad weather as came under our observation were so uncertain that it was impossible to legislate on them. Threats of a storm were so constantly unfulfilled that to have kept all hands within bounds on their account would have been irksome to individual feeling and discouraging to individual work. The only satisfactory course was to rely on the discretion of distant workers to hasten home directly the weather looked ugly, and to trust that the coming storm would not develop before they had reached a position of safety; but, needless to remark, this happy result was not always realised, and my diary throughout the two years records many hours of anxiety caused by the prolonged absence of some person, and some occasions on which search parties were rapidly organised to find such a belated worker. In the course of time this naturally became an easier task, as we all became better acquainted with the features of the tide crack and the various patches of rock and with their relative bearings. In course of time also our system of relief became better organised; and although we did not put it in practice, it may be well to record our final arrangement in this respect as a hint to those who may live under like conditions in the future. In outline our ultimate plan for searching was to spread out the search party in a very extended order, connecting them by a fine strong line, and so to sweep round the floe systematically until the object of our search was recovered.

Experiences of this sort taught us the valuable lesson of never leaving our sledges on our long sledge journeys except under the most favourable conditions. It can be imagined that one was often tempted to do this to get a better knowledge of some object which lay off the line of march, but when such a detour became necessary, wisdom suggested that the sledges should be taken as far as possible towards the object, even if the ground were rough; and although we often marched in threatening and stormy weather, it was always with our temporary home behind us.

The idea of requisitioning our large hut as a place of entertainment had occurred to us early in the winter, and in this connection it was first used for a concert given during the first week in May. Royds, who took much pains in getting up this function, arranged a long programme in order to bring forth all the available talent; but although we were not inclined to be critical of our amusements, one was fain to confess that our company had not been chosen for their musical attainments. However, there were exceptions to the mediocrity, and some exhibition of dramatic talent, which prompted the conception of a modified entertainment for a future occasion; so Barne was entrusted with the task of producing a play, and after much casting about succeeded in getting his company together. All became very diligent with rehearsals, and as these were conducted in the hut with all due secrecy, the audience remained in ignorance of even the name of the play until the night of its production. It was decided that this should be immediately after our mid-winter celebrations, and my diary for June 25 gives some account of this great night.

'At seven tonight we all journey across to the hut, forcing our way through a rather keen wind and light snowdrift. The theatre within looks bright and cheerful, but as there are no heating arrangements other than the lamps, one conquers the natural instinct to take off one's overcoat and head covering, and decides that it will be wise to retain these garments throughout the performance. On one side of the large compartment a fair-sized stage has been erected, raised some two feet above the floor; the edge is decorated with a goodly row of footlights, immediately behind which hangs a drop-curtain depicting the ship and Mount Erebus in glowing colours, and boldly informing one that this is the "Royal Terror Theatre". The remainder of the compartment forms an auditorium of ample size to accommodate all who are not performing, with a stray dog or two brought in to enliven the proceedings.

'In front stands a row of chairs for the officers, and behind several rows of benches for the men; the apartment is lighted by a large oil lamp, and when all are seated one must own to having seen theatricals under far less realistic conditions. When all are seated also, and when pipes are lit, there is a perceptible improvement in the temperature, a condition that one feels will be very welcome to the lightly clad actors.

'In due course programmes are passed round, informing us that Part I will consist of several songs rendered by popular singers, and that for Part II we shall have the *Ticket of Leave*, "a screaming comedy in one act". These programmes, I may remark, are correct at least in one respect, in that there is some difficulty in picking out the information from amongst the mass of advertisements. Presently the curtain rolls up and discloses Royds at the piano and the first singers in true concert attitude. We have a duet, followed by several solos, and occasionally a rousing chorus, when one rather fears that the roof of the Royal Terror Theatre will rise. On the whole the first part passes decorously, and we come to the interval, when the wags advertise oranges and nuts.

'Then we have Part II, which is what we are here for: the "screaming comedy" commences and proves to be fully up to its title. There is no need for the actors to speak – their appearance is

quite enough to secure the applause of the audience; and when the
representatives of the lady parts step on to the stage it is useless for
them to attempt speech for several minutes, the audience is so
hugely delighted. Thanks to Mr Clarkson and his make-up box,
the disguises are excellent, and it soon becomes evident that the
actors have regarded them as by far the most important part of the
proceedings, and hold the view that it is rather a waste of time to
learn a part when one has a good loud-voiced prompter. As the
play progresses one supposes there is a plot, but it is a little difficult
to unravel. Presently, however, we are obviously working up to a
situation; the hero, or perhaps I should say one of the heroes (for
each actor at least attacks his part with heroism), unexpectedly sees
through the window the lady on whom he has fixed his affections,
and whom, I gather, he has not seen for a long and weary time. He
is evidently a little uncertain as to her identity, and at this stirring
moment he sits very carefully on a chair – he almost dusts the seat
before he does so. Seated and barely glancing at the window, he
says with great deliberation and in the most matter-of-fact tones,
"It is – no, it isn't – yes, it is – it is my long-lost Mary Jane." The
sentiment – or the rendering of it – is greeted with shouts of
applause. Later on we work up to a climax, when it is evident that
the services of the police force will be required. This part is much
more to the taste of the players; somebody has to be chucked out;
both he and the "chuckers-out" determine to make their parts
quite realistic, and for several minutes there is practically a free
fight with imminent risk to the furniture. And so at last the curtain
falls amidst vociferous cheering, and I for one have to acknowledge that I have rarely been so gorgeously entertained. With
renewed cheers we break up and wander back to the ship, after
having witnessed what the "S. P. T." may veraciously describe as
"one of the most successful entertainments ever given within the
Polar Circle" – and indeed they might with some truth add "or
anywhere else".'

From the above it will be seen that our first essay at acting met
with very hearty approval, if it did not show us to be possessed
of great histrionic talent. We had always intended to call again on
our dramatic company, but owing to the work of several of its
members and other circumstances our plans slipped through; later
on, however, Royds undertook to organise a nigger minstrel

troupe, and towards the end of the winter succeeded in getting them together and in rehearsing their various parts through many a cold hour spent in the freezing theatre.

On August 6, the date fixed for this performance, we were in the midst of a cold snap, but although the temperature had fallen below −40°, it was decided that the programme should be carried out as intended.

'Tonight the doors of the Royal Terror Theatre opened at 7.30, and as the temperature was −40° and there was a strong wind, everybody did his best to make a record in reaching it. Even inside the temperature must have been well below zero; I wonder how the ordinary theatre-goer would appreciate sitting in stalls under such conditions.

'One was not sorry when the curtain rolled up and disclosed our twelve minstrels with blackened faces sitting in a row with "Massa Johnson" in the centre. A programme with an illustrated cover informed us that this was the "Dishcover Minstrel Troupe". There is no doubt the sailors dearly love to make up; on this occasion they had taken an infinity of trouble to prepare themselves; calicoes of all sorts had been cut up and sewn together to make suits of the most vivid colours and grotesque form; shirt fronts and enormous collars of elaborate design had been made from paper; wigs had been manufactured from tow, in some cases dipped in red ink, and an equal ingenuity had been displayed in producing the enormous boots and buttons which constitute an important part of the nigger minstrel's costume. "Bones" and "Skins" had even gone so far as to provide themselves with movable top-knots which could be worked at effective moments by pulling a string below.

'As everyone knows, a nigger minstrel performance consists of a number of songs and choruses, between which the ball of conversation is kept rolling amongst the various minstrels in the form of weighty conundrums, which, after numerous futile attempts from others, are usually answered by the propounder himself. I don't know why a joke should sound better in nigger language, but I rather think the class of joke made on these occasions does so.

'Tonight the choruses and plantation songs led by Royds were really well sung, and they repay him for the very great pains that he has taken in the rehearsals. Of course in the choruses of "Marching through Georgia", "Golden Slippers", "Suwanee River", and such songs, the audience felt that they must also "lend a hand", and did so with such a will that the rafters shook. The jokes were nearly all home-made and topical, but amused us none the less for that; everyone had some sly shaft of wit aimed at him, but all in the best of good humour, and so the merry jests went round until something had been said about the ship, the dogs, the windmill, the people, and every imaginable or unimaginable thing about us, and on the whole they afforded us a good deal of hearty laughter.

'I can remember but few of these jocular efforts; I recollect that the cook was likened to a cooper round a cask – because he was always going round "doing a tap". Another question which puzzled me for some time was, "Can you told me, Massa Bones, what am de best way to clear lower-deck in de Dishcubry?" Bones suggested that it was to turn on a southerly wind (when the stoves begin to smoke badly), but the correct answer was much truer: "You tak' an' open a tin of —'s Brussels sprouts." Another, and perhaps better, question was, "Can you told me what am de worst vegetable as we took from Englan'?" One naturally thought that some such answer as the above might have fitted here, but the proper reply was stated to be "The Dundee leak". When we got back to the ship after the performance we decided that in spite of the cold we had spent an extremely pleasant evening.'

'August 7. – The cold snap continues, and today is calm. Barne is far out with a small sledge and sounding machine; Shackleton and Hodgson still further, digging up a fish trap. Many others are scattered about in various directions, and all rejoicing in the absence of wind. The sky is clear overhead and the light fairly good, but to the north hangs a yellowish brown haze, now rather common. It seemed to grow colder as I went outwards over the floe, and a light wind persistently attacked my most vulnerable feature, my nostrils. I could feel them pricking and tingling on the road to frostbite, but as I was talking to Barne on my way back this feeling suddenly ceased, the air seemed to grow much warmer, and on going to the screen I found the temperature was −36°, whereas a short time before I had left it at −51½°. It was a striking example of the waves of temperature that occur in this comparatively calm, clear weather. Koettlitz, who has been to his thermometer off the cape, reports a minimum of −62° and a present temperature of −57.5°, which is probably the degree of cold in which Shackleton and Hodgson are now labouring to clear the latter's fish trap, a task in which they are consequently not much to be envied. The cold is pushing through the weak spots in our defences below, and makes itself known as usual by an increase of ice on the bulkheads and over the bolts, but we have not much difficulty in keeping the air in the wardroom up to 50°.'

'August 9. – Preparations for sledging are being pushed on apace; it is astonishing what a lot of time and attention it all takes.

'There is now a bright orange light to the northward at noon, and each day brings a nearer approach of the sun; in a week we shall have good light for several hours, and in a fortnight we shall be welcoming back the sun.

'The result of the snowless wind which we have had of late has been to harden and polish the surfaces of the floes and the hill slopes. I find it impossible to maintain footing on slopes which I could climb easily a fortnight ago. Seals have ceased to appear on the ice for a long time, but they are still about beneath it, and can be heard at the tide cracks and at their snow-covered breathing-holes; occasionally they come under the ship and give a prolonged whining snort, unlike any sound one can recall, but which can be distinctly heard within. In the early winter we were much puzzled by this noise, and many declared that it was caused by the ice, but we have since traced it without doubt to the seals.

'Many times lately we have heard mysterious noises on deck when the temperature is falling. Amidst the sharp crackling of the rigging which always accompanies this condition, there is occasionally a loud report like the fall of some heavy weight. In whatever cabin one may be, it seems to be immediately overhead. Again and again we have dashed on deck to discover the cause, but always without result. It is so uncanny that we now feel confident that it is the manifestation of our own particular ghost.'

'August 12. – Another blizzard, so thick that one cannot see one's hand before one's face. Two days ago we had almost cleared the snow from off the boats; now they will be completely covered again. No-one goes out on these occasions; the drifting snow has very much the effect of a sandblast – it positively pricks the skin and brings frostbites with alarming rapidity. Though it is now moderately light at noon, we could see nothing today but a whitening of the whirling cloud about us. The dogs, whose kennels were likely to be drifted up, were brought on board early in the storm; they are generally rather sad and subdued on such occasions, and can be safely huddled together without fear of a fight, always excepting the redoubtable "Nigger", who is given a corner to himself. With him action follows so quickly on thought, and is so immediately effective, that it is considered advisable to take no risks.'

'August 13. – ... Walked today round the cape to Pram Point; it is between three and four miles from the ship, and is a spot that has been visited by us often throughout the winter. A little beyond this point lies the limiting line up to which the sea-ice broke away in the autumn, and consequently on the farther side of this line lies ice of an unknown age whose surface gradually rises to the level of the barrier, whereas on the near side the ice is all of recent formation. The centre of interest lies in the ridges which have formed and are continuing to form in this region. The coastline beyond the point runs towards Erebus, only slightly curving, and fringed with steep ice-cliffs and crevassed slopes.

'The ridges in the ice are parallel to each other and to the coastline, and extend for a considerable distance along it. From the heights above they look like heavy, round-crested rollers of the sea that are preparing to fling themselves on the shore, so smooth and regular do their undulations appear, and so gradually are they lost in the plain beyond; and from the same heights also they have frequently been counted, and I think most of us have made their number to be seventeen. But amongst the ridges it is possible to see that their summits are cracked in an irregular fashion, and that they are by no means regular in height. This may well be accounted for by the varying amount of snow which has fallen in the hollows. Today I measured two of these ridges from crest to hollow, and found one to be 18 feet, whilst another nearer the shore was 14 feet. There can be little doubt that this formation is due to the ice-sheet pressing up from the south; and, large as the disturbance is, when the mighty nature of the cause is considered, it vanishes into insignificance.

'Whatever the cause may be, it is still active, for the freshly formed ice to the southward is gradually being waved up in the same fashion. The whole thing is puzzling, because one is at a loss to account for the absence of ridges further to the north, and because, if this is a measure of the movement of the great ice-sheet, that movement must be extremely small, as the whole extent of the pressing-up of the new sea-ice cannot be more than a collapse of twenty or thirty yards at the outside. In any case it will be an interesting thing to watch for further developments in this movement, and to see whether there is any difference in its rate in summer.'

What was at this time comparatively new sea-ice remained fast throughout the following winter, and we saw the ridges in it gradually rising in a slow, silent, uncanny fashion, until they presented a huge confusion of upreared ice-blocks.

'August 16. – . . . We have now three litters of puppies in various stages of development. "Vincka", Armitage's pet Samoyede, has four which were born a month ago and are now capable of snarling and snapping on their own account. "Blanco" produced five on the 11th. She has since succeeded in killing two, but the remainder of her family are just opening their eyes on this strange new world and rolling about their warm nest with shrill squeals. Today "Nell" has added seven to the puppy population; they look like seven little blind rats, but she guards them very jealously with ominous growls when anyone approaches. We shall probably reduce this last litter to four or five, and so remain the possessors of about a dozen in all.

'Each mother has her own comfortable nest under the shelter of the forecastle, and gets sufficient warmth from the straw and sacking which are plentifully distributed about it. "Vincka" takes her maternal duties very lightly, and spends the day in teasing her offspring, apparently under the impression that they exist to romp with her. But her pups don't see it in the same light: their small minds are seriously bent on exploration, and they become so annoyed at their mother's levity that they growl and snap at all her playful efforts, and occasionally fly into paroxysms of rage. "Blanco" is a lady possessed of much low cunning, which has made her very unpopular with the men. It was not expected that she would prove a good mother, and she certainly is not; her three small mites would find it hard to get a living without human assistance. But "Nell" promises to be in all respects a model parent. She has always possessed a very uncertain temper, and the responsibilities of a family have rendered her absolutely fierce.

One has to approach her nest with great caution and be extremely careful not to do anything that she may consider suspicious; but when she is assured that one's intentions are friendly, she will condescend to accept ministrations to her wants.

'We have had "Brownie", another of the dogs, under shelter for some time; he is a very handsome beast, with nice affectionate manners which make him rather a pet with all, so that when he was found shivering violently in the cold, pity was taken on him and he was brought under the forecastle. Careful observation, however, showed that he is really rather a rascal, and that he is in the habit of putting on his shivering fits when anyone appears in sight; he is evidently aware that if he is taken on board he will not only get a warmer nest, but certain tit-bits which his soul desires. So today we have hardened our hearts and put him out again.

'There is a world of character in these animals of ours. One of the greatest pities is that they cannot be made to follow or to obey a word of command unless they are in harness. They are great losers by it in missing many a walk. To lead them continually about on a string is very trying, as they pull hard the whole time, and it is odds that the dog rather than the man directs the course of the walk; at other times they will be particularly meek and ingratiating, trotting alongside and pressing their noses into one's mit, all in the most companionable spirit, until one rashly slips the leash, when in a moment they are off on their own devices, and are seen no more until a wild hubbub at the kennels signifies their return, and someone has to rush out to prevent a fight.

'The sport they most dearly love is to worry a seal. The hunting instinct is paramount; the most listless, weary, bored-looking dog or team of dogs has only to catch sight of the black dots afar off over the snow which signify the presence of seals, to become electrified into a state of wild excitement. If a person has a single animal on leash, the chances are that he is caught unprepared and the next moment finds himself without a dog or being dragged violently along on his stomach: if he is with a team harnessed to a heavy sledge, a load which a moment before appeared to be taking all heart out of the animals, becomes the merest bagatelle, and he is lucky if he has time to add his own weight and so prevent himself from being left behind.

'In the early part of the winter, when the seals came up frequently, loose dogs immediately made for their haunts, and the distant furious barking would soon tell what was going forward. We did our best to capture these stray animals and prevent the slaughter of the unfortunate seals, but of course we were not always successful, and more than one lifeless form was found to tell the tale of these ravages. In each case the wretched seal had been literally worried to death; there were no wounds on the body worth mentioning – in fact, the hide is far too thick and tough for a dog's teeth to penetrate. The fiends must have danced round their unfortunate victim, rushing in and snapping at him from every side and giving him not an instant's peace until life was extinct. The tormentors did not attempt, and in fact it is doubtful if they would have been able, to feed off their victim. Soon after he ceased to show sport they must have quietly trotted away in search of fresh excitement. The fact that they cannot get food in this manner is a distinct advantage, as it means that they are forced eventually to come back to the ship.'

Later on a rather curious incident occurred in this connection. A few days before the dog-team was required for a sledge trip to the south, the masters of two dogs – 'Birdie', a powerful, timid, nervous beast, and 'Snatcher', a lighter-built animal – took them for a walk on leash, and after a time somewhat stupidly let them run with their chains, thinking that thus handicapped they could be caught again without difficulty; but the animals, rejoicing in their freedom, soon disappeared from sight. Days went by and there was no sign of them, and finally, much to my annoyance, I had to start without them. On my return a fortnight later, I learnt that after a long absence 'Snatcher' had suddenly appeared, very worn out, thin, and hungry; and guessing seals were at the bottom of the trouble, a search party had gone some way along the coast to the north and eventually discovered 'Birdie' in a starving condition and pinned close down to the snow by his chain, which was solidly frozen beneath the body of a huge dead seal. The dogs must have worried the seal to death, and in the scrimmage the latter must have rolled over 'Birdie's' chain, holding him a fast prisoner; but it is curious that he lay there and starved within reach of plenty, and one wonders also how long the other animal voluntarily submitted to starvation rather than desert his companion. One never quite learns what are the rights of a story like this in real life.

'August 19. – From the hills today I was astonished to see that there was open water within nine or ten miles of us. It cuts round close to the islets in Erebus Bay, and sweeps in a curve across the strait; and although young ice is again forming, not a scrap of the old can be seen beyond this line. I do not think that a ship was ever frozen in in polar regions with the sea so constantly and completely clearing within view; and wholly ignorant as we were of these conditions on our arrival, it is certainly providential that we should have fallen on such a secure spot for our winter quarters. Except, perhaps, for New Harbour on the opposite side of the strait, I doubt if there is a place for many miles where we could have lain without being subject to appalling dangers and difficulties. During the gales our over-bold members have had difficulty in finding their way back to the ship over the solid firm floe: what would have been their case if these same gales had broken up the floe and swept it away to the north?

'Shackleton has invented a new sledge, or rather a vehicle to answer the same purpose, much to the amusement of his messmates, who scoff unmercifully. The manufacture of this strange machine has been kept the profoundest secret between the inventor and the maker, our excellent carpenter. It was to burst suddenly on our awestruck world, to carry immediate conviction as it trundled easily over the floe, to revolutionise all ideas of polar travelling, and once and for all to wipe the obsolete sledge from off the surface of the snow. An inventor in our community can make certain of receiving critical attention and outspoken advice, and in this case there was no reticence at all. Advice was most freely given, but it was generally to the effect that it would be kind to remove such an eyesore by immediate burial and oblivion. But the inventor refused to be drawn, and rolled his machine with difficulty, but with the light of enthusiasm still burning in his eye. It was the queerest sort of arrangement, consisting of two rum-barrels placed one in front of the other and acting as wheels to a framework on which the load was intended to be placed; the manner in which the whole machine wobbled as it was pushed forward on such ungainly rollers can be well imagined. This new toy continued to give pleasure to the inventor, and incidentally to many others, for some hours; and as I came in, Barne was assisting Shackleton to rig it with the dinghy's sails – I do not know with what success, but I can very well imagine.'

Of course this machine was very soon neglected and forgotten, but in justice to the inventor it ought to be added that there were times when the snow surface about us was so hard that it would have been quite possible to resort to wheeled traffic, and I am sure that for many purposes a very light cart with broad-tyred wheels would have been extremely useful. But I cannot conceive that a rum-cask would ever prove a desirable addition to a vehicle!

'August 21. – . . . The sun returns to us today, but, alas and alack! we could get no sight of it. A few hours of calm in the morning were succeeded by whirling snow-squalls from the south, and each lull was followed by a wild burst of wind. I was glad enough to have everyone on board under such unsettled conditions, and at noon when we had hoped to be far over the hills, we could see only vast sheets of gleaming snow.'

'August 22. – . . . An ideal day for our first view of the long-absent sun: the sky was gloriously clear, and in its vaulted arch the strong returning light of day hid all except the brightest stars, and these wore but a pale semblance of their winter aspect. The air was mild and the temperature ranging up to 5°, as, in high spirits, many of the officers started to mount the steep hill-slopes, determined to have a good look at our long-absent friend. I went myself to the top of Crater Hill, a thousand feet above the floe, to watch for the returning orb; at noon, when it was due north, it rested behind the long foot-slope of Erebus, but as it travelled westward its altitude decreased far less rapidly than that of the slope, and gradually the refracted glowing ellipse crept from behind that obstacle and stood clear, dazzling our unaccustomed sight with its brilliancy. For long our blinking eyes remained fixed on that golden ball and on the fiery track of its reflection; we seemed to bathe in that brilliant flood of light, and from its flashing rays to drink in new life, new strength, and new hope. This glorious sun was bringing the light of day and some measure of warmth to the bleak, desolate region about us, and heaven only knows how far prophetic thoughts took us over its trackless wastes before those beneficent rays should again vanish and sombre darkness once more descend. And so we gazed, saying little but thinking much, until the chill of the air reminded us that, however great the promise, summer itself was not yet upon us.

'With full daylight each detail of our landscape once more stands clear, and the view from Crater Hill is magnificent.

'From Arrival Bay a line of rocky ridges runs towards Castle Rock, facing the north-west and gradually rising in height, with four distinct eminences, of which two are well-formed craters; the fourth is almost on a level with Crater Hill, and therefore nearly touches the skyline; behind it Castle Rock, rising to 1,350 feet, shows in sharp precipitous outline, a black shadow against the snowy background of Erebus. It is a high, hilly country, this foreground, with many a black mass of rock and many a slope of smooth white snow; in itself it might be called a fine rugged scene, but how dwarfed it all is by that mighty mountain behind, which, in spite of its twenty geographical miles of distance, seems to frown down on us. Even Castle Rock, with its near bold eminence, is but a pigmy to this giant mass, which from its broad spreading foot-slopes rises, with fold on fold of snowy whiteness, to its crater summit, where, 13,000 feet above the sea, it is crowned with a golden cloud of rolling vapour.

'The eastern slope of Erebus dips to a high saddle-backed divide, beyond which the snowy outline rises to the summit of Terror, whence a long slope runs gradually down to sea-level far to the east. From point to point these two huge mountains fill up nearly 90° of our horizon, and from this southern side offer almost a complete prospect of snow-covered land. Beyond Castle Rock commences the low isthmus which connects our small peninsula to the main island, and as it bends slightly to the east it can be seen from Crater Hill. In running towards the right slope of Erebus and gradually broadening to its foot-slopes, it sweeps out on either side a huge bay.

'The eastern bay is filled with the perpetual level plain of the fast barrier-ice; scarce a vestige of bare rock is to be seen in the vast extent of its coastline, and it would appear that climatic conditions have rendered it a focus for snow, though an area little swept by wind; the mere view in this direction suggests the idea, and the experience of the Terror sledge party goes far to substantiate it.

'The western bay is cleared of ice in the summer; its northern limit is marked by a bare rocky cape, and in a few other spots on its coastline the bare rock stands boldly out. Three black volcanic islets stand well within its shelter, and it is to these that the open water has extended since the late gales. This open water is now again frozen over, but the dark colour of the young ice forms a strong contrast to the older snow-covered surface, and this darker shade stretches to the north-west beyond sight.

'Looking to the eastward from Crater Hill, one has Pram Point almost beneath one's feet, and one gets a good view of the regular parallel ridges that fringe the coast; beyond these ridges stretches the immeasurable barrier surface, limited to the eye by one long clear sweep of perfectly regular horizon stretching from the eastern slopes of Terror through more than 70° of arc to the eastern slope of White Island. Beyond this long stretch of uniformity the eye can follow the skyline over the three comparatively low craters of the White Island, till it dips once more for a short space to the horizontal, and rises over the sharp steep end of the distant bluff. One is now looking south, in the direction which involves most of our hopes and fears; and as one gazes on the light shades of the distant snowfields, one realises the impotence of speculating on what may lie beyond, and grows ever more impatient for the hour when we shall march forth with the high hope of solving the mystery.

'Leaving the south once more, the eye, following the skyline, passes on over the high outline of Black Island, if island it is, and then rises and traverses the lofty peaked cone of Mount Discovery, from which it falls slightly to an elevated saddleback; and then suddenly it travels to a far greater distance, and towards the south-west it rests on very distant hills in front of which a huge glacier descends to sea-level. Here one pauses to consider, for this also may be a direction of promise. Can this be the road to the west, the path by which we shall pierce that rock-bound coastline? Again one sees the futility of speculation: we must go and see.

'Meanwhile the eye has passed on to scan that great frowning range of mountains to the west which has looked down on us in such ghostly, weird fashion throughout the winter months. Seen now in the daylight, what a wild confusion of peaks and precipices, foothills, snowfields, and glaciers it presents! How vast it all is! and how magnificent must be those mountains when one is close beneath them! But what of our travellers to the west? Here the skyline runs from peak to peak with ridges that can rarely dip below 12,000 feet, and it is beyond hope that they can scale to such heights.

'But northward of west these lofty ridges fall again, and the ranges which stretch on beyond till they are lost in the fiery glow of the sun are lower than this monstrous pile to the west. Perhaps it is in this direction that we shall conquer the western land. It is to the west more than anywhere one realises the impossibility of understanding the conditions until our parties have been forth to face them; that there will be immense difficulties there can be little doubt. To expect to find a smooth and even road in that great chaos of hills and glaciers would be to expect the impossible, and I feel that if we ever do get beyond those mountains we shall have deserved well of our country.

'Not more than fifteen miles away in this direction one can see the long shadow marking the decayed pinnacled ice which puzzled us so much as we approached our winter quarters. One cannot trace the position and direction of its origin, but if, as we suppose, it is a discharge of the inland-ice, and if it continues as we saw it at the end, it is certain to form a most formidable obstacle to our western exploration.

'Finally, from the vantage point of Crater Hill one can now obtain an excellent bird's-eye view of our own snug winter quarters. Even from this distance the accumulation of snow which has caused us so much trouble can be seen; the ship looks to be half-buried, and a white mantle has spread over the signs of our autumn labours and over the masses of refuse ahead of the ship. Hodgson's biological shelters show as faint shadowed spots, and numerous sharp black dots show that our people are abroad and that work is being pushed ahead.

'Over all the magnificent view the sunlight spreads with gorgeous effect after its long absence; a soft pink envelops the western ranges, a brilliant red gold covers the northern sky; to the north also each crystal of snow sparkles with reflected light. The sky shows every gradation of light and shade; little flakes of golden sunlit cloud float against the pale blue heaven, and seem to hover in the middle heights, whilst far above them a feathery white cirrus shades to grey on its unlit sides.

'Returning to the floes about one o'clock, inspired by the scenes which we had just witnessed, we informed the men that the sun could now be seen from Hut Point. To our astonishment there was little or no enthusiasm. Everyone seemed extremely pleased to hear it was there, and glad to think that it had kept its appointment so punctually; but, after all, they had seen the sun a good many times before, and in the next few months they were likely to see it a good many times again, there was no object in getting excited about it; so a few set off at a run for the point, some followed at a walk, as it seemed the right thing to do, but a good number remained on board and had their dinner. It is perhaps as well that we do not all take our pleasures in the same way or rejoice in the same sentiments, and, at any rate, it is evident that those who can so passively observe the coming day cannot have been deeply affected by the vanishing night.'

'August 23. – A glorious morning; have been away over the hills, clambering along Arrival ridges on the sharp angular stones heedless of the wear of my finneskoes, and sliding down the snow-slopes regardless of the wear on other articles of clothing. This latter has been a very common practice of mine during the winter; on the smooth hard snow one can get up a capital speed without the assistance of a toboggan, but the practice has meant the frequent renewal of a patch behind.

'The air today was splendidly exhilarating, with a temperature of −10° and a wind just sufficiently keen to make climbing a pleasure. Erebus showed a column of golden smoke rising perpendicularly for about five hundred feet and then streaming horizontally to the east; to have had this splendid beacon giving throughout our winter a continuous record of the upper air currents is luck indeed.

'What unique and glorious mountains we have about us! Nowhere else can there be such vast masses snowed to the base, and hence possibly nowhere such great altitudes above the snow-line. One wonders when the mountaineer, having conquered all the peaks of the known world, will descend on this lonely region, for here indeed lies a field where the boldness of man might have play for many a year; as parties could be left and relieved in successive seasons with practical certainty, the idea is by no means inconceivable.

'Today one could see the islets to the north looking very black and grim; besides the group of three or four some ten miles away, there is a curious turtle-backed rock not more than three or four miles from Castle Rock, and far across the strait I could count five distinct islets bearing about W. by N. A low bank of cloud to the north shut out the sun, whose position was only marked by the intensity of the golden-red glow above: small fleecy intermediate clouds were floating about Erebus, golden or grey as they passed from light to shadow.

'The scene is so rarely beautiful that on the hilltops one seems to breathe inspiration from the keen air, and one's thoughts are compelled to soar out of the common groove; but as one descends to the ship they fall back on the more practical details of our life, and little remains in the memory. Here below the broad light of day has revealed not a little that is ugly. The ugliness lay concealed under the glamour of the dim mysterious twilight, but now the traces of man are all too obvious: here is a little heap of dirty rubbish, there an empty tin with a gaudy label, and everywhere the soil of traffic staining the purity of the snow. It is all a little too much like a Bank-holiday picnic.

'It is a curious fact that throughout the winter most of the officers have preferred to take their walks alone. Many, no doubt, would think that the fact was by no means curious, and that one would naturally wish to escape from companionship which he was so constantly forced to endure; and, indeed, before we sailed I constantly heard the remark, "How sick you will get of one another!" As a matter of fact, we are not at all sick of each other's company, and if it transpires that the plans of two individuals coincide as regards the day's walk, they are only too delighted to go together. The real reason for separation is that plans rarely do coincide. Nearly everyone likes to walk with an object, and no two people have precisely the same object, and if they have, it is probably not convenient to their work to leave the ship at the same hour. It has also to be remembered that when two persons are muffled up with little showing but their noses, conversation can only be carried on with difficulty, and an argument is impossible.'

'August 25. – . . . Yesterday we kept the Feast of the Sun, and celebrated it with an excellent dinner. Turtle soup, tinned fish, seal cutlets, and mutton, washed down with Heidsieck '95. The warrant officers joined us at dinner, and afterwards we had the usual small concert, and proceedings were kept up late and with the greatest hilarity. Armitage brewed punch, but after previous experience few were rash enough to partake of it, and the few are repenting heartily today.

'Everywhere on board now is stir and excitement; sledges are being put together, provisions weighed out, dog-harness prepared, fur clothing overhauled, and each item of equipment carefully reconsidered. Everything is being pushed forward for a start on Monday next; the first party away, others will quickly follow, and soon, it is to be hoped, our travelling will be in full swing.'

'August 29. – . . . For some time past it has been amusing on entering the warm, comfortable living-quarters, to see the table strewn with garments, reels of cotton, skeins of thread, tape, thimbles, packets of needles, and every other necessary of the tailor's art, and to see gathered around the table our whole company plying their needles as though they were being sweated by some iron-handed taskmaster. Indeed, I am not sure that this is not the case: if we consider "King Frost" as a taskmaster, he is certainly an exacting one. This sort of thing is bound to go on until we actually start on our journeys, because no-one is ever quite satisfied with what he has made, and when a garment is completed there is always some suggested alteration that promises to be a slight improvement; and after the spring journeys, when we have had more experience, the probability is that nearly everything will be altered again. However, it is very cheering to see so much enthusiasm displayed, and it augurs well for our work that every-one should be taking it so seriously, and should be so evidently bent on making it a success.

'So our only sewing-machine clatters away all day long, whilst bent fingers are stitching busily, and the whole ship is alive with the bustle of our active preparations. I have issued orders for sledging to commence next week, and for the gear to be ready for packing on Monday.'

'Monday, September 1. – . . . All will be ready for a start to-morrow. The wind has sprung up again, but it is comparatively mild, and we are packing the sledges. Tomorrow at this hour I hope we shall be spinning along to the north with the dogs, to test our arrangements, the climatic conditions, and the discipline of the animals; whilst Armitage and Barne, with a party of ten men, go forth on a similar errand, as well as to bring back the depot which we established last year under such uncomfortable conditions. From this commencement we shall work up to our more ambitious projects.'

So now the long winter, with its darkness and forced inactivity, was at an end. Although our faces looked pale and white in the glare of the returning day, beneath the pallor lay every evidence of unimpaired vitality; and believing ourselves to be in the perfection of health, as we were of spirits, all thoughts turned to the coming season and to prospects which could look nothing but bright and hopeful.

History and development of sledge-travelling

> Much more in this great work should we survey
> The plot of situation, and its model,
> Question surveyors, know our estate,
> How able such a work to undertake. — SHAKESPEARE

It may be fairly claimed that polar sledging is an English production; it is the direct outcome of that feverish energy in exploration which has distinguished our race for so many centuries and has led them to the performance of such glorious pioneer work within the Arctic Circle. To give my readers some idea of the history of sledge-travelling, I cannot do better than quote the words of one who had perhaps the largest share in its making, and who gave more care and attention to the subject than has anyone before or since. The following words were written by Sir Leopold McClintock more than thirty years ago, and give a good idea of the conditions under which this mode of travelling was evolved, the objects it sought to accomplish, and the state of perfection to which it had then been brought.

'In early Arctic voyaging the ship alone was relied upon for penetrating into unknown seas; it was not until the second and third voyages of Parry and the second voyage of Sir John Ross – that is, between 1821 and 1834 – that sledging was commenced and a number of short journeys were made, mainly by the assistance of the Esquimaux, whose methods were closely observed and more or less imitated.

'But our seamen had not yet familiarised themselves with the idea that it was quite possible for well-equipped Europeans not only to exist, but to travel in an Arctic climate, as well as the Esquimaux themselves; and it was not until the Franklin Search Expeditions were sent out, between 1848 and 1854, that men seriously reflected upon the possibility of any extensive exploration on foot; and no more powerful incentive could have been imagined to rouse the utmost energies of the searchers than the protracted absence of the missing expedition.

'The endurance of the hardiest was called forth, and the talent of invention evoked and stimulated, until at length a system of sledging was elaborated such as I will now proceed to describe.

' . . . The late Sir James Ross, who had served with very great credit in all the six voyages of Parry and John Ross from 1818 to 1834, formed the connecting link between them and the searching expeditions which commenced in 1848, and the first of which he commanded. He was acquainted with the flat sledges of the Hudson Bay Territory, which alone can be used in deep soft snow, gliding as they do over its surface; he was also acquainted with the Greenland dog sledge, with its high narrow runners shod with ivory or bone, and which cuts down through the usually thin layer of snow and runs upon the ice beneath; he was familiar with the various modifications of these typical forms which had been used in the Arctic expeditions of Parry and John Ross.

'He had moreover made several journeys with the natives of Boothia Felix, culminating in his discovery of the Magnetic Pole, and on one of these journeys he was absent from his ship for the then unprecedented period of twenty-nine days. It was under his directions that our sledges and tents were made in 1848; and these designs, with comparatively slight modifications, have continued in favour in all subsequent expeditions.

'The tent requires little description. It is a pent-roof about seven feet high along the ridge, supported on boarding pikes or poles crossed at each end, and covering an oblong space sufficient to enclose the party when closely packed together; its duty is merely to afford shelter from the wind and snowdrift. . . . The sledge is a more important article of equipment. That which our experience has proved to be the most suitable is a large runner sledge; the runners are rather broad – that is, three inches – and they stand high, carrying the lading about a foot above the ice. An average sledge is three feet wide and ten feet long, and is drawn by seven men. It is constructed with only just so much strength as is absolutely necessary, since every pound of weight saved in wood and iron enables so much more provisions to be carried. All our sledges have been drawn by the seamen, and the labour of doing so is most excessive. The first sledge expedition in the search for Franklin was led by Sir James Ross in person. By very great efforts a distance out and home of 500 statute miles was accomplished in forty days; but out of the twelve picked men by whom the two sledges were drawn five were completely knocked up, and every man required a considerable time under medical care to recruit his strength after this lengthened period of intense labour, constant exposure, and insufficient food.

'It is necessary to apprehend clearly the nature of the surface over which our sledges had to travel. People unacquainted with the subject commonly fall into one or the other extreme, and suppose that we either skate over glassy ice or walk on snow-shoes over snow of any conceivable depth. Salt-water ice is not so smooth as to be slippery; to skate upon it is very possible, though very fatiguing. But hardly is the sea frozen over when the snow falls and remains upon it all the winter. When it first falls the snow is soft and perhaps a foot or fifteen inches deep; but it is blown about by every wind until, having become like the finest sand and hardened under a severe temperature, it consolidates into a covering of a few inches in depth and becomes so compact that the sledge-runner does not sink more than an inch or so. . . . This expanse of snow is rarely smooth; its surface is broken into ridges or furrows by the strong winds. These ridges are the sastrugi of Admiral Wrangell; and although the inequalities are seldom more than a foot high, they add greatly to the labour of travelling, especially when obliged to cross them at right angles. . . .

' . . . Having accompanied Sir James Ross on his sledge journey in 1849, I was entrusted with the preparations for sledge-travelling in the second and third search expeditions under Austin and Belcher; and this method now became recognised as an important feature of these voyages.

'The utmost attention was devoted to the travelling equipments and the methods adopted by Wrangell and other distinguished

Arctic travellers; and the spring parties of the second expedition set out in 1851 on April 15, instead of May 15 as in 1849, and sledges carrying forty days' provisions were dragged with less labour than thirty days' rations had previously occasioned. Moreover, the allowance was a more liberal one. The result was a corresponding increase of work done – one party remaining absent for eighty days and making a journey of 900 miles. But in 1853 and 1854 the sledge parties of the third searching expedition did still better service – one party accomplished about 1,400 miles in 105 days. Another party, having several depots along its line of route and favourable circumstances generally, travelled nearly 1,350 miles in seventy days.'

From the above it will be clearly seen that to the English explorers of the early nineteenth century belong the honour of being the first to discover that, again to quote Sir Leopold, 'the ice which arrests the progress of the ship forms the highway for the sledge'; they were the first civilised beings to use that highway, and on it they accomplished work which has remained, and will probably remain, unsurpassed. Of his own share in this development Sir Leopold speaks most modestly but a comparison of the periods of absence and the distances covered by the parties of the 1853 expedition with similar records in 1849 are sufficient to show how great it was, more especially when it is known that it was he himself who conducted the longest journey of the later expedition.

To realise the great revolution which had been effected in Arctic exploration, it has but to be considered that in 1820 the fact of an explorer venturing beyond his ice-bound ship had barely been considered, whereas little more than thirty years later it could be written of these far Northern regions: 'It is now a comparatively easy matter to start with six or eight men and six or seven weeks' provisions, and to travel some 600 miles across snowy wastes and frozen seas from which no sustenance can be obtained.'

Although these sledging records of half a century ago have not been surpassed, it would be incorrect to say that there has been no improvement in sledging methods; with the march of the times and the advance of mechanical skill many details have been improved, whilst the comfort of the sledge-traveller has been increased and his hardships mitigated; but that the fundamental principles have remained unaltered is sufficiently proved by the figures.

Since the high-tide mark of 1853 England has not maintained her reputation in the sledging world; one effort of importance alone has been made – when in 1875 the *Alert* and *Discovery* were sent forth. The sledging outfit of this expedition was again arranged by Sir Leopold McClintock, but the margins of strength and safety were rather enlarged, so that in many respects the equipment had retrograded. In spite of this, long journeys were made in very adverse circumstances; and had the expedition been able to continue its work for more than a single year, improvements in the outfit would doubtless have been tried and further advancements suggested. In the last years of the century the Jackson-Harmsworth expedition spent three winters in Franz-Josef Land and carried out several sledge expeditions with dogs and ponies; but here, again, the effort was not sufficiently sustained to add greatly to our knowledge.

Since 1853 whatever improvement has been made in sledging methods has been developed abroad, and it is abroad therefore that the modern traveller must look for all that is latest and best in this respect. But here also he is met by a want of continuity and system; and whilst he pauses to admire the splendid efforts of individual travellers he cannot but deplore the absence of a more systematic correlation of their experiences, enabling each to benefit more fully by the difficulties which his predecessor conquered. Notwithstanding this drawback, however, there is much to be learnt from these experiences: the inquirer will at least have embarked on a history of absorbing interest, and he cannot but emerge a wiser man if he follows it through the wild and sometimes tragic expeditions of the latter half of the nineteenth century and studies the historic journeys of such great explorers as Peary and Fridtjof Nansen.

The sledge equipment which we took to the South was the result of much consultation; in arranging it, I had to depend largely on the experience of others, and especially on the experience of one, Mr Armitage, whose interests were identified with the expedition. From the commencement of that busy year of preparation which preceded the departure of the expedition, when on my own inexperienced shoulders alone rested the responsibility of every department of an undertaking of such considerable magnitude, I realised the primary importance of an efficient sledging outfit, and I strove to glean from every source such information as should serve to see us properly provided in this respect.

The difficulties were great. In England a quarter of a century had elapsed since sledging expeditions of magnitude had been accomplished, and during that time not a single sledge, and very few portions of a sledge equipment, had been made in this country. The popular accounts of former expeditions were not written with a view to supply the minute detail that was required, and no memory could be expected to retain these details after the lapse of such a time: the art was lost. But, fortunately, the genius of Nansen had transferred it or built up a new art in Norway. Having modernised the methods of the older English sledge-travellers, he had gathered about him a small body of tradesmen cognisant of his ideas and capable of carrying them out. Christiania had become, so to speak, the centre of the sledging industry, and within easy reach of the city lived and worked the man who had made it so, always ready to give advice and assistance to all who needed it, and always ready to help those who, like myself, were embarking on the field of exploration in which he had played so eminent a part.

In the autumn of 1900 I visited Christiania, and in Nansen's company interviewed the various tradesmen who worked under his superintendence, whilst obtaining many a practical hint from the explorer himself. But now, as always, Nansen was an extremely busy man, and, kind and considerate as he was, it was impossible not to realise that one was robbing him of hours which he could ill afford to spare.

Moreover, my own work was of such a nature as to necessitate haste; with so much to be done in England delay was not permissible, and much as I should have liked to linger and increase my knowledge in this province, I was forced to curtail my visit to the shortest possible limits. However, I had learnt enough to give me a practical idea of the basis on which our equipment should be collected. It seemed evident that we should have to purchase in Norway some important part of our outfit, but I saw no reason why the main portion should not be made under our own superintendence in England, provided we could supply patterns or full instructions to the makers. Sledges, ski, and furs could be made and supplied from Norway at a price and of a quality which we could not hope to equal in England, even had we been prepared to issue the fullest instructions and specifications, which we were not. On the other hand, tents, clothing, cooking-apparatus, and other details could be obtained in London if the necessary super-intendence were available.

Having some ideas and notes as to what our requirements were, the question now in my mind was how these ideas should be put into effect; with such a vast amount of work connected with other departments, I could not possibly devote the necessary time to these details, and even had I attempted to do so I should have been handicapped at every turn by my want of practical experience. I was for some time in this dilemma before Sir Clements Markham forwarded me a letter written by Mr Armitage, who was at that time serving in the P. and O. service in the Far East. Armitage, as I knew, had served in the Jackson-Harmsworth Expedition, but it was not until I read this letter that I realised how invaluable such an experience might be; the letter was written with the intention of suggesting the lines on which our sledging outfit should be pre-pared, and I saw at once that it contained the ideas at which I had been so ineffectually attempting to grasp. Armitage met me on his return to England, and agreed to serve as second in command of the expedition, provided the permission of his directors could be obtained. This was granted, and within the month, after numerous consultations, Armitage was in full direction of that important part of our preparation, the sledging outfit. Time was all too short for the excessive care and attention that were needed, but, thanks to untiring efforts, we had collected all that was necessary in this respect before the expedition left the London Docks in July 1901.

In describing the various articles of this equipment, I shall explain in some detail their origin, and endeavour to point out in what respects they suited our purpose, and in what respects they failed. It must be remembered that in making long sledge journeys in the South we had no previous experience to go on except that which had been gained in the North; we were forced to assume that Southern conditions were more or less similar to those of the North, and in so far as they proved different our sledging outfit ran the risk of failure.

We found, in fact, that in many respects our sledging con-ditions differed from those in the North, and it is just to consider all our sledge journeys as pioneer efforts. It is perhaps as well to indicate these differences here; they are essentially climatic and geographical.

In regard to climate, the conditions in the South are more severe than those in the North; the spring temperatures are lower, and the summer temperatures far lower. The early spring travellers in the North have rarely recorded a temperature below −50°, whereas with our early parties the thermometer frequently fell below −60°, and at its lowest stood at −68°; in the Arctic summer travellers have experienced temperatures of +40° and even +50°, whilst in the height of our Southern summer the thermometer rarely rose above freezing-point, even on the great snow-plains adjacent to the sea-level; and when we were forced to explore at great altitudes, we were fortunate if it showed higher than −10° at this season.

The effect of these generally low temperatures was naturally to increase the hardships to which the sledge-travellers were exposed, and of which so much has been written, while it is doubtful whether we could have so well withstood this greater intensity of cold had we not been possessed of those improvements to the sledging outfit which have been added in the years that have elapsed since the great English journeys of 1850. But the low summer temperature has one advantage, although we were not fated to gain greatly by it, in that the snowy surface of the sea-ice never gets into that sodden, slushy condition which obtains in the latter part of the Northern summer, and which prevents sledging operations being undertaken after the month of June in the Arctic Regions. Except in a few places where dust or grit has been blown on to it, the surface of the Southern sea-ice remains hard throughout the summer; and as there are many places where it does not break up until the latter part of February, it is quite possible to conceive sledging being carried on over its surface until that month, which corresponds with the Northern August.

A circumstance, however, that is far more objectionable to the Southern traveller than the extremity of temperature is the frequency of wind. It is perhaps too broad a generalisation to say that Arctic journeys have usually been made under fine-weather conditions, but few, if any, Arctic travellers have been subjected to the distressing frequency of blizzards and strong winds that added so much to our discomfort in the South. Here again, therefore, the Southern traveller is at a disadvantage from a climatic point of view, and the effect is to increase his discomforts and reduce the distance he is able to march, for it is only on the very rare occasions on which a sail may be used that wind brings any compensating advantage. In general, therefore, from a climatic point of view, the South is at a considerable disadvantage as compared with the North in sledge-travelling.

The geographical difference between the work of the Northern and the Southern sledge-traveller is as great as the climatic, if not greater. With the exception of Nansen's and Peary's journeys into the interior of Greenland, the sledge journeys of the North have almost invariably been performed over level if not smooth sea-ice, and it is especially to be remembered that those record journeys to which Sir Leopold McClintock refers were made amongst the frozen channels of an archipelago. If sea-ice is much broken up and hummocked, it may constitute one of the worst travelling surfaces, but if it is smooth it is undoubtedly the best that exists. In very general terms, therefore, with the exceptions I have mentioned, the travelling of the North has been carried on over a comparatively good surface, and those travellers who constitute the exception in having ventured on the inland surfaces have made it abundantly clear that the difficulties are far more formidable than are found on anything but the most hummocked sea-ice. Turning now to the South, it will be seen that everywhere the explorer's ship is brought up by solid land or by some mighty wall resembling that of the Great Ice Barrier; to pass beyond his ship, therefore, the explorer must either travel over land or over great and ancient snowfields which possess a similar surface. Judging from our present knowledge of the Antarctic Regions, it is doubtful whether extensive journeys will ever be made over the sea-ice.

We have, therefore, this great geographical difference between the North and the South: the greater part of Northern travelling has been and will be done on sea-ice, but the greater part of Southern travelling has been and will be done over land surfaces, or what in this respect are their equivalents.

The relative merits of these surfaces, always excepting the very rough hummocked sea-ice, is a matter which has been placed beyond doubt by travellers in the North, and hence it is of interest to relate our own experience with regard to it. On travelling over the Great Barrier to the south, I was constantly impressed by recognising the difficulties of surface so graphically described by

Nansen in his *First Crossing of Greenland*, and I came to the conclusion that the conditions were very similar. But I was still more impressed by the obvious impossibility of dragging a sledge over such a surface at the rate maintained by the old English travellers on the Northern sea-ice. I was so exercised on this score that I was forced to wonder whether it might not be our own incapacity for walking that caused us to fall so far short of those old records, and the thought that the British race of explorers had deteriorated so rapidly and so completely in stamina was by no means a pleasant one. In the following year, in carrying out our exploration to the west, I made no fewer than six crossings over the sea-ice of the strait, a distance of about forty-five statute miles, and the mystery was revealed when we found that we could cover this distance with full weights in two and a half days, while with light weights we actually got across in one and a half day, covering over thirty-six miles in a single day.

It was consoling to be free from immediate alarm in regard to our racial stamina, but a flood of light was thrown on the comparatively difficult nature of the barrier surface; we saw that the difficulties we had met in crossing it were by no means existent only in our imagination. The barrier surface varied greatly, but, taking an average condition, I doubt whether we should have approached twenty miles over it by expending an equal amount of energy to that which gave us the thirty-six miles over the sea-ice. This argues a great difference, and it is one that cannot be wholly explained. Of course the primary condition of importance on which the excellence of a surface depends is its relative hardness. The snow surface of the sea-ice, when we crossed it so rapidly, was so hard that the sledges left but a faint track; at the same time, it was not too hard to prevent one's fur-clad foot from getting some grip at each step. On the other hand, the sledges always left a well-marked track in the barrier surface, and at each step one sank ankle-deep and sometimes even deeper. But this is by no means the only factor that governs a surface; wind, sun, temperature, and the age of the snowfall are all elements that affect it, increasing or decreasing the friction on the sledge-runners in a manner that is often inexplicable and sometimes exasperating. All such changes, however, will be dealt with in the accounts of our sledge journeys; for the present it is only necessary to point out that it is difficult to define exactly what constitutes a good or a bad sledging surface.

Besides being dependent on the climatic conditions and on the nature of the snow over which he journeys, the sledge-traveller has to consider other obstructions which more obviously hinder his progress. On the sea-ice he may meet with those elevated fragments pressed up by the movement and distortion of the ice-sheet, which are commonly called hummocks; on sea or on land he may encounter regions where the wind has ploughed the snow into furrows, the waves between which are technically termed sastrugi; on the land-ice he may meet vast ridges and chasms, cracks and crevasses, mild and gentle undulations, or any other resultant of the irresistible movement of an ice-sheet. All such obstacles are very obvious deterrents, and exist both in the North and in the South, but to a different degree. Sea-ice in the South, as far as we know it, is extraordinarily free from hummocks, and such is its geographical situation that the probability is there are few places in the Antarctic Regions where the ice will be found much pressed up; while in the North hummocks have been the bane of many a sledge journey. In regard to sastrugi, it is probable that such a windswept area as the Antarctic outvies the more placid North; indeed, I doubt whether snow-waves have ever been seen before of such giant size as some which we observed abreast of our windiest gullies or on the high plateau of Victoria Land. In regard to the disturbances of the vast land ice-sheets it is difficult to institute any comparison with the North, but these formed a sufficiently solid obstruction to many of our sledging efforts.

A general comparison of the sledging conditions met with in the North and in the South cannot be said, therefore, to be in favour of the latter, and it must be conceded that the Antarctic sledge-traveller journeys under considerable relative disadvantages: he has to meet severer climatic conditions, he has to pull his sledges over heavier surfaces, and he is not likely to encounter fewer obstacles in his path. Hence it is probable that the distances recorded by the Northern travellers will never be exceeded in the South.

I do not wish it to be inferred from what I have written that the sledge-traveller does or should go forth in order to make marching records; but whatever his objectives may be, it is obvious that they are best achieved by speed on the march; and hence where conditions are equal, speed and the distance travelled are a direct gauge of the efficiency of sledging preparations and of the spirit of those who undertake this arduous service.

From the summary, necessarily brief, of the history of the development of sledge-travelling which I have given, and the equally brief account of the physical conditions under which it is conducted, the reader will see that the object of the traveller is to journey as far as possible beyond the limit to which his ship can attain, and some idea of the problems that are encountered in pursuit of this object will have been conveyed. The weight which can be dragged by a party is limited by the draught-power they possess, but it is also dependent on the surface, the state of the sledge-runners, the manner in which the sledges are loaded, and many other details. The greater the proportion of food in this weight, the longer is the possibility of absence; but sledges must possess strength, and therefore weight; man must be sheltered and clothed, and this cannot be done without weight; and civilised man requires hot food, and must therefore drag the weight of his cooking-apparatus and fuel.

The less that is eaten by any individual, the longer the food will last; but there is a limit where economy ceases, and insufficient food produces loss of strength and reduction of marches. The longer the marches, the greater the distance covered; but staleness awaits the over-pressed marcher.

Good sledging is the nicest balance of all these conflicting elements, and it is clear that it can only be accomplished by the utmost attention to detail in preparation, the complete exclusion of all but the bare necessities of life, and, above all things, by the display of an unconquerable determination to carry it through in face of all risks, dangers, or hardships.

Perhaps the most important part of the sledge-traveller's outfit is the sledge itself. Our sledges had been made in Christiania, to comprise all those modifications and improvements which had been suggested by the experience of Nansen, and on the whole it is doubtful if we could have provided ourselves with sledges more suitable to our various purposes. The main differences between these sledges and those used by older explorers were a decrease in breadth and an increase in runner surface.

Such a sledge as we used consists of two long runners, slightly rounded beneath, with a strengthening rib above, and curved up at each end. The strengthening rib is pierced with holes at intervals, into which are tenoned the uprights, short pillars of wood about four inches in length; adjacent uprights are joined by crossbars, and the heads of the uprights on each side are connected by long thin strips of wood, which end in junction with the upturned ends of the runners. There are four, five, or six pairs of uprights and crossbars, according to the length of the sledge.

In the numerous joints thus created only those which connect the uprights to the crossbars are rigid, and these are strengthened by small steel stays bound to the frame with wire. It is of the utmost importance that all other joints should be flexible, in order that the sledge may have the fullest play over a rough surface, and therefore all these joints are made with lashings of either hide or tarred hemp. Hence the sledge, when put together, is by no means a rigid structure. Lifted by one corner, it can be distinctly seen to sag in the centre; and as it is dragged over a rough snow surface it is rarely possible to see any portion of the runner which is not in contact with the snow – in fact, it is very fascinating to watch a heavily laden sledge winding its way over rough ground in this snake-like manner. The load being distributed over a great area, no part sinks too deeply.

Measured across from the centre of one runner to the centre of the other, our sledges were all, with one exception, 1 foot 5 inches. The runners themselves were 3¾ inches across, so that the sledge track from side to side measured about 1 foot 8¾ inches. In all we had twenty sledges when we began, and this allowance proved barely sufficient for our two years' work; we could, indeed, well have done with half as many again, but this was owing to much of the travelling being over extremely rough country. These sledges were of various lengths; we had two of 12 feet, six of 11 feet, nine of 9 feet, and three of 7 feet; of these the 11-foot sledges proved by far the most convenient for our work, though the 9-foot were much used. A length of 12 feet seemed to pass just beyond the limit of handiness; whereas the very short sledges were comparatively stiff, and skidded about so much on a rough surface that they were often more troublesome to pull than the heavier and longer ones.

Taking 11 feet as about the best length for this type, it will be seen that we have a comparatively long and narrow sledge at considerable variance with the old Arctic type, which was 10 feet long and 3 feet broad. The advantages gained by the longer sledge are an increased strength against racking strains and an easier motion over inequalities of surface; on the other hand, the broader type has more stability and a greater and more convenient stowage capacity. Our own sledges had to be stowed with great care so as to bring the weight low, and even thus over rough sastrugi they would frequently capsize; in spite of such disadvantages, however, I am inclined to favour the longer and narrower form. The increase of runner surface which was adopted by Nansen in what he named his 'ski runners', was a comparatively natural outcome of the new condition of surface for which he prepared on his inland journey, and as our conditions were very similar, it is a fortunate thing that we possessed broad runners. There were many occasions on which they were not needed, and when a light narrow runner would have been all that was required; but there were others when we needed every inch of bearing surface we possessed to support the sledges on the light soft snow.

The weight of an 11-foot sledge such as I have described may be anything between 40 and 47 lbs., and this was none too light for some of our purposes where the full strength of the structure was required; but on the level barrier I think it would be possible to travel with a considerably lighter sledge. The weight which can be placed on such a sledge varies according to circumstance, but in general the full load may be said to be about 600 lbs.

These sledges are made of ash, and it is of great importance that the wood should be thoroughly well selected and seasoned. In some of our sledges the wood was not above suspicion, and caused some inconvenience. The most important part is the runner, in which the grain should be perfectly straight and even, otherwise it will splinter even when running over snow. It is surprising what a lot of wear a good wood runner will stand provided it is only taken over snow. Some of our 9-foot sledges must have travelled over 1,000 miles, and there was still plenty of wear left in the runners.

The older Northern sledges were shod with iron or steel, and Nansen covered his Greenland sledge-runners with the same material. The drawback to this is that it is liable to rust, and in a rusty state the friction is of course much increased. In his Northern journey Nansen substituted German silver, a non-corrosive metal, for steel, and reported the result as satisfactory; in consequence the runners of all our sledges were covered with this metal, which added considerably to their weight, though that quoted for the 11-foot sledge includes this item This shoeing gives rise to a difficulty, since there are certain conditions of surface when German silver offers great friction, whereas it is impossible to strip the runners to meet these conditions and then to replace the metal. To get over this difficulty Nansen devised thin under-runners of wood with light steel attachments, thus providing for the condition when a wooden surface for the runner would be desirable, but again adding to the weights carried. As far as our experience went, both the German-silver shoeing and the wood under-runner proved unsatisfactory; in nine cases out of ten on the snow surfaces over which we travelled, wood runners offered less resistance than metal, and though the idea of the under-runner is theoretically good, we found that practically the thing was too flimsy; the snow tended to pack above it, and it was liable to become loose and distorted. Moreover, it introduced a complication where simplicity should be the first consideration. As far as all our journeys made over the flat on snow surfaces were concerned, the plain wood runner of the sledge itself, without any covering, would have been amply sufficient, and in fact, as I have pointed out, well-seasoned wood would stand far more wear than could well be given it in the course of a single expedition.

But many of our journeys lay over hard rough ice or places where sand and grit had been blown over the snow, and where an unprotected wood runner would soon be torn to shreds. It was here that the German silver should have served us, and to some extent it did; but in the main we found it altogether too soft – grit was liable to score it deeply, and the metal once pierced, the runner gave an infinity of trouble.

The difficulties we were put to on account of our sledges and sledge-runners will be mentioned in due course, but it is as well to lay down here, for the guidance of future travellers in these regions, such recommendations as arise out of our experience.

It may be safely said that the 11-foot ski-runner sledge is a good type for general purposes in the Antarctic Regions, whether it is to be hauled by men or dogs. It would be a good plan to have sledges made of different weights to suit special circumstances. Under ordinary conditions such sledges may be allowed to run on their wood runners, but if it is desired to ascend glaciers or travel over rough ice, a steel-protected runner is necessary. As a general rule, such a protection would only be required for a limited part of the journey, and I do not think it would be difficult to devise one which could be temporarily secured by clamps and detached when no longer of use. The importance of selecting the wood of which the sledges are made cannot be too strongly urged. Though ash has been mostly used, I understand the American hickory is also an excellently tough wood for the purpose. Sledge-runners have also been made of elm and maple, either of which offers little friction to the snow.

Before leaving the subject of sledges it is well to mention the necessity of providing strong heavy ones for the ordinary work about headquarters, for the travelling sledges would soon be knocked to pieces at this. Three or four heavy rough sledges with narrow iron-bound runners did all our heavy work about the ship during her stay in the ice.

In point of numbers the *Discovery*'s crew was far behind the old Northern expeditions; it was this fact that first decided us, in arranging a sledge equipment for a condition where men, and not dogs, would do most of the haulage, to divide our parties into the smallest workable units. The old Northern plan had allowed for parties of twelve, or at the least eight, who were in all respects self-contained, but, having a common tent and cooking arrangements, could not be subdivided. Without necessarily limiting the number of men in our parties, the system we aimed at was to divide them into units of three, which should be self-contained, so that whenever it was advisable a party could be split up into threes, or three could be detached from it, or, again, three people could leave the ship without carrying more than was necessary for their requirements. It is obvious that with such a system each unit of three must have its own tent, its own sleeping-bag, cooker, and so on; and herein lies a disadvantage, as economy of material and weight can be better carried out with a large unit than with a small one. It has also to be remembered that the risk of accident is increased in a small party by the diminishing of its capacity for mutual assistance.

But with our small crew it was clearly advisable that we should be able to break up into small numbers, and in the course of events we frequently did so. It will be understood, therefore, why each article which I am about to describe was designed to satisfy the requirements of three men, and this fact should be remembered in comparing any weights I may quote with those carried by former expeditions.

The object of a tent is to provide shelter from the wind and drifting snow. Those we used were bell-shaped. Some were made of the lightest green Willesden canvas, and others of thin gaberdine; we rather preferred the former, as they let in more light, and the green tint was especially grateful to the eye.

Each tent was spread on five bamboo poles; the poles were seven feet in length, and united at the top, and when spread the tent was about five feet six inches in height and about six feet in diameter on the floor. It was kept more or less tight down on the poles by digging out and piling blocks of snow on its vallance, or skirting edge – a device which also effectually prevented the wind and snowdrift from getting in beneath it. The entrance was a hole about two and a half feet in diameter, and the funnel-shaped door was sewn around its edge, so fitted that the material of which it was composed could be gathered up into a bunch and tied from the inside. This bunch once tied up, the entrance was practically drift-proof. There was one other hole in the tent close to the top which was named the ventilator, but would have been more correctly called the chimney, as it was rarely opened except to allow the steam of the cooking to pass away, instead of being condensed and frozen on the sides of the tent. This orifice was closed in a similar manner to the entrance.

On the floor inside the tent was spread a stout square or waterproof canvas which prevented the sleeping-bag or the occupants from coming into immediate contact with the snow surface. This floorcloth spread on bamboos likewise made an excellent sail, but could be used in this capacity only when the wind was abaft the beam.

Such a tent, with poles and floorcloth complete, weighed about 30 lbs., and I do not think it would be safe to use a tent of less weight in the Antarctic Regions owing to the heavy strains which are brought on it by the frequent gales. In this respect our tents deserve a high meed of praise. When we first travelled with them in windy weather, and in their shelter were forced to listen to the thunderous flapping of the canvas as gust after gust swept across the plain, we were not a little alarmed for their safety and our own; it seemed impossible that a thin shred of canvas could withstand attacks of such violence. We went so far as to fit extra guys on the principle of what is known to the sailor as a euphroe, to assist in preserving the stability of the erection, and when it was possible we built snow walls as a further protection against the extreme force of the wind. But with greater experience we gained more confidence in our tents, till finally we realised that if they were properly secured with snow it would take little less than a hurricane to uproot them. Before the second year, the constant flapping had worn the canvas very thin and threadbare, and as far as appearances went in the second season they presented the most dilapidated aspect from the numerous patches of various colours which we had been forced to insert in the weak places. It was when in this condition they still offered a bold front to the wind, and saved us from the rigours of many a storm, that we realised their excellent design and complete suitability for Antarctic purposes. A tent made to contain more persons would naturally economise material and save weight, but I have already explained why we chose ours of such small dimensions. Silk is a possible substitute for the heavier material we employed, but, strong as it is, I doubt whether it would have equal wearing qualities, and should it fail in this respect one might pay dearly for the saving in weight.

Experience teaches that the comfort of a tent depends largely on banishing loose snow and snowdrift. People learn to take the most extraordinary precautions in brushing their clothes and their boots before entering, and in having the floorcloth well swept within – precautions which are a great aid in keeping the equipment free from ice, and thus decreasing the weights carried as well as the discomforts of the journey. But this care is largely a question of personality; and just as in a house it is generally some particular person who deposits mud on the carpets, so in a tent it is generally some particular person who seems incurably desirous of adding to the snow within. The qualities of a sledging companion, however, are compounded of too many elements for him to be condemned on such a trait alone, and in that small community of three, where nothing can be hidden, and good and bad must alike be judged, it is not improbable that this very carelessness may serve to make the delinquent the more beloved.

Though it may not appear so on the surface, the sleeping-bag is really a more important article of equipment than the tent. In the bitter blast of an Antarctic storm it would be possible to exist without a tent, but it is doubtful if one could remain alive without the shelter of 'the bag', or some additional clothing which corresponded to it. All our fur clothing had been purchased in Norway; we had some suits and mits made of wolf-skin, but the greater proportion of the furs were of reindeer-skin. The pelt of the reindeer does not possess a fur in the sense which might be understood by ladies who are accustomed to dress themselves in the soft expensive productions of a London furrier; the reindeer possesses only coarse hair, but the hair is closer and thicker than on any other animal, and therefore, for reasons which are rather too technical to be given here, the skin is better suited for the polar traveller than any other. We had never contemplated dressing in furs for our journeys, but the many troubles to which sleeping-bags give rise had induced us to consider the possibility of replacing them by fur suits which would be adopted for night wear only. Our autumn journeys had very soon shown us the error of our ways. The sleeping-suits soon got into such a hard, stiff state that it was almost impossible to get into them, and, once in, one was practically incapable of motion; in fact, we thought the discomfort of a night where three persons thus clad were striving for rest in a small tent would be difficult to equal.

When the winter set in, therefore, our men were soon busy converting the reindeer suits into sleeping-bags; and as besides the suits we had a quantity of unsewn skins, there was plenty of material for the change.

As can be imagined, the actual work of turning out the bags, after a suitable design had been fixed upon, gave little trouble to men who were accustomed to the use of sail needles; but this fact serves to indicate a point which I hope to make abundantly clear – namely, that there is no class of men so eminently adapted by training to cope with the troubles and trials of sledging life as sailors.

In this manner a few single sleeping-bags were made, but the greater number were designed as 'three-man bags', so that all the occupants of a tent could sleep in the same bed. The single bag had certain advantages: in particular, when the temperature rose it was pleasant to have shelter which was all one's own, and for officers the single bag served as a receptacle in which they could keep their diaries and notebooks; but from a point of view of weight the advantage lay all on the side of the 'three-man bag', a consideration so important that eventually everyone used these bags on the longer journeys.

The 'three-man bag' was made with the fur inside and with an overlap at the head and at the sides, in addition to a large flap which could be drawn up over the occupants when they had settled themselves within. This flap completely covered the entrance, and could be secured to the top and sides with beckets and toggles.

In the springtime these toggles were all rigidly secured, and every effort was made to stop up the gaps which might be left between the flap and the bag; one felt and found that it was impossible to be too tightly sealed up, and many a pipe smoked under these conditions showed that the icy draughts from without could not be wholly banished. The warmest position in the bag was naturally the middle, but it was not always preferred. As an offset for his increased comfort it was the duty of the centre occupant to toggle up the bag – a task which, with bare cold fingers, was by no means pleasant, and generally occupied a considerable time.

Our three-man sleeping-bags weighed a little over 40 lbs. on starting from the ship; on their return from the spring journeys they were often found to be more than twice that weight from the accumulation of ice which they carried.

It would be possible to make such bags lighter by using the skins of younger animals; and here, again, it is of importance that great care should be taken in choosing the skins intended for use in an expedition. In our case, the haste of our preparations prevented sufficient care being taken, and in consequence we found a good number of our skins unsatisfactory. Nearly all had come from older animals, on which, whilst the fur is heavier, it is not necessarily warmer. To be stowed on the sledge each day the sleeping-bag had to be doubled over, rolled up, and secured with rope – no easy job when it was stiff and hard and the weather was cold. As may be imagined, also, when snow was drifting in the air very great caution was needed to prevent it from getting inside the bag.

The most difficult matter to arrange on a sledge-journey, and the matter on which there is likely to be the greatest difference of opinion and the most controversy, is the food.

The issue is clear enough: one desires to provide a man each day with just sufficient food to keep up his strength, and not an ounce beyond. It is certainly suggestive of a normally overfed condition in civilised mankind that when it is reduced to this allowance it is conscious of much inconvenience from the pangs of hunger. The great difficulty for the sledge organiser is to arrive at this happy mean, more especially as it can be regulated by no food allowance given in other parts of the world which enjoy a less rigorous climate. The sledge-traveller seems to need not only a special allowance, but also a specially proportioned allowance. If one really goes into this matter with some thoroughness, as I had the leisure to do, one is involved in a bewildering array of facts and figures which it would be hopeless to attempt to display with clearness to the reader; but there are a few facts which may be quoted with advantage, not only on the chance of their being of interest, but because they show the exceptional requirements of the sledge-traveller. And it must be remembered that, apart from all theoretical conceptions in fixing the ultimate allowance for our travellers, I had the benefit of a great deal of practical experience, and can therefore speak with some knowledge of the subject.

The following is a physiological estimate of the proportionate energy expended by an average man in a day who does eight hours of hard mechanical labour.

Heart action and respiration expend	62,100	kilogramme metres
Bodily heat produced expends	620,000	,, ,,
Mechanical work for eight hours	125,000	,, ,,
Total	807,100	,, ,,

Assuming these figures to be even approximately correct, the absurd disproportion of the energy expended on work is noticeable, and hence man cannot be treated like a machine and fed in proportion to the amount of work he does. It has a very practical bearing on our subject, since it has been remarked by even experienced sledge-travellers that if a party are forced to remain in their tents for a day they ought to go on half-food allowance, and I have seen some of our own officers rather chagrined to find that appetites remained almost as keen during a period of forced inaction as when a long day's work was being performed.

The above, therefore, shows that food cannot be materially reduced whilst parties remain in camp, and that the sooner they are on the march again the better it is for the distance they will eventually be able to travel. The figures which I have quoted also tend to show why it is that a man requires more food in a polar climate than in a temperate one, for it is evident that the expenditure on bodily heat will be larger.

During our second year in the South I very carefully calculated the food which was provided for my own party, but I allowed other officers to modify this allowance according to their own ideas. I then calculated the result of my own and Barne's ideas to rank in the following table. It is now pretty generally known that our ordinary food can be placed under three headings – the proteids, or nitrogenous food, such as is mainly supplied by meats; the fats; and the carbohydrates, or farinaceous foods. It is known also that man ordinarily assimilates a given proportion of these various natures of food. I do not vouch for the exact accuracy of this table, more especially as I find authorities differ much as to actual requirements in this respect; the table purports to give the number of ounces of water-free food required under the different headings, and I have neglected salts.

	Amount required for man in full work according to different authorities			Prisoner on hard labour	Army on war footing	My own allowance	Barne's allowance
Proteid	4.5	4.8	4.4	4.0	4.8	8.6	7.9
Fats	3.0	4.1	2.0	1.5	1.0	4.4	4.2
Carbohydrates	14.2	12.4	17.6	19.0	18.8	15.6	17.0
Total	21.7	21.3	24.0	24.5	24.6	28.6	29.1

In my first year of sledging work I went south with something considerably under the allowance given above, when my party suffered much from hunger and grew decidedly weaker; in the second year, with the allowance shown, our strength was fairly well maintained, but there was still no doubt about our hunger. There can be little question, therefore, that polar sledging ranks an easy first as a hunger-producing employment, and inferentially from that fact one can draw some conclusion as to the arduous nature of the work.

But from the foregoing I do not wish it to be thought that we were able to maintain our daily life on an allowance of twenty-nine ounces of food per man. This figure represents the water-free weight. Whereas absolute freedom from water can only be calculated, it is never achieved; and herein lies one of the greatest difficulties that faces the sledge-traveller, since it is obvious that the water is a dead and useless addition to his weights. Some idea of the difficulty can be gathered from the statement that ordinary cooked meat contains no less than 54 per cent. of moisture. Hence, to the sledger, to reduce the water in his food is of as much importance as to curb his appetite. It is therefore of interest to quote the actual nature and weight of food carried on the occasions which I have taken for examples.

	Ounces per day per man	
	Self	Barne
Biscuit	12.0	14.5
Oatmeal	1.5	1.5
Pemmican	7.6	7.6
Red Ration	1.1	1.1
Plasmon	2.0	1.5
Pea Flour	1.5	0.7
Cheese	2.0	1.5
Chocolate	1.1	1.1
Cocoa	0.7	0.7
Sugar	3.8	3.8
	33.3	34.0

One or two articles in this list need explanation. Pemmican was, I believe, the name given in the Hudson Bay Territory to a compound of dry buffalo meat and lard. It was transferred to the dried beef and lard carried by the Northern sledgers, and in that sense it is still retained. The best of our pemmican came from Messrs. Beauvais, of Copenhagen, and contained 50 per cent. of lard and, what was not so pleasing, 20 per cent. of moisture; later on we received from the *Morning* some good pemmican made by the Bovril Company. The red ration was a nondescript compound of bacon and pea-flour. I am not very sure as to its food value, and it was retained because it was starchy enough to thicken our nightly soup and make it a mixture which, as the sailors said, 'stuck to your ribs'.

The remaining articles need no comment, but I should not forget to add that the following were also carried, though for purposes of comparison I have omitted them from the first list. Each tent was allowed per week:

> 0.75 lb. of tea
> 0.5 lb. of onion powder
> 0.25 lb. of pepper
> 0.4 lb. of salt

The totals compared with the figures given before show the amount of water which was unavoidably present, and without going into details I can assure the reader that when one obtains over twenty-nine ounces of food value out of thirty-four ounces of weight carried, one can congratulate oneself on having one's food in an exceedingly concentrated form.

Including the smaller matters which I have mentioned, this total would be brought up to thirty-five and a half ounces as the daily allowance per man. It is interesting to compare this with the allowance given in Northern expeditions. Greely allowed thirty-six ounces; McClintock, forty-two ounces; Nares, forty ounces; whereas Parry, in the early days, allowed only twenty-two ounces. The journeys of the latter were not of great length, but one can imagine how famished his party must have been.

The trouble taken in apportioning the different natures of food has an extremely practical bearing. The object aimed at is that, whilst the traveller develops a craving for food, it should not be for any particular form of food. I have heard it said by members of the older expeditions, 'The thing we craved for was sugar', or 'The thing we craved for was fat', and without doubt this argues that the party would have been better provided had they carried a greater proportion of these articles and less of something else.

In this connection I may point out that Barne's allowance contained more biscuit than mine, and I am not sure that he was not right, as our biscuit was certainly on the short side, and we had a distinct craving for more. On the whole, however, our parties went well in this respect. Our people on getting back to the ship wanted food and plenty of it, but did not especially demand it in any particular form.

From the above list it will be seen that our variety of food was not a very large one. Nansen seems to have been of opinion that variety was of great importance, but in this I cannot agree. During our long absences our food was pretty much the same day after day, and though we sighed for greater quantity we were never particularly desirous of changing the quality. The great drawback to a large variety is the complication which is introduced into the packing arrangements; that these should be as simple as possible with a party of men is of the greatest importance. Our biscuit was packed on the sledges in boxes or in canvas tanks specially made on board for the purpose, but although the boxes were of the lightest Venesta packing material, the additional weight involved by either tank or box was considerable. The packing of biscuit is especially difficult, because if packed loosely it will grind itself into fine powder with the movement of the sledge, so that probably much will be lost.

All the remaining provisions were carefully weighed out into amounts which constituted the allowance for three men for one week; this amount was placed in a small light bag, and then all the small bags were placed in a canvas tank on the sledge.

In addition to this, each tent party of three men possessed a ready-use bag containing all the small bags allowed for the week. It will be seen that this was an extremely simple arrangement; all the trouble and care had been taken on board the ship, and when once away the arrangements went like clockwork. Each member of the group of three living together in a tent would take it in turn to be cook for the week. On the stated day he would go to the provision tank and take out his allowance of small bags; these he would place in the ready-use bag, which was always kept handy on the sledge. When camping-time came and the tent was up, the cook would get inside, with his provision bag and cooking-apparatus, and with everything under his hand he was able to prepare supper in the shortest possible space of time. Of course the cook was responsible for the weekly allowance lasting out its proper time; if it ran short before, the inmates of the tent had to go hungry, and this made the cook unpopular.

I have said there was little variety in our provisions, but a good cook had some chance of showing his abilities. Even in such a ménage he could vary the ingredients of his hoosh each night, provided he did not outrun the constable, and a very wily cook would save a bit here and there during his term of office so as to end it up with one really thick 'stick to the ribs' hoosh, which kept his memory green for several days.

The weekly allowance of food for a tent I called a provision unit, and I find I had to allow at least 6 lbs. for the packing of each unit.

The habit of heating his food is about the only one possessed by the sledge-traveller which can be said to go beyond the bare necessity of life. Theoretically I believe the food would be as nourishing and sustaining were it swallowed cold; it would only lose its immediate stimulating effect. Hence to some extent fuel is a luxury, but even from this point of view not entirely, for it would always be necessary to carry some fuel and some vessel in order to obtain water for drinking. As regards the heating of food, I can only say that I should prefer to be absent from a party who had decided to forego it. The prospect of a cold supper after a long and tiring march through the snow, with the thermometer below zero, would hold out no allurements, and indeed, from my small experience of a shortage of fuel under these conditions, I believe that few, if any, sledge-travellers could continue long without hot food.

So, at any rate for me, the sledge cooker is a matter of great importance, and it is here, if anywhere, that an immense advance has been made of late years in the sledging equipment. The cooking-apparatus we adopted was Nansen's, who, I consider, in devising this and adapting to it a modern form of heating-lamp, consuming paraffin in a vaporised state, made his greatest contribution to the sledge-traveller's requirements.

The principal requirement of a good cooking-apparatus is that it should allow a minimum wastage of heat, and though it is difficult to arrive at an exact figure, it is probably stated with some reason that the Nansen cooker expends usefully nearly 90 per cent. of the heat supplied by the lamp beneath it. The design of the apparatus provides that the heated gases circulate about the central cooking-pot, and after passing up inside the annular container, which we termed the outer cooker, descend again on the outside and thus give up most of their heat before reaching the open air. The greater part of the apparatus is constructed of aluminium, and the whole is made as thin as is compatible with the necessary strength in order to save weight.

I have already mentioned how at camping time the tent would be erected and the cook would retire inside with his provision bag and lamp; whilst he was lighting the latter one of the other members would fill the inner and outer cookers with snow and pass them into the tent, so that a very few minutes after the tent was up the lamp could be heard giving forth its pleasant music, and one knew that its heat was already acting on the frozen snow within the cookers.

Without wishing to take the reader into abstruse problems, I must here mention one of the physical properties of ice, which has a very practical bearing on the sledge-traveller. It may possibly be overlooked that it requires nearly as much heat to turn ice into water as it does to raise the resultant water to boiling-point. In other words, if the snow that is put into the cookers is at a temperature of $-36°$, it will take just as much heat to turn it into water as it does subsequently to raise the water to boiling-point.

The practical bearing is obvious: it means that the sledge-traveller requires nearly double the amount of fuel for cooking his meals that would be necessary if he could fill his cookers with water. Here again, therefore, he is handicapped in his struggle for existence.

The cook, having started his lamp under the cooker, proceeded to prepare the ingredients of the hoosh, by which term the hot, thick soup that constituted the sledging meal was generally known. Whilst he ladled out a spoonful from one small bag and two from another, and added a little pepper and a little salt, he kept a watchful eye for the first spurt of steam which should signify that the water was on the boil. Directly this appeared, off came the covers and in went the assortment of food; in a very few minutes there was a bubbling and spluttering, and the tent was filled with the savoury odour of the coming meal. Not a moment was lost; with the steady hand of the expert handling a priceless possession, the steaming contents of the cooking-pot were soon being poured into the several pannikins. Then came the cleaning of the pot by the cook, whose perquisite this was; all that would not pour out in a fluid state was rapidly scraped out with a spoon and transferred to the cook's mouth. Without again employing the word 'cleaning', I may say I have known worse ways of emptying a pot. In the meanwhile the snow in the outer cooker had melted, and so the water was all ready for transference to the inner vessel for the final brew of cocoa. As soon as this was on the boil the lamp was extinguished.

The excellence of this cooking-apparatus can only be gleaned from a citation of figures. With it, boiling water could be made from snow in twelve minutes; a simple one-course meal could be prepared in less than twenty minutes; and a two-course meal – that is, a hoosh with hot cocoa to follow – could be provided with a lapse of less than half an hour between the time the lamp was lighted and its extinction. Except for further economy of fuel, a more rapid apparatus would have given no advantage, for, as it was, the supper was generally ready before all the outside camp work, such as securing the tent and sledges, &c., could be fully accomplished.

The immense advantage which we possessed in this respect can be gauged when it is recalled that McClintock speaks of the inevitable wait of two hours which his parties had to endure, after a long day's march, before they could hope to get warmed food; or, again, when it is stated that the records of the Arctic sledge journeys of 1875 show that the cook was always called two hours before the remainder of the party. With us, on more than one occasion, a very rapidly prepared brew of tea has saved serious trouble from freezing, and this alone made possible those exceptional efforts of marching in which we occasionally indulged.

In our rapid cooking the lamp was, of course, an even greater factor than the cooker; after some consideration we had adopted the Primus lamp which Nansen had found so useful. When in good working order nothing could exceed the efficiency of this lamp. The oil, which is pressed up into the upper tubes, is vaporised by the heat, and the vapour, emerging through a small pinhole, burns with a flame of intense heat, and effects the most complete combustion of the oil. In the rapidity and completeness of the combustion lies its great advantage. It has serious disadvantages: it is complicated and difficult to repair; it is likely to get out of order unless both the lamp and the oil used in it are kept absolutely free from dirt and grit; and when out of order it is quite useless. Moreover, the vaporisation has to be started by outside artificial means, the correct method being to fill a small outside cup with spirit. From these various defects we had at first much trouble, more especially as the sailor is inclined to be rather heavy-handed and careless with delicate mechanism. Later on, however, the men realised how much depended on keeping the lamps in good working order, and in consequence became very expert in handling them. Our confidence in them grew as we came to understand them better, and in spite of their defects we ultimately placed such reliance on them that we never thought of taking an alternative lamp. On two occasions, in fact, my party were away on very extended journeys with nothing to fall back on had our lamp failed.

As may have been gathered, the cooking and eating utensils of our sledge parties were not numerous. Besides the cooker and lamp, a folding pannikin of aluminium was provided for each man, one-half of which could be used for his hoosh and the other for his cocoa. In addition each person had a dessert-spoon.

Pannikins and spoons could be conveniently stowed inside the cooker for transport, and the latter then added 15 lbs. to the load, beyond which an extra weight of 2½ to 3 lbs. had to be allowed for the Primus lamp.

The oil was carried in small rectangular tins, which fitted close to one another on a light platform on the sledge. Some of these tins had been made in England, but we had considerably to increase our supply by others made on board the ship. Each tin had a small cork bung, which was a decided weakness; paraffin creeps in the most annoying manner, and a good deal of oil was wasted in this way, especially when the sledges were travelling over rough ground and were shaken or, as frequently happened, capsized. It was impossible to make these bungs quite tight, however closely they were jammed down, so that in spite of a trifling extra weight a much better fitting would have been a metallic screwed bung. To find on opening a fresh tin of oil that it was only three-parts full was very distressing, and of course meant that the cooker had to be used with still greater care.

A full tin of oil weighed 10 lbs. and contained exactly a gallon, and this quantity, as a general rule, was the allowance for ten days for three persons. With care this was amply sufficient, and on the southern journey when our stock was somewhat short a gallon was made to last fourteen and even sixteen days, but this meant very short commons.

The incidental weights of a sledge party were numerous, and depended greatly on the direction in which the party were going and on the nature of their work. Those who journeyed to the mountainous regions of the west were forced to go most fully equipped in this respect, and in planning a sledge journey in that direction it was especially maddening to see how the weights of indispensable articles mounted up, and ever cut away from the margin which remained for food.

The weights of a party naturally divide themselves under two headings: the permanent, which will not diminish throughout the trip, and the consumable, including food, oil, &c. The following is a list of permanent weights carried on my own journey to the west; it will give some idea of the variety of articles which were taken exclusive of provisions; the party numbered six:

	lbs.		lbs.
2 Sledges with fittings complete	130	3 Ice-axes	8
Trace	5	Bamboos and marks	11.5
2 Cookers, pannikins, & spoons	30	Instruments and camera	50
2 Primus lamps, filled	10	Alpine rope	9
2 Tents complete	60	Repair and tool bags, sounding-line,	
2 Spades	9	tape, sledge brakes	15
2 Sleeping-bags with night-gear	100	Ski boots for party	15
Sleeping-jackets, crampons, spare		Ski for party	60
finneskoes	50		
Medical bag	6	Total	568.5

Although our sledges weighed little over 40 lbs. each, by the time they had been fitted with tanks for the provisions, platforms for the oil, boxes for the instruments and for the Primus lamps, and straps for other articles, it will be seen by how much their weight had risen.

Some of the other items may need a word or two of explanation. The spades were of course needed for digging up the snow to secure the tents. The night-gear consisted of warm footwear for the night, and a small bag containing one or two spare pairs of socks, a spare pair of mits, possibly a small amount of tobacco, and some extra grass for filling fur boots. This bag was always kept in the sleeping-bag, and was used by the owner as a pillow as well as a receptacle for diaries and the few oddments that constitute private property on such an occasion.

The heavy labour of marching made it possible to undertake it in comparatively light clothing; but on coming to camp it was generally necessary to put on something extra. In this garment also we slept, wherefore it figures as the sleeping-jacket. It was usually made from a woollen pyjama jacket, and lined with some extra woollen material. Of course all personal property was strictly limited by a given weight, and if a man chose to forego a pair of socks and take out the weight in tobacco, he was at liberty to do so. I remember gazing at my spare mits and wishing to heaven I'd brought tobacco instead.

The crampons were a necessity for travelling over smooth ice or very hard wind-blown snow. For the second year we invented and made a particular pattern of our own, which suited us admirably, and which I shall describe in due course.

Our medical bag contained bandages, sticking-plaster, an emulsion for sprains, a few phials containing medicines in the tabloid form, and a tube of hazeline cream. The general health of our sledge-travellers was so good that I believe, with the exception of two, the medicine phials were never required; the two exceptions contained zinc sulphate and cocaine, the first to cure and the second to deaden the pain of snow-blindness. As this disease was a constant companion, these tabloids were very frequently needed.

The ice-axes mentioned above were of the ordinary Alpine type; they came in very handy for various work on the glaciers, but they were seldom absolutely necessary.

The title 'bamboos and marks' includes sticks and flags taken to measure the movement of the ice of the glaciers and to mark the positions at which we left our depots of provisions.

The contents of our instrument-box were an extraordinarily heavy item, and yet there was nothing which we could have spared. They consisted of a small three-inch theodolite in its case, for taking observations of the sun and bearings, two small aneroids, a compass, two thermometers, a hypsometer, a small book containing logarithmic tables, and a camera, with plates. On this journey we took the half-plate camera with its slide-box, and although one almost groaned on seeing the weight it added, there can be little source of regret when one contemplates the pictures which Mr Skelton managed to produce with its assistance.

Alpine rope was a thing one scarcely liked to be without when travelling in a country where crevasses abounded; the thought of a companion possibly hung up in one of these and his fellow men unable to reach him for lack of rope, was too grim to be thrust aside. The repair-bag was an important item; it contained the housewife, with needles, thread, &c., to repair our garments, a few strips of material to patch the tent, with sail needles and a palm, some hide thongs, some tough pieces of reindeer-skin for boots, and some spun yarn for lashings. A tool-bag was also very necessary, and contained pliers, files, a bradawl, a gimlet, &c., with some screws, nails, and binding wire for the repair of the sledges. The sounding-line and lead were provided for sounding and taking temperatures in crevasses, but it was rarely possible to use them. The tape was also for glacier measurements, whilst the sledge brakes were introduced in hopes of saving the sledges on the down grade over slippery ice. They were of hemp, and proved of very little use.

We took ski boots on this journey in hopes of being able to use ski, and thinking they might be of service on the glacier; we used neither the ski nor the boots, and 'depoted' the latter at a very early stage in the journey. The ski we took on, thinking always they might be required, but never finding that they were so.

And here I should like to explain my attitude towards ski, more especially as since Nansen's journeys it has been very generally thought that they have revolutionised the methods of polar travel. I have mentioned in former chapters how delighted we were with our ski practice, and I have also called attention to an incident where some officers were able to push on with a journey because they possessed ski. The latter is really an extraordinary exception, and it is still more extraordinary that it should have been our first experience of Antarctic travelling. It naturally biassed us all in favour of ski, so that although a few remained sceptical, the majority thought them an unmixed blessing. Bit by bit, however, the inevitable truth came to light: it was found that in spite of all appearance to the contrary, a party on foot invariably beat a party on ski, even if the former were sinking ankle-deep at each step; while, to add to this, when the surface was hard, ski could not be used, and had to be carried as an extra weight and a great encumbrance on the sledges. The ski party still made a stand in their favour by stating that they saved labour, but even this could not be admitted when the facts were thoroughly known. It stands true to some extent for a party out of condition, but the fact we gradually came to appreciate was that after a week's marching our legs got so hard that it troubled us little to plod on throughout the day whether the snow was soft or hard.

It will be seen, therefore, that our experience has led me to believe that for sledge work in the Antarctic Regions there is nothing to equal the honest and customary use of one's own legs. Progress may be slow and dull, but it is steady and sure. On my western journey, having no knowledge of the inland surface, I took ski. They remained on the sledge from start to finish. As we were contemplating them just before our return to the ship, one of my companions remarked, 'They've had a nice cheap ride', and that about summed up the situation.

In the list of permanent weights which I have taken as an example of a sledge-load for six men, the reader will see that the various articles total 568 lbs.; roughly speaking a man can drag from 200 to 240 lbs., but we rarely loaded our sledge parties much above 200 lbs.; this for six men would give a total carrying capacity of 1,200 lbs and hence about 630 lbs. which could be devoted to provisions. Speaking again very roughly, this amounts to about six weeks' provisions for the party, so that this party, dragging at the start 200 lbs. per man, can go away for forty-two days and throughout that time remain entirely self-supporting. If the party is increased to twelve men, for reasons which I need not detail, the absence can be increased to seven weeks, or about fifty days. But neither of these terms is long enough to suit the ambitious sledge-traveller, so that he is forced to organise means by which he can prolong his journey. This can be done in two ways: he may go out earlier in the season and lay out a depot at a considerable distance towards his goal, or he may arrange to receive assistance from a supporting party, which on a prearranged plan accompanies him for a certain distance on his road and helps his advance party to drag a heavier load than it is able to accomplish alone.

Both these plans were adopted on our longer journeys, and thus some of us were able to be absent from the ship for long periods and to travel long distances.

I have endeavoured to describe how a sledge party is housed and fed; it remains to conclude this chapter by giving some idea of how it is clothed, and this can be done very briefly. The sledge-traveller takes little more clothing than that in which he stands at starting; in fact, I have already mentioned the articles of which his spare wardrobe consists. They do not include a change of clothing, so that he sleeps and lives in the one costume until his return.

In our case officers and men were clothed in a similar manner, save for such touches as the fancy of the individual might suggest. Each wore a warm thick suit of underclothing, one or two flannel shirts, a jersey, or sweater, a pair of pilot-cloth breeches, and a pyjama jacket. A pilot-cloth coat or any stiff garment about the upper part of the body was unpopular, and personally I cut off the sleeves of my pyjama jacket so that it was practically a very free-and-easy outer waistcoat. Some wore woollen comforters, but others, like myself, found the collar of the pyjama jacket sufficient covering for the neck.

Of great importance we found it to have many pockets, and a large breast-pocket was very generally adopted. It was here that in hard times by day one dried one's night socks, and by night those which one had worn during the day. Besides this, one's pockets contained a collection of miscellaneous articles: a knife, a match-box, goggles, a whistle, and odds and ends such as string, thongs, and so forth.

Braces were another matter on which there was difference of opinion. Some thought them indispensable, but I, with others, found that a leather belt served all needful purposes in this respect.

But one of the most important parts of our sledging-costume was the complete outer suit of thin gaberdine, a material manufactured by Messrs Burberry for use in many climates. It purports to be watertight, but of this we had little chance of judging; we required it only to keep out the keen edge of the wind and the drifting snow, and for this it was admirably adapted.

We found it very desirable that this suit should be very easily put on or off. On fine days it was convenient to march without it; but when the wind sprang up or the sky looked threatening it was wise to don it at once. But to construct a suit which had this desirable quality and at the same time was impervious to snowdrift was by no means easy. The suit consisted of a blouse, breeches, and leggings, but whether the leggings should be attached to the breeches, and how exactly the neck, sleeves, and other parts of the blouse should be fitted were matters of keen controversy, eventually decided according to individual taste. It is impossible, therefore, to give any very definite opinion as to the best form for these garments; subject to their being easy to put on and off, one great thing is that they should fit as closely as possible about the neck, wrists, and ankles, and that there should be no admittance for snowdrift between the blouse and trousers. It is almost equally important that there should be as few creases as possible, especially about the legs, as the snow which lodges in these is bound to be brought into the tent.

The parts of the body which need the most careful protection are the extremities, and here, again, everyone had his own ideas and his own patent devices. To face the cold of the early spring we had thick camel-wool helmets provided with gaberdine covers, but many of us found these too heavy, and when they became coated with ice they were particularly unmanageable. A better plan was to use one or two ordinary woollen Balaclava helmets under the gaberdine cover. Personally, I used one, provided with an extra thickness of material to cover those most sensitive organs, the ears. I have already described the wind-guard which most of us wore to protect the face.

In summer, when the glare was very great, we wore broad-rimmed felt hats, either over a Balaclava or fitted with a special protection for the ears and back of the neck, which could be lowered or tucked into the crown according to circumstances. It is a great mistake to have too heavy a head-covering; the ice which inevitably forms on it in cold weather is sufficient to make a light helmet comparatively warm.

On our hands, when sledging, we wore either fur or felt mits over long woollen half-mits which extended from the elbows to the knuckles. These half-mits were excellent things, as one could draw them forward to assist one in handling the cold metal cooking-utensils or could curl one's fingers back under their protection when the tips became particularly cold. Personally I swore by our wolfskin fur mits. We wore them with the fur outside, and I lined mine with light wool and found that one pair lasted me throughout each of my extended sledge journeys. The most convenient plan was to have these mits slung round the neck, as one could then withdraw one's hands at will without the prospect of finding the mits gone when one wished to resume them. For taking observations and for other trying tasks it was very convenient to have a pair of light woollen mits or gloves, but of these there was a great scarcity on board.

Of all parts of the person of which it is necessary to have care the feet are the most important, and for clothing the feet in cold weather there can be nothing to excel the reindeer-fur boot or finnesko, which is made in Norway. It behoves the traveller to be most careful in the selection of these articles, as, though many are made for wear, many also are made for a tourist market and will prove quite unsuitable for his purpose. Here, again, a lack of time had prevented a sufficient care being taken in selecting the large supply which we purchased, and though we had a good number of excellent articles, others were weak and unsatisfactory. The difference is most marked – a good pair of finneskoes will stand many weeks of hard wear on snow, whereas a poor pair will be gone in a few days; the importance of selecting good pairs for a sledge journey is therefore obvious. Luckily we soon became fairly good judges, and so never actually ran out of footwear on our journeys, though we came very close to it.

The sole of the finnesko is made of the forehead skin or the hard skin of the legs of the reindeer; it is important that it should have a twist in the natural growth of the hair, as this gives a better foothold. The upper sides are made of softer skin from the neck or legs; all the joints are very carefully sewn with gut, and the boot is worn with the fur outside.

To examine a pair it is necessary to turn them inside out, and this is not easy to do until they are made damp. With experience it is then possible to see the quality of the sewing and the probable lasting power of the sole. The Laps make a nest of grass inside these boots and place their foot in this nest without further covering. There is an advantage in this in the fact that the grass can be taken out and the frozen perspiration shaken clear, but the custom probably springs from the absence of wool. This grass is called sennegraes. We had provided ourselves with a good quantity; but we wore two pairs of socks inside the finneskoes, and only used the grass to pad out the toes and sides. Finneskoes are provided with a draw-string at the top, but we found that the best means of securing them was with a long strip of lamp-wick, which was wound about the ankle and covered the joint between the legging and the boot. Instances of seriously cold feet in finneskoes were extremely rare, and usually after an hour's marching one's feet perspired freely in the coldest weather. One great advantage is that there is absolutely no restraint to the circulation.

Before leaving the subject of dress one ought to mention the goggles, which were worn almost as constantly as many of the articles I have described. A few men preferred the ordinary wire-gauze type with smoked glass, but a drawback to these was their liability to become frosted over. The alternatives were to have a piece of leather with a slit in place of the glass, or to have goggles cut out from a slip of wood. Personally I much preferred the latter, and in the end invariably used them; mine were very carefully shaped to fit over the nose and eyes, had a considerable cross-shaped aperture, and were blackened outside and in.

One other article of sledge furniture deserves notice – the harness. Each man had a broad band of webbing passing round his waist and supported by braces over the shoulders; the two ends of the band joined in an iron ring, to which a rope was attached which could be secured to the sledge or the trace. In the old days men were accustomed to pull from the shoulder, and thus of necessity assumed a somewhat lopsided attitude; with our arrangement, by adjusting the braces the weight could be distributed very evenly over the upper part of the body, and this I believe made the pulling easier and gave greater freedom for breathing.

From the foregoing the reader will, I hope, have gathered some general idea of the objects and methods of sledge-travelling. He will see how varied is the assortment of articles with which the traveller provides himself; he will understand something of the rigid nature of the sledging routine and the simplicity of the sledging life; he will perceive how the sledge party are housed, and fed, and clothed, and how their absence is prolonged. Above all, he will realise how dependent is a sledging expedition on the efficiency of its organisation and the care of its preparation.

CHAPTER II

Typical sledging experiences

Use of Dogs for Sledging – A Discussion of their Merits – History of our Dog-Team – Discomforts of Sledge-travelling – Typical Experiences – The Ordinary Routine – Result of a Blizzard – Benefit of Summer Temperatures – Disadvantages of Summer – The Fascination of Sledging

> By mutual confidence and mutual aid
> Great deeds are done and great discoveries made. – ANON.

> 'Tis a weary round to which we are bound
> The same thing over and over again;
> Much toil and trouble. – LINDSAY GORDON

From the outline of our sledging arrangements which I have given in the previous chapter, the reader will understand the occupation of our time and thoughts throughout the later months of the dark season. Yet this outline has been necessarily of a fragmentary nature, and I am conscious of having missed many points of importance. To one of these, at least, I ought to refer, since the chapter has made no mention of our four-footed friends, who were to play so important and tragic a part in our longest journey.

The use of dogs for sledging is a subject about which there has been much controversy. Broadly speaking, there are two ways in which dogs may be used – they may be taken with the idea of bringing them all back safe and sound, or they may be treated as pawns in the game, from which the best value is to be got regardless of their lives.

In the first case their value is indicated by a direct comparison of their pulling power and food requirement with that of the man. McClintock, who had much experience in this matter, has said: 'Two dogs require the same weight of food as one man, and they will draw a man's full load for about one-fourth a greater distance than the man would. If both man and dogs are but lightly loaded, the dogs will almost double the distance which the man could do.'

To this may be added that the dog requires no sleeping-bag, tent, or cooking-apparatus, nor, indeed, any of those articles which figured so largely as the permanent weights of a sledge party. Most authorities agree that 100 lbs. is about the maximum load for a dog, and few place its food for a long journey at less than 1½ lb. per diem, or something over half the weight consumed by a man.

So far, then, it would appear that a dog is a more efficient machine than a man; but, on the other hand, it has to be remembered that the dogs cannot travel without man, and they have therefore, in addition to their own food, to carry the food and impedimenta of their drivers. Moreover, the dog is fickle and unstable: its best performance, which has sometimes fallen little short of the marvellous, has been on short journeys, over beaten tracks, and with a light load; sustained effort with a heavy load over a new track seems always to have shown the dog in a much less favourable light. Difficult as it is to ascertain the reason exactly, the fact remains that no very long journey has ever been made by a wholly detached dog-team in the Arctic Regions, from which the animals have returned alive. The subject is complicated, and I am aware of treating it somewhat summarily, but I am inclined to state my belief that in the polar regions properly organised parties of men will perform as extended journeys as teams of dogs, provided always that it is intended to preserve the lives of the dogs.

But if, on the other hand, it is decided to sacrifice the dogs to the supreme object of the journey, the matter is placed on a different footing, and the dog-team is invested with a capacity for work which is beyond the emulation of a party of men. To appreciate this is a matter of simple arithmetic. We can suppose a party of three men starting on a journey dependent on their own labours, and we can suppose the same party starting with the assistance of twelve dogs which they intend should feed on one another. In the latter case, although the party start with heavier weights than in the former, the dogs not only draw this heavier load but carry their own food on their own legs. It is obvious, therefore, that the dog-assisted party will have the radius of the simple man party plus the distance added by the dogs' energy. This is not quoted as a practical case, but merely to show the clear gain which the dog offers.

This method of using dogs is one which can only be adopted with reluctance. One cannot calmly contemplate the murder of animals which possess such intelligence and individuality, which have frequently such endearing qualities, and which very possibly one has learnt to regard as friends and companions. On the other hand, it may be pointed out with good reason that to forego the great objects which may be achieved by the sacrifice of dog-life is carrying sentiment to undue length. It is a case, if ever there was one, where the end justifies the means. There is no real reason why the life of a dog should be considered more than that of a sheep, and no-one would pause to consider the cruelty of driving a diminishing flock of sheep to supply the wants and aid the movements of travellers in more temperate climates.

If one comes to look into this matter, one sees that the real cruelty to a dog lies in over-working or under-feeding it, and it is in avoiding this as far as possible that the sledge-traveller most truly shows his humanity. The avoidance of unnecessary pain should be the aim, and suddenly and painlessly to end the life of an animal which has been well fed and well cared for is not cruelty. Unfortunately, it is not always possible to avoid pain, and it was this fact more than the actual killing that weighed heavily on us when, as I shall relate, we had gradually and completely to efface the patient companions of our southern sledge journey.

My plan for utilising our dog-team was compounded of the two methods which I have sketched above. We faced the situation that the weaker animals must be sacrificed to the exigencies of the work, though we hoped that a remnant of the larger and stronger beasts would survive to enjoy again a life of luxury and ease; but, as events turned out, we saved none: all were lost under the unavoidable pressure of circumstances.

Probably our experience was an exceptionally sad one in this respect, but it left in each one of our small party an unconquerable aversion to the employment of dogs in this ruthless fashion. We knew well that they had served their end, that they had carried us much farther than we could have got by our own exertions; but we all felt that we would never willingly face a repetition of such incidents, and when in the following year I stepped forth in my own harness, one of a party which was dependent on human labour alone, it would not be easy adequately to convey the sense of relief which I felt in the knowledge that there could be no recurrence of the horrors of the previous season.

I have endeavoured to give a just view of the use of dogs in polar enterprises. To say that they do not greatly increase the radius of action is absurd; to pretend that they can be worked to this end without pain, suffering, and death is equally futile. The question is whether the latter can be justified by the gain, and I think that logically it may be; but the introduction of such sordid necessity must and does rob sledge-travelling of much of its glory. In my mind no journey ever made with dogs can approach the height of that fine conception which is realised when a party of men go forth to face hardships, dangers, and difficulties with their own unaided efforts, and by days and weeks of hard physical labour succeed in solving some problem of the great unknown. Surely in this case the conquest is more nobly and splendidly won.

It must not be forgotten, however, that few expeditions can command the numerical strength to perform extended journeys with men alone. A large party of men is not only a great responsibility, but a great expense; the dog gives little anxiety, requires no housing, and draws no wages.

There is one other point which must not be omitted in considering the relative services of dogs and men. There are places where men can go but dogs cannot. The greater part of polar travelling has lain over flat sea-ice or comparatively flat land-ice, and this is a condition suitable to the dog; but on steep slopes and over uneven country the dog is practically useless. It will be seen that a great deal of our travelling lay over uneven country. Everywhere but on the barrier surface we had inequalities to contend with, and in rising to the steep mountain ranges to the west we had to ascend rough uneven glaciers and to traverse surfaces of smooth glassy ice, where dogs would have been a hopeless encumbrance; men, and men alone, could have dragged our sledges over these rugged tracts. As we were situated, therefore, the services of dogs could only have been utilised to a limited extent, nor is it at all improbable that a similar experience awaits future Antarctic travellers.

For some time before the start of our sledging season we had strained inventive talent in the hope of devising the best form of harness for our dog-team, one which would give them the best chance of utilising their strength; but in this respect a dog is a most uncanny animal to suit. Except after an exhausting march he is never still: he will leap about and turn and twist in a manner calculated to tangle the simplest harness, and to this he adds an ineradicable habit of gnawing at his trace.

The harness, as regards the dog itself, we kept a permanency. Each dog was measured for his suit, and then it was sewn securely about him. It consisted of a broad breast-band secured to a girth about the forepart of the body. The trace could be secured on either side of this arrangement. At first we tried a double trace to equalise the pull, using some small steel rope, impervious to the animals' teeth. This promised well, and, fitted with swivels, it was a really ingenious contrivance; but we found later that the wire, though very flexible, was liable to chafe, and when the small, sharp strands stuck out at all angles it was not pleasant to handle. Finally we had to revert to the single trace of rope, which was secured to the harness with a hitch and to the main trace with a toggle; whilst half-way along it was a swivel, which helped to counteract the constant restless twisting of the animal.

We also had many trials to find out how the dogs should be placed with regard to the sledge, finally arranging a long central trace, along which they were secured in pairs. Thus arranged our dog-team trailed out to rather a long procession. First came the leading dog, led by one of the party; after him, two by two, the remainder of the team, the 'wheelers' being close back on the sledge. Even with this simple arrangement the traces would sometimes be worked into a bad tangle, which it was only possible to unravel with bare fingers – a task that was not looked forward to with any pleasure, especially in the early morning. In this respect there is a curious habit in dogs, which appears to be some survival of a remote wild age, and which most people will doubtless have noticed: a dog rarely coils himself down to sleep without turning round several times, as though arranging some imaginary lair. However pleasing this habit may be to watch on ordinary occasions, one does not contemplate it with delight in a sledge dog, knowing that one will eventually have to disentangle the twisted confusion that results.

It may be of interest perhaps to explain briefly how we came to be possessed of a dog-team. In the early days of preparation which preceded our departure from London the subject of dogs very naturally arose, and it became evident that if we were to obtain a team arrangements would have to be made in good time. The German expedition, which was to start simultaneously with our own, had already secured a team in Eastern Siberia, where, it is reported, the dogs are both larger and stronger than in the West. It was too late for us to copy this example, but I shortly got into communication with an agent, Mr Wilton, who was then in Archangel, and who undertook to fulfil our requirements. At this time a Russian named Trontheim had been commissioned to obtain between 300 and 400 dogs for an American expedition, then about to start for Franz-Josef Land. It was Trontheim who in 1891 had secured the dogs carried on Nansen's famous voyage, and, as he was in all respects fitted for collecting the animals, our agent added our modest requirement of twenty to the number of his commission, on condition that we, through our agent, should be allowed first pick of the crowd collected. The particulars of Trontheim's wanderings are not in my knowledge, but it is certain that he must have travelled over a great portion of the country inhabited by the Ostiak and Samoyede tribes of Northern Russia to fulfil his contract. On his return to Archangel Mr Wilton selected twenty dogs and three bitches for our expedition, and duly brought them to London, where they were housed in the Zoo until such time as we could make arrangements for their transport to New Zealand and provide for their care on the voyage. I really do not think I ever had an opportunity of thoroughly examining the dogs until we came to rest in our winter quarters, but then, of course, one not only saw them, but rapidly grew to know their individual characteristics.

Notwithstanding the care with which they had been brought together, though the majority were fine, strong dogs, there was a distinct tail to our team, and several young dogs which had evidently never been in harness before. One of the most noticeable points about the team was the difference of breed. There were three distinct types, besides many modifications of these types. The first was a big, strong-limbed dog of nondescript colour, with a very thick but comparatively short coat; these animals formed the best pulling element in the team. Next came a short-legged, thick-set dog, with a long, shaggy coat, and black-and-white in colour; it was one of these who kept up the traditions of his race by pulling to the last gasp. The third type was in form and colour so near to the grey wolf that one felt confident that his blood relationship was extremely close. These dogs were by far the most unattractive in the pack; timid, cunning, and uncertain in temper, they possessed all the sneaking distrust of the wild animal and none of the good humour and boisterous affection which were so marked a characteristic of the rest. And all this mixed team had come to us unnamed and unknown; we had not a scrap of their history, nor could we tell within a thousand miles whence they came. But what mattered that? They had now good Anglo-Saxon names, and their value lay in their future, and not in their past.

One fact only had been borne by word of mouth – the king and ruler of our pack had held the same high office when he had travelled amongst 400 of his kind. And well he might. His new name of 'Nigger' wholly failed to convey the grandeur of his nature. In peace he was gentle and dignified, but in war, as we knew to our cost, he was swift and terrible.

When we opened our spring campaign with the dogs in 1902, the original team had sadly diminished. One had been lost with poor Vince in the disaster of March; two had been murdered under our very eyes, and two others had come to an untimely end during the winter.

To what remained, for our southern journey, were added the three ladies and poor 'Joe', who had been the private property of Mr Bernacchi, bringing their number up to a total of nineteen, of which all but one, who was dismissed at an early period in the journey, left their bones on the great southern plains. This in brief is the history of our dogs, but of the circumstances in which they met their end I shall speak at greater length.

A mere description, such as I have given, of the organisation of sledge-travelling and the paraphernalia which accompanies a sledge party can give no idea of the actual life of the sledge-traveller or the difficulties and hardships which he has to face, so that it is necessary to point out wherein the latter lie. The worst time for sledging is the coldest time; not so much on account of the cold itself as on account of the effects produced by the cold. The most troublesome of these is the absence of evaporation. Very cold air will only contain the minutest quantities of moisture, and consequently there is in it little or no drying effect, while the human body is always giving off moisture, much passing away in the breath, but much issuing through the pores of the skin. It is not difficult to see what will happen under such conditions, and how much the traveller will be inconvenienced. Though the greater proportion of the moisture will pass away with air artificially heated by the body a small quantity will remain as ice on one's garments, and this ice will gradually and surely increase until one is completely enclosed in it. There is ice everywhere: one's garments are covered with it; one's helmet is encrusted with it; one's boots are full of it; and all these things which on board the ship were so caressingly soft to the touch will have become as hard as boards. Worse still, this ice will be found plastered as thickly on everything that makes for comfort at night: sleeping-bag, night-jacket, and night foot-gear will have grown equally hard and chill; one's life seems to be spent in thawing things out.

Some idea of these discomforts may be gathered from the description of a day's sledging under severe conditions of temperature. We will imagine ourselves of a party who have been a week or more out, and first observe ourselves as we are plodding along through the snow towards our evening camping place. The exertion of the march has sent the blood coursing freely through our veins, and each man inside his heavy clothing has a grateful sense of warmth; but the day has been a long one, in the last half-hour the sledges have grown decidedly heavier, and legs and back are already giving warning that the camping hour ought to be at hand. Breath is now coming gustily; it has frozen thick under the wind-guards and hangs in long icicles from the unshaven chins; eyelashes are thickly encrusted with it, and now and again a bared hand has to thaw out a sealed eyelid and restore the sense of vision to its owner.

Half an hour ago the leader looked at his watch and announced, 'Thirty-five minutes to camp'; by this time we can gauge shrewdly the passage of time and the watch has not been seen again until now, when it is followed by the caution, 'Three minutes more.' Heads go up; it is time to look for the camping spot. But we are now travelling over rough sastrugi; we cannot camp on these with any hope of comfort. Suddenly the owner of a keen eye says, 'There we are, sir'; he has detected a smooth patch just large enough for our tents, and we make for it. We march to the site and up goes the leader's hand. The sledges stop dead; traces and harness fall with a clatter on the snow, and without a moment's delay the heavily clad figures turn towards the sledges. There must be no standing about in this weather; we must be constantly active until we can creep into the shelter of our thin tent. Everyone is soon wrenching at the straps of the neatly packed sledges and running busily to and fro with various articles of the equipment. In each group of three, one man seizes the tent-poles and after some struggling succeeds in planting them firmly in the snow over the smoothest site he can find; his two companions advance with the tent, and whilst he holds grimly to the poles they whisk it over his head and straighten it till it hangs squarely on its support. One now pulls out and arranges the skirting, whilst the other has seized the shovel and is cutting out large slabs of snow as though his life depended on it.

I may here add that this was not always an easy task. Sometimes the snow was brittle and crystalline and difficult to work; at others there was very little of it, especially when we camped on glaciers; but the worst condition was when it was excessively hard. It may seem almost incredible that we occasionally found wind-blown snow so hard that, except in the strongest hands, a solid sharp shovel made no impression on it. To prise out pieces at such times was really expert work, and it was lucky that we only came on this condition after we had had some experience.

But to return to our tent. Whilst the others are delving and securing the tent without, the cook has spread the floorcloth within, and is now seated on it with his Primus lamp and provision bag. He handles the first with care, pours spirit from a tiny flask into the outer cup, and laying in it a small piece of wick proceeds to light it. His matches are produced with great care from an inner pocket. Herein lies great danger, for on no account must moisture be allowed to condense in that box; the contents of many a match-box have been wasted by incaution. If he has been sufficiently careful, however, the lamp-wick is soon sputtering and thin blue flame creeps up about the burner of the lamp; with bated breath he waits for the psychological moment, and suddenly gives a sharp stroke to the plunger of the lamp. If he has hit it off, small shafts of blue flame shoot out beneath the caps, and in a minute, as he works away at the pump, the top of the lamp is surrounded by a hissing, roaring flame. If, however, he has not hit it off, the yellow flame of free oil alone shoots up, and all has to be done over again. Meanwhile the cooker has been filled by those outside and handed in through the door. Directly the lamp is lit the various vessels are placed on top of it; the lamp takes a deeper note as it gets to its work, and those without breathe a sigh of relief as they realise that supper is now really in sight.

The cook now gets ahead with the contents of the provision bag and continues to suffer in comparative silence, for indeed all this time he has suffered; he has had to work with bared hands and to seize one by one all these chilled metal articles, where a moment's delay will convey a tingling, burning shock to the fingers. Of such work it may be truly said:

> Ah me! what perils do environ
> The man who meddles with cold iron.

In our spring journeys it was impossible to avoid this trouble with cold metal; our fingers became to a certain extent callous, but only when each fingertip terminated in a large horny blister. Except that they burnt and tingled, these blisters did not give much trouble during a short journey, but were very sore when they burst after one's return. On a long cold journey one's fingers were liable to split and crack about the nails, and this was both painful and troublesome.

As soon as the tent is well secured without, those who have been at work on it demand admittance; the door is unfastened and they come tumbling in with a confused medley of night-coats and foot-gear. All now squat round the hissing cooker, and we gain what comfort we can from the heat that escapes from it. The confined space within is now filled to repletion, and elbows and knees have to be managed with caution to avoid disaster to the cooker. By this time, in the spring, the sun has sunk below the horizon, and the gloom of the tent is lightened only by the flickering rays of a candle placed in a collapsible lantern which hangs from a tent-pole. So small is the space that an incautious movement often sends this contrivance flying, and there is much groping and imprecation before light can be produced again on the scene.

Whilst the cook devotes his attention to the all-important supper we others make shift to change our foot-gear; in the narrow, cramped space we tug and pull at sodden finneskoes and ice-covered socks, and, diving into our warm breast-pockets, hasten to cover bared feet with the night-socks which have been dried in that receptacle. Suddenly, without warning, a leg shoots out whilst the owner exclaims loudly under the sharp pain of violent cramp. The cooking-pot rocks wildly, but in the confusion the ever-watchful cook rises to the occasion and prevents a catastrophe.

A few moments more, and little spurts of steam rise from the centre of interest; snow has been converted into boiling water, and the cook's busiest moment has arrived. Off come the lids and covers, and in a moment all is hidden in a dense cloud of steam, through which one can dimly perceive that the cook has seized the candle and with its aid is conveying the frozen ingredients of the supper into the boiling pot. Soon, as he stirs, the most fragrant odour in the world greets our nostrils. All other work ceases as the pot is lifted and its precious contents poured into the ready pannikins. The cook takes his perquisites by scraping out, with his spoon, all that remains; this done he refills the empty pot from the outer cooker and sets it once more to boil. Then follows an interregnum of comparative silence, broken only by the crunch of biscuit or the smack of lips which have closed on a succulent spoonful of hoosh.

This is a moment to be lived for – one of the brief incidents of the day to which we can look forward with real pleasure. The hot food seems to give new life, its grateful warmth appears to run out to every limb, exhaustion vanishes, and gradually that demon within, which has gripped so tightly for the past hour or two, is appeased. The hoosh is followed by an equally delightful drink of boiling hot cocoa, but even as we gulp it down we feel that pleasure is drawing to an end, for the Primus is now out, the steam of cooking that has not passed away through the ventilator has frozen in glistening crystals on the side of the tent, and the chill of the outer air is again finding its way through the thin canvas.

There is no time to be wasted; the door is opened, and two people plunge out into the open air, the cooker and provision bag are hastily packed together, passed outside, and made secure from the wind by heavy lumps of snow; the floor is swept, and the miscellaneous assortment of clothing is collected with as much discrimination as possible into the corners allotted to the various individuals. Meanwhile the sleeping-bag is dragged to the door of the tent, and by dint of much coaxing it is eventually got inside. By this time it is quite stiff and hard; it crackles as it is forced open, and has to be flattened out with the full weight of the body. What was once the soft covering flap will now stand erect and rigid, so stiffened is it with ice. Inside, the hair is matted together and hard frozen – so hard in places that under the raps of one's knuckles it resounds like a wooden door. Could any bed be more uninviting?

Before we enter it we must have a look round. The sun is skimming round below the southern horizon; there is a deep red flare in its wake. The sky is clear save in the south-east, where lies a rather ominous bank of cloud. Are we in for a blizzard? Now and again a puff of wind sweeps over the snow; as it passes, the fine ice-crystals of the surface-drift patter against the sledges and our legs and gather in little sandy heaps beyond; the tent, which has been flapping idly, shivers violently as the blast sweeps by; a last look at the thermometer shows that the temperature has fallen to $-48°$; we wonder how much lower it is going, and make for the tent door.

It doesn't do to dive straight in, for we may land in the centre of someone else's anatomy, so we shout, 'All right for coming in?' There is a scuffling, then 'Right, oh!' and we dive with a blind lurch towards our own corner; the last-comer gathers up the loose folds of the door and ties them up tightly; then we all sit round on the sleeping-bag and complete our costume for the night. It is breathless work this, dealing with hard frozen garments in such a cramped space. Conversation is kept up in gasps, and now and again some struggling figure has to pause for a rest; but at length all are ready, and, sweeping away the loose snow as far as possible, we lift the flap of the sleeping-bag and step inside.

But the day's work is not yet over: this is the time for diaries, meteorological records, casual repairs, and pipes. The last-named, being the only attractive part of this programme, is the first to be considered, and each smoker's hand dives into the inner recesses of the pocket in which pipe, matches, and his meagre allowance of tobacco are cherished. Experience soon teaches that a pipe must be kept in a very warm place, otherwise the stem will be found choked with ice, with which nothing but a stiff bit of wire will cope.

A diary is a great nuisance when the nights are dark: the writer is obliged to secure the flickering lantern close beside his book, and when the tent is being shaken by the wind the fitful motion of the light can be imagined. As he pores over his task his breath forms a film of ice over the paper, on which the pencil frequently skids, and sometimes after writing a few lines he will turn the page to the light and find half of it illegible, so that he has to go painfully over each word afresh. Now and again his bare fingers will refuse duty, and he must wait awhile until they are nursed back to life. This sort of thing does not help one's ideas to flow, and altogether the keeping of diaries and records is no joke in this cold weather. Sewing is a still less pleasant job, and the garment must be badly rent indeed before its owner undertakes its repair on a spring journey.

As these tasks are finished, one by one the inhabitants of the sleeping-bag wriggle down into its horny depths. The last to lower himself is the centre man, who has still some duties to perform. When the others have reported themselves fixed, he laboriously wrestles with the fastenings of the bag over their heads; these secured, he 'dowses the glim' and works himself down as best he can between his companions, and finally seals the opening above his own head. Ere this dreaded night commences, the leader has again consulted his watch and found that between two and three hours have elapsed since the party halted.

The time consumed in all these simple operations of camping puzzled us greatly at first. There was no particular delay anywhere; from start to finish one was busy, and there was every incentive to hurry, yet even with experience the interval was very little shortened. The secret lies in the fact that the simplest operation becomes complicated in intensely cold weather. Even to change a pair of socks takes nearer five minutes than one. The continuous thawing-out is the real cause of delay, but the difficulty shows that the sledge-traveller has much to occupy him in cold weather beyond dragging his sledge over the snow.

A night in such a sleeping-bag as we are picturing, with the temperature below $-40°$, cannot be said to be less than horribly uncomfortable. We are rarely conscious of sleeping; certainly not oftener than one night in three can we realise that several hours have passed in oblivion, and these seem only to be bought at the price. of extreme exhaustion. Ordinarily we sleep in the fitful, broken, comfortless fashion of which the mere recollection is a nightmare, and even this poor apology for slumber does not come until we have lain broad awake and shivering for an hour or two.

With the temperature at −48° we can make a shrewd guess as to the sort of night that is before us. The first half-hour is spent in constant shifting and turning as each inmate of the bag tries to make the best of his hard mattress or to draw the equally hard covering closer about him. There is a desultory muffled conversation broken by the chattering of teeth. Suddenly the bag begins to vibrate, and we know that someone has got the shivers. It is very contagious, this shivering, and paroxysm after paroxysm passes through the whole party. We do not try to check it: the violent shaking has a decidedly warming effect; besides, it is a necessary part of the programme, and must be got through before we can hope for sleep. Presently we hear our neighbour marking time, and we rather unnecessarily ask him if his feet are cold; he explains their exact state in the most forcible language at his command.

All this time we are mentally surveying our own recumbent figure and wondering whether the parts that feel so cold are really properly covered or whether our garments have got rucked up in the struggle for ease. Our hands are tucked away in some complicated fashion that experience has commended; they are useless for exploring. Besides, we know of old how far imagination can lead one. Our thoughts, taking flying journeys round the world, flit past the tropics to log-wood firesides, but they stop nowhere until they have raced back to present discomfort. The last squirm brought the wind-guard of our helmet across our face. It is crusted with the ice of the day's march; this is now gently thawing, and presently a drop trickles down our nose. Our thoughts become fixed on that drop. It is very irritating; we long to wipe it away, but that means taking out one hand and disarranging the whole scheme of defence against the cold. We are debating the question when a second drop descends. Flesh and blood cannot stand this: out comes our hand, and for the next quarter of an hour we are pitching and tossing about to try to regain the old position.

It is all very small, very trivial; yet there are probably few who have not passed sufficiently restless nights to appreciate how these trivialities weigh on such an occasion, and here we have in their most concrete form the greater part of those elements which go to disturb the rest of man.

We start to count those imaginary sheep jumping over their imaginary hurdles for the hundredth time as the shivering lessens. The last half-hour has brought a change; we are no longer encased with ice. There are signs of a thaw; above and below the bag is less rocky; it is becoming damp and coldly clammy, but it covers us better. There is just a suspicion of somnolence, when suddenly the whole bag is shaken violently and we hear the most harrowing groans. It is only another attack of the cramp, an enemy that is never far away. We try to sympathise with the victim as we start the sheep jumping afresh.

And so this wearisome night passes on, with its round of trivial detail and its complete absence of peace and comfort. It was the same last night, and it will be the same tomorrow.

It is not an exaggeration to say that we dreaded these nights, yet it is worthy of record that none passed without a jest; the more cheerless and uncomfortable the conditions became, the more lighthearted grew the men.

I have mentioned only some of their ills. Besides cramp, cold feet, and general discomfort, many were attacked by rheumatism; later, snow-blindness intervened. Another great source of trouble was indigestion and heartburn. I, with several others, had never known this ailment under ordinary conditions, but during the earlier sledging days it attacked us most fiercely. Also, of course, frostbites were common, with painfully blistered faces and hands; feet were likewise blistered on the long, fatiguing marches.

To all these ills were our sailors regularly and constantly exposed on their sledge journeys, and not only did they hate to forego their share, but never an evil fell on them but they made so light of it that one would have thought they were engaged in the most humorous occupation imaginable. Their conversation either on the journey or after their return could have conveyed only one impression – that the whole thing was a glorified picnic. It was not that the jokes were of a high order. The acknowledged humorists were in the minority, and even they were reduced to the feeblest witticisms: the striking thing was their capacity for finding amuse-ment, not only in the dull and prosaic, but in the physically miserable. There are few people, I take it, who will not appreciate the saving qualities of this sense of humour, or who have not at some time experienced the advantage of meeting misfortune with a smile; there are few, therefore, who will not realise that one would have to search far for a better sledge-companion than the British bluejacket.

If refreshing sleep comes at all on a spring sledge journey it will be in the early morning hours, when the sleeping-bag has thawed down on its occupants, and they, though damp, can get better protection from its folds; it is now, therefore, that we doze for brief intervals and wake in fitful starts. The leader, who alone possesses a watch, is conscious of his responsibility for rousing the party, and wonders vaguely in his waking moments what the time may be. To look at his watch is a thing only to be done when all other evidence as to the passage of time has been duly considered, for it means that his present attitude has to be disturbed; he must struggle with his garments to produce the watch, and, worse still, he must slightly open the sleeping-bag so that the grey outer light may fall on its face. Therefore before he moves he recalls the incidents of the night and sums up in imagination the intervals of time which have elapsed between them; he arrives at the conclusion that another half-hour may well pass before he disturbs himself.

Then the deed has to be done, and he shuffles the watch-face up to the light. As he peers into it his breath freezes on the face, and he has to rub again before he can mark the position of the hands, but finally they show that there is still a quarter of an hour to the time of rising. He tucks away his timekeeper and lies wakefully counting the minutes. When he thinks the fifteen have elapsed he shouts, 'Time to get up!' It is evident the others have been waiting for the signal. There is no lagging; even the morning hours have not made the bag sufficiently comfortable for anyone to desire to linger in it. The toggles are soon undone, and we all hoist ourselves into a sitting position and search about us for mits and other articles of attire. A prolonged howl is sent forth into the dim morning light, 'Rouse out! Rouse out! Time to get up!' and presently one hears the muffled response from the other tents, 'A' right, sir!' A moment or two more, and all are busy again.

The murmur of conversation in the other tents comes to our ears, and occasionally some remark intended for the whole camp. Two of us have tumbled out through the door of the tent, and the moist sleeping-bag is dragged through to be rolled up outside. The cook has already dashed for his Primus lamp; the cooker is filled and passed in, and soon the hissing sound in each tent tells that breakfast preparations have commenced.

We take a swift run round to the other tents to inquire the news of the night and make a rapid survey of the various ailments; then on to the thermometer to find the spirit column resting at −45°, though the indicator shows that it has been colder in the night; its upper end is resting more than 50° below zero (in fact, on spring journeys it was often found below −60°). The temperature is slowly rising, but it is still bitter enough as we seek again the shelter of the tent.

It is lucky that the watched pot does occasionally boil, for all eyes are now glued on the cooker, and, thanks to its efficiency, no long time passes before the pemmican can be thrown in and the savoury smell of breakfast arises. With breakfast, peace and comfort again reign for a short spell, and whilst its grateful warmth is still felt we puff again at our pipe and collect as best we can our boots and other articles necessary for the day's march. The sun has just risen above the horizon, but the wind has come with it, and its golden rays are reddened by the low driving snowdrift. Some of the worst ordeals of the day are before us, and to venture into the open in the wind is not a pleasing prospect. Faces take rather a grim expression, but delay doesn't help matters; things have to be done, and they are done somehow. With the coming of the sun the flickering lantern can be dispensed with, and now we can see well to put on our marching boots.

It is very trying work. With a caution born of experience we took immense care last night in freezing them to conform as nearly as possible to the shape of our feet. After the march they had been wet through, and came off in a soft and flabby condition; we knew that this would only last for a few minutes, and as they froze we had carefully supported and kneaded them into the required shape. Half an hour later they were so hard that we could throw them about without risk of altering it; they are still in this condition, and we are about to test the result of our labours. They clatter like wooden sabots as they are deposited on the floorcloth.

We squat down and withdraw one foot from its night-clothing, grope in our breast for our day-socks, produce one of them still very wet but moderately warm, jam our foot into it, and with many gasps proceed to wedge it into a wooden finnesko. The finnesko has been prepared by placing in it a sole cut from reindeer-skin and a little padding of sennegraes. This grass is soft, but the sole is as wooden as the boot, and has needed much pushing to get it in place. We are lucky if our foot gets half-way into its rocky cover at the first attempt. We leave it at that for the moment, and proceed with the other; by the time it is in a similar position, an inch can be gained on the first, and so inch by inch these tiresome boots are pulled on. Meanwhile our feet have got alarmingly cold, and with a groan we are obliged to start up and stamp about.

There is no exaggeration in the above picture. The putting on of our finneskoes in very cold weather was generally a matter of excruciating agony; it often brought tears to the eyes and always strong expressions to the lips, and all this with footwear that on board the ship could be put on as easily as one's hat. Yet even when one was fuming in this discomfort, a glance at one's writhing companions made it impossible not to appreciate the humorous side of the situation, and we have often paused in the midst of our trying labours to indulge in a real hearty laugh.

Heaven help the man who had failed in caution on the previous night! At first, from want of experience, and later from carelessness or by accident, a boot would be found in the morning squeezed flat and frozen hard in that impossible shape. There was nothing for the owner to do but to thaw it into shape with his foot, which had to be withdrawn at intervals and rubbed violently to restore the circulation. The least time in which one could hope to cope with a boot of this description was half an hour.

By this time all have their foot-gear on, and have readjusted all their clothes ready for the march. Considerably over two hours have elapsed since we roused out of the sleeping-bag. When all is ready comes the order, 'Pack up.' Out tumble all the thickly clad figures; lamps, cookers, and sleeping-bags are bundled into their proper places on the sledges, the snow is shovelled off the tent, and the latter is whisked off its poles, shaken, and folded up; the floorcloth is rolled up or secured to a bamboo to serve as a sail. All these articles are soon piled on the sledges and securely strapped down; the camp has disappeared as though by magic, and all that is left to mark the spot is the weird circles of snow-blocks which held the tents.

The warming effect of breakfast has long since vanished, and now all is eagerness to be on the march. The harness is soon picked up from the snow and adjusted about the body; then, with a final look to see that nothing has been left behind, we bend to the traces and the leader says, 'Off.'

There is rarely much conversation on the march, especially in cold weather; and, starting with a quick, warming step, it is not long before we have fallen into our regular stride – that steady rhythmic plod before which the miles come slowly but surely. In half an hour's time the blood is flowing freely, garments are hanging more easily, and our boots have thawed sufficiently to give to the step. A halt is called to tighten up our lamp-wick straps and to readjust the folds about our legs to the new conditions; then we are off once more.

And now hour after hour creeps on whilst we seem to have turned into a machine – a machine that must keep moving with that regular swinging step, and now, thank heaven, a machine that can do so without straining its parts. A week ago things were very different; we vividly remember the start of the journey, when, in spite of the temperature, the perspiration ran off us, when our legs seemed uncontrollable members, and our back one huge ache. Since that, day by day we have grown stronger on the trail, until now the early hours of the march are almost a physical pleasure, and it is only towards its end that we feel the weight of the sledges. Yet withal progress is not rapid; one and three-quarter mile an hour is good going. Sometimes we come down to one and a half or less, and if we exceed two we seem to be racing. Still, even a mile and a half an hour produces a fair total for the day, if we can keep it going for nine hours or more. So we plod along mechanically, each footfall but little in advance of the last, whilst the sledges come jerkily in our wake and leave the long, snaky furrows behind.

At one o'clock there is a halt for lunch. Here we score, for in the old days with ponderous, dilatory cooking-apparatus the sledge-traveller could not afford to take his luncheon hot; but with us the cooker is singing ten minutes after we halt, and in less than half an hour we have hot tea or cocoa; and whilst we munch our modest allowance of biscuit and cheese, the hot fluid once more sends the blood coursing through our veins.

I think there can be no doubt as to the benefit of this hot meal in the middle of the day, though possibly some hardened travellers may consider it an unnecessary luxury; it forms an oasis in the long desert of the day's march, it breathes new vigour and spirit into a flagging party. For lack of fuel I have been long spells without a hot drink at midday, and therefore I know well the difference it makes to the afternoon march; and though I know the case is not strong scientifically, I am prepared to affirm that the distance gained on the marches more than compensates for the extra weight of fuel required. Personally I always preferred cocoa to tea for this meal, mainly because tea is not a food, and can only stimulate. The fact that we took tea on our sledge journeys was rather a concession to the men, who from habit are much attached to this beverage; indeed, there were one or two men who posit-ively disliked cocoa. The best marching hours were always those which succeeded the lunch hour.

But an hour under these conditions literally flies, and we have barely swallowed our lunch and drawn a whiff or two from our pipes when the order comes to 'pack up'; tents and cookers are again packed on the sledge, harness is resumed, and we are once more on the march.

So mechanically and evenly go these marching hours that I have sometimes had to collect my thoughts to remember whether it is morning or afternoon, or even where I am and what I am doing. It is easy to go into reverie and fly away to the ends of the earth; nothing disturbs the silence but the regular crunch of the snow-crust and the swish of the sledge-runner.

But now the wind is springing up again. Throughout the day the clouds have been banking up from the south; they are now travelling fast overhead, a low flying scud. The sun peeps through at rarer and rarer intervals, the sky and the mountains look very black and sombre, and throw up the intense whiteness of the snow; the surface drift comes whirling along in ghostly wreaths, and patters about our feet. The outlook is threatening, but we don't want to lose our miles if we can help it, so we plod along as before. As the wind grows stronger, one by one out go the face-guards, and we march with heads turned slightly to the right, away from it. We must keep our eye open for frostbites now: they will give no warning. Presently the leader calls a halt; everyone knows what it is for, and each peers into the face of his next-door neighbour. Apparently all is well, and off we go again; a quarter of an hour later there is another halt and we hear, 'Your cheek's gone, Jim', and Jim immediately extracts his hand from his mit and places it over the offending feature. Also Jim knows that there will be a blister there tomorrow.

Once more we resume the march, and for long it is only interrupted by the occasional search for frostbites. To the south the outlook appears still more gloomy, and presently some adjacent hill-spur disappears as though it had fallen through the earth, completely blotted out by a sheet of deep grey which is rushing towards us. This is the threatened storm, and the sooner we are in camp the better. We cast round for a camping ground and rush for the likeliest spot; we halt and dash for the sledges; we think of nothing but getting the tents up in time. But alas! we have marched just five minutes too long, and we have scarcely placed the tent-poles before the storm is upon us.

The air is thick with driving snow-crystals; they lash at our face like a sand blast. It is impossible to face them directly, and we rush to and fro with averted head. So thick is the air that we can scarcely see the sledges from the tent position, though only six or seven yards lie between. It is each party for itself now with a vengeance. One of our three hangs on like grim death to the tent-poles, whilst the others bear the fluttering, straining canvas to windward and strive to envelop him. Once or twice they fail, but at last the tent is over, and whilst to windward it is stretched taut on the bending bamboos, to leeward it is flapping madly in the rising gale. One of us sits on the weather skirt, and the other flies for the shovel and returns to dig with wild haste. It is a long and difficult job this, to set up a tent in a heavy wind whilst the snow curls and bites into our face and creeps into our mits and into every hole and crevice it can find in our garments. That wildly flapping skirting is only conquered inch by inch by the united efforts of the whole party. But it is bound to be done, and the sooner the better, so we work with all the strength that remains to us.

We must have everything handy now, so when the tent is secured we fly for sleeping-bag, cooker, and anything else we may need, and bundle them all indiscriminately into the interior, following ourselves with all the haste we can compass. Only when door and ventilator are tied have we time to look about us, and then the sight is not pleasant. The powdery snow-dust lies inches deep everywhere; it has covered everything we possess, and lies thick in every crack of the sleeping-bag. We ourselves are white from head to foot, and none of us but is keenly frostbitten about the face, whilst one has two of his fingers white to the knuckles. Something hot is what all need, and we set about to get it with the least possible waste of time, whilst we brush the snow as best we can from our belongings.

Supper makes one feel better, and immediately after we unroll the sleeping-bag and commence to prepare ourselves for entering it. We know from experience what all this snow will mean; we cannot wholly banish it, and the icy condition of our belongings is nothing to what it will be; yet we sweep and sweep as diligently as may be with our fur mits to make the best of a bad job, till finally we lift the cover of the bag and settle ourselves with all possible care within.

It is curious to lie like this in a blizzard; luckily the temperature has gone up, as it always does on these occasions. The rise is apparent in every way; we can handle things more easily, our breath does not rise in such steaming clouds; but, above all, there is a milder and easier feel in the air once one is out of the lash of the wind. Our discomforts now come more from the miserably chilly wetness of everything than from the actual cold.

Meanwhile the storm without is raging unabated, and the thin canvas of the tent is flapping with a continuous roar that drowns all noise within; conversation can only be carried on by shouting. Still, the main point is that we are all in the sleeping-bag and safe and sound if not very comfortable, so in due course we settle ourselves in its depths and draw over us the protecting flap. There will be no shivering tonight at any rate, and we can smoke our pipes with greater ease in consequence; here, in the depths of the bag, the mad flapping of the tent has sunk to distant thunder.

The chances are that on the following day the blizzard will not have gone down; our blizzards usually last for more than twenty-four hours, and therefore next morning one is not surprised to hear the tent flogging away as wildly as ever. Breakfast is deferred for an hour, but man must live, and it is better to keep one's strength up at all times, so at last we all get out of the bag, roll it up carefully, and prepare our meal.

The meal over, the bag is spread again, and in it we while away the hours as best we can. It is an admirable lesson of patience, since we are absolutely incapable of bettering matters till the clouds roll by. We only allow ourselves two hot meals – a late breakfast, and then supper as darkness is again descending on us. During these meals the bag is rolled up, but lunch, with its scraps of biscuit, cheese, sugar, and chocolate, is eaten inside it; one keeps all these luxuries in a warm breast pocket and munches away at them at intervals.

How unutterably wearisome these long daylight hours are! The smoker looks ruefully at his small stock of tobacco; to smoke now is to rob the future, but the temptation is great, and he argues that just half a pipe will not make much difference, so he lights up, but in a quarter of an hour finds himself sucking at an empty bowl. The inside of the bag has grown moist where it comes into contact with the body, whilst the ice is still hard in the corners; the damp has worked through to the skin, and we seem to be swathed in wet bandages. It is horribly cold and clammy, and we think of what joy it would be to be able to walk into our comfortable wardroom, to rub ourselves with a rough towel, don dry clothing, and bask in the rays of the glowing fire.

Now and again conversation breaks out; someone tells a droll legend of his infancy; the tale carries us away to other places and other times for a space, forgetful of our miserable surroundings; but the effort flickers and dies, and gradually thought creeps back to the present. The small aneroid barometers are consulted again and again; there has been a slight fall for the gale, not more than two or three tenths of an inch, but we eagerly look for a rise; occasionally a head is raised out of the bag to contemplate the green canopy above, but no-one cares to look long at the shivering canvas and trembling bamboos; a glance is sufficient to show that the conditions without are unchanged. And as the long day goes by and the second night creeps on we eat our modest supper and once more resort to the bag. As we settle ourselves for the night we are conscious of the first sign of break in the gale. The wind is becoming more squally; during the furious gusts the tent flaps more madly than ever, but between whiles there is a sensible indication of peace, and we shut ourselves in with hopes that we are approaching the end of our imprisonment.

By the early hours of the morning the improvement is very marked; we are conscious that for brief spells the canvas is still, and that even in the squalls it is less violently agitated. This is the beginning of the end; the air is probably still full of flying snow-crystals, but in a few hours they will be settling and the nimbus clouds will have passed us by. When we rise at the first streaks of dawn it is to a brighter prospect; the light which penetrates the green walls of the tent is sufficient to show that there must be a clear sky. These walls are fluttering only at rare intervals and in gentle fashion, chiefly because the wind has fallen, but partly also because they are banked high with drift snow which has caused them to sag in on every side until the inner space is narrowed by some feet. The door is completely drifted up by a heavy bank.

After rolling up the sleeping-bag the first thing to be done is to effect an exit, and this we do by lying on our backs and kicking for all we are worth at the snow-banked canvas. After a bit we can untie the door, and, still kicking, force our way out; then the shovel is found, and with its aid the drifts are soon diminished.

We drop at once into our usual camping routine, but as the cook prepares the breakfast we have time to look about us and to note the havoc wrought by the gale. The sledges are almost covered, and we know well that the boxes and tanks on them will be found partly, if not wholly, filled. Our tent is covered with ice, the sleeping-bag is filled with it, and there is not a single article of our equipment which has not had pounds added to its weight. It is a gruesome thought; the temperature is falling again, and we shall soon have the normal condition of intense cold, with an accumulation of ice which will double each separate discomfort. We realise we are in for a 'high old time', and that the effects of this gale will be felt to the bitter end of the journey; there will be no drying, and the ice which we have gathered will remain with us throughout. However, it is no use inveighing against the inevitable, and we start to dig out our sledges, and afterwards books, instruments, and provisions are taken out and brushed, whilst the tanks and boxes in which they have reposed are freed as far as possible from the sandy deposit. Then we go back to the tent for our well-earned breakfast, and in due course step forth once more on the march.

As can well be imagined, the diaries which record the doings of a sledge party, and which are written in such adverse circumstances as I have described, do not enter into the hardships and discomforts which are inevitable to the day's work, but in the main are devoted to the special incidents of the particular day. Such references to the normal conditions as they contain are rather in the form of hasty and incomplete entries which would convey little to the outsider, though they may amply stimulate the memory of the writer, who possesses the key to the situation. It will not be difficult to understand, however, that the person who has actually been through sledging experiences will have little trouble in recalling their general nature. The daily recurrence of discomforts and hardships leaves an impression which is not easily dispelled, and his memory affords him ample material for drawing a typical picture of the sledge-traveller's daily round.

It would be impossible in describing the special incidents of our journeys always to supply the detail which would make the circumstances clear. I have therefore in this chapter endeavoured to describe what may be considered the normal experiences and environment of the spring sledging parties, and thus to provide a general background for the more varied adventures of our individual excursions. I am not conscious of colouring the picture highly – the discomforts are far too real to need imaginative treatment – nor is it conceivable that anyone would willingly face such conditions without some sufficient object to compensate for the hardships endured.

But it must be remembered that all these conditions which I have described are a result of the severe temperatures and storms of the spring. Fortunately for the sledge-traveller, as the season advances, the climatic conditions become milder, and in summer the sledging life may become not only bearable but pleasant. It has always seemed to me that scarcely sufficient stress is laid on this difference in Arctic books of travel. One is apt to overlook the fact that the conditions described in the earlier journeys have passed away during the more extended efforts, and that in some of the latter the travellers have actually suffered more from the sun and the heat than from the cold. In point of fact, summer sledging is so different from spring sledging that it might well be considered a separate employment, and therefore the description of a day's travelling in spring can convey no impression of the summer traveller's experiences, unless, of course, he is journeying on a high plateau (such as the summit of Victoria Land), where the climate is continuously severe.

In the South, as compared with the North, we were much handicapped by the late advent of our improved temperature conditions. There is generally a considerable rise in the Northern April; in May the air can be mild and pleasant, and in June it is sometimes disagreeably warm. In the South we got no marked improvement until the early part of November, which corresponds to the Northern May. December was the finest and mildest month, though the temperature rarely rose above the freezing-point, but even then we had sometimes cause to complain of the heat.

It would not be possible to describe a typical summer day's sledging, because two days were rarely alike, and so much depended on the direction in which we travelled and on the object of the journey; but it is perhaps as well to point out wherein it differed from such experiences as I have already described. In summer, of course, there was full daylight; one lived and slept and ate with the sun circling above the horizon, and the flickering candle formed no part of one's equipment. During the night one's boots had reposed near the tent: much of the damp had dried from them, and although they were frozen, there was little difficulty in thawing them – they could be put on and secured neatly whilst the breakfast was being prepared.

On a fine day in summer the first task is to drag the sleeping-bag out into the open, to turn it inside out and support it facing the sun; by this means much of the moisture is evaporated out and much forms in tiny crystals on the hair and can be brushed away. Sometimes it is carried on top of the sledge in this way, so that the drying process may continue, but if the weather is unsettled it is thoroughly beaten and turned again before packing. Except during blizzards and cold snaps, this sleeping-bag has become a really pleasant resort. There may be a little ice under each person's body, but the greater part of the material is soft and pliable, and after a hard day's march one snuggles comfortably into its folds and is soon away in dreamland.

The cooking-things can be handled now without much difficulty, and the ends of one's fingers no longer display a row of horny blisters, though in many places they have dried and split and there are deep cuts about the nails.

We start on the march without our wind-clothes; in fact, we rarely wear them now except when it is blowing or snowing. In place of our helmets we now wear a broad-brimmed hat, for the glare of the sun is great, and with its reflection on the white snow it has already burnt us all to a deep chocolate colour; while at night we wear a simple Balaclava. Soon after the march starts we are perspiring freely; the labour is very heavy, and we are not sorry to be able to throw open our coat. We scarcely realise that the air is chill until a halt shows it is necessary to button up again. Mits are still slung around our necks, but we usually march with our hands free and yet with pleasantly pink fingers.

On coming to camp we can take things coolly – and as the march has been carried to its utmost length, we are capable of little else. Except for the cook, no-one enters the tent now until supper is ready; for the rest there is plenty to be done in thoroughly securing the tent, opening out the sleeping-bag, and spreading out damp articles to dry. The cook calls us when supper is ready, and we are not slow in answering the call. After supper we leisurely change our foot-gear and spread out the sleeping-bag, but instead of jumping into the latter at once we carry our sodden boots and stockings into the open and distribute them about the sledges, taking care to secure them with string or safety pins that no unkind gust may waft them away whilst we sleep.

After this, with the memory of supper still fresh, it is comfortable enough to sit in the sleeping-bag, smoke our pipes, write up our diaries, and stitch away at some torn garment; then, perhaps, as the chill of the air creeps in or the fatigue of the day overcomes us, we creep down into our berths and are soon asleep. If it is calm and the sun shines directly on the canvas side, it can be quite warm within the tent; sometimes we have to sleep with our heads in the open, and on rarer occasions we have even had to leave the bag and sleep on top of it.

But there are troubles in the summer travelling as well as in the spring, though they are of a somewhat different nature.

There are blizzards and winds still to be contended with; either will cover us with snow and put a stop to the drying, and we have several days of damp misery before we can recover from its effects. We leave our socks out to dry in a bright sun. The wind springs up in the night, and they are covered with drift; the sun melts this into the fabric, and in the morning, instead of dry footwear, we have to grapple with masses of ice. The same sun melts the snow on the tent and covers it with a sheet of ice. Though the temperature may be below freezing, snow incautiously left in the provision tank will melt and render everything soft and sodden.

From start to finish of the march we have to wear goggles for protection against the intense glare, but we grow inexpressibly sick of these safeguards, and weary of always seeing the world through a tiny aperture. In spite of this protection, too, snow-blindness is common, and rarely a night goes by but someone needs doctoring; the solution of zinc sulphate is thawed out, and the sufferer lies flat on his back whilst a ministering companion drops the remedy into his eyes with the end of a match. It is one of those remedies which might be thought worse than the disease, for it gives the victim what he calls 'gyp', and generally keeps him awake for the next hour or two with throbbing eyeballs.

In the spring journeys the marches had to be suited to the conditions, but in the summer we live to march; there is no excuse for dawdling in the morning now, and we are soon on the go. Hour after hour passes till the welcome halt for lunch, and then again hour after hour till the night camp is pitched. It is very toilsome work. Day after day we put forth our best efforts, but though physically fit and hard, it is impossible not to feel stale at times and to long for the hands of the watch to go faster; the number of miles to show for a long day's work seems ridiculously inadequate to the exertion expended. When camping time comes, we feel almost inclined to drop in our tracks and wish to goodness there was someone else to pitch the tent or do the cooking. The march has been arranged to absorb the maximum portion of our energy, but there is not much present satisfaction in contemplating the limp condition that results. With the most desperate desire to sit or lie down, we remember that it is our duty to fix the position, and, with a groan, plod away to the instrument box, produce theodolite, watch, and notebook, and endeavour to collect all our faculties to start on the dreary round of observations.

But our most poignant suffering during the summer season comes to us by reason of our hunger. The spring absence was not long enough fully to develop the pangs, but now, as week follows week, we become more famished until our thoughts turn to little else but food. The effects of breakfast have passed in an hour, or at the most two, and we plod on with unsatisfied longings during the morning. Lunch has become almost an insult in its insufficiency; it is gone in a twinkling, and we gaze at the provision bag, frown at the cook, and wonder if he has not cut our allowance too fine with a misplaced ardour for saving. The end of the afternoon is sometimes really painful; tired and worn, we feel a positive gnawing in the middle and begin to doubt if supper-time will ever come.

When at length the halt is called there is no need to hurry the cook, though the conversation takes a personal turn if he is clumsy with the Primus. Our sensations from the moment that the first savoury scent of cooking issues from the tent till the last drop of hoosh is poured down our craving throats are beyond description; they can only be imagined, and not even that by such as have not known what hunger really is. It is well to be asleep before the effects of supper wear off, but this is rarely possible, and it is always a wise precaution to haul one's belt quite tight for the night.

Summer sledging is, in fact, a grind; it is a grind because only by putting forth one's utmost can one hope to achieve success, and because a self-imposed task can be carried to whatever lengths one chooses. Although it is conducted under far less severe conditions than those of the spring journeys, it has drawbacks and difficulties of its own, which are increased in proportion to the serious nature of the effort which is being made.

At perhaps too tedious a length I have set forth the objects of sledging, the manner in which it is organised and conducted, and the difficulties with which it has to contend. I cannot conclude without calling momentary attention to it as an occupation for men, apart from the more practical results which it purports to achieve.

Sledging draws men into a closer companionship than can any other mode of life. In its light the fraud must be quickly exposed, but in its light also the true man stands out in all his natural strength.

Sledging therefore is a sure test of a man's character, and daily calls for the highest qualities of which he is possessed. Throughout my sledging experience it has been my lot to observe innumerable instances of self-sacrifice, of devotion to duty, and of cheerfulness under adversity; such qualities appeared naturally in my comrades because they were demanded by the life.

It is in considering this that perhaps the reader will see that there is a charm and fascination in the sledging life despite its hardships and trials.

CHAPTER 12

The spring journeys of 1902

> And the deed of high endeavour
> Was no more to the favoured few,
> But brain and heart were the measure
> Of what every man might do. – RENNELL RODD

Tired of the long winter's inaction, impatient to be away on our travels, and anxious to submit our diligent preparations to a practical test, we waited restlessly during the latter end of August 1902 for the sun to achieve a sufficient altitude to give us light for a reasonable proportion of the twenty-four hours. So ignorant were we of our surroundings, and so formidable appeared many of the obstacles which we could view from our neighbouring heights, that it seemed desirable to devote our first efforts principally to reconnaissance.

In accordance with a plan which had long been conceived, Armitage was to conduct a party to the west, and, travelling light, was to explore the region of New Harbour and endeavour to find some route whereby the inland ice might be reached to the northward of that forbidding range of mountains which faced the ship. It was realised that he would have to cross the sea-ice and turn slightly to the north to avoid the decayed glacier tongue on which we had landed from the ship. At the same time, with the sea-ice so constantly being broken up by the heavy gales, the party would have to be extremely cautious in their movements in order to avoid all risk of being carried away on a broken floe. Yet as long as the sea-ice held firm, it would afford a smooth and easy road, possibly the only one on which the obstacles would not prove insuperable.

Royds, with another light travelling party, was to journey to the south-west. Here our lofty mountain range again fell, and though snow-covered peaks could be seen in the far distance, there appeared to be a glacier of great volume descending into the strait. Here, then, was another possibility of finding a road to the inland. All depended on what lay between, and whilst the prospect was not hopeful, it was quite possible that by turning and twisting amongst the various obstructions a clear road could be found.

To have laden either of these parties with sufficient food to make a depot for future journeys would have been to limit their ability for exploration; obviously the first step was to find the road. I had entrusted the western exploration to Armitage, and it would be for him, after the return of these parties, to decide on the best route to be taken.

I had decided in the very early winter months to undertake the southern work myself, and as every consideration seemed to point to this being the best route for the dogs, I had determined that all these animals should be commandeered for it, making the journey essentially a dog-sledging trip. For a long time I contemplated taking only one companion, thinking that two persons would be sufficient to manage the animals, while the saving of weight would compensate for the extra trouble; but in considering the difficulties which might arise from the unknown nature of the route and the risk of sickness, I finally decided on increasing the number to three. Long before this my two chosen companions, Barne and Shackleton, had been training themselves for the work.

From our hills we could see two possible roads to the south. One lay outside the White Island and promised the smoother travelling, but necessitated a considerable detour. The other was more direct, and led towards the high black cape which we commonly called the Bluff; it passed between the 'White' and 'Black' islands, and though it seemed to contain some rough places, I thought it worth exploring, on the chance of saving the longer distance.

But in making a spring journey to observe these routes it was obvious that as one or the other must eventually be taken by the main party, in either case that party must pass around the Bluff, so that it was advisable that the southern reconnaissance party should carry enough food to be able to establish a depot at the Bluff.

Besides these early efforts at clearing the routes for the main journeys, one other matter claimed our attention in the spring programme: we had still to communicate with the record at Cape Crozier. It was advisable that this should be done before the longer journeys were undertaken, but I thought it might be left until after the reconnaissance parties had returned.

As a preliminary to the commencement of the spring pro-gramme, I decided to make a short trip to the north with the dogs and a party of six officers and men, mainly in order to test the various forms of harness which we had on trial, and to find out whether the dogs pulled best in large or small teams; but incid-entally there were many minor topographical features in this direction which we could not see clearly from the hills, and which we now wished to make sure of.

On September 2 we started in a blizzard and camped in con-ditions of some discomfort; on the following day we pushed on past the Turtle Rock and found ourselves brought up by the long tongue of a glacier. Although this was but eight miles from the ship, from our hills we had only been able to make out a wavy, indistinct shadow, showing how extraordinarily limited is the distance at which one can detect ice disturbances.

This glacier tongue is worthy of a short description, because it is typical of other ice formations in the Ross Sea, and has puzzling characteristics for which, even to this day, we have not been able to account. It consisted of a thin tongue of ice, about five miles long, which shot out directly into the bay and thus into a position where the sea-ice annually formed and broke up on each side of it. It was little broader at its base than at its end, but both sides of the tongue were deeply serrated, so that a man walking along the top would find it might narrow to a quarter of a mile, or broaden out to nearly three-quarters. Moreover, thus pursuing his way along the top he would gradually rise and fall in level perhaps as much as ten or twenty feet, the outer higher parts being separated by many valleys from the inner. If the reader considers this shape, he will see that it suggests itself as an impossible form for an active ice-stream to take, and though it led directly away from the higher southern snow-slopes of Mount Erebus, one could not conceive that it had been actually formed by those snow-slopes in their present condition.

Later on we sounded around the end and for some way on each side of this glacier; we found that the ice-tongue, or at least the end of it, regularly rose and fell with the tide, and nowhere about it could we get anything but deep soundings. Now, not far to the north were some rugged volcanic islets, showing that the bottom of the bay may be very irregular; but if some irregularity kept this long fragile tongue in position, why should it rise and fall with the tide? To all intents and purposes we seemed to have a peninsula of ice floating in the sea, and yet for year after year failing to break away from its source. For this phenomenon we could never find a reason, but for the general shape of this ice-formation I shall hope to advance an explanation in a later chapter. Before we left our winter quarters we spent a long time camped in its vicinity, and in consequence had many an argument concerning it.

On September 5 we crossed this glacier tongue and explored the islets beyond. They were of little interest, being merely masses of volcanic rubble, but as we crossed we noticed that the ice underfoot was of very recent growth; evidently the sea had been swept clear beyond the snout of the glacier quite lately. What we had seen from the hilltop latterly was no figment of our imagination, for whilst we lay snug and secure in our winter quarters the sea had been open, and probably tempestuous, within seven or eight miles of us.

On this journey we took our four sledges independently, with four dogs harnessed to each. We found that if the first team got away all right, the others did pretty well at 'follow my leader'. Sometimes there was even some competition for place, and on one occasion two competing teams gradually converged, with the natural result that when they got close enough to see what was happening it occurred to them that much the easiest way to settle the matter would be by a free fight; the teams therefore turned inwards with one accord and met with a mighty shock. In a moment there was a writhing mass of fur and teeth and an almost inextricable confusion of dog traces. Even in the short interval that elapsed before the drivers were amongst them, beating right and left, it was possible to see that the code was observed; each dog confined his attentions to the 'enemy', and did not attempt to attack his comrades. It was rather surprising to find even this amount of honour amongst such unscrupulous creatures.

On the afternoon of the 5th we turned homewards, and arrived on board just before dusk. Even in this short trip of four days we had gained some experience. There were evidently good reasons for not dividing the dogs into small teams. We had learnt also to distinguish between the strong and the weak, and, what was of more importance, the willing and the lazy; and we saw that we should require a good deal of alteration in our harness and in some of the fittings of our sledges.

For the few days which now intervened before my party started for the south, I call on my diary once again.

'September 5. – Armitage returned tonight with a party of twelve. They have fetched in the depot which we left out last year; it was no use having provisions out at such a short distance, but it is rather amusing to think that this deliberately wipes out the only result of our autumn trip. This party camped at the depot last night and dragged it right in today. It is only about eight or nine miles, but I calculate they must have been dragging nearly 280 lbs. per man, and they are all terribly out of condition. As a result, when they arrived at the ship they were positively cooked, and tonight they are fighting their battles over again, and the conversation is highly entertaining. They all agree that if sledging is always going to be like this, there will be reason deeply to deplore the fact that they ever left a comfortable home and came to sea.'

'September 10. – Royds and Koettlitz started away today with Evans, Quartley, Lashly, and Wild. The party looked very work-manlike, and one could see at a glance the vast improvement that has been made since last year. The sledges were uniformly packed. Everything was in its right place and ready to hand, and all looked neat and business-like. One shudders now to think of the slovenly manner in which we conducted things last autumn; at any rate, here is a first result of the care and attention of the winter.

'Tonight it has been bright and clear, and we saw in more perfect form a phenomenon which we have occasionally wit-nessed before. High in the northern sky were some light, wavy cirrus clouds, carrying the most perfect prismatic colouring. They

seemed like twisted fragments of a rainbow, and were very beautiful against the pale blue sky; we watched until the lights paled
with the dying sun.'

'September 11. – This morning Armitage left for the west.
He takes one other officer, Ferrar, and four men, Cross, Scott,
Walker, and Heald. The party introduced the novelty of systematically pulling on ski, at which they have been practising lately,
much to the amusement of the onlookers. There is not much
difficulty in the pulling after the first start; the great thing is to
swing together and keep in perfect time. I am inclined to reserve
my opinion of the innovation. The "Terror" trip may have proved
their use in soft snow, but a hard surface is a different matter. The
men seem rather in their favour, but that is natural with any
novelty, and however this party may have got on later in the day,
their starting pace was very slow.

'I was thinking today as I looked up at our masts and yards that
my preconceived notion of a polar winter always pictured them
covered with snow, and perhaps with long icicles depending; as a
matter of fact, they have been generally quite free from snow, and
throughout the long night nearly always looked black and grim.
But, curiously enough, this afternoon, when ice-crystals were
falling, they became frosted over, though a strong wind was
blowing; and, oddly too, the wind seemed to have quite a different
note as it blew through the frosted rigging.'

'September 12. – Hodgson has made quite a discovery; he finds
that his ropes and nets whilst under water become coated with ice-
crystals. He tells me he noticed this fact some time ago, and that
the effect has been gradually growing, presumably as the water has
become colder. This morning I went out to see some lines which
he was hauling up. It is certainly a very curious phenomenon, and
one that is difficult to describe; one small line only an inch in
circumference came up covered with a cylinder of flaky ice nearly
a foot in diameter, and this cylinder extended five or six fathoms
below the surface, after which it gradually dwindled away. The
formation is very delicate, and in the flaky structure the axes of the
leaves are at right angles to the rope, whilst their planes are
inclined and intersect at the angle of crystallisation, 60°. The
whole thing looks like some beautiful lace fabric, and held up to
the light one can see through it the most gorgeous prismatic

colouring. It falls to pieces at a touch, and each leaf can be split to the thinnest layers. Shackleton took some photographs and Wilson attempted a sketch, but I doubt if either will produce a picture which is anything like the delicate original.

'Somewhat similar crystals are formed on the tow-nets, but here each minute fibre which stands out from the fabric has formed a nucleus for the ice to form, and the net, with its hanging icicles, looks like nothing so much as an old-time candelabrum with crystal pendants. We do not know quite how to account for these formations; our thermometers show the temperature of the water as something below its freezing-point, but I do not know that they are very reliable for such small differences. In any case, I do not know of this sort of thing having been recorded elsewhere.'

It has been since explained that these crystals were probably due to the super-cooling of the sea, and that with the sea in this condition ice will only form about such nuclei as were afforded by the ropes and the nets, just as a supersaturated solution can be made to crystallise in much the same manner in a simple laboratory experiment. In this light it would be natural enough that the effect should increase as the water grew colder towards the spring, and it is interesting to note that Hodgson found that at one time these crystals formed as deep as seventeen fathoms below the surface.

Owing to some delay in making fresh harness for our dogs, and in rearranging the manner of their pulling, followed by the intervention of a most tantalising blizzard, it was not until September 17 that I was able to make a start on the southern reconnaissance journey. On the morning of that day we got away fairly early, my two comrades being Barne and Shackleton. We had with us only thirteen dogs, divided into two teams. The sledges carried food for a fortnight for all concerned, together with a quantity of stores to form a depot, the whole giving a load of about 90 lbs. per dog. My diary for this journey continues:

'Left the ship at 9 a.m., dogs at first pulling well. Bright clear sky with sunshine, fluctuating temperature. Came to the old ice-rise (about fifteen feet in height, four miles south of the ship). 1.15, camped for lunch, having covered about ten miles; wind turned to east, very cold, thermometer −43°, haze near surface and now slight wind-drift. Land mostly obscured, but high points giving general direction. Dogs find loads heavy, but pulling fairly well; a few cases of sore feet; made good evolution of packing tent, and away again. Saw magnificent parhelion showing prismatic colours on each side from horizon to about 20° of altitude. About 3.30 observed black specks far over the snow to the right front; proved to be Royds's party; soon came up with them. Heard they had had a very rough time, low temperatures with much wind. They had found road to the S.W. quite impossible, strewn with enormous boulders and all sorts of ice obstructions; failing to pass to the north of Black Island, they had tried to the south, but without much result. It was far too cold to stop and discuss details. One gathers that there is no hope of making a long journey in this direction, which is a nuisance; the rest must remain till we get back. After about twenty minutes we parted, Royds steering for ship, mist still obscuring land; head wind sprang up, very biting (temperature −45°), frostbites coming rather fast, dogs wearying. About 5.30 decided to camp, none too soon; excellent supper; have turned my finneskoes inside out for sleeping in, to make trial of this plan. Struggled into sleeping-bags about 7.30, where now writing. Have travelled 12½ geographical miles (14¼ statute); last temperature reading −48°, keen wind from S.E.'

From the above extract it will be seen that the sledging diary gives a very laconic record of the day's events. It is drafted somewhat after the fashion of a telegram, where each word has to be considered – and, indeed, on such occasions, if one does not pay in cash, one pays in kind for superfluous verbiage. It is therefore from such a daily record as this that the sledge-traveller is able to reconstruct the history of his wanderings in very severe weather, though of course when the temperatures rise and his hand is no longer paralysed with the cold, he is inclined to amplify his sentences and enlarge on his ideas.

But on this occasion with the above entry my sledge diary comes to an abrupt conclusion, as, contrary to expectation, the next time I took up my pen to write I was once more comfortably seated in my cabin on board the ship.

'September 19. – . . . I suppose it was our want of condition that made us all so very exhausted on Wednesday night (17th), and that it was in consequence of this that we did not heap enough snow on the skirting of our tent and that we became so utterly unconscious of the change that was taking place in the weather. At any rate, I remember nothing until Thursday morning, when I woke up to find myself in the open. At first, as I lifted the flap of my sleeping bag, I could not think what had happened. I gazed forth on a white sheet of drifting snow, with no sign of the tent or my companions. For a moment I wondered what in the world it could mean, but the lashing of the snow in my face very quickly awoke me to full consciousness, and I sat up to find that in some extraordinary way I had rolled out of the tent. A violent gale was raging and the air was filled with thick, blinding snow. I could only just make out the tent, though it was flapping wildly across the foot of my bag; it was evident that it still stood upright, and that the sooner I was in its shelter the better. I started to wriggle in, bag and all, and at length got beneath it, and could see more clearly what had happened. The bamboos were still secure and the skirting of the tent was still held down on the weather side, but to leeward the snow had been flung off it, and on this side the canvas was flapping loosely, leaving an interval beneath through which I must have rolled.

'I do not think this state of things can have obtained for long, as Barne and Shackleton had only just realised it, but of course by this time the snow was whirling as freely inside the tent as without, our sleeping-bags were covered, and we ourselves were powdered with it. The tent was straining so madly at what remained of its securing that evidently something must be done at once to prevent its flying away altogether. With freezing fingers we gripped the skirting and gradually pulled it inwards, and, half sitting on it, half grasping it, endeavoured to hold it against the wild efforts of the storm whilst we discussed ways and means. Discussion led us nowhere; to have attempted to secure the tent properly in such weather would have been useless, even to venture outside would be dangerous, whilst we felt that if we once let go it might be goodbye to our tent.

'As we clung on in this horrid position the skirt would gradually pull out beneath us and suddenly fly out, flapping wildly again, and we were forced to get a fresh hold and lever ourselves over it once more. Without exception this was the most miserable day I have ever spent; our sleeping-bags became more and more snow-filled until we were lying in masses of chilling slush; our mits were filled in a similar manner, the slippery canvas would pull through their grasp, one was obliged to bare one's fingers to haul it in again, and one could not possibly get through such a job without having some of them frostbitten.

'Thus we remained for hour after hour, grimly hanging on and warning each other of frostbitten features. We waited longingly for a lull, but the first did not come until midday. Then we made a desperate effort to get to the sledges; my companions ventured out whilst I clung to the canvas; they succeeded in getting hold of two provision bags, and returned with a rush. Their absence was certainly not longer than two minutes, yet both faces were quite white with frostbite when they came in, and it was several moments before they regained their natural colour.

'In the afternoon we were beginning to feel a bit spent, and realising that something more must be done, we waited for a lull and again ventured out. This time we managed to get hold of two heavy bags of biscuit. It was not until 6 p.m. that by continued exertions we had so far conquered matters as to have no further need to hold the tent except with the weight of our sleeping-bags, and for the first time our arms were released for other purposes. An inspection of hands showed that we had all been pretty badly frostbitten, but the worst was poor Barne, whose fingers have never recovered from the accident of last year, when he so nearly lost them. To have hung on to the tent through all those hours must have been positive agony to him, yet he never uttered a word of complaint.

'We were now able to wriggle down a little further into our wretchedly wet bags and to eat some cold pemmican and chocolate, whilst we waited for the storm to pass, with a growing stiffness in the backs of our necks from the never-ceasing flap of the canvas against which we leaned. More miserable conditions could scarce be imagined.

'Throughout the day we had not been able to spare a thought for the dogs, but we imagined that they would long ere this have been covered with snow, and therefore comfortable enough; but about this time we heard a sad whimpering at our door and found poor "Brownie", a very miserable shivering object, whining piteously with cramp, so he was allowed to pass the night inside, where he seemed to make himself very happy, especially when he got some of our supper. The rest never uttered a sound till we roused them out of their soft nests on the following morning.

'As darkness descended on us again we lay in our bags with the snow four inches thick on the floorcloth about us, and our clothes becoming more and more saturated with moisture; but at seven o'clock the snow ceased to fall, at nine the wind came in violent squalls, and at ten it was evident that the worst of the storm was passed. Stiff and sore, we set about making our position more comfortable, and then endeavoured to snatch a few hours' sleep.

'This morning we roused out at 3 a.m., cooked our first meal for thirty hours, and briefly discussed the situation. Our sleeping-bags and clothes were literally covered with ice, and we could only push on under the most abject discomfort; by returning to the ship we should only lose one day's march and everything could be dried afresh. We did not hesitate long before deciding to return, and after a grand hot meal of cocoa and pemmican we gradually collected our scattered belongings and packed them on the sledges.

'As we started on the homeward march, the sun was rising in great magnificence, lighting the east with brilliant red and bathing the western hills in the softest pink. It was hard to think that a gale had raged here but a few hours before.

'I think this must have been the coldest blizzard we have had; our minimum thermometer was drifted up with snow and stood at $-43°$, but possibly this recorded a temperature prior to the blizzard. Whilst it was blowing we could not reach the thermometer, but judging by temperatures taken elsewhere, and our own sensations, I do not think it could have risen above $-30°$ throughout, which is most exceptional with a strong wind. When we got up this morning the spirit column stood below $-50°$, and Royds, five miles to the north, recorded $-53°$. The effect of such a temperature on our wet clothing may be imagined. I shall remember the condition of my trousers for a long while; they might have been cut out of sheet iron. It was some time before I could walk with any sort of ease, and even when we reached the ship I was conscious of carrying an armour plate behind me.

'So here we all are, back again, having accomplished nothing except the acquisition of wisdom. It will certainly be a very long time before I go to sleep again in a tent which is not properly secured.

'Royds and his party weathered the gale five miles north of us; they had no trouble at all with their tent, thanks to plenty of snow on the skirt. They have had a severe trip, but are all pretty fit. It appears they came to very rough ground to the north of Black Island, and advanced for some distance by portage, but finding little improvement they turned back. At one place a gust of wind swept one of their single sleeping-bags away; luckily, there was a three-man sleeping-bag, and they managed to squeeze four people into that, but all four agree that such a tight squeeze banished all chance of sleep. Two days later they found the missing bag some four miles from the spot at which it had been lost. Koettlitz thinks that it will be quite possible to circumnavigate the Black Island in spite of the rough ground, so I have given him permission to try.

'I hear that the late gale was very severely felt in the ship: the temperature fell to −32°, no work could be done outside on Thursday, the stove pipes were bent, and heavy planks were swept off the skid beams by the wind.'

'September 23. − . . . We are preparing to be off again, but some fatality seems to ensure bad weather on the date fixed for our departure. Barne's fingers suffered so severely in our recent adventure that he has had to be replaced by the boatswain, Feather. The latter has worked so splendidly all through, and has taken such a keen interest in every detail of the sledging, that I am glad to give him the chance of accompanying us.'

Early on September 24 we got away; travelling with light sledges, we reached our desolation camp, fifteen miles to the south, before we called a halt, and, increasing our loads to full weights, camped for the night at a distance of twenty-three miles from the ship. On the following day we were forced to face a bitter southerly wind with drift and a temperature of −30°. After a few miles the dogs refused duty, and we were obliged to camp.

Proceeding later, when the wind had dropped somewhat, we found ourselves climbing a stiff incline between the two islands, and we had risen at least 180 feet before we reached the top. Across the slope there ran two or three well-marked cracks which I think can only have been tide cracks, and which went to show that the ice-sheet over which we had been travelling was afloat. On the other side of this crest there was a slight descent, but not for much more than fifty feet, after which the surface stretched horizontally ahead of us and was undoubtedly at about the general level of the barrier. I came to the conclusion that the two islands were joined, at least by a shallow bank, if not by land above the water level, and that the barrier sheet was overriding this and pouring slowly into the sea to the north.

On the 26th we had a beautifully clear day, and pushed on towards the Bluff, which now loomed high above us. We were much struck by the fact that all the wind-furrows in this region lay in a south-westerly direction, showing that the prevalent wind is from that quarter, although at the ship we had known little but south-easterly winds. When we camped at the close of this day, after a fifteen mile march, we were within a short distance of the north side of the Bluff, and already there were signs of obstacles ahead. Here and there in the snow surface rose a dome-shaped mound of blue ice, and beyond these we could see little heaps of rubble. It behoved us to be cautious if we would avoid injury to our sledge-runners.

The ice-mounds deserve notice; they are a very typical form of disturbance on the surface of any glacier, but are probably rarely so well developed as we saw them. They are caused by surface melting, the water freezing again below the ice, when the expansion on regelation gradually lifts the surface. To stand amongst a number of these domes is very impressive, especially when they are uniformly rounded. They rise but a short distance before they are cracked in all directions on top, and the cracks gradually open into broad, deep fissures. We found domes as high as seven and eight feet in this region, and saw mounds which in attempting to rise further had lost the dome form and stood up like irregular-shaped craters. It was on the surface of one of these, far from the land, that Mr Ferrar found a large quantity of crystals of sodium or magnesium sulphate. I am not chemist enough to suggest a reason.

'September 27. – Started with promise of a fine day, temperature –46°. Soon after, the sky became overcast and the temperature rose. The travelling changed altogether in character; the ice-mounds grew thicker, and reached a height of eight to ten feet, with broad, ugly cracks all over them. Later they seemed to assemble in ridges running more or less east and west, and hence right across our tracks; the dogs could make no show of crossing them, so we had to turn outwards in hopes of getting better travelling. Instead of this it got worse, and after lunch we passed into a turmoil of torn and twisted ice, forming ranges of hillocks twenty and thirty feet high, sometimes rounded on top and sometimes rising in sharp ridges. The higher parts were swept clear of snow and showed bare blue ice, whilst in the hollows the snow lay in high, hard sastrugi; the contrast was plain even in a bad light.

'Travelling now became a regular scramble up hill and down dale. The dogs did not appreciate it at all; they had to be helped up the stiff bits, and when the sledge came skidding down the descents they almost howled with terror. The wind has increased to half a gale from the S.S.W., but it is astonishingly warm; the temperature has risen above zero, so we have built a good snow-wall to protect our tents.'

'September 28. – Awoke to find a gale with heavy drift, but our tent very snug and comfortable. The temperature has gone up to +7°, and our sleeping-bags are pleasantly warm and comfortable. The most extraordinary thing is that in spite of the flying snow outside our things are actually drying, and for the first time in our experience we find ourselves in a weather-bound camp becoming drier instead of wetter. Not being at all cold, we find time to be bored, and, by ill-luck, no-one thought of bringing a book or a pack of cards; but who could suppose that it would be possible to use them during a spring journey? We could really get on now but for the light, but that is so bad that to move over this rough country would be a great risk.'

'September 29. – Wind dropped in night, and was succeeded by flat calm with rapidly falling temperature. We were away by 7 a.m., but shortly after a fresh bank of cloud came up from the south, with more wind and drift. We were all too impatient to stop again, so pushed on, myself leading, with orders to the two teams to follow rigidly in my wake, in spite of any turns and twists I might make.

'Notwithstanding the bad light I could see the bridged crevasses where they ran across the bare ice surface by slight differences in shade, and where they dived into the valleys, though I could not see them, I found that the bridges were strong enough to bear. I stuck as much as possible to the snowy patches, but this necessitated a very irregular course and the dogs invariably tried to cut corners. In this manner we proceeded for some time, but suddenly I heard a shout behind, and, looking round, to my horror saw that the boatswain had disappeared; there stood the dog-team and sledges but no leader. I hurried back and saw that the trace disappeared down a formidable crevasse, and to my relief the boatswain was at the end of the trace.

'I soon hauled him up and inquired if he was hurt, to which, being a man of few words, his only reply was, "D—n the dog!" from which I gathered that "Nigger" had tried to cut a corner and so pulled his leader at the wrong moment, and, incidentally, that the boatswain wasn't much hurt. This evening the boatswain has shown me his harness; one strand was cut clean through where it fell across the ice-edge. Altogether he had a pretty close call.

'After this accident we joined our dog-teams, and, loath to give up the march, pushed on again. About half an hour later there was another shout, and, looking round, I found this time that it was not a man, but a sledge, that had disappeared. It was the last of the four, and I found it hanging vertically up and down in an ugly-looking chasm. To the credit of our packing, although it had fallen with a jerk into this uncomfortable position, not a single thing had come off. It was too heavy for us to haul up as it was, so, after some consultation, our indefatigable boatswain suggested that he should be let down to unpack it. He was therefore slung with one end of our Alpine rope, whilst the other was used for hauling up the various packages. It must have been a mighty cold job, but at last all the load was got up, and the lightened sledge soon followed. After getting everything in order again we found that we had sustained no greater damage than a broken ski.

'After this incident we thought it would be wise to treat these numerous crevasses with more respect, so on proceeding we roped ourselves together, and whilst I went ahead the boatswain led the dog-team and Shackleton brought up the rear to look after things in general. But we had not gone far like this when the light became thoroughly bad; we could see nothing at all under foot, and have been obliged to camp early. The effect of this light on our surroundings is very curious, making everything appear of gigantic size; the smallest wind-furrow looms up like a heavy bank, and the larger ice-hillocks look like ranges of high mountains.'

Looking back on this day, I cannot but think our procedure was extremely rash. I have not the least doubt now that this region was a very dangerous one, and the fact that we essayed to cross it in this lighthearted fashion can only be ascribed to our ignorance. With us, I am afraid, there were not a few occasions when one might have applied the proverb that 'Fools rush in where angels fear to tread.'

The bad light to which I have referred was a very constant source of trouble to us on our travels. It came when the sky – as was very usual – was completely overcast with a uniform pall of stratus cloud; under such a sky there would only be diffused light, and no direct rays to cast a shadow. It can be easily understood that on a snow surface the only thing that can indicate an inequality is shadow; consequently on these grey days it was impossible, within limits, to see what was coming next. Bad light does not, therefore, mean insufficiency of light, because on such occasions one could see dark objects at a long distance, and there was quite enough light both outside and inside the tent for all camping purposes.

'September 29 (continued). – . . . After lunch the sun peeped through the cloudy mantle, and with some difficulty we managed to push out a mile or two, when the undulations and upheavals of ice gradually disappeared, though the crevasses remained. The broader ones were safe to cross, being filled with snow, except at the edges, where a leg was likely to disappear with a false step. This seems to show that they are ever widening. The dangerous crevasses are those from three to four feet in width, as they are covered only with light snow-bridges, which, when broken away, disclose chasms between perpendicular blue ice-walls of unknown depth. These walls are crusted with branching growths of ice-crystals, very beautiful in form, but which prevent one from seeing more than a few fathoms down.

'Tonight when we camped I warmed a thermometer, ran up its indicator and lowered it at the end of our Alpine rope to a depth of sixteen fathoms; on hauling it up I found both spirit and indicator stood at $-10°$, so I imagine this to be about the mean temperature of the ice masses in this region.

'When we halted tonight our dog-trace lay across one of these crevasses, and little "Kid" promptly coiled himself down on the middle of the snow-bridge; had he been allowed to remain he would certainly have melted himself through in an hour or two, and would have become a very surprised dog. Luckily, we saw his position, and rescued him in time.'

'September 30. – Starting at 7.15, and still steering east, we soon passed out of the region of crevasses and turned to the south. The weather was brilliant, the sun shone forth in a cloudless sky, and the temperature was exceptionally high at −20°. At lunch we were about ten miles east of the extremity of the Bluff, and the scene was very impressive. Far to the north, clothed in soft white folds of snow, lay the imposing mass of Erebus and Terror; to the north-west towered Mount Discovery and the Western Range, whilst behind us also lay the various islands and foothills on which we have gazed throughout the winter. To the west we could see that the Bluff ended abruptly, being but a long peninsula thrust out into the great ice-sheet. Beyond the Bluff our eyes rested searchingly on the new country that rose above our snowy horizon. It seemed to stretch in isolated masses ever increasing in distance; but beyond the fact that the coast curves sharply away to the west we could make little of it.

'But the most impressive fact of all was that from this new western land through the south, through the east, and away to the slopes of Terror, there stretched an unbroken horizon line, and as the eye ranged through this immense arc and met nothing but the level snow-carpet below and the cloudless sky above, one seemed to realise an almost limitless possibility to the extent of the great snow-plain on which we travel.

'Hope of finding land beyond the Bluff to which we could advance our depot was now at an end, and this afternoon we steered south-west to close the Bluff and to look for landmarks. An excellent line was at length suggested by Shackleton, who, pointing to a small sharp crater on the end of the Bluff, proposed that we should bring it in line with the sharp cone of Mount Discovery. This was done, and tonight we are encamped on the line and about five or six miles from the land. One has but to walk a hundred yards either way to throw the alignment off, so that there should be little difficulty in finding any stores we may leave here provided the weather is clear. We have just been gazing with curious eyes on the road to the south. We have passed out of the region of high snow-furrows, and it seems probable that even those which we have would be lost as one advances to the south. One conceives a plain with the surface growing smoother and possibly softer; but what will it be like to tramp on, day after day and week after week, over such a plain?'

'October 1. – . . . We made our depot this morning, leaving six weeks' provisions for our men and 150 lbs. of dog-food; the whole was marked with a large black flag, and I took careful angles with a prismatic compass to all the points I could see, after which we packed up our traps and faced homewards. The dogs knew at once what was meant, and there is no longer any need to drive them. The weather has been overcast, with a heavy deposition of snow-crystals; but we have already covered several miles on the home-ward track, steering to pass outside the White Island to see how the route promises in that direction.'

On our homeward march we went for all we were worth; the weather was persistently overcast, but this kept the temperature above −30° though it brought a continuous fall of very light powdery snow to add to the friction of the runners. Underneath this powdery snow the surface was in good condition, having been swept very hard with the wind, but the loose crystals seemed to cling badly to the metal runners.

'October 3. – Got away at seven again; mist as thick as a hedge, so steered in towards the island; stumbled on rocks at about ten and gained some idea of position. Evidently passing over a slope succeeded by some ridges, a few crevasses, and some clear blue ice. Guessed by this we must have passed the corner of the island and steered for the ship. At 12.30 passed clear of broken surface, and camped for lunch at one o'clock. After tea, cheese, and jam, prepared to start, and found fog had lifted in rear showing island at our back. In afternoon were able to steer by sun, though still very thick ahead; suddenly Erebus appeared above fog, and ten minutes later we found ourselves within a mile of Observation Hill and going directly for it. The tired dogs set up a yap of delight and sprang forward with fresh energy, and soon we were home.

'We have covered eighty-five statute miles in less than three days, which is not bad going, especially as we have almost had to feel our way along. However, there is no longer a doubt that our road to the south should lie outside, and not inside, the White Island.

'I did not realise that the ship could be such a delightful place as I have found it tonight; the sense of having done what one wanted to do, and the knowledge that we have a far clearer problem before us in the south, have much to do with one's feelings of satisfaction, but it is the actual physical comfort of everything that affects one most; a bath and a change into warm dry clothing have worked wonders. The knowledge that one can sit at ease in warmth and comfort, without being swathed to the chin in clothing, is an immense relief, and the prospect of creeping into a bed without the usual accompaniment of ice is an even greater one; but the greatest delight of all is to possess the sledging appetite in the midst of plenty.'

The joy of this possession was beyond description, and the feats of food-consumption which were performed by the possessors might well be beyond ordinary belief. For many days after we returned from our sledging trips we retained a hunger which it seemed impossible to satisfy. The ordinary frugal meals served at our table seemed to us to be heaven-sent feasts; at each meal one partook ravenously of everything, and though one ate to repletion, half-an-hour later one would be searching for bread and butter and chocolate. For the first few days, when this sledging appetite was keenest, the returned traveller would demand supper to succeed the more solid dinner; he would wake in the night to devour a stick of chocolate or to forage for better fare in the pantry; and he could be seen glancing anxiously at the clock a full hour before each meal. It seemed almost worth going a sledge journey to experience the delight of satisfying such a hunger.

'October 3 (continued). – . . . At dinner tonight I felt especially pleased with myself and the world in general. Armitage and Koettlitz had returned from their journeys, and were able to give a rough outline of their movements, and altogether our meal went very merrily; nor was it till towards the end that I had a suspicion that something was being kept back: about one or two members there seemed to be a sort of unnatural restraint, and I didn't know what to make of it.

'So after dinner I called Armitage into my cabin and asked him what was the trouble. He looked very grave and said that he had not meant to worry me until the morning, but the fact was there had been an outbreak of scurvy. This was indeed a shock! At one blow it upset all one's sense of peace and comfort. Of course one could not allow it to rest at that, so the whole story had to be told.

It is not a pleasant thing to go to bed on, and I do not feel like writing it tonight; possibly also things may look brighter in the morning when one is not so "done".'

'October 4. – . . . The history of our outbreak of scurvy is more or less contained in the history of Armitage's journey, into which I have been therefore with some detail. It appears that after leaving the ship on September 11, the party made a pretty straight line for the end of the decayed glacier tongue in the middle of the strait. Their progress was not very rapid, as they stuck as closely as possible to the old worn ice for the sake of safety. Even as it was, this course took them within a mile of the open water. They reached the glacier snout on the 13th, and camped securely on it. The ice beyond the snout, and from thence to the westward, had only recently been formed; there was practically no snow on it, and its dark colour was only relieved by the briny ice-flowers.

'Apart from the danger of this ice being broken up again, it was impossible to camp on it, as no snow could have been obtained for cooking or for securing the tents; the party were obliged, there-fore, to skirt the edge of older ice to the south, and this added to the length of the journey. During this time the open water was never far from them, and, besides numerous seals and penguins, they constantly saw whales (probably killer whales) spouting in the offing. On the night of the 16th they camped on the slope of the foothills of the mainland; not far to the north of them was the New Harbour, whilst immediately to the south was an immense pile of morainic material which they have called the "Eskers". This it is that looks like a small range of hills from the heights above us and which we have often been puzzled to account for.'

I should add that this formation was really an old lateral moraine, and, as we soon discovered, it was quite wrongfully called the Eskers, a name properly given to deposits formed by glacial streams; but a name once given is a very hard thing to change, and after this first journey no-one could be brought to refer to this formation otherwise than as the Eskers, and I have no doubt this name crops up many times in my journal in spite of my knowledge of the error.

'On the 17th they hauled their sledges to a height of 500 feet up the snow-slope and pitched a camp there, with the intention of making excursions from it. Since their start from the ship the weather had been very changeable, and they had experienced a great deal of wind with low temperatures. On some days the wind had been so violent that they had been forced to stop in their tents; such a day was the 18th, but on the 19th five of the party left the camp and crossed the long snow-slope which bounds our view on the south side of New Harbour. From this they could get a good view of the valley beyond, and saw that it cut deeply into the mountain range and contained a huge glacier. Looking up the valley, they were faced by a high single-peaked mountain, and the glacier appeared to turn to the right as it reached its foot. As far as the upper parts of the glacier were concerned, there appeared to be good travelling, but from the foot of the descent, for some seven miles outwards, they looked down upon a confusion of ice which they had never seen equalled. Armitage describes huge masses broken and fissured and standing nearly fifty feet above the general level. Interspersed with the ice are vast heaps of morainic material, and the whole forms a chaotic obstruction across which he thinks it is impossible that sledges can be taken.

'Skirting along this rough disturbance they advanced up the valley, but it was now getting towards midnight and some of the party were beginning to tire from the long exposure. Mr Ferrar and Heald had been sent back some hours before, and now the remaining two turned also. Armitage says that on his return he came across the tracks of two people, which he followed, expecting them to lead to the camp, but later discovering that they certainly did not he became very alarmed, thinking that Ferrar and Heald had missed their way. Still following these tracks, he now and again came across a mark in the snow as though one of the two had been obliged to take frequent rests. At last, to his relief, the tracks suddenly turned about and now led directly towards the camp, which he eventually reached at 5 a.m., after an absence of twenty hours.

'He found that Ferrar and Heald had made the tracks he had seen, and that by losing their way they had been three hours late in arriving back; furthermore, that on the way Ferrar had collapsed several times and on each occasion had been overcome by an irresistible desire to sleep. He was only kept awake by the persistence of his companion, Heald, who, although almost worn out himself, realised the danger they were running and showed the greatest determination in pushing on. As the temperature at the time was −45°, there seems litttle doubt that Ferrar practically owes his life to his companion's exertions.

'Hoping to find out more about the New Harbour glacier, on the 21st they dragged their sledges over a rise of 1,000 feet towards its entrance. They had great difficulty with the steep descents, but eventually made their way down safely. A second examination of this region did not give any more promising results than the first, and Armitage came to the conclusion that to attempt to reach the mainland by this route was impracticable. On the 22nd they started their homeward journey, skirting now around the base of the long snow-slope on recently formed sea-ice. It was about this time that, in cogitating over recent events in the journey, Armitage began to suspect that there was something wrong with the health of the party. Several men had complained of sprains and bruises which seemed to give pain without much cause; he thought, too, that they tired more easily than strong men should have done, and it seemed especially curious that such an active officer as Ferrar should have collapsed under a hard day's work. The thought of scurvy, however, did not enter the leader's head, and he was inclined to put the troubles down to the horrible weather conditions and to the fact that so few of them had been able to sleep.

'As the party gradually made their way back to the ship, things got worse and his alarm grew. The light sledges hung heavily on the men, and though there were no complaints, several seemed only to keep themselves going with an effort. The evening of the 25th found them within a few miles of the ship, and in such a crippled state that Armitage thought it wiser to struggle right on till they reached her, which they did at 6 a.m. on the 26th.

'The result of Wilson's medical examination of this party on their return has been handed to me; the gist of it is that Heald, Mr Ferrar and Cross have very badly swollen legs, whilst Heald's are discoloured as well. Heald and Cross have also swollen and spongy gums. The remainder of the party seem fairly well, but not above suspicion; Walker's ankles are slightly swollen.

'Of course there is no good blinking our eyes to the fact that this is neither more nor less than scurvy, but whence it has come, or why it has come with all the precautions that have been taken, is beyond our ability to explain. The evil having come, the great thing now is to banish it. In my absence, Armitage, in consultation with the doctors, has already taken steps to remedy matters by serving out fresh meat regularly and by increasing the allowance of bottled fruits, and he has done an even greater service by taking the cook in hand. I don't know whether he threatened to hang him at the yardarm or used more persuasive measures, but, whatever it was, there is a marked improvement in the cooking.

'Koettlitz has only been back a few days from his second trip, but has made an examination of everyone on board. He tells me there are signs of scurvy in a good many, but in most cases it is only the merest indication, and probably we should not have known anything about it had it not been for this searching examination. The worst cases are those which I have named above, and they, as well as the rest, are improving by leaps and bounds – in fact the disease is vanishing rapidly. He confesses himself unable to suggest any cause for the outbreak.

'The signs of improvement are hopeful, and there seems little doubt that we shall banish the disease; but one cannot be too cautious, and we must lay ourselves out to make arrangements which will not only banish it for the present, but will prevent all chance of its recurrence in the future.

'Royds was to have started for the "Record" at Cape Crozier on the 2nd, but deferred his departure till my return. I saw no reason for delaying further, and the doctors report his party to be in first-rate condition, so they went off this morning. With the leader go Skelton, Lashly, Evans, Quartley, and Wild – practically the same party that went to the south-west, so they ought to know what they are up to. Though there is not much else but scurvy in my thoughts just at present, the great thing is to pretend that there is nothing to be alarmed at.'

'October 15. – The determination to have everything above suspicion, and not to give our dread enemy another chance to break out, has kept all hands pretty busy of late.

'With the idea of giving everyone on the mess-deck a change of air in turn, we have built up a space in the main hut by packing cases around the stove. In this space each mess are to live for a week; they have breakfast and dinner on board, but are allowed to cook their supper in the hut. The present occupants enjoy this sort of picnic-life immensely.

'We have had a thorough clearance of the holds, disinfected the bilges, whitewashed the sides, and generally made them sweet and clean.

'As a next step I tackled the clothes and hammocks. One knows how easily garments collect, and especially under such conditions as ours; however, they have all been cleared out now, except those actually in use. The hammocks and bedding I found quite dry and comfortable, but we have had them all thoroughly aired. We have cleared all the deck-lights so as to get more daylight below, and we have scrubbed the decks and cleaned out all the holes and corners until everything is as clean as a new pin. I am bound to confess there was no very radical change in all this; we found very little dirt, and our outbreak cannot possibly have come from insanitary conditions of living; our men are far too much alive to their own comfort for that. But now we do everything for the safe side, and from the conviction that one cannot be too careful.

'We have had great difficulties in trying to live on fresh meat alone, as our stock of seal-meat had run short. It is not easy to supply so large a company; a large seal barely lasts two days at the present rate of consumption. Just as our stock ran out, one or two seals happened to come up on the ice close to the ship, and these kept us going until, at Wilson's suggestion, we organised a large seal-killing party to go further afield. This party, consisting of Barne, Wilson, and four men, girt about with knives and other murderous implements, journeyed away to the north with all the dogs on Thursday (9th); they camped under the glacier tongue, weathered a blizzard on the following day, and started their operations on Saturday. After a long and hard day's work, they started homewards, and arrived here on Sunday morning with over a thousand pounds of meat, and having left a large quantity ready to be brought in.

'They report that the seals are plentiful near the glacier, and that there is also a colony below Castle Rock, not more than three miles from the ship; we ought to have little trouble, therefore, in keeping up our supply in future.

'On Monday I was able to give the satisfactory order that no tinned meat of any description should be issued, and one may reasonably hope that this order can be observed throughout the remainder of our stay in these regions.

'Regular outdoor exercise is the only other circumstance that can affect our physical well-being, and with regard to that I am glad to say there has been no need to issue an order. There is a great deal of outdoor work, and every evening after tea the men either go for long ski runs or walks, or play football. As for the spirits of our party, they have never been cast down for a single minute; with the daylight and the increased activity there has been more chaff and laughter than ever, and certainly no-one who walked into the living-quarters at night would guess that we were in the act of dispelling a very dreaded disease. To whichever or to what combination of the steps we have taken this is due, it is impossible to say, but the fact remains that within a fortnight of the outbreak there is scarcely a sign of it remaining, and certainly all cause for anxiety has vanished. Heald's is the only case that hung at all, and since fomentations have been applied to his legs he also has made rapid strides towards recovery, and is now able to get about once more. Cross's recovery was so rapid that he was able to join the seal-killing party last week.

'Koettlitz has taken advantage of the returning daylight to grow a crop of mustard and cress. He has raised some on flannel, and with chemicals, but the best result has been obtained from our own Antarctic soil, which is evidently most productive. The wardroom skylight does not make a very large garden, but enough cress has been produced for one good feed for all hands.'

'October 19. – The weather conditions have not been too favourable to our changes, though of course they have not delayed the return of full daylight, which has the most cheering effect. On the 12th commenced one of the thickest and longest blizzards we have yet had. Except for a calm interval of six hours on the 13th, the snow was whirling about us continually till midday on the 16th. The wind as usual commenced in the south and gradually worked round to the east, and the temperature rose at one time to +2°. This blizzard seems to have cleared the air for the time, as the weather since has been bright and clear, and we have had the most gorgeous light effects.

'On Saturday night between ten and eleven we witnessed an especially curious sight. The sun was behind Mount Discovery, and cast a clear shadow of its cone on a bank of cirro-stratus cloud on the near side. This effect was very curious; there appeared to be a clearly defined inverted cone superimposed on the top of the mountain.'

'October 20. – I think it may safely be said that our scurvy is at an end, and unless it is produced again in the sledge parties we shall hear no more of it. I do not think the milder conditions of the future sledging season are likely to reproduce it, but so as to avoid the risk I have been arranging to replace the pemmican by a proportion of cooked seal-meat. The difficulty here is to get it free from water, and the only way is to cook it again and again, but with all our efforts I doubt whether we shall get quite the same value for weight as we do in the pemmican.'

It may be of interest here to quote the result of some of our experiments in this line, though, of course, they rest on estimation, as we had no facilities for chemical analysis.

We took 140 lbs. of seal-meat, and cooked it in 20 lbs. of margarine, producing as a result 60 lbs. of cooked meat; or, in other words, we evaporated off a little under two-thirds of the original weight. Raw meat contains about 75 per cent. of moisture, and we estimated our margarine to contain about 20 per cent.; so speaking very roughly, something under three-quarters of the original weight of our seal and margarine was water.

Again very roughly, therefore, in the cooked meat which remained there was water equal to about a twelfth of its original weight, or about a fourth of its present weight. We estimated that we eventually reduced this moisture to 20 per cent., and in this state we calculated that 12 lbs. of seal-meat was equal to 10 lbs. of pemmican.

'October 20 (continued). – . . . We have come to the end of our fresh mutton, except a small quantity kept for possible sickness; this makes a difference to Sunday, but our seal-meat is now so well served that the loss is not greatly felt. In this matter of seal-meat there has been an extraordinary change throughout the ship. There is no getting over the fact that none of us really enjoyed the seal in the winter, and when tinned meat was stopped there were not a few downcast faces; but within a fortnight all that has been altered: everyone now eats the seal with relish, and I do not think there is a single man who would go back to tinned meat, even if he had the chance. The consumption is so great that we have all our work to keep up the supply, and appetites seem to be increasing rather than lessening. Somewhere in this, but not wholly revealed, lies the root of our scurvy trouble; one would fain be able to trace it more clearly.'

In the extracts which I have given from my diary it is possible to trace the history of our scurvy from its outbreak to the time when it vanished from amongst us, but they show also that we were in the unsatisfactory state of being unable to trace the cause of the evil, and in that state we still remain, for amongst the various circumstances of our daily life we can find none that definitely contributed to it. The surprise which this unpleasant discovery brought us has not been lessened by time. We are still unconscious of any element in our surroundings which might have fostered the disease, or of the neglect of any precaution which modern medical science suggests for its prevention.

It is well known that scurvy is a world-wide disease, and that, whilst it has attacked all sorts and conditions of men, it has proved an especial scourge to those who, by force of circumstances, have been deprived of fresh food for any length of time. This last has been so often the lot of the polar traveller that the disease has played a particularly important, and often a tragic, part in his enterprises, and one cannot read the history of polar adventure without realising the gravity of the evil and the urgency of precautionary measures. It was natural, therefore, that this subject should have been one of the first to be considered by one, like myself, on whom fell the responsibility of equipping an expedition for Antarctic research, and I felt at once that, however efficient might be the medical staff, it was highly desirable that I also should know something of it. Needless to say, I could only approach the matter as a layman, and therefore it is only in that capacity that I offer the following remarks, though I had the advantage of excellent medical advice in forming my opinions.

The symptoms of scurvy do not necessarily occur in a regular order, but generally the first sign is an inflamed, swollen condition of the gums. The whitish pink tinge next the teeth is replaced by an angry red; as the disease gains ground the gums become more spongy and turn to a purplish colour, the teeth become loose and the gums sore. Spots appear on the legs, and pain is felt in old wounds and bruises; later, from a slight oedema, the legs, and then the arms, swell to a great size and become blackened behind the joints. After this the patient is soon incapacitated, and the last horrible stages of the disease set in, from which death is a merciful release. Curiously enough, I believe that the appetite is rarely lost even towards the end, and the rapidity with which the disease spreads is excelled by the rapidity of recovery if circumstances allow the proper remedies to be applied.

For centuries, and until quite recently, it was believed that the antidote to scurvy lay in vegetable acids; scurvy grass was sought by the older voyagers, and finally lime-juice was made, and remains, a legal necessity for ships travelling on the high seas. Behind this belief lies a vast amount of evidence, but a full consideration of this evidence is beset with immense difficulties. For instance, although it is an undoubted fact that with the introduction of lime-juice scurvy was largely diminished, yet it is apt to be forgotten that there were other causes which might have contributed to this result; for at the same time sea voyages were being largely reduced by steam power, and owners were forced to provide much better food for their men.

It is beyond the scope of these pages to deal with such evidence, and it is sufficient to remark that modern medical thought finds it inconclusive, taking the view that the only antidote to scurvy is to banish its cause. Thus put, it is easy to see that many cures might have been attributed to the virtues of a supposed antidote which were really due to a discontinuance of the article of food that caused the disease.

I understand that scurvy is now believed to be ptomaine poisoning, caused by the virus of the bacterium of decay in meat, and, in plain language, as long as a man continues to assimilate this poison he is bound to get worse, and when he ceases to add to the quantity taken the system tends to throw it off, and the patient recovers. The practical point, therefore, is to obtain meat which does not contain this poison, and herein lies the whole difficulty of the case, for danger lurks everywhere. Tainted fresh meat may be virulent, but in the ordinary course of events one eats it rarely and so is saved from any disastrous result. The risk of a taint in tinned meat is greater because of the process involved in its manufacture, and with salt meat the risk is greater still for the same reason. To what extent meat must be tainted to produce scurvy is unknown, but there is reason to suppose that the taint can be so slight as to escape the notice of one's senses; in other words, poison may lurk in a tin of meat which to the sight, taste, and smell appears to be in perfect condition. Such a supposition alone shows the difficulty of tracing an outbreak of the disease to its exact source.

It is important to lay stress on the foregoing remarks because it is very commonly thought that unwholesome tinned meat can be detected at once by the proportion of tins that are 'blown'. Such a test must, of course, be a good rough guide as between good and bad, but it does not achieve the delicacy necessary to detect food which may cause scurvy. As having achieved an unsurpassed feat in the prevention of scurvy, Dr Nansen may well be taken as an authority in this matter; and more or less to this point he relates a story where a party of men found a depot of provisions, selected the best tins, ate of them, and got scurvy; his comment is that they would have done better to have selected the worst tins.

On the many points of importance with regard to the selection of tinned provisions I am not able to dwell – it is sufficient to show that the question is more complicated than appears at first sight; and, further, it must be remembered that there is no service where excellence is demanded so fully as on polar service. The ordinary traveller may be obliged to subsist on tinned food for weeks or months, but the polar voyager may be forced to extend these periods to months and years.

One great practical certainty arises, however, out of this complicated problem: one cannot be too careful; without being able to ensure perfection in one's tinned provisions, one can go a long way towards it by very careful selection and by preparing with all the safeguards which modern science can suggest. Such a preparation requires time, and therefore it becomes still more evident that ample time should be allowed for the equipment of a polar expedition.

With these few general remarks I would briefly trace the history of such circumstances as may have led to the outbreak of scurvy in the *Discovery*. I commence by giving some account of the provisions which we carried. Owing to facts which can be well understood from the shortness of time at our disposal, it was not until the spring of 1901 that our provision list was finally drawn up and the necessary orders given; the orders were distributed over a large number of firms, and deliveries were directed to be made to the East India Docks, where a shed had been placed at our disposal. At the same time, by the courtesy of the Health Office of the City of London, it was arranged that all the tinned food collected in the shed should be examined by one of their officials before it was transmitted to the *Discovery*. The examination showed that, as far as could be seen, everything was of good quality with the exception of one delivery, and it became a question whether we should reject the whole of this delivery and seek a fresh contractor, or whether we should reject only the portion that was unsatisfactory and demand its renewal. Urgency decided in favour of the latter alternative. It must be understood that the food supplied after this rejection, and indeed all the food that actually sailed in the *Discovery*, was examined, but such an examination has obvious limitations. The suspicious circumstance was that *anything* ordered for the *Discovery* should have been unsatisfactory, and the inference was that if there were shortcomings in this delivery which the examination could detect, there would probably be others which it could not.

On our arrival in New Zealand we shipped a large addition to our stock of tinned food, some on a consignment from Australia, and some on purchase in the colony itself; both deliveries were excellent as far as we had any power of judging.

I have already given some idea of our routine in winter quarters with regard to meals. It will be recalled that we had seal-meat twice a week, mutton once, and tinned meat on the remaining days; the problem is, which of these gave us the scurvy?

As regards the seal-meat, I think we may at once reject the idea. The animals had to be skinned immediately after they were killed, and carcases were thus frozen within a very short space of time.

The mutton is more doubtful. It was killed inside the Antarctic circle, but I am not sure that the meat was wholly above suspicion of taint, as the sun may have raised the darker portions of the carcases above the freezing-point; but it is to be remembered that though we ate very heartily of it we only enjoyed this luxury once a week.

The grave suspicion naturally rests on the tinned meats, and therefore it becomes necessary to examine a little more closely into them. In nine cases out of ten our solid food on ordinary 'tinned meat' days consisted of plain tinned beef or mutton made up into some dish on board. It was the rarest thing for us to open tins containing made-up dishes, mainly because these were part of the consignment which I mentioned as being unsatisfactory. Without exception the plain beef and mutton came from Australian and New Zealand firms, and I have no doubt that it was as good as such things can be; the excellent state of preservation of that which we brought back is alone sufficient to prove this. I cannot think, therefore, that we have a right to suspect these tinned meats. In considering all facts in connection with this elusive disease, it must not be forgotten also that we regularly opened tins of milk and less regularly other 'kickshaws' in which it may have been hidden; but as we continued this practice during our second winter, without ill result, it is reasonable to consider that its effect may be discounted.

The main fact, however, that makes it so difficult to trace our scurvy to faulty provisions is that not a single tin of any sort or description was served out in the *Discovery* until it had been opened and examined by one of the doctors, and in this respect no risks were taken. The least suspicion was sufficient to ensure rejection, and therefore it is certain that no food which bore any outward sign of being unsafe was ever consumed in the ship.

It has been pointed out that scurvy depends largely on environment, and there can be no doubt that severe or insanitary conditions of life contribute to the ravages of the disease. Indeed, we saw how this might be from the outbreak in our western party, but I do not think such conditions can be regarded as the prime cause.

In summing up this brief survey of our outbreak of scurvy, I may point out that the evidence shows it was caused by the food the discontinuance of which led to recovery, and that this food consisted of tinned meats which were to all appearances of the best quality, and of apparently fresh mutton taken in small quantity. Beyond this it seems impossible to go, and consequently, as far as the investigation of the disease is concerned, we are left in an unsatisfactory position of doubt.

Our scurvy came to us as a great surprise. Fully alive to the danger of the disease, we seemed to have taken every precaution that the experience of others could suggest, and when the end of our long winter found everyone in apparently good health and high spirits, we naturally congratulated ourselves on the efficacy of our measures. How rudely we were awakened from this pleasing attitude I have shown, and, though the disease was banished with astonishing rapidity, the incident could not fail to leave an impression that in some manner we had been unwittingly culpable. Quite apart from the benefit lost to medical science, therefore, it was extremely grievous that, for our own personal satisfaction, we could not put our finger on the spot, and definitely state whence the evil sprang.

Yet, inconclusive as our experience was, it serves to emphasise the lessons taught by former experiences. It shows that too much care and attention cannot be paid to the provisioning of a polar expedition; it indicates that in this connection the ordinary methods of food examination are not sufficiently refined, but should be supplemented by chemical analyses and every test that modern science can suggest; and it again points clearly to the inestimable advantage of fresh food.

In this last respect there lies the most invaluable safeguard for the welfare of future Antarctic expeditions; it seems evident that the whole circle of the Antarctic seas is abundantly provided with animal life. It is not conceivable, therefore, that any party wintering in the Antarctic Regions will have great difficulty in providing themselves with fresh food; and, as we have proved, where such conditions exist there need be no fear of the dreaded word 'scurvy'.

CHAPTER 13

Journey to the Farthest South

Future Plans Modified by Reconnaissance Journeys — Trip to Cape Crozier —
Start of the Southern Journey — Depot A — Description of the Dog-Team —
Equipment of Sledges — Return of Supporting Party — Failure of the Dogs — Relay
Work — Dog-driving — Dog-food — Atmospheric Phenomenon — Cracking of
the Surface Crust — New Land in Sight — Beautiful Effects Produced by
Snow-crystals — Dogs Weakening — Slow Progress — Depot B — The Chasm —
Pushing Southward — Increase of Hunger — Further Land — Scurvy Appearing —
Cooking-arrangements — Soft Snow — Experiences with the Dogs — Christmas
Day and its Good Cheer

> Hold hard the breath and bend up every spirit
> To his full height. . . .
>   . . . Shew us here
> That you are worth your breeding, which I doubt not.
> For there is none so mean or base
> That have not noble lustre in your eyes.
> I see you stand like greyhounds in the slips,
> Straining upon the start.   — SHAKESPEARE

Although the gravity of our outbreak of scurvy was not under-rated, and we had been busied in measures for the prevention of its recurrence, it must not be supposed that we had allowed it in any way to interfere with our plans for the future. Our preparations were pushed on as vigorously as though no such cloud had come to overshadow the brightness of our outlook.

The general results of the spring journeys had enabled us to lay our plans for the summer with greater definition. Our reconnaissance to the south had indicated that the main party, after leaving the Bluff, would have to travel directly over the snow-plain at a long distance from, and possibly out of sight of, land; the probability was that no further depots could be established, and hence it was desirable that the party should be supported as far as possible on their route. This theory added another object for our sledging efforts, for if the coast ran sharply to the west after rounding the

Bluff it was evidently desirable that we should gain some information concerning it. To meet these requirements it was decided that
Barne, with a party of twelve men, should accompany the dog-team
until the weights were reduced to an amount which the latter could
drag without assistance. He was then to return to the ship, and,
after a short rest, to start again, with a party of six, and endeavour
to follow the coastline west of the Bluff. With such a plan as I have
outlined it was hoped that there would be a good chance of solving
the mysteries in a southerly direction; and as soon as this was in train
Armitage was to have at his disposal all the resources of men and
material in the ship for his attack on the western region.

In considering his earlier observations, Armitage had come to the
conclusion that it was impossible to force a way through the
entrance to New Harbour, where for so many miles he had seemed
to see a chaos of ice and morainic material, and he thought his best
chance lay in ascending to the foothill plateau, in the neighbourhood of the so-called 'Eskers', as from this he hoped to find a pass
which would lead him over the main ridge of mountains.

In busily preparing for this programme we did not forget the
advantage we possessed in the fact that our surfaces and general
travelling conditions were likely to improve rather than otherwise
as the summer advanced; we should have little of the sea-ice to
cross, and we knew that with our cold summer this would not
develop into the same treacherous condition that it does in the
North, whilst the surfaces to the south or inland could not possibly
grow moist and sludgy. With these conditions we could arrange our
movements to take advantage of what we hoped to find the warmest and finest summer months; and since there was no chance of the
ship being released from the ice until February, there was little
object in our sledge parties being back much before that date, while
we should travel during the time that the sun was circling at its
greatest altitude.

As a further result of our reconnaissance journeys, we were now
better able to judge of the requirements of each individual party as
far as smaller matters of equipment were concerned. It was evident
that the western travellers would have to be provided with ice-
axes, crampons, ropes, and other necessaries for climbing; but it
seemed that in going to the south we should be safe in omitting
these accessories, and in preparing for a journey in which there was

no formidable obstruction. As we proposed to begin our journey to the south at the end of October, it can be imagined that, with so many minor details to be attended to, the last weeks of the month were not a slack season for any of us.

On Friday, October 24, Royds and his party returned to the ship, having achieved the object of communicating with our 'Record' post at Cape Crozier. We now had the satisfaction of knowing that we had done all in our power to guide a possible relief ship to our winter quarters; should she make a diligent search on the northern slopes of Terror, as had been arranged, she would at least have a good prospect of receiving the latest information concerning us. It was also a very great source of satisfaction to find that the party returned in excellent health, for they had left us almost immediately after the outbreak of scurvy, and that they should have come back safe and well went far to show that hard sledging work would not necessarily cause a return of the disease.

From our experience of the previous season we had concluded that Terror Point, as the eastern extremity of the land mass was called, was an extremely windy region, and the adventures of this party left the matter beyond much doubt. Skirting the large bay south of Erebus to avoid the deeper snow, they had carried fine but cold weather with them on the outward march, and until October 10, when they were able to make their most advanced camp, ready to proceed over the bare rocks towards the rookery. The 11th proved a beautifully calm, bright day, and Royds, having injured his ankle, deputed the task of reaching the 'Record' to Skelton. The latter left the camp at noon with Evans, and by 6 p.m returned, having accomplished his errand; in the bright, clear afternoon he had little difficulty in finding the spot, and came to the conclusion that they must have been within a very short distance of it in their autumn wanderings.

On the 12th Skelton set out again with two companions, this time intent on photographing the immense ice disturbance caused by the barrier pushing around the land. After taking several photographs he returned, and the homeward route brought him close to the edge of the Crozier cliffs, where they rise with magnificent grandeur and form a frowning precipice more than 800 feet sheer above the sea; from this point of vantage he looked down directly on the barrier edge and into the small bay which breaks its outline near the land. Whilst he was admiring the beauty of the scene, his quick eye caught sight of numerous small dots on the sea-ice far below; it was not long before he decided that they must be Emperor penguins. He asked himself what they could be doing here in such numbers, and wondered if it were possible that at last the breeding-place of these mysterious birds had been discovered – it seemed almost too good to be true. Assurance must wait for some future occasion, and in the meanwhile he returned to the camp in no small state of excitement.

Tomorrow the mystery must be cleared up; but tomorrow brought the wind, and not a yard from their tents could the party stir. This was the 13th. On the 14th the weather proved equally bad, save for a short lull, when they were able to prepare a hot meal; directly afterwards, the blizzard swept down on them again and continued without intermission throughout the 15th, 16th, and 17th.

Before the gale they had built elaborate protecting snow walls to windward of the tents, and these almost proved their undoing; for the never-ceasing drift collected deeper and deeper behind these walls, and the occupants of the tents were conscious that the snow was gradually accumulating around them and that they were now powerless to prevent it. It soon reduced the light within to a mere glimmer, and then, becoming heavier and heavier on every fold of canvas, it diminished their interior space to such an extent that all were obliged to lie with their knees bent double. In the end they were practically buried in the heart of a snowdrift; but whilst the stout bamboos bent under the load and still further narrowed the space within, they luckily withstood the strain to the end.

It was now only by observing the extreme summit of their tents that the prisoners had any indication of what was happening without. Though in some respects this was a relief, yet for want of space they were unable to cook any food, they could barely turn from side to side, and they suffered a martyrdom from cramp. Their enclosed position brought them comparative warmth, but what advantage they gained in this way was largely discounted by the sodden dampness of articles which had thawed.

On the 17th the snow ceased to drift. The occupants of one tent were able to free themselves after some difficulty, but the other tent had literally to be dug out before its imprisoned members could be got into the open; whilst the sledges and all that had been left without were buried completely out of sight. The tale of five days spent in the manner which I have described is soon told – Mr Royds dismisses it in half a page of his report – but I, and I believe the reader may, find that no great effort of imagination is needed to grasp the horrible discomforts that it involved; and yet when this party were recounting their adventures on board the ship, one might have imagined that the incident was all extremely amusing. The hardships had been forgotten, and all that the men seemed to remember was how So-and-so had launched out with the cramp and kicked someone else fair in the middle, or how the occupants of one tent had declared that they had been awakened by the snoring of some particular member in the other.

It was not until the 18th that the wind ceased, and they were able to make shift to dry their equipment and to look out on the scene about them. When they had arrived the whole Ross Sea had been frozen over as far as their eyes could see, and now they gazed on a sheet of open water. Not a scrap of ice remained in sight, except in the bay to which Skelton had directed his footsteps at an early hour; in this bay the ice still hung, and it was doubtless the permanency of this sheet which had caused the Emperor penguins to adopt it as a breeding-place.

For Skelton had not been deceived in his observation: on reaching the sea-ice in this bay, after a stiff climb over the high-pressure ridges, he found again his colony of Emperors, numbering some four hundred, and, to his delight, amongst them several that were nursing chicks.

Upon the great interest of this find, and upon the many important notes made concerning the colony, both at this time and later, I will not dwell, as these facts are dealt with in the appendix contributed by our zoologist, Dr Wilson, to the two-volume edition of this work which is easily available. He described the habits of these birds more clearly than I could hope to do; I will only testify to the joy which greeted this discovery on board the ship. We had felt that this penguin was the truest type of our region. All other birds fled north when the severity of winter descended upon us: the Emperor alone was prepared to face the extremest rigours of our climate: and we gathered no small satisfaction from being the first to throw light on the habits of a creature that so far surpasses in hardihood all others of the feathered tribe.

Full of their exploits the party started for home on the 19th, and, as I have said, reached the ship on the 24th.

Before the end of the month everything was prepared for the southern journey, instructions for various sledge parties and for the custody of the ship had been given, details of the conduct of affairs had been discussed and rediscussed. Every eventuality seemed to be provided for, and nothing now remained but to wait for the date which had been fixed for our departure.

The southern supporting party, as I have said, consisted of Mr Barne with eleven men; and as it was expected that at first, at any rate, the dogs would outstrip the men, it was decided that this party should start on October 30, but that the dog-team should not leave until a few days later. All were to meet at the depot which I had laid out, and which was now known as Depot A.

Accordingly, on October 30, I record: 'The supporting party started this morning, amidst a scene of much enthusiasm; all hands had a day off, and employed it in helping to drag the sledges for several miles. The sledges carried some decorations: Barne's banner floated on the first, the next bore a Union Jack, and another carried a flag with a large device stating "No dogs need apply"; the reference was obvious. It was an inspiriting sight to see nearly the whole of our small company step out on the march with ringing cheers, and to think that all work of this kind promised to be done as heartily. Later Shackleton had a trial trip with the dogs to get our runners in better order, and the animals started so strongly that they carried away the central trace and started to gallop off; but luckily they all wanted to go in different directions, and so didn't get far, and, luckily also, there were a few of us about to prevent the worst effect of the inevitable fights.'

'November 2. – . . . We are off at last. By ten this morning the dogs were harnessed and all was ready for a start; the overcast sky was showing signs of a break in the south. Every soul was gathered on the floe to bid us farewell, and many were prepared to accompany us for the first few miles. A last look was given to our securings, the traces were finally cleared, and away we went amidst the wild cheers of our comrades. The dogs have never been in such form; despite the heavy load, for the first two miles two men had to sit on the sledges to check them, and even thus it was as much as the rest of us could do to keep up by running alongside.

E. H. Shackleton   R. F. Scott   E. A. Wilson
The Southern Party

One by one our followers tailed off, and by noon we three were alone with our animals and still breathlessly trying to keep pace with them. Soon after lunch we saw a dark spot far ahead, and about 5 p.m. we made this out to be our supporting party; we caught them up just as they were rounding the corner of White Island, and learnt that they had had very bad weather which had confined them to their tents. Relieving them of some of their loads, we camped, whilst they pushed on to get the advantage of a night march.'

'November 3. – . . . At 2 p.m. we came up with Barne's people. They are doing their best, but making very slow progress. The difficulty is the slipperiness of the windswept snow, the surface being particularly hard amongst the sastrugi opposite the gullies of the island. They can get no hold with their fur boots, and find their leather ski boots dreadfully cold for the feet; the result is that they scarcely cover a mile an hour. The only thing is for us to take life easy whilst they go on in the best manner possible; we have relieved them of over 150 lbs. of weight, so that they now only help us to the extent of 500 lbs. I have told Barne to go on quite independently of us.'

In this manner we journeyed slowly to the south outside the White Island, the parties constantly passing and repassing; it was impossible at this part to keep together, as men and dogs took the march at quite a different pace. To add to the slowness of our journey, the weather proved very unpropitious, for the wind constantly sprang up and obliged us to camp, and we were forced to lie up during the greater part of the 8th and 9th, whilst a heavy blizzard passed over us.

On the 9th I wrote: 'The wind still blows with exasperating persistence, though the sun has been peeping out all day; it adds to the trying nature of this inactivity to watch the sun pass pole after pole of our tent and to know that the supporting party are cut off from their slow daily progress. We are now south of the Bluff, and cannot be more than eight miles from the depot. Tonight the wind is dying; the cloud mantle on the Bluff has vanished, and for the first time for many days one can catch a view of the western lands.

'On our outward track we have kept rather too close to the White Island, and consequently have had to traverse a good many undulations; it was curious to watch the supporting party dipping out of sight on what appeared to the eye to be a plain surface. Disturbed by much barking from the dogs, we crawled out of our bags tonight about eleven o'clock, to find, much to our satisfaction, that our supporting party had arrived; they camped close by, and Barne tells me they have had a hard, cold pull up against the wind.'

'November 10. – Started early this morning, leaving the supporting party quietly slumbering. Had much difficulty in forcing the dogs along in face of a low drift and cutting wind, but managed to make good progress. At one o'clock, sighted the depot and were soon camped beside it, when the wind died away, the sky cleared, and we have again the whole splendid panorama of the northern and western mountains in full view.

'On the march today a small snow petrel suddenly appeared hovering above us, and later it was joined by a second; these are the first birds we have seen since the departure of the skuas in the autumn, and form a very pleasant reminder of summer. We are left in wonder as to why they should be so far from the sea. We were first apprised of their coming by the conduct of the dogs, and for a moment or two we could not understand why these animals should suddenly begin to leap about and bark furiously, but their wild dashes soon drew attention to our fluttering visitors.

'Already it seems to me that the dogs feel the monotony of a long march over the snow more than we do; they seem easily to get dispirited, and that it is not due to fatigue is shown when they catch a glimpse of anything novel. On seeing the men ahead they are always eager to get up with them, and even a shadowy ice disturbance or anything unusual will excite their curiosity. Today, for instance, they required some driving until they caught sight of the depot flag, when they gave tongue loudly and dashed off as though they barely felt the load behind them.'

It would perhaps be as well to introduce the reader to our dog-team, as they played so important a part in this journey, and before the tale of its ending will have disappeared from the scene for ever. Their origin and the names by which they had been formerly known are, as I have explained, mysteries which we could not penetrate, but long before the commencement of this journey each had learnt to answer to his own title in the following list:

'Nigger'	'Birdie'	'Wolfe'
'Jim'	'Nell'	'Vic'
'Spud'	'Blanco'	'Bismarck'
'Snatcher'	'Grannie'	'Kid'
'FitzClarence'	'Lewis'	'Boss'
'Stripes'	'Gus'	'Brownie'
	'Joe'	

Each of these dogs had his own peculiar characteristics, and altogether they displayed as great a variety as could well be comprehended in a team of the size; it can be imagined that what we did not know concerning their individuality we had ample opportunities of learning during the weeks that followed.

I have already given some idea of the dignity of character of our leader, 'Nigger'. He was a black dog with some tawny markings, and possessed the most magnificent head and chest, though falling off a little in the hinder quarters. A more perfect sledge dog could scarcely be imagined; he chose his place naturally as the leader, and if put into any other position would make himself so unpleasant to his neighbours, and generally behave so ill, that he was very quickly shifted. In the happy times before sickness fell on our team, it was a delight to watch 'Nigger' at his work: he seemed to know the meaning of every move. He would lie still as a graven image till he saw the snow being shovelled from the skirting of the tent, when up he would spring and pace to and fro at his picket, giving out a low throaty bark of welcome as any of us approached, and now and again turning towards his neighbours to express his opinion of them in the most bloodthirsty snarl. A few minutes later, as the leading man came to uproot his picket, his keen eye would watch each movement, and a slow wagging of his tail would quite obviously signify approval; then as the word came to start, he would push affectionately against the leader, as much as to say, 'Now, come along', and brace his powerful chest to the harness. At the evening halt after a long day he would drop straight in his tracks and remain perfectly still with his great head resting on his paws; other dogs might clamour for food, but 'Nigger' knew perfectly well that the tent had to be put up first. Afterwards, however, when one of us approached the dog-food, above the howling chorus that arose one could always distinguish the deep bell-like note of the leading dog, and knew that if disturbance was to be avoided, it was well to go to the front end of the trace first.

'Lewis' was a big, thick-coated, brindled dog, a very powerful but not a consistent puller; always noisily affectionate and hopelessly clumsy, he would prance at one and generally all but succeed in bowling one over with boisterous affection. He was very popular with everyone, as such a big, blustering, good-natured animal deserved to be.

'Jim' was a sleek, lazy, greedy villain, up to all the tricks of the trade; he could pull splendidly when he chose, but generally preferred to pretend to pull, and at this he was extraordinarily cunning. During the march his eye never left the man with the whip, on whose approach 'Jim' could be seen panting and labouring as though he felt sure that everything depended on his efforts; but a moment or two later, when the danger had passed, the watchful eye would detect Master 'Jim' with a trace that had a very palpable sag in it. Yet with all his faults it was impossible not to retain a certain affection for this fat culprit, who was so constantly getting himself into hot water.

The general opinion of 'Spud' was that he was daft – there was something wanting in the upper storey. In the middle of a long and monotonous march he would suddenly whimper and begin to prance about in his traces; in dog-language this is a signal that there is something in sight, and it always had an electrical effect on the others, however tired they might be. As a rule they would set off at a trot with heads raised to look around and noses sniffing the breeze. It was 'Spud' alone who gave this signal without any cause, and, curiously enough, the rest never discovered the fraud; to the end he openly gulled them. On ordinary occasions 'Spud' would give one the impression of being intensely busy; he was always stepping over imaginary obstacles, and all his pulling was done in a jerky, irregular fashion. He was a big, strong, black dog, and perhaps the principal sign of his mental incapacity was the ease with which others could rob him of his food.

Amongst the team there had been one animal who was conspicuous for his ugliness: with a snubbish nose, a torn ear, an ungainly body, ribs that could be easily counted through a dirty, tattered coat, and uncompromisingly vulgar manners, he was at first an object of derision to all; and being obviously of the most plebeian origin, he was named 'FitzClarence'. Kindness and good food worked wonders for 'Clarence', and although he never developed into a thing of beauty or of refined habits, he became a very passable sledge dog.

'Kid' and 'Bismarck' were the only two dogs of the team that bore an outward resemblance, both being short-legged animals with long, fleecy, black-and-white coats. But the likeness was only superficial. Inwardly they differed much, for whereas Bismarck was counted amongst the lazy eye-servers, 'Kid' was the most indefatigable worker in the team; from morn to night he would set forth his best effort. The whip was never applied to his panting little form, and when he stopped it was to die from exhaustion.

With all our efforts we could never quite tame 'Birdie', who had evidently been treated with scant respect in his youth. At the ship he would retire into his kennel and growl at all except those who brought him food, and to the end he remained distrustful and suspicious of all attempts to pet him. He was a large, reddish-brown dog, very wolfish in appearance, but a powerful puller when he got to understand what was required of him.

Of the rest of the team, 'Gus', 'Stripes', 'Snatcher', and 'Vic' were nice, pleasant-mannered dogs, and good average pullers.

'Brownie' was a very handsome animal, but rather light in build. He was charming as a pet, but less gifted as a sledge-puller, and always appealed to one as being a little too refined and ladylike for the hardest work; nor did he ever lose a chance of utilising his pleasing appearance and persuasive ways to lighten his afflictions.

'Wolf' was the most hopelessly ill-tempered animal; his character seemed to possess no redeeming virtue. Every advance was met with the same sullen, irreconcilable humour, and the whip alone was capable of reducing him to subjection. On the principle that you can lead a horse to the water but you cannot make him drink, 'Wolf' had evidently decided that we might lead him to the traces but nothing could make him pull; and, as a consequence, from start to finish no efforts of ours could make him do even a reasonable share of his work. We should have saved ourselves much trouble and annoyance had we left him behind in the first place.

To the effort to swell the numbers of our team Bernacchi had sacrificed his own property, 'Joe', and poor 'Joe' had a history. He had been born in the Antarctic Regions at Cape Adare; later in life he had learnt to behave himself with proper decorum in a London drawing-room; and now he had returned, no doubt much against his will, to finish his career in the land of his birth. He was a very light dog, with a deceptively thick coat; much pulling could not be expected from his weight, and he certainly gave but little.

Such was our team as regards the dog element; but a word may be added about the three of the other sex, whom at first I was very reluctant to take. 'Nell' was a pretty black animal with a snappish little temper but attractive ways; 'Blanco', so called because she ought to have been white, had few attractions, and was of such little use that she was sent back with the supporting party; and poor 'Grannie' was old and toothless, but lived and died game on the traces.

Whilst the loads for this dog-team had been heavy from the start, it had not been proposed to bring them up to full weights till after our departure from Depot A, and from that spot we proposed to assist by pulling ourselves; it may be of some interest, therefore, to note the weights which we actually dragged.

The table given on page 389 was one of a number of sheets which I prepared in order that we might know at each place exactly how we stood, and it seemed to simplify matters to draw

*Weights on leaving
Depot A*

	lbs.
Dog-food	400
Tank	8
Sledge	35
Bamboo	4
Tomahawk	3
	450

Dotted
lines
show
plans of
sledges
and
straps

	lbs.
Dog-food	400
Tank	8
Sledge	35
Bamboo	3
	446

Ready provision bag	16
Kit bag	20
Spare foot-gear bag	10
Five biscuit cases	217
Tent	29
Ice-axe, shovel, and dog pickets	10
Three blouses	15
Sledge	35
Bamboo and straps	5
	357

Three sleeping-bags	45
Tank	6
Contents 9 provision bags	227
Seal-meat	70
Alpine rope	5
All ski on top	30
Sledge	35
Bamboo and straps	4
	422

Repair bag	12
Instrument box	40
Cooker, Primus, &c.	34
Oil	60
Sledge	28
Securings	3
	177
	1,852

rough diagrams of the sledges on the margin. The total of 1,850 lbs. was of course a heavy load for our team of nineteen, especially as the team possessed a few animals which were of little account; but it must be remembered that we expected to pull ourselves, and that each night, after the first start, would see a reduction of between thirty and forty pounds by the time all creature comforts had been attended to.

The load here shown allows for nine weeks only for our own food, and it was in order that we might increase this allowance to thirteen that the supporting party was arranged to accompany us for some part of our journey.

On the afternoon of the 11th the supporting party hove in sight, and we were soon busily engaged in arranging matters for an early start on the morrow.

The 12th proved a misty, raw, cold day – not a happy omen for our start – but we got away betimes, and with a cheer set off for the first time on a due south course. The dogs were in such high feather that they quickly caught up the men, and little by little we had to increase their load until they were drawing no less than 2,100 lbs. When we camped for the night we had made 11½ miles, and, in the slightly misty weather, already appeared to be lost on the great open plain. I note in my diary: 'The feeling at first is somewhat weird; there is absolutely nothing to break the grey monotone about us, and yet we know that the mist is not thick, but that our isolation comes from the immense expanse of the plain. The excellent pulling of the dogs is likely to modify our plans, and I think of sending half the supports back tomorrow.'

'November 13. – Sights today showed us to be nearly up to the 79th parallel, and therefore farther south than anyone has yet been. The announcement of the fact caused great jubilation, and I am extremely glad that there are no fewer than fifteen of us to enjoy this privilege of having broken the record. Shackleton suggested that all should be photographed, whereat the men were much delighted, and we all gathered about the sledges with our flags fluttering over us. Then half our supporting party started to return, bearing the good news of our present success, and the other half stepped out once more on a due south line, with the dogs following.

'This morning it was very bright and sunny except to the far north, where probably those on board the ship are not enjoying such delightful weather; behind us only the Bluff showed against a dark background, and that was already growing small in the distance. Away to the west the view was perfectly clear, and we now know that there is land beyond our western horizon; it is very distant, and appears in detached masses, but it is evident that the general trend of it is in a more southerly direction than we had supposed. At this great distance it looks to be completely snow-covered; we can only catch the high lights and shadows due to irregularity of shape, and can only say definitely that there must be many lofty mountains. I took a round of bearings with the prismatic compass, and then asked Barne to do the same; he got different readings, and on trying again myself I got a third result. The observations only differed by a few degrees, but it shows that these compasses are not to be relied upon where the directive force is so small.'

The needle of the prismatic compass carries a weighty graduated circle with it; it therefore bears heavily on the pivot, and the friction produced is sufficient to prevent accuracy of reading where the earth has such small influence on the needle. After this I depended for all bearings on the compass attached to our small theodolite, which possessed a simple light needle and seemed to give greater accuracy. I record this fact, because it was important that we should obtain accurate observations on our extended sledge journeys, and it would be well that this point should be more carefully considered in future expeditions.

On the 13th and 14th we pushed on to the south in spite of thick snowy weather which followed the fine morning of the 13th, and during those two days we managed to add fifteen miles to our southing. On the afternoon of the 14th I record: 'The men go ahead, and when they have got a good start we cheer on our animals, who work hard until they have caught up with them; in this manner we get over the ground fairly well. The day has been murky and dull with a bad light, and we have come upon a new form of *sastrugus*: instead of the clean-cut waves about the Bluff, we have heaped-up mounds of snow with steepish edges. Heavily laden as they are, it is difficult work for the dogs when they come across the sudden rises. Now and then the clouds have lifted, showing the horizon line and glimpses of the land to the north, but for the main part the sky and snow-surface have been merged in a terrible sameness of grey, and it has been impossible to see the spot on which one's foot was next to be placed; falls have been plentiful. The surface itself is getting softer, but the sledges run fairly easily. The dogs were pretty "done" when we camped tonight, but we are feeding them up, and I do not propose to overwork them whilst the load remains as heavy as at present. That we are travelling over a practically level surface was evident from our view of the supporting party today; though we were often some distance apart they were always clearly in view, which would not have been the case had there been undulations.'

'November 15. – A beautifully bright, calm morning; the sun shone warmly on our tents, making them most cheerful and comfortable within. To the north the land has become dim, to the west we have the same prospect of distant detached snow-covered ranges, and in all other directions the apparently limitless snow-plain.

'We were very busy this morning making arrangements for our last parting: the loads had to be readjusted, the dog-harness attended to, observations taken, and notes of farewell written. All this was not finished till after noon, when many willing hands helped us to pack up our tent and make all ready for our final start. If former moments of parting have seemed unpropitious, the same cannot be said of today; the sun shone brightly on our last farewells, and whilst behind us we left all in good health and spirits, it is scarcely to be wondered at that our hopes ran high for the future. We are already beyond the utmost limit to which man has attained: each footstep will be a fresh conquest of the great unknown. Confident in ourselves, confident in our equipment, and confident in our dog-team, we can but feel elated with the prospect that is before us.

'The day's work has cast a shadow on our highest aspirations, however, and already it is evident that if we are to achieve much it will be only by extreme toil, for the dogs have not pulled well today; possibly it may be something to do with the surface, which seems to get softer, possibly something to do with the absence of the men in front to cheer them on, and possibly something to do with the temperature, which rose at one time to $+20°$ and made the heavy pulling very warm work. Whatever the reason may be, by five o'clock we had only covered about three miles, and this is by no means up to expectation. We have decided that if things have not improved in the morning we will take on half the load at a time; after a few days of this sort of thing the loads will be sufficiently lightened for us to continue in the old way again.'

The above extract shows that our troubles were already beginning, but as yet we had no suspicion that they were likely to be as grievous as they soon became. On the following day we attempted once more to start our heavy loads, but after a few yards of struggling the dogs seemed to lose all heart, and many looked round with the most pathetic expression as much as to say we were really expecting too much of them; there was but one thing to be done – namely, to divide the load into two portions and take on half at a time. This meant, of course, that each mile had to be traversed three times, but as there was no alternative we were forced to start on this tedious form of advance. With this, even, we should have been content had the dogs shown their former vigour; but now, for some reason which we could not fathom, they seemed to be losing all their spirit, and they made as much fuss over drawing the half-load as a few days before they had done over the whole one.

On November 18 I write: 'A dull day again, but we plodded on in the same monotonous style. Starting at 11 a.m., we pushed on for two and a half miles by our sledge-meter, with half the load, then returned for the second half; the whole operation took about four hours and a half, after which we had lunch and then repeated the same performance. It was 11 p.m. before we were in our sleeping-bags, and at the end of the march the dogs were practically "done". What can be the cause it is almost impossible to guess. It cannot be wholly the surface, though this is certainly much worse; not only is it softer, but all day long snow-crystals are falling, and these loose, light crystals enormously increase the friction on the runners; nor can it be altogether the temperature, for even when it falls very chill there is no sign of improvement in the pace. I fear there must be another reason which is at present beyond us. We gained five miles today, but to do it we had to cover fifteen.'

These miles to which I refer are geographical, and not statute miles: in all our journeys we calculated in the former unit, for ease of reference to the degrees and minutes of latitude, but it must be explained that there is a considerable difference in these measurements: seven geographical miles are equal to a little more than eight statute. In many cases I have reduced the mileage in this book to the better-known statute mile for the convenience of the reader, but in some of my quotations I leave the original figure unaltered; I think with this explanation it will be clear when either is used.

A word may be added concerning the sledge-meter. Our engine-room staff cleverly manufactured these instruments by applying the counter apparatus of some recording blocks to wheels of a certain definite diameter, and thus as one of these wheels trundled behind the sledge it revolved the mechanism of the counter so as to show the number of yards travelled. As I think I have said, at first we all thought we were walking very long distances through the snow, and when we adopted the sledge-meter and it showed us the chilling truth, many were inclined to be sceptical of its accuracy until it was found that when there was a difference of opinion between the party and the sledge-meter, astronomical observations invariably decided in favour of the latter, so that we were obliged to acknowledge that it was we, and not the sledge-meter, who were going too slowly.

After our experience one cannot help thinking that not a few sledging records would have been modified had this truth-telling instrument always been available; it is to be recommended to future expeditions, not only for this reason, but on account of the excellent check it affords to the position of a sledge party for geographical purposes.

'November 19. – The sun was shining when we started today, and the fine snow was falling continuously; it is a drizzle of tiny crystals, which settle on the sledges and quickly evaporate. The effect on the surface is very bad, and the dogs are growing more and more listless. We could only advance four and three-quarter miles, and that only by hard driving and going longer than we have yet gone. Two of us always pull on the traces whilst the third drives; the latter task is by far the most dreaded. In going to the rear for the second half-load, we always carry an empty sledge, and up to the present, to prevent confusion of the traces, someone has sat on the sledge, but today even this appeared to be a perceptible drag on our poor animals.

'It is very tiring work. When one goes out in the morning there is now no joyous clamour of welcome; one or two of the animals have to be roused up out of their nests, then we start in a spiritless fashion. We take our duties in turns; one of us attaches his harness to the head of the trace, and whilst he pulls he endeavours to cheer on the flagging team. A second takes the best position, which is to pull alongside the sledges, in silence; the third does not pull, but carries the whip and has to use it all too frequently. Thus our weary caravan winds its slow way along until the sledge-meter has reeled off the required distance. When we halt, the dogs drop at once, but when the lightened sledge is attached and we start to wheel them round, they wake up and for the first time display a little energy in trying to fight as they circle about; but this show of spirit soon fails, though we naturally get back at a brisker pace. Then the second half-load is joined up, and the whole thing has to be done over again. When the dogs sight the advanced load, however, there is a distinct improvement; they know that to get there means rest, and, encouraging this spirit as much as we can, the last half-mile is done almost at a trot. The afternoon march is of the same nature as that of the forenoon, but is made worse by the increased fatigue of our wretched animals. It is all very heart-breaking work.

'This morning we sighted further land to the south-west, and like the rest it appears as a detached fragment. We now see three distinct gaps between the several land masses, and the distance is too great for us to make out any detail of the latter; to the south and round through east to the north we have still the unbroken snow horizon.

'Tonight we have been discussing our position again; it is evidently going from bad to worse. We have scarcely liked to acknowledge to ourselves that the fish diet is having a permanently bad effect on the dogs, but it looks very much like it; we saw that it disagreed with them at first, but we have tried to persuade ourselves that the effect is only temporary. It will be a terrible calamity if this is the cause of all our distress, for there is no possible change of diet except to feed the poor things on each other, and yet it is difficult to account in any other way for the fact that whilst they are receiving an ample amount of food they should daily be growing weaker. One of the most trying circumstances in our position is that we are forced to spend hours in our tent which might be devoted to marching; it is the dogs, and not we, who call the halt each night.'

Though it was only gradually that we could convince ourselves that the dog-food was at the bottom of our trouble, subsequent events proved it beyond a doubt, and therefore it may be of interest to give some account of that food. Originally, I had intended to take ordinary dog-biscuits for our animals, but in an evil moment I was persuaded by one who had had great experience in dog-driving to take fish. Fish has been used continually in the north for feeding dogs, and the particular article which we ordered was the Norwegian stockfish such as is split, dried, and exported from that country in great quantities for human food. There is no doubt about the excellent food-value of this fish, and in every way it seemed well adapted to our purpose; and yet it was this very fish that poisoned our poor animals.

It is easy to be wise after the event, and on looking back now one sees the great probability of its suffering deterioration on passage through the Tropics, and, doubtless, had it been designed for human food we should have considered that point; but, unfortunately for our dogs, this probability escaped our notice, and as there was no outward sign of deterioration it was carried on our sledge journey. As a result the dogs sickened, and in some cases died, from what one can only suppose was a species of scurvy. The lesson to future travellers in the South is obvious, in that they should safeguard their dogs as surely as they do their men. The dog is such a terrible scavenger that one is apt to overlook this necessity.

'November 21. – This morning the sun was shining in a cloudless sky, and to our surprise we found land extending all along our right; probably it appears deceptively close owing to the mirage. At any rate, things are growing so bad that we have decided to edge towards it, and have altered our course to S.S.W. All things considered, this seems the best course, as our prospect of reaching a high latitude is steadily melting away. Our method of advance gives us at least the advantage of gauging the level nature of the surface over which we are travelling. To judge by one's feelings on the march, one might be climbing the steepest of hills all day, but the fact that we can always see our advanced or rear sledges from the other end shows that there must be an absence of inequality;

even the man who sits on the returning sledge with his eye not more than three feet above the surface rarely loses sight of these tiny black dots. It is surprising that although a sledge appears as a very minute object at two and a half miles, it can generally be seen clearly against the white background. On dull days, however, I am not sure but that it is a risk to advance them so far.'

'November 22. – The surface is becoming smoother, with less sastrugi, but the snow covering is, if anything, thicker; one sinks deeper, and there is no reduction of friction on the sledge-runners. After lunch we made a trial to start with full loads; the dogs made a gallant effort, but could scarcely move the sledges, and we had to proceed as before. With this land ahead we ought to get some variation of the monotony of our present travelling, but there is a fear that the snow may get still softer as we approach it.

'We are growing very sunburnt, and noses and lips are getting blistered and cracked and extremely sore; lips are especially pain-ful, as one cannot help licking them on the march, and this makes them worse. With the constant variations of temperature and the necessary application of the hot rim of the pannikin they get no chance to heal; hazeline cream is in much request at night to deaden the burning. We have also had some trouble with our eyes, though we wear goggles very regularly. Our appetites seem to be increasing by leaps and bounds: it is almost alarming, and the only thing to be looked to on our long marches is the prospect of the next meal.'

'November 23. – . . . There was a distinct improvement in the surface today, with a N.N.E. wind rolling the snow along like fine sand; in this way the old hard surface crust became exposed in patches, and the sledges drew easily over these. Altogether we have advanced 5⅕ miles, travelling over 15½ miles to do it. We raised the land considerably, and were able to see something more of the bold black headland for which we are making.'

'November 24. – . . . Today we started a new routine, which eases us and gives a chance for odd jobs to be done. After pushing on the first half-load one of us stops with it, gets up the tent, and prepares for lunch or supper, as the case may be, whilst the other two bring up the second half-load.

'The land which appeared to be rising so quickly yesterday was evidently thrown up by mirage; I fear it is farther off than we thought.'

'November 25. – Before starting today I took a meridian altitude, and to my delight found the latitude to be 80° 1'. All our charts of the Antarctic Regions show a plain white circle beyond the eightieth parallel; the most imaginative cartographer has not dared to cross this limit, and even the meridional lines end at the circle. It has always been our ambition to get inside that white space, and now we are there the space can no longer be a blank; this compensates for a lot of trouble.'

'November 26. – Last night we had almost decided to give our poor team a day's rest, and today there is a blizzard which has made it necessary. We had warning in the heavy stratus clouds that came over fast from the south yesterday, and still more in Wilson's rheumatism; this comes on with the greatest regularity before every snowstorm, and he suffers considerably. Up to the present it has been in his knee, but last night it appeared in his foot, and though he ought to have known its significance, he attributed it to the heavy walking. Today it has passed away with the breaking of the storm, and there can be no longer a doubt that it is due to change of weather, and that he, poor chap, serves as a very effective though unwilling barometer.'

'November 27. – Today it is beautifully bright, clear, and warm, the temperature up to +20°; but, alas! this morning we found that the dogs seemed to have derived no benefit from their rest. They were all snugly curled up beneath the snow when we went out, but in spite of their long rest we had to drag them out of their nests; some were so cramped that it was several minutes before they could stand. However, we shook some life into them and started with the full load, but very soon we had to change back into our old routine, and, if anything, the march was more trying than ever. It becomes a necessity now to reach the land soon in hopes of making a depot, so our course has been laid to the westward of S.W., and this brings the bold bluff cape on our port bow. I imagine it to be about fifty miles off, but hope it is not so much; nine hours' work today has only given us a bare four miles.

'It was my turn to drive today; Shackleton led and Wilson pulled at the side. The whole proceedings would have been laughable enough but for the grim sickness that holds so tight a grip on our poor team: Shackleton in front, with harness slung over his shoulder, was bent forward with his whole weight on the trace; in spite

JOURNEY TO THE FARTHEST SOUTH

of his breathless work, now and again he would raise and half-turn his head in an effort to cheer on the team. "Hi, dogs", "Now then", "Hi lo-lo-lo . . . " or any other string of syllables which were supposed to produce an encouraging effect, but which were soon brought to a conclusion by sheer want of breath. Behind him, and obviously deaf to these allurements, shambled the long string of depressed animals, those in rear doing their best to tread in the deep footprints of the leaders, but all by their low-carried heads and trailing tails showing an utter weariness of life. Behind these, again, came myself with the whip, giving forth one long string of threats and occasionally bringing the lash down with a crack on the snow or across the back of some laggard. By this time all the lazy dogs know their names, as well they ought; I should not like to count the number of times I have said, "Ah, you, 'Wolf'," or "Get on there, 'Jim'," or " 'Bismarck', you brute"; but it is enough to have made me quite hoarse tonight, for each remark has to be produced in a violent manner or else it produces no effect, and things have now got so bad that if the driver ceases his flow of objurgation for a moment there is a slackening of the traces. Some names lend themselves to this style of language better than others; "Boss" can be hissed out with very telling effect, whereas it is hard to make "Brownie" very emphatic. On the opposite side of the leading sledge was Wilson, pulling away in grim silence. We dare not talk on such occasions as the dogs detect the change of tone at once; they seize upon the least excuse to stop pulling. There are six or eight animals who give little trouble, and these have been placed in the front, so that the others may be more immediately under the lash; but the loafers are growing rather than diminishing in numbers. This, then, is the manner in which we have pro-ceeded for nine hours today − entreaties in front and threats behind − and so we went on yesterday, and so we shall go on tomorrow. It is sickening work, but it is the only way; we cannot stop, we cannot go back, we must go on, and there is no altern-ative but to harden our hearts and drive. Luckily, the turn for doing the actual driving only comes once in three days, but even thus it is almost as bad to witness the driving as to have to do it.

'Tonight we discussed the possibility of getting some benefit by marching at night; it was very warm today in the sun, and the air temperature was up to +25°.'

On the days which followed we gradually made our starting-hour later until we dropped into a regular night-marching routine; we then used to breakfast between 4 and 5 p.m., start marching at 6 p.m., and come to camp somewhere about three or four in the morning. Thus while the sun was at its greatest altitude we were taking our rest, and during the chiller night hours we marched. There were some advantages in this arrangement which scarcely need notice, but it was curious that with it we never quite got rid of the idea that there was something amiss, and it will be seen that it was likely to lead to confusion as to the date of any particular occurrence. Other drawbacks were that we were often obliged to march with the sun in our faces at midnight, and that sometimes the tent was unpleasantly warm during the hours of sleep.

'November 29. – Shortly after four o'clock today we observed the most striking atmospheric phenomenon we have yet seen in these regions. We were enveloped in a light, thin stratus cloud of small ice-crystals; it could not have extended to any height, as the sun was only lightly veiled. From these drifting crystals above, the sun's rays were reflected in such an extraordinary manner that the whole arch of the heavens was traced with circles and lines of brilliant prismatic or white light. The coloured circles of a bright double halo were touched or intersected by one which ran about us parallel to the horizon; above this, again, a gorgeous prismatic ring encircled the zenith; away from the sun was a white fog-bow, with two bright mock suns where it intersected the horizon circle. The whole effect was almost bewildering, and its beauty is far beyond the descriptive powers of my sledging pencil. We have often seen double halos, fog-bows, mock suns, and even indications of other circles, but we have never been privileged to witness a display that approaches in splendour that of today. We stopped, whilst Wilson took notes of the artistic composition, and I altitudes and bearings of the various light effects. If it is robbed of some of the beauties of a milder climate, our region has certainly pictures of its own to display.'

On our return to the ship I could find no account, in such reference books as we had, of anything to equal this scene, nor have I since heard of its having been witnessed elsewhere.

'November 29 (continued). – Both in the first and second advance today we noticed that the points of starting and finishing were in view of one another, but that in travelling between them either end was temporarily lost to sight for a short time. This undoubtedly indicates undulation in the surface, but I should think of slight amount, probably not more than seven or eight feet, the length of the waves being doubtful, as we cannot be certain of the angle at which we are crossing them; they cannot exceed two miles from crest to crest, and are probably about one.

'We had rather a scare tonight on its suddenly coming over very thick just as Wilson and I were coupling up the second load to bring it on; all our food and personal equipment had been left with Shackleton in the advanced position, and, of course, we could see nothing of it through the haze. We followed the old tracks for some way, until the light got so bad that we repeatedly lost sight of them, when we were obliged to halt and grope round for them. So far we were only in danger of annoying delays, but a little later a brisk breeze sprang up, and to our consternation rapidly drifted up the old tracks; there was nothing for it but to strike out a fresh course of our own in the direction in which we supposed the camp to lie, which we did, and, getting on as fast as possible, had the satisfaction of sighting the camp in about half an hour. "All's well that ends well", and luckily the fog was not very thick; but the incident has set us thinking that if very thick weather were to come on, the party away from the camp might be very unpleasantly situated, so in future we shall plant one or two flags as we advance with the first load, and pick them up as we come on with the second.'

'December 2. – We noticed again today the cracking of the snow-crust; sometimes the whole team with the sledges get on an area when it cracks around us as sharply and as loudly as a pistol shot, and this is followed by a long-drawn sigh as the area sinks. When this first happened the dogs were terrified, and sprang forward with tails between their legs and heads screwed round as though the threatened danger was behind; and, indeed, it gave me rather a shock the first time – it was so unexpected, and the sharp report was followed by a distinct subsidence. Though probably one dropped only an inch or two, there was an instantaneous feeling of insecurity which is not pleasant. Digging down tonight Shackleton found a comparatively hard crust two or three inches under the soft snow surface; beneath this was an air space of about

an inch, then came about a foot of loose snow in large crystals, and
then a second crust. There is a good deal that is puzzling about
these crusts.'

During the following year on our sledge journeys we frequently
dug into the snow surface to see what lay below, and though we
always found a succession of crusts with soft snow between, the
arrangement was very irregular and gave us no very definite
information.

'December 3. – . . . Our pemmican bag for this week by an
oversight has been slung alongside a tin of paraffin, and is consequently strongly impregnated with the oil; one can both smell
and taste the latter strongly; it is some proof of the state of our
appetites that we really don't much mind!

'We are now sufficiently close to the land to make out some of
its details. On our right is a magnificent range of mountains,
which we are gradually opening out, and which must therefore
run more or less in an east-and-west direction. My rough calculations show them to be at least fifty miles from us, and, if so, their
angle of altitude gives a height of over 10,000 feet. The eastern
end of this range descends to a high snow-covered plateau,
through which arise a number of isolated minor peaks, which I
think must be volcanic; beyond these, again, is a long, rounded,
sloping snow-cape, merging into the barrier. These rounded
snow-capes are a great feature of the coast; they can be seen dimly
in many places, both north and south of us. They are peculiar as
presenting from all points of view a perfectly straight line inclined
at a slight angle to the horizon. North of this range the land still
seems to run on, but it has that detached appearance, due to great
distance, which we noted before, and we can make little of it.
The south side of the range seems to descend comparatively
abruptly, and in many cases it is bordered by splendid high cliffs,
very dark in colour, though we cannot make out the exact shade.
Each cliff has a band of white along its top where the ice-cap ends
abruptly; at this distance it has a rather whimsical resemblance to
the sugaring of a Christmas cake. The cliffs and foothills of the
high range form the northern limit of what appears to be an
enormous strait; we do not look up this strait, and therefore
cannot say what is beyond, but the snow-cape on this side is
evidently a great many miles from the high range, and there

appears to be nothing between. This near snow-cape seems to be more or less isolated. It is an immense and almost dome-shaped, snow-covered mass; only quite lately could we see any rock at all, but now a few patches are to be made out towards the summit, and one or two at intervals along the foot. It is for one of these that we have now decided to make, so that we may establish our depot there, but at present rate of going we shall be a long time before we reach it.

'South of this isolated snow-cape, which is by far the nearest point of land to us, we can see a further high mountainous country; but this also is so distant that we can say little of it. One thing seems evident – that the high bluff cape we were making for is not a cape at all, but a curiously bold spur of the lofty mountain ranges, which is high above the level of the coastline, and must be many miles inland. It is difficult to say whether this land is more heavily glaciated than that which we have seen to the north; on the whole, I think the steeper surfaces seem equally bare. There is a consolation for the heavier surface and harder labour we are experiencing in the fact that each day the scene gets more interesting and more beautiful.

'Today, in lighting the Primus, I very stupidly burnt a hole in the tent; I did not heat the top sufficiently before I began to pump, and a long yellow flame shot up and set light to the canvas. I do not think I should have noticed what had happened at first, but luckily the others were just approaching and rushed forward to prevent further damage. As it was, there was a large hole which poor Shackleton had to make shift to repair during our last lap; it is not much fun working with a needle in the open at the midnight hours, even though the season happens to be summer.'

'December 4. – After a sunshiny day and with the cooler night hours there comes now a regular fall of snow-crystals. On a calm night there is nothing to indicate the falling crystals save a faint haze around the horizon; overhead it is quite clear. Suddenly, and apparently from nowhere, a small shimmering body floats gently down in front of one and rests as lightly as thistledown on the white surface below. If one stoops to examine it as we have done many times, one finds that it is a six-pointed feathery star, quite flat and smooth on either side. We find them sometimes as large as a shilling, and at a short distance they might be small hexagonal pieces of glass; it is only on looking closely that one discovers the intricate and delicate beauty of their design.

'The effect of these en masse is equally wonderful; they rest in all positions, and therefore receive the sun's rays at all angles, and in breaking them up reflect in turn each colour of the spectrum. As one plods along towards the midnight sun, one's eyes naturally fall on the plain ahead, and one realises that the simile of a gem-strewn carpet could never be more aptly employed than in describing the radiant path of the sun on the snowy surface. It sparkles with a myriad points of brilliant light, comprehensive of every colour the rainbow can show, and is so realistic and near that it often seems one has but to stoop to pick up some glistening jewel.

'We find a difficulty now in gaining even four miles a day; the struggle gets harder and harder. We should not make any progress if we did not pull hard ourselves; several of the dogs do practically nothing, and none work without an effort. Slowly but surely, however, we are "rising" the land. Our sastrugi today, from the recent confused state, have developed into a W.N.W. direction; it looks as though there was a local wind out of the strait.'

'December 5. – At breakfast we decided that our oil is going too fast; there has been some wastage from the capsizing of the sledge, and at first we were far too careless of the amount we used. When we came to look up dates, there was no doubt that in this respect we have outrun the constable. We started with the idea that a gallon was to last twelve days; ours have averaged little over ten. As a result we calculate that those which remain must be made to last fourteen. This is a distinct blow, as we shall have to sacrifice our hot luncheon meal and to economise greatly at both the others. We started the new routine tonight, and for lunch ate some frozen seal-meat and our allowance of sugar and biscuit. The new conditions do not smile on us at present, but I suppose we shall get used to them.

'The events of the day's march are now becoming so dreary and dispiriting that one longs to forget them when we camp; it is an effort even to record them in a diary. Tonight has been worse than usual. Our utmost efforts could not produce more than three miles for the whole march, and it would be impossible to describe how tiring the effort was to gain even this small advance. We have an idea we are rising in level slightly, but it is impossible to say so with certainty.

'Shackleton broke the glass of his watch yesterday afternoon; the watch still goes, but one cannot further rely on it, and I am therefore left with the only accurate time-keeper. It is a nuisance to lose a possible check on future observations, but luckily my watch seems to be a very trustworthy instrument; its rate on board the ship was excellent, and I have no reason to suppose that it has altered much since we left. My watch was presented to me by Messrs. Smith & Son, of the Strand, and I believe it to be an exceptionally good one, but the important observations which we take ought not to depend on a single watch, and future expeditions should be supplied with a larger number than we carry.'

'December 6. – . . . A dire calamity today. When I went outside before breakfast I noticed that "Spud" was absent from his place. I looked round and discovered him lying on the sledge with his head on the open mouth of the seal-meat bag; one glance at his balloon-like appearance was sufficient to show what had happened. As one contemplated the impossibility of repairing the mischief and of making him restore his ill-gotten provender, it was impossible not to laugh; but the matter is really serious enough: he has made away with quite a week's allowance of our precious seal-meat. How he could have swallowed it all is the wonder, yet, though somewhat sedate and somnolent, he appeared to suffer no particular discomfort from the enormously increased size of his waist. We found of course that he had gnawed through his trace, but the seal-meat bag will be very carefully closed in future.

'Whilst we were making preparations for a start last night we were overtaken by a blizzard and had to camp again in a hurry. The barometer has been falling for two days, and Wilson has had twinges of rheumatism; the former we took for a sign that we were rising in altitude, but we ought to have been warned by a further drop of two-tenths of an inch whilst we were in camp. The blizzard was ushered in with light flaky snow and an increasing wind, and a quarter of an hour later there was a heavy drift with strong wind. We have been completing our calculations of what is to be left at the depot and what carried on to the south.'

'December 8. – . . . Our poor team are going steadily downhill; six or seven scarcely pull at all, perhaps five or six do some steady work, and the remainder make spasmodic efforts. The lightening of the load is more than counter-balanced by the weakening of the animals, and I can see no time in which we can hope to get the sledges along without pulling ourselves. Of late we have altered our marching arrangements; we now take the first half-load on for four miles, then return for the other half, eating our cold luncheon on the way back. Today it took us three and a half hours to get the advance load on, and I who remained with it had to wait another five and a half before the others came back – nine hours' work to gain four miles.

'Before supper we all had a wash and brush-up. We each carry a toothbrush and a pocket-comb, and there is one cake of soap and one pocket looking-glass amongst the party; we use our toothbrushes fairly frequently, with snow, but the soap and comb are not often in request, and the looking-glass is principally used to dress our mangled lips. Snow and soap are rather a cold compound, but there is freshness in the glowing reaction, and we should probably use them oftener if the marches were not so tiring. Tonight the tent smells of soap and hazeline cream.'

'December 10. – Yesterday we only covered two miles, and to get on the second load at all we had to resort to the ignominious device of carrying food ahead of the dogs.

' "Snatcher" died yesterday; others are getting feeble – it is terrible to see them. The coast cannot be more than ten or twelve miles, but shall we ever reach it? and in what state shall we be to go on? The dogs have had no hesitation in eating their comrade; the majority clamoured for his flesh this evening, and neglected their fish in favour of it. There is the chance that this change of diet may save the better animals.

'This evening we were surprised by the visit of a skua gull; even our poor dogs became excited. We are nearly 180 miles from any possible feeding-ground it may have, and it is impossible to say how it found us, but it is curious that it should have come so soon after poor "Snatcher" has been cut up.'

'December 11. – Last night I had a terrible headache from the hot work in the sun and the closeness of the tent. I couldn't sleep for a long time, though we had the tent open and our bags wide; sleep eventually banished the headache, and I awoke quite fit. The weather has improved, for although still hot a southerly breeze has cooled the air. In covering three and a half miles we have altered several bearings of the land, so that it cannot now be far off. As we travel inward the snow-covered ridges of our cape are blocking out the higher range to the north.

'About 1 a.m. a bank of stratus cloud came rapidly up from the south; it looked white and fleecy towards the sun and a peculiar chocolate-brown as it passed to the northward and disappeared. It must have been travelling very fast and about two or three thousand feet above us; in an hour we had a completely clear sky.

'Hunger is beginning to nip us all, and we have many conversations as to the dainties we could devour if they were within reach.'

'December 14. – We have arrived at a place where I think we can depot our dog-food, and none too soon; I doubt if we could go on another day as we have been going. We have just completed the worst march we have had, and only managed to advance two miles by the most strenuous exertions. The snow grows softer as we approach the land; the sledge-runners sink from three to four inches, and one's feet well over the ankles at each step. After going a little over a mile things got so bad that we dropped one sledge and pushed on to bring some leading marks in line. Then Shackleton and I brought up the second half-load with the dogs somehow; after which, leaving the dogs, we all three started back for the sledge that had been dropped. Its weight was only 250 lbs., yet such was the state of the surface that we could not drag it at the rate of a mile an hour.

'The air temperature has gone up to +27°, and it feels hot and stuffy; the snow surface is +22°. It would be difficult to convey an idea of what marching is like under present conditions. The heel of the advanced foot is never planted beyond the toe of the other, and of this small gain with each pace, two or three inches are lost by back-slipping as the weight is brought forward. When we come to any particularly soft patch we do little more than mark time.

'The bearings of our present position are good but distant. To the west we have a conspicuous rocky patch in line with one of three distant peaks, and to the north another small patch in line with a curious scar on the northern range. The back marks in each case are perhaps twenty or thirty miles from us, and, though they will be easy enough to see in clear weather, one cannot hope to recognise them when it is misty. It is for this reason that I propose tomorrow to take our own food, on which our safety depends, closer in to the land, so that there may be no chance of our missing it.'

'December 15 (3.15 a.m.). – As soon as we had lightened our load last night we started steering straight for the rocky patch to the westward. The sky was overcast and the light bad, and after proceeding about a quarter of a mile we found that we were crossing well-marked undulations. Still pushing on, we topped a steep ridge to be fronted by an enormous chasm filled with a chaotic confusion of ice-blocks. It was obvious that we could go no further with the sledges, so we halted and pitched camp, and after eating our meagre lunch set forth to explore. The light was very bad, but we roped ourselves together, and, taking our only ice-axe and the meat-chopper, descended cautiously over a steep slope into the rougher ice below. Taking advantage of the snow between the ice-blocks we wended our way amongst them for some distance, now and again stepping on some treacherous spot and finding ourselves suddenly prone with our legs down a crevasse and very little breath left.

'At first we could get some idea of where these bad places lay, but later the light grew so bad that we came on them quite without warning, and our difficulties were much greater, whilst the huge ice-blocks about us swelled to mountainous size in the grey gloom, and it was obvious that we could make no useful observations in such weather. We stumbled our way back with difficulty, and, cutting steps up the slope, at length caught a welcome view of the camp.

'The dogs were more excited than they have been for many a day; poor things, they must have been quite nonplussed when we suddenly vanished from sight. We can make little out of the chasm so far, except that it quite cuts us off from a nearer approach to the land with our sledges, so that we shall have to depot our own food with the rest of the dog food and trust to fortune to give us clear weather when we return.'

'December 16. – There was bright, clear sunshine when we awoke yesterday afternoon, and we not only had a good view of the chasm, but Shackleton was able to photograph it. It looks like a great rift in the barrier which has been partly filled up with irregular ice-blocks; from our level to the lowest point in the valley may be about a hundred feet, and the peaks of some of the larger blocks rise almost to our level. The rift is perhaps three-quarters of a mile broad opposite to us, but it seems to narrow towards the south, and there is rather a suggestion that it ends within a few miles. The general lie of the rift is N.N.W. and S.S.E.; on the other side the surface appears to be level again, and probably it continues so for five or six miles to the land; however, it is certainly not worth our while to delay to ascertain this fact. In the sunlight the lights and shadows of the ice-blocks are in strong contrast, and where the sun has shone on blue walls, caverns have been melted and icicles hang over glassy, frozen pools. We found some of the icicles still dripping.

'Intent on wasting no more of our precious time, we got back to our depot as quickly as possible, and set about rearranging the loads, taking stock, and fixing up the depot. Whilst we were thus employed a very chill wind came up from the south, and we did not escape without some frostbitten fingers; however, after luncheon we got away and started head to wind and driving snow at 11 p.m. At midnight I got an altitude which gives the latitude as 80.30, and at 1.30 we camped, as we have decided now to start our marches earlier every day until we get back into day routine.

'As I write I scarcely know how to describe the blessed relief it is to be free from our relay work. For one-and-thirty awful days have we been at it, and whilst I doubt if our human endurance could have stood it much more, I am quite sure the dogs could not. It seems now like a nightmare, which grew more and more terrible towards its end.

'I do not like to think of the difference between the state of our party now and as it was before we commenced this dreadful task; it is almost equally painful to think of the gain, for during all this time we have advanced little more than half a degree of latitude, though I calculate we have covered 330 miles (380 statute miles).

'But it is little use thinking of the past; the great thing is to make the best of the future. We carry with us provisions for four weeks and an odd day or two, a little dog-food, our camp equipment, and, for clothing, exactly what we stand in.

'At the depot, which I have now called Depot B, we have left three weeks' provision and a quantity of dog-food. This should tide us over the homeward march, so that the present stock can all be expended before we return to Depot B; and all will be well if we can get back within four weeks, and if we have a clear day to find the spot.

'Poor "Vic" was sacrificed tonight for the common good.'

'December 17. – We roused out yesterday afternoon at 3 p.m. in very bright sunshine. To our astonishment, a couple of hundred yards behind us lay the end of the chasm which stood between us and the coast; it gradually narrows to a crevasse, which in places is bridged over with snow, but in others displays a yawning gulf. We must have crossed it within a few feet of such a gulf; our sledge track could be seen quite clearly leading across the bridge. Not suspecting anything of this sort we were quite regardless of danger during our last march, and unconsciously passed within an ace of destruction. It certainly has been a very close shave, as we could scarcely have escaped at the best without broken limbs had we fallen into the hole, and one doesn't like to contemplate broken limbs out here.

'This new light on the chasm seems to show that it is caused by a stream of ice pressing out through the strait to the north against the main mass of the barrier; this would naturally have such a rending effect on either side of the entrance. We have got the dogs on seven miles tonight; they need a lot of driving, especially as the surface has become irregular, with wavy undulations. It is almost impossible to make out how these waves run. As the chill of the evening comes on now, a mist arises along the whole coastline and obscures the land; for this reason we are the more anxious to get back into day-marches, and we shall make a much earlier start tomorrow.'

'December 18. – Started at 5 p.m. and finished at midnight. The short hours are to get to earlier marches, but I begin to doubt whether we shall ever be able to work the dogs for much more than eight hours again; the poor creatures are generally in a healthier state with the fresh food, but all are very weak and thin. With such a load as we now have there would have been no holding them when we left the ship; as someone said today, "If only we could come across some good, fat seals, we could camp for a week and start fair again." It is curious to think that there is possibly not a living thing within two hundred miles of us. Bad as the dog-driving is, however, the fact that each mile is an advance, and has not to be covered three times, is an inexpressible relief.

'We are gradually passing from the hungry to the ravenous; we cannot drag our thoughts from food, and we talk of little else. The worst times are the later hours of the march and the nights; on the march one sometimes gets almost a sickly feeling from want of food, and the others declare they have an actual gnawing sensation. At night one wakes with the most distressing feeling of emptiness, and then to reflect that there are probably four or five hours more before breakfast is positively dreadful. We have all proved the efficacy of hauling our belts quite tight before we go to sleep, and I have a theory that I am saved some of the worst pangs by my pipe. The others are non-smokers, and, although they do not own it, I often catch a wistful glance directed at my comforting friend; but, alas! two pipes a day do not go far, even on such a journey as ours.'

'December 19. – We are now about ten miles from the land, but even at this distance the foothills cut off our view of the higher mountains behind, save to the north and south. Abreast of us the skyline is not more than three or four thousand feet high, though we know there are loftier peaks behind. The lower country which we see strongly resembles the coastal land far to the north; it is a fine scene of a lofty snow-cap, whose smooth rounded outline is broken by the sharper bared peaks, or by the steep disturbing fall of some valley. Here and there local glaciers descend to barrier level; the coastline itself winds greatly, forming numerous headlands and bays; we are skirting these and keeping our direct course, a little to the east of south. The coast is fringed with white snow-slopes, glaciers, and broken ice-cascades; but in many places black rocky headlands and precipitous uncovered cliffs serve more clearly to mark its windings. Perhaps one of the most impressive facts is that we see all this above a perfectly level horizon line. Everywhere apparently there is as sharp and definite a line between the land and the level surface of the barrier as exists on an ordinary coastline between land and water. When it becomes at all thick or gloomy the rocks stand out and the white, snowy surfaces recede, giving rise to curious optical illusions. The high, curiously shaped rocky patches seem to be suspended in mid-air; there was one a few days ago, long and flat in shape, which appeared to be so wholly un-supported that it was named "Mahomet's Coffin", but when the weather cleared we could see that the snow about it was really closer than the rock itself.

'Wilson is the most indefatigable person. When it is fine and clear, at the end of our fatiguing days he will spend two or three hours seated in the door of the tent sketching each detail of the splendid mountainous coast-scene to the west. His sketches are most astonishingly accurate; I have tested his proportions by actual angular measurement and found them correct. If the fine weather continues we shall at least have a unique record of this coastline. But these long hours in the glare are very bad for the eyes; we have all suffered a good deal from snow-blindness of late, though we generally march with goggles, but Wilson gets the worst bouts, and I fear it is mainly due to his sketching.

' "Wolf" was the victim tonight. I cannot say "poor 'Wolf'", for he has been a thorn in the flesh, and has scarcely pulled a pound the whole journey. We have fifteen dogs left, and have decided to devote our energies to the preservation of the nine best; we have done nearly eight miles today, but at such an expenditure of energy that I am left in doubt as to whether we should not have done better without any dogs at all.'

'December 20. – . . . Poor "Grannie" has been ailing for some time. She dropped today. We put her on the sledge, hoping she might recover, and there she breathed her last; she will last the others three days. It is little wonder that we grow more and more sick of our dog-driving.

'The sky has been overcast with low stratus cloud, but it is wonderfully clear below; we have had this sort of weather for some time. One looks aloft and to the east and finds the outlook dull and apparently foggy, when it is surprising to turn to the west and get a comparatively clear view of all the low-lying rocks and snow-slopes which are now ten or a dozen miles from us.

'My tobacco supply is at such "low water" that today I have been trying tea-leaves: they can be described as nothing less than horrid.'

'December 21. – We are now crossing a deep bay, but the sky is still overcast and our view obscured; the surface was particularly heavy today, and our poor dogs had an especially bad time. After a few miles we determined to stop and go on at night again, as the heat was very great; the thermometer showed 27°, but inside the instrument-box, which is covered with white canvas, it showed 52°. There must be an astonishing amount of radiation, even with the sun obscured. Starting again at 8 p.m., we found that matters were not improved at all. Very few of the dogs pulled, whilst "Stripes" and "Brownie" were vomiting. Things began to look very hopeless, so we thought it would be wise to see what we could do alone without assistance from our team. We found that on ski we could just move our own sledges, but only just; on foot, after going for ten minutes, we found we were doing something under a mile an hour, but only with much exertion. After this experiment we camped again, and have been discussing matters. We calculate we were pulling about 170 lbs. per man; either the surface is extraordinarily bad or we are growing weak. It is no use blinding ourselves to facts: we cannot put any further reliance on the dogs. Any day they might all give out and leave us entirely dependent on ourselves. In such a case, if things were to remain just as they are, we should have about as much as we could do to get home; on the other hand, will things remain just as they are? It seems reasonable to hope for improvement, we have seen so many changes in the surface; at any rate, we have discussed this matter out, and I am glad to say that all agree in taking the risk of pushing on.

'Misfortunes never come singly; since starting we have always had a regular examination of gums and legs on Sunday morning, and at first it seemed to show us to be in a very satisfactory condition of health, but tonight Wilson told me that Shackleton has decidedly angry-looking gums, and that for some time they have been slowly but surely getting worse. He says there is nothing yet to be alarmed at, but he now thought it serious enough to tell me in view of our future plans. We have decided not to tell Shackleton for the present; it is a matter which must be thought out. Certainly this is a black night, but things must look blacker yet before we decide to turn.'

'December 22. – . . . This morning we had bright sunshine and a clear view of the land; the coastline has receded some way back in a deep bay, beyond which the land rises to the magnificent mountain ranges which evidently form the backbone of the whole continent. There are no longer high snow-covered foothills to intercept our view of the loftier background; it is as though at this portion of the coast they had been wiped out as a feature of the country, though farther to the south where the coastline again advances they seem to recur.

'But just here we get an excellent view of the clean-cut mountain range. Abreast of us is the most splendid specimen of a pyramidal mountain; it raises a sharp apex to a height of nine thousand feet or more, and its precisely carved facets seem to rest on a base of more irregular country, fully four thousand feet below. With its extraordinary uniformity and great altitude it is a wonderfully good landmark. Close to the south of this is an equally lofty table mountain, the top of which is perfectly flat though dipping slightly towards the north; this tabular structure is carried on, less perfectly, in other lofty mountain regions to the south; we have not seen it so well marked on any part of the coast since the land we discovered south of Cape Washington, which seems to indicate some geological alliance with that part. We can now see also the high land that lies beyond the foothills we have lately been skirting; it is more irregular in outline, with high snow-ridges between the sharper peaks. To the south one particular conical mountain stands much closer to the coast than the main ranges. It looks to be of great height, but may not be so distant as we imagine; it will form our principal landmark for the next week. It is noticeable that along all this stretch of coast we can see no deep valley that could contain a glacier from the interior ice-cap (if there is one).

'The beauty of the scene before us is much enhanced when the sun circles low to the south: we get then the most delicate blue shadows and purest tones of pink and violet on the hill-slopes. There is rarely any intensity of shade – the charm lies in the subtlety and delicacy of the colouring and in the clear softness of the distant outline.

'We have decided to cease using our bacon and to increase the seal allowance, as the former seems the most likely cause of the scurvy symptoms. To Shackleton it was represented as a preventive measure, but I am not sure that he does not smell a rat. The exchange is not quite equal in weight; we again lose a little. We cannot certainly afford to lose more, as we are already reduced to starvation rations. Our allowance on leaving the ship ran to about 1.9 lb. per man per day, but various causes have reduced this. At first we went too heavy on our biscuit; then we determined to lay by two extra weeks out of eleven; then "Spud" had his share of the seal-meat bag; altogether I calculate we are existing on about a pound and a half of food a day; it is not enough, and hunger is gripping us very tightly. I never knew what it was like before, and I shall not be particularly keen on trying it again.

'Our meals come regularly enough, but they are the poorest stopgaps, both from want of food and want of fuel. At breakfast now we first make tea – that is to say, we put the tea in long before the water boils, and lift and pour out with the first bubbling. The moment this is over we heap the pemmican and biscuit into the pot and make what we call a "fry"; it takes much less time than a hoosh. The cook works by the watch, and in twenty minutes from the time it is lighted the Primus lamp is out; in two or three more the breakfast is finished. Then we serve out luncheon, which consists of a small piece of seal-meat, half a biscuit, and eight to ten lumps of sugar. Each of us keeps a small bag which, when it contains the precious luncheon, is stowed away in the warmth of a breast-pocket, where it thaws out during the first march. Absurd as it may sound, it is terribly difficult not to filch from this bag during the hours of the march. We have become absolutely childish in this. We know so perfectly the contents of the bags that one will find oneself arguing that today's piece of seal is half an inch longer than yesterday's; ergo, if one nibbles half an inch off, one will still have the same lunch as yesterday.

'Supper is of course the best meal; we then have a hoosh which runs from between three-quarters to a whole pannikin apiece, but even at this we cannot afford to make it thick. Whilst it is being heated in the central cooker, cocoa is made in the outer. The lamp is turned out directly the hoosh boils, usually from twenty-eight to thirty minutes after it has been lighted; by this time the chill is barely off the contents of the outer cooker, and of course the cocoa is not properly dissolved, but such as it is, it is the only drink we can afford. We have long ceased criticising the quality of our food; all we clamour for now is something to fill up, but, needless to say, we never get it. Half an hour after supper one seems as hard set as ever.

'My companions get very bad "food dreams"; in fact, these have become the regular breakfast conversation. It appears to be a sort of nightmare; they are either sitting at a well-spread table with their arms tied, or they grasp at a dish and it slips out of their hand, or they are in the act of lifting a dainty morsel to their mouth when they fall over a precipice. Whatever the details may be, something interferes at the last moment and they wake. So far, I have not had these dreams myself, but I suppose they will come.

'When we started from the ship we had a sort of idea that we could go as we pleased with regard to food, hauling in automatically if things were going too fast; but we soon found that this would not do at all – there must be some rigid system of shares. After this we used to take it in turns to divide things into three equal portions; it is not an easy thing to do by eye, and of course the man who made the division felt called upon to make certain that he had the smallest share. It was when we found that this led to all sorts of absurd remonstrances and arguments that Shackleton invented the noble game of "shut-eye", which has solved all our difficulties in this respect. The shares are divided as equally as possible by anyone; then one of the other two turns his head away, the divider points at a "whack" and says, "Whose is this?" He of the averted head names the owner, and so on. It is a very simple but very efficacious game, as it leaves the matter entirely to chance. We play it at every meal now as a matter of course, and from practice we do it very speedily; but one cannot help thinking how queer it would appear for a casual onlooker to see three civilised beings employed at it.'

'December 23. – We have been getting on rather faster than we thought, though we had a suspicion that the sledge-meter was clogging in the very soft snow. Our latitude is now about 81½° S. Today I had to shift the balance-weight on the theodolite compass needle; the dip must be decreasing rapidly. Theodolite observations are now difficult, as the tripod legs cannot be solidly planted. I find it a good plan to leave it up for the night, as in the morning there is always a little cake of ice under each leg. The surface is so soft that one can push the shaft of the ice-axe down with a finger.

'The dogs of course feel it much, but the leaders have the worst time, for they have to make the footprints; the others step carefully into them, and are saved the trouble of making their own. Several times lately, and especially today, the dogs have raised their heads together and sniffed at the breeze; with a northerly wind one might suppose that their keen scent might detect something, but it is difficult to imagine what they can find in air coming from the south. Shackleton, who always declares that he believes there is either open water or an oasis ahead, says that the dogs merely confirm his opinion.

'We felt the chill wind in our faces much, owing to their very blistered state. We have especial trouble with our nostrils and lips, which are always bare of skin; all our fingers, too, are in a very chapped, cracked condition. We have to be very economical with our eyes also, after frequent attacks of snow-blindness; all three of us today had one eye completely shaded, and could see only by peering with the other through a goggle. But all our ailments together are as nothing beside our hunger, which gets steadily worse day by day.'

'December 24. – Wilson examined us again this morning. I asked him quietly the result, and he said, "A little more." It is trying, but we both agree that it is not time yet to say "Turn". But we have one fact to comfort us tonight – we have passed on to a much harder surface, and though it still holds a layer of an inch or two of feathery snow, beneath that it is comparatively firm, and we are encamped on quite a hard spot; the sastrugi are all from the S.S.E. parallel to the land. If the dogs have not improved, they have not grown much worse during the past day or two; their relative strength alters a good deal, as the following tale will show: "Stripes" and "Gus" pull next one another; a week ago one had great difficulty in preventing "Stripes" from leaping across and seizing "Gus's" food. He was very cunning about it; he waited till one's back was turned, and then was over and back in a moment. Time has its revenges: now "Gus" is the stronger, and tonight he leapt across and seized "Stripes's" choicest morsel. At other times they are not bad friends these two; loser and winner seem to regard this sort of thing as part of the game. After all, it is but "the good old rule, the simple plan", but of course we right matters when we detect such thefts.

'Tonight is Christmas Eve. We have been thinking and talking about the folk at home, and also much about our plans for tomorrow.'

'December 25, Christmas Day. – . . . For a week we have looked forward to this day with childish delight and, long before that, we decided that it would be a crime to go to bed hungry on Christmas night; so the week went in planning a gorgeous feed. Each meal and each item of each meal we discussed and rediscussed. The breakfast was to be a glorious spread; the Primus was to be kept going ten or even fifteen minutes longer than usual. Lunch for once was to be warm and comforting; and supper! – well, supper was to be what supper has been.

'In fact, we meant this to be a wonderful day, and everything has conspired to make it so.

'When we awoke to wish each other "A merry Christmas" the sun was shining warmly through our green canvas roof. We were outside in a twinkling, to find the sky gloriously clear and bright, with not a single cloud in its vast arch. Away to the westward stretched the long line of gleaming coastline; the sunlight danced and sparkled in the snow beneath our feet, and not a breath of wind disturbed the serenity of the scene. It was a glorious morning, but we did not stay to contemplate it, for we had even more interesting facts to occupy us, and were soon inside the tent sniffing at the savoury steam of the cooking-pot. Then breakfast was ready, and before each of us lay a whole pannikin-full of biscuit and seal-liver, fried in bacon and pemmican fat. It was gone in no time, but this and a large spoonful of jam to follow left a sense of comfort which we had not experienced for weeks, and we started to pack up in a frame of mind that was wholly joyful.

'After this we started on the march, and felt at once the improvement of surface that came to us last night; so great was it that we found we three alone could draw the sledges, and for once the driver was silent and the whip but rarely applied. The dogs merely walked along with slack traces, and we did not attempt to get more out of them. No doubt an outsider would have thought our procession funereal enough, but to us the relief was inexpressible; and so we trudged on from 11.30 to 4 p.m., when we thoroughly enjoyed our lunch, which consisted of hot cocoa and plasmon with a whole biscuit and another spoonful of jam. We were off again at 5.30, and marched on till 8.30, when we camped in warmth and comfort and with the additional satisfaction of having covered nearly eleven miles, the longest march we have made for a long time.

'Then we laid ourselves out for supper, reckless of consequences, having first had a Christmas wash and brush-up. Redolent of soap, we sat around the cooking-pot, whilst into its boiling contents was poured a double "whack" of everything. In the hoosh that followed one could stand one's spoon with ease, and still the Primus hissed on, as once again our cocoa was brought to the boiling-point. Meanwhile I had observed Shackleton ferreting about in his bundle, out of which he presently produced a spare sock, and stowed away in the toe of that sock was a small round object about the size of a cricket ball, which when brought to light, proved to be a noble "plum-pudding". Another dive into his lucky-bag and out came a crumpled piece of artificial holly. Heated in the cocoa, our plum-pudding was soon steaming hot, and stood on the cooker-lid crowned with its decoration. For once we divided food without "shut-eye".

'I am writing over my second pipe. The sun is still slowly circling our small tent in a cloudless sky, the air is warm and quiet, all is pleasant without, and within we have a sense of comfort we have not known for many a day; we shall sleep well tonight – no dreams, no tightening of the belt.

'We have been chattering away gaily, and not once has the conversation turned to food. We have been wondering what Christmas is like in England – possibly very damp, gloomy, and unpleasant, we think; we have been wondering, too, how our friends picture us. They will guess that we are away on our sledge journey, and will perhaps think of us on plains of snow; but few, I think, will imagine the truth, that for us this has been the reddest of all red-letter days.'

CHAPTER 14

Return from the Far South

Result of Shortage of Food – Nature of the Coastline – Snow-blindness – Approaching the Limit of our Journey – View to the South – New Mountains – Blizzard at our Extreme South – Turning Homeward – Attempt to Reach the Land – The Passing of our Dog-Team – Help from our Sail – Difficult Surfaces – Running before a Storm – Finding Depot B – Scurvy Again – Shackleton Becomes Ill – The Last of our Dog-Team – Bad Light for Steering – Anxious Days – Depot A – Overeating – The Last Lap – Home Again – Our Welcome

> How many weary steps
> Of many weary miles you have o'ergone,
> Are numbered to the travel of one mile. – SHAKESPEARE

'An' we talks about our rations and a lot of other things.'

– KIPLING

Our Christmas Day had proved a delightful break in the otherwise uninterrupted spell of semi-starvation. Some days elapsed before its pleasing effects wore off, and for long it remained green in our memories. We knew by this time that we had cut ourselves too short in the matter of food, but it was too late to alter our arrangements now without curtailing our journey, and we all decided that, sooner than do the latter, we would cheerfully face the pangs that our too meagre fare would cost.

Looking back now on the incidents of this journey, the original mistake is evident, and even at the time, apart from the physical distress which it caused us, it is clear that we suspected, what was indeed the case, that we were slowly but surely sapping our energies and reducing ourselves to the condition of our more willing dogs, who, with every desire to throw their weight on the traces, were incapable of doing so. Of course we never sank into the deplorable state of these poor animals, but there is no doubt that from this time on we were gradually wearing out, and the increasing weariness of the homeward marches showed that we were expending our energies at a greater rate than we were able to renew them with our inadequate supply of food, and thus drawing on a capital stock which must obviously have restricted limits.

Such a state of affairs is, as I have pointed out elsewhere, a false economy, and the additional weight which we should have carried in taking a proper allowance of food would have amply repaid us on this occasion by the maintenance of our full vigour.

A shortage of food has another great disadvantage which we experienced to the full: our exceptionally hungry condition caused our thoughts and conversation to run in a groove from which it was almost impossible to lift them. We knew perfectly well how ridiculous this was, and appreciated that it was likely to increase rather than diminish the evil, but we seemed powerless to prevent it. After supper, and before its pleasing effects had passed, some detachment was possible, and for half an hour or more a desultory conversation would be maintained concerning far-removed subjects; but it was ludicrous to observe the manner in which remarks gradually crept back to the old channel, and it was odds that before we slept each one of us gave, all over again, a detailed description of what he would now consider an ideal feast.

On the march it was even worse; one's thoughts were reduced to the most trivial details of the one unsatisfying subject. One would find oneself calculating how many footsteps went to the minute, and how many, therefore, must be paced before lunch; then, with a sinking heart, one would begin to count them, suddenly lose count, and find oneself mentally scanning the contents of the pemmican bag and wondering exactly how much could be allowed for tonight's hoosh. This would lead to the stock of pemmican on board the ship, and a recollection of the gorgeous yellow fat with which it was incorporated; the ship would recall feasts of seal, thick soup, and thicker porridge, and on one would speed to the recollection of special nights when our fare had been still more bountiful, and on again to all the resources of civilised life; the farewell dinner at So-and-so, what would it be like if it was spread out here on the barrier? One remembers declining a particularly succulent dish; what an extraordinary thing to do! What a different being one must have been in those days! And so one's thoughts travelled on from place to place, but always through the one medium of creature comfort.

It is natural that a diary kept through these long weeks should have reflected the subject that most fully occupied our thoughts and our conversation, and, as the weakness of the dogs curtailed our marches and left ample time for writing, I find copious allusions to the somewhat distressing circumstances which attended our experiences in this respect.

But it must not be supposed that we were wholly absorbed by this subject; if there were trials and tribulations in our daily life at this time, there were also compensating circumstances whose import we fully realised. Day by day, as we journeyed on, we knew we were penetrating farther and farther into the unknown; each footstep was a gain, and made the result of our labour more solid. It would be difficult to describe with what eagerness we studied the slowly revolving sledge-meter, or looked for the calculated results of our observations, while ever before our eyes was the line which we were now drawing on the white space of the Antarctic chart. Day by day, too, though somewhat slowly, there passed on that magnificent panorama of the western land. Rarely a march passed without the disclosure of some new feature, something on which the eye of man had never yet rested; we should have been poor souls indeed had we not been elated at the privilege of being the first to gaze on these splendid scenes.

On December 26 we had another brilliant, calm and cloudless day, with a clear view to the west; the coastal ice-cape again obscured our view of the higher ranges behind, but now it rose to a more considerable altitude, being at least three or four thousand feet above our level; it undulated in long sweeping curves, with here and there a black jagged outcrop of rock, and elsewhere a steep crevassed fall. Our track had been taking us close to the coast, and as we had skirted along, past pointed snow-capes and rocky headlands, we had gradually blocked out the remarkable tabular and pyramidal mountains which had been abreast of us a week before; behind us also we had left the sharp conical peak which had been our principal landmark for many days.

When, far to the north, we had first seen this mountain, we had exaggerated both height and distance, and when things had gone badly with us we had wondered if our fortunes would ever allow us to pass it. On Christmas Day, however, we were abreast of it, and though I calculated its height to be under seven thousand feet, this was no mean altitude for so remarkable a peak. Since in preserving its uniform, sharp, conical appearance, it was still the most salient feature in our view, we dubbed it 'Christmas Mountain' in honour of the day. We passed within eighteen miles of it, according to my calculations, and by the 26th it was 'abaft the beam'. Whilst still retaining its pointed appearance, it seemed from this new aspect to have assumed a certain resemblance to the higher pyramidal hills of the north.

Perhaps the most interesting part of our view just at this time was the coastline itself. We were from eight to ten miles from it, and at such a distance one could see very distinctly in that clear air; it was comparatively steep all along — that is to say, the undulating ice-cap fell gradually to a height of one or two thousand feet and then abruptly to the barrier level. In a few places this fall was taken by steep but comparatively smooth snow-slopes, in others the snow seemed to pour over in beautiful cascades of immense ice-blocks, and in others, again, the coast was fringed by huge perpendicular cliffs of bare rock. On this day we were abreast of the highest cliffs we had seen and my angles, roughly computed, gave a height of 1,800 feet between their base and the white snow-line on top, and they were so impressive even in the distance that I cannot believe them to have been much under. In many places the rock-face must have been sheer to this great height, for where it fell away a white splash showed where the snow had found lodgment.

Even at a distance of ten miles these cliffs were magnificent, and how grand they would have appeared had we been able to get close beneath them we could well imagine. In colour they were a rich, deep red, though a little farther to the south this rock was confusingly bedded with a darker, almost black one; this alternation of black and red occurred along the whole coast south of our position at this time, always in the same irregular fashion, but always with a definite line between the red and the black. At this time we were all under the impression that these rocks were of the same recent volcanic nature as those about the ship, but later on, after my visit to the western hills, I came to doubt this belief. It is possible that if at this time we had known more of the structure of the mainland to the north we should have been able to note points of similarity or difference which threw more light on this southern land, but it is doubtful whether in any case we could have discovered much that was definite at the distance from which we saw it.

It can be imagined that as we travelled onward our eyes were most frequently lifted towards the south. It is always bewildering to look along a coastline at such an oblique angle. Shortly before this the south had meant a long succession of dark rock-masses and hazy snow-capes, but during the last few days we had 'risen' a feature of noticeable distinction, and now we knew that we looked on a lofty mountain whose eastern slopes fell to the long snow-cape which for the present bounded our view.

The very gradual unfolding of its details told us that this mass of land was both distant and lofty, and as we approached the limit of safe endeavour we knew that here was an object that we could not hope to reach; though we might approach it by many miles and be able to examine it with care, we should never know definitely what lay beyond. We felt that it was the most southerly land to which we should be able to apply a name, and we thought that the fine peak which for the present must remain the southerly outpost of all known lands could bear no more fitting title than one derived from the contributor whose generous donation had alone made our expedition possible. On the night of the 26th, therefore, we christened this distant peak 'Mount Longstaff', but it was only on our return to the ship that I was able to fix its position as well beyond the 83rd parallel.

From a point of view of further exploration our position on the 26th did not promise great things. On our right lay the high undulating snow-cap and the steep irregular coastline; to the south lay a cape, beyond which we could not hope to pass; and to all appearance these conditions must remain unaltered to the end of our journey. We argued, however, that one never knows what may turn up, and we determined, in spite of the unpromising outlook, to push on to our utmost limit. As events proved, we argued most wisely, for had we turned at this point we should have missed one of the most important features of the whole coastline; it was only one more instance of the happening of the unexpected.

In spite of the comforting nature of our Christmas festivities, worry was never long absent from what was now becoming rather a forlorn party, as the following extract shows.

'December 26. – . . . Poor Wilson has had an attack of snow-blindness, in comparison with which our former attacks may be considered as nothing; we were forced to camp early on account of it, and during the whole afternoon he has been writhing in horrible agony. It is distressing enough to see, knowing that one can do nothing to help. Cocaine has only a very temporary effect, and in the end seems to make matters worse. I have never seen an eye so terribly bloodshot and inflamed as that which is causing the trouble, and the inflammation has spread to the eyelid. He describes the worst part as an almost intolerable stabbing and burning of the eyeball; it is the nearest approach to illness we have had, and one can only hope that it is not going to remain serious.

'Shackleton did butcher tonight, and "Brownie" was victim. Poor little dog! his life has been very careworn of late, and it is probably a happy release.'

'December 27. – Late last night Wilson got some sleep, and this morning he was better; all day he has been pulling alongside the sledges with his eyes completely covered. It is tiresome enough to see our snowy world through the slit of a goggle, but to march blindfolded with an empty stomach for long hours touches a pitch of monotony which I shall be glad to avoid. We covered a good ten miles today by sledge-meter, though I think that instrument is clogging and showing short measure. The dogs have done little, but they have all walked, except "Stripes", who broke down and had to be carried on the sledge; he was quite limp when I picked him up, and his thick coat poorly hides the fact that he is nothing but skin and bone. Yesterday I noticed that we were approaching what appeared to be a deeper bay than usual, and this afternoon this opening developed in the most interesting manner.

'On the near side is a bold, rocky, snow-covered cape, and all day we have been drawing abreast of this; as we rapidly altered its bearing this afternoon it seemed to roll back like some vast sliding gate, and gradually there stood revealed one of the most glorious mountain scenes we have yet witnessed. Walking opposite to Wilson I was trying to keep him posted with regard to the changes, and I think my reports of this part must have sounded curious. It was with some excitement I noticed that new mountain ridges were appearing as high as anything we had seen to the north, but, to my surprise, as we advanced the ridges grew still higher, as no doubt did my tones. Then, instead of a downward turn in the distant outline came a steep upward line; Pelion was heaped on Ossa, and it can be imagined that we pressed the pace to see what would happen next, till the end came in a gloriously sharp double peak crowned with a few flecks of cirrus cloud.

'We can no longer call this opening a bay; it runs for many miles in to the foot of the great range, and is more in the nature of an inlet. But all our thoughts in camp tonight turn to this splendid twin-peaked mountain, which, even in such a lofty country, seems as a giant among pigmies. We all agree that from Sabine to the south the grandest eminences cannot compare in dignity with this monster. We have decided that at last we have found something which is fitting to bear the name of him whom we must always the most delight to honour, and "Mount Markham" it shall be called in memory of the father of the expedition.'

'December 28. – Sights today put us well over the 82nd parallel (82.11 S.). We have almost shot our bolt. If the weather holds fine tomorrow, we intend to drop our sledges at the midday halt and push on as far as possible on ski. We stopped early this afternoon in order to take photographs and make sketches. Wilson, in spite of his recent experiences, refuses to give in; whatever is left unsketched, and however his eyes may suffer, this last part must be done.

'It is a glorious evening, and fortune could not have provided us with a more perfect view of our surroundings. We are looking up a broad, deep inlet or strait which stretches away to the south-west for thirty or forty miles before it reaches its boundary of cliff and snow-slope. Beyond, rising fold on fold, are the great névé fields that clothe the distant range; against the pale blue sky the outline of the mountain ridge rises and falls over numerous peaks till, with a sharp turn upward, it culminates in the lofty summit of Mount Markham. To the north it descends again, to be lost behind the bluff extremity of the near cape. It seems more than likely that the vast inlet before us takes a sharp turn to the right beyond the cape and in front of the mountains, and we hope to determine this fact tomorrow.

'The eastern foothills of the high range form the southern limit of the strait; they are fringed with high cliffs and steep snow-slopes, and even at this distance we can see that some of the rocks are of the deep-red colour, whilst others are black. Between the high range and the barrier there must lie immense undulating snow-plateaux covering the lesser foothills, which seem rather to increase in height to the left until they fall sharply to the barrier level almost due south of us.

'To the eastward of this, again, we get our view to the farthest south, and we have been studying it again and again to gather fresh information with the changing bearings of the sun. Mount Longstaff we calculate as 10,000 feet. It is formed by the meeting of two long and comparatively regular slopes; that to the east stretches out into the barrier and ends in a long snow-cape which bears about S. 14 E.; that to the west is lost behind the nearer foothills, but now fresh features have developed about these slopes. Over the western ridge can be seen two new peaks which must lie considerably to the south of the mountain, and, more interesting still, beyond the eastern cape we catch a glimpse of an extended coastline; the land is thrown up by mirage and appears in small white patches against a pale sky.

'We know well this appearance of a snow-covered country; it is the normal view in these regions of a very distant lofty land, and it indicates with certainty that a mountainous country continues beyond Mount Longstaff for nearly fifty miles. The direction of the extreme land thrown up in this manner is S. 17 E., and hence we can now say with certainty that the coastline after passing Mount Longstaff continues in this direction for at least a degree of latitude. Of course one cannot add that the level barrier surface likewise continues, as one's view of it is limited to a very narrow horizon; but anyone who had travelled over it as we have done, and who now, like us, could gaze on these distant lands beyond its level margin, could have little doubt that it does so.

'It is fortunate to have had such glorious weather to give us a clear view of this magnificent scene, for very soon now we must be turning, and though we may advance a few miles we cannot hope to add largely to our store of information.'

'It has been a busy evening, what with taking angles, sketching, and attending to our camp duties, but hours so full of interest have passed rapidly; and now the sun is well to the south, and from all the coast is rising the thin night mist exactly as it does after a hot day in England, so we are preparing to settle down in our sleeping-bags, in the hope that tomorrow may prove equally fine.

'A great relief comes to us in this distant spot at finding that our slight change of diet is already giving a beneficial result; late tonight we had another examination of our scurvy symptoms, and there is now no doubt that they are lessening.'

'December 29. – Instead of our proposed advance we have spent the day in our tent, whilst a strong southerly blizzard has raged without. It is very trying to the patience, and tonight, though the wind has dropped, the old well-known sheet of stratus cloud is closing over us, and there is every prospect of another spell of overcast weather which will obscure the land. This afternoon for the third time we have seen the heavens traced with bands and circles of prismatic light, and, if anything, the phenomenon has been more complicated than before; it was a very beautiful sight.

'Only occasionally today have we caught glimpses of the land, and it is not inspiriting to lie hour after hour in a sleeping-bag, chill and hungry, and with the knowledge that one is so far from the region of plenty.'

'December 30. – We got up at six this morning, to find a thick fog and nothing in sight; to leave the camp was out of the question, so we packed up our traps and started to march to the S.S.W. This brought us directly towards the mouth of the strait, and after an hour we found ourselves travelling over a disturbed surface with numerous cracks which seemed to radiate from the cape we were rounding. After stumbling on for some time, the disturbance became so great that we were obliged to camp. If the fates are kind and give us another view of the land, we are far enough advanced now to see the inner recesses of our strait.

'After our modest lunch Wilson and I started off on ski to the S.S.W. We lost sight of the camp almost immediately, and were left with only our tracks to guide us back to it, but we pushed on for perhaps a mile or more in hopes that the weather would clear; then, as there was no sign of this, and we could see little more than a hundred yards, we realised there might be considerable risk and could be no advantage in proceeding, and so turned and retraced our footsteps to the camp.

'This camp we have now decided must be our last, for we have less than a fortnight's provision to take us back to Depot B, and with the dogs in their present state it would be impossible to make forced marches; we have, therefore, reached our southerly limit.

Observations give it as between 82.16 S. and 82.17 S.; if this compares poorly with our hopes and expectations on leaving the ship, it is a more favourable result than we anticipated when those hopes were first blighted by the failure of the dog-team.

'Whilst one cannot help a deep sense of disappointment in reflecting on the "might have been" had our team remained in good health, one cannot but remember that even as it is we have made a greater advance towards a pole of the earth than has ever yet been achieved by a sledge party.

'We feel a little inclined to grumble at the thick weather that surrounds us; it has a depressing effect, and in our state of hunger we feel the cold though the temperature is +15°; but we must not forget that we had great luck in the fine weather which gave us such a clear view of the land two days ago.'

'December 31. – As we rose this morning the sun was still obscured by low stratus cloud, which rapidly rolled away, however; first the headlands and then the mountains stood out, and we could see that we had achieved our object of yesterday in opening out the inlet; but in this direction the cloud continued to hang persistently, so that it was to little purpose that we had obtained such a position. We could see now that the inlet certainly turned to the north of west; on either side the irregular outlines of the mountains were clear against a blue sky, and, descending gradually towards the level, left a broad gap between, but low in this gap hung the tantalising bank of fog, screening all that lay beyond. By turning towards the strait we had partly obscured our clear view of Mount Longstaff and quite cut off the miraged images of the more distant land, but we had approached the high cliffs which formed the southern limit of the strait, and in the morning sun could clearly see the irregular distribution of red and black rock in the steep cliff faces.

'In hope that the fog-bank to the west would clear, we proceeded with our packing in a leisurely manner, and when all was ready, turned our faces homewards. It was significant of the terrible condition of our team that the turn produced no excitement. It appears to make no difference to them now in which direction they bend their weary footsteps; it almost seems that most of them guess how poor a chance they have of ever seeing the ship again. And so we started our homeward march, slowly at first, and then more briskly as we realised that all chance of a clearance over the strait was gone.

'In the flood of sunlight which now illumined the snow about us, we were able to see something of the vast ice upheavals caused by the outflow of ice from the strait; pushing around the cape, it is raised in undulations which seem to run parallel to the land. We directed our course towards the cape with the hopes of getting to the land, but were obliged to keep outwards to avoid the worst disturbances; this brought us obliquely across the undulation, and as we travelled onward they rose in height and became ridged and broken on the summit. Now, too, we came upon numerous crevasses which appeared to extend radially from the cape, and these, with the cracks and ridges, formed a network of obstruction across our path through which we were forced to take a very winding course.

'We extended our march until we had passed the worst of this disturbance, and by that time we were well to the north of the cape and abreast of one of the curious rocky groins that occur at intervals along the coast. This showed samples of both the red and the black rock, which seem to constitute the geological structure of the whole coast, and we decided to pitch our camp and make an excursion to the land on our ski. By the time that we had swallowed our luncheon the clouds had rolled away, leaving us in the same brilliant sunshine that we have enjoyed so frequently of late, and in which even at a distance of five or six miles every detail of the high groin could be distinctly seen.

'Not knowing what adventures we might encounter, we thought it wise to provide ourselves with a second luncheon, which we safely stowed in our breast-pockets, and taking our ice-axe and Alpine rope, we set out for the shore. It looked deceptively near, nor was it until we had marched for nearly an hour without making any marked difference in its appearance that we realised we were in for a long job.

'By this time we were again crossing long undulations which increased in height as we advanced; soon from the summits of the waves we could see signs of greater disturbances ahead, and at five o'clock we found ourselves at the edge of a chasm resembling that which had prevented us from reaching the shore farther to the north. This was not an encouraging spectacle, but on the opposite side, a mile or so away, we could see that a gentle slope led to the rocks, and that once across this disturbance we should have no difficulty in proceeding. On the near side the spaces between the ice-blocks had been much drifted up with snow, so that we found no great difficulty in descending or in starting our climb amongst the ice-blocks; but as we advanced the snow became lighter and the climbing steeper. We could get no hold with our finneskoes on the harder places, and in the softer we sank knee-deep, whilst the lightly-bridged crevasses became more difficult to avoid, and once or twice we were only saved from a bad fall by the fact of being roped together. Constantly after circling a large block with difficulty we found in front of us some unclimbable place, and were obliged to retrace our steps and try in some new direction; but we now knew that we must be approaching the opposite side, and so we struggled on.

'At length, however, when we thought our troubles must surely be ending, we cut steps around a sharp corner to find the opposite bank of the chasm close to us, but instead of the rough slopes by which we had descended, we found here a steep, overhanging face of ice, towering some fifty feet above us. To climb this face was obviously impossible, and we were reluctantly forced to confess that all our trouble had been in vain. It was a great disappointment, as we had confidently hoped to get some rock specimens from this far south land, and now I do not see that we shall have a chance to do so.

'Before starting our homeward climb we sat down to rest, and, of course, someone mentioned the provisions – it was tomorrow's lunch that we carried – and someone else added that it would be absurd to take it back to the camp. Then the temptation became too great; though we knew it was wrong, our famished condition swept us away, and in five minutes not a remnant remained. After this we started our return climb, and at ten o'clock we reached the camp pretty well "done".

'There can be little doubt, I think, that the chasm we have seen today is caused by the ice pushing out of the southern strait against the barrier, and possibly it may end a little farther to the north, but I could not see any signs of its ending; the blocks of ice within seem to have been split off from the sloping ice-foot – in fact, we saw some in the process of being broken away – and the fact that there is so much less snow towards the land seems to show that the inner ones are of more recent origin. The ice-foot is fed by the ice-cap on the hills above, which at this part flows over in a steep cascade. I do not see that we can make another attempt to reach the land before we get back to Depot B; in fact, we shall have none too easy a task in doing that alone. We shall have to average more than seven miles a day, and the dogs are now practically useless; but, what is worse, I cannot help feeling that we ourselves are not so strong as we were. Our walk today has tired us more than it ought.

'Tonight Shackleton upset the hoosh pot. There was an awful moment when we thought some of it was going to run away on to the snow; luckily it all remained on our waterproof floorcloth, and by the time we had done scraping I do not think that any was wasted.'

'January 1, 1903. – We have opened the new year with a march which is likely to be a sample of those which will follow for many a day to come. The state of our dog-team is now quite pitiable; with a very few exceptions they cannot pretend to pull; at the start of the march some have to be lifted on to their feet and held up for a minute or two before their limbs become stiff enough to support them. Poor "Spud" fell in his tracks today; we carried him for a long way on the sledge, and then tried him once more, but he fell again, and had to be carried for the rest of the journey tucked away inside the canvas tank. Towards the end of our day's march it has always been possible to get a semblance of spirit into our poor animals by saying, "Up for supper". They learnt early what the words meant, and it has generally been "Spud" who gave the first responsive whimper. This afternoon it was most pathetic; the cheering shout for the last half-mile was raised as usual, but there was no response, until suddenly from the interior of the sledge-tank came the muffled ghost of a whimper. It was "Spud's" last effort: on halting we carried him back to his place, but in an hour he was dead.

'The whole team are in a truly lamentable condition; "Gus" and "Bismarck" are tottering; "Lewis" and "Birdie" may fail any moment; "Jim" is probably the strongest – he had reserves of fat to draw on, and has been a great thief; "Nigger" is something of a mystery: he is weak, but not reduced to the same straits as the others, and seems capable of surprising efforts.

'This afternoon a southerly breeze sprang up, and we improvised a sail out of our tent floorcloth; it makes an excellent spread of canvas. Some time ago I fixed up our bamboo mast as a permanency by stepping it in the runner and binding it with wire to one of the standards. On this we hoisted our sail, spreading it with two bamboo ski-poles. This evening we saw the last of Mount Markham, and Mount Longstaff is already growing small in the distance.'

'January 3. – We are not finding our homeward march so easy as we expected, and we are not clearing a large margin over the distances which are actually necessary for each day; it is plain that if there are blizzards now we must go on right through them. But today we have done rather better than before. This morning there was a hot sun, which brought the snow-surface nearly up to freezing-point, and we found the sledge drew easily. This afternoon there was a fresh breeze, when we got a great deal of help from our sail. The dogs have not pulled throughout the day – we do not expect it of them now – and this afternoon Shackleton was ahead dragging on those who could not walk. Wilson was carrying their long trace in rear to prevent it getting foul of the sledges, whilst I was employed in keeping the latter straight before the wind and in helping them over the rough places; the sail did most of the pulling. We have only two sledges left now, as we find this is sufficient to carry our much-lightened load.

'To walk eight or nine miles in a day does not sound much of a task for even a tired dog, yet it is too much for ours, and they are dropping daily. Yesterday poor little "Nell" fell on the march, tried to rise, and fell again, looking round with a most pathetic expression. She was carried till the night, but this morning was as bad as ever, and at lunch-time was put out of her misery. This afternoon, shortly after starting, "Gus" fell, quite played out, and just before our halt, to our greater grief, "Kid" caved in. One could almost weep over this last case; he has pulled like a Trojan throughout, and his stout little heart bore him up till his legs failed beneath him, and he fell never to rise again.

'It is useless to carry all this dog-food, so we have decided to serve it out freely, and the seven animals that remain are now lying about quite replete; at any rate, poor things, they will not die of starvation.

'Save for a glimpse of the sun this morning, a high stratus cloud has hung over us all day. We see the land, but not very clearly; we are inside our course in passing down the coast, and about ten miles from the remarkable cliffs we then noticed. To the north-west we recognise well-known landmarks. In spite of our troubles we managed to keep going for seven hours today, but we feel that this is the utmost that we can do at present owing to our poor team.'

'January 6. – This morning saw us start off in overcast weather, but with a high temperature making very wet snow, and in consequence a comparatively easy surface. By lunch-time it had commenced to snow in large flakes, and the temperature had risen to $+33°$ by the sling thermometer; this is the first time the air-temperature has been above freezing; the snow falling on us or on the sledges immediately melted, so that the effect was precisely the same as a shower of rain; and it was ludicrous to see us trying to push things into holes and corners where they would not get sopping wet. We wore our gaberdine blouses this afternoon, and they had the appearance and the effect of mackintoshes. All this is a strangely new experience to us, and certainly one would never have dreamt that an umbrella might be a desirable thing on the Great Barrier. This wave of heat with thick foggy snow came from the south with a fairish breeze.

'We have been trying once or twice lately to go on ski as the snow is very soft and we sink deeply, but we find that we cannot put the same weight on the traces as we do on foot. On the whole our ski so far have been of little value. They have saved us labour on the rare occasions on which we have not had to pull, such as when we returned for the second load at our relay work; but the labour thus saved is a doubtful compensation for the extra weight which they add to the load. Another thing to be remembered is that one gets used to plodding, even in heavy snow, and, though it is very tiring at first, one's capacity for performance on foot ought not to be judged until one is thoroughly accustomed to the work.

'We have passed our old track once or twice lately; it is partly obliterated but much clearer than I expected to find it after the recent winds. We made sail again this afternoon, and the dogs, which have now become only a hindrance, were hitched on behind the sledges – a very striking example of the cart before the horse. "Boss" fell, and was put on the sledge.'

'January 7. – We have had a very warm and uncommonly pleasant day. The temperature at noon rose to 34° and the snow surface was just on the melting-point, a condition that is excellent for the sledge-runners. We dropped all the dogs out of the traces and pulled steadily ourselves for seven hours, covering ten good miles by sledge-meter. "Boss", when we left, turned back to the old camp; later he was seen following, but he has not turned up tonight, though supper-hour is long past. The rest of the animals walked pretty steadily alongside the sledges. It is a queer ending for our team; I do not suppose they will ever go into harness again, unless it is to help them along.

'But who could describe the relief this is to us? No more cheering and dragging in front, no more shouting and yelling behind, no more clearing of tangled traces, no more dismal stoppages, and no more whip. All day we have been steadily plodding on with the one purpose of covering the miles by our own unaided efforts, and one feels that one would sooner have ten such days than one with the harrowing necessity of driving a worn-out dog-team. For the first time we were able to converse freely on the march, and in consequence the time passed much more rapidly.

'We have seen little of the land of late, though occasionally our landmarks show up. The sun has been flickering in and out all day. Much cloud hangs above the coast; this afternoon it developed into masses of rolled cumulus which clung about the higher peaks like rolls of cotton wool. It is the first time we have seen these to the south, and they are pleasantly reminiscent of milder climates; they would certainly appear to have some connection with the wave of heat that is passing over us.

'We have been arguing tonight that if we can only get to the depot in good time we can afford to have an extra feed, a sort of revival of Christmas Day; at present we have gained a day on our allowance. We are positively ravenous, but this thought is sending us to bed in a much happier frame of mind.'

'January 8. – Truly our travelling is full of surprises. Last night we had a mild snowstorm depositing flaky crystals, but none of us guessed what the result would be. This morning the air temperature had fallen to 22°, the snow surface was 23°, and below the upper layer 26°; after breakfast the fog gradually cleared, the sun came out, and a brisk northerly breeze sprang up. We got into our harness in good time, and, lo! and behold, found we could scarcely move the sledges. We scraped the runners and tried again without any difference; somewhat alarmed, we buckled to with all our energy, and after three hours of the hardest work succeeded in advancing one mile and a quarter; then we camped to discuss the matter. It was evident that the surface had completely changed: last night we could have dragged double our present load with ease; this morning each step was a severe strain, we were constantly brought to a standstill and had to break the sledges away with a jerk. As the wind came up, the loose snow settled into little sandy heaps, and seemed actually to grip at the runners. We have decided to remain in camp until the surface changes, but the question one cannot help asking is, Will it change? I suppose it is bound to come right, but we have less than a week's provisions and are at least fifty miles from the depot. Consequently the prospect of a daily rate of one mile and a quarter does not smile on us – in fact, we are none of us very cheerful tonight; and to add to his discomfort poor Shackleton has another bad attack of snow-blindness.

'We got a clear view of the land this afternoon, and I was able to get an excellent round of angles. We are opposite the high pyramidal and tabular mountains once more, and get a good idea of the general loftiness of the country.

' "Birdie" remained behind at the camp this morning, but came on later; "Boss" has never rejoined – he must have sunk like the rest from sheer exhaustion, but with no-one by to give him the last merciful quietus; "Joe" was sacrificed for the common good tonight. It is fortunate that numbers will not permit these massacres to continue much longer; yet, after all, one cannot help being struck with the extraordinary and merciful lack of intelligence that these beasts display in such tragic moments. We have had the most impressive examples of this.

'When a decree has gone forth against any poor wretch, it has been our custom to lead him some way to the rear of the sledges and there, of course, to put an end to him as painlessly as possible. As the intended victim has been led away, the rest of the team have known at once what is going to happen, and as far as their feeble state has allowed they have raised the same chorus of barks as they used to do when they knew that we were going to fetch their food. Of course the cause is precisely the same; they know in some way that this means food. But the astonishing fact is that the victim himself has never known: he has always followed willingly with his tail wagging, evidently under the impression that he is going to be taken to the place where the food comes from, nor, until the last, has he ever shown the least suspicion of his end.

'Thus we have seen an animal howling with joy at seeing his comrade led to the slaughter, and the next night going on the same road himself with every sign of pleasure; it has a distinctly pathetic side, but it is good to know clearly that they have not the intelligence to anticipate their fate.

'I have used the pronoun "we" above, but I must confess that I personally have taken no part in the slaughter; it is a moral cowardice of which I am heartily ashamed, and I know perfectly well that my companions hate the whole thing as much as I do. At the first this horrid duty was performed by Wilson, because it was tacitly agreed that he would be by far the most expert; and later, when I was perfectly capable of taking a share, I suppose I must have shrunk from it so obviously that he, with his usual self-sacrifice, volunteered to do the whole thing throughout. And so it has been arranged, and I occupy the somewhat unenviable position of allowing someone else to do my share of the dirty work.'

'January 9. – Late last night I was awakened by a flapping of wings, and found a solitary skua gull hovering round the camp. One cannot guess how the creature can have spotted us, especially as we had a northerly wind yesterday; but whatever has brought him, it is cheering to see a sign of life once more, as it is more than a month since we saw the last. It was anxious work trying the surface this morning, and we hurried over the breakfast to get into harness. We found the pulling hard work, but very much better than yesterday, and in the afternoon we were able to set our sail again. We have made a fairly good march, but now, unfortunately, cannot tell the exact distance covered, as this morning we found that the sledge-meter had refused duty. An examination showed that one of the cog-wheels had dropped off, so we detached the counter mechanism and abandoned the rest; it has done us good service, and we shall miss its exact record of our work.

'Our four remaining dogs roam around the sledges all day, sometimes lying down for a spell, but never dropping far behind. "Nigger" and "Jim" are moderately well, but "Birdie" and "Lewis" are very weak and emaciated. Poor "Nigger" seems rather lost out of harness; he will sometimes get close to our traces and march along as though he was still doing his share of the pulling.'

'January 10. – We started this morning at 8.25, with a moderately bright outlook and the land clear; the surface was a trifle better than yesterday, but with no helping wind we found it heavy enough until at eleven o'clock a high stratus cloud drifted up from the south and plunged us into gloom. With this the temperature rose and the surface improved as if by magic, and for the last hour before lunch we were able to step out briskly. Soon after this the wind came, and as we started our afternoon march it became evident that a blizzard was beginning. It is the first time we have marched in a blizzard, and though it has been very trying work, it has given us several extra miles.

'Almost immediately after lunch the sledges began to outrun us, and soon we were obliged to reef our sail, and even with reduced canvas the mast was bending like a whip. The great difficulties were to keep the course and to run the sledges straight. At first we tried to steer by the direction of the wind, and only discovered how wildly we were going by the sail suddenly flying flat aback on either tack. The air was so thick with driving snow that one could not see more than twenty or thirty yards, and against the grey background it was impossible to see the direction in which the snow was driving. After this we tried steering by compass; Shackleton and Wilson pushed on before the wind, whilst I rested the compass in the snow, and when the needle had steadied directed them by shouting; then as they were disappearing in the gloom, I had to pick up the compass and fly after them. It can be imagined how tiring this sort of thing was to all concerned. At length I made up my mind that we could only hope to hold an approximate course, and getting Shackleton well ahead of me, I observed the manner in which the snow was drifting against his back, and for the remainder of the day I directed him according to this rough guide.

'As it was evident that, although we were not steering straight, we were covering the ground quickly, we decided to go on for two hours extra and take every advantage we could from the wind.

It was as much as we could do to hold out for this time, and when at length the halt was called we were all thoroughly exhausted. We had difficulty in getting our tent up in the heavy gale that was now blowing, and, as luck would have it, our wretched Primus lamp chose this occasion to refuse work, so that it was late before we could prepare our hot meal.

'The march has been the most tiring we have done; we are more or less used to steady plodding, but today we have sometimes had to run, sometimes to pull forward, sometimes backward, and sometimes sideways, and always with our senses keenly on the alert and our muscles strung up for instant action. Wilson and I are very much 'done', though only to the extent that needs a night's rest; but Shackleton is a good deal worse, I think, and I am not feeling happy about his condition.

'We could very rarely spare our attention for the dogs today. Poor "Birdie" gave out early, and was carried on the sledge; as tonight he could not stand, we have had to give up hope of saving him, and he has breathed his last. "Nigger" and "Jim" have kept up well, but "Lewis" has only done so with great difficulty, and has sometimes dropped a long way behind.

'We cannot now be far from our depot, but then we do not exactly know where we are; there is not many days' food left, and if this thick weather continues we shall possibly not be able to find it.'

'January 11. – The surface has been truly awful today; with the wind swelling our sail and our united efforts we could scarcely budge the sledges. Nothing could be seen; not a sign of land; cold snow was driving at our backs, and it was most difficult to steer anything like a straight course. At noon the sun peeped out for a few minutes, and I got an altitude which gives the latitude as 80.44 S.; tonight, therefore, we cannot be more than ten or twelve miles from the depot.

'Our loads are ridiculously light, and that we should be making such heavy weather of them is very discouraging. It may be because we are overdone, but I cannot help thinking that the surface is getting consistently worse; and with no knowledge of our climate we have certain dismal forebodings that a snowy season has set in, which may be a regular thing at this time of year. With no sight of landmarks and nothing about one but the unchanging grey it is impossible to avoid a sense of being lost;

never before have we entirely lost sight of the land for more than twenty-four consecutive hours, and looking at the diminished food-bag we are obliged to realise that we are running things very close. However, it is no use meeting troubles half-way; the only thing now is to push on all we can.

'We are not very comfortable in our camping equipment, as everything is wet through – clothes, sleeping-bags, and tent-gear. The canvas tanks and covers of the sledges are shrunk and sodden; the snow was melted as it drifted against one side of our sail today, and from the other hung long icicles.

' "Lewis" dropped farther and farther astern this morning, and as he has not come up tonight I fear we shall not see him again.'

'January 12. – This morning as we breakfasted there was just a glimpse of landmarks, but before we could properly recognise them the pall of cloud descended once more; we saw enough to show us that we cannot be very far from the depot. Thanks to a good southerly breeze we have done a good march, and with the help of another latitude sight I calculate the depot must be within a very few miles, but the continuance of this thick weather naturally damps our spirits.

'There is no doubt we are approaching a very critical time. The depot is a very small spot on a very big ocean of snow; with luck one might see it at a mile and a half or two miles, and fortune may direct our course within this radius of it; but, on the other hand, it is impossible not to contemplate the ease with which such a small spot can be missed. In a blizzard we should certainly miss it; of course we must stop to search when we know we have passed its latitude, but the low tide in the provision-tank shows that the search cannot be prolonged for any time, though we still have the two dogs to fall back on if the worst comes to the worst. The annoying thing is that one good clear sight of the land would solve all our difficulties.

'For a long time we have been discussing the possible advantage of stripping the German silver off the sledge-runners. Once off it cannot be replaced, and therefore to strip them is a serious step; the only way in which we have been able to guess the relative merits of the wood and metal runners is by contrasting the sledges and the ski, and it has always seemed to us that the latter are as likely to clog as the former, but the differing conditions of their use make the comparison difficult. However, the pulling has been so severe lately that I cannot but think that, however bad the wood may be, it cannot be worse than the German silver, and, though we may not gain by stripping our runners, we cannot very well lose; so tomorrow morning I intend to strip one of the sledges for trial, and we are looking forward with some anxiety to the result of the experiment.'

'January 13, noon. – This morning we stripped a sledge and then started on our march. Everything was as bad as it could be. There was not a sign of the land; the whole outlook was one monotonous grey, and when we started to march we found the surface in the most trying condition. Steering could only be done by one person pulling behind, catching the shadow of the others on the light sastrugi, and constantly directing right or left; we were obliged to put every ounce of our strength on the traces, and even thus advanced at a rate which was something less than three-quarters of a mile an hour. The whole thing was heartbreaking, and after three hours of incessant labour we decided to halt. I am now writing in the tent, and, I am bound to say, in no very cheerful frame of mind. We have thought it wise to reduce our meals still further, so that luncheon has been the very poorest ray of comfort.

'And so here we lie, again waiting for a favourable change. Little has been said, but I have no doubt we have all been thinking a good deal. The food-bag is a mere trifle to lift; we could finish all that remains in it at one sitting and still rise hungry; the depot cannot be far away, but where is it in this terrible expanse of grey? And with this surface, even if we pick it up, how are we to carry its extra weight when we cannot even make headway with our light sledges?

'I have been staring up at the green canvas and asking myself these questions with no very cheering result.'

'January 13, midnight. – Catching a glimpse of the sun in the tent today, I tumbled out of my sleeping-bag in hopes of getting a meridional altitude; it was one of those cases which have been common of late when observation is very difficult. Light, ragged clouds were drifting across the face of the sun, and through the theodolite telescope at one moment one saw its blurred, indistinguishable image, and at the next was blinded with the full force of its rays. After getting the best result that I could, I casually lowered the telescope and swept it round the horizon; suddenly a speck seemed to flash by, and a wild hope sprang up. Slowly I brought the telescope back; yes, there it was again; yes, and on either side of it two smaller specks – the depot, without the shadow of a doubt. I sprang up and shouted, "Boys, there's the depot." We are not a demonstrative party, but I think we excused ourselves for the wild cheer that greeted this announcement. It could not have been more than five minutes before everything was packed on the sledges and we were stepping out for those distant specks. The work was as heavy as before, but we were in a very different mood to undertake it. Throughout the morning we had marched in dogged silence; now every tongue was clattering and all minor troubles were forgotten in knowledge that we were going to have a fat hoosh at last. It took us nearly two hours to get up, and we found everything as we had left it, and not much drifted up with snow.

'We have had our fat hoosh, and again, after a long interval, have a grateful sense of comfort in the inner man. After supper we completed our experimental comparison of the two sledges, which have respectively metal and wood runners; we equalised the weights as nearly as possible, and started to tow the sledges round singly; we found that there was an astonishing difference: two of us could barely move the metalled sledge as fast as one could drag the other. We are wholly at a loss to account for this difference; one would have thought that if metal was ever to give a good running surface it would be now when the temperatures are high; but though the result puzzles us, we have of course decided to strip the second sledge.

'On the whole things stand favourably for us; we have perhaps 130 miles to cover to our next depot, but we have a full three weeks' provisions, and it looks as though we should not have great difficulties with our load, now that we are on wood runners. On the other hand, I am not altogether satisfied with the state of our health. There is no doubt that we are not as fit as we were: we are all a bit "done". In Shackleton's case especially I feel uneasy; his scorbutic signs are increasing, and he was again terribly done up when we camped tonight. All things considered, without knowledge of what may be before us, it is safer not to increase our food allowance for the present, more especially as in going north I want to steer inwards so as to examine more closely those masses of land which we have seen only in the far distance. But in spite of all, our circumstances are very different tonight from what they were last night; the finding of the depot has lifted a load of anxiety, and I think we shall all sleep the better for it.

'We are all terrible-looking ruffians now; the sun has burnt us quite black, and for many days our only bit of soap has remained untouched. It is some time, too, since we clipped our beards, and our hair has grown uncomfortably long; our faces have developed new lines and wrinkles, and look haggard and worn – in fact, our general appearance and tattered clothing have been a source of some amusement to us of late.'

'January 14. – This morning we had a thorough medical examination, and the result was distinctly unsatisfactory. Shackleton has very angry-looking gums – swollen and dark; he is also suffering greatly from shortness of breath; his throat seems to be congested, and he gets fits of coughing, when he is obliged to spit, and once or twice today he has spat blood. I myself have distinctly red gums, and a very slight swelling in the ankles. Wilson's gums are affected in one spot, where there is a large plum-coloured lump; otherwise he seems free from symptoms. Both he and I feel quite fit and well, and as far as we are concerned I think a breakdown is very far removed.

'Early this morning we reorganised our load, dropping everything that was unnecessary, overhauling mast and sail and generally putting everything ship-shape. When we got away at last we carried, besides our own belongings, a small quantity of food for our two remaining dogs, the whole amounting to a weight of 510 lbs., or 170 lbs. per man. We made a fairly good march, and to our surprise the sledges came easily; the only marring element was poor Shackleton's heavy breathing. The sky has been overcast all day, but for a short time we had a good view of the lower land and could very clearly see the leading marks on which we had placed the depot, a sight which would have meant much to us a day or two ago.

'Soon after coming to camp I went to the sledges to feed the dogs, and, looking round, found that Wilson had followed me; his face was very serious, and his news still more so. He told me that he was distinctly alarmed about Shackleton's condition; he did not know that the breakdown would come at once, but he felt sure that it was not far removed. The conversation could only be conducted in the most fragmentary fashion for fear it should be overheard, but it was sufficiently impressive to make our supper a very thoughtful meal. It's a bad case, but we must make the best of it and trust to its not getting worse; now that human life is at stake all other objects must be sacrificed. It is plain that we must make a bee-line for the next depot regardless of the northern coast; it is plain also that we must travel as lightly as possible.

'It went to my heart to give the order, but it had to be done, and the dogs are to be killed in the morning. I have thought of the instruments, which are a heavy item, but some of them may be needed again, and I am loath to leave any until it is absolutely necessary.

'One of the difficulties we foresee with Shackleton, with his restless, energetic temperament, is to keep him idle in camp, so tonight I have talked seriously to him. He is not to do any camping work, but to allow everything to be done for him; he is not to pull on the march, but to walk as easily as possible, and he is to let us know directly he feels tired. I have tried to impress on him the folly of pretending to be stronger than he is, and have pointed out how likely he is to aggravate the evil if he does not consent to nurse himself. We have decided to increase our seal-meat allowance in another effort to drive back the scurvy.

'More than this I do not see that we can do at present. Every effort must be devoted to keeping Shackleton on his legs, and we must trust to luck to bring him through. In case he should break down soon and be unable to walk, I can think of absolutely no workable scheme; we could only carry him by doing relay work, and I doubt if Wilson or I am up to covering the distance in that fashion; it is a knotty problem which is best left till the contingency arises.

'It looks as though life for the next week or two is not going to be pleasant for any of us, and it is rather curious because we have always looked forward to this part of the journey as promising an easier time.'

'January 15. – This morning "Nigger" and "Jim" were taken a short distance from the camp and killed. This was the saddest scene of all; I think we could all have wept. And so this is the last of our dog-team, the finale to a tale of tragedy; I scarcely like to write of it. Through our most troublous time we always looked forward to getting some of our animals home. At first it was to have been nine, then seven, then five, and at the last we thought that surely we should be able to bring back these two.

'After the completion of this sad business we got into our harness, where another shock awaited us, for we put our weights on the traces without the least effect, and it was only when we jerked the sledges sideways the least movement followed. It was evident that something was wrong, and on turning the sledges up we found the runners solidly crusted with ice. It took us twenty minutes to clear them; but afterwards we got on well and have covered nearly eight miles. As this caking of the runners is likely to happen whenever our sledges are left long in one position, we have decided to lift them off the snow every night.

'In the morning march we had bright sunlight, and it cheered us all wonderfully after its long absence. We could see the northern side of the high rounded snow-cape abreast of which we left our depot, and which we have always known as "Cape A". This northern side forms the southern boundary of the great glacier which occupies the strait, and it is very steep, with high frowning cliffs. We are now crossing more directly across the mouth of the strait, and there are already indications of ice disturbances; we have been travelling over slight undulations and most confused sastrugi.

'Shackleton's state last night was highly alarming; he scarcely slept at all, and had violent paroxysms of coughing, between which he was forced to gasp for breath. This morning to our relief he was better, and this evening he is rather better than last, though very fagged with the day's work. We try to make him do as little pulling as possible until the pace is settled, and he can lean steadily forward in his harness.

'It is early to judge, but the double ration of seal-meat seems already to have a good effect: gums seem a trifle better. On the other hand, I have some stiffness in the right foot, which I suppose is caused by the taint, but at present I have not mentioned it, as my gums look so well that I am in hopes it will pass away.'

'January 16. – The sledges have been running easily, and we have made a good march, but the surface is getting more uneven, and under the dark, gloomy sky we could not see the inequalities and stumbled frequently. This sort of thing is very bad for Shackleton; twice he slipped his leg down a deep crack and fell heavily, and on each occasion we had to stop several minutes for him to recover. He has been coughing and spitting up blood again, and at lunch time was very "groggy". With his excitable temperament it is especially difficult for him to take things quietly, and at the end of each march he is panting, dizzy, and exhausted.

'It is all very dreadful to watch, knowing that we can do nothing to relieve him; if at the ship, he would be sent straight to bed, but here every effort must be made to keep him on his feet during the marches. There is now no doubt that the scorbutic symptoms are diminishing; both Wilson and I have much cleaner gums, and my leg is vastly improved. Our seal-meat at the present rate will last another fifteen days, by which time we ought to be within reach of safety. Six weeks ago we were very much inclined to swear at the cook, who had been careless enough to leave a good deal of blubber in our seal-meat, but now we bless his carelessness, and are only too eager to discover that our "whack" has a streak of yellow running through the dark flesh. I could not have believed it possible that I should ever have enjoyed blubber, and the fact that we do is an eloquent testimony to our famished condition.

'This afternoon we have had some glimpses of the land and have got some bearings, but there are still masses of cloud over the mountains. We can see the steep cliffs on the northern side of Cape A, and similar cliffs fringing the foothills on the opposite side of the strait, but what stands behind we cannot hope to know, unless the weather clears. So far as exploring is concerned, on these overcast days one might just as well be blindfolded.

'The sunlight this afternoon showed that we are crossing a very peculiar surface of hard, cracked, lateral ridges, with softish snow between, due no doubt to the pressure of the ice-mass pushing out through the strait.'

'January 17. — . . . The continuance of our overcast weather has brought a trouble which is now becoming a serious matter, and that is the difficulty of steering. I take it on myself to do most of it now, sometimes by a cloud, sometimes by the sun, and sometimes by sastrugi, and in half an hour it often happens that each of these methods has to be employed in turn.'

It would perhaps be as well here to make a short digression to explain the difficulties connected with this matter in such a journey as ours. It will be understood that we carried a compass in our instrument-box, but to have held this in one's hand as one marched would have been quite useless, as it was not until several minutes after it was placed firmly on the snow that the card ceased to swing and indicated a definite direction; the compass was therefore of little use to us on the march.

Knowing that this would be so, and expecting to travel out of sight of land, I had prepared a device for steering by the sun, and as this was constantly in use, and can be highly recommended to future expeditions, it deserves a short description. It consisted of a small wooden dial in the centre of which was a shadow-pin. The edge was marked with two circles, one showing the points of the compass and the other a twenty-four hour clock-face subdivided to half-hours; the relation of these circles involved a consideration of mean latitude and equation of time, details which are somewhat technical, but will be understood by the navigator.

The use of the instrument was extremely simple. It was held in the hand in such a position that the shadow of the pin fell on the hour, and when so held the outer circle showed the true north and south, or the true bearing of any object. Thus one could march straight on in any required direction by occasionally consulting one's watch and more frequently the dial. Whenever the sun was out, therefore, with this instrument we had no difficulty at all in keeping a straight course; and it served yet another practically useful purpose, for when it was put down correctly at night, it gave the time to anyone leaving the tent later on.

But when the sun disappeared this instrument was useless. Then it was that our troubles began, and we were reduced to all sorts of shifts and devices to steer a course. When possible we would take the bearing of a cloud and march on this for some time until we were conscious that its direction was altered and a fresh mark must be sought. Occasionally the low, rocky patches on the distant coastline formed a guide, but on the majority of overcast days the land was not visible, and the cloud-forms had no definite shape. At such times one looked on a monotonous, uniform sheet of grey which extended from under foot to the zenith. The leader could see nothing, but others might catch an idea of the direction of the snow-waves in his shadow. But the expedients to which we were reduced and the troubles they brought can be gathered from my tale, and it will be understood why the continuance of overcast weather should have caused them to be so frequently mentioned at this time.

'January 17 (continued). – This morning we started with an overcast sky and an unshaded wall of grey ahead. A rapidly closing bright patch on our starboard beam was the only guide. After two hours I had to give up leading; Wilson went ahead, but by lunch his eyes had had enough, and I finished the afternoon. It is difficult to describe the trying nature of this work; for hours one plods on, ever searching for some more definite sign. Sometimes the eye picks up a shade on the surface or a cloud slightly lighter or darker than its surroundings; these may occur at any angle, and have often to be kept in the corner of the eye. Frequently there comes a minute or two of absolute confusion, when one may be going in any direction and for the time the mind seems blank. It can scarcely be imagined how tiring this is or how trying to the eyes; one's whole attention must be given to it, without relaxing for a moment the strain on the harness. At lunch today I fixed up a new device by securing a small teased-out shred of wool to the end of a light bamboo to act as a wind vane. The wind was light and shifty, but the vane relieved my eyes.'

'January 18. – We started today on another abominable "blind" march. For half an hour I could just see some ridges and the slightest gleam in the sky to the north; for another spell, a very light easterly breeze kept my vane on the flutter. The sastrugi under foot are light and confused, and when at last the wind fell we were left with no guide at all, and were forced to camp; for the last ten minutes we had been four points off our course. Wilson says his eyes are on the point of going; mine, on which I see the party must principally depend, are not quite right, but not yet painful. The situation is startling, but we have not yet exhausted our resources. If there is no improvement after lunch, Shackleton will start on ahead with a flag, and when he has been directed for half a mile, Wilson and I propose to bring on the sledges; it promises to be slow work, but we must get on somehow.'

'Midnight. – All was going well with our march this afternoon, when Shackleton gave out. He had a bad attack of breathlessness,

and we are forced to camp in a hurry; tonight matters are serious
with him again. He is very plucky about it, for he does not
complain, though there is no doubt he is suffering badly.'

'January 19. – Another long "blind" march. It is very distressing
work, and the gloom does not tend to enliven our spirits; but
Shackleton was better this morning and is still better tonight. We
have now had overcast weather almost continuously for ten days.'

'January 20. – At luncheon we found ourselves in latitude
79.51 S., and on coming out of the tent were rejoiced to find a
sight of the land on our left, though as yet but hazy. It rapidly
cleared as we resumed our march, and soon a new scene was
unfolded to our view. An opportunity of this sort was not to be
missed, and we camped early, since which we have been busy
taking angles and sketching. The temperature has fallen to zero, so
that both these tasks have been pretty "nippy". The beautiful
feathery hexagonal ice-crystals are falling again, and came floating
down on our books and instruments as we worked.

'The land is a long way from us, but much closer than it was on
the outward march; the detached appearance which it then had is
still maintained to some extent, but there is now every indication
that a still closer view would show a continuous coastline, and that
in the gaps between the nearer high mountain ranges would be
found lower and perhaps more distant hills.

'Cape A is far behind us; we get a distant view up the strait on its
northern side, and see only enough to show that it must penetrate
deeply into the land before it rises in altitude to any extent. If, as
one cannot but suppose, it contains a glacier, that glacier must be
the largest yet known in the world; but with ice disturbance
commencing nearly thirty miles from its mouth, one can imagine
that to travel up it would not be an easy task. Through the gap of
the strait we get a distant view of more mountains – in fact, at any
place on this coastline one is struck with the vast numbers of peaks
that are within sight at the same moment. There are far more than
one could hope to fix on such a journey as ours: to plot the coastal
ranges alone would be a big task, but wherever we get a view
behind them it is to see a confusion of more distant hills.

'Northward of the strait we again see the high flanking range
end on; northward of this, again, are three distinct coastal ranges.
The farthest may possibly be the Royal Society range, though of

this we cannot be sure at present; but perhaps the most pleasing sight tonight is the glimpse we get of Mount Discovery; its conical peak rises just above our horizon, and the sight of that well-known landmark has seemed to bring us miles nearer to home and safety.'

'January 21. – The clouds have drawn down on us again, shutting out the land, but we have had a brisk southerly breeze, and, setting our sail, got along at a fine rate. For a time Shackleton was carried on the sledges, but for most of the march he walked along independently, taking things as easily as possible. Our sail did most of the pulling. I, hitched to the bow of the front sledge, kept it straight, and helped it over the rough places; Wilson hitched to the back of the rear sledge, and by hauling sideways acted as a sort of rudder. We got on fast, but it was by no means easy work, being so extraordinarily jerky and irregular. Shackleton is improving, but takes his breakdown much to heart.'

'January 22. – The southerly wind continued today; it is a godsend, and is taking us to the north faster than we ever hoped for. The masses of low heavy cumulus and stratus cloud and the higher cirro-cumulus, all hurrying to the north, have given us the most beautiful cloud effects. The sun has peeped forth occasionally, but the land is still heavily overcast. We are beginning to hope that we shall soon be able slightly to increase our food allowance.'

'January 23. – I think the fates have decided in our favour. We got off another excellent march today. The wind holds from the south, sometimes falling light, but on the whole giving us great help. This wind is the greater blessing because it was so wholly unexpected.

'We have slightly increased our food allowance, but we feel that it would take weeks of such feeding to make up for arrears. I went out late tonight and, as usual, inspected our biscuit tank; it looked so healthy that I suggested a biscuit all round. There was loud applause from the tent, and we munched away at our small extra meal with immense joy.

'Ever since the warmer weather set in we have had to be very careful to keep our provisions out of the sun's rays. Our first warning was when an ominous splash on the canvas showed where the grease of the pemmican had melted its way through. Since then this class of food has been put in the middle and banked round with sugar and other non-meltable articles; and after supper every night the ready provision-bag is buried under the snow. In spite of such precautions, we are rather afraid that our seal-meat has suffered from the heat, and that it is not so anti-scorbutic as it was; our scurvy symptoms for the last few days have remained about the same, no better and no worse.'

'January 24. – Things are still looking well. Shackleton remains about the same; he is having a cruel time, but each march brings us nearer safety. The overcast weather still holds, and we cannot see the main land, although, to our great joy, we caught a glimpse of the Bluff to the north this afternoon.

'We have got on to a new form of surface which makes the pulling very wearisome. There is a thin crust an inch or so beneath the soft snow surface; this crust is almost sufficient to bear our weight, but not quite; the consequence is that as one steps on it, one is held up until the whole weight comes on the advanced foot, when the crust breaks and one is let down some three or four inches. To go on breaking the surface like this throughout a long day is extremely tiring. Such work would finish Shackleton in no time, but luckily he is able to go on ski and avoid the jars altogether. In spite of our present disbelief in ski, one is bound to confess that if we get back safely Shackleton will owe much to the pair he is now using.'

'January 25. – At last we have sunshine again and a grand opportunity for sketches and angles. The surface is bad and the work increasingly heavy, but Wilson and I are determined to leave as little as possible to chance and to get our invalid along as quickly as his state will allow. We start him off directly our breakfast is over, and whilst we are packing up camp he gets well ahead, so that he is able to take things easy; we follow on and gradually catch him up, and after lunch the same procedure is adopted. At the night halt he sits quietly while the tent is pitched, and only goes into it when all is prepared. He feels his inactivity very keenly, poor chap, and longs to do his share of the work, but luckily he has sense enough to see the necessity of such precaution.

'The Bluff looks delightfully close in the bright sunshine, but the depot must still be twenty or thirty miles away. Just before we camped tonight we could see a little round cloud over the centre of the Bluff ridge, and as we "rose" it further, we made it out to be the smoke of Erebus; it was cheerful to think that here was something which was beyond the ship; it is more than a hundred miles away from us, but we are too well accustomed to see things at a distance to treat this fact as wonderful.'

'January 26. – Plodding on in our usual style this afternoon we suddenly saw a white line ahead, and drawing closer found a sledge track; it must have been Barne's, on his return from his survey work to the west. Thinking over it tonight, it is wonderful what that track told us. We could see that there had been six men with two sledges, and that all the former had been going sound and well on ski; the sledge-runners had been slightly clogged. From the state of the track it was evident that they had passed about four days before on the homeward route, and from the zigzagging of the course we argued that the weather must have been thick at the time. Slight discolouration of the snow showed that two or three had been wearing leather boots, and so on: every imprint in the soft snow added some small fact, and the whole made an excellent detective study. The main point is that we know now, as certainly as if we had been told, that Barne and his party are safe and in good health, and this is no small relief after our own experiences.'

'January 27. – The temperature has again fallen to zero, but it has been brisk and pleasant in the sun. Old and familiar landmarks have been showing up one by one. Erebus raised its head above the Bluff range; Terror opened out to the east; the western range developed into better-known shape. It has been grand to watch it all. We calculate to get to the depot tomorrow, and have been wondering whether we shall find all the good things we expect.'

'January 28. – Things did not look so bright this morning; low, suspicious-looking clouds came up from the south with a bitterly cold wind, and soon they were about us, obscuring everything. Shackleton had a bad return of his cough, but said he thought he could manage to get along; so we spread our sail and proceeded. One has to be prepared for very quick changes in these parts, and by nine o'clock the whole sky had cleared again, and the wind had gone round to W.S.W.; this was an awkward angle for our sail, and resulted in frequent capsizes of the sledges, which brought a considerable strain on our tempers. We hoped to reach the depot by lunch, but it was an hour after that meal before Shackleton, who was ahead, spotted the flag, and we turned our course to make for it. As can be imagined, the last of the march was as near a rush as our tired legs could command. At length and at last we have reached the land of plenty; the one great and pressing evil will grip us no more.

'Directly our tent was up we started our search amongst the snow-heaps with childish glee. One after another our treasures were brought forth: oil enough for the most lavish expenditure, biscuit that might have lasted us for a month, and, finally, a large brown provision-bag which we knew would contain more than food alone. We have just opened this provision-bag and feasted our eyes on the contents. There are two tins of sardines, a large tin of marmalade, soup squares, pea soup, and many another delight that already make our mouths water. For each one of us there is some special trifle which the forethought of our kind people has provided, mine being an extra packet of tobacco; and last, but not least, there are a whole heap of folded letters and notes – billets-doux indeed. I wonder if a mail was ever more acceptable.

'All the news seems to be good; the weather at the ship has been wonderfully warm and fine, and the glare of the sun so great that our people have had to wear goggles at their work. After long and trying labour Royds tells me he has succeeded in rescuing all the boats, though not without damage. Armitage has not returned, but is expected soon. So far there has been no sign of a return of scurvy. Blissett has discovered an Emperor penguin's egg, and his messmates expect him to be knighted. With all this to gossip about, we are a pretty cheerful party tonight, and I can only write scrappily. Meanwhile our hoosh is preparing; we are putting a double "whack" of everything into the cooking-pot, and when in doubt as to what is double, we put in treble. The smell of this savoury mess is already arising, so I cease.'

'January 29. – I intended to finish writing up my diary last night, but I couldn't, and I'm afraid it's no use trying to disguise the fact that this was due to nothing but a condition of horrible surfeit. The tale is really lamentable; we have got into a habit of eating our food in the most wolfish fashion, and last night no sooner was our first pannikin of hoosh served out than it was gone, the unusual second pannikin vanished almost as quickly, and even when it came to the hitherto unknown third, there was not much slackening in the pace. Then, having exhausted the contents of the inner cooking-pot, in almost less time than it takes to tell, we passed on to the thickest brew of cocoa with "lashings" of jam and biscuit. Supper did not last more than twenty minutes, but the amount we put away in that time would have excited the envy of any gourmand.

'For the first half-hour everything was pure joy; we revelled in the sense of repletion, and read once more all the good news that had come from the ship. But after this there slowly crept on us a feeling that something was going wrong; our clothes seemed to be getting extraordinarily tight, and the only conclusion we could come to was that the concentrated food was continuing to swell.

'For me at least discomfort speedily gave place to acute suffering. From a sitting position I lowered myself until I was stretched out at full length, but this did not ease matters at all, and, with many groans, I was obliged to hoist myself to my knees, and, later, to as near a standing position as I could assume in the confined space of our small tent. In this trying attitude I remained until explosion seemed so imminent that I was forced to gasp, "For heaven's sake, undo the door," and directly the string was untied I dived out with a feeling that nothing less than the vault of heaven could hold me.

'But if I expected relief outside it was very slow in coming. Round and round our small tent I paced with measured tread until the minutes grew into hours, a well-beaten track had been worn, and I began to wonder whether I should ever return to a sense of normal dimensions. I don't think I have ever spent a more unpleasant time, and it did not make matters easier to know that it was entirely the result of my own greediness. Moreover, although Shackleton had not been in a fit state to over-indulge himself as I had done, I felt distinctly aggrieved that Wilson had not been obliged to join me in my midnight walk, and such sympathy as I got from these others very thinly disguised their inclination to find the whole incident extremely amusing.

'However, when at length my pangs subsided sufficiently to allow me to return to the tent I had some revenge, for as I was about to enter, Wilson realised that his acutest suffering had only been deferred, and as I approached he burst into the open with a pea-green face, and I had some consolation in knowing that we had changed places. It will be a long time before any of us over-eat ourselves again, and it is certainly an object-lesson on the effects of hunger; but one of the most curious points is that at the worst, when we felt that we carried a great deal more than we ought, and were suffering in consequence, we still craved for more. Our appetites are in a state which it seems impossible to satisfy, and this morning we are as hungry as ever.

'A few hours of fitful sleep followed this uncomfortable experience, and we awoke to find a heavy blizzard and the usual obscurity without. The first thought of pushing onward was speedily abandoned when we found that Shackleton had relapsed into the worst condition. To the reaction from the excitement of last night is added the most trying condition of weather. The result is very dreadful. Our poor patient is again shaken with violent fits of coughing and is gasping for breath; it looks very serious.'

'Later. – There is no doubt Shackleton is extremely ill; his breathing has become more stertorous and laboured, his face looks pinched and worn, his strength is very much reduced, and for the first time he has lost his spirit and grown despondent. It is terrible to have to remain idle knowing that we can do nothing to help. I have talked to Wilson tonight, who thinks matters are very critical, and advises pushing on to the ship at all hazards. The only chance of improvement lies in a change of weather, and if this blizzard continues the worst consequences may ensue. We have enough food now to carry him on the sledge, but tonight one may well doubt whether he will be well enough for that. It is a great disappointment; last night we thought ourselves out of the wood with all our troubles behind us, and tonight matters seem worse than ever. Luckily Wilson and I are pretty fit, and we have lots of food.'

'January 30. – Shackleton scarcely slept at all last night; his paroxysms of coughing grew less only from his increasing weakness. This morning he was livid and speechless, and his spirits were very low. He revived a little after breakfast, and we felt that our only chance was to get him going again. It took him nearly twenty minutes to get out of the tent and on to his ski; everything was done in the most laboured fashion, painful to watch. Luckily the weather had cleared, and, though there was a stiff southwesterly breeze and some drift, the sun was shining brightly. At last he was got away, and we watched him almost tottering along with frequent painful halts.

'Re-sorting our provisions, in half an hour we had packed our camp, set our sail, and started with the sledges. It was not long before we caught our invalid, who was so exhausted that we thought it wiser he should sit on the sledges, where for the remainder of the forenoon, with the help of our sail, we carried him. After lunch he was better, and in one way and another we have brought off a very long march. If he can only sleep tonight there is a chance of further improvement; much depends on this. It is all very anxious work; if there is no improvement I half think of pushing on to the ship for assistance. Wilson thinks that the relapse is mainly due to the blizzard, and doubts if he can stand another; one would give much to ensure three or four fine days. Nothing could be better than the weather tonight, and the surface is excellent. Just here it is swept hard by the wind, and the relief of treading on something solid and firm is enormous. I did not fully realise what terribly bad surfaces we had been struggling with until we got back on this hard one.'

'February 1. – For two days the weather has been glorious, and has had a wonderful effect on our invalid, who certainly has great recuperative powers. He managed to sleep a little last night, and today has kept going on his ski. After the last halt he had an attack of vertigo and fell outside the tent, which alarmed us greatly; but after about ten minutes it passed off, and tonight he is better again.

'All day we have been travelling along outside the White Island. So many parties have passed to and fro to the depot that there is now a regular beaten track, and one's eye can follow this highway for miles with a very cheering effect. This afternoon to the north we had a glorious view of Erebus and Terror; the smoke of the former trailed away in a long streamer to the east, and most curiously a second similar streamer floated away from the summit of Terror; one could have sworn that both mountains were active.'

'February 2. – Awaking to another fine day, we saw at last the prospect of an end to our troubles, and since that we have got off a long march and cannot now be more than ten or twelve miles from home. It was not till the afternoon that we surmounted a slight rise and altered our course in passing around the corner of the White Island; as we did so the old familiar outline of our friendly peninsula burst on our view; there stood Castle Rock like some great boulder dropped from the skies, and there to the left the sharp cone of Observation Hill. Almost one could imagine the figures on it looking eagerly out in our direction. Away to the west were all the well-known landmarks which led back to the vast western range, and tonight, therefore, on every side we have suggestions of home.

'That it is none too soon is evident. We are as near spent as three persons can well be. If Shackleton has shown a temporary improvement, we know by experience how little confidence we can place in it, and how near he has been and still is to a total collapse. As for Wilson and myself, we have scarcely liked to own how "done" we are, and how greatly the last week or two has tried us. We have known that our scurvy has been advancing again with rapid strides, but as we could do nothing more to prevent it, we have not looked beyond the signs that have made themselves obvious. Wilson has suffered from lameness for many a day; the cause was plain, and we knew it must increase. Each morning he has vainly attempted to disguise a limp, and his set face has shown me that there is much to be gone through before the first stiffness wears off. As for myself, for some time I have hurried through the task of changing my foot-gear in an attempt to forget that my ankles are considerably swollen. One and all we want rest and peace, and, all being well, tomorrow, thank Heaven, we shall get them.'

At this point my sledge diary comes to an end, for on the following day I had neither time nor inclination to write, but the incidents of such a day leave too deep an impression to need the aid of any note to recall them.

Nature wore its brightest aspect to welcome us home, and early in the brilliant, cloudless morning we packed up our camp for the last time, and set our faces towards Observation Hill. We had plodded on for some hours when two specks appeared ahead, which at first we took to be penguins, but soon made out were persons hurrying towards us. They proved to be Skelton and Bernacchi. We had been reported early by watchers on the hills; these two had hastened out to meet us, and soon we were gathered in our small tent whilst cocoa was made, and we listened to a ceaseless stream of news, for now not only had all our other travellers returned safe and sound with many a tale to tell, but our relief-ship, the *Morning*, had arrived, bringing a whole year's news of the civilised world.

And so at our last sledging lunch, and during the easy march which followed, we gradually gathered those doings of the great world which had happened between December 1901 and December 1902, and, as can be imagined, these kept our thoughts full until we rounded the cape to see once more our beloved ship.

Though still held fast in her icy prison, our good vessel looked trim and neat. She was fully prepared to face again the open seas, and the freshly painted side glistened in the sunlight. A fairer sight could scarcely meet our snow-tried eyes; and to mark the especial nature of the occasion a brave display of bunting floated gently in the breeze, while, as we approached, the side and the rigging were thronged with our cheering comrades.

But how can I describe this homecoming; how we again clasped the hands of our friends; how our eyes wandered about amongst familiar faces and objects; how we dived into our comfortable quarters to find every want forestalled and every trouble lifted from our shoulders by our kind companions; how for the first time for three months we shaved our ragged chins and sponged ourselves in steaming hot water; how in the unwonted luxury of clean raiment we sat at a feast which realised the glories of our daydreams; how in the intervals of chatter and gossip we scanned again the glad tidings of the homeland; and how at last in the comfort of our bunks, the closely written sheets fluttered from our hands, and we sank into the dreamless sleep of exhaustion?

It was a welcome home indeed, yet at the time to our worn and dulled senses it appeared unreal: it seemed too good to be true that all our anxieties had so completely ended, and that rest for brain and limb was ours at last.

And so our southern sledge journey came to an end on February 3, 1903, when for ninety-three days we had plodded with ever-varying fortune over a vast snowfield and slept beneath the fluttering canvas of a tent. During that time we had covered 960 statute miles, with a combination of success and failure in our objects which I have endeavoured to set forth in these pages.

If we had not achieved such great results as at one time we had hoped for, we knew at least that we had striven and endured with all our might.

CHAPTER 15

What had happened during our absence in the South

Royds's Journey to Cape Crozier – The King's Birthday – Athletic Sports – The Western Journey – Difficulties amongst the Mountains – Ascent of the Ferrar Glacier – Approaching the Summit – First Party on the Interior of Victoria Land – Return of Western Party – Summer Thawing – About the Islands to the South-West – Curious Ice Formations – Recovery of the Boats – Preparing for Sea – History of the Relief Expedition – Arrival of the 'Morning'

> Up along the hostile mountains where the
> Hair-poised snow-slide shivers. – KIPLING

> As cold waters to a thirsty soul,
> So is good news from a far country. – PROVERBS

During our long absence in the south much work had been done both on board the ship and by parties travelling in various directions, wherefore it can be imagined that I set myself with no little eagerness to gather the particulars of this employment, and especially to learn how it had fared with those who had undertaken the more extended journey to the west.

It was soon evident that since our departure the sledging resources of the ship had been utilised to the fullest extent; the ship herself had become the centre of the busiest activity, and throughout the summer parties had been going and coming, ever adding something to the knowledge of our surroundings.

On November 2, Royds had again journeyed to Cape Crozier to see how matters went with the Emperor penguins, and this short trip produced one or two interesting results. It can be seen from the chart* that from the elevated land at this cape an excellent view of the Ross Sea can be obtained, and it will be remembered that Royds on his last visit, little more than a fortnight before, had seen this sheet of water swept clear of ice. We had thought that this was the last of the ice in this direction, and that it would have

---

* Not reproduced in this edition.

continued to drift to the north; but now, to his astonishment, he found the whole sea thickly packed, and although the pack sometimes drifted away from the land, leaving some miles of open water, it was evident that no general exodus had yet commenced.

Descending to the Emperor rookery, he found several hundred adult birds, but not a single chick except those which lay dead on the floe; this was a most surprising fact, as it seemed impossible that the small downy chicks of a fortnight before could have already taken to the sea. It was not until the following year that we learnt the interesting manner in which these small creatures leave their birthplace.

Pushing farther on, Royds found that he must have just missed the occupation of the Adélie penguin rookery. These small birds had returned in their thousands, and were just commencing to lay their eggs; a few had laid their second, a larger number their first, but the majority had as yet laid none at all. From one point of view the moment could not have been more opportune, and it was not long before the party were enjoying the greatest delicacy which the Antarctic Regions can afford. In their good fortune, moreover, they did not forget their comrades, but loaded their sledges with a supply of eggs sufficient to provide at least one feast for those on board the ship. It was on taking a last look at the spot where the Emperor penguins had reared their young that Blissett called Royds's attention to a rounded object almost buried in the snow, which on being dug out proved to be an egg – the first that had been found. The joy was great, and soon after the party hastened back with their treasure.

Meanwhile on board the ship all efforts were devoted to the preparations of the western party, and it was hoped that in spite of the difficulties of providing for the large numbers who were to be employed, all would be ready before the end of the month. Progress was so satisfactory that it was decided that, November 9 being the King's birthday, there should be a general holiday, and it seemed no more fitting occasion could present itself for holding the athletic sports which we had often discussed. Accordingly, in the early morning the ship was dressed with flags, the large silken Union Jack was hoisted at Hut Point, and marks were placed and arrangements made for the various competitions. The events were entered into with the keenest delight, and as they were of a somewhat novel character for English sports, some of them deserve notice.

Since our men had become expert on ski, competitions connected with them were bound to be included; in the flat ski race it was impossible to say who would win, as so many could now go at a great pace; for the first half mile this event was wildly exciting, the leaders passing and repassing one another; but after that, staying powers showed up, and the race was won by Evans 'in a canter'. Next came a ski race down one of the steep hill-slopes which had given us so much amusement in the previous autumn; here of course it was skill and dexterity rather than strength which won the prize.

A very sporting event was the half-mile race on foot between teams of officers and men dragging heavy loaded sledges; at the start the teams went off at a gallop, but this pace was very soon reduced, and as the officers staggered back and won by a small margin they felt that they had had enough racing to last them for a long time.

Perhaps the keenest interest had been taken in the toboggan race. For this the men had entered in pairs, and each pair had been obliged to provide their own toboggan, subject to the rule that no sledge, or part of a sledge, and no ski could be used. The start was to be made from high up the hillside, and as the time for it approached there were gradually assembled perhaps the queerest lot of toboggans that had ever been seen together. The greater number were made from old boxes and cask staves, but the manner in which these were put together and the ideas they embodied were widely divergent; at last our canny Scotch carpenter's mate arrived with a far more pretentious article, though fashioned from the same material. He had devoted his skill in secret to making what was really a very passable sledge, and when he and his companion proceeded to secure themselves to this dark horse the result seemed a foregone conclusion. But after the start it was seen that these worthies had overrreached themselves, for though at first they shot ahead, the speed was altogether too great; in a brief space they lost control of their machine, and a moment after were rolling head-over-heels in clouds of snow, and whilst the hare thus disported itself the tortoises slid past and won the race.

Another competition that had to be arranged and managed with care was the rifle-shooting match. On this occasion there was keen competition to hit the bull's-eye, and amongst the competitors was our redoubtable cook, who claimed to be a marksman of the highest order. But by this time the cook's capacity for the narration of fables had become proverbial. It first became evident from varying accounts of the number of places in which he had been born, and later, when the long hours of the winter had given him an opportunity of relating his adventures in many countries, one of the sailors computed that the sum total of these thrilling experiences must have extended over a period of five hundred and ninety years, which, as he said, was a fair age even for a cook. So when this winner of many competitions possessed himself of a rifle at the firing-point, the markers disappeared with extraordinary promptitude behind the butt, and after the first two bullets had buried themselves in that obstruction the cook was informed that whoever won the prize the honours of the day were certainly his, and it would be quite unnecessary for him to exert himself further.

And so the King's birthday was kept merrily on board the *Discovery*, and the first Antarctic athletic meeting was pronounced by all to have been a distinct success.

By November 29 the preparations for the western journey had been completed, and it was a formidable party that set out on that day to cross McMurdo Sound and attack the mainland. In Armitage's own party were included Skelton and ten men, whilst the supports consisted of Koettlitz, Ferrar, and Dellbridge, with six men. In all twenty-one souls went forth to try to surmount that grim-looking barrier to the west. I have already pointed out that Armitage's plan, formed on the observations of his reconnaissance journey, was to attempt an ascent of the mountain region in the vicinity of that vast pile of morainic material which had erroneously been termed the 'Eskers'.

In pursuance of this plan, late on December 2, the party started to ascend the steep snow-slope which, as can be seen on the chart,* divides two masses of bare, rocky foothills, and rises to a plateau separating them from the higher mountains beyond.

As the party ascended the gradient became steeper, and it was soon necessary to divide the loads and make double journeys in the usual tedious manner of relay work. It was not until the 7th that they reached the summit of the slope and found themselves on a plateau with the lofty mountain range in front and the high granite foothills behind. They were now at a height of 5,000 feet.

* Not reproduced in this edition.

The *mer de glace* on which they stood seemed to have an outlet far to the south; there was another over which they had ascended, and yet a third to the north-west, which appeared to them the most hopeful direction in which to find a pass to the west. To the south of this outlet there rose a mass of magnificent rocky cliffs, which Armitage named the Cathedral Rocks, and which he thought he recognised as being the southern boundary of the New Harbour Glacier; it was this glacier which had appeared to him so unpromising in the lower reaches, and which he now hoped to reach at some higher point.

Advancing over a wavy, uneven surface of névé, they reached the vicinity of the outlet by the 9th. It was evident that it descended steeply into the New Harbour Glacier, which in future I shall call by its subsequent name, the Ferrar Glacier; but, in order to see its details more clearly, the officers were obliged to leave the camp and travel some distance to a more elevated position. On reaching this, they looked directly down on the Ferrar Glacier, and saw that it wound its way between high rocky cliffs far to the inland; but the prospect of reaching this and of travelling on its surface did not at this time look hopeful.

To quote Armitage's report: 'After putting on the rope, which Koettlitz held, I went as close to the edge of the slope overlooking the pass as possible. It certainly did not look promising. Unfortunately, I could not see its juncture with the glacier. After consulting Dr Koettlitz, I came to the conclusion that it would be best to seek a passage across the western range. . . . If we find it impossible to drag the sledges over the mountains, we must try the glacier, although Koettlitz considers that it would be madness to attempt it.' This was an unfortunate decision, and delayed the party greatly. It appears that in addition to the uncertainty of the steep road which led to it, the observers on this occasion were very distrustful of the appearance of the glacier itself; the blue ice, with no snow on its surface, apparently promised great dangers and difficulties. However, the decision being made, on the 10th the parties separated, the supports turning towards the ship, whilst the main party continued to ascend the rising snow-slopes which led towards the higher mountains.

The slopes quickly increased in gradient, and the ascent became the most arduous and toilsome work. Armitage's report says: 'The following was our mode of procedure: two men carried the crowbar and two ice-axes up the slope to the available length of rope (about 180 feet). The crowbar was then driven into the ice, and the ice-axes served as a backing; a strong lashing connected the three. A small tailed block was made fast to the crowbar, the Alpine rope rove through it, and the other end made fast to a sledge. Eight hands then walked downwards with the upper end of the rope, hauling the sledge upwards as they did so; two men guided the up-going sledge, and when it arrived at the top it was secured, and another was hauled up. Three hauls made one fleet of the four sledges.' After proceeding for two days in this fashion and reaching a height of 6,000 feet, they suddenly found further progress barred by an outcrop of rock; 'beyond this was an undulating plain in which we could see large ugly-looking crevasses and holes. To my intense disappointment there was no route by which I could justifiably lead my party.' They had little difficulty in descending the steep hillside towards their former camps, but, delayed by blizzards, it was not until the 16th that they could make a fresh examination of the pass to the Ferrar Glacier, which they were now obliged to consider the only possible route to the west.

At this time the party were by no means in a pleasant position. The plateau on which they stood was 1,800 feet above the glacier which they wished to reach; it was evident that the pass which lay between, and which they now called 'Descent Pass', was filled with snow, but how steep the slope might be, or how broken and crevassed its surface, they could not guess. They attempted to make a reconnaissance without the sledges, but after descending a few hundred feet found the valley so filled with cloud that they could see little except that the slope appeared to get steeper as they proceeded. In this quandary they determined to take their fortunes in their hands, and, starting blindly with the sledges above, to trust to fortune to land them safely in the valley below.

Armitage says: 'I had the sledges lashed two and two, abreast of one another, rope breaks on each runner, and I told the teams to use the bridles as extra breaks on the steeper parts. Four men were told off to each sledge; Skelton, Allan, Macfarlane, and I led the way. We started slowly, but the pace gradually increased until we were beyond all power of stopping; it seemed but a moment before we were brought to rest on a much more gradual slope, and

I stood up to find that we had descended 630 feet by aneroid. The other sledges came down after us with equal speed, and all arrived safely abreast of us. From this spot there was a long gentle slope, and then another fall of 400 feet, which, however, was not so steep as the first.' And so at length the party stood safely on the Ferrar Glacier at a spot whence its valley could be seen cutting deeply through the mountains, while its surface seemed to offer a gradual ascent to the interior. The place on which they stood was barely 2,000 feet above the sea level, but, as will be seen, in their pioneer efforts to reach it they had been forced to drag their heavy sledges over much difficult country, and had at one time reached an altitude of 6,000 feet.

The route taken by the party from this point was one which, as I shall relate in due course, I travelled myself in the following season. I was enabled then not only to observe it at first hand, but with much enlightenment which further experience had given us. The result of personal observation must ever be more satisfactory than an attempt to reproduce the impressions of others, and although this party were the first to see and describe the magnificent scenes of this glacial valley, I reserve an account of them until I can tell of that which I saw with my own eyes.

In the following year I was able to traverse this glacier at considerable speed and to treat its difficulties and obstacles lightly, but this, of course, was largely due to the fact that I was travelling over a route which was to some extent known. One is apt to forget the benefits conferred by the experience of others, and therefore, before recounting the slow and laborious progress of this party, I take the opportunity of acknowledging the debt which we owed to it.

On December 18 a start was made to ascend the glacier, and during the following days the party proceeded with great caution; before the new track was broken Armitage went ahead, sounding at every other footstep with his ice-axe. Their route gradually ascended, but though the gradient was irregular it was never steep; sometimes they were travelling over long stretches of blue ice where cracks and crevasses could be seen and avoided, but at others, the surface was covered with a thin and treacherous layer of soft snow, and here the greatest care had to be taken, as it was obvious that all dangers would be hidden. On such soft places, too, even a small gradient meant very heavy labour with the sledges, and nearly every day it was necessary to divide the loads and take the sledges on singly. The difficulty of advance was greatly hampered by the weather; though temperatures were high, the wind and snowdrift constantly swept down the valley with great force, and on many occasions masses of cloud hung about the valley and shut off all view of the surroundings. In bad weather it was almost impossible to proceed in a country which was so utterly unknown, and where it was necessary to direct a course with a view to avoiding obstacles which were sometimes seen a great distance ahead.

On the 23rd they had reached a plateau some 4,500 feet above the sea. Here the glacier, as may be seen on the chart,* opens out into a broad basin turning towards the right; from this point a slight descent led them to a lower level, where a moraine of immense boulders ran transversely across the basin. Christmas Day was spent amongst the huge rocks of this moraine, but instead of the bright, cloudless weather which at this time we were experiencing in the south, here the sky was overcast with heavy nimbus cloud and all day long fierce squalls swept down the valley; nor had this party the sauce of hunger to give that full enjoyment of their Christmas fare which went so far to mark this day in our southern calendar. But in spite of these facts the season seems to have been celebrated with much merriment.

From this time the party still continued to ascend: at first over very rough wavy ice, where the sledges skidded but could be pulled with ease, and where neither fur nor leather boot could get a hold, and crampons armed with steel points had to be worn; later they came again to snow surfaces, and on these they turned the corner and faced once more to the west to rise over the last stretch of the widening glacier. The rocky boundaries of the glacier were now comparatively lower. They had no longer frowning cliffs on each side; gradually the bare land seemed to be sinking beneath the level of the great ice mass, and only the higher mountains showed as nunataks above the vast névé fields.

On December 31 they were abreast of one of the last of these isolated summits, and as it formed a most conspicuous landmark they determined to leave at its foot a depot of a week's provision.

---

* Not reproduced in this edition.

They were able to approach the high weathered basaltic cliffs with ease, and found a sheltered position amongst the rough talus heaps at its base. Continuing to the west, they were faced by a steep rise over which the surface was much broken; but, selecting the smoothest route, they were able to surmount this obstacle, when, after crossing some wide bridged crevasses, they found themselves on a plateau which continued for many miles to a second steep rise.

New Year's Day found them on this plateau at a height of 7,500 feet; the temperature had fallen to −2°, and a strong wind was blowing from the W.S.W. It was whilst they were marching under these conditions that one of their number, Macfarlane, suddenly collapsed. Armitage says: 'At first I was very much alarmed; he could neither move nor speak, and his face, which had turned to a dull grey, looked positively ghastly. I had a tent pitched immediately, and soon the colour began to flow back into his face. He then complained of pains under his heart and shortness of breath, but these troubles gradually subsided. Being anxious to push on, after waiting some time, I decided to leave half the party in camp and continue to the west with the remainder. I came to the conclusion that Macfarlane's breakdown was due to some form of mountain sickness.'

Proceeding to the westward the advance party ascended another very steep rise, and then travelled over a gradual slope, at the top of which they camped on the night of January 3. This Armitage decided should be his last camp. They had now reached a height of 8,900 feet, and as far as they could see in every direction to the westward of them there extended a level plateau; to the south and north could be seen isolated nunataks, and behind them showed the high mountains which they had passed. On the 5th the party left their camp and proceeded to the south-west for some miles on ski. Armitage says: 'We ascended seventy feet in the first two miles; this was the highest elevation we reached, being about 9,000 feet. We then proceeded along a dead level for two miles, then we gradually descended thirty feet in a mile. At this point we stopped; the weather was beautifully clear, and observations showed that the horizon was rather below our level in every direction except to the north and north-east, whence we had come. On all sides the surface was quite smooth, and there was very little sign of wind; it looked as though the plateau on which we stood was the summit of the ice-cap.'

On the 6th the party started to return, and whilst descending the upper falls met with an incident which shows the treacherous nature of the irregular snow-slopes over which they were travelling. I quote the story from Armitage's report: 'We descended the upper falls with ease, and whilst crossing the smooth ice at their foot I was talking casually to Skelton when I suddenly became conscious that I was taking a dive, then I felt a violent blow on my right thigh, and all the breath seemed to be shaken out of my body. Instinctively I thrust out my elbows and knees, and then saw that I was some little way down a crevasse. It was about four feet wide where I was, but broadened to the right and left of me; below it widened into a huge fathomless cavern. Skelton sang out that my harness had held, and threw down the end of the Alpine rope with a bowline in it. I slipped this over my shoulders, and was hauled up with a series of jerks, and landed on the surface, feeling rather as though I had been cut in two and with not a gasp left in me. They told me that below my face had appeared to them to be covered in blood; the force of my fall had scattered everyone right and left and pulled the sledges up to the brink of the chasm, so that I was let down about twelve feet. It shook me up very much, and I could only hobble very lamely after the sledges as we proceeded on towards the camp where Macfarlane had been left.' After this the party continued to descend, following more or less the track by which they had come. Macfarlane, who had shown some signs of improvement, had further trouble with his breathing, and was carried for most of the way on the sledges; but it soon became evident that there was nothing very wrong with him, and that he was more alarmed about himself than others were for him.

On the way down, visits were made to the cliffs on each side, and specimens of the rock were obtained *in situ* as well as from the various moraines which were passed. By January 11 the party were well on towards the lower reaches of the glacier, and they found that the temperature of the valley had risen considerably; it was frequently above 40°, and the air inside the tents was often oppressively warm. This led to several minor and unexpected troubles; for instance, it was found that the sleeping-bags gradually melted the surface of ice or snow on which they were laid, and in the morning were surrounded with a pool of water.

The high temperatures also gave rise to a very great amount of thawing in the valley. We never again found it in this condition, and it is probable that it only lasts for a period of a fortnight, or at the most three weeks. This season of thaw is an extremely interesting matter, and no doubt it plays an important part in the denudation of the country. It will be remembered that before our arrival in winter quarters, in February 1902, we had landed on the tongue of a glacier and observed the beds of considerable glacial streams, though at that time the thaw had ceased. It may therefore be worth while to quote some remarks from a report made by Skelton, who, as a member of this party, saw the glacier in its most melting mood. Skelton writes: 'During the hot days of the latter part of December and early in January an immense amount of melting goes on in the valley. On the glacier surface there is quite a loud "buzzing" sound, caused by the air bubbles confined in the ice being freed and coming to the surface through water. On the way back we found every boulder in the moraines standing in a large pool of water, often three or four feet deep, and during the night frequent rumblings could be heard as the boulders lost their equilibrium and shifted their positions. Some boulders could be seen in the clear ice several feet below the surface, having melted their way down. There was quite a torrent of water running down past the Cathedral Rocks, where it flowed into a lake nearly half a mile in diameter; from there it ran in a rapid stream past Descent Pass towards the sea. The water in this stream was about nine inches deep and seven feet across, and on measuring its speed I calculated the flow of water to be about fifty-three tons per minute; this was only one of many streams.'

On January 12 the party began to climb the steep slopes of Descent Pass, and had to resort to their old device of hauling the sledges up with the help of ropes and blocks. As some parts of these slopes stood at an average angle of 45°, the task proved so laborious that they did not reach the summit of the pass till the evening of the 14th. From this time their work was easy, and by the 17th they had again reached the sea level. Here they were fortunate enough to find numerous seals basking on the ice, and it was not long before they regaled themselves on fresh meat.

The remainder of the journey was uneventful, and on the nineteenth, when the party reached the ship, Macfarlane had practically recovered, whilst the remainder were in the best of health and condition. Some months elapsed before I was able to go closely into the results of this journey, and by that time unexpected circumstances had made it evident that we should have a further chance of exploring the interesting region which it had brought to our knowledge. By that time also the several rock specimens which had been secured had passed into the hands of the geologist. A rough map had been constructed and a series of photographs taken by Skelton had been developed, all going to show the valuable information which the party had collected, and opening an exceptionally interesting field of investigation for a second visit to the region.

There was no doubt that a practicable road to the interior had been discovered and traversed, and that the grim barrier of mountains which had seemed so formidable an obstruction from the ship had been conquered, but the portion of this road which led over the foothill plateau and down the steep slopes of Descent Pass still appeared as a serious impediment in the way of speedy approach to the ice-cap. It remained to be seen whether some easier route might not be found to the base of Cathedral Rocks, and, in spite of Armitage's observations, I could not help thinking that there must be some way by which sledges could be dragged from the New Harbour over the foot of the Ferrar Glacier.

It was evident that this party had reached the inland ice-cap and could claim to be the first to set foot on the interior of Victoria Land; but it was clear, too, that they had been forced to terminate their advance at an extremely interesting point, and to return without being able to supply very definite information with regard to the ice-cap. As I have already pointed out, the view of the sledge-traveller on a plain is limited to an horizon of three or four miles; beyond this he cannot say definitely what occurs. This party appeared to have been on a lofty plateau, but the very short advance they had been able to make over it could not give a clear indication of what might lie to the westward; the nature of the interior of this great country was therefore still wrapped in mystery.

The photographs, the rock specimens, and the enthusiastic descriptions of the rugged cliffs which bordered the glacier valley showed that here lay the most promising field for geological investigations that we could possibly hope to find, and that at all hazards our geologist must be given the chance of exploring it. In the original programme it had been impossible to guess in what direction this important officer should direct his footsteps, and it had been decided that his ends would best be served by making short journeys in various directions. It was now evident that this deep glacier valley cutting a section through the mountain ranges was incomparably more interesting than any other region known to us, and what could be learnt of it from the returned travellers only went to show more clearly the extreme importance of a second visit. But perhaps the most promising circumstance of all that pointed to the interest of this region was that amongst the rock specimens brought back were fragments of quartz-grits. These, with other observations, showed the strong probability of the existence of sedimentary deposits which might be reached and examined, and which alone could serve to reveal the geological history of this great Southern continent.

On the whole, therefore, the western party had done excellent pioneer work; they had fulfilled their main object, and in doing so had disclosed problems which caused the greater part of our interest to be focussed in this direction throughout the remainder of our stay in the South.

The extensive preparations for the western journey had almost denuded the ship of sledge equipment, and the travellers who embarked on the shorter journeys in the vicinity of the ship were obliged to do as best they could with the little that remained. It was of course a rule that everything must give way to the extended efforts. However, this did not baulk the energies of other travellers, who were willing to resort to all sorts of shifts and devices rather than forego their share of exploration, and, in consequence, many short journeys were made which added much to our knowledge of the very interesting region about the ship.

A glance at the chart* will give some small idea of the confused conditions which existed to the south-west of our winter quarters, and it can be imagined that before our sledging commenced this district, on which we gazed at a distance of twenty or thirty miles, seemed to hold many mysteries. We could not tell whether the closer masses of land were connected, or whether, as seemed more

* Not reproduced in this edition.

probable, they were detached islands. Far away we could see long lines of irregular debris-strewn ice, but we could not say whence they came or what they indicated.

Taken as a whole, from the point of view of the map-maker, the general outline of the coast of Victoria Land is simple. The land is bold and well marked, and the coast is of a nature that lends itself to rough contouring; but, in marked distinction, the region of Ross Island has very intricate geographical features. The complication seems to start with that very curious formation which we called the Bluff, and which runs out in such a singularly thin, straight strip from the isolated volcanic cone of Mount Discovery. North of this, as will be seen, there are three large volcanic islands and a number of smaller islets, amongst which lie the rock-strewn remains of an ancient ice-sheet, with numerous vast and partly hidden moraines; while finally comes the great upheaval of Ross Island itself. The land masses as a whole, with their thousands of craters, great and small, show the result of a very remarkable volcanic outburst. For such light as was thrown on this region during the summer of 1902–3 we had to thank Koettlitz, Ferrar, Hodgson, Bernacchi, and others, who managed from time to time to collect a rough sledging outfit and to make short trips of a week or ten days towards the various points of interest. In this manner Koettlitz proved the insularity of the Black Island by surmounting the obstacles which had checked the first reconnaissance party, and succeeded in walking completely round it. On another occasion he examined the northern side of the Bluff, and on a third traversed much rough ice and ascended to the summit of Brown Island (2,750 feet), whence he and his companions were able to get some idea of what lay beyond.

In journeying to the south-west our travellers found it advisable to make for the northern coast of Black Island. As I have mentioned before, on such a track after crossing some four or five miles of recently formed ice, they rose from ten to fifteen feet in level to the surface of an older ice-sheet. The travelling continued good till within two or three miles of the island, when disturbances were met with, and it was necessary to cross lines of morainic material which streamed north from the eastern end of the island. This morainic material was principally composed of the black volcanic rock of the island, but amongst it could be found numerous blocks of granite, altogether foreign to the region. The island was surrounded by a well-marked tide-crack, which showed that the ancient sheet of rubble-strewn ice to the north was afloat. Amongst the huge heaps of rock material which it bore were found numerous remains of marine organisms, shells, polyzoa, worm-casts, and sponge spicules. There could be no doubt that in some manner the movement of the ice had lifted this material from below the water-level to its present elevation of perhaps fifteen or twenty feet above; but precisely how this had been accomplished it was impossible to say.

From any of the small peaks which fringed the Black Island the travellers could get a good view of the surface of the strait which separated them from the Brown Island, and this was a very impressive sight. From the base of Mount Discovery in the south, long ridges of morainic material spread out and entirely filled the strait, where they were disposed in wonderfully regular parallel lines which at first ran towards the north-east, but later swept round with perfectly uniform curves towards the north, in which direction they continued for some fifteen miles to the sea. Here, then, was the origin of that rough, water-worn tongue on which we had landed on our way to winter quarters.

The finer material of these long lines of rock debris was naturally blown by the wind in all directions, and, settling liberally between the lines, it had caught the rays of the sun, melted deep and irregular channels, and left standing a wild confusion of fantastic columns and pinnacles of ice. Seen from the distance the whole, as Koettlitz says, 'appeared like a tumultuous frozen sea with high crested waves curling towards us'.

To cross this confusion was no easy matter: long distances had to be done by portage, and in the thaw season the travellers had sometimes to take off shoes and stockings to cross rapid streams of water two and three feet in depth.

Whilst Black Island was formed of a very hard black volcanic rock, Brown Island was principally composed of lava and volcanic ash. The rock was much weathered, and had a deep, reddish-brown appearance, while scattered over this island to a height of 500 or 600 feet were found erratic blocks of granite.

There seemed every reason to suppose that Brown Island is joined to Mount Discovery, and at least our travellers were certain that there was no flow of ice between the two; away to the west they could see the long sweep of the Koettlitz Glacier growing rough and disturbed as it fell to the level of the sea.

The snow plateau to the south of Black Island was found to be from 100 to 150 feet above the level to the north, rising to the general barrier level; it afforded a comparatively smooth, easy crossing, undisturbed until within two miles of the Bluff, to reach which the travellers had again to cross lines of morainic material in which the volcanic rocks of the region were mixed with numerous boulders of granite. Taken together, these various observations gave a moderately clear outline of the ice condition in this region. The space inside the Brown Island is governed locally by the Koettlitz Glacier, but it is evident that the ice of the barrier itself is moving, or has moved, around the end of the Bluff, and close along its northern shore; thence it is pressing, or has pressed, northward through the two channels which separate the islands, the greater part passing round to the west of Black Island.

All this led up to a highly important and interesting discovery. We could not doubt that the decayed and water-worn ice on which we had landed on February 8, 1902, marked what was nothing less than the end of the lateral moraine of the Great Ice Barrier. When it is considered what a colossal agent for transportation this moraine must be, it is curious to find that it ends in such a tame manner.

Whilst these efforts at exploration had been going on in various directions, the ship had been left in the charge of Mr Royds. With people constantly going and coming, the numbers on board varied much; sometimes there might be ten or a dozen hands available for work, at others no more than four or five could be got together; but, whatever the number, all were kept steadily employed on the one most important task – that of freeing the boats.

I have already explained the calamity that had befallen us in this respect – how these indispensable articles of the ship's furniture had been placed on the ice, how they sank below the water level, and how we were forced to shovel away the snow to prevent them from going still deeper. This work of clearance was continued well on into the sledging season, as it was hopeless to attempt extrication until the night temperature had risen sufficiently to prevent the work of the day being wasted. This condition was not reached until the middle of December, and even then it was rarely that the thermometer stood above the freezing-point of salt water through-out the whole of the twenty-four hours, so that the work was greatly retarded.

When it was decided that the time had come to make an effort to free the boats, many shifts and expedients were tried. At first it was thought that something might be done by sprinkling ashes and dark volcanic soil over the ice, but it was found that the sun's rays were not sufficiently powerful or constant to make this device a success. As a next step, after all the snow was cleared off the surface of the floe, the ice-saw was brought into action, and a complete cut was made around that part of the ice-sheet in which the boats were embedded; but when this cut was finished it was found that, contrary to our hopes, the centre square refused to rise. Then efforts were concentrated on a single boat; the saw-cut was com-pleted about it, not altogether without injury to the boat, but even this small detached piece was held down in some inexplicable manner. Finally, in order to bring it up, small tins of gun-cotton had to be employed, and it was only after several explosions that the block was successfully brought to the surface.

In this position, the men, working knee-deep in slush, were able to dig out the inside of the boat, and bit by bit to clear away the ice which clung to the outside; then with shears and tackles she was slowly dragged from her icy bed. In this manner the first boat was got out, and then one by one the rest were extricated in like fashion.

As can be imagined, with so much sawing and blasting going on in the unseen depths of the ice below, it was not likely that the task could be accomplished without considerable injury to the boats, and when at length they had all been brought to the surface they presented a very dilapidated appearance, very different from that which they had possessed when first they had been incautiously placed on the floe. Of all our staunch whale-boats two only were in a condition to float, and it was evident that there would be many weeks of work for our carpenter before the remainder could be made seaworthy. Still, even the skeleton of a boat is better than no boat at all, and when on January 17 the last had been raised it was justly felt that a big load of anxiety had been removed.

Long before my departure to the south I had given instructions that the *Discovery* should be prepared for sea by the end of January; consequently after the boats had been freed, and as the sledge parties returned, everyone was very busily employed. To the non-nautical reader it may not be very clear what preparations for sea may mean in such circumstances, nor is he likely to understand what a lot of work they entailed on the few men who were available.

From the deck, tons and tons of snow had to be dug out with pickaxes and shovelled over the side; aloft, sails and ropes had to be looked to, the running-gear re-rove, and everything got ready for handling the ship under sail; many things which we had displaced or landed near the shore-station had to be brought on board and secured in position; thirty tons of ice had to be fetched, melted, and run into the boilers; below, steam-pipes had to be rejointed, glands repacked, engines turned by hand, and steam raised to see that all was in working order. But, not doubting that the ice would soon break up and release us, all this work was pushed forward vigorously, and in consequence, as I have remarked, on returning to the ship I found her looking trim and smart, and was told that all was ready for us to put to sea again.

But meanwhile the great event of the season had happened. The *Morning*, our relief ship, had arrived; and here, perhaps, I may be permitted to make a digression in order to explain how this had come about.

I have already shown the manner in which the necessary funds were raised for the *Discovery*, and how, after arduous efforts, enough money was collected to equip our expedition in a thoroughly efficient manner. This being the case, and there being no reason to suppose that the *Discovery* was in distress, it may not be quite clear why it was thought necessary to send a relief ship in the following year. Indeed, the reason will probably not be plain to anyone who is incapable of putting himself into the position of those who bore the responsibility of the expedition.

Taking any general case where an expedition is sent forth to the polar regions, it is evident that when it has passed beyond the limits of communication, the authorities who despatched it must bear some burden of anxiety for its safety; whilst they may hope that all will be accomplished without disaster, they cannot blind themselves to the risks that have been taken, and must inevitably ask themselves whether on their part they have done everything possible to avert mischance. If the expedition has departed without any definite plan, or has passed into a region in which it would be hopeless to search, those at home can do nothing; if, on the other hand, it has planned to pass by known but unvisited places, then it is obvious that its footsteps can be traced with the possibility of ascertaining its condition and of relieving distress. In this last case the proper action of the authorities is clear: they must endeavour to take no risk of their relief arriving too late, but do their utmost to despatch it as early as possible in the track of the first venture. Such has always been the attitude of those responsible for North Polar voyages, and in the South there is a further reason for its observance in the fact that the Antarctic Regions are surrounded by a belt of tempestuous ocean, across which it would be impossible for explorers to retreat should they have suffered the loss of their ship.

As soon as the *Discovery* had departed on her long voyage all these facts began to be practically considered, and the necessity of safeguarding the enterprise by the early despatch of relief was realised.

To raise the necessary funds for this second venture was no light task, but the Geographical Society recognised its responsibility and energetically supported its President in the campaign which he immediately opened with his customary energy and pertinacity. Urgent appeals were issued; a subscription list was opened and graciously headed by H.M. the King and H.R.H. the Prince of Wales; Mr Longstaff again came to the front with an addition of 5,000*l.* to his former munificent donation; Mr Edgar Speyer most generously subscribed a like sum.

From this start the fund gradually grew by the arrival of gifts from the most diverse and interesting quarters – from five great City Companies,* from boys at school, from members of the Stock Exchange collected by Mr Newall, from sub-lieutenants at Greenwich, from officers of a Gurkha regiment in Chitral, from the New Zealand Government, from officers in South Africa, and from a thousand private individuals who gave what they could afford. But, great as was the interest shown, as always on such occasions, its manifestation was slow, and there were times when it seemed almost impossible that the urgency of the case could be met. Sir Clements Markham, however, refused to acknowledge

* Goldsmiths, Fishmongers, Drapers, Mercers, and Skinners.

defeat; as usual, having set his shoulder to the wheel, he worked on in good times or bad with the same untiring zeal and singleness of purpose, and, as all who know of this troublous time most freely acknowledge, it was due to this alone that the sum of 22,600*l.* was eventually raised in time to make the despatch of the projected relief expedition possible.

Even this sum did not admit of elaborate plans in the equipment of the relief expedition; the greatest economy was necessary.

A stout wooden whaler named the *Morgenen*, or *Morning*, was purchased in Norway, and after being thoroughly refitted and overhauled by Messrs. Green, of Poplar, was stored with the requisites for the voyage.

At an early date her commander had been appointed, and this proved in every respect a most fortunate selection. Lieutenant William Colbeck, R.N.R., was at this time in the employment of Messrs. Wilson, of Hull, who generously lent his services; he had already been in the Antarctic Regions, having spent a winter at Cape Adare with Sir George Newnes's expedition, and he was therefore chosen as the most fitting person to command this new venture. Colbeck selected some of his officers and most of his men from amongst those with whom he was personally acquainted; many had served at one time or another in the Wilson Line. The Admiralty showed their interest in the enterprise by permitting two naval officers to join the expedition.

At length, all being prepared, the *Morning* left the London Docks on July 9, 1902, and after a long sea voyage, in which she rounded the Cape of Good Hope without touching land, on November 16 she duly arrived at Lyttelton, New Zealand, the base of all our operations. Here she received the same generous treatment which had been accorded to the *Discovery*, and on December 6 made her final departure for the South, stored with many an additional present supplied by the kindly thought of our New Zealand friends.

Here perhaps it is necessary to pause for a moment to consider the work which lay before Captain Colbeck and his crew.

Long before the *Discovery* had left New Zealand the idea of a relief ship had been mooted, and although I saw the great difficulties that were to be overcome in sending her, I felt confident that if the thing was to be done, Sir Clements Markham would do it. From any point of view it was desirable to leave as much information as possible in our track, and with this idea I had fore-shadowed the positions at which I hoped to be able to leave records, and had laid down a rough programme for any ship which might follow us. These instructions could only be indefinite; but such as they were, they stated that attempts would be made to leave information at one or more of a number of places – Cape Adare, Possession Islands, Coulman Island, Wood Bay, Frank-lin Island, and Cape Crozier. Especially in the last place, as the most southerly, I hinted that news of us might be looked for; the relief ship was to endeavour to pick up such clues as might be found in this way, but if this was unproductive or signified that we had passed to the eastward without returning, she was to turn homeward after having landed provisions and stores at certain definite spots.

It will be seen, therefore, that it was in order to act up to this pre-arranged plan that we had left records at such of the named places as we could approach, and that I had been so anxious to establish sledge communication with the record at Cape Crozier. For this enabled me to start south with the knowledge that a relief ship might gather meagre information at Cape Adare and Coul-man Island, whilst, should she recover the Cape Crozier record, she would at once ascertain our whereabouts.

Captain Colbeck's instructions were to fall in with the purport of my letter, but the manner in which he should do so was left entirely to his discretion, and wisely, for with such slender inform-ation as was available no-one could have acted more promptly or with greater discretion.

Thus it came about that whilst we were surmounting the diffic-ulties of the great snow-plain and finding a way amongst the mountain ranges, the gallant little *Morning* was hurrying towards us, eager to perform her helpful mission and bring us news of our distant home.

Small as she was, and without the ability to force a way through heavy pack-ice, her voyage to the South was full of adventure, and is a record of difficulties overcome by sturdy perseverance; but of this I hope that Captain Colbeck will himself tell one day. On December 25 he crossed the Antarctic Circle, and a short way to the south, to his great surprise, discovered some small islands which he has since done me the great honour of naming the Scott Islands. The pack was negotiated successfully, if slowly, and on January 8 a landing was effected at Cape Adare, where the notice of the *Discovery*'s safe arrival in the South was found. The Possession Islands were drawn blank, since we had not been able to land there. South of this the whole coast was found thickly packed; it was impossible to approach Coulman Island or Wood Bay, and the ship was obliged to keep well to the eastward to get any chance of an ice-free sea.

Franklin Island was visited on January 14, but without result, and again quantities of pack had to be skirted in making a way to Cape Crozier, so that it was not until 1 a.m. on the 18th that a landing was effected at this spot. Captain Colbeck himself joined the landing party, which spent some hours in searching for a sign of us. He had almost given the matter up in despair, and was despondently wondering what to do next, when suddenly our small post was seen against the horizon; a rush was made for it, and in a few minutes the contents of the tin cylinder were being eagerly scanned. It can be imagined with what joy the searchers gathered all the good news concerning us and learnt that they had but to steer into the mysterious depths of McMurdo Sound to find the *Discovery* herself; their work seemed practically accomplished.

But though they got hastily back to their ship, and started westward with a full head of steam, the goal was not yet reached. The channel between Beaufort Island and Ross Island was filled with an ugly pack in which the *Morning* could do little more than drift idly along, but fortunately this drift carried her steadily to the west, and on the 23rd our friends were able to free themselves from the ice, and, turning south, to round Cape Royds and recognise the landmarks which had been described and sketched for their instruction.

On board the *Discovery* the idea that a relief ship would come had steadily grown. For no very clear reason the men had gradually convinced themselves that it was a certainty, and at this time it was not uncommon for wild rumours to be spread that smoke had been seen to the north. It was therefore without much excitement that such a report was received on the night of the 23rd; but when, shortly after, a messenger came running down the hill to say that there was a veritable ship in sight, it was a very different matter, and few found much sleep that night whilst waiting and wondering what news that distant vessel might bear.

Early on the 24th a large party set out over the floe, and after marching a few miles could see clearly the masts and yards of the relieving vessel, which lay at the limit of the fast ice some ten miles north of the *Discovery*, and comparatively close to the Dellbridge Islets. The last mile was covered with difficulty, as here the ice was only a thin sludgy sheet which had formed since August, and which would only bear those who were fortunate enough to be wearing ski. There was much shouting and gesticulation, and one or two of the most eager, sinking waist-deep in the treacherous surface, had to be rescued with boards and ropes; but at last our party stood on the deck of the *Morning*, and the greetings which followed can be well imagined. Those who had remained in the *Discovery* were not forgotten, and soon the sledges were speeding back, dragged by willing hands and stacked high with the welcome mail-bags.

During the last week of the month the weather remained gloriously fine; some of the treacherous thin ice broke away, allowing the *Morning* to approach us by about a mile; otherwise all was placid. In the bright sunshine parties were constantly passing to and fro, and all gave themselves up to the passing hour in the delight of fresh companionship and the joy of good news from the home country, and with an unshaken confidence that the *Discovery* would soon be freed from her icy prison.

It was thus that I found things on my return on February 3, and when I and my companions, the last to open our letters, could report that all was well, we had the satisfaction of knowing that the *Morning* had brought nothing but good news.

CHAPTER 16

Our second winter

> And so without more circumstance at all
> I hold it fit that we shake hands and part. – SHAKESPEARE

> Come what come may
> Time and the hour runs through the darkest day.
> – SHAKESPEARE

It was a curious coincidence that Colbeck should have chosen the night of our return for his first visit to the *Discovery*. Up to this time he had felt reluctant to leave his ship, not knowing when a change of weather might occur, but on this day he had decided to visit the company to which he had brought such welcome intelligence, and soon after I had emerged from my first delicious bath and was revelling in the delights of clean garments, I had the pleasure of welcoming him on board.

In those last weary marches over the barrier I had little expected that the first feast in our home quarters would be taken with strange faces gathered about our festive table, but so it was, and I can well remember the look of astonishment that dawned on those faces when we gradually displayed our power of absorbing food. As we ate on long after the appetites of our visitors had been satisfied, there was at first mild surprise; then we could see politeness struggling with bewilderment; and finally the sense of the ludicrous overcame all forms, and our guests were forced to ask whether this sort of thing often happened, and whether we had had anything at all to eat on our southern journey.

But although we found our appetites very difficult to appease, for a fortnight after our return from the south our party were in a very sorry condition. Shackleton at once took to his bed, and although he soon made an effort to be out and about again, he found that the least exertion caused a return of his breathlessness, and more than once on entering or leaving the living-quarters he had a return of those violent fits of coughing which had given him so much trouble on the journey; now, however, after such attacks, he could creep into his cabin and there rest until the strain had worn off and some measure of his strength returned. With Wilson, who at one time had shown the least signs of scurvy, the disease had increased very rapidly towards the end. He had slightly strained his leg early in the journey, and here the symptoms were most evident, causing swelling and discolouration behind the knee; his gums also had dropped into a bad state, so he wisely decided to take to his bed, where he remained perfectly quiet for ten days. This final collapse showed the grim determination which alone must have upheld him during the last marches.

If I was the least affected of the party, I was by no means fit and well: although I was able to struggle about during the daytime, I had both legs much swollen and very uncomfortable gums. But the worst result of the tremendous reaction which overcame us, I found to be the extraordinary feeling of lassitude which it produced; it was an effort to move, and during the shortest walks abroad I had an almost unconquerable inclination to sit down wherever a seat could be found. And this lassitude was not physical only; to write, or even to think, had become wholly distasteful, and sometimes quite impossible. At this time I seemed to be incapable of all but eating or sleeping or lounging in the depths of an armchair, whilst I lazily scanned the files of the newspapers which had grown so unfamiliar. Many days passed before I could rouse myself from this slothful humour, and it was many weeks before I had returned to a normally vigorous condition.

It was probably this exceptionally relaxed state of health that made me so slow to realise that the ice conditions were very different from what they had been in the previous season. I was vaguely surprised to learn that the *Morning* had experienced so much obstruction in the Ross Sea, and I was astonished to hear that the pack was still hanging in the entrance of the Sound, and as yet showed no sign of clearing away to the north; but it was long before I connected these facts with circumstances likely to have an adverse bearing on our position, and the prospect of the ice about us remaining fast throughout the season never once entered my head.

My diary for this month shows a gradual awakening to the true state of affairs, and I therefore give some extracts from it, more especially as when the news of our detention first reached England it was half suspected that the delay was intentional, and it is doubtful whether that view has been entirely dissipated even yet.

'February 8. – We are expecting a general break-up of the ice every day, but for some reason it is hanging fire. This is the date of our arrival at Hut Point last year, and then the open water extended as far as the Point; it is evident that this season is very backward, and I do not like the way in which the pack is hanging about in sight of the *Morning*. It must go far to damp all prospects of the swell necessary for a general break-up. The *Morning* is eight miles away; very slowly she is creeping closer, but I do not think that she has advanced more than a quarter of a mile in the last week. We have been arranging the stores which are to be transferred, but it will be rather a waste of labour to transport them whilst the distance remains so great.

'Today England, Evans, and nine men came from the *Morning*, bringing us a fresh load of papers and some more luxuries, especially potatoes. At present I feel that if I had the power of poetic expression I should certainly write an ode to the potato. Can one ever forget that first fresh "hot and floury" after so long a course of the miserable preserved article?'

'February 10. – Today we gave a dinner party, the invitation being delivered across six miles of ice through the medium of the semaphore. Colbeck, Doorly, Morrison, and Davidson arrived as guests clad in good stout canvas suits and quite ready for the feast. They brought good news, for they reported that more than a mile of ice has broken away yesterday and this morning. We entertained our guests principally on the luxuries they had brought us, and there was little to be complained of in the fare; we had giblet soup, skua gull as an entrée, then our one and only turkey, and a joint of beef, with plum-pudding and jellies to follow. Truly we are living high in these days, and I ask myself whether it was really

I who was eating seal blubber a fortnight ago. After dinner we had the usual musical gathering, to which our guests brought a great deal of fresh talent. We have had a right merry night, and now all are coiled down to sleep; those who cannot find berths are snoring happily on the wardroom table.'

'February 12. – The weather has changed very much for the worse. The day of our return seemed to mark the last of the fine sunny summer; since that it has been almost continuously overcast, and our old enemy the wind returns at all too frequent intervals. Colbeck was weather-bound yesterday, but it gave us an opportunity of discussing the situation. If the ice is to be very late in breaking up, I think it is advisable that the *Morning* should not delay to await our release; she at least should run no risk of being detained, and it is to be remembered that she has little power to push through the young ice. We have decided to commence the transport of stores tomorrow; it will be tiresome work, but we ought to get it over in less than a fortnight.'

On February 13 the work of transferring the stores was commenced; it was arranged that the loads should be taken half-way by the *Morning*'s men, and from thence brought in by our own. It seemed at first that the *Morning*, with her smaller company, would have the heavier task, but this was avoided by a very liberal interpretation of the half-way point; in fact, the distance they covered gradually became little more than a quarter of the whole, whilst our parties took 3¾ hours to fetch the load in from the junction. The loads ran from 1,500 lbs. to 1,800 lbs., and in good weather two could be got across in the day, but the biting cold east wind was a great hindrance, and was felt more keenly at the *Discovery* end. It was in general especially strong about Hut Point, showing that, as we had suspected, chance had placed our winter quarters in the most windy spot in the vicinity.

Owing to this interference of the weather, by the 20th only eight loads had been brought in; on that day, therefore, we started an extra party, which went to the *Morning* in the forenoon and returned with a whole load in the afternoon. In this manner ten more loads were transported by the evening of the 23rd, and this completed the work except for sundry light articles. The manner in which the officers and men of the relief ship stuck to this very monotonous task was beyond praise; if anything had been wanting to show their ardent desire to assist us by every means in their power, this surely would have proved it. On our side, our people laboured for their own comfort, though, whatever the cause, they were little likely to jib at hard work; in fact, on this occasion there were not a few who, like Mr Barne, volunteered to make the double journey each day – a matter involving eleven or twelve hours of solid marching.

The goods which we thus obtained from our relief ship were none of them necessary to our continued existence in the South, but they were such as added greatly to the comfort of our position, and I do not use the word 'necessary' here in its strictest sense; as far as food is concerned, the absolute necessities of life are very limited, and in the South they were amply provided by the region in which we lived, for life could have been maintained on the seals alone. But although existence may be supported in this simple fashion, it is scarcely to be supposed that civilised beings would willingly subject themselves to such limitations, and therefore it is reasonable to include as necessaries such articles as not only make existence possible, but life tolerable.

From this broader point of view we were well equipped in the *Discovery*, and experience had taught us that we could continue to live with comparative comfort on very modest requirements. We had an ample stock of flour – enough to have lasted us for at least three years. To this might be added a large store of biscuit, which had been rarely used except on our sledge journeys. We were well provided with sugar, butter, pea-flour, tea, chocolate, jam, and marmalade, and had a moderate supply of lard, bottled fruits, pickles, cheese, and milk. With our holds thus stored we should have had little cause for anxiety for at least two or three years to come, but with the relief ship so well stocked it can be imagined that we were not long in considering how we might still further increase our comfort and provide for a greater variety in our fare. Our vegetables, both tinned and dried, had been a distinct failure, and it was in this, therefore, that we made our first call on the resources of the *Morning*. But besides this we had run very short of sauces, herbs, tinned soups, and articles of this nature, which were particularly desirable for cooking and seasoning our dishes of seal-meat. Our cheese, too, was not very satisfactory, whereas that brought by the *Morning* from New Zealand was in excellent condition; and although our tinned butter was very good, we were not long in discovering that the fresh New Zealand butter brought by the *Morning* was a great deal better.

The sledge loads which were dragged across the ice with so much hard labour during this month of February went, therefore, as far as food was concerned, to supplying minor deficiencies and to ensuring for us in the second winter a greater degree of comfort than we had enjoyed in the first; but, besides food, they contained other stores which, although we could have done without, we were exceedingly glad to have. In this manner we took the small quantity of engine-oil which the utmost generosity could spare, nearly a hundred gallons of paraffin, some finneskoes, mits, and socks, and some canvas and light material to repair our tattered garments.

'February 18. – . . . Yesterday I paid my first visit to the *Morning*, and although I took the journey very slowly, I found it an awful grind. Hodgson accompanied me and shared in a royal welcome. During the night the ship broke away twice and had to steam up and re-secure to the floe; it was strange to feel the throb of the engines once more. A few small pieces of ice are breaking away, but there is practically no swell, and the pack can still be seen on the northern horizon. At this time last year we had a constant swell rolling into the strait, but as I returned today the ice conditions were so stagnant that one begins to wonder whether our floe is going to break up at all. It is rather late in the day, but I have arranged to send some people down to the ice-edge to try the effect of explosions.'

'February 22. – Yesterday I took the explosive party down to the *Morning*. We made a hole about three hundred yards from the ice-edge, and sank a charge of 19 lbs. of gun-cotton about six feet below the surface. It blew up a hole about twenty feet in diameter, but the effect was altogether local; there were no extending cracks. We next tried closer to the edge, and sank the charge about thirty feet. The effect was better: a similar hole was made, but from it a few long cracks ran to right and left. Today two more charges were exploded near the cracks already formed; the cracks were increased in length and number, but no part of the floe was detached. I came to the conclusion that it was only a waste of material to continue these experiments further, and sent the party back. On the whole, I think, something might be done in this way towards breaking up the ice, but, if so, the business must be undertaken in a thoroughly systematic manner; we must be prepared to employ everyone at the work, and to expend gun-cotton with a lavish hand; it is far too late to commence such a big undertaking this year.'

'February 25. – . . . There is no doubt things are looking serious. The ice is as stagnant as ever; there has been scarcely any change in the last week. I have had to rouse myself to face the situation. The *Morning* must go in less than a week, and it seems now impossible that we shall be free by that time, though I still hope the break-up may come after she has departed. I have been busy all day writing despatches, and have drawn up a summary of our proceedings, as well as a more detailed description of our present position.

'Some time ago I decided that, if we are to remain on here, it will be with a reduced ship's company, and certainly without the one or two undesirables that we possess.

'Yesterday I had a talk to the men. I put the whole situation before them; I told them that I thought we should probably get out after the *Morning* had left, but it was necessary to consider the possibility of our not being able to do so, and to make arrangements for such a contingency at once. I said that I wished nobody to stop on board who did not do so voluntarily, and I hinted that I should be glad for a reduction in our numbers; anyone who wished to leave would be given a passage in the *Morning*.

'Today a list has been sent round for the names of those who desire to quit, and the result is curiously satisfactory. I had decided to reduce our number by eight, and there are eight names on the list, and not only that, but these names are precisely those which I should have placed there had I undertaken the selection myself.

'As regards the mess-deck, therefore, we shall be left with the pick of our company, all on good terms, and all ready, as they say, to stand by the ship whatever betides. Of course, all the officers wish to remain; but here, with much reluctance, I have had to pick out the name of one who, in my opinion, is not fitted to do so. It has been a great blow to poor Shackleton, but I have had to tell him that I think he must go; he ought not to risk further hard-ships in his present state of health. But we cannot afford to lose officers, and Colbeck has already kindly consented to replace Shackleton by his Naval sub-lieutenant, Mulock, and the latter is most anxious to join us.'

'February 26. – We have 84 tons of coal left in the *Discovery*. This will be enough for more than one winter, but will not be sufficient to allow us to do any further exploration if, as I hope, we get out of the ice; so I asked Colbeck to leave 20 tons on the Erebus glacier tongue. He came on board tonight with Skelton and Davidson to say that this was done yesterday. It appears that they had a great excitement last night, for as they came back to the ice-edge, for the first time they found a northerly swell rolling into the strait, and the ice was breaking up with extraordinary rapidity. In little more than half an hour nearly a mile and a quarter went out, and bets were being freely made that they would be up to Hut Point in the morning; but, alas! the swell lasted little beyond the half-hour, and after that all was quiet again.'

'February 28. – Colbeck has spent the last few days with us; he goes back tomorrow early, and with him go those of our party who are homeward bound. Then in the evening we are invited to a last feast before our gallant little relief ship turns her bows to the north.'

'March 2. – . . . Yesterday early our guests left us, and our returning members soon followed with their baggage. In the afternoon all our company, except two or three men and Wilson, set forth for the *Morning*, there to be entertained for the last time by our good friends; there was much revelry on the small mess-deck forward, and at the eight o'clock dinner aft seats had to be found for no fewer than sixteen; as the utmost seating capacity of the wardroom table was eight, the overflow had to be accommodated in the tiny cabins at the side, but this in no way detracted from the excellence of the dinner or the merriment of the evening. After a most satisfying meal we all gathered about the piano, the air became thick with tobacco smoke, and for the last time we raised our voices in the now familiar choruses. It was well into the small hours before this final merry-making came to an end, and the occupants of the crowded wardroom rolled themselves into blankets to snatch a few hours' rest.

'During the night the temperature had fallen to zero, and young ice had formed over the open water; it needed no great experience to see that it was quite time that our farewells were said. The morning proved overcast and gloomy, and as we snatched a hasty breakfast a strong south-easterly wind sprang up, drifting thick clouds of snow across the floe and dissipating the young ice to seaward. It was not a cheering scene for our leave-taking, but delay was impossible.

'At length we of the *Discovery*, with our belongings, were mustered on the floe; the last goodbyes had been said, and the last messages were being shouted as the *Morning* slowly backed away from the ice-edge; in a few minutes she was turning to the north, every rope and spar outlined against the black northern sky. Cheer after cheer was raised as she gradually gathered way, and long after she had passed out of earshot our forlorn little band stood gazing at her receding hull, following in our minds her homeward course and wondering when we too should be permitted to take that northern track.

'Then we turned our faces to the south, and, after a long and tiring walk against the keen wind, have reached our own good ship; so now we must settle down again into our old routine. If the ice does not break up we are cut off from civilisation for at least another year, but I do not think that prospect troubles anyone very much. We are prepared to take things as they come, but one wonders what the future has in store for us.'

'March 13. – I have abandoned all hope of the ice going out. The most optimistic members of our community still climb up the Arrival Heights in hopes of bringing back favourable reports, but it is long since they have been able to return with cheerful faces. We had a strong north-easterly blow on the 5th and 6th, during which hope ran high, and was followed by much excitement when Dellbridge dashed on board to say that nearly all the ice had gone out, and that the open water was little more than a mile from us. We ran out to see this pleasing prospect, but only to find that the report was based on a curious mirage effect, and that it would have been nearer the mark to have given four miles instead of one as the distance of the open sea. Since this incident there has been no change; heavy pack has again been seen to the north, and it is evident that there is no swell entering the strait.

'The weather is a great deal worse than it was last year; we have had much more wind and much lower temperatures; the thermometer has not been above zero since the 6th, but possibly this is due to the absence of open water about us. We were frozen in last year on the 24th, but the old ice had ceased to break away some time before that, and so I fear the chance of more ice going out now is very small.

'But meanwhile we have not been idle; we have determined to stick rigidly to our fresh-meat routine throughout the winter, and whenever the weather has permitted, our seal-killing parties have been away on their murderous errand. Already the snow-trench larder contains 116 frozen carcases. We have now thirty-seven mouths to feed, and an average seal lasts about a day and a half; later, when appetites fall off, it ought to run to two or two and a half days, so that we shall be safe in allowing an average of two days per seal.

'Our sportsmen, too, have been adding to our food supply, and have succeeded in killing over five hundred skuas; one would not have thought there were so many to be killed. These birds will form a good change to the regulation seal. Our ideas and customs have certainly changed: last year we regarded the skua as an unclean, carrion-feeding bird. It was Skelton who first discovered the error of our ways. Whilst sledging to the west he caught one in a noose, and promptly put it into the pot; the result was so satisfactory that the skua has figured largely on our menu ever since. In summer each appetite demands its whole skua, but in winter a single bird ought to do for two people; the legs and wings are skinny, but the breast is full and plump. Like all polar animals it is protected with blubber, and unusual precautions have to be taken to prevent the meat being impregnated with its rancid taste. The birds that have been shot for the winter have been cleaned and hung in the rigging, with their skins and plumage still on. It is found that when they are taken below and thawed out the skin can be removed without difficulty.

'Summing up our food supply for the winter, therefore, we seem to be in pretty good case.

> 116 seals should last about 230 days
> 551 skuas   ,,   ,,   ,,   25 ,,
> 20 sheep   ,,   ,,   ,,   20 ,,
>   Total 275 ,,

Of course some of the seal-meat will be required for sledging operations, and we must allow margins for accidents, but on the whole I think we ought to steer through the winter without difficulty. We deplore very heartily that we cannot add penguins to the variety of our fare, but it is long since any have approached the ship, and they are not likely to come now, across so many miles of ice.'

'March 14. – We have admitted the certainty of a second winter, and today orders have been given to prepare the ship for it. It is like putting the clock back: all our care and trouble in getting ready for the sea voyage are wasted. The boilers will be run down again, the engines pulled to pieces, small steam-pipes disconnected, ropes unrove and coiled away, the winter awning prepared, and snow brought in on the decks. The awning is in a very dilapidated state, and looks anything but fit to face the rigours of another season, but I suppose we shall be able to patch it up somehow. One thing we shall not do this year, and that is, place the boats out on the floe; those in the way of the awning will be carried over on to the land, in which it is to be hoped they will not sink out of sight.'

'March 20. – Today I went out on ski to Cone Hill, close to Castle Rock. The day has been fine, calm, with a bright sun, but the temperature has fallen to −20°. From the hill it was clear that the old ice had broken away a good deal since the *Morning* left, but it is still a long way from the ship – quite three and a half miles. The young ice nearly covers the sea, and must be getting pretty solid. There were a good many open leads in it, but very few seals were up, which is curious on such a fine day; yesterday we added twenty-eight to our stock, which ought now to be ample.

'On my walks I can rarely think of much else but our position and its possibilities. What does our imprisonment mean? Was it this summer or the last which was the exception? Does the ice usually break away around the cape, or does it usually stop short to the north? For us these must be the gravest possible questions, for on the answers depend our prospects of getting away next year or at all. It is little wonder that I think of these things continually and scan every nook and corner in hopes of discovering evidences to support my views; for I hold steadily to a belief that the answers are in our favour, and that our detention is due to exceptional conditions.

'The Ross Sea has certainly never been found in such a heavily packed state as it was this year, but how far this bears on the question one can only surmise. Coming more immediately to our neighbourhood, we have but one thing which can help us in the comparison of the two seasons – namely, the state of the old ice on our arrival. If this was one year's ice, as we supposed, then there must have been open water round the cape for two years in succession, and we could reasonably complain of ill fortune if there are many close seasons to follow; but the question is, Was what we found one year's ice? On our arrival we never doubted the fact, but for this reason we never looked critically at it, and now it is most difficult to remember the indications which we observed so casually more than a year ago. All sorts of complicated difficulties arise in thinking out this problem, yet if it were purely an academic one, I should long ago have given my opinion unhesitatingly in the direction I have indicated. But, alas! it is far too serious to be disposed of by the strongest expression of opinion, and no certain answer will come until we have waited to see what happens next year.

'So at the end of all my cogitations on this most important matter, I get little further than the knowledge that patience is an invaluable quality, and that it is not the least use worrying about the question now. I think this is pretty well the attitude of everyone on board, for although the subject sometimes crops up in conversation, it is generally dismissed as unprofitable: all are content to make the best of the present and hope for the best in the future.

'It is certainly a great matter for congratulation that we are rid of the undesirable members of our community; although they were far too small a minority to cause active trouble, there was always the knowledge that they were on board, mixing freely with others, ready to fan the flame of discontent and exaggerate the smallest grievance. No doubt it would have been possible to suppress this element as effectually during a second winter as during the first, but one grows tired of keeping a sharp eye on disciplinary matters, and it is an infinite relief to feel that there is no longer the necessity for it. With such an uncertain future before us, it is good to feel that there is not a single soul to mar the harmony of our relations, and to know that, whatever may befall, one can have complete confidence in one's companions.

'It is not until lately also that I realised how easily we could spare the actual services of those who have left; in fact, the manner in which the work is done now seems to show that they were a hindrance rather than a help to it. For instance, though I was unaffectedly glad to see the last of our cook, I was a little doubtful as to how we should manage in the galley department, but as things have turned out, we are doing infinitely better. It has been arranged that the cook's mate, Clarke, should be nominally the cook, and that volunteers from the crew should take spells of a fortnight or more as his assistant; this means practically that Clarke continues to make the excellent bread and cakes which we have always enjoyed, whilst the cooking is conducted more or less by a committee of taste, who collectively bring considerable knowledge to bear on the subject and take a huge delight in trying to make pleasing dishes. Of course, as is natural with such an arrangement, there are occasional failures, but on the whole it works admirably; the men are delighted with what might be termed the freedom of the galley, and at least they know now that everything is prepared with a proper regard for cleanliness.'

'March 23. – The sun is sinking rapidly, and already lamps are lit for dinner. It is curious to observe the varying effect which the summer has had on the ice about us. At the end of the winter it was from six to seven feet thick, but now at its thickest, in Arrival Bay, it is only five feet, whereas a few hundred yards away off Hut Point at one time it was almost melted through, while off Cape Armitage there was a large hole where it had disappeared altogether. Under this hole we have recently found a shallow bank of three fathoms, and we know there is another bank off Hut Point; there can be no doubt, therefore, that the melting takes place where the current runs rapidly over shallow places. In our small bay the ice is eight or nine feet thick, and in some places much more, but this is due to the quantity of snow which has fallen on its surface.

'It is strange how the tracks of footsteps remain indicated in the snow round about; as a rule, the compressed snow under each footprint remains firm, and is left like a small islet after the surrounding deposit has been swept away by the wind. In this manner the whole nature of the surface about our colony has been altered; it is surrounded by a hard trodden area from which radiate beaten highways in all directions. The hill slopes round about are quite spoiled for skiing purposes.'

'April 7. – With the exception of spreading the awning our preparations for winter are now pretty well completed. Snow has been brought in and distributed liberally over the decks, and has been banked up on each side opposite the living-quarters; guide-ropes to the screen and to the huts have been erected; one of the boats has been placed on the ice-foot, and the remainder so secured that they will be clear of the awning; leading away in various directions can be seen long lines of sticks and cask staves, which go to different fishing holes and other outlying stations for work. All these are due to the industry of Hodgson and Barne.

'The great game for the season is hockey; whenever the weather permits all hands join in the keen contests we hold on the floe. The game is played with light bandy-sticks and a hard ball made on board; it is just as well we have not the heavier sticks, as few rules are observed and figures can be seen flying about with sticks held high above their heads ready to deliver the most murderous blows, back-handed or front, as suits best. There is really no time to consider rules, and although there is the proper organisation of backs and forwards on each side, no-one wants to take the part of umpire. Occasionally there is a cry of "Offside!" but no-one pays very much attention.

'However, in spite of this, we have very exciting matches. Sometimes the officers play the men, sometimes we divide by an age limit, and sometimes in other ways. Today it has been "Married and Engaged v. Single", and as the former side lacked numbers we had to include in it those who were accused of being engaged, in spite of protest. The match was played in a temperature of −40°, and it was odd to see the players rushing about with clouds of steam about their heads and their helmets sparkling with frost. We played half-an-hour each way, which was quite enough in such weather. We shall, I hope, keep to this capital exercise until the light fails.'

'April 24. – On Wednesday the sun left us, and darkness is coming on apace; and so we are entering on the course of our second winter, but withal in the highest spirits, just as happy and contented a community as can be. It would be agreeable to know what is going to happen next year, but otherwise we have no wants. Our routine goes like clockwork; we eat, sleep, work, and play at regular hours, and are never in lack of employment. Hockey, I fear, must soon cease, for lack of light, but it has been a great diversion, although not unattended with risks, for yesterday I captured a black eye from a ball furiously driven by Royds.

'Our acetylene plant is now in full swing, and gives us light for twelve hours at an expenditure of about 3 lbs. of carbide. The winter awning is spread, and all is as snug as we can make it; but the temperature is extremely low, and we have the old trouble with the ice inside our living-spaces.'

'May 6. – A brilliant idea struck us a fortnight ago. We thought of putting our large fish-trap down on the shallow bank off the cape, and weighing it every few days to see what it contained. Visions of supplying our whole company with this delightful luxury were before our eyes. The fish-trap consists of a large pyramidal frame, six feet square on the base, and covered with wire netting, in which there are cone-shaped openings.

'In accordance with our idea, this trap was taken out to the bank, which is about a mile from the ship, and over which the ice is still comparatively thin. Here a high tripod was erected, a hole made, and the trap lowered; two days after it was got up again, and to our great joy we found it contained 105 fish. Our visions seemed realised; down went the trap again, and without a moment's delay we set about making another and digging a second hole close to the ship. This was no light task, and the workers were lost to view from above long before they reached the bottom of our solid ice, which proved to be more than eight feet thick. However, at length both traps were down, and since that we have been getting them up every other day; but, alas! there has been a most terrible falling-off in the catches. The outer trap fell from 105 to thirty, then to ten, and lately we are lucky if we find more than five or six. The inner has never had more than this last number, and sometimes comes up empty. One of the reasons for the failure of the outer trap is, I think, that the seals have found it, and feel that they ought to have first choice of the fish that it attracts, and this would naturally not be encouraging to the latter. Sometimes the seals must run full speed into the trap, because it often comes up badly dented; one can only hope it gives them a bad headache. Another great enemy to our fishing industry is the small shrimp–like amphipod; these small creatures collect in millions, and eat things up with extraordinary rapidity; they are submarine locusts, and vast armies of them settle on the bait, or even on the live fish, and in a few hours not a remnant remains of what they have attacked.

'The small bottom fish which we catch are very ugly little creatures; they have an enormous head, a protruding under lip, and a gradually tapering body – rather the shape of a whiting, only exaggerated. They are extremely good eating, but unfortunately the majority are very small; it takes two of the largest to make a decent meal for one person, and of the average size four or five will scarcely suffice. They are of the genus *Notathenia*, and I believe there is more than one species; the Weddell seals feed principally on these, but they also catch other sorts, whose present habitat we cannot discover by any of our fishing methods. Besides what we may call the Antarctic whiting, our people caught a quantity of a surface fish that frequented the pools and cracks in the ice during the summer. This was whilst I was absent from the ship, and I have neither seen nor tasted this fish, but I hear that it gave very good sport. Some of the men would go out for an hour or two with quite a short line and bread for bait, returning with a dozen or two decent-sized fish, which report declares to have been much better eating than even the whiting. Now that all the cracks are frozen over we do not get a glimpse of these fish, except when they are brought to view from the interior of a seal. We know that there must be lots of fish about from the continuance of the seals in our region, and we have strong reason for supposing that there must be some of a much greater size than any we have caught, but we have tried all sorts of methods and all sorts of baits without success in capturing anything but our whiting.

'The seal is certainly the best fisherman, and very frequently when one is captured our people have the benefit of its latest prey as well as the animal itself.

'As far as our fish-traps are concerned, I'm afraid as the darkness deepens our catches are likely to get smaller and smaller. Recently we have been saving up, so that the mess-deck should have a fish breakfast one Sunday and the officers the same on the next, but this will not continue, as we cannot hope to keep up the supply for so many months.

'Our winter routine of feeding is now pretty well fixed. We shall have mutton on Sunday as long as it will last, skua on Tuesday, seal's heart on Thursday, and plain seal on the other days. The kidneys are used to make seal-steak pie, an excellent dish; the liver comes at breakfast twice a week; and the sweetbreads I suppose pass as cook's perquisites, as we never see them aft. I am thinking of having cold tinned meat one night a week, so as to give the galley people a night off.'

'May 16. – We are getting record temperatures. Yesterday the minimum at the outer thermometer was –66°, and today I read it myself at –67.7°; the screen thermometer has not been below –55°, showing that we still enjoy the shelter of our comparatively warm corner. It would appear that this year is going to be much colder than last, but since March we have had far less wind than during the corresponding period of last year, and we could welcome a far severer cold if it assures us an absence of this scourge.

'Some of our costumes this year are very quaint. Our gaberdine wind clothes are badly worn, and what remains of them is being reserved for sledging; to take the place of these we have served out all sorts of odd scraps of material together with a large green tent which was brought south by the *Morning*. This has resulted in the most curious outer garments, and one may see a figure approaching in a pair of gaily striped and patched trousers and a bright green jumper, a combination of colour which in any other place could scarcely fail to attract marked attention.'

'June 12. – This week we have had the first blizzard for the winter, with some rather novel features. The wind has come and gone with surprising rapidity. Sometimes it has been blowing with extreme violence, harder than I have ever known it; at others it has been almost calm, with the air still filled with snow. The barometer has been hurrying down and up over a range of nearly an inch, and the thermometer rose at one time to +17½°. Last night the floor of the entrance porch was a swamp, whilst water was dripping from the sides and roof. It has never been in this state before during the winter. In many respects the gale has been the worst we have had, and yet, thanks to experience, we have weathered it without any of the minor mishaps of last year, except the temporary loss of our stove-pipe exhaust. From without the ship looks to be completely buried in snow.

'We are still at a loss for any warning of our approaching blizzards. The barometer only commences its vagaries after the storm is on us. There has been a suggestion that strong mirage is a sign of bad weather to come, but this fortunately is not the case, as very extraordinary mirage effects are constantly seen. At one time we had an idea that the electrometer might be taken as a guide, but this, again, seems to show little until the gale has actually begun.

'But although the electrometer may not serve us in this way, it has yielded some extremely interesting results. Bernacchi has continued to take regular observations with this instrument; he mounts it on a tripod and takes observations with the match conductor just above it, or hoisted on a pole fifteen feet high. He is thus able to discover the electrical potential at both these heights, though the task is not always a pleasing one, as the small screws of the instrument have to be manipulated with bared fingers. Once or twice Skelton has assisted Bernacchi in taking hourly observations over a considerable period. Perhaps the most interesting point is that there is almost continuously a negative potential in our regions, whereas in temperate regions the air is generally electro-positive to the earth.

'The observations at four feet and fifteen feet show that the difference of potential increases considerably with the altitude. During the summer months there is a perceptible daily range, with a maximum at midnight and a minimum at noon, and the potential is higher than in winter when there is no measurable range. When the air is filled with falling or drifting snow the potential becomes very large and the tension is often great enough to discharge the instrument.'

'June 23. – Our second mid-winter day has come and gone, finding us even more cheerful than the last. We made a great night of it last night; the warrant officers dined aft, and we had soup made from a real turtle sent to us by our kind friend Mr Kinsey, of Christchurch, and brought over in the last sledge-load from the *Morning*. After this came tinned halibut, roast beef with artichokes, devilled wing of skua as savoury, and the last of our special brand of champagne. On ordinary nights we are now reduced to enamelled plates and mugs, but we still hold in reserve some crockery and glass for these special occasions, and it adds to our cheer to see our table well appointed again.

'After dinner we felt we must have some novelty, so someone suggested a dance. The table was got out of the way, Royds went to the piano, and the rest of us assembled for a set of lancers, one of the most uproarious in which I have ever indulged. Then came cock-fighting and tugs of war, and altogether we had as festive an evening as we have ever spent.'

'July 3. – Our winter is speeding along in the pleasantest fashion, and all are keeping in good health and spirits. Our puppies of last year are puppies no longer, but have developed into dogs, showing all the unmerciful, bullying traits of character of their parents. In all there are eight survivors of last year's litters: "Blackie", "Nobby", "Toby", and "Violet" are descendants of poor "Nell", "Roger" and "Snowball" of "Blanco", and "Wolf " and "Tin-tacks" of "Vincka". The different families are not at all fond of one another, nor is there any wild attachment between members of the same. However, we have decided they must take care of themselves and settle their own grievances, as, although they may be useful next year, we do not propose to take them on long journeys; they are therefore allowed to roam about as they please, though kennels are provided for them, and of course they are regularly fed. The result of this freedom is that there are already new families of puppies arriving on the scene. The greater number of these must be removed, as it cannot be hoped that they will be anything but poor creatures; meanwhile there has been a searching for names, and the latest suggestion is a series including "Plasmon", "Soma-tose", and "Ptomaine"!

'I am taking rather longer walks over the hills than I did last winter, as I want to be thoroughly fit for the sledging. As a rule four or five of the dogs come with me, and my appearance outside is the signal for a chorus of welcome; as we go up the hills my companions scrimmage, playfully or otherwise, the whole time; then their delight is for me to roll stones down the steeper slopes, when they dash after them at a prodigious speed and in a smother of snow. They are wonderfully sure-footed, and will sometimes bring themselves up in mid-career with extraordinary suddenness, and come trotting up the slope as though it was the easiest of feats.'

'July 13. – Yesterday Wilson reported an eruption of Erebus, a considerable sheet of flame bursting forth and lighting up the rolls of vapour, so that he could clearly see the direction in which they were going – a fact impossible to distinguish either before or after; the flare only lasted for five or ten seconds. These eruptions have been seen before, and possibly many have occurred without being seen, but they are certainly not frequent, and never last for more than a few seconds. I myself have never seen more than a red glare on the cloud of vapour immediately over the crater.'

'July 16. – Hodgson has been working away throughout the winter in the same indefatigable manner as before. His fish-traps and tow-nets merely go down through a hole in the ice, and there is no great difficulty about working them, but the manner in which he has carried out his dredging is really very cunning, and deserves description. Now and again, and especially after a cold snap, fresh cracks are formed in the ice-sheet across the strait, and these open out perhaps two or three inches. Before the space left has time to freeze thickly, Hodgson goes out with a long line, and presses the bight down between the sides of the crack until it is hanging in a long loop between points two or three hundred yards apart. Then at each end of the loop he starts to dig a large hole; this is the work of several days, and meanwhile the ice along the crack has become solid and thick, but this does not matter when once he has got what he wants – namely, two holes connected by a line which passes underneath the ice.

'Later on, when the holes are completed and shelters have been erected about them, the more important work commences. A net is secured to the line and lowered to the bottom at one hole, whilst at the other the line is manned and gradually hauled in; thus the net is dragged along the bottom to the second hole, where it is hoisted out and its contents emptied into a vessel. Then the process is repeated by hauling the net back to the first hole. Finally the vessel, usually an old tin-lined packing-case, with its precious contents of animals buried in a mass of hardening slush, is sledged back to the ship and deposited close to the wardroom fire.

'On the following day the table is littered with an array of glass jars and dishes, with bottles of alcohol, formalin, and other preservatives, and soon we are able to examine the queer denizens of our polar sea-floor, and to watch their contortions as they are skilfully turned into specimens for the British Museum.'

'July 31. – For some days there has scarcely been any wind, and we have been able to enjoy delightful walks in the light noontide.

The northern horizon at this hour is dressed in gorgeous red and gold, and the lands about are pink and rosy with brightness of returning day. I am not sure that a polar night is not worth the living through for the mere joy of seeing the day come back.

'The latest addition to our forces, in the shape of Mulock, has been a great acquisition. In one way and another we have collected a very large amount of surveying data, but the trouble was that we none of us had sufficient knowledge to chart it. Mulock came in the nick of time to supply the deficiency; he has been trained as a surveyor, and has extraordinary natural abilities for the work. He has done an astonishing amount this winter, first in collecting and reworking all our observations, and later in constructing temporary charts. A special table was fixed up for him in my cabin, where he now spends most of his time. The result of his diligence is most useful to me, as I can now see much more clearly what we ought to try to do during our next sledging season.'

'August 1. – Walks over the hills are now delightful. However cold one may be on starting, by the time one reaches the crest one's blood is circulating freely, and the rest is wholly enjoyable. A good look at the glorious scene round about, a long trot over the hill plateau, an observation of Erebus with its gilded coil of smoke, a half slide, half shuffle down some convenient snow-slope amidst two or three scrambling, skylarking dogs, a sharp walk back over the level, and a glorious appetite for tea to follow: there is not much hardship about this sort of life.

'Perhaps Barne has enjoyed himself as much as anyone this winter in his own queer way. The improved weather has given him a chance to spend many a day at his distant sounding holes, and he has constantly departed soon after breakfast to vanish from our ken until dinner. But this winter he has rigged his small sledge with sails, and if it has not aided his work much, it has given him a deal of extra amusement. The sledge carries a small sounding machine, mounted high on a box in the centre. The box contains a miscellaneous collection of sinkers, thermometers, &c., together with the owner's light midday repast. In front of and behind the box are the main and mizzen masts, to which are hoisted a dashing suit of sails, made from the drop scene of the Terror Theatre. There is also a drop keel or lee board, made from a piece of boiler-plate, and a wooden outrigger, which can be placed on either side and weighted with a sinker to increase the stability of the machine. Barne declares that if there is any breeze his noble craft sails like a witch, on or off the wind, but this is scarcely the opinion of others who have watched his movements. However, when the *Flying Scud*, as she is called, is lying astern of the *Discovery* with sails neatly furled, or when with all canvas spread she is prepared for her voyage over the floe, she at least looks a very imposing and business-like tender.'

'August 13. – For three days we have had a furious blizzard, which has kept us closely confined. On the few occasions when we attempted to reach the ship side we found it almost impossible to stand, and there was a curious suffocating feeling in battling with the whirling drift. Some gusts were so violent that the ship was shaken, and things hanging in the wardroom were set on the swing, notwithstanding that the ice must now be from eighteen to twenty feet thick immediately around us. On Tuesday, with a lull, the glass rose three-quarters of an inch in six hours – about the steepest gradient we have known. It then fell again sharply, and the wind returned in full force. Today it is quite calm again, and we can see that there has been an immense deposition of snow; the ice-sledges are covered, and the surface has risen to the level of the meteorological screens. From the hills I could see no sign of open water – a curious difference from last year, when after such a gale the sea would certainly have been open up to the Northern Islets.'

'August 20. – Some time ago poor little "Tin-tacks", who has a litter of pups in the after deckhouse, was found with her mouth covered with blood; she was unable to eat, and on examination Wilson found that her tongue had been torn or cut off within an inch or two of the root. The only fitting theory seems to be that the poor beast got it frozen to a tin and then became frightened, and jagged or bit it off. It was a horrible accident, but it shows the astonishing vitality of these dogs that within a few days she was able to eat and ran about as though nothing had happened; she had evidently quite ceased to suffer pain. But although she can feed herself she cannot keep herself clean, and she is likely to get into such a bad state in this way that I fear we shall have to kill her.

'Wilson has found a hard, calcareous growth in the seals' hearts which appears to show that these animals suffer from gout!

'We have seen some very beautiful "mother-of-pearl" clouds to the north lately – little patches of yellowish-white close to the horizon, edged with pale green passing to red and yellow, this bordering extending all around. The prismatic colouring we have hitherto seen in the light high cirrus has been horizontal only. The Danish Lapland Expedition noted prismatic clouds as having a height of thirty miles; ours are certainly nothing like so high.'

'August 21. – The rim of the refracted sun could just be seen above the northern horizon at 12.30 today. I climbed Arrival Heights and got a view of the golden half-disc. It was a glorious day; everything was inspiriting. For the first time for many a month the sun's direct rays were gilding our surrounding hills; little warm, pink clouds floated about, growing heavier towards the south, where the deepening shadow was overspread with a rich flush; the smoke of Erebus rose straight in a spreading golden column. It was indeed a goodly scene! One feels that the return of day is beyond all power of description – that splendid view from the hills leaves one with a sense of grandeur and solemnity which no words can paint.

'And now our second long polar night has come to an end. I do not think there is a soul on board the *Discovery* who would say that it has been a hardship. All disappointment at our enforced detention has passed away, and has been replaced by a steady feeling of hopefulness. There is not one of us who does not believe that we shall be released eventually, however difficult he might find it to give his reasons. All thoughts are turned towards the work that lies before us, and it would be difficult to be blind to the possible extent of its usefulness. Each day has brought it more home to us how little we know and how much there is to be learned, and we realise fully that this second year's work may more than double the value of our observations. Life in these regions has lost any terror it ever possessed for us, for we know that, come what may, we can live, and live well, for any reasonable number of years to come.'

'August 25. – The earth shadows on the southern sky thrown by the sun as it skims along the northern horizon have been very distinct this year, and there is much that cannot be explained and therefore gives rise to hot argument. Between nine and ten in the morning a dark shaded line, inclined to the right at an acute angle to the horizon, appears to the westward of the Black Island; this line gradually rises to the vertical to the east of Black Island, and then sinks to the left with a diminishing angle. Just before noon its extremity rests on the Bluff, when it is inclined well to the east, but sometimes at about this time two other shadows spring up, one vertical and the other inclined to the west; the whole phenomenon then has the appearance of an inverted broad arrow.

'It is very curious and interesting, and we have failed to produce any sound explanation for it. It must in some way be connected with Erebus, as it is on the opposite side of it to the sun; but what particular parts of the mountain mass trace these confused shadowy lines we cannot guess. Some of us have tried to drag in the western mountains as reflecting agents, but I think this theory has little to support it. Meanwhile we have all been busy with candles and sheets of paper trying to reproduce the various effects, but so far without much success.

'Beyond the region of our bay the snow which has fallen during the winter is heaped into patches which are clearly distinguishable from the old surface, on which can still be seen in large numbers the pellets of the cartridges used in the skua battues of last autumn. We have started our hockey matches again, and had some excellent games, but the ground is in very poor condition, with patches of soft snow where the ball gets half buried.'

'September 3. – After the return of the sun there are some very pleasing signs of summer, for which we watch eagerly. Amongst these are the first records of our solar instruments, one of which, the radiation thermometer, gave its first indication on the 28th, when there was an extremely slight difference between the black and silvered bulb thermometers. This instrument faces the sun on Hut Point, and today it showed a very marked difference between the two readings; and at the same time another instrument, the sunshine recorder, gave its first sign of life. The sunshine recorder consists of a crystal sphere, by which the sun rays are focussed on a circular strip of graduated paper; when the sun is out, the track of the focus is marked by a burnt line, and in this way the hours during which the sun shows are recorded. Last year we got several papers burnt for the complete twenty-four hours, and doubtless we shall get the same again; I believe this is the first time such a record has been got.'

Such extracts as I have given from my diary show that our second winter passed away in the quietest and pleasantest fashion. Throughout the season the routine of scientific observations was carried out in the same manner as it had been during the previous year, whilst many new details of interest were added. The weather on the whole, though colder, had been far less windy, and this, together with the help which experience gave to our methods of living, had greatly added to our comfort. Whilst everything was taken calmly and easily, the work of preparation for the coming season had been steadily pushed forward. An examination of our sledge equipment showed that there was scarcely an article which did not need to be thoroughly overhauled and refitted, and throughout the winter our men had been systematically employed in repairing the sledges, sleeping-bags, tents, &c., in weighing out and packing the various provisions, and generally in preparing for the long journeys which had been arranged. With our best efforts, however, it was evident that our outfit for this season would be a somewhat tattered and makeshift affair compared with what it had been at the commencement of the last. For our sleeping-bags we were obliged to employ skins that we knew to be of inferior quality; our tents were blackened with use, threadbare in texture, and patched in many places; our cooking-apparatus were dented and shaky; our wind clothes were almost worn out; and for all the small bags which were required for our provisions we were obliged to fall back on such sheets and tablecloths as could be scraped together.

As in the previous year, the plan of campaign for the coming season had been drawn up in good time, so that everyone might have ample opportunity of preparing himself for the work; and in the peaceful quiet of the winter it had been easy to see the weak places in our former explorations and the directions in which the future journeys should be made.

Perhaps here, therefore, it would be well to mention briefly the considerations which led me to the adoption of the programme of sledging carried out during our second year.

The first point was of course to review our resources; as before, I knew that extended journeys could only be made by properly supported parties, and an easy calculation showed me that our small company would only admit of two such supported journeys, though numbers might permit of a third more or less lengthy journey without support.

The next thing was to decide in what direction these parties should go. In this connection, as I have already explained, the principal interest undoubtedly lay in the west; to explore the Ferrar Glacier from a geological point of view and to find out the nature of the interior ice-cap were matters which must be attempted at all hazards.

In the south it was evident to me that however well a party might march, or however well they might be supported, without dogs they could not hope to get beyond the point which we had reached in the previous year; but our journey had been made a long way from land, and had consequently left many unsolved problems, chief amongst which were the extraordinary straits which had appeared to us to run through the mountain ranges without rising in level. It was obviously absurd for us to pretend that we knew all about these places when we had only seen them at a distance of twenty or thirty miles; any further light thrown on these, or on the junction of the barrier with the land, must prove of immense interest to us. It was therefore with the main object of exploring one of these straits that I decided that the second supported party should set forth.

The credit for arranging the direction in which the unsupported party should go really belongs to Bernacchi, for it was he who first asked me what proof we had that the barrier surface continued on a level to the eastward. Since the previous year, and having regard to the barrier edge in this direction, we had assumed this fact, but when I came to look into it I found we really had no definite proof. The only way to obtain it was to go and see, and this was therefore named as the objective of the unsupported party, who affected to believe that they were destined to discover all sorts of interesting land arising through the monotonous snow-plains for which they were bound. Besides the longer journeys, the programme for the season included, as before, a number of short journeys for specific purposes. The most important of these were periodic visits to the Emperor penguin rookery, as we hoped that this year our zoologist would be able to observe the habits of these extraordinary creatures from the commencement of their breeding season.

The next step in this programme was the most difficult of all; it was to name the individuals for the various journeys. When all had supported me so loyally, and when all were so eager to go to the front, it can be imagined what a hard task lay before me in making a selection. However, this difficulty, like others, was gradually overcome by much thought, and the various parties were told off. The journey to the west I decided to lead myself, that to the south I entrusted to Barne and Mulock, whilst the two officers named for the south-eastern effort were Royds and Bernacchi.

Finally, it was decided that one important factor must dominate all our sledging arrangements. We knew that we were mainly at the mercy of natural causes as to whether the *Discovery* would be freed from the ice in the coming year, but at least I determined that as far as man's puny efforts could prevail, nothing should be left undone to aid in the release of the ship. At the earliest date at which we could hope to make any impression on the great ice-sheet about us, the whole force of our company must be available for the work of extrication; consequently the last of the summer must be sacrificed, and it was ordered that all sledging journeys should start at such a date as to assure their return to the ship by the middle of December.

Thus when the sun returned again in 1903 it found us ready to start on our journeys once more, and only waiting with impatience for the light which was to guide us on our way. The story of these journeys I reserve for a future chapter, but in what state of health and spirits we undertook them can be gathered from the following:

'September 6. – Tomorrow we start our sledging; the Terror party go to Cape Crozier. The ship is in a state of bustle, people flying to and fro, packing sledges, weighing loads, and inspecting each detail of equipment. To judge by the laughter and excitement we might be boys escaping from school. The word "scurvy" has not been heard this year, and the doctor tells me there is not a sign of it in the ship. Truly our prospects look bright for the sledge-work of the future.'

CHAPTER 17

Commencement of our second sledging season

Parties Starting – Away to New Harbour – We Find a Good Road, Establish a Depot, and Return – Sledging in Record Temperatures – Experiences in Different Directions – Emperor Penguin Chicks – Eclipse of the Sun – A Great Capture – Preparing for the Western Journey – Ascending Ferrar Glacier – Our Sledges Break Down – Forced to Return – Some Good Marching – Fresh Start – More Troubles with the Sledges – A Heavy Loss – Wind from the Summit – The Upper Glacier – A Week in Camp – We Break Away and Reach the Summit – Hard Conditions – Party Divided – Eight Days Onward – An Awe-inspiring Plain – We Turn as the Month Ends

> Where the great sun begins his state
> Robed in flames and amber light. – MILTON

> Path of advance! but it leads
> A long steep journey through sunk
> Gorges, o'er mountains in snow. – M. ARNOLD

When the great sun had begun his state in 1903 we were all, as I have said, eager to be off on our travels once more.

Royds and Wilson were the first to get away, on September 7; they had with them four men – Cross, Whitfield, Williamson, and Blissett; their mission lay on the old track to Cape Crozier, and the object of going thus early was to catch those mysterious Emperor penguins before they should have hatched out their young.

Barne and his party were timed to start some days later, with the idea of laying out a depot beyond the White Island, in preparation for the longer journey to come.

On the 9th I got away with my own party, which included Mr Skelton, Mr Dailey, Evans, Lashly, and Handsley. Our object was to find a new road to the Ferrar Glacier, and on it to place a depot ready for a greater effort over the ice-cap. I pause a moment to recall to the reader the position of affairs in this region. The Ferrar Glacier descends gradually to the inlet, which we named New Harbour, but it will be remembered that Mr Armitage had reported most adversely on this inlet as a route for sledges, and in conducting his own party had led it across the high foothills. I had not been to this region, but in the nature of things I could not help thinking that some practicable route must exist up the New Harbour inlet, and I knew that if it could be found our journey to the west would be made far easier. It was in this direction, therefore, that I set out with my party.

Half-way across the strait we had the misfortune to encounter a blizzard, which delayed us in our tents and effectually covered all our camping equipment with ice; then the temperature fell rapidly, and we knew that our discomfort for the trip was ensured. Owing to the delay we did not reach the New Harbour until the 13th, and it took us the whole of the daylight hours of the 14th to struggle up the south side of the inlet to the commencement of the disturbances caused by the glacier.

The night of the 14th was an anxious one, and I remember it well. On each side of us rose the great granite foothills. The light had been poor in the afternoon march, and now that the sun had sunk behind the mountains in a crimson glow, we were left with only the barest twilight. We had been forced to camp when we had suddenly found ourselves on a broken surface, and all about us loomed up gigantic ice-blocks and lofty morainic heaps. To-morrow was to decide whether or not these obstructions could be tackled; meanwhile the temperature had fallen to $-49°$, and in the frigid gloom our prospects did not look hopeful.

On the following day, however, with cheerful sunshine to aid our efforts, we proceeded for some way up the bed of a frozen stream, still on the south side of the glacier. On our right was the glacier itself, distorted into a mass of wall faces and pinnacles, which looked unscalable, whilst on our left were the steep bare hillsides; soon the glacier stream came to an end, and we were forced to consider what was next to be done.

As a result of our consultation some of the party climbed the hillside to prospect, whilst Skelton and I attacked the glacier. We fully expected to discover a mass of broken ice extending right across the inlet, but were agreeably surprised to find, first, that by carefully selecting our route we could work our way to the summit of the disturbance; and, secondly, that beyond our immediate neighbourhood the high, sharp ice-hillocks settled down into more gradual ridges. This implied that to the north things were smoother, and after our short reconnaissance and a confirming report from the hills, we occupied the rest of the day in carrying our loads and sledges in the direction we had chosen across the disturbance. It was a difficult portage, but by night we were camped in a small dip well in on the glacier surface.

Those who have seen glaciers in a mountainous country will recall the regular and beautiful curves they present in sweeping around the sharp turns of the valleys they occupy. It was such a curve that the Ferrar Glacier now showed us as we looked westward on the morning of the 16th; its surface, as we afterwards found, was comparatively regular, but in the distance it looked like a smooth polished road – a ribbon of blue down the centre of which ran a dark streak caused by a double line of boulders. On each side towered the massive cliffs and steep hillsides which limited its course. But the foot of this promising road was some way from us, and we had still four or five miles of unviewed surface to cross before we could reach it. Here, again, we were agreeably surprised, for instead of further ice disturbances we found our way gradually growing smoother, and in the afternoon we reached the incline without further difficulty.

What followed was easy. We proceeded to ascend the smooth icy surface of the glacier until we came abreast of Cathedral Rocks, and when their lofty pinnacles towered three or four thousand feet immediately above our heads we selected a conspicuous boulder in the medial moraine, about 2,000 feet above the sea, and, ascertaining its bearings, 'cached' the provisions which we had brought, and turned homeward.

The result of our short journey had been really important. It had taken the western party of the previous year three weeks to reach the spot at which we had left our depot; I knew now it would go hard with us if we could not get there well within the week, and if in the future we found a still easier road, avoiding the portage stage, we might hope to journey out in four or five days.

On our return, therefore, we steered more to the north, and to our further delight found that the route in that direction was much easier, so that eventually we reached the sea-ice without having to carry our sledges across any difficult places.

The south side of a glacier

The fact which was thus discovered, and which was amply supported by further observations, is a general one that is highly important to future explorers. In all cases in the Antarctic Regions where glaciers run more or less east and west, the south side will be found very much broken up and decayed, whilst the north side will be comparatively smooth and even. The reason is a very simple one – so simple that it seems to argue some obtuseness that we did not guess its effect. The sun of course achieves its greatest altitude in the north, and consequently its warmest and most direct rays fall on the south side of a valley, and on the loose morainic material and blown débris that rest on that side of a glacier. Here, therefore, the greater part of the summer melting takes place with irregular denudation, causing the wild chaos of ice disturbance that I have described.

At the foot of the Ferrar Glacier, Armitage had seen the disturbance on the south side, and had concluded that it must extend right across; our fortunate step had been to push over the southern disturbance and find the easier conditions beyond.

Throughout this short journey we had exceedingly low temperatures. Nearly every night the thermometer fell below −50°, and in the daytime it was very little above that mark. After the effects of our blizzard we were extraordinarily uncomfortable; it was partly for this reason, and partly to test the real marching capabilities of my party, that, our object attained, I decided to put on the speed in crossing the fifty miles of sea-ice which lay between us and our snug ship. We crossed this stretch in less than two and a half days; we were to do better marching still under better conditions, but at the time we were very pleased with this effort, and considering the excessive cold and our heavily clad and ice-encumbered condition, it was certainly worthy of note. It was on the night of the 20th, therefore, that we tramped into our small bay and saw the pleasantly familiar outlines of the ship.

We were inclined to be exceedingly self-satisfied; we had accomplished our object with unexpected ease, we had done a record march, and we had endured record temperatures – at least, we thought so, and thought also how pleasant it would be to tell of these things in front of a nice bright fire. As we approached the ship, however, Hodgson came out to greet us, and his first question was, 'What temperatures have you had?' We replied by complacently quoting our array of minus fifties, but he quickly cut us short by remarking that we were not in it. It was evident, therefore, that we should have tales to listen to as well as to tell.

For such tales I draw once more on my diary.

'September 22. – It is pleasant to be back in the ship again after our hard spring journeys. They have awakened us all and given us plenty of fresh matter to talk about, so that there is a running fire of chaff and chatter all day. Everything looks very bright and hopeful: the journeys have accomplished all that was expected of them, and there is not a sign of our old enemy the scurvy; and this in spite of the fact that our travellers have endured the hardest conditions on record.

'It is no small tribute to our sledging methods that our people have come through temperatures nearly seventy degrees below zero without accident or injury; a tent and a sleeping-bag have never protected men under such conditions before.

'Whilst we have been away there seems to have been a cold snap throughout our region. Barne with his party got the worst of it, as they were away out on the barrier, where conditions are always most severe. He was absent for eight days, and succeeded in laying out a depot to the S.E. of White Island. His party consisted of Mulock, Quartley, Smythe, Crean, and Joyce; all have tales to tell of their adventures, and agree that it was pretty "parky". The temperature was well below −40° when they left the ship; it dropped to −50° as they reached the corner of White Island, and a little way beyond to −60°; but even at this it did not stop, but continued falling until it had reached and passed −65°. At −67.7° the spirit-column of the thermometer broke, and they found it impossible to get it to unite again; we shall never know exactly, therefore, what degree of cold this party actually faced, but Barne, allowing for the broken column, is sure that it was below −70°.

'Joyce was the only one who suffered seriously from these terribly severe conditions. After his features had been frostbitten several times individually, they all went together, and he was seen with his whole face quite white. Though, of course, it is in a very bad state now, the circulation was restored in it at the time without much difficulty; but worse was to follow, for on the march he announced that one of his feet was gone, and, having pitched the tents, Barne examined it, and found that it was white to the ankle. It was quite an hour before they could get any signs of life in it, and this was only accomplished by the officers taking it in turns to nurse the frozen member in their breasts.

'All the party, and especially the owner of the frozen foot, seem to regard this incident as an excellent jest; but for my part I should be slow to see a joke when I had a frostbitten foot myself, or even when I had to undo my garments in a temperature of −70° to nurse someone else's. It appears that those who were giving the warmth found that they could keep the icy foot in contact with their bodies for nearly ten minutes, but at the end of that time they had to hand it on to the next member of the party; they own that it was not a pleasing sensation, but think that it increased their appetites. However, their ministrations have brought Joyce safely back to the ship with his full allowance of toes, which is the main point.

'Royds and his party also had very low temperatures, as their thermometer often showed −60°, and at the lowest −62°. Blissett was the chief sufferer on this journey, as he also had his face very severely frostbitten; the rest seem to have stood it well, and Whitfield is described as standing outside the tent with his pipe in his mouth, his hands in his pockets, and the air of cheerful satisfaction of one who contemplates his garden on a warm summer day at home.

'This party have had a great stroke of luck. On arriving at Cape Crozier it was found, in spite of calculations, that the Emperors had already hatched out their young; about a thousand adult birds were seen, and a good number of chicks, but at first there appeared to be no eggs. The luck came when the travellers examined the ice towards the land and found that there had been a recent fall of ice-blocks; close to this they discovered a number of deserted eggs. It seems evident that the avalanche frightened away the sitting birds, much to the benefit of our collection. Including the single find of last year we have now seventeen specimens of this new egg; some are cracked, but a good number are whole; they weigh about a pound apiece.

'As may be imagined, the party were highly elated with this find, and Wilson was glad of the opportunity of studying the chicks at a more tender age than they were seen last year. In spite of the severe temperature, Cross determined to try to bring two of these small mites home. He sacrificed his sleeping-jacket to keep them warm, and tended them with such motherly care that he has succeeded in his design, and now these small creatures are housed in Wilson's cabin, much to our amusement. They chirrup like overgrown chickens, and possess the most prodigious appetites.'

These chicks continued to afford us entertainment; they had no fear whatever, and when they thought that the time had come for more food, they clamoured loudly for it.

At first they were fed on crustaceans, and afterwards on seal-meat, but both of these were chewed up by the person who fed them, so that there should be no chance of indigestion. It was obvious from their shape that they were well designed as regards capacity for containing food, but even allowing for the fact that they did not study the symmetry of their waists, one paused aghast at the amount they swallowed. From the first we had to regard them as small tanks, but as they grew they almost seemed to be bottomless caverns, into which any quantity of material might be dropped without making any appreciable difference.

After meals their small heads would sink back on their round, distended little bodies, and they would go placidly off to sleep in their well-lined nest, when they were covered up and for the moment forgotten; but as the next meal-hour approached there would be a great 'to-do', and the box would be uncovered to show the small heads bobbing up and down and giving forth shrill demands for more food, nor was there peace till they got it.

Things went on like this until our small friends suddenly took it into their heads that there was much too long an interval between supper and breakfast, and after this they used to go off like alarum clocks in the middle of the night. There was only one way of pacifying them, and their custodian had perforce to get out of his warm bed and to chew up more seal-meat until they were satisfied.

Of course we could scarcely hope to rear these birds under such artificial conditions, and we were not surprised when one of them pined away and died; but the other lived and throve for a long time, and only met his end when the warmer weather came on and he was incautiously put in one of the deck-houses for a short time; this exposure brought on the rickets, from which he never recovered.

During the interval between the return of our spring expeditions and the start of the longer summer ones we had several small excitements on board.

In one of these we suffered a grievous disappointment. Our nautical almanac told us that there would be an eclipse of the sun on September 21. It was not to be a total eclipse for us, but nine-tenths of the sun would be obscured. Bernacchi was especially busy in preparation for this event, and all placed themselves under his orders for the occasion. When the great day came all telescopes and the spectroscopic camera were trained in the right direction, magnetic instruments were set to run at quick speed, and observers were told off to watch the meteorological instruments, the tide gauge, and everything else on which the absence of sun could possibly have a direct or indirect effect. Everything, in fact, was ready but the sun itself, which obstinately refused to come out; from early morning a thick stratus cloud hung over our heads, and as the hours went by we were forced to abandon all hope of a clearance. There may have been an eclipse of the sun on September 21, 1903, as the almanac said, but we should none of us have liked to swear to the fact.

After our return from the spring journey, appetites had increased to such an alarming extent that we began to have renewed doubts as to the adequacy of our stock of seal-meat, and by this time all the especial luxuries in the shape of livers and kidneys had entirely disappeared. Seals rarely came up on the ice, and when they did our wretched dogs, the puppies of the previous year, did their best to worry them down again. It was at this juncture that our hunters were called upon, and their chief, Skelton, devised an excellent harpoon with hinged barbs which proved the most effective weapon. With a line attached, it was kept in readiness at one of the nearer fishing holes, and the keenest sportsmen would go out and wait by the hour, harpoon in hand, ready for the first unfortunate seal which should come up to breathe. The long wait in the cold was rather a drawback, but when at last a black snout appeared on the surface and the murderous weapon was plunged downward there was great excitement, and loud shouts were raised for assistance to haul in the line. In this way our larder was kept well supplied, whilst a few obtained feasts of the fish which we had long ceased to catch by our own efforts.

There was great excitement one day when one of the men went to this hole in the ice and, seeing a disturbance in the water, plunged the harpoon down. Evidently striking something, he rushed back to the ship to say that he had hit a big fish. There was a general stampede for the hole, and the harpoon line was soon being hauled in, in spite of the very lively something at the other end; but when at last this something was landed on the floe it was found to be nothing more unusual than a large seal, and naturally there was a chorus of jeers at the expense of the man who had claimed to have struck a big fish. In spite of ridicule, however, this individual stuck to his story that there had been a fish, and soon after it was proved that he had been quite accurate, for, searching amongst the brash ice in the hole, Skelton suddenly raised a shout, and in a moment or two produced the headless body of the large fish for which we had angled so ineffectually.

It was borne back in triumph to the ship and hung up for general admiration; in its mangled condition it was three feet ten inches in length and weighed thirty-nine pounds.

The importance of this capture deserves some description. Large fish are very uncommon in polar waters: as a general rule, the colder the water the smaller the fish. We had known, however, that large fish existed in our regions, as more than once we had found the skeletal remains of one on the ice. But this was the first time we had actually seen the creature itself, and now, alas! it had no head, and therefore lacked the most important detail for its scientific classification. The most scientific, and, in fact, the only account we ever had of the missing head was from the originator of the incident, who declared that 'it was like one of Mr Barne's crampons'. This account, whilst it delighted those who not infrequently entered into discussions with Barne as to the size of his feet, failed to supply the accuracy necessary for scientific description. There was one consolation, however, in the fact that if the head had remained on, the fish would have sunk and we should have seen nothing of it.

Piecing together the facts of the capture, we came to see how it had all happened, and the whole makes a curious story. We found that the seal was a female with young, and had not had food for a long time. In this condition it had attacked the large fish, and evidently had had a tremendous tussle with it. The seal must have been almost at the end of its diving powers when it had dragged its struggling prey to the surface, and at this point the harpoon must have transfixed both it and the fish. Whether the seal had mutilated the head of the fish we could not tell, but close to the tail and on the tail-fin of the latter were found distinct wounds caused by the seal's teeth. It shows the great swimming powers of the seal that it should have been able to capture so powerful a victim.

When we had safely got our big fish on board, a dreadful fear arose that our biologist would demand its preservation in spirit. I do not know whether it was the absence of the head or his own appetite that prompted his decision on this question, but to our relief he announced that as long as he had the skeleton, the rest, after he had examined it, could go to the cook. As we had no use for the skeleton, we were perfectly contented with this arrangement, and on the following day our fish provided the most sumptuous repast for our whole company. It is difficult to say exactly what this fish tasted like. Science would, I suppose, dismiss its qualities in this respect by the single word 'edible', and we, whilst we could muster a good many adjectives to express our appreciation, found it difficult to liken it to anything we had previously tasted. It had a firm, white flesh, and a most deliciously delicate flavour, and that perhaps is all I can say of it.

Not long after this great capture the ship was once more busy with all the preparations for the coming sledging campaign. Barne and Mulock were the first to get away, on October 6. This was one of the two extended journeys of which our complement would allow. In the advance party with these two officers went the men who had accompanied them on their severe depot journey, whilst the supporting party consisted of Dellbridge, Allan, Wild, Pilbeam, and Croucher. The whole party were to journey south around the Bluff, and thence to strike across for the entrance to the big strait since called the Barne Inlet. After about a fortnight the supporting party were to turn back, whilst the advance party made the best of a ten weeks' absence from the ship.

By October 11 all preparations for my own western effort had been completed, and on the following day we started full of high hopes of penetrating far into the interior.

I have already pointed out what great interests lay to the west at this time, and how incomplete our knowledge was of this region. The long hours of our second winter had given me ample time to consider the importance of the problems which yet remained to be solved there, and these thoughts had not only resigned me to our detention in the ice, but had gradually shown me that if all went well in future, it might turn out to be an unmixed blessing.

If we could do all that I hoped in the Ferrar Glacier and beyond, during a second season's work, I knew that the value of our labours of the first year would be immensely increased. As I have said before, the interest centred in this region; there were fascinating problems elsewhere, but none now which could compare with those of the western land. It was such considerations that made me resolve to go in this direction myself, and I determined that no effort should be spared to ensure success.

Rarely, I think, has more time and attention been devoted to the preparation of a sledge journey than was given to this one. I rightly guessed that in many respects it was going to be the hardest task we had yet undertaken, but I knew also that our experience was now a thing that could be counted upon, and that it would take a good deal to stop a party of our determined, experienced sledge-travellers.

I am bound to confess that I have some pride in this journey. We met with immense difficulties, such as would have brought us hopelessly to grief in the previous year, yet now as veterans we steered through them with success; and when all circumstances are considered, the extreme severity of the climate and the obstacles that stood in our path, I cannot but believe we came near the limit of possible performance.

It is for this reason, and because the region in which much of our work lay was very beautiful and interesting, that I propose to take the reader into the details of one more sledging excursion.

The party with which I left the ship on October 12, 1903, numbered twelve members in all. It was really the combination of three separate parties. First came my own advance party, which I had selected with great care, and which included our chief engineer, Skelton, our boatswain, Feather, and three men, Evans, Lashly, and Handsley; secondly, there was a small party for our geologist, Ferrar, with whom went two men, Kennar and Weller; and thirdly, there were the supports, consisting of our carpenter, Dailey, and two other men, Williamson and Plumley.

The original scheme was that the whole party should journey together to the summit of Victoria Land, and as far beyond as could be reached within a certain limit of time; then the advance party should proceed and the remainder turn back. An absence of nine weeks was calculated for the advance party. The supports were to return direct to the ship, but stores were to be so arranged in the glacier depots that Ferrar was allowed an absence of six weeks in which to make a geological survey of the region.

We started from the ship with four eleven-foot sledges, and with an outfit of permanent stores which the reader will find on referring to the chapter dealing with sledge equipment. Altogether our loads were a little over 200 lbs. per man; but most of us were in pretty hard condition by this time, and we found little difficulty in dragging such a weight.

And so we started away with the usual cheers and good wishes, little thinking how soon we should be on board again.

As I had determined that from first to last of this trip there should be hard marching, we stretched across over the forty-five miles to New Habour at a good round pace, and by working long hours succeeded in reaching the snow-cape on the near side early on the 14th – a highly creditable performance with such heavy loads.

This snow-cape was in future to be known as 'Butter Point'. It was here that on our return journey we could first hope to obtain fresh seal-meat, and, in preparation for this great event, a tin of butter was carried and left at this point for each party.

And here I fall back on my diary as may be required to continue the thread of my tale.

'October 14. – Had to camp early tonight, as Dailey and Williamson are a bit seedy, probably a little overcome with the march. At supper the third member of this unlucky unit, Plumley, cut off the top of his thumb in trying to chop up frozen pemmican. He is quite cheerful about it, and has been showing the frozen detached piece of thumb to everyone else as an interesting curio. For the present we are comparatively comfortable; the temperature has not been below –20°, and I do not expect anything lower till we get to the upper reaches of the glacier.'

On the 15th we struck the glacier snout well on its north side, and found, as I had guessed, an easy road; from there on to the first incline of the glacier we crossed only mild undulations and had no difficulties with our sledges. It was extraordinary, after we had discovered and travelled over this easy route, to remember what a bogey it had been to us for more than twelve months.

On the 16th we reached our spring depot under the Cathedral Rocks, and after picking it up and readjusting our loads, proceeded a few miles higher to a spot where Armitage had planted some sticks in the previous year to mark the movement of the glacier. We camped in gloriously fine weather, and I wrote: 'Tonight it is difficult to imagine oneself in a polar region. If one forgets for the moment that there is ice under foot, which it is not difficult to do as it is very dark in colour and there are many boulders close about us, one might be in any climate, for nearly all around is dark bare rock. We are in a deep gorge, not narrow, as the glacier here is probably four or five miles across, but the cliffs on either side are so majestic and lofty that the broad surface of the glacier is wholly dwarfed by them.

'We are on the south side of the valley, and towering precipitously between three and four thousand feet above our heads are the high sunlit pinnacles of the Cathedral Rocks; they were

well named by Armitage, for their lofty peaks might well be the
spires of some mighty edifice. Low down the rock itself is gneiss,
I believe; in colour a greyish black, but veined and splashed with
many a lighter hue. The high weathered pinnacles have a rich
brown shade; this is basalt, which here directly overlies the gneiss.
On the further side of our valley the hills rise almost as abruptly as
on this; reddish brown is the predominant colour there also, but
where the sunlight falls on the steeper cliffs it is lightened almost
to a brick red. A little snow can be seen amongst the peaks and
gullies opposite to us, and here and there the sparkling white of
some hanging glacier is in marked contrast to the rich tones of the
bare rock.

'We are camped in the medial moraine, a long scattered line
of boulders of every form and colour. Looking east one can see
this line winding down with graceful curves over the blue surface of the glacier, towards the sea; far away beyond is the ice-
covered sea itself, pearly grey in the distance. One can follow this
highway of boulders to the west too, till it vanishes over the
undulating inclines above us; in this direction the glacier wears a
formidable aspect, for in its centre is an immense cascade. It is
exactly as though this was some river which had been suddenly
frozen in its course, with the cascade to show where its waters
had been dashing wildly over a rocky shallow; it is very beautiful,
with its gleaming white waves and deep blue shadows, but we
shall have to give it a wide berth when we travel upward. The
upper valley is perhaps our most beautiful view; the dark cliffs
form a broad V and frame the cascading glacier, and above it the
distant solitary peak of the Knob Head Mountain and a patch of
crimson sky.'

'October 17. – We have been climbing upward all day, at first
over a gentle incline on smooth, hard, glassy ice, where the sledges
came very easily but unsteadily, skidding in all directions; later the
incline increased and the surface was roughened with tiny wavelets
like those formed by a cat's paw sweeping over a placid lake. We
walked on without crampons, getting foothold in the hollow of
these wavelets. Later still we came to a stiffer rise, and transverse
cracks appeared across our path, growing more numerous and
widening out as we ascended till we found ourselves crossing
miniature crevasses lightly bridged with snow. We had to step

across these, and often it meant a long step. In this manner we steered round to the north of the cascade, and by lunch-time had ascended almost to the higher basin of the glacier.

'Immediately before lunch we had to get over a very stiff little bit, where the cracks were sometimes three or four feet across, and the ice very rough between; it was heavy work getting the sledges up, and I rather feared someone would get a strain or sprain, but we all got over it in safety. In the afternoon, at a height of 4,500 feet, we topped the last rise that led to the glacier basin; and then, on a surface covered with the usual tiny wavelets, and from which the cracks rapidly disappeared, we travelled over a stretch of seven or eight miles with a gradual fall of 600 or 700 feet, and at length reached a stream of enormous boulders which ran right across our track. This is what Armitage called the Knob Head Moraine. He was twenty-seven days out from the ship before he reached it; we have got here in six.

'The changes of scene throughout the day have been bewildering. Not one half-hour of our march has passed without some new feature bursting upon our astonished gaze. Certainly those who saw this valley last year did not exaggerate its grandeur – indeed, it would be impossible to do so. It is wonderfully beautiful. As we came up the lower gorge this morning, we passed from side to side with frowning cliffs towering over us on either hand; ahead between these dark walls the sky, perhaps by contrast, looked intensely blue, and here and there in the valley floated a little wisp of feathery white cloud; again and again these appeared under some forbidding rock-face only to melt impalpably away. As we emerged into the great ice-basin we turned towards the north to face a new aspect of this wonderful country.

'To describe the wildly beautiful scene that is about us tonight is a task that is far beyond my pen. Away behind us is the gorge by which we have come; but now above and beyond its splendid cliffs we can see rising fold on fold the white snow-clad slopes of Mount Lister. Only at the very top of its broad, blunt summit is there a sign of bare rock, and that is 11,000 feet above our present elevated position; so clear is the air that one seems to see every wrinkle and crease in the rolling masses of névé beneath.

'The great basin in which we are camped has four outlets. Opposite that by which we have come descends what we call the south-west arm; it is a prodigious ice-flow, but falls steeply and roughly between its rocky boundaries. Away ahead of us is the north-west arm; we have some twisting and turning to get to it, but shall eventually round a sharp corner and steer up it to the westward. To the right of this and ahead of us also is the north arm, which seems to descend sharply towards the sea. Besides these main outlets or inlets, there are some places to the west of us where smaller ice-flows fall into our basin with steep crevassed surfaces, and in many places around are lighter tributaries descending from the small local névé fields. But for the main part we are surrounded with steep, bare hillsides of fantastic and beautiful forms and of great variety in colour. The groundwork of the colour-scheme is a russet-brown, but to the west especially it has infinite gradations of shade, passing from bright red to dull grey, whilst here and there, and generally in banded form, occurs an almost vivid yellow. The whole forms a glorious combination of autumn tints, and few forests in their autumnal raiment could outvie it.

'The most curious feature about us is the great mass of rock immediately in front. It appears to form two islands, for the great body of ice which occupies the basin seems to join again beyond it. Armitage called these islands the "Solitary Rocks"; they are comparatively flat on top, and rich brown in colour, save where two broad bands of yellow run horizontally through them. These bands are so regular and uniform in thickness that one might almost imagine they had been painted on. Geologically all this should be of immense interest, for the bands which are broken off so sharply at the cliffs of these islands can be seen to appear again in the high hills beyond, and no doubt would appear everywhere if many of the hillsides were not covered with loose rubble. The whole structure of the country seems to be horizontal, but exactly what the rocks are, we have not yet ascertained; the brown is probably basalt, and the yellow, Ferrar hopes, is the sedimentary rock which he has found in the moraines.'

As Mr Ferrar added an appendix dealing with the geological formation of this interesting region to the earlier editions of this work which are easily available, I shall in future omit all remarks of mine which bear on the subject and refer the reader to that. Both before and after this Ferrar found in the various moraines a large variety of rocks – granites, gneisses, sandstone, quartz, &c. – but as this was all transported material it told very little. It was only as we ascended this great glacier and saw the curious horizontal stratification of the hills that the problem gradually unfolded itself before him, and he arrived at some notion of the places to be visited when he commenced his investigations.

It was on the night of the 17th, whilst we were still absorbed in the beauty and novelty of the scene about us, that the first cloud of trouble loomed above our horizon, for it was on this night the carpenter reported that the German silver had split under the runners of two of our sledges. As this matter was of the gravest import to us, it perhaps needs a little explanation. I have pointed out before that the wood runners of our sledges were quite capable of running on snow without protection; on the hard, sharp ice, however, it was a different matter. In such circumstances, a wood runner would be knocked to pieces in a very few hours, especially if the sledge was heavily laden. At all hazards, therefore, it was necessary to protect our runners over this hard ice, but unfortunately the German silver protection had already stood one season's work, and this had worn it thin without giving any outward sign. We only found out how thin it had become when it gave out on this journey, and hence the troubles which I am about to describe were quite unexpected.

From start to finish of the Ferrar Glacier there were about ninety miles in which hard ice might be expected, and the problem that soon came before us was how to get our sledges over this without damage.

On the 17th I scarcely realised myself the full importance of the carpenter's report, but on the 18th matters came to a crisis, as will be seen.

'October 18. – We got away early this morning, crossed the moraines and continued our ascent over hard, wavy ice. It was quite calm about us, with the temperature at about −20°, but a short distance ahead we could see the wind sweeping down from a gully on our left, carrying clouds of snowdrift. We did not at all like the look of this windswept area, but it had to be crossed, and we plunged into it after adjusting our wind-guards. It took us over an hour to get across, and several of us got badly frostbitten, as immediately opposite the gully the wind was extraordinarily violent, and it was as much as we could do to hold up against it.

Once past the gully, however, it was nearly calm and comparatively warm again; by lunch-time we had reached a new meandering moraine, almost abreast of the Solitary Rocks, and had achieved a height of over 6,000 feet.

'I, with my party, was some way ahead when I decided to camp, but the supports soon came up, bringing, alas! a woeful tale – another sledge had split its runners.

'After lunch I had all the sledges unpacked and the runners turned up for inspection, with horrid revelations. On two sledges the German silver was split to ribbons and the wood deeply scored, a third was only in slightly better case, whilst the fourth still remained sound. I could see nothing for it but to return home; if we had two sound sledges we might struggle on with the advance party, but with one we could do nothing. It was no use even discussing the matter – there was only one course; so we left the sound sledge with everything else except the half-week's provisions necessary to take us back, and after crossing the windy area once more, we are now back at our old encampment in the Knob Head Moraine. It is a bitter disappointment to my hopes; everything will have to be reorganised, and Heaven knows what sacrifices of time we shall have to make. However, there shall not be more than I can help, and things which have gone fast in the past, will positively have to fly in the future.'

On the following days we came as near flying as is possible with a sledge party. We had eighty-seven miles to cover on the morning of the 19th, when we were up and away with the first streak of dawn; then we started our rush, at first up the slight incline to the summit of the pass, and then down through the steeper gorge towards the sea. We did not pause to pick a road, but went straight forward, scrambling as best we could over steep places and taking all obstacles in our stride. Once only we halted to snatch a hasty lunch, and then were off again over the rugged, slippery ice.

That night we camped at sea level twenty-seven miles below our starting point. The next morning brought us a hard pull with our torn runners over the long stretch of rough snow-covered glacier tongue, but at lunch-time we had reached the end, and devoted an hour to stripping the broken, twisted metal from our sledges.

By this time I had determined to test my own party to the utmost, but I did not see that the supporting people need be dragged into our effort; so telling the latter that they might take their own time, I started away with my own detachment over the sea-ice towards the mouth of the inlet at the quickest pace we had yet attempted. When the brief night descended on us we camped with twenty-four miles to our credit for the day, and as our tents were being secured I looked round to find that the supporting party were still gallantly struggling on in our wake; seeing our tents go up, they halted about a mile and a half behind us.

At dawn on the 21st we were away once more, and stretching out directly for the ship; far away we could see Castle Rock and Observation Hill, small dots on the horizon. Hour after hour went by, but we never eased our pace till at our lunch hour we came on a fat seal and paused to eat our meal and to secure the certainty of a good supper from the animal that had been unwise enough to bask in our track. In the afternoon our home landmarks grew more distinct, and as the sun dipped we came on the last six miles of wind-tossed snow that skirted our peninsula. The semi-darkness found us struggling on over this uneven, difficult surface, but at half-past eight we were through and reached the ship, having covered thirty-six miles in the day.

We had accomplished a record for which the glow of satisfaction that we felt was excusable; but more was to follow, for later that night a shout of welcome announced that our undefeated supporting party had also struggled home. Ferrar soon told me his tale; at first they had not intended to come in at racing speed, but seeing the advance party striding off at such a pace, their feelings of emulation had been excited, and they had felt bound to follow. On camping behind us on the previous night they had determined to catch us in the early morning, but as they roused out with that intention they saw that we also were preparing to be off. Then followed the long march, when, despite all their efforts, the leading party grew more and more indistinct. It was not until late in the afternoon that they lost sight of us altogether, and then there could be no doubt of our intention to reach the ship before night.

In spite of their lame and exhausted condition, they determined to follow. Once or twice they had halted to brew tea to keep themselves going, but not one of them had suggested that the halt should be extended. In the hard struggle of the last few hours some of the men had kept things going by occasionally indulging in some dry remark which caused everyone to laugh. Kennar's attitude had been one of grieved astonishment; presumably referring to me, he had kept repeating, 'If he can do it, I don't see why I can't: my legs are as long as his.'

And so it was that this party made the record march of all, for they started more than a mile behind us, and must have covered over thirty-seven miles in the day.

In spite of our marching, it was a blow to be back in the ship so soon after we had made our first hopeful start, and, as can be imagined, I did not allow time to be wasted in preparing to be off again. Our carpenter was soon at work repairing the sledges with all the assistance that could be afforded him. Meanwhile I saw that it would be necessary to reorganise our arrangements. Without going into the reasons which guided me, I may say that I now thought the best scheme was for the advance party to start off on its own account, to pick up the glacier provisions, and to dispose of them on a new plan. I arranged that Ferrar should start with a small sledge of his own, and should be entirely independent; but as he signified his wish to remain with us as long as possible, it was still a party of nine that started out on October 26, five days after our flying return. Our material for repairing sledges was very scanty, but at length out of the parts of various broken ones we had succeeded in producing one sound eleven-foot sledge for our own party and a short seven-foot one for Ferrar's glacier work.

With these we once more started to cross the long stretch of sea-ice to the mainland. The night of the 27th found us at the end of the glacier tongue, and I wrote: 'We can fairly claim to be in good marching condition, having crossed the strait at an average of over twenty-five miles a day. This morning we met a small group of Emperor penguins; they were going south towards the "Eskers", for what reason one cannot guess, travelling on their breasts and propelling themselves with their powerful feet at a speed of at least five miles an hour. Of course when they saw us they made in our direction, and when quite close stood up and squawked loudly. They watched us for some time with every manifestation of amazement, and then started to follow in our wake, but of this they soon tired, and resuming their old course to the south, were shortly out of sight.'

In preparation for our renewed struggle with the hard ice of the glacier, we had brought with us some under-runners shod with German silver, and at the glacier tongue we picked up all the scraps of this metal which we had formerly discarded.

'October 28. – We are camped opposite Descent Pass after a hard day. This morning early we had a glorious view of the glacier valley. The sun shone brightly on the great gaunt cliffs which rose one above the other towards the inland, and every outline was sharp against the deep blue sky. Later, low sheets of stratus cloud spread across the valley and shimmered in the sunlight. This afternoon a nimbus cloud crept in over our heads, bringing a trifling snowfall; the sun struggled against it, but for the time the valley was clothed in mists.

'Troubles have already come upon us; the under-runners of our sledge split on the first incline, and we had to take them off. The metal on one of the runners on which we now rely is badly laminated, and may go at any moment. These difficulties are very annoying, but I have determined to get to the top this time, even if we have to carry our loads.'

From this time on we had constant worries with these wretched runners. On the 29th Ferrar's small sledge gave out, and we had a long delay to get it into working order again. Notwithstanding this we got within a few hundred yards of the Knob Head Moraine before we called a halt for the night. On the broad surface of this glacier there were few places in which we could camp for want of snow to secure our tents; for this reason we generally kept moderately close to the long lines of morainic boulders, as under the largest of these there was usually sufficient snow for our purpose. In a few places elsewhere we found a thin sheet or isolated patches, but this was not common.

On the night of the 29th we camped in a calm, with the sun shining brightly, and had a fair view of grand hills that surrounded the glacier basin, but now also we again observed a fact which was not so cheering. On each occasion when we were in this basin it was calm all about us, except in two regions where the wind evidently swept down with great and almost continuous violence. One of these was what we called the 'Vale of Winds', across which we had passed before, and the other was unfortunately the north-west arm, up which we proposed to go. We had never seen the latter without clouds of drift pouring down over its surface, and we shrewdly suspected that we were in for a pretty bad time when we reached it.

'October 30. – We have grown a little careless in leaving our things about outside the tent, and this morning we had a lesson. Our sleeping-bags, with socks, finneskoes, and other garments, lay scattered about on the ice whilst we were having breakfast, when suddenly the wind swept down on us; before we could move everything was skidding away over the surface of the ice. The moment we realised what was happening the tents were empty and we were flying over the ice as fast as we could after our lost garments. The incident would have been extremely funny had it not involved the possibility of such serious consequences. The sleeping-bags were well on towards the steep fall of the north arm before they were recovered, and by good luck the whole affair closed with the loss of only a few of the lighter articles.

'As soon as we had struggled back against the heavy wind that was now blowing, we packed our sledges, put on our crampons, and started onward; but by this time the wind had increased to a full gale, and we could hardly stand against it, so we steered to the westward to get under shelter. This brought us on a slope which gradually grew steeper till it ended in the perpendicular side of the glacier. Proceeding down as far as we thought safe, we entered the moraine and pitched our camp again. I do not know what to make of this moraine, which, starting from the side of the glacier, runs directly across it, and, after first rising for several hundred feet, descends again steeply down the north arm towards the sea.'

I may here mention that these crampons to which I refer were manufactured on board the ship; those used in the previous year were voted wholly unsatisfactory, and gave rise to many blisters, whereupon our chief engineer took the matter in hand, and with the assistance of the boatswain produced an article which rendered us excellent service on this journey. Each crampon had two steel plates studded with mild steel spikes, one for the sole and the other for the heel; the plates were riveted on to a canvas overall half-boot which could be put on over a finnesko and kept tight with thongs. The device was heavy, but as quite the best sort of thing in the circumstances it is well worthy of imitation by future travellers in these regions.

The moraine which at this time bewildered us so much was one of those signs of a former greater extension of the ice to which I shall refer in my final chapter.

The wind kept us in this wretched moraine for two days – a tiresome delay – but we managed to get out for an hour or two and make an interesting excursion to the side of the glacier. After a short search we found a way by which, with some aid from a rope, we could climb down the steep ice-face and visit the land beyond.

We afterwards found that the side of this glacier was more or less typical of other places. It must be understood that from the top of this wall the surface sloped rapidly up, whilst the bottom layer of ice would naturally have sloped down into the valley, so that in the middle the glacier must have been very many times as thick as at the side. The ice was curiously stratified; the white part contained numerous air vesicles, the darker parts were in many cases due to included dirt, but a broad dark band running through the middle had no dirt in it at all – it was the cleanest ice we saw. A piece split off it was like the purest crystal without a sign of grit or air bubble to obstruct its perfect transparency.

Between this ice-wall and the mountain side lay a deep trench, showing the smooth glassy surface of frozen thaw-water. The mountain side itself, except for one place lower down where there was an outcrop of red granite, was thickly strewn with boulders of every kind of rock which the region produced, whilst here and there could be seen enormous perched blocks ranging up to three or four hundred tons in weight.

All this vast quantity of débris had evidently been carried by ice, and it was now that we first realised to what vastly greater limits our glacier had once extended, for these thickly strewn boulders covered the mountain side to a height of three thousand feet above our heads, where a horizontal line signified their limit and the extent of the glacier at its maximum.

'November 1. – It was overcast and dull this morning, but the wind had fallen light and we decided to push on; although the air was comparatively still about us, close ahead the "Vale of Winds" was sending forth its snow-laden gusts as merrily as ever. Before we came to this unattractive area we passed two more carcases of

Weddell seals; the last was at the greatest altitude we have yet found one, nearly 5,000 feet above the sea; it grows more than ever wonderful how these creatures can have got so far from the sea.' We never satisfactorily explained this matter. The seal seems often to crawl to the shore or the ice to die, possibly from its instinctive dread of its marine enemies; but unless we had actually found these remains, it would have been past believing that a dying seal could have transported itself over fifty miles of rough steep glacier surface.

'We got safely past the "Vale of Winds" with only one or two frostbites, and a few miles beyond found our depot without much difficulty. At first we thought that everything was intact, but a closer examination showed us that the lid of the instrument box had been forced open and that some of the contents were missing. Evidently there has been a violent gale since we were here before. When we came to count up the missing articles, we found that Skelton had lost his goggles and that one or two other trifles had disappeared; but before we could congratulate ourselves on escaping so lightly, I found to my horror that the *Hints to Travellers* had vanished.

'The gravity of this loss can scarcely be exaggerated; but whilst I realised the blow I felt that nothing would induce me to return to the ship a second time; I thought it fair, however, to put the case to the others, and I am, as I expected, fortified by their willing consent to take the risks of pushing on.'

I must here explain what this loss signified. In travelling to the west, we expected to be, as indeed we were, for some weeks out of sight of landmarks. In such a case as this the sledge-traveller is in precisely the same position as a ship or boat at sea: he can only obtain a knowledge of his whereabouts by observations of the sun or stars, and with the help of these observations he finds his latitude and longitude. To find the latitude from an observation of a heavenly body, however, it is necessary to know the declination of that body, and to find the longitude one must have not only the declination, but certain logarithmic tables. In other words, to find either latitude or longitude, a certain amount of data is required. Now, all these necessary data are supplied in an excellent little publication issued by the Royal Geographical Society and called *Hints to Travellers*, and it was on this book that

I was relying to be able to work out my sights and accurately fix the position of my party.

When this book was lost, therefore, the reader will see how we were placed; if we did not return to the ship to make good our loss, we should be obliged to take the risk of marching away into the unknown without exactly knowing where we were or how to get back.

As will be seen, this last is precisely what happened, and if the loss of our *Hints to Travellers* did not lead us into serious trouble it caused me many a bad half-hour.

'Having decided to push on, we lost as little time as possible in packing our sledges, and in the afternoon we were off once more, steadily ascending over the rough ice. The Solitary Rocks have fallen behind us, and our camp tonight looks out on the broad amphitheatre above them where the glacier sweeps round from the upper reach. On our left is the Finger Mountain, a precipitous mass of rock showing the most extraordinary "fault" in that yellow-banded structure which now seems to surround us on every side.' The significance of this fault is explained by Mr Ferrar in appendix to the two volume edition of this work.

'Finger Mountain forms the pivot about which the glacier turns, and the great difference in the level of the ice above and below the mountain is taken by two heavy broken falls. We are encamped under the lower and smaller one, but the upper, some three or four miles beyond, is a magnificent mass of twisted, torn ice-blocks. Tomorrow we have to rise over these falls, but I propose to take a very roundabout way to avoid difficulties.

'The scene behind us is glorious; we look down now on the great glacier basin with the dark rugged mountains that surround it, and far away beyond, the summit of Mount Lister shows above a bank of twisted sunlit cloud. But, alas! pleasant as it is to look at this beautiful scene, trouble is never far from us, and this afternoon we have had our full share. First one sledge-runner gave out and then another, and we arrived at camp with three out of four disabled. Now, however, there is a fixed determination in the party to get through somehow, and each difficulty only serves to show more clearly their resourcefulness. This particular trouble has called on the metal workers, and no sooner had we halted and unpacked the sledges than Skelton and Lashly

were hard at work with pliers, files, and hammers stripping off
the torn metal and lapping fresh pieces over the weak places.
They have established a little workshop in this wild spot, and
for hours the scrape of the file and the tap of the hammer have
feebly broken the vast silence.

'We have hopes of the lapping process which is now being
effected, but it needs very careful fitting; each separate piece of
metal protection is made to overlap the piece behind it, like slates
on a roof! I should doubt whether such work could be done by
people unaccustomed to dealing with these matters.'

'November 2. – This morning it was perfectly calm and still,
with a bright sun and the temperature at +2°. There was little
difficulty in finishing off our repairing work, and when the sledges
were ready we started to march upwards again.

'We steered well to the eastward to make a wide circuit of
Finger Mountain and its dangerous ice-falls, and on this course
gradually approached the northern limit of the great amphitheatre beyond. The precipitous mountains that fringe this limit
show in the clearest and most beautiful manner the horizontal
stratification of their rocks, and now there can be no doubt that
this simple, banded structure is common to the whole region
about us, and that the sharp clear lines of the strata are singularly
free from faulting.

'In ascending we gradually passed from hard ice to snow.
Apparently there is a considerable snowfall in this amphitheatre; it
has made our pulling much harder, but, on the other hand, it
saves our sledge-runners from injury, and the more we can get of
it the better we shall be pleased. After lunch we passed on to ice
again, and the wind sprang up. Coming at first in eddying gusts, it
increased with great rapidity, and very soon we were all getting
frostbitten. It was obviously desirable to camp as soon as possible,
but never a patch of snow could be seen, and we pushed on with
all haste towards the base of the mountains and the fringing
moraines of the glacier. We had to search long amongst the latter
before we could find the least sign of snow, and when at length
we found some, it was so hard that it took us nearly an hour to
get our tents up.

'We are now at the base of the upper glacier reach. From here it
rises directly to the inland, and it is over this broad surface that the

wind seems to sweep perpetually. The whole valley is very ugly with wind and driving snow, and there cannot be a doubt that this is its usual condition, and that we shall have a hard fight with the wind in our teeth; it will be no child's play battling with this icy blast from the summit. We have had a foretaste of it this afternoon, and at the present moment it is straining our threadbare tent in no reassuring manner.'

On the following day the wind was as strong as ever, but we knew it was useless to wait, so pushed on once more. For a brief half-hour we got some shelter in a curious horseshoe bay which we entered to repair Ferrar's sledge-runners. Here the cliffs rose perpendicularly, and immediately above our heads the broad band of sandstone ran with perfect uniformity around the whole bay. On rising to the open glacier again, I struck off for the south side, hoping to get better conditions, and with very happy results, for shortly after lunch we walked out of the wind as easily as we had walked into it on the previous day. And now I made an error, for I started from this point to ascend directly upward. It is impossible to describe all the turns and twists which were taken by this glacier, or to mention the numerous undulations and disturbances which obliged us constantly to alter our course from side to side, but it must not be imagined that our route was all plain sailing and easy travelling.

From a very early time we saw that it was desirable to map out our course a long way ahead, and to do so with reference to the various land masses so as to avoid disturbances which we could not see, but at which we guessed. I mention this matter because it impressed on us a golden rule for travelling in this region, which was, 'Always take a long sweep round corners.' We were often tempted to break this rule when a shorter road looked easy, but we never did so without suffering. It was an error of this nature that I made on the afternoon of the 3rd, and which after an hour's work landed us in such a dangerously crevassed region that we were very glad to struggle back by the way we had come. The note I made at this time may perhaps be quoted: 'The whole of this glacier can be made easy by taking the right course – a course such as a steamer takes in rounding the bends of a river. The temptation to cut corners is excessive, but it is always a mistake. By walking round obstructions such as cascades, not only does one avoid danger to life and limb, but also the chance of relay work, which alone would allow the longer distance to be three times as far, without loss of time.

'Whilst we were in difficulties this afternoon there occurred one of those extraordinary climatic changes which are such a menace to sledge-travellers. The cold had been so intense that we had been walking all day in our wind clothes and with our heaviest headgear; but now we suddenly found ourselves perspiring freely, and within half an hour we had stripped off our outer garments, and the majority were walking bareheaded.'

That night we camped in gloriously fine weather, after crossing to the south side of the glacier and finding another long stream of boulders. Here we had our usual trouble in repairing our battered, torn runners; and, to add to this annoyance we had come to the end of our scraps of metal, nails, and everything else necessary for repairing work. It was evident that we could not stand many more miles of this rough ice, and that it would be touch-and-go whether we ever reached the snow above without having to carry our belongings.

We had now attained a height of 7,000 feet, and whilst the summits of the mountains on each side still stood high above our level, they no longer overawed us or conveyed that sense of grandeur which we had felt so keenly at our former camps. The majestic cliffs of the lower valley were beneath us, and we gazed over the top of many a lesser summit to the eastward. To the west the glacier still wound its way upward, and we saw that there was a stiff climb yet to come; but already the character of the valley was altering, the boundary cliffs were cut by the broad channels of tributary glaciers, the masses of dark, bare rock were becoming detached and isolated, whilst the widening snowfields were creeping upward with the ever-increasing threat to engulf all beneath their white mantle.

November 4 was such an eventful day that I quote its incidents from my diary.

'Started in bright sunshine, but with a chill, increasing wind in our teeth. At first we made good progress over hard, smooth ice, but soon came to a broad field of snow where a large tributary entered the main ice-stream. It was heavy pulling across this snow with our ragged runners, and to add to our discomfort, the wind swept down the side valley with the keenest edge. Beyond this valley lay the Depot Nunatak, a huge mass of columnar basalt, and at length we were able to get our breath beneath its shelter. Here Evans told me that one of his feet was "gone". He was foolishly wearing a single pair of socks in remembrance of the warm march of yesterday. As soon as we had got his unruly member back to life we proceeded.

'Ahead of us there showed up an immense and rugged ice-fall, one of those by which the glacier signifies its entrance into the valley; at this I knew the bare blue ice would come to an end, and with it our difficulties with the sledge-runners, so I determined to push on to the foot of this fall before camping. The way led up a steep crevassed slope of rough, blue ice, and before we had even reached this slope the weather assumed a most threatening aspect. The sun was obscured by stratus cloud, which drifted rapidly overhead, and the wind momentarily increased. We went on at our best speed, but when we were half-way up the bare icy slope, which proved much longer than I had expected, the full force of the gale burst upon us, and the air became thick with driving snow.

'We pushed on almost at a run to reach the summit of the slope, and then started to search in every direction for a camping spot. By this time things were growing serious, everyone was badly frostbitten in the face, and it was evident that the effects might be very ugly if we did not find shelter soon. I shall not forget the next hour in a hurry; we went from side to side searching vainly for a patch of snow, but everywhere finding nothing but the bare blue ice. The runners of our sledges had split again, so badly that we could barely pull them over the rough surface; we dared not leave them in the thick drift, and every minute our frostbites were increasing. At last we saw a white patch, and made a rush for it; it proved to be snow indeed, but so ancient and windswept that it was almost as hard as the solid ice itself. Nevertheless, we knew it was this or nothing, and in a minute our tents and shovels were hauled off the sledges, and we were digging for dear life.

'I seized the shovel myself, for my own tent-party, but found that I could not make the least impression on the hard surface. Luckily, at this moment the boatswain came to my relief, and managing the implement with much greater skill, succeeded in chipping out a few small blocks. Then we tried to get up the tent, but again and again it and the poles were blown flat; at last the men came to our assistance, and with our united efforts the three tents were eventually erected. All this had taken at least an hour, and when at length we found shelter it was not a moment too soon, for we were thoroughly exhausted, and fingers and feet, as well as faces, were now freezing. As soon as possible we made a brew of tea, which revived us greatly; afterwards we got our sleeping-bag in, and since that we have been coiled up within it.

'The temperature tonight is −24°, and it is blowing nearly a full gale; it is not too pleasant lying under the shelter of our thin, flapping tent under such conditions, but one cannot help remembering that we have come mighty well out of a very tight place. Nothing but experience saved us from disaster today, for I feel pretty confident that we could not have stood another hour in the open.'

Whilst we congratulated ourselves on the fortunate manner in which, in the nick of time, we had been able to find shelter in this camp, we little thought of the dismal experience that we were to suffer before we left it. It was Wednesday, November 4, when we pitched our tents so hurriedly; it was Wednesday, November 11, before we resumed our march; and if I were asked to name the most miserable week I have ever spent, I should certainly fix on this one. Throughout this whole time the gale raged unceasingly; if the wind lulled for a few brief minutes, it was to return with redoubled violence immediately after. Meanwhile not a vision of the outer world came to us; we were enveloped continuously in a thick fog of driving snow.

It is difficult to describe such a time; twenty-two hours out of each twenty-four we spent in our sleeping-bags, but regularly in the morning and in the evening we rolled these up, prepared and ate a hot meal, and then once more sought the depths of the bag. To sleep much was out of the question, and I scarcely know how the other long hours went. In our tent we had one book, Darwin's delightful *Cruise of the 'Beagle'*, and sometimes one or another would read this aloud until our freezing fingers refused to turn the pages. Often we would drop into conversation, but, as can be imagined, the circumstances were not such as to encourage much talking, and most of the commoner topics were threadbare by the end of the week. Sometimes we would gaze up at the fluttering green canvas overhead, but this was not inspiriting. I find I have written a great deal in my diary, obviously as an occupation; but the combination of all such things was far from filling a whole day, and therefore for the greater part of the time we lay quite still with our eyes open doing nothing and simply enduring. Communication between tents was only possible in the lulls; we therefore watched for these eagerly, and in the quietest, rushed round to shout greetings and learn how our comrades fared.

One task only we were able to perform throughout the time, and that on the first day of our imprisonment, when, thinking all would soon blow over, we hauled our sledges beneath one of the tents and stripped the German silver ready for the onward march.

At first, of course, we went to sleep each night with the comforting hope that the next morning would see a change for the better; but as day followed day without improvement, it was impossible to cherish this hope. And yet I do not believe we ever grew despondent; the feeling that there must be a change if we had the patience to wait, never left us.

By the fifth day of our imprisonment, however, sleep threatened to desert us, and matters in general began to take a more serious aspect. Our sleeping-bags were getting very icy; some complained that they could no longer keep their feet warm in them, and there could be no doubt that the long inactivity was telling on our circulation and health.

On the evening of this day, therefore, realising that things were beginning to go badly for us, I determined that whatever the conditions might be, we would make an attempt to start on the following morning. To show the result of this attempt I again have recourse to my diary.

'November 10. – Before breakfast this morning we shifted our foot-gear ready for the march, and during a lull the boatswain and I dug out our sledges and provisions. After breakfast the wind came down on us again, but we went out to complete our work. In ten minutes we were back in the tent; both my hands were "gone", and I had to be assisted in nursing them back. Skelton had three toes and the heel of one foot badly frostbitten, and the boatswain had lost all feeling in both feet. One could only shout an occasional inquiry to the other tents, but I gather their inmates are in pretty much the same condition. I think the wind and drift have never been quite so bad as today, and the temperature is −20°. Things are looking serious; I fear the long spell of bad weather is telling on us. The cheerfulness of the party is slowing waning; I heard the usual song from Lashly this morning, but it was very short-lived and dolorous. Luck is not with us this trip, and yet we have worked hard to make things go right. Something must be done tomorrow, but what it will be, tomorrow only can show. Weller complained of feeling giddy today, but Ferrar says it is because he eats too fast.'

'November 11. – Thank heaven we have broken away from our "Desolation Camp" at last. It is impossible to describe how awful the past week has been; it is a "nightmare" to remember. When we turned out this morning there was a lull, but the air was still as thick as a hedge. We hurried over breakfast, dreading each moment that the wind would return, then we bundled everything on to the sledges anyhow, seized our harness and were away. I had just time to give a few directions to Ferrar, who turned back to seek shelter under the Depot Nunatak. Then we started for the icefall, and since that we have got to the top, but how, I don't quite know, nor can I imagine how we have escaped accident. On starting we could not see half-a-dozen yards ahead of us; within a hundred yards of the camp we as nearly as possible walked into an enormous chasm; and when we started to ascend the slope we crossed any number of crevasses without waiting to see if the bridges would bear. I really believe that we were in a state when we none of us really cared much what happened; our sole thought was to get away from that miserable spot.

'At the top of the slope, after ascending nearly 500 feet, we passed suddenly out of the wind which we could still see sweeping down the valley behind us and here we halted for lunch, after which all six of us got in one tent whilst the other was hauled in for repairs, which it badly needed after its late ill-usage. While we were chatting over this work, it would have been difficult to recognise us as the same party which had started under such grim circumstances in the morning.'

We rose nearly 700 feet on the 11th, and over another steep fall of about the same height on the 12th, but the 13th found us on a more gradual incline, and at the end of the day we camped with our aneroids showing an elevation of 8,900 feet above the sea. We had at length won our fight and reached the summit. We had nearly five weeks' provisions in hand, and I felt that things would go hard if we could not cover a good many miles before we returned to the glacier.

During these few days the weather had been overcast and dull, but on the 14th it cleared, and we got a good view of our surroundings. We found ourselves on a great snow-plain, with a level horizon all about, but above this to the east rose the tops of mountains, many of which we could recognise. Directly to the east and to the north-east only the extreme summits of the higher hills could be seen, but to the south-east Mount Lister and the higher peaks of the Royal Society Range still showed well above our level. It was a fortunate view, for it gave me a chance of fixing our latitude by bearings and of noting the appearance of objects which would be our leading marks on returning to the glacier.

The latitude also assisted me in putting into execution a plan which I had thought out, and which, though it is somewhat technical, I give for the benefit of explorers who may be in like case in future. I have already mentioned the loss of the tables necessary for working out our observations, and the prospect which lay before us of wandering over this great snow-plain without knowing exactly where we were. The matter had naturally been much in my thoughts, and whilst I saw that there was no hope of working out our longitudes till we got back to the ship, it occurred to me that we might gather some idea of our latitude if I could improvise some method of ascertaining the daily change in the sun's declination.

With this idea I carefully ruled out a sheet of my notebook into squares with the intention of making a curve of the sun's declination. I found on reflection that I had some data for this curve, for I could calculate the declination for certain fixed days, such as the day when the sun had returned to us, and the day when it first remained above our horizon at midnight; other points were given by observations taken at known latitudes on the glacier. To make a long story short, I plotted all these points on my squared paper, and joined them with a freehand curve of which I have some reason to be proud, for on my return to the ship I found it was nowhere more than 4' in error. On the journey I did not place so much reliance on my handiwork as it deserved, for there is no doubt it gave us our latitude with as great an accuracy as we needed at the time.

We had scarcely reached the summit of the ice-cap and started our journey to the west, when troubles began to gather about us once more. Our long stay in 'Desolation Camp' had covered our sleeping-bags and night-jackets with ice, and now the falling temperature gave this ice little or no chance to evaporate, so that our camping arrangements were attended with discomforts from which there seemed little prospect of relief. Each night the thermometer fell a trifle lower, until on the 16th it had reached −44°, and although it rose slightly in the daytime, the general conditions of our work were such as we had experienced on the spring journeys at sea level. The snow surface in places became extremely hard and slippery, so that we were obliged to wear crampons, and between the hard patches lay softer areas through which we had the greatest difficulty in dragging our sledges. But the worst feature of our new conditions was the continuous wind; it was not a heavy wind − probably its force never much exceeded 3 or 4 in the Beaufort scale − but, combined with the low temperature and the rarefied air, its effect was blighting. It blew right in our teeth, and from the first it was evidently not the effect of temporary atmospheric disturbance, but was a permanent condition on this great plateau.

I do not think that it would be possible to conceive a more cheerless prospect than that which faced us at this time, when on this lofty, desolate plateau we turned our backs upon the last mountain peak that could remind us of habitable lands. Yet before us lay the unknown. What fascination lies in that word! Could anyone wonder that we determined to push on, be the outlook ever so comfortless?

And so we plodded on to the west, working long hours and straining at our harness with all our strength, but in spite of every effort our progress became slower. Up to the 17th we kept a fairly good pace, but on the 18th and 19th there was a visible slackening. By this time we had divided our sledges; Feather, Evans, and I pulled one of them, whilst Skelton, Handsley, and Lashly pulled the other. It was customary for my sledge to pull ahead whilst the other followed as best it could, but soon I found that the second sledge was only keeping up with the greatest difficulty, and it was borne in on me that the excessive strain of our labour was beginning to tell on the party.

The realisation of this fact placed me in a rather amusing but awkward predicament, because, whilst I knew my own strength was unimpaired, I was forced to admit that some of my companions were failing, and in order to find out which of them it was, I was obliged to keep a constant watch on their actions. As was natural with such men, not one of them would own that he was 'done'; they had come to see the thing through, and they would have dropped in their tracks sooner than give in. And so it was only by the keenest attention, and by playing the somewhat unattractive part of a spy, that I could detect those who from sheer incapacity were relaxing their strain on the traces. Even when the knowledge came to me, my position seemed no clearer, for how could I tell these lion-hearted people that they must turn back? Thus it came about that all six of us marched onward, though I knew that progress would have been bettered had the party been divided.

But this state of affairs came to a climax on the 20th, as the following extract shows.

'We have struggled on some miles today, but only with difficulty. Late last night Handsley came to me to ask if there was anything in the medical bag to relieve a sore throat; of course there was nothing. I asked his tent-mates about it, and they told me that for some time he had suffered from his chest, and that on getting up in the morning he had been unable to speak. This morning he could only answer my questions in a whisper, but declared that he was feeling perfectly fit and quite up to pulling all day. I didn't like the look of things, but we pushed on. After about two hours, however, Skelton ranged alongside to say that Handsley had broken down; it appears that the rear sledge party is finding it terribly hard work to keep up with us, and Handsley has been overstraining himself in attempting to do so. We camped and had lunch, after which Handsley said he felt sure he could go on, so we packed up, but this time I put all hands on a single sledge, marched it out about three miles, and leaving Handsley to pitch camp, went back to fetch the other one. This sort of thing won't do at all, but what is one to do?

'Handsley came to me tonight to beg that he might not be made an example of again. I tried to explain that I had no intention of reflecting on his conduct, but apparently nothing will persuade him but that his breakdown is in the nature of disgrace. What children these men are! and yet what splendid children! They won't give in till they break down, and then they consider their collapse disgraceful. The boatswain has been suffering agonies from his back; he has been pulling just behind me, and in some sympathy that comes through the traces I have got to know all about him, yet he has never uttered a word of complaint, and when he knows my eye is on him he straightens up and pretends he is just as fit as ever. What is one to do with such people?'

'November 21. – . . . There was nothing for it this morning but to go on with relay work. We started over heavy sastrugi, but soon came to a space where there was a smooth glazed crust, which made travelling easier. The wind blows continuously from the W.S.W., and the temperature has not been above −30° all day; conditions could not be more horrid. Handsley is better, but our whole day's work has only yielded four or five miles. Whatever disappointment it may entail, we cannot go on like this.'

'November 22. – After a night's cogitation, I determined this morning on a separation of our party. Till lunch we went on in the usual order, but at that meal I was obliged to announce my decision. Those told off to return took it extremely well; they could not disguise their disappointment, but they all seemed to understand that it had to be. The boatswain was transferred to the other tent, and Lashly to mine. After lunch the whole party manned our single sledge and marched out with us for two hours, then as the sky looked threatening, the three returning members turned back to seek their own camp, whilst I and my chosen two marched steadily on to the west.'

We had now lost sight of landmarks for several days, and were marching as straight a course as we could, principally with the aid of a small steering dial such as I described as being in use on our southern journey. The error of our compass had passed from east to west, and was nearly at its maximum of 180°; although I could not calculate it accurately at the time, I could get a good idea of its amount by observing the direction in which the sun reached its greatest altitude. The reader will see that from a magnetic point of view this was a very interesting region. We were directly south of the South Magnetic Pole, and the north end of our compass needle was pointing towards the South (geographical) Pole.

To show what a practical bearing this reversal of the compass had, I may remark that in directing Skelton on his homeward track to the eastward, I told him to steer due west by the compass card. It is only on this line or the similar one which joins the northern poles that such an order could be given, and we were not a little proud of being the first to experience this distinctly interesting physical condition in the Southern hemisphere.

From the date on which, so reluctantly, I decided that some of my party should turn homeward, there followed for us who remained, three weeks of the hardest physical work that I have ever experienced, and yet three weeks on which I cannot but look with unmixed satisfaction, for I do not think it would have been possible to have accomplished more in the time. I have little wonder when I remember the splendid qualities and physique of the two men who remained with me by such a severe process of selection. Evans was a man of Herculean strength, very long in the arm and with splendidly developed muscles. He had been a gymnastic instructor in the Navy, and had always been an easy winner in all our sports which involved tests of strength. He weighed 12 st. 10 lbs. in hard condition. Lashly, in appearance, was the most deceptive man I have ever seen. He was not above the ordinary height, nor did he look more than ordinarily broad, and yet he weighed 13 st. 8 lbs., and had one of the largest chest measurements in the ship. He had been a teetotaller and non-smoker all his life, and was never in anything but the hardest condition.

My own weight at this time was about 11 st. 6 lbs.; it fell so far short of the others that I felt I really did not deserve such a large food allowance, though I continued to take my full share.

With these two men behind me our sledge seemed to become a living thing, and the days of slow progress were numbered. We took the rough and the smooth alike, working patiently on through the long hours with scarce a word and never a halt between meal and meal. Troubles and discomforts were many, and we could only guess at the progress we made, but we knew that by sticking to our task we should have our reward when our observations came to be worked out on board the ship.

We were now so far from the edge of the plateau that our circumstances and conditions were such as must obtain over the whole of this great continental area at this season of the year. It is necessary, therefore, to give some description of them.

I used to read my aneroid with great regularity, and I find that the readings vary from 20.2 in. to 22.1 in., but both of these limits were under exceptional atmospheric conditions. By far the greater number of readings lie between 21.1 and 21.6 inches, and these differences were due to change of level to some extent, but, as will be seen, they do not admit of any considerable change in level. It was evident to us as we travelled onward that there were undulations in the plain; we could sometimes see the shadow of a rise and sometimes a marked depression, but these variations were so slight and so confused that we could make little of them, until we recognised a connection between them and the occurrence of the sastrugi. We then came to see that the summits and eastern faces of undulations were quite smooth with a very curious scaly condition of surface, whilst the hollows and the western faces were deeply furrowed with the wind. On our track, therefore, we met with great differences of surface. For long stretches we travelled over smooth glazed snow, and for others almost equally long we had to thread our way amongst a confused heap of sharp waves. I have rarely, if ever, seen higher or more formidable sastrugi than we crossed on this plateau. For instance, on November 24 I wrote: 'At first there were lanes of glazed surface leading to the W.S.W., but afterwards these disappeared, and we struggled over a sea of broken and distorted snow-waves. We were like a small boat at sea: at one moment appearing to stand still to climb some wave, and at the next diving down into a hollow. It was distressing work, but we stuck to it, though not without frequent capsizes, which are likely to have a serious effect on our stock of oil, for I fear a little is lost with each upset.'

Regularly each night, when the sun was low in the south, the temperature fell to −40° or below, whilst during the marching hours it rarely rose much above −25°, and with this low temperature we had a constant wind. At first it blew from the W. by S., and it was in this direction that most of the hard high sastrugi pointed, but we noticed that it was gradually creeping to the southward. Before we left the plateau it had gone to S.W. by W., and now and again it became still more southerly and brought a light snowfall which formed fresh waves in the new direction.

There can be little doubt, I think, that the wind blows from west to east across this plateau throughout the winter, and often with great violence, as the high snow-waves showed. What the temperature can be at that season is beyond guessing, but if the thermometer can fall to −40° in the height of summer, one can imagine that the darker months produce a terrible extremity of cold.

On November 26 I wrote: 'The wind is the plague of our lives. It has cut us to pieces. We all have deep cracks in our nostrils and cheeks, and our lips are broken and raw; our fingers are also getting in a shocking state; one of Evans's thumbs has a deep cut on either side of the nail which might have been made by a heavy slash with a knife. We can do nothing for this as long as we have to face this horrid wind. We suffer most during the first half-hour of the morning march before we have warmed up to the work, as then all these sore places get frostbitten. There is a good deal of pain also in the tent at night, and we try to keep our faces as still as possible; laughing is a really painful process, and so from this point of view jokes are not to be encouraged. The worst task of all is the taking of observations. I plant the theodolite as close as possible to the tent to gain what shelter I can, but it is impossible to get away from the wind, which punishes one badly at such times.'

'November 28. – Today we have a new development in the weather. The sky has been overcast with a bank of stratus cloud; the light has been very bad, and we have had the usual difficulty under such conditions in keeping our course. This is really serious. At this altitude I had expected at least the single advantage of a clear sky, but if we are to have overcast weather, our return journey will be a difficult matter. I almost thought of stopping today, but reflecting that days of this sort cannot be common, I resolved to push on to the appointed date.'

'November 29. – Started in moderately bad light, but in half an hour struggled through sastrugi to a decent surface and did a long march. Stopped for a minute or two to dig down in an apparent crevasse, but found, as I expected, that the resemblance was superficial. We have not seen a crack, crevasse, or sign of ice-disturbance since we reached the summit.

'Our finneskoes are getting very worn. Evans has had to take to his spare pair, but Lashly and I still have ours in reserve. One of the pair I am using, however, is scarcely good for more than two or three marches. We are all in excellent condition and health: not a sign of the scurvy fiend has appeared, though I watch narrowly for it.'

'November 30. – We have finished our last outward march, thank heaven! Nothing has kept us going during the past week but the determination to carry out our original intention of going on to the end of the month, and so here we have pitched our last camp. We made an excellent march in the forenoon, and started well after lunch, when we could see the sun gleaming on a more than ordinarily steep incline ahead. I altered course a little to take it square, and soon we were amongst heavy sastrugi. I think it must have taken an hour and a half to struggle through. It is not that it reduces our pace so much, but it shakes us up dreadfully; falls are constant, and the harness frequently brings up with a heavy jerk, which is exasperating to a tired man. At last we got through, and found on looking back that we must have descended into a hollow, as the horizon was above us on all sides. Ahead the slope was quite smooth, and, in spite of all the dreary monotony of the plain we have crossed, I felt distinctly excited to know what we should see when we got to the top. I knew it was the end of our effort, and my imagination suggested all sorts of rewards for our long labours. Perhaps there would be a gradual slope downward, perhaps more mountains to indicate a western coast for Victoria Land.

'Greenland, I remembered, would have been crossed in many places by such a track as we have made. I thought, too, what a splendid thing it would be to find a coast in this way. All very vain imaginings, of course, for after 200 miles of changeless conditions there was a poor chance indeed of finding a difference in the last one. But so it was. I journeyed up this slope with lively hopes, and had a distinct sense of disappointment when, on reaching the summit, we saw nothing beyond but a further expanse of our terrible plateau.

'Here, then, tonight we have reached the end of our tether, and all we have done is to show the immensity of this vast plain. The scene about us is the same as we have seen for many a day, and shall see for many a day to come – a scene so wildly and awfully desolate that it cannot fail to impress one with gloomy thoughts. I am not an imaginative person, but of late all sorts of stupid fancies have come into my mind. The sastrugi now got on my nerves; they are shaped like the barbs of a hook with their sharp points turned to the east, from which direction many look high and threatening, and each one now seems to suggest that, however easy we may have found it to come here, we shall have a very different task in returning.

'But, after all, it is not what we see that inspires awe, but the knowledge of what lies beyond our view. We see only a few miles of ruffled snow bounded by a vague wavy horizon, but we know that beyond that horizon are hundreds and even thousands of miles which can offer no change to the weary eye, while on the vast expanse that one's mind conceives one knows there is neither tree nor shrub, nor any living thing, nor even inanimate rock – nothing but this terrible limitless expanse of snow. It has been so for countless years, and it will be so for countless more. And we, little human insects, have started to crawl over this awful desert, and are now bent on crawling back again. Could anything be more terrible than this silent, windswept immensity when one thinks such thoughts?

'Luckily, the gloom of the outer world has not been allowed to enter the door of our tent. My companions spare no time for solemn thought; they are invariably cheerful and busy. Few of our camping hours go by without a laugh from Evans and a song from Lashly. I have not quite penetrated the latter yet; there is only one verse, which is about the plucking of a rose. It can scarcely be called a finished musical performance, but I should miss it much if it ceased.

'We are all very proud of our march out. I don't know where we are, but I know we must be a long way to the west from my rough noon observation of the compass variation; besides which we cannot have marched so many hours without covering a long distance. We have been discussing this matter at supper, and wondering whether future explorers will travel further over this inhospitable country. Evans remarked that if they did they "would have to leg it", and indeed I think they would.'

CHAPTER 18

Return from the West

Returning over the Great Plateau – Doubts about Provisions and Oil – Harrowing Effect of Fresh Snowfall – Thick Weather – No Sight of Landmarks – Sudden Descent into Glacier – Escape from a Crevasse – Exploration of North Arm – A Curious Valley – Return to the Ship – Results of other Sledging Efforts – Ferrar's Journey – Barne's Journey – Royds's Journey – Shorter Journeys – Review of Sledging Work

> Ceaseless frost round the vast solitude
> Bound its broad zone of stillness. – SHELLEY

The interior of Victoria Land must be considered the most desolate region in the world. There is none other that is at once so barren, so deserted, so piercingly cold, so windswept or so fearsomely monotonous.

I have attempted to give some idea of it in the last chapter, but I feel that my pen has poorly expressed the awe-inspiring nature of its terrible solitude. Nevertheless, when the reader considers its geographical situation, its great elevation, and the conditions to which we were subjected while travelling across it, he will, I think, agree that there can be no place on earth that is less attractive. For me the long month which we spent on the Victoria Land summit remains as some vivid but evil dream. I have a memory of continuous strain on mind and body lightened only by the unfailing courage and cheerfulness of my companions.

From first to last the month was a grim struggle with adversity, and never a trouble was overcome but some fresh one arose, until an ever-increasing load of anxiety was suddenly and finally removed. Thus it was that on turning homeward on December 1, whilst we enjoyed the relief of having the biting wind at our back, new difficulties soon appeared. Scarcely had we started our return march when the weather again grew overcast, and, though we struggled on for the first part of the day, the sky eventually became so gloomy that we were forced to camp and sacrifice more than an hour of the afternoon. On December 2, this sort of thing was still worse and landed us at one time in what seemed a most serious position, as my diary shows.

'We started at seven o'clock this morning, the sky very overcast, but the sun struggling through occasionally. All went well until ten o'clock, when the sun vanished and the light became shockingly bad. We plunged on for an hour amongst high sastrugi; our sledge capsized repeatedly and we ourselves sprawled in all directions. At length we could see nothing at all, and our falls became so frequent and heavy that I felt that we were running too great a risk of injury to our limbs, and that there was nothing for it but to camp. So here we are in our sleeping-bag in the middle of the marching-hours, and I don't like the look of things at all. We are about seventeen marches out from the glacier, but of course this includes the days when, with full numbers, we did poor distances. We have something over fourteen days' full rations left, and perhaps twelve days' oil allowance. If we could get clear weather, I believe we have not over-estimated our marching powers in supposing we can cover the longer daily distance required to reach the safety of the glacier, but this overcast weather puts an entirely new complexion on the matter; it is quite clear that we cannot afford delay. I don't like to think of half rations; we are all terribly hungry as it is, and I feel sure that we cannot cut down food without losing our strength. I try to think that at this altitude there cannot be long spells of overcast weather, but I cannot forget that if this condition should occur frequently we shall be in "Queer Street".'

The reader will remember that this same difficulty with an overcast sky had been met by my southern party of the previous year, and therefore it was not new to me; but, as I have pointed out, at the high altitude to which we had climbed, and with the low temperatures that prevailed, to find banks of cloud still above us was unexpected and added a most alarming circumstance to our situation. For, as will be seen, we had placed ourselves in a position from which we could only hope to retreat by relying on our hard condition and utilising all our marching powers; a simple arithmetic sum showed that we could not afford an hour's delay, and to be forced to lie idle in our tent was one of the most serious misfortunes that could overtake us. But this black outlook was not to remain for long, and later this day I was able to make a more cheering entry.

'After we had lain for two hours in the bag in a highly discon-solate frame of mind, Evans suddenly put his head outside and in his usual matter-of-fact tones remarked that the sun was shining. We were up in a moment. I do not believe sledges have ever been packed so quickly; it was certainly less than ten minutes before we were in our harness and away. As this meant shifting foot-gear, packing everything, and hoisting our sail, it can be imagined how we flew about. Strangely enough, by a good light we found the surface we had been struggling with in the morning was by no means bad, and now that we could see where to step, we got on at a great pace. In spite of our distressing delay we have covered a good distance. My companions are undefeatable. However tire-some our day's march or however gloomy the outlook, they always find something to jest about. In the evenings we have long arguments about naval matters, and generally agree that we could rule that Service a great deal better than any Board of Admiralty. Incidèntally I learn a greal deal about lower-deck life – more than I could hope to have done under ordinary conditions.'

'December 3. – . . . About an hour after lunch we suddenly came on one of our outward-bound night camps, and from that we followed our old track with some difficulty till we came to what I think must be our lunch camp of the 27th, which means that we have gained half a day on the outward march. Considering the bad light, this is good enough, but I shall hope to gain at a greater rate if the weather holds. The wind today was exceedingly cold, but with our backs to it it was not so much felt, except at packing and camp work, which were simply horrible. The old track we foll-owed is being rapidly drifted up; we are unlikely to see it again. Evans and Lashly have both been suffering a good deal from cold feet and fingers; my feet keep well, though fingers easily go.'

'December 4. – . . . We were up before five o'clock and away early. Started marching along the faint remains of our old track but soon lost it. We kept a good surface for two hours, then fell amongst bad sastrugi which gave us the usual trouble; by lunch we were fairly clear again. Returning now we can see more clearly the undulations of the surface; they seem irregular depressions rather than waves. We cross the hollows sometimes and seem to skirt them at others; they average anything from three to five miles across. The sledge has not capsized the whole day, which is a relief. The weather has been very threatening on several occasions during the last two days, but, thank heaven, it has come to nothing, and the sun only disappears altogether for very short intervals.'

'December 6. – . . . I am a little alarmed about our oil, so have decided to march half an hour extra each night. Tonight the weather became overcast again, but luckily not until our camping time had arrived. It is still terribly cold work, but we all feel exceedingly fit. My trouble is want of sleep, or, rather, it doesn't seem to trouble me except as regards the nuisance of lying awake in the bag. I have had extraordinarily little sleep this last week, and none of us seems to want much; after our long marches we ought to be in a fit state to go straight off into dreamland, but for some reason we are not.

'This afternoon two skua gulls were suddenly seen circling around us. It was such a pleasant sight that we could almost have cheered; but how in the world they can have found us at this great altitude and distance from the sea is beyond guessing. Hunger is growing upon us once more, though not to such an alarming extent as it did last year; still, we practise the same devices for serving out our rations, and are as keen at picking up the scraps as ever. It is curious that last year we used to think mostly of beef-steak pies and what Shackleton called "three-decker puddings", but this year there is ever before my eyes a bowl of Devon-shire cream. If it was only a reality, how ill I should be! I think Evans's idea of joy is pork, whilst Lashly dreams of vegetables, and especially apples. He tells us stories of his youth when these things, and not much else, were plentiful.'

During this time we were making excellently long marches, and gradually as the days passed we were losing much of our fear of the overcast weather in its power of delaying us, though I still saw that the greatly increased amount of cloud might make it most difficult for us to recognise our landmarks when they should appear in sight.

Certainly the ups and downs of sledging life are wonderful; for instance, on the 8th, I find my record full of hope. We had marched long hours over a comparatively easy surface; I did not know where we were, but I knew that we must be up to date, and that if conditions held as they were, we should reach the glacier in good time, even if we had to spend some time in looking for landmarks. But on the 9th came a most serious change of surface which seemed to baffle all our hopes at one blow, for we knew well that this new condition had come to stay. I found out afterwards that at this time we must have been somewhere close to the spot which we had crossed on November 16 when outward bound. I have given some description of the surface at that time; it was alternately hard and soft, but the hard places had been so slippery that we had been obliged to wear crampons to pull our sledges over them. Now all this was changed by a recent fall of snow, which had covered everything with a sandy layer of loose ice-crystals and brought terrible friction on the sledge-runners.

This layer grew heavier as we approached the edge of the plateau: apart from the difficulty which it presented to our travelling, this was an interesting observation, for it shows that the plateau snowfall takes place in December, and that it is far heavier on the edge than in the interior of the continent. Another interesting fact was observable in this connection, for whilst this light snow had been falling the wind had crept round to the south, sometimes to such an angle with our course that it was most difficult to trim our sledge sail to derive any benefit from it. In its most southerly direction it brought a desirable increase of temperature, and on some days we had a fair imitation of the mild southerly blizzards which were such a conspicuous feature at the ship. But at this time, as we plodded on with an eye on our diminishing stock of provisions, it can be imagined that we were not inclined to bless the climatic conditions which had wrought such a change in the surface. December 9, in fact, seemed to show everything going wrong for us, and the marches on that day and those which followed I can never forget. Our sledge weight was reduced almost to a minimum, and we ourselves were inured to hard marching if ever three persons were, yet by our utmost exertion we could barely exceed a pace of a mile an hour. I have done some hard pulling, but never anything to equal this. The sledge was like a log; two of us could scarcely move it, and therefore throughout the long hours we could none of us relax our efforts for a single moment – we were forced to keep a continuous strain on our harness with a tension that kept our ropes rigid and made conversation quite impossible. So heavy was the work that I may remark we once tried pulling on ski and found we simply couldn't move the sledge.

It was on the evening of the 9th that the seriousness of our position once more manifested itself, and I therefore resort again to my diary.

'. . . This afternoon the surface grew worse and worse, and at the end of the march we were all dog tired. The state of affairs is again serious, whereas this morning I thought it would only be a matter of hours before we should be able to increase our rations and satisfy the pangs of hunger, which are now growing very severe. I have had to think things out under this new development, and I don't find the task is pleasant; nothing is in sight ahead, and the prospect is gloomy. We have a week's provision in hand, but it looks mighty little in the midst of this horrible, never-ending plain; but what is more alarming is that we are well into our last can of oil, and there is only a few days' allowance left, at the rate we have been using it.

'We have had a long discussion about matters tonight. I told the men I thought we were in a pretty tight place, and that we should have to take steps accordingly. I proposed that we should increase our marching hours by one hour, go on half allowance of oil, and if we don't sight landmarks in a couple of days reduce our rations. I explained the scheme for oil economy which we adopted last year, and when I came to the cold lunch and fried breakfast poor Evans's face fell; he evidently doesn't much believe in the virtue of food unless it is in the form of a hoosh and has some chance of sticking to one's ribs. Lashly is to do all the cooking until we come to happier times, as he is far the best hand at the Primus, and can be relied upon not to exceed allowance.

'I have been struggling with my sights and deviations table, but although I believe we cannot be far off the glacier the sense of uncertainty is oppressive. We are really travelling by rule of thumb, and one cannot help all sorts of doubts creeping in when the consequences are so serious.'

'December 10. – This morning we plugged away for five mortal hours on a surface which is, if anything, worse than yesterday. The pulling is so heavy that it is impossible to drag one's thoughts away to brighter subjects, and the time passes in the most wearisome manner. Then came our new routine of cold, comfortless lunch, and we started once more. We had not been going more than an hour in the afternoon, however, when Evans's sharp eye sighted the land, and soon some isolated nunataks appeared on both bows. This was very cheering, and we struggled on through the remainder of our march with renewed hope. Later we rose several mountain peaks to the S.E., but cloud hangs so persistently about them that I cannot recognise anything. I imagine we are too far to the south, but I am not at all certain. I rather thought that when we saw the land it would bring immediate relief to all anxiety, but somehow it hasn't. I know that we must be approaching the edge of the plateau, but now the question is, where? There must be innumerable glaciers intersecting the mountains, and one cannot but see that it will be luck if we hit off our own at the first shot, and that we cannot afford to make a mistake. I hope and trust we shall soon recognise landmarks; but the sky is most unpromising, and it looks very much as though we were about to have a return of thick weather.'

On the 11th we caught only the same fleeting glimpses of the land as on the previous day, but we marched stolidly on, hoping for clearer weather, and on December 12 I wrote:

'It has been overcast all day. Now and again this morning I caught glimpses of land, which seems much closer, but I am still left in horrible uncertainty as to our whereabouts, as I could not recognise a single point. The light became very bad before lunch; everything except the sun was shut out, and that was only seen through broken clouds. Lately we have been pulling for ten hours a day; it is rather too much when the strain on the harness is so great, and we are becoming gaunt shadows of our former selves. My companions' cheeks are quite sunken and hollow, and with their stubbly untrimmed beards and numerous frostbite remains they have the wildest appearance; yet we are all fit, and there has not been a sign of sickness beyond the return of those well-remembered pangs of hunger which are now becoming exceedingly acute. We have at last finished our tobacco; for a long time Evans and I have had to be content with a half-pipe a day, but now even that small comfort has gone; it was our long stay in the blizzard camp that has reduced us to this strait. There is one blessing; the next day or two will show what is going to happen one way or the other. If we walk far enough in this direction we must come to the edge of the plateau somewhere, and anything seems better than this heavy and anxious collar work.'

'December 13. – Strong southerly wind with blinding drift when we started this morning. Marched steadily on for four hours, when Evans had his nose frostbitten. Evans's nose has always been the first thing to indicate stress of frostbiting weather. For some weeks it has been more or less constantly frostbitten, and in consequence it is now the most curious-looking object. He speaks of it with a comic forbearance, as though, whilst it scarcely belonged to him, it was something for which he was responsible, and had to make excuses. When I told him of its fault today, he said in a resigned tone, "My poor old nose again; well, there, it's chronic!" When this unruly member was brought round we found the storm increasing, and the surface changed to the hard wind-swept one which we encountered on our ascent. On this we slipped badly, and when we stopped to search for our crampons the wind had grown so strong that I thought it necessary to camp. Before this was accomplished we were all pretty badly frostbitten, and we had to make some hot tea to bring us round. After waiting for an hour there were some signs of clearance, and as we cannot now afford to waste a single moment I decided to push on. We held steadily to the east, and towards the end of our march there could be no doubt that we were commencing to descend. But it was uncanny work, for I haven't any notion where we are, and the drift was so thick about us that for aught we knew we might have been walking over the edge of a precipice at any moment. Tonight it is as thick as ever; it is positively sickening, but, good weather or bad, we must go on now.'

'December 15. – We all agree that yesterday was the most adventurous day in our lives, and we none of us want to have another like it. It seems wonderful that I should be lying here in ease and comfort to write of it, but as it is so, I can give its incidents in some detail.

'Very early in the morning I awoke to find that the storm had passed, and that the land was all around us; but the clouds hung about the higher summits, and I was still unable to recognise any peak with certainty. In this bewildered condition we packed our sledge, and I could see no better course than to continue our march due east. We had scarcely been going half an hour, however, when high ice hummocks and disturbances appeared ahead, and we found ourselves on a hard glazed surface, which was cracked in all directions. Hoping to avoid the disturbed area, we first made a circuit to the right and then another to the left, but in neither of these directions did the prospect look more hopeful; we stopped and had a council of war, but by this time the wind had sprung up again, it was bitterly cold, and the only result of our deliberations was to show more clearly that we did not know where we were. In this predicament I vaguely realised that it would be rash to go forward, as the air was once more becoming thick with snowdrift; but then to stop might mean another long spell in a blizzard camp, when starvation would soon stare us in the face. I asked the men if they were prepared to take the risk of going on; they answered promptly in the affirmative. I think that after our trying experiences we were all feeling pretty reckless.

'At any rate, we marched straight on for the ice disturbances, and were soon threading our way amongst the hummocks and across numerous crevasses. After a bit the surface became smoother, but at the same time the slope grew steeper, and our sledge began to overrun us. At this juncture I put the two men behind the sledge to hold it back whilst I continued in front to guide its course; we were all wearing crampons, which at first held well, but within a few minutes, as the inclination of the surface increased, our foothold became less secure.

'Suddenly Lashly slipped, and in an instant he was sliding downward on his back; directly the strain came on Evans, he too was thrown off his feet. It all happened in a moment, and before I had time to look the sledge and the two men hurtled past me; I braced myself to stop them, but might as well have attempted to hold an express train. With the first jerk I was whipped off my legs, and we all three lay sprawling on our backs and flying downward with an ever-increasing velocity.

'For some reason the first thought that flashed into my mind was that someone would break a limb if he attempted to stop our mad career, and I shouted something to this effect, but might as well have saved my breath. Then there came a sort of vague wonder as to what would happen next, and in the midst of this I was conscious that we had ceased to slide smoothly, and were now bounding over a rougher incline, sometimes leaving it for several yards at a time; my thoughts flew to broken limbs again, for I felt we could not stand much of such bumping. At length we gave a huge leap into the air, and yet we travelled with such velocity that I had not time to think before we came down with tremendous force on a gradual incline of rough, hard, windswept snow. Its irregularities brought us to rest in a moment or two, and I staggered to my feet in a dazed fashion, wondering what had happened.

'Then to my joy I saw the others also struggling to their legs, and in another moment I could thank heaven that no limbs were broken. But we had by no means escaped scatheless; our legs now show one black bruise from knee to thigh, and Lashly was unfortunate enough to land once on his back, which is bruised and very painful. At the time, as can be imagined, we were all much shaken. I, as the lightest, escaped the easiest, yet before the two men crawled painfully to their feet their first question was to ask if I had been hurt.

'As soon as I could pull myself together I looked round, and now to my astonishment I saw that we were well on towards the entrance of our own glacier; ahead and on either side of us appeared well-remembered landmarks, whilst behind, in the rough broken ice-wall over which we had fallen, I now recognised at once the most elevated ice cascade of our valley. In the rude fashion which I have described we must have descended some 300 feet; above us the snowdrift was still being driven along, but the wind had not yet reached our present level, so that all around us the sky was bright and clear and our eyes could roam from one familiar object to another until far away to the eastward they rested on the smoke-capped summit of Erebus.

'I cannot but think that this sudden revelation of our position was very wonderful. Half an hour before we had been lost; I could not have told whether we were making for our own glacier or for any other, or whether we were ten or fifty miles from our depot; it was more than a month since we had seen any known landmark. Now in this extraordinary manner the curtain had been raised; we found that our rule-of-thumb methods had accomplished the most accurate "land fall", and down the valley we could see the high cliffs of the Depot Nunatak where peace and plenty awaited us.

'How merciful a view this was we appreciated when we came to count up the result of our fall. Our sledge had not capsized until we all rolled over together at the end, but the jolting had scattered many of our belongings and had burst open the biscuit box, so that all that had remained in it lay distributed over the cascade; we had no provisions left except the few scraps we could pick up and the very diminished contents of our food bag. As well as our stiffening limbs would allow we hastened to collect the scattered articles, to repack the sledge, and to march on towards the depot. Before us now lay a long plateau, at the edge of which I knew we should find a second cascade, and beneath it the region of our Desolation Camp and a more gradual icy surface down to the Nunatak. By lunch-time we were well across the plateau, and we decided that our shaken condition deserved a hot meal, so we brewed cocoa and felt vastly better after swallowing it. By this time the wind had reached us again, and I had cold work in taking a round of angles, but I got through it, and in an hour we were on the march once more. We soon found ourselves at the top of the second cascade, and under conditions which prevented us from looking for an easy descent; however, fortune favoured us, and by going very slowly and carefully we managed to get down without accident.

'Though we were all much shaken and tired, we congratulated ourselves on having overcome the worst difficulties, and started off briskly to cover the last five or six miles which lay between us and our goal. Feeling quite unsuspicious of danger, we all three joined up our harness to our usual positions ahead of the sledge; this brought me in the middle and a little in advance, with Lashly on my right and Evans on my left. After we had been tramping on in this way for a quarter of an hour the wind swept across from the south, and as the sledge began to skid I told Lashly to pull wide in order to steady it. He had scarcely moved out in response to this order when Evans and I stepped on nothing and dis-appeared from his view; by a miracle he saved himself from following, and sprang back with his whole weight on the trace; the sledge flashed by him and jumped the crevasse down which we had gone, one side of its frame cracked through in the jerk which followed, but the other side mercifully held. Personally I remember absolutely nothing until I found myself dangling at the end of my trace with blue walls on either side and a very horrid

looking gulf below; large ice-crystals dislodged by our movements continued to shower down on our heads.

'As a first step I took off my goggles; I then discovered that Evans
was hanging just above me. I asked him if he was all right, and
received a reassuring reply in his usual calm, matter-of-fact tones.
Meanwhile I groped about on every side with my cramponed feet,
only to find everywhere the same slippery smooth wall. But my
struggles had set me swinging, and at one end of a swing my leg
suddenly struck a projection. In a moment I had turned, and saw at
a glance that by raising myself I could get foothold on it; with the
next swing I clutched it with my steel-shod feet, and after a short
struggle succeeded in partly transferring my weight to it. In this
position, with my feet firmly planted and my balance maintained
by my harness, I could look about me.

'I found myself standing on a thin shaft of ice which was wedged
between the walls of the chasm – how it came there I cannot
imagine, but its position was wholly providential; to the right or
left, above or below, there was not the vestige of another such
support – nothing, in fact, but the smooth walls of ice. My next
step was to get Evans into the same position as myself, and when
he had slipped his harness well up under his arms I found I could
pilot his feet to the bridge.

'All this had occupied some time and it was only now that I
realised what had happened above us, for there, some twelve feet
over our heads, was the outline of the broken sledge. I saw at once
what a frail support remained, and shouted to Lashly to ask what
he could do, and then I knew the value of such a level-headed
companion; for whilst he held on grimly to the sledge and us with
one hand, his other was busily employed in withdrawing our ski.
At length he succeeded in sliding two of these beneath the broken
sledge and so making our support more secure. The device was
well thought of, but it still left us without his active assistance; for,
as he told us, directly he relaxed his strain the sledge began to slip,
and he dared not trust only to the ski.

'There remained no other course for Evans and me but to climb
out by our own unaided efforts, and I saw that one of us would
have to make the attempt without delay, for the chill of the
crevasse was already attacking us and our faces and fingers were on
the verge of freezing. After a word with Evans I decided to try the

first climb myself, but I must confess I never expected to reach the top. It is some time since I swarmed a rope, and to have to do so in thick clothing and heavy crampons and with frostbitten fingers seemed to me in the nature of the impossible. But it was no use thinking about it, so I slung my mits over my shoulders, grasped the rope, and swung off the bridge. I don't know how long I took to climb or how I did it, but I remember I got a rest when I could plant my foot in the belt of my harness, and again when my feet held on the rings of the belt. Then came a mighty effort till I reached the stirrup formed by the rope span of the sledge, and then, mustering all the strength that remained, I reached the sledge itself and flung myself panting on to the snow beyond. Lashly said, "Thank God!" and it was perhaps then that I realised that his position had been the worst of all.

'For a full five minutes I could do nothing; my hands were white to the wrists, and I plunged them into my breast, but gradually their circulation and my strength came back, and I was able to get to work. With two of us on top and one below, things had assumed a very different aspect, and I was able to unhitch my own harness and lower it once more for Evans; then with our united efforts he also was landed on the surface, where he arrived in the same frostbitten condition as I had. For a minute or two we could only look at one another, then Evans said, "Well, I'm blowed"; it was the first sign of astonishment he had shown.

'But all this time the wind was blowing very chill, so we wasted no time in discussing our escape, but turning our broken sledge end for end, we were soon harnessed to it again and trudging on over the snow. After this, as can be imagined, we kept a pretty sharp lookout for crevasses, marching in such an order as prevented more than one of us going down at once, and so we eventually reached the bare blue ice once more, and at six o'clock found our depot beneath the towering cliffs of the Depot Nunatak.

'As long as I live I can never forget last night. Our camp was in bright sunshine, for the first time for six weeks the temperature was above zero, but what we appreciated still more was the fact that it was perfectly calm; the canvas of our tent hung limp and motionless, and the steam of our cooking rose in a thin, vertical shaft. All Nature seemed to say that our long fight was over, and that at length we had reached a haven of rest. And it has been a fight indeed; it is only now that I realise what discomforts we have endured and what a burden of anxiety we have borne during the past month. The relief of being freed from such conditions is beyond the power of my pen to describe, but perhaps what brought it home to us most completely was the fact that the worst of our troubles and adventures came at the end, and that in the brief space of half an hour we passed from abject discomfort to rest and peace.

'And so we dawdled over everything. We were bruised, sore, and weary, yet Lashly sang a merry stave as he stirred the pot, and Evans and I sat on the sledge, shifted our foot-gear, spread our garments out to dry, and chatted away merrily the whole time. Evans's astonishment at the events of the day seemed to grow ever deeper, and was exhibited in the most amusing manner. With his sock half on he would pause to think out our adventures in some new light and would say suddenly, "Well, sir, but what about that snow bridge?" or if so-and-so hadn't happened "where should we be now?" and then the soliloquy would end with "My word, but it was a close call!" Evans generally manages to sum a case up fairly pithily, and perhaps this last remark is a comprehensive description of our experiences of yesterday.

'This morning the sun shines as brightly as ever, and there is still no breath of wind. It is so warm in the tent that as I write I have had to throw open my jacket. Meanwhile outside I can hear the tap of the hammer as my companions are arming our sledge-runners for the hard ice of the glacier.'

We only found a very small quantity of food at the Depot Nunatak, but it was enough to carry us to the main depot, which lay several miles below, provided we marched hard, as we were quite prepared to do. Luckily, here also we found a new nine-foot sledge which had been left the previous year, and to which we could now transfer the greater part of our load. But one of our most pleasing discoveries at the Depot Nunatak was the small folded notes which told us of the movements of our fellow-travellers. By these I learnt to my relief that Skelton and his companions had safely reached the glacier, and that Ferrar's party was all well after it had left our Desolation Camp. According to previous arrangements I found these notes at various stated points in the glacier, and there were few pleasanter things for us returning wayfarers than to find these cheery documents.

Starting our downward march on the afternoon of the 15th, we stretched over the miles with ease. This sort of work was mere child's play to our hardened muscles, and that night we reached the broad amphitheatre below Finger Mountain. On the 16th we picked up the ample supply of food which we had left in our depot opposite the Solitary Rocks, and that evening took up our old quarters in the Knob Head Moraine. I mention these movements because at this point I had determined to do a small piece of exploration which is of some interest. The reader will see that we were now in the large glacier basin which I described, and will remember that I mentioned amongst other outlets its northern arm. This arm of the glacier descended with a very steep incline to the right of the Solitary Rocks, and then its valley seemed to turn sharply to the eastward. The direction of flow of the ice-streams in the glacier basin had always been something of a mystery for us, and we had thought that the main portion of the ice must discharge through this valley.

On the 17th, therefore, we started to descend it to see what the conditions actually were, and after rattling down over a sharp gradient for several miles we found ourselves turning to the east. We followed a long string of morainic boulders through a deep valley on a moderate incline, but early in the afternoon the descent became steeper and the surface of the ice much rougher, until at length our sledge bumped so heavily that we thought it wise to camp.

Our camp life by this time had become wholly pleasant except to poor Lashly, who had a fierce attack of snow-blindness. We pitched our tent behind a huge boulder which must have weighed at least five hundred tons, and here we were pleasantly sheltered from the wind, whilst close by us trickled a glacier stream from which we were able to fill our cooking-pot and obtain an unlimited quantity of drinking-water. We had a splendid view of the great ice masses sweeping down from above, but looking downward we were much puzzled, for the glacier surface descended steeply, and beyond it stood a lofty groin of rock which seemed a direct bar to its further passage. This sight made us very anxious to proceed with our exploration, and as we could not advance further with our sledge, it became necessary to arrange for a long absence from our camp. Accordingly we rose very early on the following day, and taking our coil of Alpine rope, with our crampons and a supply of food, we set off over the rough ice of the glacier. As this walk had several points of interest, I give its outline from my diary.

'Started at seven o'clock with a supply of pemmican, chocolate, sugar, and biscuit in our pockets, and our small provision measure to act as a drinking-cup. It is an extraordinary novelty in our sledging experience to find that one can get water by simply dipping it up. As we descended, the slope became steeper, and soon the ice grew so disturbed that we were obliged to rope ourselves together and proceed with caution. The disturbance was of very much the same nature as that which we had found on the south side of the Ferrar Glacier; the ice seemed to have broken down, leaving steep faces towards the south. Here and there we found scattered boulders and finer morainic material, and the channels of the glacial streams became visible in places, to vanish again under deep blue arches of ice.

'At length we descended into one of these watercourses and followed it for some distance, until, to our surprise, it came abruptly to an end, and with it the glacier itself, which had gradually dwindled to this insignificant termination. Before us was a shallow, frozen lake into which the thaw-water of the glacier was pouring. The channel in which we stood was about twenty feet above its surface, and the highest pinnacles of ice were not more than the same distance above our heads, whereas the terminal face of the glacier was about three or four hundred yards across. So here was the limit of the great ice-river which we had followed down from the vast basin of the interior; instead of pouring huge icebergs into the sea, it was slowly dwindling away in its steep-sided valley. It was, in fact, nothing but the remains of what had once been a mighty ice-flow from the inland.

'With a little difficulty we climbed down to the level of the lake, and then observed that the glacier rested on a deep ground moraine of mud, in some places as much as ten or twelve feet in thickness; this layer of mud extended beyond the face of the glacier, where it had been much worn by water; enough remained, however, for Lashly to remark, "What a splendid place for growing spuds!" Skirting the lake below the glacier, we found ourselves approaching the high, rocky groin which puzzled us so much last night, but we now saw that a very narrow channel wound round its base. At its narrowest this channel was only seventeen feet across, and as we traversed this part, the high cliffs on either side towered above our heads and we seemed to be passing through a massive gateway; beyond this the valley opened out again, and its floor was occupied by a frozen lake a mile in breadth and three or four miles in length. As the snow surface of this lake was very rough, we were obliged to skirt its margin; we were now 1,300 feet below our camp, and about 300 feet above sea level. The shores of the lake for several hundred feet up the hillsides were covered with a coarse granitic sand strewn with numerous boulders, and it was curious to observe that these boulders, from being rounded and sub-angular below, gradually grew to be sharper in outline as they rose in level.

'At the end of the second lake the valley turned towards the north-east; it was equally clearly cut, but the floor rose on a mass of morainic material. At first there was a general tendency for this to be distributed in long ridges, but later the distribution was disturbed, and it was easy to see that broad water-channels had made clean breaches in these vast piles of sand and boulders. Quite suddenly these moraines ceased, and we stepped out on to a long stretch of undulating sand traversed by numerous small streams, which here and there opened out into small, shallow lakes quite free from ice.

'I was so fascinated by all these strange new sights that I strode forward without thought of hunger until Evans asked if it was any use carrying our lunch further; we all decided that it wasn't, and so sat down on a small hillock of sand with a merry little stream gurgling over the pebbles at our feet. It was a very cheery meal, and certainly the most extraordinary we have had. We commanded an extensive view both up and down the valley, and yet, except about the rugged mountain summits, there was not a vestige of ice or snow to be seen; and as we ran the comparatively warm sand through our fingers and quenched our thirst at the stream, it seemed almost impossible that we could be within a hundred miles of the terrible conditions we had experienced on the summit.

'Proceeding after lunch, we found that the valley descended to a deep and splendid gorge formed by another huge groin extending from the southern side, but as we approached the high cliffs we found our way again obstructed by confused heaps of boulders, amongst which for the first time we saw the exposed rocks of the floor of the valley smoothed and striated in a manner most typical of former ice action. My object in pressing on had been to get a view of the sea, and I now thought the best plan would be to ascend the neck of the groin on our right. It was a long climb of some 700 feet over rough, sharp boulders. We eventually reached the top, but, alas! not to catch any glimpse of the sea; for the valley continued to wind its way onward through deep gorges, and some five or six miles below yet another groin shut out our further view.

'But from our elevated position we could now get an excellent view of this extraordinary valley, and a wilder or in some respects more beautiful scene it would have been difficult to imagine. Below lay the sandy stretches and confused boulder heaps of the valley floor, with here and there the gleaming white surface of a frozen lake and elsewhere the silver threads of the running water; far above us towered the weather-worn, snow-splashed mountain peaks, between which in places fell in graceful curves the folds of some hanging glacier. The rocks at our feet were of every variety of colour and form, mixed in that inextricable confusion which ice alone can accomplish. The lower slopes of the mountains were thickly clothed with similar rocks, but the variety of colour was lost in the distance, and these steep slopes had a general tone of sober grey. This colour was therefore predominant, but everywhere at a height of 3,000 feet above the valley it ended in a hard line illustrating in the most beautiful manner the maximum extent to which the ice had once spread.

'I cannot but think that this valley is a very wonderful place. We have seen today all the indications of colossal ice action and considerable water action, and yet neither of these agents is now at work. It is worthy of record, too, that we have seen no living thing, not even a moss or a lichen; all that we did find, far inland amongst the moraine heaps, was the skeleton of a Weddell seal, and how that came there is beyond guessing. It is certainly a valley of the dead; even the great glacier which once pushed through it has withered away.

'It was nearly four o'clock before we turned towards our camp, and nearly ten before we reached it, feeling that it was quite time for supper. The day's record, however, is a pretty good tribute to our marching powers, for we have walked and climbed over the roughest country for more than fourteen hours with only one brief halt for lunch.'

With this short expedition our last piece of exploration came to an end, and on the 19th we started to ascend the north arm. By the night of the 20th we had reached our second depot under Cathedral Rocks, and here for the first time, and with anxious eyes, we looked out towards the sea. Many a time we had discussed this prospect, and agreed that we should not have cared how far round we had to walk if only that stubborn sheet of ice in the strait would break away. But now, alas! it was evident that our homeward track might be as direct as we chose to make it, for the great unbroken plain of ice still bridged the whole strait. Only in the far distance could we see the open water, where a thin blue ribbon ran in from Cape Bird and ended abreast of the black rocks of Cape Royds. We saw with grief that there must be very many miles between it and our unfortunate ship.

On rounding Butter Point we had another blow on finding an entire absence of seals, but, thanks to the kindness of Skelton and his party, we were not deprived of our long-expected feast of fresh meat, for close to our tin of butter we found a buried treasure in the shape of some tit-bits of an animal which they had killed. From Butter Point we turned our course south to those curious moraine heaps which we had called the 'Eskers', and which I had not yet seen. We spent half a day in rambling amongst these steep little hills, and in trying to find skuas' eggs which were not hard set; but fortune was against us in this last respect, and we found that we were at least a week too late.

On the afternoon of the 23rd we started to cross the strait for the last time, and late on Christmas Eve we saw the masts of the *Discovery*, and were soon welcomed by the four persons who alone remained on board. And so after all our troubles and trials we spent our Christmas Day in the snug security of our home quarters, and tasted once again those delights of civilised existence to which we had so long been strangers.

And now, seated at my desk, I could quietly work out my observations, and trace the track which we had made. I found, to my relief, that my watch had kept an excellent rate, as far as my observed positions could check it. This was a matter of great importance, as the longitude of our position on the great plain of the interior depended entirely on its accuracy. This watch has since been given to me by its makers, and I value it highly; as I think few watches have done greater service; and here, for the benefit of future explorers, I must again point out the importance of the manner in which a watch is carried on such a journey. I shifted my watch-pocket several times during my earlier experiences before I decided on its best position, and throughout my travels I never failed to treat my watch with the greatest care. The pocket was eventually sewn to my inner vest, in such a position that my harness could not touch it, and I never took the watch out of this warm place unless it was necessary; when taking sights I held it in the palm of my hand, and as far as possible under the cover of a mit.

When I had worked out our various positions and calculated the distances we had travelled, I had before me an array of figures of which our party might justifiably feel proud. In our last absence of fifty-nine days we had travelled 725 miles; for nine complete days we had been forced to remain in camp, so that this distance had been accomplished in fifty marching days, and gave a daily average of 14.5 miles.

Taking the eighty-one days of absence which had constituted our whole sledging season, I found that Evans, Lashly, and I had covered 1,098 miles, at an average of 15.4 miles a day, and that, not including minor undulations, we had climbed heights which totalled to 19,800 feet.

I started my account of this journey by saying that I thought we came near the limit of possible performance in the circumstances, and I hope these figures will be considered as justifying that remark. What the circumstances were I have endeavoured to show, but when it is considered that to the rigours of a polar climate were added those which must be a necessary consequence of a great altitude, it needs little explanation to prove that they were exceptionally severe.

We may claim, therefore, to have accomplished a creditable journey under the hardest conditions on record, but for my part I devoutly hope that wherever my future wanderings may trend, they will never again lead me to the summit of Victoria Land.

The four persons whom we found on board the *Discovery* on our return were Dr Koettlitz, our ship's steward, Handsley (who had not yet fully recovered from his chest troubles), and Quartley (who had received a slight injury on the southern journey). All the remainder of our company had gone to the north, in accordance with our pre-arranged plan, to saw through the ice. I purposed shortly to go in this direction myself, but after our excessive work the usual reaction set in, and I thought that my small party had earned a few days' rest in which we might renew our energies. Communications with the northern camp were of daily occurrence, thanks to our new team of dogs, which had been brought into capital working order by their driver, Dell.

It was not long therefore before I learnt the outlines of the other sledge journeys, and was able to read the reports of the officers who had led them and study the advance which had been made in our knowledge by the sledging work of our second season. Space does not permit me to go in detail into these various journeys, nor do I think that the reader would be grateful for the minute relation of more sledging adventures. But this story would not be complete without a summary of the material facts which these efforts produced, nor could I omit to pay a well-earned tribute to those who secured them by prolonged and arduous labour and unfailing spirit.

I purpose, therefore, to give in brief the movements of other members of the expedition during our absence to the west.

It will be remembered that the party which had left the ship with me towards the end of October had eventually split into three units. At first our geologist, Ferrar, left us to explore the glacier valley, and later Skelton and I parted company on the inland ice. Skelton, returning with his overworked party, had wisely taken matters easily, but on arriving at the Depot Nunatak he had picked up the half-plate camera, and, although he had only a very limited number of plates, he succeeded in taking some excellent photographs of the valley.

Ferrar with his two companions had also come down the valley slowly, not because he had lingered on his way, but because he had crossed and recrossed the glacier to examine the rocks on each side. I was quite astonished to learn the numbers of places he had visited and the distances he had traversed in pursuit of his objects, especially when I remembered that all had been done with one rickety little sledge which I knew must have broken down repeatedly and have given endless trouble to those who dragged it. The results of this journey are told by the geologist in the appendix to the two volume edition of this work, but he has not told of all the difficulties which he had to overcome and which in themselves might well form a chapter of this book. For each specimen of rock which Ferrar brought back was obtained only by traversing long miles of rough ice, by clambering over dangerous crevassed slopes, and by scaling precipitous cliffs; and all this at a great distance from home, and where a strained limb might have led to very serious consequences.

It will be remembered that the main work of this season was thoroughly to explore this valley and the ice-cap which lay beyond; thus, when to the results of the longer journey were added Ferrar's survey and Skelton's photographic work we had the satisfaction of knowing that our object had been well accomplished.

The object before Barne and Mulock on their journey to the south has already been stated. They left the ship on October 6, and, passing around the Bluff, steered for the inlet which has since been named after the former.

But ill fortune dogged this party from the start. They were hampered by continual gales from the south, and again and again had to spend long days in their tents, as it was impossible to march onward with the wind directly in their faces. In this manner no fewer than ten days were wasted on the outward march, four of these being consecutive, and consequently it was not until the middle of November that they approached the entrance to the inlet, and here they became involved amongst numerous undulations and disturbances which greatly impeded their progress.

As they advanced these disturbances grew worse, and it was necessary to cross wide crevasses and clamber over steep ridges. On November 19, to their great disappointment, they were forced to turn, having barely passed the mouth of the inlet which they had hoped to explore. From their observations, however, it seems evident that the whole of this area is immensely disturbed, and it is doubtful whether a sledge party could ever cross it unless they were prepared to spend many weeks in the attempt. Although from their farthest position they could see no definite rise in the level of the ice in the inlet, as they travelled towards its northern side they found a moraine of large granite boulders which showed conclusively the general flow of the ice-stream and gave some indication of the nature of the land which lay beyond.

Throughout this journey Mulock was indefatigable in using the theodolite. The result of this diligence is that this stretch of coastline is more accurately plotted than any other part of Victoria Land, and by the fixing of the positions and heights of more than two hundred mountain peaks a most interesting topographical survey of this region has been achieved.

But one of the most important results of this expedition was obtained almost by an accident. The reader will remember that in my early journey in 1902 I fixed on a position off the Bluff to establish what I called Depot A. This position lay on the alignment of a small peak on the Bluff with Mount Discovery. On visiting this depot in 1903, Barne found to his astonishment that the alignment was no longer 'on', and therefore it was evident that the depot had moved. Thirteen and a half months after the establishment of the depot he measured its displacement, and found it to be 608 yards. And thus almost accidentally we obtained a very good indication of the movement of the Great Barrier ice-sheet.

To this very interesting fact I shall refer in considering the results of the expedition. Barne and his party safely reached the ship on December 13, after being absent sixty-eight days.

I have already referred to the projected trip to the south-east; it will be remembered that its object was to ascertain whether the barrier continued level in that direction. The conduct of this journey was undertaken by Royds, and with him went our physicist Bernacchi, Cross, Plumley, Scott, and Clarke; the track which was taken by the party can be seen on the chart.* It was a short journey, as it only occupied thirty days, and for those who took part in it it could not be otherwise than monotonous and dull; yet it deserves to rank very high in our sledging efforts, for every detail was carried out in the most thoroughly efficient manner.

The party went on a very short food allowance, and day after day found themselves marching over the same unutterably wearisome plain, and on a surface of such a nature as I described in my own southern journey; yet they marched steadily on, and fully accomplished the main object for which they were sent − a

---

* Not reproduced in this edition.

negative but highly important result. It was on this journey also that a most interesting series of magnetic observations were taken by Bernacchi, who carried with him the Barrow dip circle, an especially delicate instrument. The great value of these observations lies in the fact that they were taken in positions which were free from all possible disturbance either from casual iron or from land masses; the positions also run in a line which is almost directly away from the magnetic pole, and consequently the series is an invaluable aid to mapping out the magnetic conditions of the whole of this region.

To Bernacchi belongs the credit of these observations, but a certain amount of reflected glory must be allowed to those who accompanied him, for whilst he wrestled with the usual troubles of the observer within the tent, his companions had to cool their heels outside; and as they consented to do this night after night for an hour or more, it may be considered that they showed considerable practical sympathy with his scientific aims.

On December 10 Royds and his party arrived on board the ship in an extremely famished state, but with the satisfaction of having accomplished an exceedingly fine journey.

Our sledging efforts of 1903 were not confined to the longer journeys, for, as in the previous year, many shorter trips were made. From October 12 Wilson was away for more than three weeks to pay yet another visit to the Emperor penguin rookery. It was on this occasion that he observed the extraordinary manner in which these penguins migrated with their young. It will be remembered that in the previous year these birds had been found with very young chicks in down, and that on a second visit, shortly after, all the chicks had vanished, though it was evident that they could not have been prepared to take to the water. Now this mystery was explained. Soon after Wilson's arrival the ice began to break away, and he watched the parent birds and their young leave their rookery and station themselves in batches near the edge of the ice-sheet. In due course a piece of ice on which a batch stood was broken off, and slowly sailed away to the north with its freight of penguins, and there can be no doubt that in this manner these curious creatures are transported for many hundreds of miles until the chicks have attained their adult plumage and can earn their own living.

Emperor penguin rookery

Wilson spent twelve days at Cape Crozier, and probably at what is the most interesting season of the year in that region. Whilst the steady emigration of parties of Emperor penguins went on day after day, a little further to the west there was an equally steady immigration of Adélie penguins now coming south to lay their eggs on the lower slopes of Mount Terror. Both these movements were evidently dependent on the seasonal change which was taking place, for on his arrival Wilson found the Ross Sea frozen over, and on precisely the same date as on the previous year a series of S.W. gales commenced, and swept the sea clear, giving at once a chance for the Emperors to go and the Adélies to come. Such a long stay as this party made was only rendered possible by a lucky find of seals on the sea-ice, these animals providing them with food and fuel. As this was the only time that our sledge parties cooked their meals with a blubber fire, I quote from Wilson's report: 'We killed a seal and brought the whole skin to camp. It was cut into three long strips with all the blubber on, and to each was tied a piece of line. Each of us had one strip to manage in crossing the pressure ridges. When we reached camp a stove was improvised outside the tent by Whitfield and Cross; it was made out of an old tin biscuit box, which had been left on a previous journey, and some stones, and in this we eventually succeeded in lighting a blubber fire, over which we cooked our supper.'

Altogether this journey to Cape Crozier was more productive of information than any of its predecessors, for Wilson by no means confined himself to his zoological studies. He climbed high on the foothills of Mount Terror and discovered a curious ice-formed terrace 800 feet above the barrier level; he collected numerous geological specimens from this area, and found erratic boulders at great altitudes. Next he made a complete examination of the enormous and interesting pressure ridges which form the junction of the Great Barrier ice-mass with the land, and now and at a later date he spent much time in studying the curious windless area which exists to the south of Ross Island, and thus threw considerable light on meteorological facts that puzzled us, and on the ice condition of an extremely interesting region.

I cannot conclude a summary of our last sledging season without referring to an excellent little journey made by Armitage, Wilson, and Heald. This small party crossed the strait towards the end of November and then turned sharply to the south under the foothills of the mainland. In this manner they broke new ground, and reached and examined the Koettlitz Glacier. This had previously been seen only from Brown Island, and its closer examination was important not only to complete the topographical survey of our region, but to verify numerous observations taken in the Ferrar Glacier. Amidst a scene of wild beauty Armitage obtained some excellent photographs which give a good idea of the typical mountain scenery, and would alone prove the receding glacial conditions of the whole continent.

Thus it will be seen that whilst I had been away on my long journey to the west, my companions had been working diligently in every direction which promised to increase our store of information. All, however, had returned before myself, so that when I arrived at the ship on Christmas Eve, 1903, it was to ring the curtain down on the last of our sledging efforts in this Far Southern region.

When all things are considered, it must be conceded that no polar ship ever wintered in a more interesting spot than the *Discovery*. It was good fortune which had brought us to our winter quarters in February 1902, and from the first we saw what great possibilities lay before us, and determined that no effort should be spared to take advantage of our opportunities. During one long season we had laboured hard to this end, but yet its finish found us with many important gaps in our knowledge. Then fortune decided that we should be given another season to complete our work, and we started forth once more to fill in those gaps. With what success this was accomplished I have endeavoured to show, and I trust it will be agreed that after the close of our second sledging season we were justified in considering that the main part of our work was done.

CHAPTER 19

Escape from the ice

And Thor
Set his shoulder hard against the stern
To push the ship through . . .
. . . and the water gurgled in
And the ship floated on the waves and rock'd.
— M. ARNOLD

On the whole, the few days' rest which I allowed myself and my party after our return to the ship was enjoyable, and for such sensations as were not I had only myself to thank. I found that Ford had become cook for the few who remained on board, and that, as a result of studying Mrs Beeton's cookery book, he was achieving dishes of a more savoury nature than we had thought possible with the resources at our command. It was unfortunate that the highest development of the cooking art should have occurred at this season, as it found us too morally weak to resist its allurements, and, as a consequence, we suffered from the most violent indigestion. Though my limbs craved for rest, I was obliged to be up and doing to silence the worst pangs of this complaint.

The ship at this time was in a more snowed-up condition than I ever remember to have seen her, and Koettlitz told me there had been such heavy falls of snow a week earlier that they had been obliged to dig their way out of the lobby entrances. Koettlitz had remained on board to attend on the medical cases; these were now practically off his hands, but he was devoting most of his time, as he had done throughout the summer, to bacteriological studies.

He rather feared, however, that his diligence in this line would prove of little avail, as few less promising places could have been found for pursuing such investigations than the wardroom of the *Discovery*.

After two or three days on board I began to grow restless to see what was doing to the north; moreover, I saw that as I could not curb my appetite there was little chance of being rid of my indigestion until I was once more on the march. Our inactivity was also having a most obvious effect on my sledging companions. It had to be acknowledged that they were 'swelling wisibly'; each morning their faces became a more ludicrous contrast to what I remembered of them on the summit. Lashly was a man who usually changed little, and therefore he quickly fell back into his ordinary condition, but Evans continued to expand, and reached quite an alarming maximum before he slowly returned to his normal size.

On the morning of the 31st, therefore, we three, with Handsley, who was now quite recovered, packed our sledge once more, and started away for the sawing camp, some ten and a half miles to the north; in the afternoon we arrived at the camp, to be greeted with cheers and congratulations.

I may perhaps now explain how this camp came to be formed. The reader will remember that I had arranged that the sledging parties should return by the middle of December, and that in the meantime a special tent should be prepared and disposition made so that as soon as possible after this date all hands should be available for the projected attempt to saw through the great ice-sheet which intervened between the *Discovery* and the open sea. In drawing out instructions I could not foretell, of course, how broad this ice-sheet would be when operations were commenced; I could only assume that it would be about the same as in the previous year, when the open water had extended to the Dellbridge Islets, about eleven miles from the ship. I directed, therefore, that the camp should be made behind these islets, so that there might be no chance of its being swept away. I had hoped to be back in time to commence the operations myself, but the breakdown of my sledges had made this impossible, and in my absence the command devolved on Armitage. He made all preparations in accordance with my instructions, but was then met with a difficulty, for when the middle of

December came the open water, instead of being up to the islets, ended at least ten miles farther to the north. In these circumstances he thought it dangerous to take the camp out to the ice-edge, and decided to pitch it behind the islets as had been previously arranged. But this, of course, meant that the sawing work had to be commenced in the middle of the ice-sheet instead of at its edge, with the result that I shall presently describe.

When I arrived at the camp the greater number of our people had been at work for ten days; the work and the camp life had fallen into a regular routine, so that I was able to judge at once of past results and future prospects. Life at this sawing camp was led under such curious conditions that it deserves some description. The main tent was a very palatial abode judged by our standards of sledging life. It was of long pent-roof shape, the dimensions being about 50 feet long and 18 feet across, and it had a door with a small lobby at each end. The interior was divided into two compartments by a canvas screen; the smaller, about 18 feet in length, was for the officers, whilst the larger accommodated the men. Close to this screen in the men's quarters stood a small cooking-range mounted on boards. The floor of both spaces was covered with tarpaulin as far as possible, and as time went on imposing tables and stools were manufactured from packing-cases. All the fur sleeping-bags were in use, but as these were not sufficient for all hands, some slept between blankets. However, this was no hardship, as very little covering was needed and nearly everyone complained of the heat of the tent. The temperature had been extraordinarily high, sometimes rising to 35° or 36°, and when the sun shone on the dark canvas of the tent a few found the interior so oppressive that they sought outside shelter in the smaller sledging tents, or spread their sleeping-bags on a piece of canvas in the open.

Thirty people were at the camp when we arrived. They were divided into three parties of ten, which relieved one another on the saws. The work on the latter was exceedingly heavy, so that a four-hour spell was quite sufficient for one party. It took them twenty minutes to get to their work, and another twenty to get back to the tent when they were relieved; then, after cooking and eating a meal, they would coil down for five or six hours, and rise in time for a fresh meal before the next spell of work. With three parties working in this manner the preparation of meals practically never ceased throughout the twenty-four hours, and cook succeeded cook at the small range. Luckily this was a land of plenty. The tent lay within 200 yards of the largest of the islets, where the working of the ice formed spaces of open water through which hundreds of seals rose to bask on the floe. Now and again also a small troop of Adélie penguins would hurry towards the tent full of curiosity – to find their way promptly into the cooking-pot. Every other day the dog sledge came from the ship laden with flour, biscuit, sugar, butter, and jam, so that supplies of all sorts were readily available – and constant supplies were very much needed, as my earliest impressions of the camp assured me.

'It is a real treat to be amongst our people once more and to find them in such splendid condition and spirits. I do not think there is a whole garment in the party; judging by the torn and patched clothing, they might be the veriest lot of tramps, but one would have to go far to find such sturdy tramps. Everyone is burnt to a deep bronze colour by the sun, but in each dark face one has not to wait long for the smiles which show the white of teeth and clear healthy eyes. I have been sitting on a packing-case with everyone trying to tell me stories at once, and from the noise which has come from beyond the screen I know that my sledge companions have been in much the same position.

'It appears that the work on the saws was felt very much at first, and arms and backs became one huge ache. Everyone had felt that if it had been leg work there would have been no difficulty after the sledging experience, but the new departure exercised a different set of muscles altogether, so that after the first efforts people suffered much from stiffness; but this soon wore off, and then there had come the emulation of one party against another to show which could complete the longest cut in a four-hour spell. There had been no reason to be alarmed about the appetites even before this work commenced, but as soon as it had settled down into full swing, it was as much as the dog-team and the seal killers could do to keep up supplies. I could scarcely wonder at this from what I saw tonight: one of the returning parties first fell on an enormous potful of porridge, and it was gone before one could well look round; next came a dish piled high with sizzling seal steaks, and very soon the dish was empty; then came the jam course, with huge hunks of bread and "flap Johnny" cakes, the sort of thing that is produced on a griddle, and which I hear is very popular. Finally, after their light supper, this party composed themselves to sleep, and very soon other people arose and inquired how their breakfast was getting on.

'Each party have four of these meals in the day, so that twelve meals altogether are served in the tent. Barne's party seem to hold the record; it appears that they possess an excellent cook in Smythe, and that a few days ago he prepared for them a splendid stew which took seven penguins in the making; after cooking this he turned his attention to making cakes, and not until these were finished did he demand his share of the first dish, and then he discovered that there was none left! Considering that a penguin is not far off the size of a goose, I think this party deserve to retain the palm.

'But, apart from this, I do not think I ever saw such exuberant, overflowing health and spirits as now exist in this camp. It is a good advertisement for teetotallers, as there is no grog, and our strongest drinks are tea and cocoa, but of course the most potent factor is the outdoor life with the hard work and good food. Apart from the work, everyone agrees that it has been the most splendid picnic they have ever had; the weather on the whole has been very fine and the air quite mild. But it is certainly well that the conditions have been so pleasant, for I hear on all sides that the work is hopeless. This is a matter I must see for myself, however; for the present I have decided that tomorrow, being New Year's day, shall be a whole holiday; this will be a treat for all, and will give me time to think what shall be done next.'

'January 1. – Last night I was irresistibly reminded of being in a farmyard. Animals of various kinds were making the queerest noises all about us. I lay awake in my own small tent for a long while listening to these strange sounds. The Weddell seal is a great musician, and can produce any note from a shrill piping whistle to a deep moan, and between whiles he grunts and gurgles and complains in the weirdest fashion. As there were some hundreds of these animals on the ice, there was a chorus of sounds like the tuning of many instruments. To this was added the harsh, angry cawing of the skua gulls as they quarrelled over their food, and now and again one of the dogs would yap in his dreams, whilst from the main tent came the more familiar snores of humanity. At first I missed one sound from this Antarctic concert, but it came at last when the squawk of a penguin was borne from afar on the still air; then the orchestra was completed.

'Royds, Wilson, and I took a sledge and our lunch, and went out to the ice-edge. It was farther than we expected, and the sledge-meter showed close on ten miles before we came to open water. Everything looked terribly stagnant; a thick pack, two or three miles across, hung close to the fast ice. The day was beautiful, and one could not feel very depressed in such weather; but I cannot say that it is pleasing to think that there is a solid sheet of twenty miles between us and freedom.'

'January 2. – Today I had all hands on the saws, and then went out to see how matters were going.'

Perhaps it would be well to pause here to describe the nature of an ice-saw. A typical saw such as we had is about 18 feet in length, 8 or 9 inches in depth, and 1½ or 2 inches in thickness; the teeth are naturally very coarse. It has a wooden cross-handle at the top, and is worked by the aid of a tripod in a very simple and primitive fashion. A rope is attached close to the handle, and led through a block on the tripod; it then divides into numerous tails, to each of which a man is stationed. When all these men pull down together the saw is lifted, and as they release their ropes other men on the handles press the saw forward, and it makes a downward cut. From time to time as the saw-cut advances the tripod has to be shifted. The arrangement will probably be well understood when it is explained that the action of the men on the ropes is very much that of bell-ringers, and it can be imagined that four hours of this sort of thing is a very good spell.

I must now ask the reader to consider what the sawing of a channel through a solid ice-sheet actually means. It will be obvious of course that two cuts must be made, one on each side of the channel; but the rest is not so evident. It lies in the problem of how to get rid of the ice which remains in the channel. In order to do this cross-cuts must be made at intervals; but this is not sufficient, for it is impossible to make the two side-cuts exactly parallel, so that by a cross-cut alone an irregular parallelogram is left, which will be immovable without being broken up. The simplest manner in which this can be effected is to make a diagonal cut right through it. The net result of the foregoing is to show that, in order to make a channel a mile in length, it is necessary to cut through four miles of ice. What added difficulties there were in our case my diary shows.

'I found that the result of twelve solid days' work was two parallel cuts 150 yards in length, and as operations had been commenced in the middle of the ice-sheet, instead of at the edge, the ice between the cuts could not be detached, and in some places it seemed to have frozen across again. I started the saws to see how matters had been going, and was astonished at the small result of the work. The ice was between six and seven feet thick, and each stroke only advanced the saw a fraction of an inch. The plain Rule of Three sum before us was, as 150 yards is to 12 days, so is 20 miles to x; and we did not have to work this sum out to appreciate the futility of further operations. I therefore directed that everything except the large tent should be taken back to the ship. The men will attempt to make a cut round Hut Point, so as to ease matters at the end if the ice breaks up, and the officers will be freed for their usual scientific work. Our sawing efforts have been an experience, but I'm afraid nothing more.

'I have been much struck by the way in which everyone has cheerfully carried on this hopeless work until the order came to halt. There could have been no officer or man amongst them who did not see from the first how utterly useless it was, and yet there has been no faltering or complaint, simply because all have felt that, as the sailor expresses it, "Them's the orders."'

'January 3. – Most of our company went back to the ship yesterday afternoon; some officers remain in the large tent, Hodgson to do some fishing and Ferrar some rock searching. Twenty miles of ice hangs heavy upon me, and I have decided we must be prepared for another winter. We have fifty tons of coal left and an ample stock of provisions; also we can now take advantage of every resource that our region provides, for there are evidently a large number of penguins to the north which will make a most grateful addition to our usual seal-meat. I have therefore told off four of the men – Lashly, Evans, Handsley, and Clarke – to fix their headquarters in the large tent, and to make such raids on the penguins as will assure us a winter stock.

'This afternoon, after making these arrangements, I started away to the north with Wilson. We are off on a real picnic; there is to be no hard marching, and we have made ample provision for the commissariat. We know there will be numberless seals and penguins, and we have brought plenty of butter to cook our unsuspecting victims; and then also we have jam and all sorts of unheard-of sledging luxuries. Personally I want to watch the ice-edge and see what chance there is of a break-up; Wilson wants to study the life in that region. There has also been a talk of trying to get some way up Erebus, but this means hard work, for which at present we are neither of us inclined.

'Tonight we are camped near some rocks half way towards the ice-edge; there are several seals close by, and small bands of Adélie penguins are constantly passing us. It is curious there should be so many, as we know of no rookery near, and it is still more curious why they should be making south, as there is no open water beyond the few cracks near the land. It gives us the idea that they don't quite know what they are doing, especially since we watched the movements of one small band; they were travelling towards the south with every appearance of being in a desperate hurry – flippers outspread, heads bent forward, and little feet going for all they were worth. Their business-like air was intensely ludicrous; one could imagine them saying in the fussiest manner, "Can't stop to talk now, much too busy," and so we watched them until their plump little bodies were mere specks, when suddenly, for no rhyme or reason, they turned round and came hurrying back just as fussy and busy as ever. I can't tell whether they saw us, but to our surprise they showed no curiosity. When they were about twenty yards beyond us again, three of them suddenly plumped down on their breasts, drew their heads close in, shut their eyes, and apparently went fast asleep. It was the queerest performance; one can imagine that in an hour or two they will be up and off again without even giving themselves time for a shake.'

'January 4. – We pursued our leisurely way, skirting the land towards the ice-edge this morning. When within half a mile of the open water Wilson suddenly said, "There they are." I looked round, and, lo and behold! on the dark bare rocks of Cape Royds there was a red smudge dotted with thousands of little black-and-white figures – a penguin rookery without a doubt. It is wonderful that we should have been here two years without knowing of this, and it is exasperating to think of the feasts of eggs we have missed. We steered into a small bay behind the cape, climbed a steep little rock-face, and found ourselves on a small plateau, luckily to windward of the rookery. No place could be better for our camp, so we hauled our belongings up with the Alpine rope and pitched our tent on a stretch of sand.

'Words fail me to describe what a delightful and interesting spot this is. From our tent door we look out on to the open sea, deep blue but dotted with snowy-white pack-ice. Erebus towers high above us on our right, and to the left we look away over the long stretch of fast ice to the cloud-capped western mountains. We hear the constant chatter of the penguins, and find a wonderful interest in watching their queer habits; the brown fluffy chicks are still quite small, and the adult birds are constantly streaming to and from the sea. Close about us many skuas are nesting; they naturally regard us as intruders, and are terribly angry. The owners of one nest nearby are perched on a rock; whenever we move they arch their necks and scream with rage, and when we go out of the tent they sweep down on us, only turning their course as their wings brush our heads. However, if we do not disturb their nest no doubt they will soon get used to us.

'We have seen facts today which throw some light on the ferocious character of this robber gull. On returning from our walk Wilson saw one of them swoop down on the nest of another and fly off with a stolen egg in its beak. The owner of the nest was only a few yards away, and started in such hot pursuit that the thief was forced to relinquish its prize, which was dashed to pieces on the rocks. It is evident that there is not even honour amongst thieves in the skua code of morality.

'Tonight we watched another incident in connection with the domestic life of these birds. Close by us there is a nest with two tiny chicks; they might be ordinary barn-door chickens but for their already formidable bill and claws, and it is quite evident that they have not been hatched out more than a day or two. Suddenly we saw the parent bird come from the sea with a very fair-sized fish in its bill. It perched on a rock and began to tear pieces from its prey and offer them to its offspring; the latter seized these tempting morsels with avidity, and though they could scarcely stand they tore and gobbled at the food with wonderful energy. But after a bit both chicks found themselves wrestling with the same piece, and for some time there was quite a tug of war until both seemed to realise that this was not the way to settle such a matter, and, as if by mutual consent, they dropped the cause of contention and went for one another. They became perfect little furies as they staggered about clawing and pecking at each other. Of course they were too feeble to do any harm, and soon fell apart exhausted, but the struggle shows that the youthful skua possesses a very full share of original sin.

'We had a charming walk to the north side of the cape this afternoon, where the sea is lapping lazily on a shelving sandy beach, and where also there are several ponds with weeds and confervæ. How delightful it is to look on the sea once more! Yet how much more delightful it would be if one could lift the *Discovery* up and deposit her twenty miles to the north!

'On our return we got amongst the penguins, much to their annoyance. They swore at us in the vilest manner, and their feathers and tempers remained ruffled long after we had passed them.

'Before supper we took soap and towels down to a small rill of thaw-water that runs within ten yards of the tent and had a delightful wash in the warm sunlight. Then we had a dish of fried penguins' liver with seal kidneys; eaten straight out of the frying-pan this was simply delicious. I have come to the conclusion that life in the Antarctic Regions can be very pleasant.'

'January 5. – This morning we got up in the most leisurely fashion, and after a wash and our breakfast we lazily started to discuss plans for the day. Our tent door was open and framed the clear sea beyond, and I was gazing dreamily out upon this patch of blue when suddenly a ship entered my field of view. It was so unexpected that I almost rubbed my eyes before I dared to report it, but a moment after, of course, all became bustle and we began to search round for our boots and other articles necessary for the march. Whilst we were thus employed, Wilson looked up and said, "Why, there's another", and sure enough there were now two vessels framed in our doorway. We had of course taken for granted that the first ship was the *Morning*, but what in the name of fortune could be the meaning of this second one? We propounded all sorts of wild theories of which it need only be said that not one was within measurable distance of the truth.

'Meanwhile we were busily donning our garments and discussing what should be done next. The ships were making towards the ice-edge some five miles to the westward; our easiest plan would be to go straight on board, but then if we did so our companions on board the *Discovery* would know nothing of it, and it would mean a long delay before they could get their mails. Our duty seemed to be to consider first the establishment of communications, so, hastily scribbling some notes with directions for the dog-team and a sledge party to be sent down without delay, we started southward to search for the penguin hunters in order that these notes might be delivered.

'We went on for a long time without seeing a sign of them, but after travelling some six miles we caught sight of their tent, though without any signs of life about it; we had to come within a hundred yards before our shouts were answered and four very satisfied figures emerged, still munching the remains of what evidently had been a hearty meal. Of course I thought they had not seen the ships, but they had, only, as they explained, they didn't see there was any call for them to do anything in the matter. I said, "But, good heavens, you want your mails, don't you?" "Oh, yes, sir," they replied, "but we thought that would be all right." In other words, they as good as said that life was so extremely easy and pleasant that there was no possible object in worrying over such a trifle as the arrival of a relief expedition. And these are the people whom, not unnaturally, some of our friends appear to imagine in dire straits and in need of immediate transport to civilised conditions!

'However, once they got their orders they were off like the wind, and Wilson and I turned about and faced for the ships. We were quite close before figures came hurrying forth to meet us, but then we were soon surrounded with many familiar faces, and with many also that were quite strange. Of course I learnt at once that the second ship was the *Terra Nova*, and that her captain, MacKay, was an old acquaintance whom I was more than pleased to welcome in this Far South region; but it was not until I had had a long talk with my good friend Colbeck that I began to understand why a second ship had been sent and what a strangely new aspect everything must wear. Indeed, as I turn in tonight, amidst all the comfort that the kindness and forethought of my *Morning* friends have provided, I can scarcely realise the situation fully. I can only record that in spite of the good home news, and in spite of the pleasure of seeing old friends again, I was happier last night than I am tonight.'

And now I must briefly explain how it was that these vessels had descended upon us like a bolt from the blue, and what messages of comfort and discomfort they bore.

To do so I must hark back to March 2, 1903, when, as will be remembered, the *Morning* left us bearing despatches which outlined the work we had done and described our situation and the prospect of our detention for a second winter. The *Morning* arrived in New Zealand in April, and the general outline of affairs was flashed over the cables, but received in a very garbled form; it was not until six weeks later that the mails brought a clear account of the situation to those who had been so anxiously awaiting news at home. And now for a moment I must pause to explain what this account conveyed to those authorities at home who were responsible for the despatch of the expedition. My report informed them that the *Discovery* and all on board her were safe and well and prepared for a second winter, but perhaps rather unfortunately it referred to the return of the *Morning* in the following summer as a foregone conclusion and enumerated the stores which it was advisable she should bring; it spoke also of our attack of scurvy, though stating that there was little chance of its recurrence. I had been tempted to omit this matter as calculated to cause unnecessary anxiety, but, reflecting that the rumour might spread from some other source and become greatly exaggerated, I had finally decided to state the facts exactly as they were.

Such a report could leave only one impression on the minds of the authorities to which I have referred – namely, that at all hazards the *Morning* must be sent South in 1903. But this contingency, which could not easily have been foreseen, involved a serious difficulty, as the *Morning* fund was found to be wholly inadequate to meet the requirements of another year. There can be little doubt, I think, that had time permitted an appeal to the public and a full explanation of the necessities of the case, the required funds would have been raised, but, unfortunately, time was very limited, and already some weeks had elapsed since the reception of the news. In these circumstances no course was left to the Societies but to appeal to the Government, and after some correspondence the Government agreed to undertake the whole conduct of the relief expedition provided that the *Morning*, as she stood, was delivered to it. These arrangements being made, the Government naturally placed the active management of affairs in the hands of the Admiralty, and a small committee of officers was appointed by this department to deal with it.

It is scarcely necessary to point out that when the Government undertakes a matter of this sort it must be with larger responsibilities than can rest on private individuals. Had the Societies possessed the necessary funds, they would have been quite justified in relying on the *Morning* to force her way to the South as she had done before, but when the Government undertook that relief should be sent, it could not afford to entrust the fulfilment of its pledge to one small ship, which, however ably handled, might break down or become entangled in the ice before she reached her destination.

It was felt, therefore, that to support the Government pledge and ensure the relief of the *Discovery* two ships should be sent. This decision and the very short time which was left for its performance brought a heavy strain on the Admiralty Committee to which I have referred. It consisted of the Hydrographer, Sir William Wharton, Admiral Pelham Aldrich, and Admiral Boyes, and it is thanks to the unremitted labour of these officers that the relief expedition was organised to that degree of efficiency which the Government desired.

To meet the requirements of the case the *Terra Nova*, one of the finest of the whaling ships, was purchased and brought to Dundee to be thoroughly refitted; whilst there she was completely stocked with provisions and all other necessaries for the voyage, and a whaling crew, under the command of Captain Harry MacKay, was engaged to navigate her. Perhaps never before has a ship been equipped so speedily and efficiently for polar work, and it is a striking example of what can be done under able guidance and urgent requirement. Even when the *Terra Nova* had been prepared for her long voyage in this rapid manner the need for haste had not vanished, and it appeared that the time still left was quite inadequate to allow her to make the long voyage around the Cape under her own motive power. The same high pressure was therefore continued, and her course was directed through the Mediterranean and Suez Canal, on which route cruiser after cruiser took her in tow and raced her through the water at a speed which must have surprised the barnacles on her stout wooden sides.

Thanks to this haste, however, she arrived in the South in time to make the final preparations for her Antarctic voyage, and towards the end of November she lay off Hobart Town in Tasmania. In December she was joined by the *Morning*, and in the middle of the same month both ships sailed for the Ross Sea. Captain Colbeck was directed to take charge of this joint venture until such time as both ships should come under my command. And so it came about that, much to our surprise, two ships, instead of one, arrived off the edge of our fast ice on January 5, 1904.

Looking back now, I can see that everything happened in such a natural sequence that I might well have guessed that something of the sort would come about, yet it is quite certain that no such thought ever entered my head, and the first sight of the two vessels conveyed nothing but blank astonishment. But it was not the arrival of the *Terra Nova*, whose captain I saw from the first was anxious to do everything in his power to fall in with my plans, that disconcerted me and prompted that somewhat lugubrious entry in my diary which I have quoted. This was caused by quite another matter, and one which I might equally have guessed had I thought the problem out on the right lines.

When the news of our detention in the ice became known in England, it is not too much to say that the majority of those who were capable of forming a competent opinion believed that the *Discovery* would never be freed. There is no doubt the Admiralty inclined to this opinion, but whether they did so or not, it was equally their duty to see that the expense of furnishing a relief expedition on such an elaborate scale should not be incurred again in a future season, and consequently they had no other course than to issue direct instructions to me to abandon the *Discovery* if she could not be freed in time to accompany the relief ships to the North.

When I came to understand the situation I could see clearly the reason which dictated these instructions, but this did little to lighten the grievous disappointment I felt on receiving them.

It does not need much further explanation, I think, to show that the arrival of the relief ships with this mandate placed me and my companions unavoidably in a very cruel position. Under the most ordinary conditions, I take it, a sailor would go through much rather than abandon his ship. But the ties which bound us to the *Discovery* were very far beyond the ordinary; they involved a depth of sentiment which cannot be surprising when it is remembered what we had been through in her and what a comfortable home she had proved in all the rigours of this Southern region.

In spite of our long detention in the ice, the thought of leaving her had never entered our heads. Throughout the second winter we had grown ever more assured that she would be freed if we had the patience to wait; we could not bring ourselves to believe – and, as events proved, quite rightly – that the ice-sheet about us was a permanency. When the end of December came and we still found twenty miles between us and the open sea, we had small fits of depression such as my diary showed; but, as is also shown, they did not interfere with the healthy, happy course of our lives, and any one of us would have scouted the idea that hope should be abandoned. We had felt that at the worst this only opened up for us the prospect of a third winter, and we had determined that if we had to go through with it, it would not be our fault if we were not comfortable.

It was from this easy and passably contented frame of mind that we were rudely awakened. The situation we were now obliged to face was that if the twenty-mile plain of ice refused to break up within six weeks, we must bid a long farewell to our well-beloved ship and return to our homes as castaways with the sense of failure dominating the result of our labours. And so with the advent of the relief ships there fell on the *Discovery* the first and last cloud of gloom which we were destined to experience. As day followed day without improvement in the ice conditions, the gloom deepened until our faces grew so long that one might well have imagined an Antarctic expedition to be a very woeful affair.

As we were very human also, it may be confessed that not a little of our discontent arose from wounded vanity. By this time we considered ourselves very able to cope with any situation that might arise, and believed that we were quite capable of looking after ourselves. It was not a little trying, therefore, to be offered relief to an extent which seemed to suggest that we had been reduced to the direst need. No healthy man likes to be thought an invalid, and there are few of us who have not at some time felt embarrassed by an excess of consideration for our needs.

Although the month that followed the arrival of the relief ships was on the whole a very dismal one, it was by no means uneventful; in fact, it was a season which displayed the most extraordinary ups and down in our fortunes, and therefore I take up the tale once more with extracts from my diary.

'January 7. – I write again in camp at Cape Royds, where I have joined Wilson to get some quiet in order to read my letters and consider the situation. I don't know in what state the relief ships expected to find us, but I think they must have soon appreciated that we were very much alive. The messages I sent back to the *Discovery* on the 5th were carried at such speed that by 10 p.m. the dog-team arrived at the ice-edge. This meant that my orders had been conveyed forty miles in twelve hours. Early the next morning the first sledge team of men arrived and departed with a large load of parcels and presents. These by arrangement were taken to the main camp, whence another party took them to the ship, and so our friends saw teams of our distressful company coming north with a swinging march, appearing on board with very brown faces and only waiting for their sledges to be loaded before they vanished over the horizon again. The number of parcels sent by our kind friends in England and New Zealand is enormous, but as one cannot tell what each contains till the owner opens it, I decided to send all.

'Conditions at the ice-edge have been absolutely quiescent, the weather calm and bright, and the loose pack coming and going with the tide; not a single piece has broken away from the main sheet. I asked Colbeck to start his people on an ice-saw to give them an idea of what the work was like; a single day was quite enough for them. MacKay suggested that he should get up a full head of steam and attempt to break the ice up by ramming, or, as he says, "butting" it. He has little hope of success, but points out that the *Terra Nova* is a powerful steamer, and may accomplish something; for my part, except as regards damage to his ship, I think he might as well try to "butt" through Cape Royds. However, he is to make the attempt tomorrow or the next day, and it is perhaps as well that every expedient should be tried. We can but try every means in our power and leave Providence to do the rest; but it looks as though Providence will have a very large share.

'There is a light snowfall tonight; the penguins are unusually quiet, and the skuas lie low on the rocks; does this mean a blow? It is a curious irony of fate that makes one pray for a gale in these regions, but at present bad weather seems the only thing that can help us.'

'January 9. – At the main camp. Came up from Cape Royds last night intending to reach the ship this morning. This resulted in rather a curious experience. I started early and trudged on towards the ship through snow that has become rather deep and sticky. Half-way across the air grew thick and misty. I lost sight of all landmarks, but went on for some time guided by the sun, which showed faintly at my back. After a while the sun vanished, but thinking I might make some sort of general direction I turned towards the land and plodded on; for nearly an hour I saw nothing, but then suddenly came across fresh footsteps; they were my own! I naturally decided that this was not good enough, so turned to retrace the track towards the camp; a mile back I fell across a sledge party, and on inquiring where they were going was told that they had been following my footsteps to the ship. Needless to say, we are all back at the main camp again.'

'January 10. – Reached the ship this morning and this afternoon assembled all hands on the mess-deck, where I told them exactly how matters stood. There was a stony silence. I have not heard a laugh in the ship since I returned.'

'January 11. – I have decided to arrange for the transport of our collections and instruments to the relief ships. Today the officers have been busy making out lists of the things to be sent.'

'January 13. – For some time we have had a flagstaff on the Tent Islet, ten miles to the north, and a system of signals in connection with it descriptive of the changes in the ice conditions. A flag or shape is hoisted on the staff each morning which has a special meaning in our code, and each morning our telescope is anxiously trained towards it. Up to the present only one signal has been read: it signifies "No change in the ice conditions." I don't know whether it is worse to be on board the relief ships and observe the monotony of the changeless conditions or to be here and observe the terrible sameness of that signal. Our people have been steadily struggling on with the ice-saw off Hut Point; the work is even heavier than it was to the north, as the ice is thicker and more deeply covered with snow. I have kept it going more as an occupation than from any hope of useful result, but today it has been stopped.'

'January 15. – I thought for some time about the advisability of starting to transport our valuables. The distance is long, and with the recent snowfall the work will be very heavy, but what I think principally held me back was the thought that it might be taken as a sign that we are giving up hope. Bad as things are, we are not reduced to that yet. In the end, however, I reflected that, whether the *Discovery* gets out or not, there is no reason why the relief ships should not carry our collections and instruments back to civilisation, and meanwhile the work of transport will relieve the terrible monotony of waiting. There is, perhaps, nothing so trying in our situation as the sense of impotence. I have decided, therefore, to set things going; our parties will drag the loads down to the main camp, and the crews of the relief ships will share the work of taking them on. Royds has gone north to arrange the details, and also to try some experiments with explosives. I have told him not to use much of the latter, as the distance is so great that it would only be waste to undertake serious operations of this sort at present. I merely want to know exactly how to set about the work when the time comes, if it ever does come.'

'January 21. – Wilson returned to the ship tonight after a long spell at the Cape Royds camp, and told me all about his great capture. It appears that one day he strolled over to the north beach to see what he at first took for a prodigiously large seal lying asleep on it. As he got closer he saw, however, that the animal was quite different from any of the ordinary Southern seals, and his excitement can be imagined. Two of the *Morning* officers were in camp with him, and when Wilson had seized the gun the three proceeded to stalk this strange new beast. Their great fear was that they might only succeed in wounding it, and that it would escape into the sea, so in spite of the temperature of the water they waded well round it before they attacked. These tactics proved quite successful, and their quarry was soon despatched, but it was far too heavy for them to move or for Wilson to examine where it lay.

The following day, however, Colbeck came over in the *Morning*, and with the aid of boats and ropes the carcase was eventually landed on his decks.

'On close examination Wilson came to the conclusion that the animal is a sea elephant of the species commonly found at Macquarie Island, but this is the first time that such a beast has been found within the Antarctic Circle: and that it should now have been captured so many hundreds of miles beyond is a very extraordinary circumstance. The sea elephant is, I believe, a vegetarian; the stomach of this one was empty.'

I may remark that we got to know this particular sea elephant very well. As a rule, skeletons which are bound for the British Museum are not cleaned until they arrive on the premises, in order that there may be no difficulty in reassembling the parts. In accordance with this custom, the skeleton of this animal was carried on the skid beam of the *Discovery* in a partially stripped state. All went well until we arrived in the tropics, but after that we had no chance of forgetting that we carried the remains of a sea elephant. Shift it from place to place as we would, it made its presence felt everywhere. In the end the Museum came very close to losing a specimen, and I doubt if it possesses many that have caused more woe.

'January 23. – Since the start of our transporting work more than a week ago, the weather has changed. We have had a great deal of wind from the east and south-east with drifting snow, and an almost continuously overcast sky. The work has been impeded, but by steadily pushing on we have managed to accomplish a good deal. Our people go out all together and drag four heavily laden sledges down to the main camp; there they remain for the night, and return on the following day. The relief ships work the remainder of the distance in much the same way. We keep a cook at the main camp to provide the necessary meals. Hodgson, Bernacchi, and Mulock have been down to the ships to see to the storage of our belongings. Most of them will go in the *Terra Nova*, which has the greater accommodation.

'From these sources or from notes which come every other day I receive accounts of the ice. I scarcely like to write that things are looking more hopeful. Nothing happened until the 18th, but on that day some large pieces broke away, and since that the ships

have made steady but slow progress. I estimate from reports that
they are four or five miles nearer than when I was down a fortnight
ago. I learn that the *Terra Nova*'s "butting" came to naught, as I expected; she could make no impression on the solid sheet, though
she rammed it full tilt.'

'January 24. – Our people report that the ships were again on the
move last night, and this morning did not appear to be more than
three miles from the camp. I have been calculating that for things
to be as they were in the year of our arrival thirteen or fourteen
miles of ice must go out in fifteen days – nearly an average of a
mile a day, whereas I scarcely like to think what a difference this
would be from what has happened in the last fifteen days. We are
at present behind last year's date as regards the ice, but, on the
other hand, the recent winds have swept the pack away – a
condition that never happened last year.'

'January 27. – Yesterday the large tent was shifted two miles this
way, and is now this side of the glacier tongue; this is by way of
equalising the distance for the transporting parties, but our people
have still much the longer distance to travel. Advices from the
relief ships inform me that the ice is still breaking away, but not so
rapidly as at the beginning of the week. I fear, I much fear, that
things are going badly for us.'

'January 28. – This morning as I lay in my bunk, I was astonished
to hear the ship creaking. On getting up I found that she was
moving in the ice with a very slow rhythmic motion. After
breakfast we all went out to Hut Point and found that the whole
ice-sheet was swaying very slightly under the action of a long
swell; its edge against the land was rising and falling as much as
18 inches. This is the most promising event that has happened;
we have not known such a thing since our first imprisonment. It is
too thick to see what is happening to seaward, but one cannot but
regard this as a hopeful sign. We are all very restless, constantly
dashing up the hill to the lookout station or wandering from place
to place to observe the effects of the swell. But it is long since we
enjoyed such a cheerful experience as we get on watching the
loose pieces of ice jostling one another at Hut Point.'

'January 29. – Still no definite news of what is happening to
seaward. The ship worked loose yesterday, and moves an inch or
two in her icy bed. This has caused a great increase in the creaking

and groaning of the timbers. This pleasant music is now almost continuous, and one feels immensely cheered till one goes up the hill and looks out on the long miles of ice and the misty screen which hides the sea. I grow a little sceptical of reports which tell of the departure of a mile or half a mile of ice, for if all these distances could be added together the relief ships should have been at Hut Point by now.'

'January 30. – Went up the hill with Koettlitz, and saw a most cheering sight. The ice has broken away well inside the glacier, and the relief ships are not much more than eight miles away. Through the telescope one can see the hull and rigging very distinctly, and even the figures of men walking about.

'Later came full reports from the ships with excellent news. Colbeck tells me that during the last few days there has been a great change. On the 26th the open water extended to the outer islet, on the 28th to the inner one, and now it has reached inside the glacier. The ice broke away in very large sheets, and so rapidly that he was carried away to the westward. As if to show contempt for our puny efforts, the scene of our sawing labours was carried away in the centre of a large floe; our feeble scratches did not even help to form one of the cracks which broke up the ice-sheet about them. In the last five days fully six miles of ice have broken away, so that we are all inclined to be very cheerful again. There is only one drawback: the swell is slowly but surely dying away, and there is no doubt that we are entirely dependent on it.'

'February 1. – We seem to be hanging in the balance, with even chances either way. On the one hand, the swell has died away, the ice is very quiet again, and one remembers that we are not really further advanced than we were at this time last year; on the other, we hear the hopeful sign of a clear sea to the north, and the knowledge that a swell will have full freedom of action. It's a toss-up.

'The work of transport has been going on steadily, and a few more days will see its finish. The main tent is now about five miles from the ship, so that the work progresses more speedily. All our scientific collections and most of the valuable instruments were taken across some time ago; then followed the scientific library, a very heavy item; and now some of our personal effects and the pictures, &c., from the wardroom are packed for transit. Our living quarters are beginning to look bare and unfurnished, but we shall not mind that a particle if we can only get out.

'I find myself growing ridiculously superstitious, and cannot banish the notion that if we make every preparation for leaving the *Discovery*, Nature with its usual cussedness will free her.'

'February 3. – I imagine the ice all over the sound has been thinning underneath; off the various headlands it has rotted right through to a greater extent than it did last year. There is a very large open pool off Cape Armitage, and another smaller one off Hut Point, beyond which the ice is very thin and treacherous for three or four hundred yards. The sledge parties have to go a long way round to avoid this, though unloaded travellers can climb over the land and down on to the firm ice in Arrival Bay.

'For some days now there has been practically no advance in the ice conditions. Our spirits are steadily falling again, and I am just off to the *Morning* to see if anything more can be done.'

'February 4. – On board the *Morning*. The ships are lying about one and a half mile inside the glacier, where they have been without change for the last three days. I have discontinued transport work for the present. It has been a lovely calm, bright day – alas! much too calm and bright. I cannot describe how irritating it is to endure these placid conditions as the time speeds along. There being nothing else to be done, Colbeck took me round the glacier tongue in the *Morning*, and we sounded on both sides, getting most extraordinarily regular depths of 230 to 240 fathoms, except at one inlet on the north side, where we got 170. In the afternoon we climbed to the top of the Tent Islet (480 feet) and brought down the telescope and flags left by the signalling party. The ice to the westward is not broken away so far as I expected; altogether the view was not inspiriting. Spent the evening with Captain MacKay, who is excellent company for a depressed state of mind.'

'February 5. – I did not want to begin explosions whilst the distance was so great, but on considering the stagnant condition of affairs I decided to make a start today. It has been evident to me for some time that if explosives are to be of any use, they must be expended freely, and so today we experimented in this direction. To explain matters, it is necessary to describe the condition of the fast ice. Its edge starts about a mile from the end of the glacier, and after a sweep to the south turns to the west, in which direction it runs for five or six miles before it gradually turns to the north; any point along this long western line is more or less equidistant from the *Discovery*. As one approaches the open water from the south, one crosses a series of cracks which run for miles parallel to each other and to the ice-edge; this is the first step that the swell makes towards breaking up the sheet. These cracks are from 50 to 150 yards apart, and according to the dimensions of the swell there may be any number from two or three to a dozen. They are constantly working, those near the ice-edge of course more perceptibly than the others. After one of the long strips thus formed has been working for some time a transverse crack suddenly appears, and then a piece breaks away, usually at the eastern end; and very soon after it is weakened in this manner the rest of the strip peels away right across the bay. I have now seen two or three strips go in this manner, and it appears to me that what we require to do is to get ahead of Nature by forming the transverse cracks. Today, therefore, I planted the charges at intervals in line with the *Discovery*, and with a specially made electric circuit blew them up together. On the whole the result was satisfactory; we formed a transverse crack and the strip under which the charges had been placed went out within the hour. It is not a great gain, and the expenditure of material is large, but I think the result justifies an attempt to continue the work on properly organised lines. I have therefore sent to the *Discovery* for a party of our special torpedo men who will continue to fit, place and fire the charges whilst the men of the relief ships go on digging the holes. I feel that the utility of these explosives depends entirely on the swell; we can do nothing unless Nature helps us; on the other hand, we in turn may help Nature.'

'February 6. – We have started our explosive work in full swing, and all hands are working very vigorously at it. We have had eight men from the *Terra Nova* and seven from the *Morning* digging holes. I went along first and planted small sticks where these holes were to be dug; then the men set to, three at each hole.

'The ice is from five to six feet in thickness, and the work is quite easy until the hole is two or three feet deep, but then it becomes hard and tiresome, and can be continued only by chipping away with long-handled implements and occasionally clearing out the detached pieces with a shovel. The worst part comes when the water is admitted, as this happens before the bottom of the hole can be knocked out, and it is most difficult to continue the chipping under water; in fact, towards the end of the day we gave up attempting to do this, and decided that it was better to blow the bottom out with a small charge. Whilst the holes were being dug, our own *Discovery* party were busily fitting and firing charges; this is dangerous work of course, and I have been very careful to see that proper precautions are taken. The charge fitters are isolated in a tent some way from the scene of action, and the fitted charges are brought up on a sledge under proper custody, and handled only by our own experts. The battery is kept on a small sledge of its own, and can thus be taken out of reach of the electric circuits when not in use.

'We are doing things on a large scale; three charges are fired together, and each charge contains 35 lbs of gun-cotton. When three holes are finished, a charge is taken to each with a small line five fathoms long attached to it; then the electric wires are joined up and the charges are lowered under water to the extent of their lines, everyone clears away from the region and the battery is run up to the other end of the wires, a hundred and fifty yards away. When all is ready the key is pressed. Then the whole floe rises as though there were an earthquake; three mighty columns of water and ice shoot up into the sky, rising high above the masts of the ships; there is a patter of falling ice-blocks and then quiet again. One might imagine that nothing could withstand such prodigious force until one walks up and finds that beyond three gaping blackened craters there is nothing to show for that vast upheaval – at least, nothing that can be detected with a casual glance; but a close scrutiny of the surface between the holes generally shows that after all something has been effected, for from each hole a number of minute cracks radiate, and one can see that in two or three places these have joined. At first these cracks are so thin as to be scarcely discernible, but if one watches on for ten minutes or more, one can detect the fact that they are very gradually opening; half an hour later they may be a quarter of an inch in width, and then it is possible to see that the ice on each side is moving unequally. This is the beginning of the end, for in an hour or two the broken floe, small enough in area but containing many hundreds of tons of ice, will quietly detach itself and float calmly away to the north.

'It is in this manner, therefore, that we now hope to reach the *Discovery*, if only the swell will hold. We have advanced about a third of a mile today, though how much is due to our own efforts, and how much to the ordinary course of Nature, we cannot tell, nor do we much care as long as the advance is made.'

'February 7. – We certainly have curious ups and downs of fortune. This forenoon nothing happened after our explosion, and I felt very despondent, but after lunch as I was sitting in Colbeck's cabin, he suddenly rushed down to say that an enormous piece was breaking away – and sure enough when I got on deck I found that a floe from a half to three-quarters of a mile across was quietly going out to sea. The men of the relief ships are working like Trojans at the hole-digging; they are taking a keen interest in the proceedings and are especially delighted with the explosions. There is a competition in cutting the holes, and some take particular care in making them very neat and round regardless of the fact that in half an hour their handiwork will be blown to pieces. The best implement for this work is a sort of spud with a sharp cutting edge at the bottom. We are short of good tools of this sort, but the *Terra Nova*'s blacksmith and our own engineers are busy making more.'

'February 8. – Wretched luck today. It is quite calm, and the swell has almost vanished; the floes that broke away last night are still hanging about the ice-edge and damping what little swell remains. Barne has a bad attack of snow-blindness, and so Evans, of the *Morning*, relieves him for the present in the charge of explosive operations.'

'February 9. – On board the *Discovery*. Our hopes, which were high on the 7th, have fallen again to a low ebb. Last night a few of the broken floes cleared away, but the swell did not return. Explosions were continued, but with little result. However, I felt that we could do no more than work on systematically, and as that has now been arranged I saw no object in my staying on board the *Morning*, whereupon, asking Colbeck to superintend operations, I journeyed homeward again.

'At this date two years ago the ice had broken back to Hut Point, and now it is fast for six miles beyond; one never appreciates what a distance six miles is till one comes to walk over it, and as I plodded homeward for two hours today I am bound to confess my heart gradually sank into my boots. There would be nothing to worry about if we only had time on our side, but each day now the sun is sinking lower and the air getting colder. It is only a matter of days now before the season closes.'

'February 10. – Today I have done very little but walk restlessly about. Twice I have been up to the observation station on Arrival Heights. On this vantage point some 500 feet up we have a large telescope with which we can see pretty clearly what is happening at the ice-edge, and sad to relate it is very little.

'The ice about Hut Point is now so thin as to be dangerous for a long way out. Crean fell in yesterday, and had a very narrow shave, as he could not attempt to swim amongst the sodden brash-ice. Luckily he kept his head, and remained still until the others were able to run for a rope and haul him out. To avoid this in future we have constructed a roadway over the land so that sledges can be hauled up the steep snow-slope from Arrival Bay. Everyone now is making an effort to be cheerful, but it is an obvious effort.

'I have made every arrangement for abandoning the ship. I have allotted the officers and men to the relief ships and drawn up instructions for the latter. The *Morning*, I think, ought to be outside the strait by the 25th, but the *Terra Nova* with her greater power can remain perhaps a week longer. I don't think I ever had a more depressing evening's work.'

'February 11. – Awoke this morning to find a light southerly wind and the air filled with snow. We could see nothing but the dismal grey wall all around us, and, as may be imagined, the general gloom was not much lightened by the view of things without; and yet, as always seems to happen to us, when things look blackest the sun breaks through. This morning I sent the dog-team over with the laboured instructions which I wrote last night. A few hours later it returned with a note to say the ice was breaking up fast. A good deal had gone out in the night and more in the morning. At eight o'clock Doorly, of the *Morning*, arrived with a second letter to say that the afternoon had proved equally propitious, and to ask that more men might be sent to dig holes for the explosives. Half an hour later Royds was away with a party of ten men, and since that I have been able to do nothing but record these pleasant facts. I can't think that much excitement of this sort would be good for us.'

'February 12. – The weather was clearer this morning, but the sky still overcast. We were out at Hut Point early, and the difference in distance of the ships was obvious at a glance, so from there we dashed up Arrival Heights. From our observation station we could now see everything. The *Terra Nova* was just picking up our large tent, which was a little over four miles from Hut Point, but the *Morning* was to the westward and quite half a mile nearer, and it was here that the explosive work was being pushed vigorously forward; one could see the tiny groups of figures digging away at the holes. This afternoon I went down to the *Morning*, and arrived after a walk of three-quarters of an hour. I learnt that there had been a considerable swell, but that it was now decreasing rapidly and things were growing quieter again; the explosions today had not done much, and the broken ice was again hanging about the edge instead of drifting to the north. Tonight matters are not quite so pleasing again; I don't fancy another long wait for a swell, yet one has to remember that appearances are very different from what they were two nights ago.'

'February 13. – Thick weather again today; have seen or heard nothing from the ice-edge. Very anxious for a clearance.'

'February 14. – So much has happened tonight that I have some difficulty in remembering the events of the day. This morning the wind was strong from the south-east and carried a good deal of drift; although one could see the relief ships, one could not make out what was happening with regard to the work, or whether the ice was breaking away. The afternoon found us in very much the same condition, and even by dinner-time we had no definite news.

'It was not until we were quietly eating this meal that the excitement first commenced, when we heard a shout on deck and a voice sang out down the hatchway, "The ships are coming, sir!"

'There was no more dinner, and in one minute we were racing for Hut Point, where a glorious sight met our view. The ice was breaking up right across the strait, and with a rapidity which we had not thought possible. No sooner was one great floe borne away than a dark streak cut its way into the solid sheet that remained and carved out another, to feed the broad stream of pack which was hurrying away to the north-west.

'I have never witnessed a more impressive sight; the sun was low behind us, the surface of the ice-sheet in front was intensely white, and in contrast the distant sea and its forking leads looked almost black. The wind had fallen to a calm, and not a sound disturbed the stillness about us.

'Yet in the midst of this peaceful silence was an awful unseen agency rending that great ice-sheet as though it had been naught but the thinnest paper. We knew well by this time the nature of our prison bars; we had not plodded again and again over those long dreary miles of snow without realising the formidable strength of the great barrier which held us bound; we knew that the heaviest battleship would have shattered itself ineffectually against it, and we had seen a million-ton iceberg brought to rest at its edge. For weeks we had been struggling with this mighty obstacle, controlling the most powerful disruptive forces that the intelligence of man has devised, but only to realise more completely the inadequacy of our powers. Even Nature had seemed to pause before such a vast difficulty, and had hitherto delivered her attacks with such sluggish force that we had reasonably doubted her ability to conquer it before the grip of the winter arrested her efforts.

'But now without a word, without an effort on our part, it was all melting away, and we knew that in an hour or two not a vestige of it would be left, and that the open sea would be lapping on the black rocks of Hut Point.

'Fast as the ice was breaking, it was not fast enough for our gallant relief ships; already we could see them battling through the floes with a full head of steam and with their bows ever pressing forward on the yet unbroken sheet; working this way and that, they saw the long cracks shot out before them and in a moment their armoured stems were thrust into them and they forged ahead again in new and rapidly widening channels. There was evidently a race as to which should be first to pass beyond the flagstaff round which our small company had clustered, but the little *Morning*, with her bluff bows and weak engines, could scarcely expect to hold her own against her finer-built and more powerful competitor.

'By ten o'clock we could observe the details of the game and watch each turn and twist with a knowledge of its immediate cause. By 10.30 we could see the splintering of the ice as they crashed into the floes and hear the hoarse shouts of the men as, wild with excitement, they cheered each fresh success. Scarcely half a mile of ice remained between us, and now the contest became keener, and the crew of the *Terra Nova* gathered together by word of command and ran from side to side of their ship till she rolled heavily and seemed to shake herself, as the force of each rush was gradually expended and she fell back to gather way for a fresh attack; but in spite of all her efforts the persistent little *Morning*, dodging right and left and seizing every chance opening, kept doggedly at her side, and it still seemed a chance as to who should be first to reach that coveted goal, the open pool of water at our feet.

'Meanwhile our small community in their nondescript, tattered garments stood breathlessly watching this wonderful scene. For long intervals we remained almost spellbound, and then a burst of frenzied cheering broke out. It seemed to us almost too good to be real. By eleven o'clock all the thick ice had vanished, and there remained only the thin area of decayed floe which has lately made the approach to the ship so dangerous; a few minutes later the *Terra Nova* forged ahead and came crashing into the open, to be followed almost immediately by her stout little companion, and soon both ships were firmly anchored to all that remains of the *Discovery*'s prison, the wedge that still holds in our small bay.

'It seems unnecessary to describe all that has followed: how everyone has been dashing about madly from ship to ship, how everyone shook everyone else by the hand, how our small bay has become a scene of wild revelry, and how some have now reached that state which places them in doubt as to which ship they really belong to. Much can be excused on such a night.

'And so tonight the ships of our small fleet are lying almost side by side; a rope from the *Terra Nova* is actually secured to the *Discovery*. Who could have thought it possible? Certainly not we who have lived through the trying scenes of the past month.'

'February 15. – The rapid passage of events has caught us unprepared, and today all hands have been employed in making up for lost time. It has been a busy day; our own men have been on board making things ship-shape and trim, whilst parties from the other ships have been digging ice and bringing it on board to fill our boilers. The small wedge of sea-ice that still remains in our bay is cracked in many places, and no doubt it would go out of its own accord in the course of a few days, but I am now all impatience to be away, and therefore contemplate expediting matters by some explosions. To make the necessary holes in the ice I have been obliged to call in the assistance of the officers, who have been digging away busily, but it has been no light matter to get through, for the ice at the edge is twelve feet thick, whilst closer to the ship it runs from fifteen to seventeen feet. We shall work all night till our boilers are filled, but what a very different matter work is under these new conditions! Faces have regained the old cheerful expression, and already the wags are finding new subjects for their sallies.'

'February 16. – I felt much too restless to go to bed last night, and so after spending the evening with my fellow captains I wandered about to see how the work went, and presently mustered the explosion party and prepared a large charge containing 67 lbs. of gun-cotton. We lowered this carefully into a hole some fifteen yards ahead of the ship, and at 1 a.m., regardless of the feelings of the sleepers, blew it up. It shook the whole bay, and I fear awakened all those who slumbered, but its effects were much what I had hoped. The ice, which had been very solid about the *Discovery*, now showed cracks in all directions, and I knew I could go to bed with the hope of finding many of these well open when I arose. After breakfast I found this had duly happened. Nearly all had opened out an inch or two, whilst one from the stern of the ship was gaping a foot or more in width; our ship work was completed, and nothing remained but the last stroke for freedom.

'So the last explosive charge was borne out and lowered into the yawning crack astern of the ship, the wires were brought on board and everyone was directed to seek shelter. When all was ready, I pressed the firing key; there was a thunderous report which shook the ship throughout, and then all was calm again. For a brief moment one might have imagined that nothing had happened, but then one saw that each crack was slowly widening; presently there came the gurgle of water as it was sucked into our opening ice-bed, and in another minute there was a creaking aft and our stern rose with a jump as the keel was freed from the ice which had held it down. Then, as the great mass of ice on our port hand slowly glided out to sea our good ship swung gently round and lay peacefully riding to her anchors with the blue water lapping against her sides.'

Thus it was that after she had afforded us shelter and comfort for two full years, and after we had borne a heavy burden of anxiety on her behalf, our good ship was spared to take us homeward. On February 16, 1904, the *Discovery* came to her own again – the right to ride the high seas.

Homeward bound

> Now strike yr sails, yee jolly mariners,
> For we are come into a quiet rode
> Where we must land some of our passengers
> And light this wearie vessel of her lode.
> Here she awhile may make her safe abode
> Till she repaired have her tackles spent
> And wants supplied; and then again abroad
> On the long voyage whereto she is bent
> Well may she speede and fairly finish her intent. – SPENSER

I wish I could convey some idea of our feelings when the *Discovery* was once more floating freely on the sea, but I doubt if any written words could express how good it was to walk up and down the familiar bridge, to watch the gentle movement of the ship as she swung to and fro on the tide, to feel the throb of the capstan engine as we weighed one of our anchors, to glance aloft and know that sails and ropes had now some meaning, to see the men bustling about with their old sailor habit, and to know that our vessel was once more able to do those things for which a ship is built. It is sufficient to say that it would have been hard to find a prouder or happier ship's company than we were that day.

But with all our feelings of elation we did not imagine that our troubles were at an end; we knew that it was far from likely that after so long a period of disuse everything would be found to work smoothly, and we knew also that if we were to carry out the remainder of the programme which we had set ourselves there must be no delay in getting to work. It had always been my intention when the *Discovery* was freed from the ice to devote what remained of the navigable season to an exploration of that interesting region which lay to the westward of Cape North, but now, after two years' imprisonment, we lacked what constituted a primary necessity for such a scheme; our long detention had made a deep inroad into our coal supply, and after lighting fires in our main boilers and raising steam afresh we found ourselves with barely forty tons remaining – an amount on which it would have been most difficult for us to reach New Zealand, and which absolutely precluded all idea of further exploration.

One of my first inquiries, therefore, on the arrival of the relief ships had been to find out the amount of this valuable commodity with which they could afford to supply us in the event of our release. At first they had been able to name a very satisfactory figure, but after the long month of combat with ice and wind which had just passed their powers of assistance had been greatly diminished; and now I saw, to my disappointment, that even at the best we should only increase our stock by an amount which would ensure our safe return to New Zealand, without leaving any adequate margin for exploring work. However, it was no use deploring facts which could not be altered. I determined to get all that could be spared without delay, and to use it as far as possible in carrying out our original programme.

As the *Discovery* seemed to be lying very snugly at anchor, we decided to get in what we could whilst we remained in the shelter of our small bay, and on the afternoon of the 16th the *Terra Nova* came alongside us to hand over her supply. Thus a few hours after our release the two ships lay snugly berthed together, busily securing whips and yards for the transfer of coal which was to commence on the following morning. The afternoon was beauti-fully calm and bright, and the weather seemed to smile peacefully on the termination of our long and successful struggle with the ice. We little guessed what lay before us, and assuredly if ever the treacherous nature of the Antarctic climate and the need for the explorer to be constantly on guard were shown it was by our experiences of the succeeding twenty-four hours, of which my diary gives the following account.

'February 16. – We have felt that our last act before leaving the region which has been our home for so long should be one of homage to the shipmate who sacrificed his life to our work. We have had a large wooden cross prepared for some time; it bears a simple carved inscription to the memory of poor Vince, and yesterday it was erected on the summit of Hut Point, so firmly that I think in this undecaying climate it will stand for centuries. Today our small company landed together for the last time, and stood bareheaded about this memorial whilst I read some short prayers. It was calm, but the sky had become heavily overcast and light snow was falling on our heads. The little ceremony brought sad recollections, but perhaps also a feeling of gratitude for escapes from many accidents which might well have added to the single name which the memorial bears.

'The water was oily calm as we pulled back to the ship, and the sky very gloomy and threatening, but this sort of weather has been so common we thought little of it. It had been decided that as today was the first time Captain MacKay had set foot on board the *Discovery*, we should show him and his officers what an Antarctic feast was like. Accordingly by dinner-time our cooks had prepared very savoury dishes of seal and penguin, and we sat down, a very merry party, to discuss them. In the midst of dinner word came down that the wind had sprung up, and although I did not expect to find anything serious I thought it as well to go up and see how the land lay. On stepping out into the open, however, I saw we were in for a stiff blow, and had reluctantly to inform our guests of the fact. MacKay took one glance at the sky and was over the rail like a shot, followed by as many of his people as could be collected at such short notice. In a minute or two the warps were cast off, and the *Terra Nova* was steaming for the open, where she was soon lost in the drift. Since that it has been blowing very stiff, and a good deal of ice has come down upon us; but I have a pretty firm reliance on our ground tackle – the anchor weighs over two tons, and we have a fair drift of cable out. The wind is from the south, and the sea, which has risen rapidly, is dashing over the ice-bound land close astern, but we have not yet dragged. Colbeck is on board with two officers and six men of the *Terra Nova*. I don't altogether like the look of things, and shall get up steam as soon as possible; but I don't want to hurry the engine-room people, or we shall have all sorts of trouble with our steam-pipes, &c.'

'February 17. – We have had a day and no mistake; I hope I may never have such another. Early this morning the wind lulled but the sky still wore a most threatening aspect, and I sent word for steam as soon as it could possibly be raised. At about 8 a.m. the *Morning* appeared out of the gloom and sent a boat for Colbeck, who got away as quickly as he could. He had scarcely reached his ship when the wind came down on us again with redoubled fury, the sea got up like magic, and soon the *Discovery* began to jerk at her cables in the most alarming manner. I knew that in spite of our heavy anchor the holding ground was poor, and I watched anxiously to see if the ship dragged.

'It came at last, just as Skelton sent a promise of steam in half an hour. The sea was again breaking heavily on the ice-foot astern and I walked up and down wondering which was coming first, the steam or this wave-beaten cliff. It was not a pleasant situation, as the distance grew shorter every minute, until the spray of the breaking waves fell on our poop, and this was soon followed by a tremendous blow as our stern struck the ice. We rebounded and struck again, and our head was just beginning to fall off and the ship to get broadside on (heaven knows what would have happened then) when steam was announced. Skelton said he could only go slow at first, but hoped to work up. I told him to give her every ounce he could, when he could, and he fled below to do his best.

'With the engines going ahead and the windlass heaving in, we gradually pulled up to our anchor and tripped it; then we ceased to advance. The engines alone would not send the ship to windward in the teeth of the gale; we just held our own, but only just. Once around Hut Point I knew we should be safe with an open sea before us; the end of the Point was only a quarter of a mile out, but off the end, some twenty or thirty yards beyond, I knew there was a shallow patch which had also to be cleared to get safely away. So finding we could make no headway I started to edge out towards the Point. All seemed to be going well until we got opposite the Point itself, when I saw to my alarm that although there was no current in our bay there was a strong one sweeping past the Point.

'Nothing remained but to make a dash for it, and I swung the helm over and steered for the open. But the moment our bows entered the fast-running stream we were swung round like a top, and the instant after we crashed head foremost on to the shoal and stopped dead with our masts shivering. We were in the worst possible position, dead to windward of the bank with wind, sea, and current all tending to set us faster ashore.

'We took the shore thus at about 11 a.m., and the hours that followed were truly the most dreadful I have ever spent. Each moment the ship came down with a sickening thud which shook her from stem to stern, and each thud seemed to show more plainly that, strong as was her build, she could not long survive such awful blows. As soon as possible I had soundings taken all around and found the depth was 12 feet everywhere except under the stern, where the line showed 18 feet; I sent for the carpenter to know our draught of water and he reported 12½ feet at the bows and 14½ feet aft. This signified that the midship section must be very hard aground, and that the only chance of release was by the stern, a direction in which we could not hope to move under present circumstances.

'So things stood before the men's dinner, but by the time it was finished we seemed to have worked another fathom ahead and then the soundings all around were 12 feet except at the extreme bowsprit end, where 15 feet was obtained. I knew the bank must be very small in extent, and asked myself, would it be possible to force her clean over it? I determined to try, and ordered sail to be made. The wind had steadily increased in force, and it was now blowing a howling gale; the temperature was low enough to make the water slushy as it fell on board. In spite of this we got the foresail and foretop-sail spread, and at the same time rang the telegraph to full speed ahead. The ship began to move, but it was only to swing round till her bowsprit almost touched the rocks of the Point; the seas came tumbling over her starboard quarter and she herself listed heavily to port.

'In two minutes I saw that we were only making matters worse, and shouted for the sails to be clewed up; and at the same moment Skelton appeared on the bridge and reported that the inlets were choked and the engines useless. Once more we sounded around the ship, to find that there was not more than 9 to 10 feet from the bows to the mainmast or from 10 to 12 feet beyond: she seemed to be hopelessly and irretrievably ashore. After this, for a very short time, we hoped that her high position on the bank would bring less strain from the seas, but soon she had formed a new bed for herself, and within an hour she was bumping more heavily than ever.

'It was now about three o'clock. We had come to the end of our resources; nothing more could be done till the gale abated. We could only consider the situation and wait for the hours to go by.

'And the situation seemed to have no ray of comfort in it. On deck the wind was howling through our rigging, the ship was swaying helplessly and rising slightly each moment, to crash down once more on the stony bottom; the seas were breaking heavily over the stern and sending clouds of spray high up the masts; the breakers on the shore flung the back-wash over our forecastle; the water was washing to and fro on our flooded decks. Towering above us within a stone's throw was the rocky promontory of Hut Point; on its summit, and clearly outlined against the sky, stood the cross which we had erected to our shipmate. I remember thinking how hard it seemed that we had rescued our ship only to be beaten to pieces beneath its shadow.

'If the situation on deck was distressing, that below fairly rivalled it. Each time that the ship descended with a sickening thud into her rocky bed the beams and decks buckled upwards to such an extent that several of our thick glass deadlights were cracked across, every timber creaked and groaned, doors flew to and fro, crockery rattled, and every loose article was thrown into some new position. With the heavier blows one could see the whole ship temporarily distorted in shape; through all and directly beneath one's feet could be heard the horrible crunching and grinding of the keel on the stones below.

'When it was known that nothing more could be done it was curious to see how different temperaments took it. Some sat in stony silence below, some wandered about aimlessly, and some went steadily on with an ordinary task as though nothing had happened. I almost smiled when I saw our excellent marine Gilbert Scott dusting and sweeping out the wardroom and polishing up the silver as if the principal thing to be feared was an interference with the cleanly state in which he usually keeps all these things. For myself I could not remain still. How many times I wandered from the dismal scene on deck to the equally dismal one below I do not know, but what I do know is that I tasted something very near akin to despair.

'But if this afternoon was a horrible experience, it has at least shown me again how firmly I can rely on the support and intelligence of my companions. For, seeing the utter impossibility of doing anything at the time, I bethought me that the next best thing was to be prepared to act promptly when the weather moderated. Accordingly I first sent for Skelton to see by how much we could lighten the ship. I had scarcely asked him the question when he said, "I have been thinking that out, sir", and in a minute or two he produced a list of our movable weights. I next sent for the boatswain to discuss the manner in which we could lay out our anchors, and he also had his scheme cut and dried; and so it went on with everybody concerned in this knotty problem, until I knew that if the gale left us with any ship at all we should at least be able to make a bold bid to get her afloat.

'And so hour after hour went by whilst we thought and planned as well as our dejected state would allow, and the ship quivered and trembled and crashed again and again into her rocky bed.

'The first sign of a lull came at seven o'clock, and then though the seas still swept over our counter, there was a decided slackening in the wind. Soon after we all assembled for dinner – not that any of us wanted to eat, but because it never does to disturb a custom. It was a dreary meal, the dreariest and most silent I ever remember in the *Discovery*. Yet we were not more than half-way through it, when the officer of the watch, Mulock, suddenly burst in and said, "The ship's working astern, sir." I never reached the bridge in less time. I found that the wind and sea had dropped in the most extraordinary manner, but what surprised me still more was that the current, which had been running strongly to the north, had turned and was running with equal speed to the south. I took this in at a glance as I turned to get a bearing on with the shore; in a minute or two I was left without doubt that Mulock's report had been correct. Each time that the ship lifted on a wave she worked two or three inches astern, and though she was still grinding heavily she no longer struck the bottom with such terrific force. I had scarcely observed these facts when Skelton rushed up to say that the inlets were free again. Every soul was on deck, and in a moment they were massed together and running from side to side in measured time. The telegraphs were put full speed astern; soon the engines began to revolve, and the water foamed and frothed along the side. For a minute or two the ship seemed to hesitate, but then there came a steady grating under the bottom, which gradually travelled forward, and ceased as the ship, rolling heavily, slid gently into deep water.

'To this moment I do not know how it has all happened, but thinking things over tonight a fact has been recalled to my recollection which I noticed without realising its full significance. It seemed to me that the level of the water at Hut Point, as far as I could judge it in its agitated state, was abnormally low this afternoon, and taking this in connection with the change in direction of the current, I am inclined to believe that events have come about much as follows. The heavy southerly wind tended to drive the water out of the Sound and lowered its level by some feet. We must have run ashore when it was at this low ebb; then came the lull, and the water swept back again, with the happy result of floating us off.

'But whether things have come about in this natural manner or not, I cannot but regard it as little short of a miracle that I should be going to bed free from anxiety at the end of this horrid day. We were clear of our shoal none too soon, for an hour after the wind blew up from the south again. Early in the day we had caught a glimpse of the *Terra Nova* far away to the south, so we made in this direction to find her and to seek shelter. At midnight we got up to the edge of the fast ice, where we found our consort secured with ice-anchors, and where we have been able to return her officers and men. We are now anchored close by her; I do not know what has become of the *Morning*.

'We have been diligently sounding our wells for signs of extra leakage, but the carpenter reports there is nothing to speak of, and so apparently, beyond the loss of our false keel, we have suffered little damage. It is an eloquent testimony to the solid structure of the ship.'

When I subsequently came to compare the experiences of the three ships during this long gale, I found that the complete lulls, such as I have recorded, took place at different times in their various localities; and I have no doubt that by this irregular action of the wind the waters of the Sound were pressed down in some places and heaped up in others in a manner that is well known in inland lakes. But, even when all the physical facts are realised, the story of our grounding and release remains a very extraordinary one. Rarely, if ever, can a ship have appeared in such an uncomfortable plight as ours to find herself free and safe within the space of an hour. Such a sudden and complete relief of our distress seemed to argue that we had been rather unnecessarily and foolishly alarmed at our situation, but on looking back I remember that we had no reason to expect that the forces of Nature would so suddenly come to our rescue: the best we looked for was a period of calm when we might lighten the ship and attempt to drag her from her perilous position; and such a prospect, with the weather thoroughly unsettled and the season closing rapidly, was not hopeful. To be in ten feet of water in a ship that draws fourteen feet cannot be a pleasant position, nor can there be a doubt that the shocks which the *Discovery* sustained would have very seriously damaged a less stoutly built vessel.

On the 18th the wind was still blowing strong, but had gone round to the south-east, bringing smoother water in our Sound, and now, as we were most anxious to complete our coaling operations, I decided to seek shelter in the inlets of the glacier tongue to the north. So at a comparatively early hour we uprooted our ice-anchors and steered in that direction, closely followed by the *Terra Nova*. In half an hour we were passing close by Hut Point, and the small bay in which we had spent such long months, but which had tendered us such a treacherous farewell. As we sped along we looked for the last time with almost affectionate regard on the scene which had grown so familiar, on the hills of which we knew every ridge and fold, on the paths which our footsteps had so often trodden, and on the huts and other signs of human life which we were leaving behind us. One wonders what is happening now in that lonely solitude, once the scene of so much activity!

In the afternoon we ran alongside the ice-edge in an inlet on the north side of the glacier tongue; soon the *Terra Nova* was rubbing sides with us, and our whips were rigged for coaling. The weather by this time had cleared and the wind had almost dropped, but we knew that these conditions were not likely to last long, and officers and men buckled to with a will to remedy the alarmingly empty state of our bunkers. Late in the afternoon the *Morning* suddenly appeared around the corner. She had been driven far to leeward by the gale, but at length had worked up and found some shelter in the New Harbour, where also the ice had recently broken away for the first time for two years.

By midnight we had received fifty tons of coal from the *Terra Nova*, and that ship stood out in the offing. A northerly breeze had sprung up, and we were now obliged to go round to the south side of the glacier to get alongside the *Morning*. Notwithstanding the long hours which they had already worked, our people elected to go right on throughout the night, and soon more coal sacks were being tumbled on board.

Now, as always, the manner in which our people undertook a heavy task and worked on at it without rest was a sight for the gods. Perhaps the strongest support of this splendid spirit was the fact that on such occasions, by mutual consent, there was no distinction between officers and men. At such times our geologist could be seen dragging coal bags along the decks, whilst the biologist, the vertebrate zoologist, lieutenants and A.B.s, with grimed faces and chafed hands, formed an indistinguishable party on the coaling whips. It did not matter how formidable might be the scientific designation of any officer: in time of difficulty and stress he was content to be plain John Smith and to labour in common for the general good.

The *Morning* afforded us twenty-five tons of coal, and I have an ever grateful recollection of that kindly deed, for in giving us so much, Colbeck reduced himself to the narrowest margin, and voluntarily resigned himself to the necessity of having to return directly homeward without joining in any attempt at further exploration. I have already mentioned that I had determined to try to penetrate to the westward around Cape North, and now that it had become necessary to promulgate my plans, I saw that whilst the *Terra Nova* could keep pace with us wherever we went, we were likely to be much hampered by the company of the small *Morning*, with her feeble engine power. But whilst these facts were evident, I naturally felt a reluctance to except from our further adventures the ship which had stood by us so faithfully in our troubles.

But Colbeck needed no reminder to see the difficulty of my position; his practical common sense told him he could be of little use to us, and with his usual loyalty he never hesitated to act for the best, at whatever sacrifice to his own hopes and wishes.

So before we left the glacier in McMurdo Sound our programme was arranged, and it was decided that the three ships
should remain in company while we journeyed up the coast, but
that afterwards we should separate, the *Morning* proceeding to the
north, whilst the *Discovery* and the *Terra Nova* turned west. The
companies of both our relief ships expressed a strong wish that,
whatever separation took place, they might be permitted to be
with us when we entered our first civilised port; and as this seemed
to me a most reasonable desire after all their efforts on our behalf,
I fixed upon Port Ross, in the Auckland Islands, as a spot at which
we might rendezvous before our final return to New Zealand.

In accordance with these plans, before we left McMurdo Sound,
the captain of each relief ship was in possession of full instructions
providing for all such eventualities as the premature separation of
the ships or the failure of any to arrive at the rendezvous before a
certain limiting date.

We finished our coaling from the *Morning* at 6 a.m. on the
19th, and by seven were alongside the glacier for the purpose of
getting in water, as our tanks were quite empty, and we had
nothing to supply the wastage of the boilers. Our people had now
been almost continuously at work for thirty-six hours, but not a
moment was lost in setting about this fresh task. Now, however, commenced all those small difficulties which were a natural
result with complicated machinery which had so long been
idle. It was beyond expectation that things would be found to
work as efficiently as if they had been in constant use, and the
engine-room staff especially knew that, as they expressed it, they
would have to work 'double tides' to put their department in
order again.

On this particular morning it was the steam-pipes of our ice-
melters which gave out and caused a long and tantalising delay, so
that by the afternoon, when we were preparing to start work, the
wind had sprung up from the south again, making our position
untenable. We got clear of the south side of the glacier with some
difficulty, and steered round to the north side, but scarcely had we
planted our anchors when the wind increased to a gale. So swiftly
did it sweep down on us that the ship could be kept up to the
ice only by steaming full speed, and we had barely time to recover
our men and anchors before we were drifted out of the inlet

altogether. There was nothing for it now but to run to the north and hope to get our water elsewhere, and away we flew with our consorts at our heels.

And so that night, running swiftly through the water with a howling gale behind, we saw the last of McMurdo Sound. It was a fine scene, for although the wind blew with great force, the sky was comparatively clear. Away to the south-west behind the ragged storm clouds could be seen the deep red of the setting sun, against which there stood in sharp outline the dark forms of the western mountains and the familiar cone of Mount Discovery. On our right in a gloomy threatening sky rose the lofty snow-clad slopes of Erebus and the high domed summit of Cape Bird. For the last time we gazed at all these well-known landmarks with feelings that were not far removed from sadness, and yet whatever sorrow we may have felt at leaving for ever the region which had been our home, it is not surprising that after our recent experiences the last entry in my diary for this night should have been, 'Oh! but it is grand to be on the high seas once more in our good ship.'

February 20 saw us still speeding along the coastline to the north with a strong following breeze; although the sky was overcast the land was clearly in view and we were able to keep within ten miles of it in a perfectly clear sea, though we could see a fringe of pack-ice and numerous small bergs close to the coast. It will be remembered that this stretch of the coast was quite unknown until we had made our way south along it, and that even then we had been obliged to keep a long distance out in many places on account of the pack-ice. Now we were able to fill in all the gaps which had formerly been missed, and even more; for our indefatigable surveyor, Mulock, remained on deck day and night during this run, taking innumerable angles to peaks and headlands, whilst our artist, Wilson, was equally diligent in transferring this long panorama of mountain scenery to his sketch-book.

At three in the afternoon of the 20th we sighted the white cliffs of the curious glacier tongue which, as may be seen on the chart,* runs out for many miles in a strangely attenuated form. At 10 p.m. we rounded the end of this snout and bore up for Wood Bay; the high cone of Mount Melbourne and the bluff cliffs of Cape Washington could be seen in the distance.

* Not reproduced in this edition.

The main object in going to Wood Bay was to fill up our water supply, but we had also come to the conclusion that this place must be closer to the magnetic pole than had been supposed, and for a long time we had cherished the hope of being able to make a series of magnetic observations on its shores, but in this respect we were destined to be disappointed, as my diary shows.

'February 21. – At 2 a.m. the wind, still freshening from the west, brought the *Morning* up on us again. She looked very trim and snug under her canvas. As she approached she ran up a signal which we could not distinguish, but guessing that she wanted to take advantage of the breeze and get away north, I hoisted "Proceed on your voyage", and soon her answering pennant fluttered out, her helm went up, and she shot away to the north-east; and so our imposing little fleet is breaking up. At 6 a.m. we rounded the inner angle of Cape Washington, and to our surprise found the whole bay full of pack-ice. We passed through one broad stream and got well inside the headland, but beyond this from the crow's-nest I could see no open water, and it was obviously impossible to proceed into any of the inlets. Signalling to the *Terra Nova* to remain outside, we pushed in towards the southern shore, and tried to secure the ship to a small berg; but there was a considerable swell running into the bay, and after some unsuccessful efforts to reach the berg we tied up to a small but solid floe. Then all hands, officers and men, tumbled over the side and started working like demons to get the ice on board; by 3 p.m. we had finished, and I was sincerely glad, for some of our people are almost dropping with fatigue. They had little rest before we came out of the ice, but since, they have had practically none. We never quite appreciated what a lot of work there was to be done till we got to sea, but what with the bending of ropes and sails, the securing of movable articles, and the constant chipping away of ice from every conceivable place, there has not been a moment's peace for our overworked crew.

'The day has been very fine and bright, with occasional south-westerly breezes, but quite warm when the wind fell. There was a good deal of young ice in the bay when we entered, but it vanished in the course of the day. Wood Bay was looking its best. The south side is fringed by the ice-cliffs terminating the slopes of Mount Melbourne, with rocky headlands and huge masses of black morainic material occasionally occurring. The north side is limited by splendid bare rocky cliffs intersected with deep glacier valleys.

'It was 5 p.m. before we could clear the pack by standing close along the southern shore, where we saw quantities of skuas, and one small Adélie penguin rookery, showing again how these birds take advantage of every available landing place. On arriving in the open water, Armitage swung the ship, but before he could complete his task the sun disappeared. At seven we steamed out of the bay, meeting a heavy swell from the south-east, which is causing us to roll heavily. I trust this does not mean a gale, as we are by no means prepared to meet one yet.'

'February 22. – Last night we had an exceedingly unpleasant experience, with some hours of serious alarm. I suppose such things must be expected to happen under the circumstances, but I shall be extremely glad when we have settled down into sea trim. As far as I was concerned the trouble began at 1 a.m., when Skelton called me and asked permission to stop the engines, as the pumps had refused duty, and the water was gaining on the ship. When we stopped, the ship dropped broadside on the swell and commenced to roll 30° each way. This was not a pleasing condition under which to contend with any difficulty, much less with such a one as now faced us, for on looking down into the engine-room I found that the water had risen well over the stokehold plates, and with the rolling of the ship, it was washing to and fro with tremendous force. It was evident that the fires in the main boilers would soon be swamped; so to avoid accidents they were drawn, which of course put the steam pump out of action, even if it had been in working order.

'The next thing was to try the hand pumps, and the carpenter with the deck watch was soon heaving at these, but without any result. Examination showed that they were quite choked up with ice, so the next hour or two was spent in attempts to clear them. Meanwhile the water was obviously gaining, though to this moment we have failed to discover exactly why, as there is no serious leak to our knowledge. At 3 a.m. it was suggested that the small boiler under the forecastle should be lighted, and an attempt be made to work the steam pump with it. An hour later therefore one party was rushing to and fro with fuel for this boiler, and another was struggling with the refractory hand pumps, but the water was gaining as steadily as ever. Meanwhile Dellbridge, working up to his waist in water, had taken the steam pump to pieces, examined each part, and replaced it.

'It was 6 a.m. before we had steam in the small boiler, and this meant that it had been raised in the quickest time on record. At the same time Dellbridge reported the pump ready again. I asked somewhat needlessly if he thought it would work now, to which he grimly replied, "It's got to, sir." Nevertheless when it was started we found to our consternation that it did not. Then, and not till then, someone thought of examining the bilge suction, and here in a moment was found the cause of all the trouble. The pump, we discovered, had never been out of order, but the rose which drew the water from the bilges was quite choked up with fine ashes. When we left our winter quarters all this part had been a mass of ice, and it had therefore been impossible to clear out the bilges, which were still in a half-frozen condition. When this suction had been cleared we had the satisfaction of seeing a stream of water pouring out of the ship's side, and soon after the hand pumps brought their small power to aid in the relief. By eight o'clock everything was reported in working order, the fires were re-lit and I got to bed. The whole of our engine-room staff have been on duty for twenty-four hours without a spell. Our scare has been useful in one way, as we can rely on our pumps for any sudden call in future.'

The heavy swell continued throughout the 22nd, but gradually fell towards the evening. Somewhat to our surprise, it did not prove to be the forerunner of a gale, and on the 23rd the sky was comparatively clear and the wind light. In the middle of this day we approached and passed Coulman Island at a very short distance, getting a fine view of its high cliffs and of the mountainous mainland. The coast to the south of the island was heavily packed, as it had been on our former visit, and even on the outside of the island we were obliged to force our way through several loose streams, besides a quantity of young ice, broken into tiny rounded pancakes with frilled edges, caused by the chafe of the swell. In the evening a breeze sprang up from the west, which enabled us to make sail and afforded us much relief from the continual heavy rolling. We had always thought that the *Discovery* was a particularly lively ship, but we never appreciated it more than on this day, when we found ourselves lurching from side to side in the most uncomfortable fashion, while our consort followed in our wake with scarcely a movement.

After passing Coulman Island we were able to hug the coast much closer than we had done when travelling south, and it is worthy of note that, as we could see, both Tucker Inlet and another unnamed one north of Cape Hallet are much deeper than Ross supposed. Either would afford excellent shelter to a ship. The two inlets curve in such a manner that the mass of land on which Ross has placed the names of Wheatstone, Hallet, and Cotter forms a peninsula. Mowbray Bay is also a deep inlet.

Early on the 24th we sighted the Possession Islands, and later passed through the group. There are nine islands and islets, very various in size and shape. That on which Ross landed is the largest, and has a shelving beach on the western side, though it is steep and precipitous on the eastern. The smaller islets are mere rocks, but some are of very curious shape. One is an almost perfect column more than 300 feet in height; another which has a similar but broader appearance from the south, when viewed from the east or west is seen to be pierced with two huge arches, the larger of which must be nearly 150 feet in height. Altogether these islands are a curious and interesting group.

Directly after we had passed through the channels between them the carpenter came to me with a serious face to call my attention to the rudder, and I immediately went aft to inspect it. I found that the solid oak rudder-head was completely shattered, and that it was held together by little more than its weight; as the tiller was moved to the right or left the rudder followed it, but with a lag of many degrees, so that it was evident that the connection between the two was quite insecure. How we had come by such an injury I could not guess, unless it was on the freeing of the ship or from collision with some submerged spur of the glacier in McMurdo Sound; but it was obvious that in such a condition we could not hope to weather a gale without losing all control over the ship, and therefore that the sooner we got our spare rudder shipped in place of the damaged one, the better. On looking back at this incident I cannot but recognise how exceedingly fortunate it was that the sharp eyes of our carpenter should have detected the fault at this time, for, as will be seen, a few days later we were in such a position that the loss of our rudder would have been a most serious matter, and the steps which we now took would have been almost impossible in the open sea. The fault, such as it was, was not easily seen, for the injured rudder-head was below the level of the deck and partly submerged by the wash of the screw. I have had reason before to speak of the invaluable qualities of our warrant officers, and certainly this was a case that proved them. As it was, immed-iately I realised our crippled state, I determined to make for Cape Adare and to seek shelter in Robertson Bay; the events which followed I quote from my diary.

'We signalled to the *Terra Nova* that our rudder was damaged and that we should anchor in the bay. There was now a brisk breeze, and with sail, steam, and current we approached Cape Adare at a rapid pace. As we came nearer we could see a very large number of bergs scattered about off the entrance of the bay; nearly all were tabular, and they varied from 50 to 150 feet in height and from a quarter to three-quarters of a mile in length. Streams of pack were lying inshore and stretching from berg to berg. It was not altogether pleasant turning and twisting amongst these immense masses of ice with the knowledge that the rudder might give out at any moment. At the entrance of the bay we were involved in a heavy pack, but it was noticeable that the floes were decayed and water-worn to an extent which we have not seen since we first entered the Ross Sea. As we came through this pack the leadsman suddenly got a sounding of five fathoms, but though we sounded repeatedly before and after, nowhere else could we get anything but deep water. It appeared as though there must be a submarine ridge or hill at this particular spot.

'Late in the afternoon we dropped our anchor in thirteen fathoms off the beach we had formerly visited; a few officers went on shore to take magnetic observations and to secure bird speci-mens, but the majority, with the men, set to work at once to shift the rudder. In spite of the facilities which are afforded by our rudder-well, the task is not an easy one, as the rudder itself and all the fittings connected with it are very ponderous. By ten tonight, however, when the light grew dim, the damaged rudder had been hoisted on deck and the spare one prepared for lowering it into its place. Whilst we were at work the tide setting out of the bay brought down on us a heavy pack; our anchor held well, but the

Terra Nova evidently did not like the look of things, and has weighed her anchor and put out to sea.'

'February 25. – By 6 a.m. we were at work again. The weather fortunately remained quite calm and bright. At 9.30 the spare rudder was in place, and, after a hasty breakfast, at 10.15 we weighed our anchor and pushed out to sea. A snowstorm swept down upon us immediately after, and we lost sight of the *Terra Nova*, but pushing out in the direction in which she had last been seen we had the satisfaction of finding ourselves close to her when the storm passed, and soon after we were steaming north-west in company. An almost incredible amount of work has been done in the *Discovery* since we left winter quarters; it has been one long fight to bring her into sea trim, and difficulty after difficulty has arisen in the most exasperating manner; but now, I think, thanks to the determined energy of our people, we may say that all things are in order again, and that our ship is prepared to face most emergencies. The only thing I am doubtful about is the steering power of our spare rudder, as it has scarcely half the area of the old one.'

It was of great importance that our ship should be in good sea trim at this time, because according to our programme we were now about to make the attempt to penetrate a new region, and we expected to find quite enough to occupy our minds in contending with the obstacles in our path without having to consider internal troubles.

Now, therefore, we turned to the west with high hope that with our steam-power we should be able to pass beyond the point which had been reached by Sir James Ross in his sailing ships. At first all went well with us, as, except for bergs and very loose streams of pack, there seemed nothing to obstruct our course. The number of bergs was extraordinary; it would appear that the current which runs up the east coast of Victoria Land continues to the north-west after passing Cape Adare, and leaves a region of slack water to the westward of Robertson Bay, and, as a consequence, many of the bergs which stream up the coast are carried by eddies into this area where they present such a formidable accumulation.

When pack-ice is entangled amongst icebergs it has to be navigated with some caution, as amongst the floes will always be found numerous fragments of the bergs themselves; these pieces generally float low and are not easily seen, but as they are very solid and often possess sharp spurs it is eminently desirable to avoid them.

By the afternoon of the 25th we were in the thick of the bergs, and, to our disappointment, we found the pack-ice growing closer. Having but a very limited supply of coal in our bunkers, it was necessarily our policy to avoid the pack as far as possible; and as we could not afford to force our way through long stretches of it, we turned outwards in hopes of finding a clearer passage. This took us a long distance from the land, but we trusted that we should soon be able to return towards it.

With the closing of the season and our advance to the north, our days were gradually drawing in, and already we had a night of four or five hours, when navigation amongst the ice promised to be anxious work.

For the incidents of the next few days I turn to my diary once more. On the night of the 25th I wrote:

'Shortly after 8 p.m. it became thick with driving snowstorms from the east. We are still surrounded with bergs, and thick weather is undesirable; however, the snowstorms are like April showers, frequent but quickly over, and after they burst upon us it is not long before we see our consort and the bergs again. We are going half-speed for the night hoping that tomorrow will afford us a brighter outlook.'

'February 26. – I had scarcely lain down in my clothes last night, thinking of a clear sea ahead, when the pack was again reported. We pushed through several streams, hoping to escape, but to no purpose. At 5.30 we found ourselves completely embayed; then the fog came down upon us, and we were obliged to stop engines. Whilst waiting about we took the opportunity to sound, and, to my surprise, got no bottom with 1,000 fathoms of line out. It is evident that the continental plateau slopes down very steeply off this coast. We were just preparing to get a net over when the weather cleared and we saw the land and clear water for some way towards it. We decided to waste no time in pushing on in this direction, but soon after noon our channel closed in again and we found ourselves surrounded with heavy pack. The weather was now quite clear, and from the crow's-nest one could get a good idea of our surroundings.

'From the high peaks of Mounts Minto and Adam the mountains gradually descend towards the west and grow more heavily glaciated; the coastline abreast of us seems very indented and is marked with numerous dark outstanding cliffs behind which the comparatively low mountains are entirely snow-covered except where occasionally a sharp pyramidal peak thrusts its summit through the white sheet. Away to the west the land still descends, and all eminences are lost under the snowy mantle which slopes down gradually to the sea level at Cape North. A little ahead of us I could see the black headlands of Smith's Inlet, but between us and it, and, in fact, over the whole sea to the west, lay the broad expanse of a mighty field of pack-ice dotted with numberless bergs. Here and there towards the shore could be seen leads of open water, but they were nowhere continuous, and it was evident that at the best it would take us some days to reach the far cape.

'The temptation to push on was great, and I sent to learn how our coal supply stood; the reply showed me that we had little over eighty tons remaining, an amount which would allow of sixteen days' steaming at our present consumption. I reflected that at least ten of these should be allowed for the return voyage, and I knew how little we could do with the six that remained if once we became involved in the pack. Reluctantly, therefore, I decided to turn to the north-east and seek a way around this formidable barrier; we must now look for the first opening in it and reserve our small margin of coal for more promising circumstances. It is grievously disappointing to find the pack so far to the east; Ross carried the open water almost to Cape North.

'After being brought up by the pack, we sounded and obtained bottom at 610 fathoms, and then devoted the afternoon to getting a haul with our trawl. Whilst this operation was in progress a stiff breeze sprang up from the west and the glass commenced to fall rapidly. Hampered with our trawl-line we drifted alarmingly close to several small bergs, so that I was not sorry when we got our net on board again; it produced some new species, but the catch was not so satisfactory as we could have wished.

'By the time we were ready to proceed the wind had increased to a moderate gale, and the ice-streams began to move with such rapidity that we made all possible speed for the open sea. We could not reach it, however, without forcing our way through a broad belt of the heaviest pack we have seen; the floes were much hummocked, and rose almost to the level of our deck. However, with a full head of steam we forced a way through, and reached the open water just before dark. We have since made sail, and are now standing to the eastward with a strong ice-blink on our port hand, but a comparatively open sea to leeward. The sky has become very overcast and the weather threatening, but the sea is smooth.'

'February 27. – We are skirting this wretched pack; I cannot think what brings it so far to the east; last night we came through several streams, and were forced to turn to the south-east; but this morning we straightened up again, and are now going nearly due north.

'Before noon the wind gradually died away, and we now have a brisk and increasing breeze from the south. The glass, which had been steadily falling since noon yesterday, is slowly rising; we have passed away from this region of bergs, but the strong ice-blink is always on our port hand. If in no other way, we can guess our proximity to the pack-ice by the constant presence of the charming little snow petrels; they never seem to wander far from the pack. Last night we had a flight of Antarctic petrels around the ship; they came and went in the gloom in very ghostly fashion, and this morning there were still a number about us. This morning brought more of the bird friends that we have missed for so long, and we saw again the fulmar petrel, the small prion, and a sooty albatross; these indicate, without doubt, a clear sea to the north. I wish one could say the same of the west.

'Our poor dogs are made very miserable by the wet. Born in the South, they have absolutely no experience of damp conditions, and at first they were much alarmed by them; they show the same horror of a wet deck or a wet coat as a cat might do. But the most curious result of their ignorance was the fact that they had to be taught to lap; they had never quenched their thirst except by eating snow, and when water was put before them they didn't know what to do with it; in fact, they grew very thirsty before they could be persuaded to drink by thrusting their noses into the water tins.'

'February 28. – The S.E. breeze increased in force during the night, and by morning it was blowing a full gale with constant snowstorms. The night was not pleasant, as we got amongst the ice again, which kept us all on the qui vive; at midnight we found it stretching across our bows, and the snow petrels had increased in number; at 3 a.m. we passed through several loose streams, and immediately hauled to the north. With a strong breeze we now bowled along at a good rate. The *Terra Nova* was some distance astern, but turned in our wake; in order that she might come up with us, I stopped the engines, and we stood on under sail alone. At six o'clock she was some two miles astern, but soon after a heavy snow squall blotted her out, and when this had passed nothing of her could be seen. I do not think there is any cause for anxiety, as the weather remained thick, but I cannot think why she did not keep close touch with us, as she should have found it easy to catch us after we stopped our engines.

'During the forenoon it blew very hard with a rapidly rising sea. I was very anxious about our foremost spars, as the hemp rigging is now quite slack and we have had no chance of setting it up. Our foretop-gallant-mast was bending like a whip; it must be a beautiful spar to have stood the strain.

'The ship has been kicking and plunging about in the most objectionable manner: the upper deck has been awash, and water has been pouring down through the skylights and chimneys. It has been horribly stuffy below, and the majority of us have been feeling extremely seasick. Altogether it has been a very unpleasant day, but perhaps the most serious thing that it has disclosed is the uselessness of our small rudder under such conditions; it had so little effect on the ship that we could only keep our course by constantly trimming our sails. Had we met an iceberg, we should have had no choice but to throw the yards aback. This is really a grave matter, as the nights are long and we may fall across bergs at any moment. Our deck watch is reduced to five hands, moreover, and this is all too small a number to deal with any sudden emergency; as it is, they have to be constantly on the alert to stand by the braces.

'The barometer ceased to fall at seven o'clock, and the wind immediately slackened.'

'February 29. – We stood steadily on to the north last night in hopes that the *Terra Nova* would catch us up, but as there were no signs of her at 4 a.m. I determined to go about. The wind had fallen light, but there was a heavy sea running, and it was a good half-hour before we could wear the ship round. We have been standing due west all day about latitude 67½; the glass has been rising, the wind dropping and the ship kicking about most unmercifully. We passed a few bergs, mostly small and flat-topped; the seas were breaking over them, dashing the spray to a height of 200 or 300 feet. I fear there is no chance of seeing the *Terra Nova* again until we reach the rendezvous.'

'March 1. – Last night we got amongst a number of bergs and some loose streams of pack, so we hove-to and kept a sharp lookout; at four o'clock we got under way again with steam and proceeded steadily to the west. The weather has been thick, with an overcast, gloomy sky, and we have had a light breeze from the north; there has been a steady ice-blink on our lee, sometimes appearing ahead, to be quickly followed by sight of a loose stream of pack. There can be no doubt that since leaving Victoria Land we have been skirting a continuous mass of pack which must cover the whole sea south of the Balleny Islands.

'That it should have lain so far to the eastward this year is very annoying; however, if we can push on upon this course we ought to strike the islands. Birds have been plentiful all day, but tonight the albatrosses have left us; snow petrels, Antarctic and fulmar petrels are our constant companions, and this afternoon we had the very unusual sight of a small flock of black-headed terns. We have also passed two or three sea leopards asleep on the floes: one we surprised greatly by ramming the floe on which he was taking his siesta, whereat he opened his formidable jaws and threatened us in the most ferocious manner.'

'March 2. – . . . Land was reported at 5 a.m., and on the port bow we could see black rock showing streakily through the mist. By 7.30 we were close up, and found on our port bow an island of considerable size. Our course took us just to the northward of its steep northern extremity. The general aspect of the land much resembled that of Coulman Island, but the glaciation was much heavier. High, precipitous, dark cliffs were capped by the sharp edge of the ice-cap, which undulated smoothly over the lesser slopes, and lay broken and crevassed on the steeper ones; at places the vast snow-sheet descended to the sea, and spread out with immense fan-shaped glaciers fringed with high ice-cliffs. These conditions of the coast could be seen clearly, but above the height of 300 or 400 feet all was hidden in dense stratus cloud.

'By noon we were abreast of this forbidding land; the clouds showed signs of lifting, but still enveloped the summit of the island. The coast was less than two miles from us, so that we could see each detail clearly, and twice, as we passed, an immense mass of névé became detached from the cliffs and fell with a huge splash into the sea. As I write we are standing to the west of the island, and, to our astonishment, with a clear sea. Once more we are treading untrodden paths. But before we turn our thoughts to the west we are puzzling over the question as to what this island and others we can dimly see to the north really are. We are about the latitude of the Russell Islands, yet we cannot follow Ross's description of them, nor can we understand where the Balleny Group lies. One thing is certain, however: whatever these islands may be, no-one has ever seen them from this side before, and the sight of a clear sea to the west is most encouraging.'

It is as well perhaps to explain the dilemma we found ourselves in with regard to these islands. In 1839 Balleny discovered a group of islands in this region, but whilst the position of his ship was most carefully reckoned and the bearings of the land masses taken, he did not supply sufficient data accurately to fix the position of the various islands which he named. Three years later, Ross, when some way to the eastward of this position, saw land which he imagined must be to the southward of Balleny's discoveries; from the great distance at which he saw it he believed it to be divided into three distinct masses, and under this impression named them the Russell Islands. We came to this region, therefore, with the expectation of seeing two groups of islands, and were naturally much puzzled when we found that by no means could we reconcile the accounts of the two explorers to fit this theory; and at first the clouded condition of the land added much to this difficulty.

It was only after I had read the accounts many times, and compared them with what we actually saw, that the solution suddenly flashed upon me, and as is so often the case, when the key was once supplied the matter became obvious to us all. We saw then that the island which we had just passed was Balleny's Sturge Island. Balleny had seen it from the north, in which direction it presents a comparatively narrow front; he could have had no idea of its length in a north-and-south line. At a later date Ross must have seen this same island, and, as we saw was quite possible, from a great distance he must have imagined it to be divided into three, and hence made the mistake of naming it as a separate group.

Later on this same day the cloudy screen about the islands gradually vanished; we were able to see the land clearly both north and south of us, and Mulock obtained sufficient bearings to fix accurately the position of each island.

In the evening of the 2nd I wrote:

'This afternoon, as the weather cleared and the sun shone forth, we got a good view of the islands now falling behind us, and had no longer a doubt as to their identity. Looking astern, on our right was Sturge Island, more than twenty miles in length, with the lofty summit of Brown's Peak arising towards its northern end. The nearest island on the left was Buckle Island, its outline from this side being the exact reverse of that sketched by Balleny's mate from the other. The smaller island next to the north was Borrodaile Island, and this also could be recognised from the sketch. Young Island presented a high land to the left, though Peak Freeman, its highest point, was never wholly clear of cloud. The last of the group reported by Balleny, Row Island, we did not see, but this was not surprising, as it is stated to be comparatively low.

'Now that we have settled the knotty question as to the geography of these islands, our position seems extremely hopeful. This region to the westward has always been found heavily packed. We are the first to enter it, and to our delight we find an open sea; it seems as though the pack has been driven to the south-east, into that area which we skirted. The wind has fallen, and we have furled our sails; a long swell comes from the north-west, showing an absence of ice in that direction. We are standing directly to the west, towards Wilkes Land, and every eye is keenly on the alert for some new development – so keenly, in fact, that twice this afternoon has an excited person rushed up to me to report some imaginary discovery of land in the fantastical cloud forms that fringe our horizon. The night promises to be fine, though the glass is falling. Birds are gathering about us in numbers once more – the commonest today is the fulmar petrel; it looks as though it nested on the islands. Rorqual whales have been spouting in all directions, and altogether signs of life are plentiful and cheering.'

'March 3. – Early last night the sky clouded over, and towards the end of the middle watch it began to snow; by the morning we found ourselves in a thick fog. We had made sail again to a northerly breeze, and at 5.30 a.m. we hove-to in none too pleasant a position, for we could not tell where we were drifting or when some monster iceberg might appear on our lee. At 11 a.m. there was a slight clearance, and we decided to push on, which we have since done, though every now and again the fog comes down on us as thick as ever. At noon today we estimated we were in longitude 159 E., and since that we have sailed some way to the west, so that we are now practically behind Wilkes's alleged land. But as there is a long swell from the north, it is plain that there cannot be any extent of land in that direction; it is still possible that Wilkes may have seen some islands, but this we can only determine when the weather clears.

'It has cleared to some extent tonight, and has shown us more than one berg in our vicinity. At seven o'clock we passed a large one that was slowly oscillating. We could see it gradually tilt over until its flat surface was half submerged, then it slowly righted itself again; this went on for some time, the oscillations growing larger, until suddenly it got beyond the point of recovery and with a huge splash turned turtle. The sight of this immense mass rolling over in the foaming sea was very impressive, and we were grateful that it should have chosen such an opportune moment for our benefit. We are longing for clear weather; one cannot but believe there must be land somewhere in this region, especially on account of our soundings, but we know that we cannot go on like this much longer. We have only sixty tons of coal remaining, a bare sufficiency to take us north; no doubt the wisest plan would be to turn north now, but I have decided to go on as we are for another day in hopes that fortune may favour us with one clear sight of our surroundings.'

'March 4. – The wind failed us last night, and it has been calm all day. The sky has been dull, but the horizon quite clear; we could have seen land at a great distance, yet none has been in sight, and thus once and for all we have definitely disposed of Wilkes Land. Both Armitage and I got good sights, and both fixed our noon position to be in latitude 67.23 S., longitude 155.30 E. We have been standing N.W. true, and on such a course we should have sighted Eld's Peak and Ringold's Knoll on our right had these places existed. It is therefore quite evident that they do not, nor can there be any land in this direction, as the long ocean swell has never ceased to roll steadily in from the north, and we have other signs of bird life which show a clear sea in that direction. Tonight

Cape Hudson should be in sight on the port bow, but that also is conspicuous by its absence. After reading Wilkes's report again, I must conclude that as these places are non-existent, there is no case for any land eastward of Adélie Land. It is a great disappointment to have to turn north at such an interesting time, but I feel that it is imperative; we have scarcely coal enough for ten days steaming, and our late experiences have shown clearly how unmanageable the ship is under sail alone with our small spare rudder. There is nothing for it but to turn homeward, and even as it is we shall have to rely on favouring winds to reach our rendezvous.

'It is a curious fact that although we have sighted no land we are still on the edge of a continental plateau, and in comparatively shallow water. This morning we got 250 fathoms, and this afternoon 254 fathoms; the continental shelf would seem to extend as far as the Balleny Islands. This afternoon we put over a trawl and got a haul which delighted the heart of our biologist with quite a number of new species.'

'March 5. – During the night we passed close to the supposed position of Cape Hudson – except for a few bergs, in a perfectly clear sea. We had a full moon which, although usually hidden by clouds, gave a good light by which objects – and certainly land – could have been seen at a great distance. This morning there is not a sign of land, and remarkably few bergs. At 3.30 we got soundings in 245 fathoms, and at eight in 260 fathoms. The continental plateau must be extensive, and Wilkes certainly had the chance of being misled by his soundings. At noon today we were in latitude 66.23 S., longitude 154.7 E., and so we have crossed the Antarctic Circle again after an interval of two years and sixty two days.

'This morning the breeze sprang up from the north-west, and we made sail, standing close-hauled to the N.N.E. Throughout the day the wind has freshened and hauled round to the west, so that we are now standing almost due north. I hoped to sound again tonight, but it is blowing too hard; I think we are in for a gale.'

On March 5, 1904, therefore, our exploring work came to an end, and we found ourselves entering once more that storm-swept area of the 'Westerlies' which separated us from civilisation. The programme with which I had hoped to close the season had been much hampered by our lack of coal, but if we had been unable to carry out our cherished plan of rounding Cape North, we had at least cleared up some geographical misconceptions in a more northerly latitude.

Two days later we saw the last of the Antarctic ice under conditions which made us exceeding grateful that it was the last, as my diary shows.

'March 7. – . . . Since we shut off steam yesterday we have been progressing to the north, but in a very curious manner. In spite of all head sails being set, the ship has such a tendency to come up in the wind that the helm has to be kept hard up, and so we plunge along about five knots, with no power of control over the ship except to stop her by throwing the yards aback. This is not so bad as long as there are no bergs in sight, and yesterday I thought we had seen the last of these unwelcome neighbours; but this morning, when it was blowing great guns, the boatswain came down and reported a berg on the lee bow, and I dashed on deck to see a huge mass of ice showing under the foot of the foresail. We had either to go on or to "heave-to", as I knew we could not alter course to pass to leeward. I decided finally to go on, but the ship was labouring so heavily that it was fully twenty minutes before we could be certain that the bearing was changing in the right direction, and that we stood a good prospect of weathering it. In another ten minutes we passed close to windward of it, and could see the mountainous waves dashing over its lofty pinnacles and imagine the condition of the unfortunate vessel that should run foul of it. It was an impressive farewell to the Southern ice, for since that gaunt, wave-beaten mass has dropped astern we have seen no more.'

With our last view of these formidable Southern bergs my tale draws to a close, for what remains is little more than the story of ordinary life on the high seas, and may be told briefly.

The month of March is the most stormy season of the year in the Southern Seas, and during the days which we spent in travelling to the north the weather made no exception in our favour. From the 6th to the 14th we had continuous gales with conditions of greater physical discomfort than we had ever experienced on board the *Discovery*. The ship was in very light trim and was tossed about on the mountainous seas like a cork. There are few things more exasperating than the unceasing pitching and plunging of a very lively ship. Many of us were very seasick, and, to add to our distress, our decks were leaking badly, so that we lived in a perpetual drip below. The wind blew almost constantly northward of west, so that we were obliged to remain close-hauled. Our crab-like motion under sail soon showed us that we should be drifted to leeward of our rendezvous, and on the 9th we were obliged to start our engines again. Even with steam and sail it was touch and go whether we lay our course until the 13th, when a lucky slant of wind sent us well to windward. On the 14th we sighted the Auckland Islands on our lee bow, and early on the following morning we furled our sails off the entrance of Ross Harbour, and steamed into the calm waters of the bay.

It is not easy to forget that morning when, weary and worn with all our long struggle with the ice and the tempests of the South, we steered into this placid shelter and, for the first time for more than two years, feasted our eyes on hillsides clothed with the green of luxuriant vegetation.

Ross Harbour is a splendidly protected winding inlet, and it was in its deepest arm, shut off from all view of the sea, that we finally came to an anchor, within a hundred yards of the thick scrub which grows down to the water's edge. A glance at our bunkers was alone sufficient to show by how narrow a margin we had accomplished our work, for less than ten tons remained of our stock of coal, and yet not an ounce had been wasted on our northward voyage. Our plans had barely carried us to this uninhabited island, and with such a remnant we could not have made the longer journey to New Zealand.

It was with great surprise, and not altogether without anxiety, that I found neither of our consorts had yet arrived at the rendezvous. However, I reflected that it was quite possible that by going to the west we had achieved a windward position and thus got ahead of them in spite of their long start, and this conjecture proved to be correct.

Meanwhile we settled ourselves down to wait, determined to enjoy our new surroundings thoroughly, and to make our ship as smart as possible for her first appearance to the eyes of the multitude. It was a curious idea this last, but it was very strongly held by us all; it seemed a point of pride with us that the good ship which had carried us so well should not be allowed to display any untidiness in public, and so all hands fell to with a will. There was much scrubbing of decks and cleaning of paintwork; then came a fresh coat of paint to cover up all the travel stains, and in a few days the *Discovery* looked as though she had spent her three adventurous years in some peaceful harbour.

On March 19 the *Terra Nova* hove in sight, and on the following day we were still more relieved by the safe arrival of the *Morning*. Both ships had the same tale to tell – a tale of continuous adverse gales which had blown so heavily that at times they had been obliged to 'heave-to', and throughout had had a long and hard struggle in beating up to the islands. The little *Morning* had had an especially dismal experience. She had been nearly a month fighting this terribly hard weather, with all sorts of added troubles in connection with her ramshackle engines and pumps, and her ill-ballasted condition. Captain Colbeck will no doubt tell of the adventurous incidents of this month, but none of us is likely to forget the utterly worn-out condition in which his small company arrived at Ross Harbour, or the universal testimony of officers and men that disaster had only been averted by the consummate seamanship with which their small vessel had been handled.

The few days which we remained in Ross Harbour after the arrival of our consorts were spent in ballasting the *Morning* and in giving a much-needed rest to her crew; we were also able to obtain from the *Terra Nova* the addition to our coal supply necessary for the last stage of our journey to civilisation.

On March 29 our small fleet set sail once more, and now everything favoured our prosperous voyage; with a strong breeze from the south-west and a moderate sea, we set all our canvas and ran rapidly to the north. On the 30th we sighted Stewart Island, and later the coast of the mainland; the following day found us running up the coast, and at length with the well-remembered outline of the Bankes Peninsula before us.

At daybreak on Good Friday, April 1, we were off the Heads of Lyttelton Harbour, and before noon we were safely berthed alongside the jetty from which we had sailed with such hearty good wishes more than two years before.

I have found my pen inadequate to describe many an incident in this narrative, but perhaps I never realised its inadequacy so completely as when I set about to picture the warmth of the welcome which we received on our arrival in New Zealand. Those who have been patient enough to follow the course of this story will remember the kindness with which our small party of adventurers were treated before our departure for the South, and how each visit of the relief ship brought us not only welcome news from the Old Country, but greetings and presents from this newer land. It is little wonder, therefore, that as we entered Lyttelton Heads after so long an absence, each one of us felt that we were returning to what was very nearly our home – to a place where we should find rest and peace after our wanderings, and to people who would greet us with sympathetic friendship. And all this we found in fullest measure; New Zealand welcomed us as its own, and showered on us a wealth of hospitality and kindness which assuredly we can never forget, however difficult we may have found it to express our thanks. In these delightful conditions, with everything that could make for perfect rest and comfort, we abode for two full months before we set out on our last long voyage; and even though that voyage was to carry us to our homeland, there was many a sad heart when for the last time we steamed out of Lyttelton Harbour and waved our farewells to those who had taken so deep an interest in our fortunes.

June 8 found us at sea again. The *Morning* sailed with us, but soon parted company; the *Terra Nova* had left more than a fortnight earlier. We did not sight land again until July 6, when we first saw the mountains of Tierra del Fuego. Meanwhile, however, our voyage had not been without interest as it had enabled us to accomplish some tasks of importance. Amongst these was the completion of our magnetic survey, which was thus carried about the greater part of the circumference of the Antarctic area, as well as to such regions as we had visited within it.

After leaving New Zealand we gradually increased our latitude until the greater part of our track lay between the parallels of 56° and 60°. This was a route which had often been taken by ships, but one in which the depth of the ocean was entirely unknown. So far as the weather and the circumstances of the voyage would permit, we endeavoured to supply this deficiency, and although we were not able to sound so frequently as I had hoped, the few soundings which we took are of great interest, as they constitute our only knowledge of the depth of the Pacific in high southern latitudes. On the whole, these soundings showed a fairly uniform depth of something over 2,000 fathoms. The shallowest, 1,710 fathoms, was obtained on the meridian of 136 W., whilst the deepest, 2,738 fathoms, occurred on that of 106 W. close down on the 60th parallel. This is only a step, and a very small one, towards what is greatly needed – namely, a complete oceanographic survey of the seas about the Antarctic Circle.

Another point of geographical interest occurring in this voyage may be noted: on two occasions an island named Dogherty Island has been reported approximately in latitude 59 S., longitude 120 W., but later observations have thrown some doubt upon its existence. On June 25 we arrived on the supposed position of this land, and found a depth of 2,318 fathoms. It was remarkably clear both before and after we took this sounding, and had there been an island within any reasonable limits of its assigned position we could not have failed to see it. The case for the retention of an oceanic island on the chart after it has been proved absent from its supposed position is that the original discoverer may have largely miscalculated that position, but the evidence against the existence of Dogherty Island is now too strong to allow of this explanation.

I had originally intended to round Cape Horn on our homeward voyage, but as we approached this longitude we were driven to the northward by S.E. winds, and consequently altered our plans to pass through the Magellan Strait. We entered this beautiful channel on the evening of July 6, and on the following night anchored off Puntas Arenas; the 9th found us racing out through the Eastern Narrows on the strong ebb tide, and three days later we anchored in Port Stanley (Falkland Islands). Here we replenished our stock of coal and took the last series of magnetic observations in connection with our Southern Survey.

On the 20th we put to sea and turned our head to the north, to face the last long stage of our journey; and now for the first time we found our life on board contained the elements of monotony. Our work was done – nothing remained but to hasten homeward – and we realised how poor a show of haste the *Discovery* was capable of displaying. We would willingly have spirited our good ship from the Southern to the Northern hemisphere, and chafed at the long weeks at sea which resulted from our slow progress.

And so our passage to the north was somewhat wearisome, but slowly and surely the miles were traversed, and we passed from the wild and stormy seas of the Westerlies to the mild regions of the gentle S.E. trade wind, and from this to the sweltering heat of the Doldrums.

On August 13 we recrossed the line, and a week later struggled slowly through the N.E. trade towards the Azores; here I decided to take in a small stock of coal, and on the last day of the month we anchored off Punta Delgada, in the island of San Miguel.

On September 2 we put to sea for the last time, and now, with favouring breezes, made comparatively rapid progress towards the Channel.

Early on the morning of the 9th we sighted the homeland once more, after an interval of three years and one month, and as we slowly steamed up the Channel it can be imagined there were not many eyes that did not gaze longingly over our port bulwarks. All Nature was smiling to welcome us, and all day long we passed in clear view of that glorious panorama of the south coast which every sailor knows so well; one wonders how many hearts have swelled at that sight!

At daylight on the 10th we were south of the Isle of Wight, and before noon the *Discovery* lay at Spithead, surrounded by many craft, whilst on board we welcomed those who had waited so long and so patiently for this moment.

There seems little to add. To attempt to describe the hearty welcome which we received from our countrymen, and the generous tributes which have been paid to our efforts, would be beyond the scope of this book, which purports to deal only with the simple narrative of our voyage. For me, and for the small band who laboured so faithfully together in the *Discovery*, there has been one cloud to dim the joy of this homecoming, for there was not one of us, I think, who did not feel the sadness of the day which brought the end of our close companionship and the scattering of those ties which had held us together for so long.

Yet although this inevitable parting has taken place, we hope that as the years roll on we may meet again, and we know that when such meetings come they will renew old friendships and recall some of the pleasantest memories of our lives.

INDEX OF NAMES